## Power

Power = work divided by time; measured in horsepower (HP), watts, etc.

1 HP = 33,000 ft-lbs/min = 4,564 kg-m/min = 746 watts.

1 watt = 44.22 ft-lbs/min = 6.118 kg-m/min = 0.0013 HP.

1 ft-lb per minute (ft-lb/min) = 0.1383 kg-m/min = 0.00003 HP = 0.0226 watt.

1 kg-m/min. = 7.23 ft-lbs/min = 0.00022 HP = 0.1635 watt.

## Velocity

1 ft per second (ft/sec) = 0.3048 m/sec = 18.3 m/min = 1.1 km per hour (km/hr) = 0.68 mile/hr (mph)

1 mph = 88 ft/min = 1.47 ft/sec = 0.45 m/sec = 26.8 m/min = 1.61 km/hr

1 km/hr = 16.7 m/min = 0.28 m/sec = 0.91 ft/sec = 0.62 mph.

## Weights

1 ounce (oz) = 0.0625 lb = 28.35 grams (g) = 0.028 kg

1 pound (lb) = 16 oz = 454 g = 0.454 kg

1 g = 0.035 oz = 0.0022 lb = 0.001 kg

1 kg = 35.27 oz = 2.2 lb = 1000 g

## Temperature

$$0°C = 32°F$$
$$100°C = 212°F$$
$$273°K = 0°C = 32°F$$
$$°C = (°F - 32) \times \tfrac{5}{9}$$
$$°F = (\tfrac{9}{5}\,°C) + 32$$

1111178    $1495

**SECOND EDITION**

# The Physiological Basis of Physical Education and Athletics

DONALD K. MATHEWS

EDWARD L. FOX

*Both of Ohio State University*

Illustrated by Nancy Allison Close

W. B. SAUNDERS COMPANY
Philadelphia • London • Toronto

W. B. Saunders Company:  West Washington Square
Philadelphia, PA 19105

1 St. Anne's Road
Eastbourne, East Sussex BN21 3UN, England

1 Goldthorne Avenue
Toronto, Ontario M8Z 5T9, Canada

**Library of Congress Cataloging in Publication Data**

Mathews, Donald K

The physiological basis of physical education and athletics.

Includes bibliographies and index.

1. Sports—Physiological aspects.  I. Fox, Edward L.,
   joint author.  II. Title. [DNLM: 1. Physical education
   and training.  2. Sport medicine. QT260 M429p]

RC1235.M36 1976    613.7'1    75-10385

ISBN 0-7216-6184-X

The Physiological Basis of Physical Education and Athletics    ISBN  0-7216-6184-X

Last digit is the print number:    9    8    7    6    5    4

Dedicated
to
Ann Roberts Fox

# PREFACE

A *completely* revised text, the second edition contains 12 new chapters, a glossary, and an appendix which describes an interval training program for college women.

The 22 chapters have been collected into 7 sections: Bioenergetics, Neuromuscular Concepts, Cardiorespiratory Considerations, Physical Training, Environmental Aspects, Nutrition and Body Composition, and Special Considerations, which includes a fine chapter on the female athlete and one on the effects of ergogenic aids. Each chapter is summarized and well documented with a recent bibliography, and contains pertinent discussion questions.

As with the first edition, we have written this text for the physical educator and coach. The primary purpose has been to present those essential materials that will help to ensure the safe conduct of sport and physical education programs.

A secondary purpose has been to approach this body of knowledge from a practical standpoint. We have attempted to accomplish this by showing direct applications of the concepts to practical problems that occur on the playing fields and in the gymnasia. Those students with little background in chemistry and physics should not be handicapped. On the other hand, those with competence in the basic science area should find new challenges in the application of their science background to the problems encountered in physical education and athletics.

As in many other fields, a number of old wives' tales are handed down from one generation to the next—a few harmless, some tragic. All should be dispensed with. For example: (1) the boy or girl who lifts weights will become muscle bound; (2) swimmers should not exercise with weights; (3) don't allow water on the playing field; and (4) give salt tablets freely, but withhold water. The latter is especially unfortunate and has precipitated tragedies in sports. The materials covered in this text should allow students to know the scientific or physiological reasons why they do certain things — not simply because their coach before them did it that way.

DONALD K. MATHEWS
EDWARD L. FOX

# CONTENTS

**Section 2**
**NEUROMUSCULAR CONCEPTS**

## Section 4
## PHYSICAL TRAINING

## Section 5
## ENVIRONMENTAL ASPECTS

### Chapter 14
### DIFFUSION, OSMOSIS, AND DROWNING .............................. 319

### Chapter 15
### EXERCISE AND ACID-BASE BALANCE ................................. 332

### Chapter 16
### SCUBA AND PERFORMANCE AT ALTITUDE ......................... 339

## Chapter 17

## HEAT BALANCE: PREVENTION OF HEAT STROKE
## IN ATHLETICS ..................................................................... 362

# Chapter 1

# INTRODUCTION

Today more than ever before it is necessary for the physical educator and coach to recognize the vital part *science* plays in the successful conduct of physical education and athletic programs. Over the past twenty years the number of laboratories dealing with the physiology of exercise has increased. As a result much new knowledge dealing with how best to train teams and develop fitness has appeared in the scientific literature.

Further evidence of advancement in the scientific area was the formation of the American College of Sports Medicine in 1954. The College membership is made up primarily of physiologists, physicians, physical educators, and coaches. This organization meets once a year, at which time research papers covering all aspects of the science of sports are presented. *Medicine and Science in Sports,* published by the College, is a journal containing articles dealing with this broad area.

The Committee on the Medical Aspects of Sports, formed in 1959, is an organization of the American Medical Association. This group does an excellent job in disseminating literature concerned with protecting the health of the athlete as well as holding seminars for coaches, trainers, and physicians.

For you to contribute to the best of your ability to all aspects of physical education and athletics will require a good understanding of the available scientific knowledge. Not only will such understanding result in better teams and better programs of activities but it will also enable you to guard the health of your charges—your primary responsibility! Then too, knowing the reasons *why* you select a particular training program for accomplishing a specific task immediately establishes you as a professional person rather than a mere technician.

In writing the chapters that follow we have worked hard to eliminate those aspects of physiology which from your standpoint might be considered of academic interest only. Our concern has been to cover materials you will be able to put to immediate use in the gymnasium and on the athletic field. In other words, we have tried to keep *you* in mind rather than your professor.

It might be wise at this time to present somewhat of an overview of the chapters which are to follow. This will permit you to obtain a more general understanding as to what we plan to cover. Let us begin by asking you to select a term that might be considered a common denominator for all phases of physical education and athletics. After a little deliberation we hope you would agree with us that *energy* is the term most appropriate. It is for this reason that we consider Chapter 2 as one of the most important for you to master; let us see why this may be true.

It is through the release of energy that a muscle is enabled to contract. The way in which energy stores are depleted depends essentially on the fitness of the person and on the physical activity being performed. You can significantly improve performance through training programs. In other words, you can modify or increase energy stores. The type of program you design will require knowledge about depletion and replacement of these energy stores for the specific activity to be performed.

Food is our *indirect* source of energy. In the body it goes through a profound series of chemical reactions that we will speak of only as chemical or metabolic pathways to form a compound which is our *direct* source of energy. We have depicted these pathways as models or figures. Studying these models will allow you to make valid judgments regarding the training table. Specifically, you will want to know the foods that result in maximum energy yield.

These are a few of the important reasons for comprehending well the information dealing with energy in Chapter 2. Of passing interest, we might mention that the term energy appears in *every* chapter of this book, for after all this is truly what you deal with throughout the field of physical education and athletics.

During activity, energy stores become depleted. Fatigue results. Chapter 3 is devoted to the important metabolic considerations such as the alactacid oxygen debt and the lactacid oxygen debt following exercise which enable the body to recharge its energy systems.

In Chapter 4, our primary mission will be to tell you how energy is *measured* in the exercise physiology laboratory. Knowing the quantity of energy required to perform an activity enables us to report this in units of work or power (if we wish to express the amount of work done in a given period of time). The information contained in Chapter 4 will also permit you to make accurate judgments regarding the strenuousness of a given activity. It will leave you with a basic understanding of how measurement of oxygen consumption indirectly but accurately reflects the energy required in performing an activity. Of interest to you might be knowing how we measure indirectly the energy being expended while an athlete runs a mile or the manner in which scientists at NASA measure the energy required by the astronaut walking in space.

All movement is dependent upon muscular contractions. Teaching skills can be facilitated if the teacher more completely comprehends the *nervous control of muscular movement.* It is especially for this reason that Chapter 5 helps us, the teacher, to better understand what fundamental neural muscular processes are involved as the child commences to learn how to throw, skip, run, and jump.

Once you are reasonably familiar with the way in which nerves and muscles, working together, cause movement, the next consideration is the anatomical organization of a skeletal muscle. Chapter 6 includes not only structure but function of the muscle as well.

What is the best way to develop strength? What equipment is most appropriate for my school or college, e.g., Nautilus? barbells, Mini Gym? Are isometric exercises better than isotonic programs? What is this new term *isokinetic contraction*? These and a number of other questions are answered in Chapter 7. Included are a discussion of flexibility and its relationship to performance, the definition and examples of levers, and suggestions for the formulation of weight lifting programs using the progressive overload principle.

Ventilation (moving the air in and out of the lungs) depends greatly on the physical activity being performed. During rest, the volume may be 5 to 6 liters of air per minute; while at exercise it may reach as high as 170 liters per minute! Chapter 8 helps us understand the physiology and mechanics of pulmonary ventilation during rest and exercise.

Moving oxygen into our bodies for the manufacture of ATP and removing $CO_2$, the by-product of metabolism, constitutes the main ingredients of Chapter 9. Exercise and training may modify the $O_2$ and $CO_2$ exchange systems. Consequently, such knowledge concerning how these modifications may take place becomes important to the coach and the athlete.

Just as the mechanisms for gaseous exchange may be modified through training, blood flow and gas transport mechanisms are likewise affected. Changes in cardiac output, distribution of blood flow, and hemodynamics are covered in Chapter 10.

Through the combined efforts of the respiratory and circulatory centers located in the brain, regulation of pulmonary ventilation and blood flow is enacted. Changes in heart rate, stroke volume, blood distribution to various organs, and venous return are the important circulatory effects considered in Chapter 11, Cardiorespiratory Control.

It is important for you to be familiar with the principles of *interval training,* which are presented in Chapter 12. This knowledge is vital to the training schedule, whether it is track and field, swimming, basketball, or conditioning of the most poorly fit individuals. Other conditioning methods include: sprint training, continuous slow-running and fast-running training, repetition training, and others. However, one thing must be made clear: without a good comprehension of Chapter 2 you will not realize the greatest possible profit from Chapter 12.

A number of anthropometric and physiological changes are brought about through an exercise program: the body loses fat and gains muscular tone; it uses less oxygen in performing light work loads and becomes more efficient; the heart rate is lower during moderate exercise; blood pressure returns to normal more quickly following work. Also, the fit person has greater aerobic and anaerobic power than the unfit person. These and other consequences of training are detailed in Chapter 13.

Chapter 14 considers osmosis, diffusion, and drowning. Although it appears that these subjects are not directly applicable to our interests, nothing could be farther from the truth. Life is maintained at the cellular level and knowledge concerning how particles move into and out of the cell will help us to understand much about the physiology of sport. You will appreciate the sequential events that are likely to occur in a situation of near drowning. As a consequence, you will be better prepared in first-aid procedures. Most important, Chapter 14 lays the foundation for understanding water and electrolyte balance and the hazards involved in severely dehydrating the athlete prior to performance.

The acid-base balance within the body fluids is very carefully regulated. During strenuous work, lactic acid is formed, upsetting this delicate balance temporarily and allowing body fluids to become highly acidic. In Chapter 15, we learn how pulmonary ventilation and the kidney function to maintain a proper acid-base medium.

Exploring appears to be a very natural part of man's heritage. In the fifteenth century Columbus was "in the headlines"; today we read about the exploits of astronauts probing the mysteries of space and aquanauts exploring the depths of the oceans and seas. Once man moves from his habitual environment physical and physiological considerations must be examined and properly dealt with to insure safety and peak performance. In Chapter 16 we will study these considerations, which confront man both under the sea and at altitude. As a result, you should be able to counsel the scuba diver as well as recognize problems which will confront the athlete who performs at altitude (elevations exceeding 5000 feet).

It is a fact that lack of knowledge concerning the heat balance of the athlete is responsible for 25 per cent of the fatalities in football. Mastery of the material covered in Chapter 17 will help to guard against water and salt (electrolyte) imbalance in the athlete. If such imbalances do occur, the ability of teams to operate at peak efficiency will be significantly diminished, and the danger of heat illness will be greatly increased.

You will learn how easy it is to condition or *acclimatize* athletes to work more efficiently in hot environments. We will also discuss the problems associated with the individual's ability to lose heat because of protective clothing as well as how to guard against the cold.

To perform at peak efficiency, an athlete (or anyone for that matter) must be well nourished. The material in Chapter 18 not only helps you to teach proper dietary practices, but includes suggestions for nutrition before, during, and following participation. You will find a suggested dietary regimen to increase glycogen stores for endurance events. The subject of obesity—its definition and suggestions for contending with the problem—completes the chapter.

Success in performance to some extent is related to the person's body type. Football players are heavily muscular (mesomorphs), while gymnasts and skiers for example are more lithe (ectomorphs). Two methods of appraising physiques (somatotyping) are discussed in Chapter 19. Instructions for determining certain skinfolds and other anthropometric measures are also covered. Methods for computing lean body mass and predicting minimal weights for high school wrestlers are highlights of this chapter.

Sometimes, a coach or an athlete resorts to measures other than conditioning and skill practice to improve athletic performance. Such work aids (ergogenic aids) may include music, shouting words of encouragement, and psychological aids including hypnosis. Too often, drugs are used as ergogenic aids with the hope that they will improve performance. In Chapter 20, you will learn what scientific studies have shown about such practices as: blood doping, the use of amphetamines, breathing oxygen, the use of steroids and others.

Today, female athletics have reached a status of prominence heretofore unheard of, and their popularity continues to grow. A most extensive coverage dealing with exercise and training of the female appears in Chapter 21. Body size, composition, energy systems, strength, and performance records of the female, with some comparisons with the male, make this a valuable chapter. A fine bibliography containing more than 70 scientific studies helps make this one of the better chapters in the book.

Our final chapter, Chapter 22, includes a number of tests and measurements that can be used to quantitate some of the materials we have studied. Their use will help you implement in a more objective manner the information contained in the various chapters. For example, the measurement of weight can be an extremely important index of the athlete's health status. We will also consider the physiological principles fundamental to weight gain and loss. Understanding measurement of temperature, humidity, and solar radiation will give you a greater appreciation of how such environmental conditions may affect performance. Power too is very important to athletic success. We have defined several ways in which this can be measured. Finally, the most valid test for measuring fitness—the maximal amount of oxygen a person can consume—is included.

There is a glossary plus five appendices. Appendix A is a list of symbols and abbreviations used by physiologists in this country and elsewhere; also included are a number of typical resting values for selected respiratory tests. Appendix B is a comprehensive discussion of gas laws and their application to exercise physiology. Appendix C gives the calculation of oxygen consumption and carbon dioxide production. Appendix D provides a basic weight lifting program; Appendix E includes examples of interval training programs for college men and women. The models were developed as a consequence of sponsored research at Ohio State University.

## SELECTED READINGS

Periodicals dealing predominantly with the science of exercise physiology, physical education, and athletics:

Ergonomics

The European Journal of Applied Physiology (Europ. J. Appl. Physiol., formerly Arbeitsphysiologie (Arbeitsphysiol.) and Internationale Zeitschrift fur Angewandte Physiologie Einschlesslich Arbeitsphysiologie (Int. Z. Angew. Physiol.)

Journal of Applied Physiology (J. Appl. Physiol.)

Journal of Sports Medicine and Physical Fitness (J. Sports Med.)

Medicine and Science in Sports (Med. Sci. Sports)

The Physician and Sportsmedicine (Phys. Sports Med.)

Research Quarterly (Res. Quart.)

Books dealing with the physiology of exercise and human performance:

Åstrand, P.-O., and Rodahl, K.: Textbook of Work Physiology. New York, McGraw-Hill Book Co., 1970.

Brown, R., and Kenyon, G. (eds.): Classical Studies on Physical Activity. Englewood Cliffs, N.J., Prentice-Hall, Inc., 1968.

deVries, H.: Physiology of Exercise for Physical Education and Athletics. 2nd ed., Dubuque, Iowa, Wm. C. Brown Co., Inc., 1974.

Encyclopedia of Sport Sciences and Medicine. The Am. College of Sports Med. New York, Macmillan Publishing Co., Inc., 1971.

Falls, H. (ed.): Exercise Physiology. New York, Academic Press, Inc., 1968.

Horvath, S., and Horvath, E.: The Harvard Fatigue Laboratory: Its History and Contributions. Englewood Cliffs, N. J., Prentice-Hall, Inc., 1973.

Jensen, C., and Fisher, A.: Scientific Basis of Athletic Conditioning. Philadelphia, Lea & Febiger, 1972.

Johnson, E., and Buskirk, E. (eds.): Science and Medicine of Exercise and Sports. 2nd ed., New York, Harper and Row Publishers, Inc., 1973.

Karpovich, P., and Sinning, W.: Physiology of Muscular Activity. 7th ed., Philadelphia, W. B. Saunders Co., 1971.

Larson, L. (ed.): Fitness, Health, and Work Capacity: International Standards For Assessment. New York, Macmillan Publishing Co., Inc., 1974.

Mathews, D. K., Stacy, R., and Hoover, G.: Physiology of Muscular Activity and Exercise. New York, The Ronald Press Company, 1964.

Morehouse, L. E., and Miller, A. T.: Physiology of Exercise. 6th ed., St. Louis, C. V. Mosby Co., 1971.

Rarick, G. (ed.): Physical Activity: Human Growth and Development. New York, Academic Press, Inc., 1973.

Ricci, B.: Physiological Basis of Human Performance. Philadelphia, Lea & Febiger, 1967.

Robinson, S.: Physiology of Muscular Exercise. In Mountcastle, V. (ed.): Medical Physiology. 13th ed., vol 2, Chap. 55, St. Louis, C. V. Mosby Co., 1974.

Ryan, J. A., and Allman, F. L., Jr. (eds.): Sports Medicine. New York, Academic Press, Inc., 1974.

Shephard, R.: Alive Man! The Physiology of Physical Activity. Springfield, Ill., Charles C Thomas, 1972.

Simonson, E.: Physiology of Work Capacity and Fatigue. Springfield, Ill., Charles C Thomas, 1971.

Wilmore, J. (ed.): Exercise and Sport Sciences Reviews. vol. 1, New York, Academic Press, Inc., 1973.

# SECTION 1 _____

# BIOENERGETICS

# ENERGY SOURCES

The main theme of this chapter is energy—what it is, where it comes from, and how it is used. The objective is to enable you, as a physical educator and coach, to apply in the gymnasia, on the athletic fields, and in the classrooms the knowledge gained from its understanding. Perhaps the most important information you will learn in this chapter is the scientific basis for the development of athletic training and conditioning programs. For example, has the thought ever occurred to you that there is an important reason why the sprinter should be trained differently from the distance runner? Have you ever thought about what fatigue is and how its onset may be delayed in certain activities? As our primary concern is energy sources, the materials contained in this chapter will also enable you to better understand statements regarding the training table and the values of so-called high energy foods. These are but a few of the extremely important reasons for understanding energy sources or the *bioenergetics of physical education.*

## ENERGY DEFINED

Before much meaning can be given to a discussion of energy sources, we need to define energy. Probably all of us have some idea of the nature of energy. Such common words as force, power, strength, vigor, movement, life, and even spirit more or less suggest the idea of energy. These terms, however, do not give us a satisfactory description

**9**

of the exact meaning of energy. Furthermore, they do not lend themselves to scientific quantitation. Scientists, therefore, define energy as the *capacity to perform work. Work* they define as the application of a force through a distance. As a result, energy and work are inseparable. We will be concerned with the relationships between energy and work in Chapter 4. Right now, let us continue with our discussion of energy.

There are six forms of energy: (1) chemical, (2) mechanical, (3) heat, (4) light, (5) electrical, and (6) nuclear. Each can be converted from one form to another. This "transformation of energy" is a fascinating and exciting story, particularly as applied to the biological world. Specifically, we are interested in the transformation of chemical energy into mechanical energy because mechanical energy finds its manifestations in human movement, the source of which comes from converting food to chemical energy within our body.

## THE BIOLOGICAL ENERGY CYCLE

All energy in our solar system originates in the sun. Where does this energy, called solar energy, come from? Solar energy actually arises from nuclear energy. Some of this nuclear energy reaches the earth as sunlight or light energy. The millions of green plants that populate our earth store a portion of this energy from the sunlight in still another form—chemical energy. In turn, this chemical energy is utilized by green plants to build food molecules such as glucose, cellulose, proteins, and lipids from carbon dioxide ($CO_2$) and water ($H_2O$). This process whereby green plants manufacture their own food is called *photosynthesis.* We, on the other hand, are not capable of doing this; we must eat plants and other animals for our food supplies. We are, therefore, directly dependent on plant life, and ultimately on the sun, for our energy.

Food in the presence of $O_2$ is broken down to $CO_2$ and $H_2O$ with the liberation of chemical energy by a process called *respiration.* The sole purpose of respiration is to supply the energy we need to carry out such biological processes as the chemical work of growth and the mechanical work of muscular contraction. This entire process is called the biological energy cycle (Fig. 2–1).

## ATP

We now know what energy is, where it originates, and that it is supplied to man by the foods he eats. Our next problem is to understand how this energy is used to perform work; in our case, the mechanical work of muscular contraction. The energy liberated during the breakdown of food is *not directly* used to do work. Rather, it is

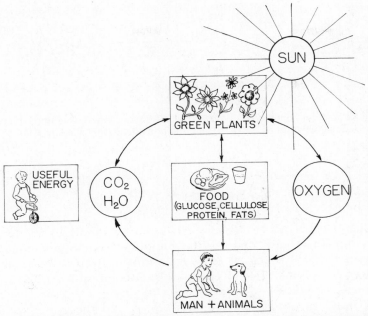

**Figure 2–1** The biological energy cycle. Energy from sunlight is used by plants to build food molecules from $CO_2$ and $H_2O$, with oxygen being given off. Both plants and animals in turn use oxygen to break down foods for the energy they need to live.

employed to manufacture another chemical compound called *adenosine triphosphate* or, more simply, *ATP*, which is stored in all muscle cells. Only from the energy released by the breakdown of this compound can the cell perform its specialized work.

The structure of ATP consists of one very complex component, adenosine, and three less complicated parts called phosphate groups. For our purposes, its chemical importance lies in the phosphate groups. In Figure 2–2A, a simplified structure of ATP is shown. The bonds between the two terminal phosphate groups represent so-called high energy bonds. When one of these phosphate bonds is broken, i.e., removed from the rest of the molecule, 7000 to 12,000 calories* of energy are liberated and adenosine diphosphate (ADP) plus free phosphate (Pi) are formed (Fig. 2–2, *B*). *This energy released during the breakdown of ATP represents the immediate source of energy that can be used by the muscle cell to perform its work.*

---

*Calorie (cal.) is the amount of heat energy required to raise 1 gram (gm.) of water 1 degree Centigrade (°C.). The large calorie or kilocalorie (kcal.) is the amount of heat required to raise 1 kilogram (kg.) of water 1° C. The latter will be the caloric term used most often in this text.

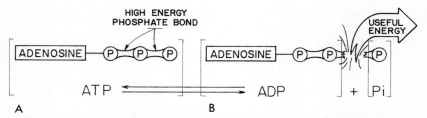

**Figure 2–2** *A,* Simplified structure of ATP, showing high energy phosphate bonds. *B,* Breakdown of ATP to ADP and free phosphate (Pi), with liberation of useful energy.

# Sources of ATP

The fact that ATP is the immediate source of energy for contraction prompts us to ask, "How is this important compound supplied to each muscle cell?" There are three ways in which this is accomplished. The least complicated from a chemical standpoint is the *ATP-PC system.* It involves the breakdown of only one compound, *phosphocreatine* (PC). In the other two ways (the *lactic acid system* and the *oxygen system*), a series of complicated chemical reactions involving the breakdown of foodstuffs provides the main source of energy for ATP formation. These two mechanisms are referred to as the *chemical* or *metabolic pathways.* However, all three suppliers of ATP operate in the same general manner. The energy liberated from the breakdown of foodstuffs and the energy released when PC is broken down are used to put the ATP molecule back together again, that is, the energy is used to "drive" the reaction shown in Figure 2–2, *B* from right to left. In other words, the energy released from one series of reactions is *coupled* with the energy needs of another series of reactions. Biochemically, this is referred to as *coupled reactions.*

## The ATP-PC System

Since this mechanism is least complicated (but in no way least important), we will discuss it first. Phosphocreatine, like ATP, is stored in muscle cells. It is also similar to ATP in that when its phosphate group is removed, a large amount of energy is liberated (Fig. 2–3). The end products of this breakdown are creatine and free phosphate. This energy is immediately available and is used directly to resynthesize ATP. For example, as rapidly as ATP is broken down during muscular contraction, it is continuously re-formed from ADP and Pi by the energy liberated during the breakdown of the stored PC. Ironically, the only means by which PC can be re-formed from Pi and creatine is from the energy released by the breakdown of ATP! The primary source of

ATP for this, however, comes from that obtained through the break-down of foodstuffs. We will discuss this in more detail later.

In Table 2–1, there is a summary of the ATP-PC system with respect to the body's total energy content. Note that storage of PC in the muscle exceeds that of ATP; this makes sense because PC is used to resynthesize ATP. From the table we can determine how much oxygen per kilogram of muscle is required to produce a given amount of ATP plus PC. For example, it requires 66 to 81 ml. oxygen per kilogram of muscle to manufacture 19 to 23 millimoles (mM.) ATP plus PC (collectively ATP and PC are called phosphagens). For your total muscle mass, this is about the amount of oxygen you would consume reading this book for 8 to 10 minutes.

The importance of the ATP-PC system to physical education and athletics is exemplified by the powerful, quick starts of sprinters, football players, high jumpers, and shot putters, and by similar feats that require only a few seconds to complete (running all-out up a flight of stairs). This system is not dependent on a series of reactions nor on the oxygen we breathe and for this reason *it represents the most rapid available source of ATP for use by the muscle.*

### The Chemical or Metabolic Pathways

One of the chemical pathways in which ATP is formed involves an incomplete breakdown of food to lactic acid, while in the other the foodstuffs are broken down completely to $CO_2$ and $H_2O$. Both, however, occur within the muscle cell. The pathway in which lactic acid is formed, i.e., the *lactic acid system:* (1) does *not* require the use of oxygen, (2) uses *only* carbohydrates (glycogen and glucose) as its food fuel, and (3) produces relatively *few* ATP molecules. The food fuel enters the pathway in its simple form as glucose but is stored in the muscle and liver as glycogen.

On the other hand, the pathway in which $CO_2$ and $H_2O$ are formed, i.e., the *oxygen system:* (1) *requires* the presence of oxygen, (2)

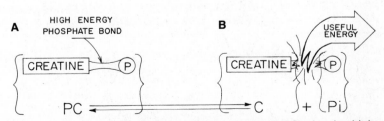

**Figure 2–3** *A,* Simplified structure of phosphocreatine (PC), showing high energy phosphate bond. *B,* Breakdown of PC to creatine (C) and free phosphate (Pi), with liberation of energy to resynthesize ATP.

**Table 2–1  ESTIMATION OF THE ENERGY AVAILABLE IN THE BODY THROUGH THE ATP-PC SYSTEM**

|  | ATP | PC | ATP + PC |
|---|---|---|---|
| 1. Muscular concentration |  |  |  |
| a. mM./kg. muscle* | 4–6 | 15–17 | 19–23 |
| b. mM. total muscle mass† | 120–180 | 450–510 | 570–690 |
| 2. Useful energy‡ |  |  |  |
| a. kcal./kg. muscle | 0.04–0.06 | 0.15–0.17 | 0.19–0.23 |
| b. kcal. total muscle mass | 1.2–1.8 | 4.5–5.1 | 5.7–6.9 |
| 3. Oxygen equivalence** |  |  |  |
| a. ml./kg. muscle | 14–21 | 53–60 | 67–81 |
| b. ml. total muscle mass | 420–630 | 1590–1800 | 2010–2430 |

*Based on data from Hultman[7] and Karlsson.[8]
†Assuming 30 kg. of muscle in a 70-kg. man.
‡Assuming 10 kcal. per mole ATP.
**Assuming 3.5 liters $O_2$ required to aerobically manufacture one mole of ATP (see p. 18).

can use *all three foodstuffs* (fats, proteins, carbohydrates) as fuel, and (3) yields a relatively *large* amount of ATP. Since the former pathway, like the ATP-PC system, does not require oxygen, it is defined as an *anaerobic pathway* or an anaerobic source of energy (ATP). The latter pathway, which requires oxygen, is called an *aerobic pathway* and thus an aerobic source of energy (ATP). Some general characteristics of the three mechanisms by which ATP is formed are contained in Table 2–2.

## The Anaerobic Pathway (Lactic Acid System)

The anaerobic pathway was discovered in the 1930's by two German scientists, Gustav Embden and Otto Meyerhof. For this reason, it is often called the Embden-Meyerhof cycle. More commonly, it is referred to as glycolysis, which simply means the "dissolving of sugar." The reason for this, as you will recall, is that this pathway uses glucose (sugar) exclusively for the manufacture of ATP.

**Table 2–2  GENERAL CHARACTERISTICS OF THE THREE MECHANISMS BY WHICH ATP IS FORMED**

| MECHANISM | FOOD OR CHEMICAL FUEL | $O_2$ REQUIRED | RELATIVE ATP PRODUCTION |
|---|---|---|---|
| ANAEROBIC |  |  |  |
| ATP-PC system | Phosphocreatine | No | Few; limited |
| Lactic acid system | Glycogen (glucose) | No | Few; limited |
| AEROBIC |  |  |  |
| Oxygen system | Glycogen, fats, proteins | Yes | Many; unlimited |

What becomes of this glucose? In the absence of oxygen, glucose is only partially broken down by a very complicated series of reactions. In man the end product is *lactic acid;* ATP is also formed in a coupled reaction. Lactic acid is actually a by-product, and when it accumulates to high levels, it causes muscular fatigue. This latter point is fundamental to the understanding of fatigue; more will be said about it later. The production of ATP, on the other hand, is the sole purpose of glycolysis. For every glucose molecule that undergoes glycolysis, a net of 2 ATP molecules is produced. This yield represents only about 5 per cent of the total yield possible when the same amount of glucose is completely broken down to $CO_2$ and $H_2O$ in the presence of oxygen (aerobic pathway). However, this anaerobic pathway, like the ATP-PC system, is extremely important to us, primarily because it also provides a very rapid supply of ATP. For example, exercises that can be performed at maximum rate for only about 2 or 3 minutes, such as sprints and underwater swimming (breath holding), depend primarily upon the ATP-PC and lactic acid systems for ATP formation.

The total energy available in the body through the lactic acid system is estimated in Table 2–3. Notice that if the muscles can tolerate 2.0 to 2.3 grams of lactic acid per kilogram of muscle, or 60 grams for the total muscle mass, then the maximal amount of ATP manufactured by glycolysis would be between 1.0 and 1.2 moles (1000 to 1200 millimoles). This is about twice as much ATP as that which is obtainable from the ATP-PC system. Also, notice that in order to manufacture the equivalent ATP via the consumption of oxygen, it would take about 15 minutes of rest.

### The Aerobic Pathway (Oxygen System)

In the presence of oxygen, a glucose molecule is completely broken down to $CO_2$ and $H_2O$ and a total of 38 molecules of ATP is

**Table 2–3  ESTIMATION OF THE ENERGY AVAILABLE IN THE BODY THROUGH THE LACTIC ACID SYSTEM***

|  | PER KG. MUSCLE | TOTAL MUSCLE MASS |
|---|---|---|
| 1. Maximal lactic acid tolerance (grams)† | 2.0–2.3 | 60–70 |
| 2. ATP formation (millimoles) | 33–38 | 1000–1200 |
| 3. Useful energy (kilocalories) | 0.33–0.38 | 10.0–12.0 |
| 4. Oxygen equivalence (milliliters) | 115.5–133.0 | 3500–4200 |

*Assumptions same as in Table 2–1.
†Based on data from Karlsson.[8]

produced. Two of these molecules of ATP come from glycolysis. This may come as a surprise to you since we just said that glycolysis is an anaerobic pathway. Actually, there is only one difference between the anaerobic glycolysis we discussed earlier and the glycolysis that occurs when there is a sufficient supply of oxygen—*lactic acid does not accumulate in the presence of oxygen*. In other words, the presence of oxygen inhibits the accumulation of lactic acid but not the formation of ATP. Oxygen does this by diverting the majority of the lactic acid precursor, pyruvic acid, into the aerobic pathway *after* the ATP is formed. It is in the aerobic pathway that glucose, which has already been broken down to pyruvic acid, is further broken down to $CO_2$ and $H_2O$, with the simultaneous production of additional ATP (Fig. 2–4). There are two series of reactions involved in the oxygen system: (1) the Krebs cycle and (2) the electron transport system.

**The Krebs Cycle.** One of the specific series of complex reactions within the oxygen system is called the *Krebs cycle* after its discoverer, Sir Hans Krebs. For this important discovery, he won a Nobel Prize in 1953. This cycle is also known as the tricarboxylic acid (TCA) cycle and as the citric acid cycle. It takes place in all aerobic cells (like skeletal muscle) in a specialized subcellular compartment called the *mitochondrion*. There are two main chemical changes that occur during the Krebs cycle: (1) the production of $CO_2$ and (2) the removal of electrons (oxidation). The $CO_2$ produced is eliminated from the body by the respiratory system (lungs). The electrons removed are in the form of

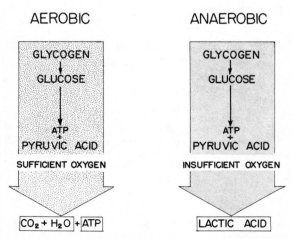

**Figure 2–4** Aerobic and anaerobic pathways. Note that breakdown of glycogen to pyruvic acid with ATP formation does not require oxygen. With oxygen present, pyruvic acid is further broken down to $CO_2$ and $H_2O$ with more ATP formation; without oxygen, pyruvic acid is converted to lactic acid with no further ATP formation.

a hydrogen atom, which contains a positive charge (called a proton) and a negative charge called an *electron*. In other words:

$$H \longrightarrow H^+ \qquad + \qquad e^-$$

hydrogen atom        hydrogen ion            electron

The Krebs cycle is shown schematically in Figure 2–5.

**The Electron Transport System (ETS).** The end product, $H_2O$, is formed from the hydrogen ions and electrons that are removed in the Krebs cycle and the *oxygen* we breathe. The specific series of reactions in which $H_2O$ is formed is called the *electron transport system or the respiratory chain;* this also takes place in mitochondria. Essentially what happens in the ETS is that the hydrogen ions and electrons are "transported" to oxygen by a series of enzymatic reactions, the end product of which is water. In other words:

$$4H^+ + 4e^- + O_2 \rightarrow 2H_2O$$

that is, 4 hydrogen ions plus 4 electrons plus oxygen yields 2 moles of water.

You may have noticed by now that we have not yet mentioned the formation of ATP. After all, this is the sole purpose of metabolism. ATP is formed by coupled reactions at the same time water is formed, i.e., when the hydrogen ions and electrons are transported by the ETS. This is true because as the electrons are transported, energy is released. The energy released is then coupled with the energy needs of the reaction in which ATP is formed (ADP + Pi → ATP). This is analogous to a waterfall, in which the water at the top of the falls (the hydrogen

**Figure 2–5** The Krebs cycle. Pyruvic acid, the end-product of aerobic glycolysis, enters the Krebs cycle after a slight chemical alteration. Once in the cycle, two further chemical events take place: (1) the release of $CO_2$, which eventually is eliminated by the lungs; and (2) oxidation, i.e., the removal of hydrogen ions ($H^+$) and electrons ($e^-$), which ultimately enter the electron transport system for further chemical alterations.

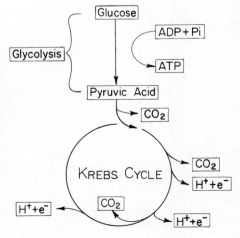

ions and electrons as removed by the Krebs cycle) possesses its highest energy level and the water at the bottom of the falls (formation of water), its lowest. As the water plunges, energy is released for the formation of ATP. This is shown in Figure 2–6.

The summary equation for the aerobic breakdown of one mole of glucose (180 grams, or about 6 ounces) is as follows:

$$C_6H_{12}O_6 + 6O_2 + 38ADP + 38Pi \rightarrow 6CO_2 + 6H_2O + 38ATP$$
(glucose)

From this equation, we can see that for one mole of glucose it requires on the average 3.5 liters of oxygen to aerobically manufacture one mole of ATP (1 mole of $O_2$ = 22.4 liters, therefore, 6 moles of $O_2$ = 6 × 22.4 = 134.4 liters $O_2$; 134.4 liters $O_2$ ÷ 38 moles ATP = 3.5 liters $O_2$ per mole ATP).

It is difficult to estimate the total muscular energy that can be manufactured through the oxygen system. This is true because the Krebs cycle and the electron transport system also serve as pathways for the

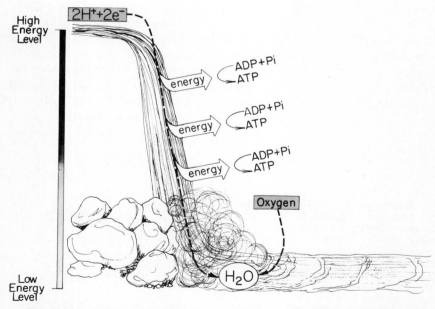

**Figure 2–6**  The electron transport system. The hydrogen ions (H⁺) and electrons (e⁻) removed in the Krebs cycle have a high energy level as they enter the electron transport system. Here, two major chemical events take place. First, the hydrogen ions and electrons are "transported" to the oxygen we breathe to form water ($H_2O$) by a series of enzymatic reactions and, second, at the same time, ATP is formed in coupled reactions from the energy released.

final breakdown of fats and protein to $CO_2$ and $H_2O$, with ATP formation. However, as a basis for comparison with the other two systems, the total aerobic energy available in the muscles from glycogen alone is given in Table 2–4. It is easily seen that the oxygen system is by far the most efficient with respect to ATP production. For example, the amount of ATP available from the aerobic breakdown of all the muscle glycogen in the body is between 87 and 98 moles! This is nearly 50 times more than that made available by the other two systems combined and requires nearly an entire day of rest (20–23 hours) to generate.

The aerobic pathway is predominantly used during long-term exercises which are performed at a submaximal rate. This is so because during such activities there is ample time for the oxygen transport system to supply the muscle cells with enough oxygen, which in turn can supply most of the ATP demanded by the exercise. A summary of the oxygen system is shown in Figure 2–7.

As a final consideration, let us compare the maximal capacity and power of the three energy systems. Capacity refers to an amount independent of time, while power refers to a rate, i.e., an amount in a given time period. From what we have already said concerning the energy systems, you should be able to rank them with respect to both their relative capacities and powers. To check your answers, consult Table 2–5.

## The Aerobic and Anaerobic Pathways During Rest and Exercise

There are at least three important features of the anaerobic and aerobic pathways under conditions of rest and exercise that need further consideration: (1) the types of foodstuffs being metabolized, (2) the relative roles played by each pathway, and (3) the presence and accumulation of lactic acid in the blood.

### Table 2–4  ESTIMATION OF THE ENERGY AVAILABLE FROM MUSCLE GLYCOGEN THROUGH THE OXYGEN SYSTEM*

| | MUSCLE GLYCOGEN | |
|---|---|---|
| | *Per kg. Muscle* | *Total Muscle Mass* |
| 1. Muscular concentration (grams) | 13–15† | 400–450 |
| 2. ATP formation (moles) | 2.8–3.2 | 87–98 |
| 3. Useful energy (kcal.) | 28–32 | 870–980 |
| 4. $O_2$ equivalence (liters) | 9.8–11.2 | 304–343 |

*Assumptions the same as in Table 2–1.
†Based on data from Hultman.[7]

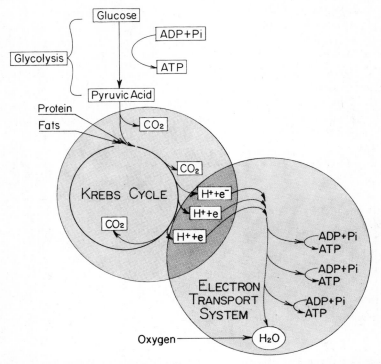

**Figure 2–7** Summary of the oxygen system. Glucose is oxidized in two major series of chemical reactions; the Krebs cycle where $CO_2$ is produced and $H^+$ and $e^-$ are removed, and the electron transport system where $H_2O$ and ATP are formed. Fats and proteins, when used for ATP production, also go through the Krebs cycle and electron transport system.

## Rest

From Figure 2–8, *A*, we see that under resting conditions about two-thirds of the food fuel is contributed by fats, and the other one-third by glucose. Although protein is shown in the diagram, its contribution as a food fuel is negligible. Also, as is indicated, the aerobic pathway is the

**Table 2–5  MAXIMAL CAPACITY AND POWER OF THE THREE ENERGY SYSTEMS**

| SYSTEM | MAXIMAL POWER (MOLES OF ATP PER MINUTE) | MAXIMAL CAPACITY (TOTAL MOLES ATP AVAILABLE) |
|---|---|---|
| ATP-PC | 3.6 | 0.7 |
| Lactic acid | 1.6 | 1.2 |
| Oxygen (from glycogen only) | 1.0 | 90.0 |

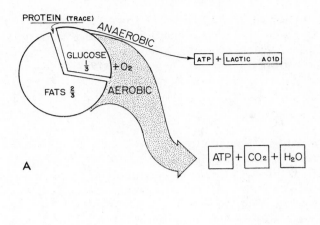

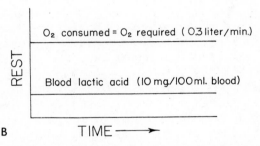

**Figure 2-8**  *A*, The aerobic pathway supplies all the ATP required in the resting state. *B*, During rest, oxygen consumption (0.3 liter/minute) remains constant and is adequate to supply the required ATP; as a consequence, blood lactic acid level remains within the normal range (10 mg./100 ml.). The combination of these factors indicates that metabolism is aerobic.

only pathway in operation. This is true because our oxygen transport system is capable of supplying each cell with sufficient oxygen and, therefore, with adequate ATP to satisfy all the energy requirements of the resting state (Fig. 2–8, *B*). The 2 ATP molecules shown coming from the anaerobic pathway are considered as part of the aerobic yield since, as we indicated earlier, they are likewise formed in the presence of oxygen.

Although the aerobic pathway is the only one in operation, perhaps you have noticed (Fig. 2–8, *B*) that there is a small but constant amount of lactic acid present in the blood (about 10 mg. for every 100 ml. of blood).* The reason for this is rather complicated and a thorough understanding would require considerable knowledge of the

---

*Ten milligrams (mg.) in 100 milliliters (ml.) of blood is usually expressed as milligrams per cent (mg. per cent). Another example: 15 gm. of hemoglobin in 100 ml. of blood would be read as 15 gm. per cent.

chemistry of the individual reactions involved. For our purposes, the fact that the lactic acid level remains constant and does not accumulate tells us that anaerobic glycolysis is *not* operating. We see, then, that at rest the foodstuffs utilized are fats and glucose and the necessary ATP is supplied solely by the aerobic pathway.

## Exercise

Both pathways contribute ATP molecules during exercise; however-er, their relative roles are dependent upon the types of exercises performed. To begin our discussion, we can divide the many types of exercises into two categories: (1) exercises that can be performed for only short periods of time but which require maximal effort, and (2) exercises that can be performed for relatively long periods of time but which require submaximal effort. Later we will point out the interaction and significance of the roles played by both pathways in exercises that do not easily fit into one or the other of these categories. The understanding of this concept is vitally important to you in planning training programs.

**Exercises of Short Duration.** Exercises in this category include sprinting events such as the 100-, 220-, and 440-yard dashes, the 880-yard run, push-ups, and other events in which the required rate of work can be maintained only for 2 or possibly 3 minutes.

Figure 2–9, *A* shows the relative roles of the metabolic pathways when performing these types of exercises. Here we see that the major food fuel is glucose, with fats minor, and proteins—once again—negligible contributors. We also see that the predominant pathway is anaerobic. This does not mean to imply, however, that it is the *only* pathway operating. It merely indicates that the energy or ATP required for these types of exercises cannot be supplied via the aerobic pathway alone. As a consequence, most of the ATP must be supplied anaerobically by the ATP-PC and lactic acid systems.

There are two reasons why there is a limitation of the aerobic pathway in supplying adequate ATP during the performance of any exercise: (1) Each of us has a ceiling for his or her aerobic capacity or the maximum rate at which we can consume oxygen; and (2) it takes at least 2 or 3 minutes for oxygen consumption to increase to a new, higher level. For example, trained athletes have aerobic capacities of between 3.0 and 5.0 liters of $O_2$ per minute, for females[3] and males,[10] respectively, whereas the maximum for the untrained female[4] is around 2.2 liters per minute and for the untrained male,[5] 3.2 liters per minute. These levels of $O_2$ consumption are not nearly enough in either case to supply all the ATP needed for such an effort as the 100-yard dash, which may require between 45 to 60 liters per minute (8 to 10 liters of $O_2$ per 100 yards or per 10 seconds).

Even if it were possible to consume oxygen at a rate that would alone meet the energy or ATP requirement, it would take the first 2 or 3 minutes of exercise to accelerate the oxygen consumption to the required level. The reason for this delayed increase in oxygen consumption deals with the time it takes for adequate biochemical and physiological adjustments to become manifest. This holds true during the transition from rest to an exercise of any intensity and from an exercise of lower intensity to one of greater intensity. The period during which the level of oxygen consumption is below that necessary to supply all the ATP required of any exercise is called the *oxygen deficit* (Fig. 2–9, *B*). It is during this oxygen deficit period that the ATP-PC and lactic acid systems are called upon to supply most of the ATP required for the exercise. This means that during short term but high intensity exercises such as those mentioned before, there will always be an oxygen deficit throughout the duration of the exercise, with the major source of ATP from the two anaerobic systems. Later we will see that this is not necessarily true for prolonged but lower intensity exercises.

From Figure 2–9, *C* we see that the rapid acceleration in anaerobic glycolysis is accompanied by an equally rapid accumulation of lactic acid. As the glycogen stores, which supply glucose for glycolysis, are used, lactic acid accumulation reaches maximum levels in the muscles and blood. With high lactic acid levels, muscular contraction is inhibited and the depletion of glycogen stores means the muscle has run out of fuel. These changes cause *fatigue* and either the exercise must be terminated or its intensity greatly reduced. This is why the ability to tolerate high levels of lactic acid and endure the discomforts of fatigue in general are prerequisites for success in most athletic events. Blood lactic acid levels as high as 200 mg. per cent have been recorded during competitive sprinting events in track and in swimming.[9] Such high levels are some 20 times greater than those normally found under resting conditions (10 mg. per cent).

The level of blood lactic acid, then, is an excellent indicator of which pathway is predominantly used during exercise. If the level is high, the primary pathway used must have been the anaerobic; if the level is low, the aerobic pathway predominated.

**Prolonged Exercises.**    Any exercise that can be maintained for relatively long periods of time should be included under this category. By relatively long periods of time, we mean 5 minutes or longer. In such cases, the major foodstuffs are again glucose and fats (Fig. 2–10, *A*). However, at the beginning of an exercise, such as an hour or two of running, the major foodstuff used is glucose, whereas by the end of exercise, fats have assumed the major role. This changeover in fuel gradually occurs as the glycogen stores are depleted.

In these types of exercises, the major source of ATP is supplied by the aerobic pathway. The lactic acid and ATP-PC systems also contrib-

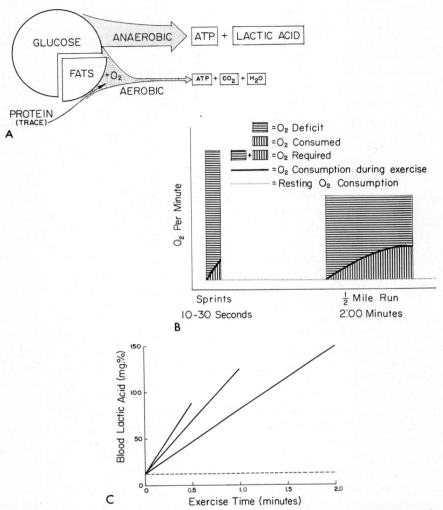

**Figure 2–9** *A,* During all-out exercises of short duration the anaerobic pathway along with the ATP-PC system (not shown) supplies most of the required ATP. *B,* Relationship among oxygen deficit, oxygen consumed, and oxygen required during exhaustive exercises of short duration. *C,* Accumulation of lactic acid in the blood during all-out exercises lasting from 30 seconds to 2 minutes.

ute, but only at the *beginning* of the exercise, before oxygen consumption reaches a new steady state level; during this time an oxygen deficit is incurred. Once oxygen consumption reaches a new steady state level (in about 2 or 3 minutes) it is sufficient to supply all the energy required for the exercise (Fig. 2–10, *B*). For this reason, blood lactic acid does not accumulate to very high levels. Anaerobic glycolysis shuts down once steady state is reached and the small amount of lactic acid accumulated prior to this time remains relatively constant until the end of the exercise (Fig. 2–10, C). A good example of this is during marathon running.[2, 6] These athletes run 26.2 miles in about 2.5 hours, but at the end of the race their blood lactic acid levels are only about two to three times those found at rest. The fatigue experienced by these run-

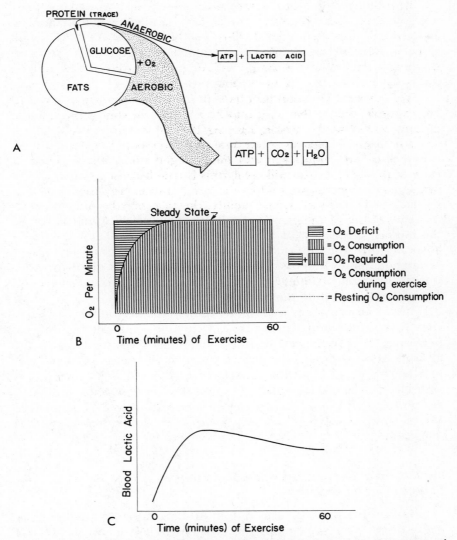

**Figure 2–10** *A,* During prolonged submaximal exercises, the major source of ATP is the aerobic pathway. *B,* The lactic acid and ATP-PC systems also contribute ATP, but only at the beginning of submaximal exercise ($O_2$ deficit), before oxygen consumption reaches a steady state. *C,* Once a steady-state oxygen consumption is reached, the small amount of lactic acid accumulated during the $O_2$ deficit period remains relatively constant until the end of exercise.

ners at the end of a race is, therefore, due to factors other than high blood lactic acid levels. Some of the more important factors leading to this type of fatigue are: (1) low blood glucose levels due to depletion of liver and muscle glycogen stores; (2) loss of water (dehydration) and electrolytes, which leads to high body temperature; and (3) boredom and the physical beating in general that the body has sustained.[1]

In prolonged activities of very low intensity, such as walking, playing golf, and certain industrial tasks, lactic acid does not accumulate above the normal resting level. This is so because the ATP-PC system alone is sufficient to supply the additional energy needed prior to reaching a steady state of oxygen consumption. In these cases, fatigue can be delayed up to 6 hours or more.

The above information can be extremely useful to you as a coach. For example, one of the most important aspects of competitive middle distance and distance running is pacing. If an athlete starts an endurance race too fast or begins his or her final sprint too soon, lactic acid will accumulate to very high levels and the glycogen stores will be depleted early in the race. As you will recall, this is true because as the intensity of the exercise increases, so does the amount of energy required from the anaerobic pathway. Consequently, the race may be lost, owing to this early onset of fatigue. The well informed coach would never let this happen. Instead, from a physiological standpoint, he or she would advocate that the athlete maintain a steady, but sufficient, pace throughout most of the race, then finish with an all-out effort. In other words, the onset of fatigue due to lactic acid and glycogen depletion should be delayed until the end of the race.

Just as anaerobic capacity is important in the performance of exercises of short duration, the aerobic capacity is a significant factor in the performance of prolonged activities. This stems from the fact that the aerobic pathway supplies the majority of energy required of these types of exercises. Maximal aerobic capacity is defined as the maximal rate at which oxygen can be consumed. *The higher an athlete's maximal aerobic capacity, the more successfully he or she will perform in endurance events, provided all other factors that contribute to a championship performance are present* (Fig. 2–11).

### Interaction of Aerobic and Anaerobic Energy Sources During Exercise

As mentioned earlier, it is difficult to determine the predominant pathway (aerobic vs. anaerobic) in activities which require between 3 and 10 minutes to perform. This can be clearly illustrated by observing Figure 2–12. For example, in the 1500-meter and 2-mile (3200-meter) events, the percentage of the total energy supplied both anaerobically and aerobically is about equal—in the 1500-meter race a little more of

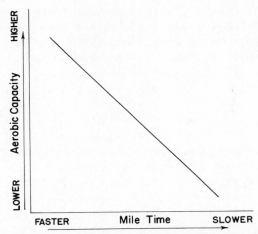

**Figure 2-11** The higher an athlete's maximal aerobic capacity, the more successfully he will perform in endurance events, provided all other factors contributing to a championship performance are present.

the energy is supplied anaerobically. Why is this important for the coach to understand?

Although the amount of energy from the aerobic and anaerobic mechanisms shows little difference, just look at the time difference—3:45 to 9:00 minutes! During this period you have events requiring that *both* aerobic and anaerobic sources be of equal importance. This is in contrast to events on either side of the zone between 3:45 and 9:00 minutes. The events to the left of the zone are predominantly anaerobic and the ones to the right of the zone are predominantly aerobic. Consequently, the coach is well advised to conduct training programs that concentrate on the development of either aerobic or anaerobic sources. Events within the "gray" zone are the

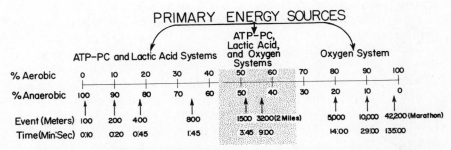

**Figure 2-12** The approximate percentage of contribution of aerobic and anaerobic energy sources in selected track events. Nonshaded areas represent predominance of one pathway over the other. The shaded area represents events in which both pathways are of nearly equal importance.

most difficult for the athlete to perform because *both* energy sources are of equal importance. The coach should employ principles of both aerobic and anaerobic training. The training method that should receive the greatest emphasis will depend upon the proximity of the event to the borders of the gray zone.

## Summary

The primary concern of this chapter is energy sources. Our sun is the ultimate source of all energy, for it is through solar radiation that glucose in plants is formed. Animals eat the plants and each other for food; in our bodies, food is used to manufacture ATP—the chemical source of energy used to contract a muscle.

The energy used to develop power (for athletic events such as standing long jump, shot put, fast starts, and sprints) comes from the ATP-PC system, which amazingly enough does *not* require oxygen to form ATP. As a matter of fact, neither does the lactic acid mechanism (another pathway used to form ATP) employ oxygen. Carbohydrate (in the form of glucose) is the only food used in this metabolic sequence. Essentially, glucose is broken down to pyruvate and then to lactic acid. Lactic acid is formed during exercise when sufficient oxygen is not available. The third pathway employed for the formation of ATP is called the oxygen system (Krebs or TCA cycle, and the electron transport system). All three foods may be used in the oxygen system to form ATP.

The first two pathways used to form ATP are referred to as anaerobic (without oxygen), while the third pathway is called aerobic (with oxygen). Activities of long duration (exceeding 5 minutes) are called aerobic, for the energy required to perform the activity is derived primarily from the oxygen system. In exercises of short duration the energy sources are predominantly the ATP-PC and the lactic acid systems, and hence these are called anaerobic activities.

It is difficult to claim any one pathway (aerobic vs. anaerobic) predominating in events that require between 3 and 10 minutes to perform. For example, in the 1500-meter and 2-mile events, the contribution of each pathway in the formation of ATP is about equal. The coach must be acutely aware of this fact, for his or her training programs should depend on the predominant pathway(s) being employed.

## QUESTIONS

1. How is energy defined?

2. Name the six forms of energy.

3. Diagram the biological energy cycle.

4. What is the immediate source of energy for a muscular contraction?

5. Describe each of the three ways by which ATP is formed.

6. Define anaerobic and aerobic.

7. How is lactic acid formed?

8. What are the functions of the Krebs cycle and the electron transport system?

9. What are the capacities and powers of the three energy systems?

10. Under conditions of either rest or exercise, what are the three important features of the anaerobic and aerobic pathways which we must consider?

11. Discuss each of these considerations as they would apply during rest and exercise.

12. Identify the predominant energy sources (ATP-PC, lactic acid, or oxygen system) used during the following activities: (A) 100-yard dash, (B) 440-yard dash, (C) mile run, and (D) marathon.

## REFERENCES

1. Costill, D.L.: Muscular exhaustion during distance running. Phys. Sports Med., 2 (10):36–41, 1974.
2. Costill, D.L., and Fox, E.L.: Energetics of marathon running. Med. Sci. Sports, 1:81–86, 1969.
3. Drinkwater, B.L.: Physiological responses of women to exercise. *In* Wilmore, J.L. (ed.): Exercise and Sport Sciences Reviews. vol. 1, pp. 125–153, New York, Academic Press, Inc., 1973.
4. Drinkwater, B.L., Horvath, S.M., and Wells, C.L.: Aerobic power of females, ages 10 to 68. J. Gerontol., 30(4): 385–394, 1975.
5. Fox, E.L., Billings, C.E., Bartels, R.L., Bason, R., and Mathews, D.K.: Fitness standards for male college students. Int. Z. Angew Physiol., 31:231–236, 1973.
6. Fox, E.L., and Costill, D.L.: Estimated cardiorespiratory responses during marathon running. Arch. Environ. Health., 24:315–324, 1972.
7. Hultman, E.: Studies on muscle metabolism of glycogen and active phosphate in man with special reference to exercise and diet. Scand. J. Clin. Lab. Invest. (Suppl. 94), 19:1–63, 1967.
8. Karlsson, J.: Lactate and phosphagen concentrations in working muscle of man. Acta Physiol. Scand. (Suppl.) 358:1–72, 1971.
9. Robinson, S.: Physiology of muscular exercise. *In* Mountcastle, V.B. (ed.): Medical Physiology. 13th ed., vol. 2, St. Louis, C. V. Mosby Co., p. 1279, 1974.
10. Saltin, B., and Åstrand, P.-O.: Maximal oxygen uptake in athletes. J. Appl. Physiol., 23:353–358, 1967.

## SELECTED READINGS

Gollnick, P.D., and Hermansen, L.: Biochemical adaptations to exercise: anaerobic metabolism. *In* Wilmore, J. H. (ed.): Exercise and Sport Sciences Reviews. vol. 1, pp. 1–43, New York, Academic Press, Inc., 1973.

Gollnick, P.D., and King, D.W.: Energy release in the muscle cell. Med. Sci. Sports, 1:23–31, 1969.

Hermansen, L.: Anaerobic energy release. Med. Sci. Sports, 1:32–38, 1969.

Holloszy, J.O.: Biochemical adaptations to exercise: aerobic metabolism. *In* Wilmore, J.H. (ed.): Exercise and Sport Sciences Reviews. vol. 1, New York, Academic Press, Inc., pp. 45–71, 1973.

Howald, H., and Poortmans, J.R. (eds.): Metabolic Adaptations to Prolonged Physical Exercise. Basel, Switzerland, Birkhauser Verlag, 1975.

Keul, J.E. Doll, and Keppler, D.: Energy Metabolism of Human Muscle (Translated by J.S. Skinner). Baltimore, University Park Press, 1972.

Lehninger, A.L.: Bioenergetics. 2nd ed., New York, W.A. Benjamin, Inc., 1971.

Pernow, B., and Saltin, B. (eds.): Muscle Metabolism During Exercise. New York, Plenum Press, 1971.

Poortmans, J.R. (ed.): Biochemistry of Exercise. Baltimore, University Park Press, 1968.

# RECOVERY FROM EXERCISE

THE OXYGEN DEBT
  Replenishment of Energy Stores
    *Restoration of ATP + PC and the*
    *Alactacid Oxygen Debt*
  *Glycogen Resynthesis, Lactic*
    *Acid Removal, and the Lactacid*
    *Oxygen Debt*

The different roles played by the metabolic pathways during the transition from rest to exercise constitute only half of the energy picture. We need to understand in addition how these pathways function during the reverse transition, i.e., from exercise to rest. We can start by saying that the sole purpose during this transition, more commonly called the *recovery period,* is to restore the body to its pre-exercise condition. This includes replenishing any energy stores that were depleted and removing any lactic acid that was accumulated during exercise. The energy needed for this task is furnished by the aerobic pathway.

## THE OXYGEN DEBT

We all know that during recovery our energy demand is considerably less since we are no longer exercising. However, our oxygen consumption continues at a relatively high level for a period of time, the length of which is dependent on the intensity of the preceding exercise. The amount of oxygen consumed during recovery—above that which would have ordinarily been consumed at rest in the same time—is called the *oxygen debt.* This is shown schematically in Figure 3–1. The term oxygen debt was first used in 1922 by the eminent British physiologist A. V. Hill.[9] This was the same year that he, jointly with O. Meyerhof, received a Nobel Prize for Physiology and Medicine.

The concept of oxygen debt, as originally developed by Hill, means that the oxygen consumed above the resting level during recovery

**31**

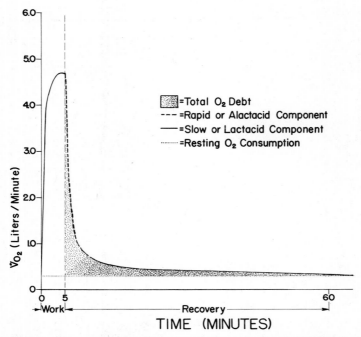

Figure 3–1 The oxygen debt. The amount of oxygen consumed during recovery, above that which would have ordinarily been consumed at rest in the same time, is called the oxygen debt. The oxygen debt repayment consists of a rapid or alactacid component, and a slow or lactacid component.

is used to provide energy, as mentioned earlier, for restoring the body to its pre-exercise condition, including replenishing the energy stores that were depleted during exercise. Many erroneously interpret the oxygen debt to mean that the extra oxygen consumed during recovery is being used to replace oxygen that was borrowed from somewhere within the body during exercise. Actually, during maximal exercise, depletion of the oxygen stored in the muscle itself (in combination with myoglobin) and in the venous blood would amount to only about 0.6 liter. Oxygen debts, on the other hand, have been found to be nearly 30 times larger than this in athletes during maximal exercise. This gives rise to several important questions: (1) "What energy stores are depleted," during exercise; (2) "How are they replenished," and (3) "What happens to the lactic acid accumulated during exercise?"

The first question should be easy for you to answer. You will recall that there are two sources of energy that are depleted to various extents during exercise: (1) the ATP and PC stored in the muscle cells, and (2) the glycogen stored in large amounts in muscle as well as in the liver, which serves as our source of glucose. If you are wondering why fats have not been included in our list, the reason is that they are not replenished directly during recovery but instead are rebuilt indirectly through the replenishment of glucose. We will not concern ourselves too much with this latter point, but will, in answering the second question, concentrate on the replenishment of the other two sources — ATP-PC and glycogen.

### Replenishment of Energy Stores and Removal of Lactic Acid

The fact that the two energy sources depleted during exercise come from two very different series of reactions has led investigators to look for two distinctly different oxygen debt components. You will notice in Figure 3–1 that oxygen consumption following exhaustive exercise decreases exponentially with time. That is to say, the rate at which oxygen is consumed is not constant throughout the recovery period. During the first 2 or 3 minutes of recovery, oxygen consumption decreases very rapidly, then more slowly until a steady rate is reached. The extra oxygen consumed during this initial phase, i.e., when the rate of oxygen consumption is decreasing very rapidly, provides the energy necessary to replenish the ATP and PC stored in the muscles.[4, 17, 18] It was once thought that the extra oxygen consumed over the time when the rate of oxygen consumption is much slower supplied the energy needed to replenish the glycogen stored in the muscles as well as in the liver. It is now known that this is not true. As we shall soon see, this energy is related, at least in part, to the removal of lactic acid which accumulates during exercise.

The initial rapid portion of the oxygen debt has been named the *alactacid oxygen debt component,* whereas the slower phase has been named the *lactacid oxygen debt component.*[15] The lactacid component was so named because at the time it was thought that the glycogen which was presumed to be resynthesized was derived from the lactic acid accumulated during exercise. The term alactacid (the prefix *a* means "not") is used because replenishment of the ATP and PC stores is apparently independent of the removal of lactic acid during recovery. At one time, it was thought that the entire oxygen debt was lactacid in nature; i.e., that it resulted from the removal of the lactic acid accumulated during exercise.[8] When it was first shown in 1933 that an oxygen debt could be incurred without lactic acid accumulation, the term alactacid oxygen debt was used[15] (Fig. 3–2).

**Restoration of ATP + PC and the Alactacid Debt.** The ATP and PC stores depleted during exercise are restored within a few minutes following exercise.[11] This is shown in Figure 3–3. Notice that the phosphagen restoration is 70 per cent completed in 30 seconds and 100 per cent completed within 3 minutes. As mentioned earlier, the fast or

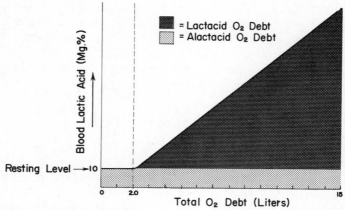

**Figure 3-2** The relationship between blood lactic acid accumulation during exercise and the total oxygen debt repayment during recovery. Note that the alactacid component is independent of blood lactic acid levels, whereas the lactacid component increases linearly as the blood lactic acid increases.

alactacid portion of the oxygen debt provides the oxygen and thus the energy necessary to replenish the ATP and PC stores. As shown in Figure 3–4, the energy made available for this replenishment comes about from the aerobic breakdown of foodstuffs (and perhaps a small amount of lactic acid) to $CO_2$ and $H_2O$ via the Krebs cycle and the electron

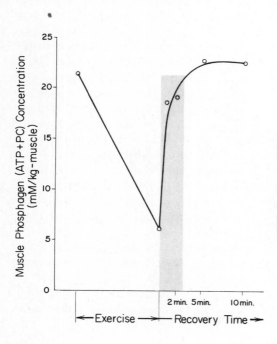

**Figure 3-3** The muscular stores of ATP + PC that were depleted during exercise are restored within a few minutes following exercise. Notice that the phosphagen restoration is 70 per cent completed in 30 seconds and essentially 100 per cent completed within about 3 minutes. (Based on data from Hultman et al.[11])

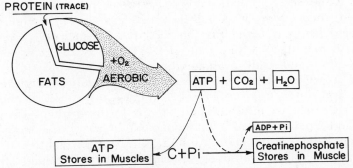

**Figure 3–4** The alactacid portion of the oxygen debt repayment provides the energy necessary to replenish the stores of ATP and PC in muscle that were depleted during exercise. Some of the ATP formed is directly stored in the muscle, whereas some is broken down immediately and used to resynthesize PC (phosphocreatine or creatinephosphate), which is then stored in the muscle.

transport system. Some of the ATP that is thus formed is stored in the muscle, whereas some is broken down immediately and used to re-synthesize PC, which is also stored in the muscle.

Since the energy for phosphagen restoration comes from the alact-acid oxygen debt, it too is repaid very rapidly and takes at most only about 3 minutes to be completed (see Fig. 3–1). Its speed of repayment can be estimated from analysis of the oxygen consumption curve during the first 2 or 3 minutes of recovery. When estimated in this manner, the half-reaction time of repayment is about 30 seconds.[14] This means that in 30 seconds, one-half of the total alactacid debt is repaid; in 1 minute, three-fourths; in one and one-half minutes, seven-eighths; and in 3 minutes, 63/64. However, as just pointed out, the actual rate at which the ATP and PC stores are replenished is somewhat greater; i.e., with 70 per cent rather than 50 per cent restored in 30 seconds. The reason for this discrepancy is the amount of oxygen consumed during recovery includes not only the amount of oxygen required to replenish the ATP and PC stores, but also: (1) a certain amount of oxygen needed to replace the depleted oxygen stores (about 0.6 liter of oxygen in maximal exercise); and (2) about 50 ml. of oxygen used by muscles not directly involved in the performance of external work, such as the heart and respiratory muscles.[12, 13] With these corrections, the half-reaction time is around 20 seconds, which is in close agreement with the actual phosphagen restoration rate.[4, 14, 15]

Since the alactacid portion of the oxygen debt supplies aerobic energy for the restoration of the muscle phosphagen (ATP + PC) stores that were depleted during the oxygen deficit period of exercise, these two quantities should be related. In other words, the greater the phosphagen depletion, the greater the oxygen required for their restoration. While such a relationship has not been experimentally determined, theoretically it should look like that shown in Figure 3–5. The relationship is based on the fact that it requires 3.5 liters of oxygen to manufacture one mole of ATP (see p. 18). This idea has been used to indirectly evaluate the maximal phosphagen capacity in men[5] as well as in women (see Fig. 21–4). Maximal values for the phosphagen stores (as given on p. 14) and maximal values for the alactacid oxygen debt are indicated in the figure by the shaded areas.

As indicated in Figure 3–5, the maximum size of the alactacid oxygen debt ranges from about 2.0 to 2.5 liters of oxygen in untrained males; higher values would be associated with well-trained athletes. This has important applications in physical education and athletics because the sprinter who can incur an alactacid oxygen debt of 3 liters will be more successful, generally speaking, than one who incurs an alactacid debt of only 2 liters. As we learned in the last chapter, the amount of ATP-PC available and its rate of utilization are directly related to the athlete's ability to generate power. Through a properly designed training program you can improve the ATP-PC system and hence performance. On page 498 you will find a practical way in which to measure indirectly the ATP-PC stores of your athletes.

**Glycogen Resynthesis, Lactic Acid Removal, and the Lactacid Oxygen Debt.** As mentioned earlier, it was believed for nearly 50 years that the muscular stores of glycogen depleted during exercise were resynthesized from lactic acid during the immediate recovery period (1½ to 2 hours) following exercise. In Figure 3–6, it is clear this is not true.[10, 16] One can observe from the figure that:

1. Only an insignificant amount of muscle glycogen is resynthesized within the immediate recovery period following exercise.

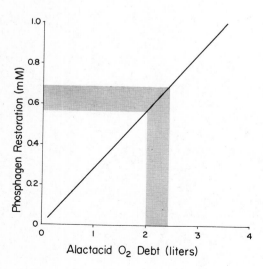

**Figure 3–5** The greater the phosphagen depletion during exercise, the greater the amount of oxygen required during recovery for restoration. This relationship between the alactacid $O_2$ debt and phosphagen restoration in muscle is based on the fact that 3.5 liters of oxygen are required to manufacture one mole of ATP. Maximal values of phosphagen stores and maximal values for the alactacid $O_2$ debt are illustrated by the shaded areas.

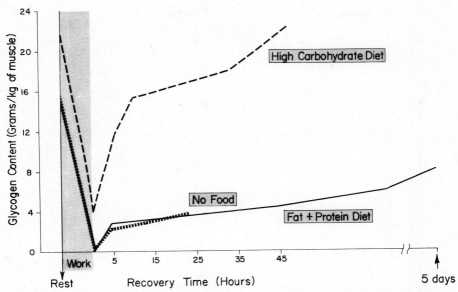

**Figure 3–6** Only an insignificant amount of muscle glycogen is resynthesized within the immediate recovery period following exercise. The complete resynthesis of muscle glycogen following exercise requires a high dietary intake of carbohydrate over at least a 2-day period. Without carbohydrate intake, only a small amount of glycogen is resynthesized even over a 5-day period. (Based on data from Hultman and Bergström[10] and Piehl.[16])

2. The complete resynthesis of muscle glycogen following exercise requires a high dietary intake of carbohydrate over a two-day time period. Without carbohydrate, only a small amount of glycogen is resynthesized even over a five-day period.

It follows from these findings that the aerobic energy provided from the lactacid oxygen debt component is *not* used to resynthesize muscle glycogen from lactic acid.

It should be mentioned at this time that the amount and rate of glycogen resynthesis in skeletal muscle can be increased to values much higher than normal,[1] as follows: (1) The muscle is first depleted of its glycogen stores through exhaustive exercise; (2) then during the next two or three days, a high carbohydrate diet is given (and a little or only light exercise is performed) and the glycogen stores of the muscles previously depleted will increase to levels two to three times normal (see Fig. 3–7). Further increases in glycogen stores can be stimulated if a day or so before beginning the high carbohydrate diet, the subject fasts or undertakes a low carbohydrate diet. This information should prove to be extremely useful to the coach insofar as the training table is concerned, for such a diet significantly elevates muscle glycogen stores and hence increases muscular performance. The diet and more detailed information appear in Chapter 18.

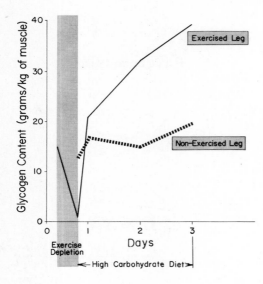

**Figure 3–7** The amount of muscle glycogen stored can be increased by first depleting the muscle of its glycogen through exercise, then for 2 or 3 days thereafter, consuming a high carbohydrate diet. (Based on data from Bergström and Hultman.[1])

Since, as shown in Figure 3–8, lactic acid is removed during the immediate recovery period and because it is not reconverted to muscle glycogen, the question is raised, "What happens to the lactic acid?" There are three possible answers to this question, all of which deal with the idea that lactic acid is absorbed by the liver. Here it can be (1) used to resynthesize the liver glycogen stores that may have been depleted during exercise and/or (2) converted to glucose and released into the blood as blood glucose and/or (3) in the presence of oxygen converted to pyruvic acid and then sent through the Krebs cycle and electron

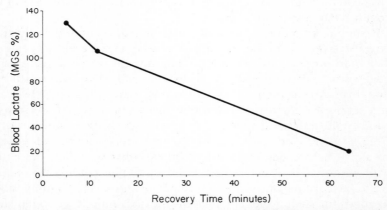

**Figure 3–8** During the immediate recovery period following exercise, lactic acid is removed from the blood. However, it is *not* reconverted to muscle and liver glycogen as was once thought. (Based on data from Fox et al.[6])

transport system with $CO_2$, $H_2O$ and ATP emerging. In addition to the liver, the skeletal muscle, the heart, and the kidney are also capable of this latter function.

It has been demonstrated that the stores of liver glycogen depleted during exercise take about the same length of time to be replenished as do the muscle glycogen stores, thus ruling out the immediate resynthesis of lactic acid to liver glycogen.[2] With respect to the other two possibilities, it has been found that approximately 10 per cent of the lactic acid removed during the immediate recovery period is converted to blood glucose[3] and 75 per cent is oxidized via the oxygen system to $CO_2$ and $H_2O$.[2] Presumably, at least part of the oxygen required for these conversions comes from the oxygen consumed during the lactacid portion of the debt. As shown in Figure 3–9, a relationship has been experimentally determined between the oxygen consumed during the lactacid oxygen debt period (horizontal axis) and the removal of lactic acid from the blood (vertical axis). However, the exact amount of oxygen required to remove a given quantity of lactic acid varies considerably.[19] Furthermore, you may have noticed that as much as 15 per cent of the lactic acid removed during recovery is unaccounted for; obviously, more research on this problem is needed. A summary of the fate of lactic acid is shown in Figure 3–10.

The repayment of the lactacid oxygen debt is slow compared with that of the alactacid. The former has a half-reaction time of 15 minutes, about 30 times slower than that of the latter.[14] This is related to the fact that it takes a much longer time to remove lactic acid than to restore the phosphagens. However, it has been shown that lactic acid can be removed more rapidly following exhaustive exercise by doing light work (walking or jogging) rather than by resting during recovery.[7] This also results in a 1- to 2-liter reduction in the size of the lactacid ox-

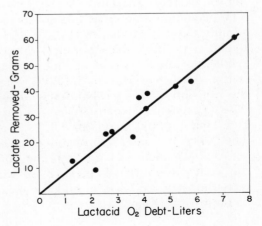

**Figure 3–9** A relationship exists between the oxygen consumed during the lactacid $O_2$ debt period and the removal of lactic acid from the blood. However, whether there is a direct cause and effect relationship is not definitely known. (Based on data from Fox et al.[6])

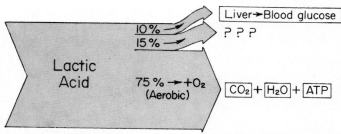

**Figure 3–10**  The fate of lactic acid. So far as is known, about 75 per cent of the lactic acid removed during recovery from exercise is oxidized to $CO_2$ and $H_2O$ (with the production of ATP); another 10 per cent is probably converted to glucose in the liver and released into the blood as blood glucose. This leaves 15 per cent of the lactic acid which was removed during recovery unaccounted for.

ygen debt. There are two reasons why the rate of lactic acid removed is increased under these conditions: (1) a more rapid distribution of lactic acid to the liver for oxidation to $CO_2$ and $H_2O$ or reconversion to glucose or both, and (2) an increased utilization of lactic acid as a fuel by the heart and working skeletal muscles. These findings provide a physiological basis for the practice by most athletes of walking or jogging intermittently between competitive events rather than resting throughout recovery. They have apparently learned through experience that this will allow them to recover more quickly and thus perform better in their second event. This method of hastening recovery is important in any situation in which a quick recovery between bouts of severe work is essential.

The significance of the lactacid oxygen debt as related to exercise performance lies in the amount of lactic acid that can be accumulated during maximal effort. The more lactic acid accumulated, the greater the amount of energy made available through anaerobic glycolysis during the exercise; therefore the larger will be the lactacid oxygen debt. The maximum amount of energy obtainable from the lactacid mechanism is about twice that of the alactacid or ATP-PC system. However, to obtain a comparable amount of energy from the lactacid mechanism requires a longer period of time and, therefore, supplies only about half as much power as the ATP-PC system (see p. 19). During exercise the function of this mechanism is to sustain maximal effort after the ATP-PC system is exhausted. For example, champion athletes can run 100, 200, and 400 meters in 9.9, 19.8, and 43.8 seconds, respectively. The ATP-PC system is probably exhausted at the end of 100 meters, yet each 100 meters of the 200- and 400-meter events is run at about the same speed. In Chapter 12 we will learn how conditioning affects the lactic acid system and the means by which performance can be improved.

# Summary

Following exercise, oxygen consumption remains elevated above resting values. The additional oxygen consumed above rest is termed *oxygen debt*. Strenuousness of the exercise and duration and condition of the subject affect the size of the debt.

For the first two to three minutes following exercise, there is a high rate of oxygen consumption followed by a gradual decline to near pre-exercise levels. The initial rapid portion of the oxygen debt has been named the *alactacid oxygen debt component*, whereas the slower phase is the *lactacid oxygen debt component*.

Oxygen consumed during the alactacid portion of the debt is used to replenish the muscular stores of ATP and PC within three minutes following exercise.

For years it was thought that the latter portion of the debt was employed in resynthesizing glycogen from lactic acid. Apparently this is not true. Only an insignificant amount of muscle glycogen is formed during the immediate recovery period. Additionally, diet plays an important role in muscle glycogen resynthesis. It takes at least two days with a high carbohydrate diet to replenish the muscle glycogen.

Muscle glycogen content can be increased two to three times above normal first by depleting the muscle glycogen through exercise and a low carbohydrate diet; this is then followed by rest and a high carbohydrate diet.

Because we now understand that lactic acid is *not* used in the synthesis of glycogen, where does it go? Approximately 10 per cent of the lactic acid removed during the recovery period is converted to blood glucose and 75 per cent is oxidized via the oxygen system to $CO_2$ and $H_2O$. Fifteen per cent remains unaccounted for; the answer to this fascinating mystery awaits the future.

Alactacid debts range from 2 to 2½ liters. Therefore, the athlete incurring the greater debt will unquestionably generate greater power, for power comes from ATP-PC utilization.

Repayment of the lactacid oxygen debt is about 30 times slower than that of the alactacid debt because it takes longer to metabolize the lactic acid than to restore phosphagens. However, lactic acid removal can be increased by performing light work, e.g., walking and jogging.

## QUESTIONS

1. Define the oxygen debt and oxygen debt components.

2. Where does the energy come from for the restoration of the muscular stores of ATP and PC?

3.  Explain how muscle glycogen is restored.

4.  How would you increase the muscle glycogen stores of your athletes?

5.  What is the practical meaning of being able to incur a large oxygen debt?

6.  What is the fate of the lactic acid removed during the immediate recovery period?

7.  Suppose an athlete were to compete first in the half-mile run, then about an hour or so later in the one-mile run. What would you as a coach tell the athlete concerning the fastest way to recover between events?

## REFERENCES

1.  Bergström, J., and Hultman, E.: Muscle glycogen synthesis after exercise: an enhancing factor localized to the muscle cells in man. Nature, 210:309–310, 1966.
2.  Brooks, G.A., Brauner, K.E., and Cassens, R.G.: Glycogen synthesis and metabolism of lactic acid after exercise. Am. J. Physiol., 224:1162–1166, 1973.
3.  Depocas, F., Minaire, Y., and Charonnet, J.: Rates of formation and oxidation of lactic acid in dogs at rest and during moderate exercise. Canad. J. Physiol. Pharmacol., 47:603–610, 1969.
4.  diPrampero, P.E., and Margaria, R.: Relationship between $O_2$ consumption, high energy phosphates and the kinetics of the $O_2$ debt in exercise. Plugers Arch., 304:11–19, 1968.
5.  Fox, E.L., Measurement of the maximal alactic (phosphagen) capacity in man. Med. Sci. Sports, 5:66, 1973.
6.  Fox, E.L., Robinson, S., and Wiegman, D.: Metabolic energy sources during continuous and interval running. J. Appl. Physiol., 27:174–178, 1969.
7.  Gisolfi, C., Robinson, S., and Turrell, E.S.: Effects of aerobic work performed during recovery from exhausting work. J. Appl. Physiol., 21:1767–1772, 1966.
8.  Hill, A.V., Long, C.N.H., and Lupton, H.: Muscular exercise, lactic acid and the supply and utilization of oxygen. I-III. Proc. Roy. Soc. (London), Series B, 96:438–475, 1924.
9.  Hill, A.V., and Lupton, H.: The oxygen consumption during running. J. Physiol., 56:xxxii-xxxiii, 1922.
10. Hultman, E., and Bergström, J.: Muscle glycogen synthesis in relation to diet studied in normal subjects. Acta Med. Scand., 182:109–117, 1967.
11. Hultman, E., Bergström, J., and McLennan Anderson, N.: Breakdown and resynthesis of phosphorylcreatine and adenosine triphosphate in connection with muscular work in man. Scand. J. Clin. Lab. Invest., 19:56–66, 1967.
12. Karlsson, J.: Lactate and phosphagen concentrations in working muscle of man. Acta Physiol. Scand. (Suppl.), 358:1–72, 1971.
13. Margaria, R.: Aerobic and anaerobic energy sources in muscular exercise. *In* Margaria, R. (ed.): Exercise at Altitude. pp. 15–32, New York, Excerpta Medica Foundation, 1967.
14. Margaria, R., Cerretelli, P., diPrampero, P.E., Massari, C., and Torelli, G.: Kinetics and mechanism of oxygen debt contraction in man. J. Appl. Physiol., 18:371–377, 1963.
15. Margaria, R., Edwards, H.T., and Dill, D.B.: The possible mechanism of contracting and paying the oxygen debt and the role of lactic acid in muscular contraction. Am. J. Physiol., 106:687–714, 1933.
16. Piehl, K.: Time course for refilling of glycogen stores in human muscle fibers following exercise-induced glycogen depletion. Acta Physiol. Scand., 90:297–302, 1974.

17. Piiper, J., diPrampero, P.E., and Cerretelli, P.: Oxygen debt and high-energy phosphates in gastrocnemius muscle of the dog. Am. J. Physiol., 215:523–531, 1968.
18. Piiper, J., and Spiller, P.: Repayment of $O_2$ debt and resynthesis of high energy phosphates in gastrocnemius muscle of the dog. J. Appl. Physiol., 28:657–662, 1970.
19. Rowell, L.B., Kraning, K.K., Evans, T.O., Kennedy, J.W., Blackmon, J.R., and Kusumi, F.: Splanchnic removal of lactate and pyruvate during prolonged exercise in man. J. Appl. Physiol., 21:1773–1783, 1966.

## SELECTED READINGS

diPrampero, P.E.: The alactic oxygen debt: its power, capacity and efficiency. *In* Pernow, B., and Saltin, B. (eds.): Muscle Metabolism During Exercise. pp. 371–382, New York, Plenum Press, 1971.
diPrampero, P.E., Peeters, L., and Margaria, R.: Alactic $O_2$ debt and lactic acid production after exhausting exercise in man. J. Appl. Physiol., 34:628–632, 1973.
Knuttgen, H.G.: Lactate and oxygen debt: an introduction. *In* Pernow, B., and Saltin, B. (eds.): Muscle Metabolism During Exercise. pp. 361–369, New York, Plenum Press, 1971.
Knuttgen, H.G.: Oxygen debt after submaximal physical exercise. J. Appl. Physiol., 29:651–657, 1970.
Knuttgen, H.G.: Oxygen debt, lactate, pyruvate and excess lactate after muscular work. J. Appl. Physiol., 17:639, 1962.
Margaria, R., Cerretelli, P., and Mangile, F.: Balance and kinetics of anaerobic energy release during strenuous exercise in man. J. Appl. Physiol., 19:623–628, 1964.
Poortmans, J.R. (ed.): Biochemistry of Exercise. Baltimore, University Park Press, 1968.

# ENERGY, WORK, AND POWER

One of the most valid means of determining a person's ability to perform physically is to measure the maximal amount of energy he or she can expend. This can be done indirectly by determining the maximal ability to consume oxygen while doing extremely heavy work. The work is usually performed using a bicycle ergometer or treadmill, which permits varying the work load from moderate to exhaustive. The amount of oxygen consumed by the individual during maximal work (usually expressed in liters*) can be converted into work units such as foot-pounds.

Understanding energy expenditure and how it is measured will make you much more knowledgeable about your subject, whether it be physical education or athletics; for as we learned in the last two chapters, it is *energy* and the way in which it is expended that results in human movement. In order to fully appreciate the whole of our subject, energy cost of performance, we need know the meaning of and relationship among (1) energy, (2) work, and (3) power.

————————————————————

*A liter equals about a quart.

# ENERGY

How often we have heard the expressions, "I haven't a bit of energy left," or "He is bursting at the seams with energy." Such everyday sayings carry a substance of meaning but fall short in defining the term. Actually, no one has ever seen energy or handled it. However, all have felt its effects. For example, a fall or being hit with a physiology book causes pain. In other words, energy and its effects are all around us—the moving auto, the sun, the atomic bomb, and even the children and athletes on the playing field—all are illustrative of energy. Energy may be described as the *capacity to perform work.*

Generally, we recognize six forms of energy: mechanical, heat, light, chemical, electrical, and nuclear. Each can readily be converted from one form to another. The child exercising or playing softball is converting chemical (foodstuffs) to mechanical energy—for every single human movement, whether it be the contraction of the viscera within the body or the punting of a football, the energy (ATP) needed to perform it is derived from food. Our bodies also convert chemical into electrical energy: the stimulus to contract a muscle is electrical. The electrocardiogram is actually a recording on paper of the electrical stimulation of the heart muscle, just as the electromyogram is the tracing of the electrical impulse across the skeletal muscle.

The source of energy in a chemical reaction, which is our primary concern, comes from either breaking up a molecule or putting it back together. Regardless of which occurs, the same amount of energy (heat) will be given off from the reaction. For example, if hydrogen reacting with oxygen produces water and 68.4 kcal., it will require exactly 68.4 kcal. to pull the water molecule apart to form hydrogen and oxygen. This is called the "first law of thermodynamics" and will be discussed later in more detail.

# WORK

The physicist defines work in a restricted sense; that is, work is the application of a force through a distance. For example, if you raised a book weighing 2 pounds *vertically* 2 feet, the work performed would have been 4 foot-pounds. One foot-pound would be defined as the work done when a constant force of 1 pound is exerted on a body that moves a distance of 1 foot in the same direction as the force. This may be expressed in the following formula:

$$W = F \times D$$

Where W = work

     F = force (remember, the force must be constant)

     D = distance through which the force is moved (distance is the length of the path through which the body moves in the same direction as the force and while the force is acting on it)

Work may be expressed in different terms. Table 4–1 contains a number of work and energy units that enable us to convert one to another depending upon how we wish to express our final measurement.

## POWER

Power is used to express work done in a unit of time. It may be written as:

$$Power = \frac{Work}{Time}, or$$

$$Power = \frac{F \times D}{t}$$

In the aforementioned example, if the book weighing 2 pounds were raised 2 feet in 1 second, power would be expressed as 4 foot-pounds per second. Table 4–2 contains a number of ways in which power may be expressed.

It is important for us to understand from the above discussion both the meaning of energy, work, and power and that the six forms of energy can be converted from one to another. The importance of these concepts can be demonstrated when describing: (1) how work by a person can be measured directly through the amount of heat the body gives off while performing various tasks; (2) how measurement of heat is employed in determining energy values of food, i.e., how much energy or, more precisely, the number of kilocalories, in a bottle of

**Table 4–1  ENERGY AND WORK UNITS**

| | |
|---|---|
| 1 foot-pound | = 0.13825 kg.-meter* |
| 1 kg.-meter | = 7.23 foot-pounds |
| 1 kcal. | = 3086 foot-pounds |
| 1 kcal. | = 426.4 kg.-meter |

*A kilogram-meter is the distance through which 1 kilogram (2.2 pounds) moves 1 meter (3.28 feet).

## Table 4–2  RELATIONSHIPS AMONG POWER UNITS
### (POWER EQUALS WORK PER UNIT TIME)

| | HORSE-POWER | KG.-METERS/ MINUTE | KG.-METERS/ SECOND | FOOT-POUNDS/ MINUTE | FOOT-POUNDS/ SECOND | WATTS | KCAL./ MINUTE | KCAL./ SECOND |
|---|---|---|---|---|---|---|---|---|
| 1 horsepower | 1.0 | 4,564.0 | 76.07 | 33,000.0 | 550.0 | 746.0 | 10.694 | 0.178 |
| 1 kg.-meter/minute | 0.000219 | 1.0 | 0.016667 | 7.23 | 0.1205 | 0.16345 | 0.00234 | 0.000039 |
| 1 foot-pound/minute | 0.00003 | 0.1383 | 0.0023 | 1.0 | 0.016667 | 0.0226 | 0.000324 | 0.0000054 |
| 1 watt | 0.001341 | 6.118 | 0.10197 | 44.236 | 0.7373 | 1.0 | 0.014335 | 0.000239 |
| 1 kcal./minute | 0.09355 | 426.78 | 7.113 | 3086.0 | 51.43 | 69.759 | 1.0 | 0.01667 |

Coke, average sized potato, or slice of bread (we will see that this latter information is vital to the understanding of weight control programs); and (3) how the exercise physiologist uses an indirect method of measuring energy by determining the amount of oxygen used — in other words, the fuel required to metabolize foodstuffs, a process that furnishes the energy to perform work.

### *Direct Measurement of Energy: The Bomb Calorimeter*

When energy is expended by the human body in performing work or the basic motions of life, heat is liberated from the working muscles. Hence, the metabolism of foodstuff (caloric value) should be equivalent to the amount of heat the body liberates. As was mentioned earlier, this demonstrates the first law of thermodynamics: *When mechanical energy is transformed into heat energy or heat energy into mechanical energy, the ratio of the two energies is a constant quantity (the principle of the conservation of energy).* It becomes a fact, then, that the expenditure of a fixed amount of energy will always result in the production of the same amount of heat. To demonstrate with animals this first law of thermodynamics, a clever scientist, Max Rubner, in the latter part of the 1800's built a chamber containing circulating water on the outside (Fig. 4–1). A dog was placed inside the chamber in an attempt to measure both metabolism and heat production of the animal. Metabolism was indirectly determined by measuring the oxygen consumed by the dog in breaking down the foodstuffs. Heat production by the dog in the chamber (which is called a bomb calorimeter) was measured by noting the change (increase) in temperature of the circulating water. Each in-

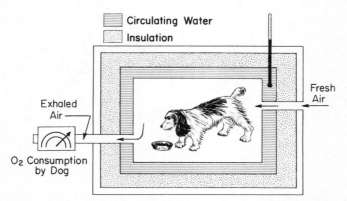

**Figure 4–1** Calorimeter for measuring heat energy. The calorimeter allows simultaneous measurement of metabolism and heat production. Oxygen consumption (indirect measurement of metabolism) equals heat production by the animal as reflected in an increase of temperature of the circulating water.

crease in water temperature of 1° C. per kilogram of water is equivalent to 1 kcal. of energy. The term *bomb* comes from the shape of the chamber (bomb) and *calorimeter* is used because energy measurement (heat) is expressed in calories.

Amazingly enough, the results of these early experiments demonstrated unequivocally that energy produced by the metabolism of foodstuffs was equal to the heat produced by the body. We can conclude, then, that energy expended by a man doing any kind of work is exactly equal to the energy set free through body metabolism. For example, if we were to measure the oxygen consumption of a man riding a bicycle or exercising in a human bomb calorimeter and then converted the oxygen utilized to heat equivalents (Table 4–3), we would find that the amount of energy employed in metabolism would equal the amount of heat given off by the body during the exercise.

By the same token, if we were to determine the amount of energy contained in an average sized potato, bottle of Coke, or medium sized pizza, we would simply burn the food item in the calorimeter. The increase in temperature of the circulating water would be equivalent to the energy or caloric value of the food. It is in this manner that caloric values for various foods are determined.

The use of the bomb calorimeter is referred to as the *direct method* in the measurement of energy. This is true because heat production, a specific form of energy, is being directly determined. On the other hand, when we measure the oxygen consumption required in metabolizing food, we use an *indirect method* in determining energy.

### Indirect Measurement of Energy

Many scientists have demonstrated that the amount of oxygen consumed at rest or while performing work (indirect method) when expressed in heat equivalents will be equal to the heat produced by the body (direct method, using calorimeter).

In order to express the amount of oxygen consumed in heat equivalents (i.e., kilocalories), it becomes necessary to know what type of food (carbohydrate, fat, or protein) is being metabolized. The reason for this deals with the energy equivalents of the particular food being metabolized. For example, when these foods are placed in a bomb calorimeter and 1 liter of oxygen is used in breaking down the foodstuffs, the following heat energy equivalents would be obtained (Table 4–3): carbohydrate (glucose), 5.05 kcal.; protein (meat), 4.46 kcal.; and lipid (fat), 4.74 kcal. From the same table in terms of kcal. per gram of food metabolized, there is a slight difference in values between the results when the food is metabolized (physiologically) in the body compared with the bomb calorimeter. The minute losses of energy as noted at the

## Table 4–3  ENERGY EQUIVALENTS OF FOOD AND ALCOHOL

| FOOD | ENERGY (BOMB CALORIMETER) kcal./gm. | ENERGY (PHYSIOLOGICAL VALUES)* kcal./gm. | RESPIRATORY EQUIVALENT $O_2$, kcal./liter | $CO_2$, kcal./liter | $R = \dfrac{\dot{V}CO_2}{\dot{V}O_2}$ | $O_2$, liter/gm. | $CO_2$, liter/gm. |
|---|---|---|---|---|---|---|---|
| Carbohydrate | 4.1 | 4.02 | 5.05 | 5.05 | 1.00 | 0.81 | 0.81 |
| Protein | 5.65 | 5.20 | 4.46 | 5.57 | 0.80 | 0.94 | 0.75 |
| Fat | 9.45 | 8.98 | 4.74 | 6.67 | 0.71 | 1.96 | 1.39 |
| Alcohol | 7.1 | 7.0 | 4.86 | 7.25 | 0.67 | 1.46 | 0.98 |
| Mixed diet | | | 4.83 | 5.89 | 0.82 | | |

*In the body there is a loss of kcal. to digestion as follows: carbohydrate, 2%; fat, 5%; protein, 8% plus a 17% loss in urine. For alcohol there is a small loss in urine and exhalation.

bottom of the table are due to digestion and some protein loss in the urine.

Note also from Table 4–3 that in terms of kilocalories per gram of food metabolized, fats (lipids) release 9.45 kcal. of energy per gram, proteins, 5.65 kcal./gm., and carbohydrates, 4.1 kcal./gm. We drew your attention first to the energy released in terms of kilocalories per liter of oxygen because the hard-working athlete is confronted primarily with getting sufficient oxygen and only secondarily with quantity of food. Why more heat or energy is liberated from fats as compared to carbohydrates on a per-gram basis is easy to explain. Remember, energy ultimately comes from the formation of water (combining hydrogen and oxygen) in metabolism of foods. There are fewer oxygen atoms per hydrogen atom in fat than in sugar. For example, sugar has the formula $C_6H_{12}O_6$ and a typical fat is $C_{57}H_{104}O_6$. As a consequence, there are more hydrogen atoms in fat to combine with oxygen in building water ($H_2O$). Therefore, when the body uses a given amount of fat, more energy results than when it metabolizes the same amount of carbohydrates. You can see from Table 4–3 that there are more than twice the number of kilocalories in a gram of fat than in a gram of carbohydrate.

Because all proteins contain nitrogen in addition to carbon, hydrogen, and oxygen, they are not as rich in energy as is fat. This is true because when proteins are used, the body must get rid of the nitrogen and it is disposed of not as a free gas, like carbon dioxide, but rather as urea. It is excreted in the urine and as a result, a portion of the energy from the protein molecule is lost.

The question that logically should confront us at this time is: If we have measured or been told the number of liters of oxygen used in performing a given task, such as 2-minute sit-ups, how do we know which food was being metabolized so that we might assign the proper caloric value to the oxygen being consumed? In the first place, it would be rare indeed if a person were using fat, protein, or carbohydrate exclusively. Rather, a person works on a mixed diet (predominantly glucose and fats), and it is through measuring not only the oxygen consumed but also the carbon dioxide produced that permits us to know the mixture of foods being metabolized and hence to properly assign the correct caloric value to each liter of oxygen consumed (Table 4–4).

### The Respiratory Exchange Ratio (R)

The quantity of oxygen required in metabolism depends on which type of food is being metabolized. The ratio of the volume of carbon dioxide expired per minute ($\dot{V}_{CO_2}$) to the volume of oxygen consumed

### Table 4-4  CALORIC VALUES FOR NONPROTEIN R*

| R.Q. | CALORIES PER LITER $O_2$ |
|:---:|:---:|
| 0.707 | 4.686 |
| 0.71 | 4.690 |
| 0.72 | 4.702 |
| 0.73 | 4.714 |
| 0.74 | 4.727 |
| 0.75 | 4.739 |
| 0.76 | 4.751 |
| 0.77 | 4.764 |
| 0.78 | 4.776 |
| 0.79 | 4.788 |
| 0.80 | 4.801 |
| 0.81 | 4.813 |
| 0.82 | 4.825 |
| 0.83 | 4.838 |
| 0.84 | 4.850 |
| 0.85 | 4.862 |
| 0.86 | 4.875 |
| 0.87 | 4.887 |
| 0.88 | 4.899 |
| 0.89 | 4.911 |
| 0.90 | 4.924 |
| 0.91 | 4.936 |
| 0.92 | 4.948 |
| 0.93 | 4.961 |
| 0.94 | 4.973 |
| 0.95 | 4.985 |
| 0.96 | 4.998 |
| 0.97 | 5.010 |
| 0.98 | 5.022 |
| 0.99 | 5.035 |
| 1.00 | 5.047 |

*From Lusk.[5]

during the same time interval ($\dot{V}_{O_2}$) is called the respiratory exchange ratio (R).*

**Carbohydrate.**  At this time let us draw our attention to carbohydrate—a foodstuff that contains hydrogen and oxygen in proper proportions (two hydrogen atoms for every oxygen atom) to form water within the molecule. Because of this, all consumed oxygen can be employed in the oxidation of carbon. At the same time, remember that equal volumes of gases at the same temperature and pressure contain an equal number of molecules (Law of Avogadro). Therefore, on a

---

*A cell respires while the animal breathes. It is usual to refer to $\dot{V}_{CO_2}/\dot{V}_{O_2}$ at the cellular level as the respiratory quotient (RQ) and from the lungs as the respiratory exchange ratio (R).

pure diet of carbohydrate we would expect $R$ to equal 1 or unity. For example:

$$C_6H_{12}O_6 + 6\,O_2 = 6\,CO_2 + 6\,H_2O$$
Sugar

$$R = \frac{\dot{V}CO_2}{\dot{V}O_2} = \frac{6}{6} = 1$$

It can readily be observed 6 $CO_2$ molecules are produced as a consequence of 6 $O_2$ molecules being used in the oxidation of the sugar. The ratio $\frac{6\,CO_2}{6\,O_2} = 1$. One liter of oxygen will release 5.05 kcal. of energy (heat), whether it is metabolized in the body or burned in the bomb calorimeter.

**Fat.**   When fat is oxidized, oxygen not only combines with carbon to form carbon dioxide but it also combines with hydrogen to form water. Therefore, we would expect $R$ to be less than unity and so it is:

Fat                                          $C_{51}H_{98}O_6$

To simplify                       $-H_{12}O_6$
(water within the
fat molecule can                _____
be deducted)                        $C_{51}H_{86}$

Upon oxidation $2(C_{51}H_{86}) + 145\,O_2 = 102\,CO_2 + 86\,H_2O$

Fat less water $(R) = \dfrac{102}{145} = 0.703$

Although fat contains more than twice the potential energy of carbohydrate per gram, it requires considerably more oxygen to release each calorie of energy.

**Proteins.**   Proteins are completely burned in the bomb calorimeter, yielding 5.65 kcal. per gram. However, when metabolized in the body, the nitrogen and small amount of sulfur residue is excreted in the urine and feces, as previously mentioned. Consequently, less energy is available when the protein is metabolized in the body than when it is burned in the calorimeter, where complete oxidation of the nitrogen and sulfur takes place. As a consequence, the energy production in the body is about 5.20 kcal. per gram of protein, whereas in the calorimeter it averages 5.65 kcal. per gram of protein. Because of this factor, special consideration must be taken when employing $R$ as representative of the food types being metabolized. This is of added significance when using $R$ to assign the caloric value for each liter of oxygen the body is using.

It would be most convenient if the body metabolized only fats and carbohydrates, for then $R$ would represent the relative proportions of the foods being used, since there is only a negligible loss of energy due to digestion. For example, an $R$ of 1.00 would indicate to us that only carbohydrate was being burned; an $R$ of 0.71, only fats; and any ratio between these two values would give us the relative combinations of the two foods being metabolized. In this manner, we could assign the proper caloric value to each liter of oxygen being consumed by the individual.

Fortunately, scientists before us have measured the excretion of nitrogen and determined the amount of protein that was oxidized. Subtracting the oxygen required and the carbon dioxide produced from the total oxygen consumption yields an $R$ value commonly referred to as the *nonprotein* $R$. How fortunate for us in the field of exercise physiology and physical education that we can merely measure the $O_2$ used and the $CO_2$ produced, then consult a table of nonprotein $R$ to arrive at the proper caloric value for each liter of oxygen consumed. If this were not the case, nitrogen excretion values would have to be obtained and more cumbersome calculations made. Table 4–4 contains the efforts of earlier scientists for our benefit. Under steady state conditions (when sufficient oxygen is available) $R$ will equal 0.82 to 0.84, provided that the person's energy is being derived from a mixed diet.

There are times when $R$ can be affected by factors other than oxidation of food. These factors are worthwhile to consider when interpreting $R$.

(1) Hyperventilation (overventilating the lungs), which may be voluntary or may sometimes occur under psychiatric stress, results in excessive carbon dioxide loss. In such an instance, $R$ would exceed unity.

(2) During the first minute or so of submaximal exercise (aerobic) the apparent stimulating effects result in hyperventilation to the extent that the person blows off more carbon dioxide than he or she consumes oxygen, causing $R$ to approach or exceed unity. After about 3 minutes, the individual would more than likely be producing sufficient carbon dioxide as a result of the exercise to return $R$ to within normal limits, more accurately reflecting the food being metabolized.

(3) During exhaustive exercise, $R$ will exceed 1 as the buffering of lactic acid causes large quantities of $CO_2$ to be released. It is common practice in this case to consider $R$ as equal to 1. In other words, carbohydrate is the primary food source and each liter of oxygen would be equivalent to 5.05 kcal.

(4) During recovery from exercise, $CO_2$ is retained, resulting in a lowered $R$.

To measure the amount of energy expended in doing work, it is apparent that we must know the value of $R$ if we are to determine the caloric value for the amount of oxygen consumed. As an illustration, let us assume that 2 liters of oxygen were consumed in performing 80 sit-ups in 2 minutes. From Table 4–3, if the person's diet were carbohydrate ($R = 1.0$), the caloric value of 2 liters of oxygen would equal 10.10 kcal. ($2 \times 5.05$) of energy expended. In cases where $R$ is not known, it can be assumed to be 0.83, which means a liter of oxygen consumed is equivalent to 4.83 kcal. (Can you convert the 10.10 kcal. used in doing the sit-ups to foot-pounds, watts, horse-power, kilogram-meters?) Approximately how much weight would be lost from the exercise assuming 1 pound of fat is equivalent to 4000 kcal?*

### Protocol for Indirectly Measuring Energy Cost

Let us imagine we were given the problem of measuring the energy expenditure of a given exercise. How shall we proceed? Three measurements are required: (1) the resting oxygen consumption; (2) the oxygen consumed during the exercise; and (3) the oxygen consumed during the recovery period (oxygen debt — see Chapter 3).

Resting oxygen consumption measurement is necessary as this value must be deducted from the oxygen measured during exercise and recovery in order to determine oxygen cost of the exercise alone (net oxygen cost of exercise). The recovery oxygen consumption value is needed because the amount consumed during exercise reflects only the energy supplied through the aerobic pathway. The oxygen debt, on the other hand, indicates the amount of energy supplied through the anaerobic pathways. Therefore:

Net cost of the exercise = exercise + recovery − resting

**Determination of Net Cost of Exercise.** In exercises of maximal intensity or those in which the *net cost of the exercise* is to be determined, Douglas bags are most often used to collect the exhaled gas for purposes of volume measurement and analysis. The bags are rubber lined and covered with canvas, and were named after a famous physiologist, C. G. Douglas. In Figure 4–2 *A*, *B*, and *C* we observe that the resting sample is obtained first, then the exercise is commenced. Throughout the entire exercise period the exhaled gas is directed into the Douglas bag and finally at the conclusion of the exercise, the recovery gas is

---

*Answer: 0.0025 pound.

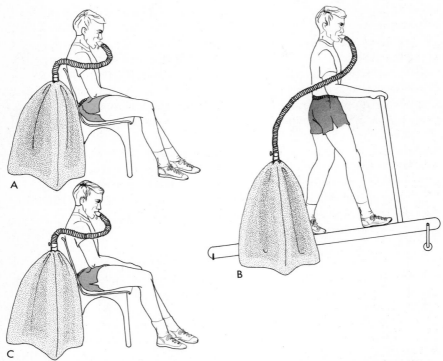

**Figure 4–2**  Indirect measurement of the net cost of exercise. *A*, Determination of resting oxygen consumption by the Douglas bag method. *B*, Determination of oxygen consumption during exercise while man walks on treadmill. *C*, Determination of oxygen consumption during recovery from exercise (oxygen debt). Net cost of the exercise equals the oxygen consumed during exercise plus recovery minus resting oxygen consumption for the same period of time.

collected. Though depending, of course, upon the strenuosity of the exercise, recovery periods seldom exceed 30 minutes. All three collections are maintained and analyzed separately. Gas samples are first taken from each of the three bags and are analyzed for $CO_2$ and $O_2$. Following sampling, the volume in each bag is determined by passing the gas through a gas meter or by drawing it into a wet spirometer (see Fig. 4–4).

Let us assume that upon analysis of the gas in the bags, we found that during a 5-minute rest period the subject consumed 1500 ml. of oxygen; during a 10 minute period of exercise he used 20,000 ml. of oxygen; and during a 15-minute recovery period he consumed 6000 ml. of oxygen. How do we compute net cost of the exercise?

During the 10 minute exercise period the subject consumed 20,000 ml. of oxygen (20 liters). From this amount must be subtracted what would have been consumed during the same period if he were resting;

in other words, the exercise or net consumption is over and above that consumed during rest. Therefore, 20,000 ml. $-$ 3000 ml. $=$ 17,000 ml. Note that the 3000 ml. was obtained by converting the resting consumption to a per-minute basis (1500/5 $=$ 300 ml. of $O_2$) and multiplying by the time period of the exercise (10 minutes).

From the recovery oxygen (6000 ml.) we must also subtract that amount which would have been used if the subject were resting for that particular time period; or 6000 ml. $-$ (15 minutes $\times$ 300 ml.), which equals 1500 ml. (net oxygen debt).

Therefore the *net cost of the exercise* would be equal to the exercise plus the recovery oxygen after the resting oxygen had been subtracted from each one; or 17,000 ml. $+$ 1500 ml. $=$ 18.5 liters of oxygen.

**Determination of Net Cost of Exercise in Liters per Minute.** If the exercise is submaximal, that is, if it can be performed aerobically, measurement of energy cost may be considerably simplified. During *submaximal* exercise, we realize a steady state of oxygen consumption occurs as noted in Figure 4–3, and that it indicates that at this time all the energy required for the exercise is being supplied aerobically. The oxygen cost of the steady state exercise in *liters per minute* can be determined simply by measuring for 1 minute the oxygen consumed during the steady state period. Therefore:

Net cost of submaximal exercise in liters per minute $=$ steady state $O_2$ consumption, liters per minute, $-$ resting $O_2$ consumption, liters per minute.

Recognizing these basic physiological considerations, let us proceed with the actual determination of oxygen consumption in liters per minute while running on a treadmill at 6 miles per hour (submaximal exercise).

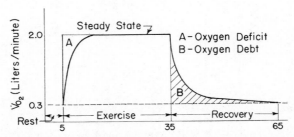

**Figure 4–3** Time course of oxygen consumption during rest, submaximal exercise, and recovery. $\dot{V}o_2$ (volume of oxygen used per unit of time) can be measured any time during steady state. Subtracting resting $\dot{V}o_2$ from this amount permits us to report the net cost of the exercise in liters per minute.

(1) Subject is weighed nude and dry, so if we wish, oxygen consumption can be expressed per unit of body weight, i.e., milliliters per kilogram of body weight. (1 liter = 1000 ml.).

(2) Seated comfortably in a chair on a treadmill, nose clip and mouthpiece in place, the subject inhales room air and exhales into the spirometer. During minutes 2 and 3, the spirometer is washed out with subject's expired gas to assure that the dead space in spirometer, hoses, and mouthpiece contains a reliable sample of subject's exhaled gas (Fig. 4–4 *A, B*). It is generally considered that during *laminar air flow* (as would be the case at rest), five times the dead space volume is adequate to flush the mouthpiece, hoses, and spirometer. For example, in Figure 4–4, *B* there are approximately 2 liters of dead space; therefore, at best 10 liters would be necessary to wash out the spirometer. During *turbulent flow* (as would be the case during exercise), three times the dead space volume should be adequate (at rest a person moves 6 to 8 liters of air per minute).

(3) During minutes 4 and 5, the subject's exhaled gas is collected in the spriometer. The timed volume is then read from the meter stick on the spirometer or from the kymograph.

(4) Temperature of the gas is read and samples are measured for $CO_2$ and $O_2$ concentration.

(5) Exercise is begun and any time after 3 minutes — for example, during minutes 5 and 6 — the spirometer is washed with the exhaled air to assure that the dead space has been adequately flushed.

(6) Collection can be made during minute 8 or, for that matter, at any time the subject is in steady state and for any desired period of time.

(7) Volume and gas temperature are recorded.

(8) Sample is analyzed for $CO_2$ and $O_2$.

(9) Barometer is read before and/or following the exercise so that correction of gas volumes may be made. Appendix B contains information as to how gas is corrected for Standard Temperature and Pressure, Dry (STPD), and Appendix C the method by which $\dot{V}O_2$ is calculated.

---

**Figure 4–4** *A,* Wet spirometer method for measuring net cost of exercise. Subject inhales room air and exhales into the wet spirometer. Either a kymograph or meter stick attached to the spirometer (not shown) permits one to measure the gas volume. *B,* A cutaway of the wet spirometer shows dead space, which first must be washed out before any gas collections are made. If this is not done, the collected gas will be contaminated and analysis for $CO_2$ and $O_2$ content will be unreliable. With the Douglas bag method (see Fig. 4–2) dead space is no problem as the bag is first evacuated and gas samples are taken prior to measuring the gas volume in a spirometer or gas meter.
*See illustration on the opposite page.*

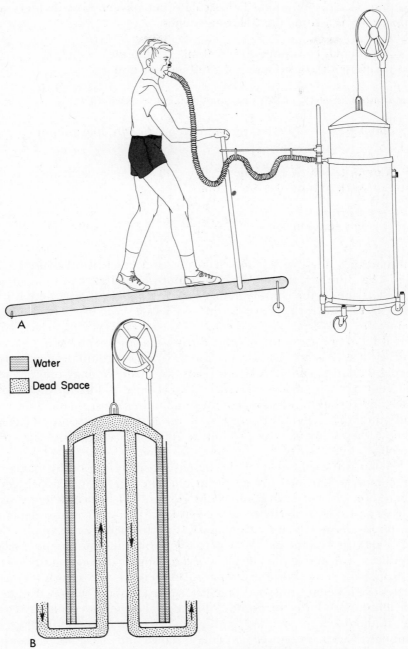

■ Water

▨ Dead Space

A

B

**Figure 4–4** *See legend on the opposite page.*

In summary, we determined (1) resting $O_2$ consumption; and (2) exercise $O_2$ consumption. To calculate net oxygen cost in liters per minute let us assume the following values:

Resting $O_2$ consumption = 300 ml. per minute
Exercise $O_2$ consumption = 2800 ml. per minute

Remember: Net $O_2$ consumption = Exercise − Resting

2800 − 300 = 2500 ml. per minute or 2.5 liters per minute

**Computation of Efficiency.** Per cent efficiency is defined as the ratio of work output over input times 100, or:

$$\text{Per cent efficiency} = \frac{\text{Useful work output}}{\text{Energy expended}} \times 100$$

All machines must be less than 100 per cent efficient because of friction. That is to say, the *useful* work output will be less than work input. The doctrine of the conservation of energy implies that although it is possible to transform energies, *one can neither create nor destroy energy.* Remember, machines do *not* create or destroy energy, they merely convert it from one form to another; during the conversion, some energy is *always* lost (wasted). If this were not the case, we could develop a perpetual motion machine. A steam plant, for example, may operate at 5 per cent or at even less efficiency because heat is lost up the smoke stack and through radiation, conduction, and exhaust steam. Turbines and automobile engines operate at about 20 to 25 per cent efficiency, while a diesel engine may produce an output-input ratio of approximately 30 to 35 per cent.

What is the efficiency of the human? Usually the performance of large muscle activities results in an efficiency of 20 to 25 per cent. There are, of course, individual differences, which include body size, fitness, and skill in performing a given task. Efficiency is also dependent upon the speed with which a task is performed. For example, riding a bicycle ergometer at 60 revolutions per minute at the pedals produces near maximum efficiency. Increasing or decreasing the speed of work will cause efficiency to decrease. Figure 4–5 clearly demonstrates the influence of speed on efficiency in climbing stairs. Fifty steps per minute produces the highest efficiency and the lowest energy cost.

It should be mentioned at this time that there is a difference in running efficiencies between middle-distance and marathon runners.[2] This is shown in Figure 4–6. Marathon runners are about 5 to 10 per cent more efficient on the average than middle-distance runners. This

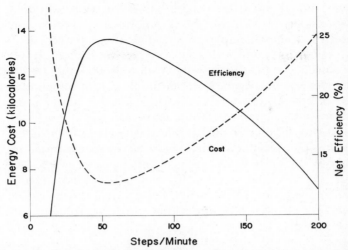

**Figure 4–5** Influence of speed in climbing stairs on energy cost and efficiency. The cost is lowest and efficiency highest when 50 steps per minute were climbed. (Data from Lupton, H.[4])

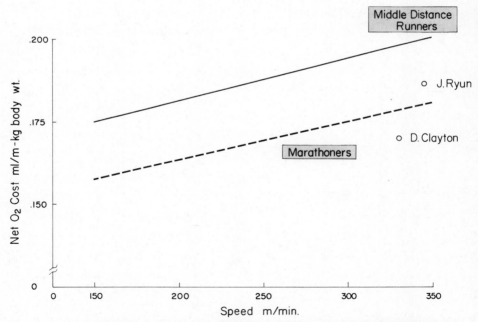

**Figure 4–6** Differences in running efficiencies between middle-distance runners and marathon runners. Marathon runners are about 5 to 10 per cent more efficient than middle distance runners. Notice that the great miler J. Ryun is the most efficient of the middle-distance runners and that D. Clayton, the world's best marathoner, is the most efficient among the marathon runners. (Based on data from various sources as compiled by Fox and Costill.[2])

advantage, though small for runs of short duration, would be an important consideration during the 2½ hours required to run a good marathon race. For example, a 10 per cent greater efficiency would mean a savings of about 60 liters of oxygen consumed or 300 kcal. of heat produced per marathon race! Also, note that the great half-mile and mile runner, Jim Ryun, is the most efficient of the middle-distance runners, and Derek Clayton, the world's best marathon runner, is the most efficient among the marathon runners.

**Measuring Efficiency on Bicycle Ergometer.**   Figure 4–7 depicts the friction type bicycle, which was the most common ergometer employed by the early work physiologists, many of whom constructed their own. To the front wheel of the bicycle is welded a heavy piece of metal weighing about 40 pounds. This is called the flywheel; around the flywheel is a leather belt, one end of which is attached to a scale and the other end to a tray to hold weights (the resistance). As the subject commences to pedal, the leather belt will cause friction against the flywheel. The resistance against which the subject works as he pedals will be equal to the weight in the tray less the reading on the scale. For computing the efficiency we need know both the work performed by the subject (input) and work accomplished (output). When using the friction type bicycle, work output may be determined as follows. Remembering that work equals force times distance, the distance (D)

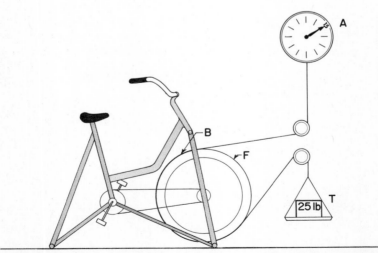

**Figure 4–7**  Friction type bicycle ergometer. With no frictional resistance, the spring scale (A) will record the weight in the tray (T). As the subject pedals, the belt (B) will cause friction against the flywheel (F). The reading on the spring scale will be reduced by an amount equal to the resistance. Therefore the work output will equal the weight in the tray minus the spring scale reading; in this example it is 10 pounds.

which the subject rides is found by multiplying the circumference of the flywheel by the number of revolutions; for example:

$W = F \times D$
$F$ = Weight in tray — reading on scale
$D$ = $2\pi r$ (circumference of flywheel) × number of flywheel revolutions

Given:

| | |
|---|---|
| Bicycle resistance (F) | = 10 pounds |
| Radius of flywheel | = 12 inches |
| $\pi$ | = 22/7 or 3.14 |
| Circumference | = $2\pi r$ or (2) (3.14) (12 inches) |
| Circumference | = 75.4 inches |
| Flywheel revolutions | = 1000 |

Therefore:

| | |
|---|---|
| Distance | = (1000) (75.4 inches) = 75,400 inches or 6283 feet |
| Work | = (Force) (Distance) |
| | = (10 pounds) (6,283 feet) |
| Work | = 62,830 foot-pounds |

*Work input* is determined by measuring the energy ($\dot{V}O_2$) used by the subject in performing submaximal work and converting this to foot-pounds.* (The numerator and denominator in the efficiency formula must be in the same unit.) If the subject's $R$ during submaximal exercise were 0.82, then each liter of oxygen consumed is equal to 4.83 kcal. (Table 4–4). Let us imagine he rode the bicycle for 10 minutes, which required 20 liters of oxygen, or (20) (4.83) = 96.60 kcal. From Table 4–1 we can convert the 96.60 kcal. to foot-pounds: (96.60 kcal.) (3086 foot-pounds/kcal.) = 298,108 foot-pounds.

$$\text{Efficiency} = \frac{\text{Work output}}{\text{Work input}} \times 100$$

$$\text{Efficiency} = \frac{62,830 \text{ foot-pounds}}{298,108 \text{ foot-pounds}} \times 100 = 21 \text{ per cent}$$

Many of the newer bicycles are calibrated to give a direct readout in power units (i.e., watts or kilogram-meters per unit of time). Efficiency may still be computed as was previously mentioned, so long as

---

*During maximal exercise, work input would be determined by measuring net $\dot{V}O_2$ during *both* work and recovery (p. 55).

the numerator and denominator are expressed in identical units (power or work).

**Measuring Efficiency on a Treadmill.**    If the subject were walking or running horizontally on the treadmill (0° slope) he or she is not performing "useful" work and therefore efficiency cannot be computed. Sometimes this is difficult for a student to resolve because you and I know it requires *energy* to walk or run—but according to the physicist, we are not doing any *work*. Recall that work is moving an object through a distance. The subject walking along a horizontal is raising and lowering the center of gravity the same distance; therefore, one cancels the other. All the energy expended by the subject is degraded as heat without performing any useful work. The same is true if you hold a weight at arm's length in front; because you are not moving the weight, no useful work is being performed, even though you are expending energy. As a consequence, the treadmill must be positioned so the subject walks up a grade; in other words, the angle of the treadmill with the horizontal must be greater than 0°. Usually the slope or incline of the treadmill is reported as per cent grade rather than in degrees. Per cent grade may be defined as units (feet) of rise per 100 horizontal units (feet); it may be determined by multiplying the tangent of the angle times 100, as can be observed in Table 4–5. To determine efficiency while walking on an elevated treadmill, we need to know (1) work output, and (2) work input.

*Determination of Work Output*

Work output is equal to the weight of the subject times the vertical distance he would have raised himself in walking up the incline of the

**Table 4–5   ANGLES OF INCLINE AND CORRESPONDING PER CENT GRADE**\*

| $\theta$ (DEGREES) | TANGENT $\theta$ | SINE $\theta$ | PER CENT GRADE |
|---|---|---|---|
| 1 | 0.0175 | .0175 | 1.75 |
| 2 | 0.0349 | .0349 | 3.49 |
| 3 | 0.0524 | .0523 | 5.24 |
| 4 | 0.0699 | .0698 | 6.99 |
| 5 | 0.0875 | .0872 | 8.75 |
| 6 | 0.1051 | .1045 | 10.51 |
| 7 | 0.1228 | .1219 | 12.28 |
| 8 | 0.1405 | .1392 | 14.05 |
| 9 | 0.1584 | .1564 | 15.84 |
| 10 | 0.1763 | .1736 | 17.63 |

\*Note that the sine and the tangent are equal for the first two degrees; as the angle increases, the difference between sine and tangent increases.

treadmill, i.e., work equals force (weight of subject) times distance. Measuring the weight of the subject poses no problem; however, computing vertical distance is somewhat more involved. Referring to Figure 4–8, the measurements and computations are made in the following manner:

The vertical distance $X$ is equal to the sine of angle theta ($\Theta$) times $B$, which is the distance traveled along the incline, or:

$$X = (\text{Sine } \Theta)\ (B)$$

For example, assume angle $\Theta$ is 2 degrees. The angle may be measured with an inclinometer at point $C$, Figure 4–8. Sine $\Theta$ of 2 degrees (from Table 4–5) equals 0.0349. The value of $B$ is calculated by knowing the speed of the treadmill belt and duration of exercise. For example, the distance traveled on the incline while walking at 3 miles per hour for 30 minutes (0.5 hours) is 1.5 miles, or:

$$B = (3 \text{ miles per hour})\ (0.5 \text{ hour}) = 1.5 \text{ miles}$$

$$\text{or}$$

$$X = (0.0349)\ (1.5 \text{ miles}) = 0.05235 \text{ mile}$$

Changing $X$ to feet: (0.05235 mile) (5280 feet per mile)
$$= 276.4 \text{ feet}$$

Therefore, work output (W) becomes:

$$W = (160 \text{ pounds})\ (276.4 \text{ feet}) = 44{,}224 \text{ foot-pounds of}$$
work accomplished during 30 minutes

Efficiency may be expressed in power units (work per unit of time) or net work. For power calculation, convert net work output to work per unit of time, or:

$$\text{Power} = \frac{44{,}224 \text{ foot-pounds}}{30 \text{ minutes}} = 1474 \text{ foot-pounds per minute}$$

### Determination of Work Input

Work input during submaximal exercise (aerobic) is expressed in terms of net oxygen consumption per unit of time. The subject must be in a steady state, as was previously discussed. Assuming the net $\dot{V}O_2$ of the subject while walking is 0.5 liter per minute, we must convert this measurement to identical units of work output; that is, liters of oxygen per minute must be expressed in foot-pounds per minute.

The first consideration is to convert liters of oxygen per minute to kilocalories per minute. This is done by determining $R$ and then referring to Table 4–4 to obtain the proper caloric equivalent. Or:

Assuming $R = 0.82$
1 liter of $O_2 = 4.83$ kcal., or

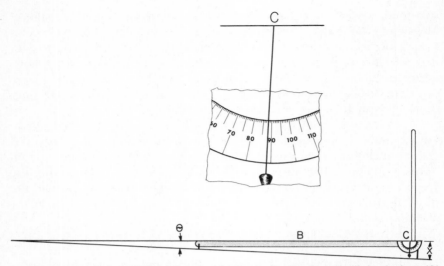

**Figure 4-8** Determination of work output using inclined treadmill. Angle theta (Θ) is determined by use of inclinometer at point *C*. The reading of 88° at point *C* on the treadmill is equivalent to 2° at angle Θ (180° − [90° + 88°] = 2°). The vertical distance the subject would travel (*X*) is computed as outlined in the text.

(0.5 liter/minute) (4.83 kcal./liter) = 2.41 kcal./minute
1 kcal. = 3086 foot-pounds per minute (Table 4–2)
(2.41 kcal./minute) (3086 foot-pounds/kcal.) = 7437
   foot-pounds/minute

$$\text{Net efficiency} = \frac{1474 \text{ foot-pounds/minute}}{7437 \text{ foot-pounds/minute}} \times 100 = 19.8 \text{ per cent}$$

Sometimes the efficiency of walking up an incline is represented as the ratio of useful work performed to the energy expended in walking up the grade less the energy expended walking the same distance on a horizontal plane, times 100.

$$\text{Net efficiency} = \frac{(\text{Vertical distance})(\text{weight of subject})}{\text{Energy expended climbing} - \text{energy expended on horizontal}} \times 100$$

## Ancillary Considerations in Measuring Energy

The indirect physiological measurement of energy is quite well standardized in the laboratory. The methods we have already discussed are applicable in most cases. However, there are certain ancillary considerations which are well to keep in mind when measuring and interpreting the energy cost of activities:

(1) Effect of body size on $O_2$ consumption.

(2) Values to be expected when measuring $O_2$ consumption, ventilation, and heart rate under conditions of light, moderate, and heavy work.

(3) Some obtained values of work cost for various physical activities.

(4) Modified methods of reflecting work cost.

**Body Size and Work Cost.**   A larger person in moving the body a given distance will certainly expend more energy than will a smaller one. As a result, it is usually more appropriate to express energy expenditure in terms of body weight, particularly when making comparisons. For example:

Work:   Kilogram-meters per kilogram of body weight
          Foot-pounds per pound of body weight

Energy: $\dot{V}o_2$ in milliliters per kilogram of body weight

On occasion, the scientist may choose units of surface area rather than of weight. Figure 4–9, which is a nomogram, permits us to calculate surface area if we know height and weight. For example, we have a subject weighing 150 pounds, who is 5 feet 8 inches in height. His surface area equals 1.8 square meters.

$$\text{Energy expenditure} = \frac{\dot{V}o_2}{\text{Surface area}} = \text{Cost per square meter of body surface area}$$

**Average Work Values.**   To be well oriented in the physiology of work and athletics, certain common values should be committed to memory. For example, one should remember that in sitting and reading this book, about 300 ml. per minute of oxygen are being consumed; at the same time, about 6 to 8 liters of air are being ventilated per minute. The resting heart rate is approximately 80 beats per minute.

Knowing such values forms a baseline for comprehending strenuosity of work. For example, work resulting in 4.5 liters per minute would mean little if one did not realize that 0.3 liter (300 ml.) is required at rest. Work requiring such a high consumption is 15 times more strenuous than resting. So, too, a person ventilating 140 liters per minute is

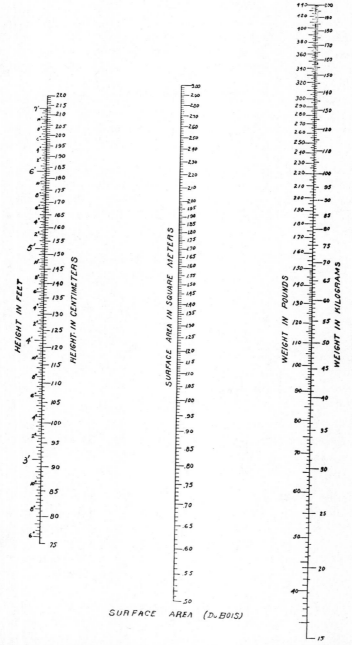

**Figure 4–9** Nomographic chart for computing surface area. (Copyright 1920 by W. M. Boothby and R. B. Sandiford.)

moving about 20 times more air than that required for resting metabolism.

Table 4–6 contains average values, which permit us better understanding of the physiological requirements of performance. Memorizing a few of these values will be well worthwhile.

## Modified Methods of Reflecting Energy Cost

Situations occur when the work physiologist must employ a somewhat different approach in measuring energy expenditure. There are three methods that can yield satisfactory results; these are perhaps best illustrated with examples.

**Measurement of Energy Cost for the 100-Yard Dash.** One might consider it rather difficult to run along the track holding a Douglas bag or wet spirometer in order to gather a sprinter's exhaled air. Instead, resting $\dot{V}o_2$ is determined; then, during the race, the subject holds his breath until the finish, at which time he holds his nose and directs all exhaled air into a series of Douglas bags.

This method was employed in measuring the cost of the open and closed swimming turn.[1] The six male swimmers were tested in a postabsorptive state (12 hours following the last meal). Resting metabolic rates were determined, then the swimmers swam 70 feet, performing either the closed or the open turn without taking a breath. Immediately upon completion of the swim, they exhaled into a Douglas bag for 15 minutes. Net energy cost of the exercise was determined by subtracting oxygen consumed during 15 minutes of rest from that obtained during the 15 minutes of recovery. The data showed no significant difference between the two turns in regard to the net energy cost, but the closed turn was performed significantly faster.

**Measurement of Energy Cost for the 440-Yard Race.** Again a difficult situation arises: finding an experimenter physically qualified to run alongside an athlete with utensils in hand in order to collect that valued exhaled air! Furthermore, what athlete can hold his breath throughout the 440 yards? In this instance, the $O_2$ debt may be used as a reliable indication of the strenuosity for the event. After resting $\dot{V}o_2$ is determined, the stage is set so that immediately following the race, all exhaled air is collected. The resting value subtracted from the recovery value represents the oxygen debt (page 31).

This method was employed in comparing the oxygen debts accumulated in swimming the 400-yard free style, using the open and closed turns.[3] The subjects were 5 Ohio State University varsity swimmers who were actively engaged in competitive swimming. Upon entering the pool area in a postabsorptive state, the swimmers lay on a training table for 20 minutes, covered with a blanket. During the last 5 minutes of rest, exhaled air was directed into a Douglas bag. The sub-

## Table 4-6 CLASSIFICATION OF PHYSICAL WORK BY WORK CAPACITY TEST*

| CLASSIFICATION OF WORK | PULSE RATE PER MINUTE | METABOLIC RATE | | VENTILATION | | RQ | LACTIC ACID IN MULTIPLES OF RESTING VALUE | LENGTH OF TIME WORK CAN BE SUSTAINED |
|---|---|---|---|---|---|---|---|---|
| | | $O_2$ ml./ Minute | kcal./ Minute | Volume, Liters/ Minute | Rate, Breaths/ Minute | | | |
| I. Light | | | | | | | | |
| A. Mild | <100 | <750 | 4 | <20 | <14 | 0.85 | Normal | Indefinite |
| B. Moderate | <120 | <1500 | <7.5 | <35 | <15 | 0.85 | Within normal limits | 8 hours daily on the job |
| II. Heavy | | | | | | | | |
| C. Optimal | <140 | <2000 | <10 | <50 | <16 | 0.9 | 1.5× | 8 hours daily for few weeks (seasonal work, military maneuvers, etc.) |
| D. Strenuous | <160 | <2500 | <12.5 | <60 | <20 | 0.95 | 2× | 4 hours two or three times a week for few weeks (special physical training) |
| III. Severe | | | | | | | | |
| E. Maximal | <180 | <3000 | <15 | <80 | <25 | <1.0 | 5–6× | 1 to 2 hours occasionally (usually in competitive sports) |
| F. Exhausting | >180 | >3000 | >15 | <120 | <30 | >1.0 | >6× or more | Few minutes; rarely |

*From Wells, et al.

jects then entered the pool and were required to swim 400 yards in 4:50, plus or minus 5 seconds. Recovery gas was collected for 30 minutes following the exercise. Average oxygen debts for the open and closed turns were 4.7 and 5.1 liters of oxygen, respectively. Although the open turn resulted in a smaller oxygen debt, the difference was not statistically significant.

**Measurement of Energy Cost Using Telemetry.** The scientists of the National Aeronautics and Space Administration (NASA), prior to initiating programs designed to probe an organism's physiological reactions to space, devised instrumentation that could radio back to the space center such information as respiration, heart rate, and blood pressure. Today, the field of physiological radio transmission—that is, telemetry—is so well advanced that most college laboratories are equipped for telemetering numerous physiological variables. Of special interest to us is the telemetering of heart rate, for under submaximal work loads this variable is linearly related to the work load and the $O_2$ consumption values. Figure 4–10 graphically illustrates these relationships.

The use of telemetry allows us to estimate the $\dot{V}o_2$ of numerous physical and sports activities which otherwise would be impossible to determine. Two physical education students telemetered the heart rate of a college basketball coach during a game. If one can use heart rate as an index of stress, these men found as the game situation became critical the coach responded with an increased heart rate. Men about to be released in the X-15 experimental aircraft responded with extremely high heart rates, even though the physical effort was of little consequence; the same is true of the astronauts when they are placed in critical situations such as liftoff and moon landing.

If we were presented with the problem of evaluating energy cost while playing handball, for instance, we would proceed as follows:

(1) Have the subject walk on the treadmill at gradually increasing work loads.

(2) At each work load, measure heart rate and oxygen consumption.

(3) Plot this relationship on a graph, as indicated in Figure 4–10.

The subject is then fitted with a transmitter, as shown in Figure 4–11. This instrument, which is fitted about the subject's waist, radios the heart rate to a recorder. Any time during the handball game heart rate can be measured. In this manner, $\dot{V}o_2$ while playing can be indirectly determined. For example, if heart rate were 155 beats per minute then $\dot{V}o_2$ would equal about 2 liters per minute at that particular time (see Fig. 4–10). Each person must be so "titrated," as the relationship is in-

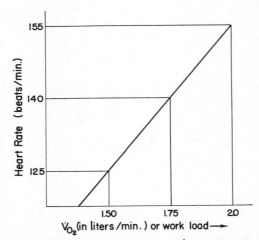

**Figure 4–10** Relationships among work load, $\dot{V}O_2$, and heart rate. As the work load or $\dot{V}O_2$ increases, so does heart rate in a linear (straight line) manner.

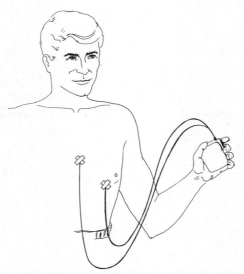

**Figure 4–11** Subject fitted to transmitter for telemetering heart rate. The instrument picks up the subject's heart rate and transmits it to a receiver and recorder. This compact and light piece of equipment allows the subject to perform activity unencumbered and at a distance from the recording equipment. Such instrumentation is used in recording the physiological data received from the astronauts.

dividualistic—the primary variables are skill, physical fitness, and work load.

## Summary

The primary purpose of this chapter is to enlighten you as to how energy requirements of human performance are determined in the laboratory. Recall that we measured oxygen consumption during performance, ascertained what food was being metabolized by determining $R$, and converted this to work equivalents. From Table 4–4, if $R$ were 0.82, then each liter of oxygen would be equivalent to 4.825 kcal. From Table 4–1 we could then convert this to the work unit we desired. By noting time of performing the work, units in Table 4–2 allow us to express our final answer in power if we should so desire.

Efficiency of performance was discussed and its measurement demonstrated; finally, the mathematical relationships among work, heart rate, and oxygen consumption were shown.

Even though you may never work in a laboratory, information contained in this chapter will form the basis for making more valid judgments regarding energy requirements of exercise and sport. After all, as has been demonstrated in Chapter 2, energy and its expenditure permit physical education. Without a successful marriage of the two, we would have to look elsewhere for a profession.

## QUESTIONS

1. Define work and power. Express each by a formula.

2. What is the principle of the conservation of energy?

3. Explain the difference between direct and indirect calorimetry.

4. What is the respiratory exchange ratio?

5. How is the respiratory exchange ratio used in the indirect measurement of energy?

6. What three fundamental measurements are needed when indirectly measuring the energy expenditure of a given exercise?

7. In what situation would it be more appropriate to use Douglas bags rather than the wet spirometer when indirectly measuring the energy cost of exercise?

8. Explain efficiency and indicate how the efficiency of a human is measured.

9. How does body size affect the performance of work?

10. How might you proceed in measuring the energy cost of running the 100-yard dash?

11. What are the physiological considerations which allow you to estimate energy cost through telemetering heart rate?

## REFERENCES

1. Fox, E.L., Bartels, R.L., and Bowers, R.W.: Comparison of speed and energy expenditure for two swimming turns. Res. Quart., 34:322–326, 1963.
2. Fox, E.L., and Costill, D.L.: Estimated cardiorespiratory responses during marathon running. Arch. Environ. Health, 24:315–324, 1972.
3. Hagerman, F.C.: A Comparison of Oxygen Debts in Swimming the 400-Yard Free-Style While Using the Open and Closed Turns. Master's Thesis. The Ohio State University, 1962.
4. Lupton, H.: Analysis of effects of speed on mechanical efficiency of human movement. J. Physiol., 57:337, 1923.
5. Lusk, G.: Science of Nutrition. 4th ed. p. 65, Philadelphia, W. B. Saunders Co., 1928.
6. Wells, J.G., Balke, B., and Van Fossan, D.D.: Lactic acid accumulation during work. A suggested standardization of work classification. J. Appl. Physiol., 10:51–55, 1957.

## SELECTED READINGS

Bogert, L.J., Briggs, G.M., and Calloway, D.H.: Nutrition and physical fitness. 9th ed., Philadelphia, W. B. Saunders Co., 1973.
Consolazio, C.F., Johnson, R.E., and Pecora, L.J.: Physiological Measurements of Metabolic Functions in Man. pp. 1–11, New York, McGraw-Hill Book Co., Inc., 1963.
Kleiber, M.: The Fire Of Life. New York, John Wiley and Sons, Inc., 1961.

# SECTION 2

# NEUROMUSCULAR CONCEPTS

*Chapter 5* ─────────────────────────────

# NERVOUS CONTROL OF MUSCULAR MOVEMENT

Our primary purpose in studying neuromuscular physiology is to learn how muscles respond to stimuli and in particular to gain some understanding about the way in which we learn motor skills. Such information should help us to become better teachers, coaches, and trainers, to say nothing of allowing us to better appreciate the masterful computerized communication system that belongs to each of us.

## INTRODUCTION

Absolutely nothing on this earth is more complex than the nervous system. Neuroanatomists and physiologists spend their entire professional careers attempting to untangle a tiny part of this complex system. Understandably, therefore, we as coaches and physical educators will study only the most pertinent parts of this complex field.

For purpose of study we may first divide the nervous system into the sensory, central, and motor portions. Sensory nerves receive stimuli from such areas as the surface of the skin (pain, cold, heat, pressure), the eyes, nose, ears, and tongue.

The spinal cord, which extends from the base of the skull to the second lumbar vertebra, and the brain compose the central portion of the nervous system, which is called the *central nervous system* (CNS). The primary functions here are to integrate incoming stimuli, to modify these stimuli if necessary, to execute motor movements, to store information (memory), and to generate thoughts or ideas.

Connections are made from the CNS to the motor portion of the nervous system. It is here that muscles receive their incoming signals and execute the desired motor event whether it be kicking a football or throwing a baseball.

The *autonomic* (meaning self-controlled, or functioning independently) *nervous system* is generally considered by itself and is that portion of the nervous system which helps to control activities such as those involving movement and secretion by the visceral organs, urinary output, body temperature, heart rate, adrenal secretion, and blood pressure. Although involuntary, many of these functions are influenced by emotions. For example, secretions and movements of the digestive organs, movement of the bowels, and secretion of sweat are modified during periods of excitement. All of us have experienced increases in heart rate as we become scared or emotionally aroused. Breaking out into a cold sweat is another example of an involuntary act (one which we cannot turn on or off at will) caused by an excited emotional state such as fear.

We might suggest at this time that the overall organization of the nervous system performs three basic functions: (1) *excitability,* which results in a signal from a receptor—for example, the retina of the eye becomes excited from a light source, and the inner ear is stimulated by a sound wave; (2) *conduction* takes place as the stimulus or signal is transmitted over nerve fibers to the CNS; and (3) *integration,* which takes place within the CNS. Here numerous stimuli or signals are received, sorted out, and integrated into the proper response(s). The response may be to throw a ball, to volley in tennis, or simply reflexively to remove your finger from a hot stove.

It is our purpose in this chapter to describe how excitation takes place, the method whereby stimuli or signals are conducted, and how the CNS integrates all messages into coordinated performance. This information will give us a better understanding of *how* children learn a motor skill, stores such information, and recalls the skill when the appropriate stimulus is applied.

# SENSORY RECEPTORS

Transmission of information throughout the nervous system is dependent upon nerve fibers as the medium and electrical impulses as the form of energy. Examples of sensory nerves are those excited by sound, pain, light, and taste. The following descriptions illustrate the way in which peripheral receptor nerves become stimulated and how this information is transmitted to the CNS.

## Smell

Located within the nostrils are millions of tiny *olfactory* cells. From these cells grow tiny cilia (olfactory hairs, about 3 microns in length) which react to various odors. For example, let's say that a bottle of perfume is opened in your presence. The odor molecules diffuse from the open bottle to the nerve receptors in your nose. A chemical reaction takes place at the site of the receptors, energizing the system that causes a signal to be sent along interconnecting nerves to the CNS. In the brain the sensation of smell is interpreted to be either pleasant (floral ) or distasteful (putrid or pungent).

## Sound

The sound waves reaching the ear activate electrical impulses in a somewhat different manner. As the sound wave reaches the ear drum, the small bones of the middle ear are set into motion. Such movement causes displacement of nerve cells, which in turn generate an electrical potential (current). In this manner the ear converts sound waves into an electrical current which proceeds toward the CNS by way of afferent nerve fibers.

## Balance

In addition to receiving sound impulses, the inner ear (containing the vestibular apparatus) functions in helping us to maintain our equilibrium (physical orientation to the space about us). Running, throwing, tumbling, and all physical motor events would be impossible without a system to keep us constantly informed of our position. Within the semicircular canals of the ears are tiny hairs cells bathed in a liquid and connected to the vestibular nerve. Movement causes pressure upon these vestibular receptor cells which transmit impulses to the brain, thereby controlling equilibrium. The three semicircular canals in each ear are arranged at right angles to one another so that physical movements, regardless of direction, stimulate the tiny receptor cells, which in turn apprise the brain of our environmental position. As soon as an imbalance occurs or is about to occur, stimuli from the semicircular canals inform the CNS, which makes proper and preventive adjustments so that we do not fall.

## THE REFLEX ARC

What happens to the electrical stimulus once it is sent along to the CNS? The simplest illustration and explanation is the reflex arc (Fig. 5–1). Let us examine what occurs when your finger touches a lighted candle. The pain receptors (sensory) in the finger receive the stimulus (heat from the flame), which is then transmitted by means of an afferent nerve fiber to the spinal cord. Entering the spinal cord through the dorsal root, the sensation of pain is transferred through one or more synapses to the motor or efferent nerve fiber. This efferent nerve fiber transmits the impulse to the appropriate muscle(s), and the hand is withdrawn from the flame.

The means by which impulses are transferred from one nerve fiber to another and nerve fiber to muscle fiber and the mechanism of inhibition between nerve fibers are important concepts when studying movement. We shall begin by examining how impulses are transferred from one nerve to another.

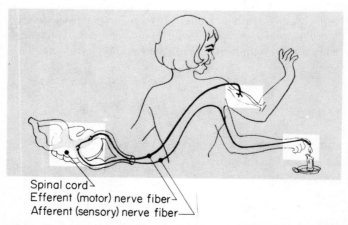

Spinal cord
Efferent (motor) nerve fiber
Afferent (sensory) nerve fiber

**Figure 5–1**   The reflex arc. When your fingers touch a flame, the pain receptors in the fingers receive the stimulus, which is then transmitted by means of the afferent (sensory) nerve fiber to the spinal cord. The efferent (motor) fiber then transmits impulses to the appropriate muscles, and the hand is withdrawn from the flame.

## NERVE-TO-NERVE SYNAPSES

A nerve cell is composed of an *axon*, the long fiber which conducts the impulse away from the cell body; the *soma* or body of the cell; and *dendrites*, numerous short projections from the body of the cell which receive impulses at their periphery and conduct them toward the soma or cell body (Fig. 5–2). Nerve cells are stimulated at one set of terminals and therefore conduct the impulse in one direction only—that is, away from the origin of stimulation. Nerve fibers that conduct impulses toward a designated place are termed *afferent; efferent* fibers carry impulses away from a specified location. Dorsal roots of the spinal cord are composed of afferent fibers; those transmitting impulses from the spinal cord to a skeletal muscle are *efferent* fibers.

Throughout the CNS are billions of these nerves; the connection of one to another is called a *synapse.* As it approaches the nerve cell, the fiber makes a *presynaptic* connection. Across the gap or *synaptic cleft* the impulse is transmitted to another neuron called the *postsynaptic* neuron. Transmission across the synaptic cleft is by means of a chemical transmitter, probably acetylcholine (ACh). Neuronal synaptic clefts are located at points where fine branches of one neuron are in contact with the cell body or with processes of another neuron.

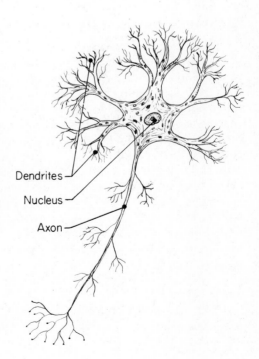

**Figure 5–2** A nerve cell (neuron) composed of an axon, the long fiber that conducts impulses away from the cell body; the soma or body of the cell, containing the nucleus; and the dendrites, numerous short projections from the body of the cell that receive impulses from other neurons.

Dendrites

Nucleus

Axon

As an impulse reaches the synaptic cleft, the chemical transmitter (ACh) is discharged and as a result, an action potential is created in the postsynaptic neuron. The increase in electrical potential (millivolts) in this neuron from its resting membrane potential is called the *excitatory postsynaptic membrane potential* (EPSP). If the voltage increase is adequate (increase of about 11 millivolts above the resting potential), the neuron will discharge, sending the impulse on its way. If the EPSP is less than about 11 millivolts, the motoneuron will not discharge and consequently the stimulus will be lost. The minimal electrical level at which this neuron will transmit is called the *threshold for excitation.*

## Spatial and Temporal Summation

Provided that a minimal number of stimuli are received from various presynaptic terminals at the synaptic cleft simultaneously or within a short time period of one another, they will summate, eliciting an increased EPSP and permitting a postsynaptic neuronal discharge. The additive effect of these various stimuli is called *spatial summation.* So, too, if successive discharges from the *same* presynaptic terminal occur within 15 milliseconds of one another, they will summate and, if strong enough, cause a neuronal discharge. This is called *temporal summation.*

## Inhibition at the Neuronal Synapse

Most neurons start and end within the brain and spinal cord. The motor and sensory neurons, however, reside both inside and outside the CNS. A message arising from prior neuron activity is transmitted to other neurons called *interneurons* or *internuncial neurons* until the impulse reaches its destination. These interneurons act as middlemen between incoming and outgoing impulses. Between each neuron is the synaptic connection discussed earlier. A strong impulse or a summation of impulses results in an excitatory postsynaptic potential in the adjoining nerve fiber and causes a neuronal discharge. There are occasions when you might wish to *inhibit* an impulse. For example, you may (foolishly!) wish to leave your hand on a hot stove. At the synaptic junction, an *inhibitory* postsynaptic potential (IPSP) is generated. Whenever an inhibitory neuron delivers its impulse to the synapse, an impulse with an electrical sign opposite to that of an excitatory neuron is created. When an IPSP occurs simultaneously with an EPSP they cancel each other: EPSPs oppose IPSPs.

The function of inhibitory neurons is not only to allow us to overcome impulses which we consciously wish to oppose (e.g., leaving your hand on a hot stove) but also more importantly to exclude unimportant nonconscious stimuli, especially those elicited through the sensory receptors. Just imagine the number of impulses which would have to be processed by the CNS if inhibition were absent. To mention a few:

1. Continual sensations of pressure from sitting, standing, and lying.
2. Sensations of touch from our clothing.
3. Innumerable sounds we do not care to be bothered with.
4. Light alone sends tremendous numbers of impulses to the retina which are of no concern (we see only what we wish to see!).
5. Stimulation from minor variations in heat and cold are ignored by the CNS through the inhibitory neuronal mechanism.
6. Odors are about us constantly and perhaps only those coming from the kitchen before dinner are worthy of processing; many others are inhibited and should be.

Stop for a moment and look about you; listen and then ponder the countless number of stimuli coming to the CNS from the environment and from your peripheral nerve endings that should be inhibited. Inhibition of extraneous impulses allows you to concentrate on the contents of this book, thus enabling you to become a better exercise physiologist, coach, and physical educator—we hope!

In addition to postsynaptic inhibition, it has been demonstrated recently that there also is a presynaptic inhibition mechanism. Perhaps upon a given stimulus the presynaptic neuronal terminals in some manner release inadequate amounts of the transmitter chemical acetylcholine. It is of paramount importance at this time to mention that inhibition has thus far been shown to occur at nerve-to-nerve synapses only and not at *nerve-to-muscle synapses.*

Without the inhibitory mechanism the poor brain probably would be stimulated right out of its cranium!

## ACTIVITY AT THE NEUROMUSCULAR JUNCTION

Figure 5–3 illustrates anatomical features of a nerve imbedded into a muscle fiber. This union is called the *neuromuscular* or *myoneural junction* or *motor endplate.* Transmission of the neuronal impulse across the synaptic cleft is made possible through the secretion of acetylcholine. As the stimulus reaches the muscle fiber, cholinesterase is secreted which deactivates the acetylcholine by absorbing it. This prevents further excitation of the muscle fiber following stimulation for that immediate time period.

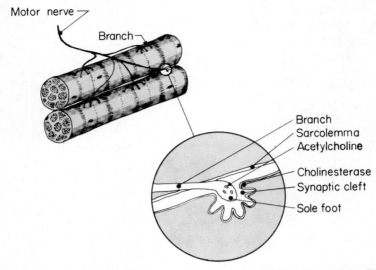

Motor nerve
Branch
Branch
Sarcolemma
Acetylcholine
Cholinesterase
Synaptic cleft
Sole foot

**Figure 5–3** The neuromuscular junction. The point at which the nerve fiber invaginates the muscle fiber is called the end-plate (enlargement). Transmission of the neuronal impulse across the synaptic cleft is made possible through the secretion of acetylcholine. The cholinesterase absorbs acetylcholine, thus preventing further excitation of the muscle following stimulation for that immediate time period.

The manner in which a stimulus is transmitted from the nerve to the muscle fiber is very similar, as you will see, to the way in which an impulse is transmitted from nerve to nerve through the neuronal synapse. Apparently, the major difference is that there is no inhibition mechanism at the neuromuscular junction.

In general, a muscle fiber receives only one nerve fiber. However, the large fibers of an efferent (motor) nerve divide into numerous smaller fibers servicing as many as 200 muscle fibers. An individual nerve fiber plus all the muscle fibers it innervates is called a *motor unit.* As an impulse arrives at the neuromuscular junction acetylcholine is released; the impulse is then able to cross the synapse, creating a potential in the muscle fiber (Fig. 5–4). Such a potential, as we just learned in our discussion of the neuronal synapse, is called an *excitatory postsynaptic potential* (EPSP). The neuron activating the muscle fiber may receive impulses from several nerve fibers (Fig. 5–4). If the postsynaptic potential is too small the fiber will not contract; but when the EPSP rises to a certain level, discharge takes place and the muscle fiber contracts.

As previously illustrated in the description of the neuronal synapse, this progressive increase in size of the EPSP as a result of a number of impulses is called *spatial summation.* In addition, successive discharges from the same presynaptic terminal will summate, eliciting

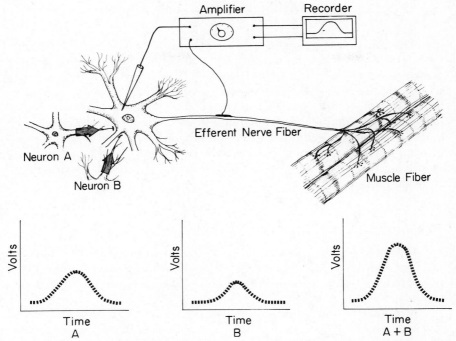

**Figure 5-4** Diagram demonstrating measurement of a nerve impulse. One electrode is placed in the soma, the other on the efferent nerve fiber. Upon stimulation from either neuron A and/or neuron B, the impulse is amplified and printed on the recorder. For example, the impulse from neuron A is recorded and appears in the insert, as does the impulse from neuron B; the combined effect results in the summation of both impulses (A + B).

an increased EPSP, provided that the discharges occur in rapid succession (within 15 milliseconds of each other). This mechanism is called *temporal summation.*

To illustrate, suppose impulse A is initiated in the brain and impulse B comes from a pain receptor in the skin. For example, you decide to get a tan from a sun lamp and in a few minutes impulses from A + B inform you that the heat is too great; you turn off the lamp or perhaps move farther from it. However, you might fall asleep while under the lamp, in which case impulse A, which originated in the brain, could not be activated. Impulse B is not sufficiently strong by itself to arouse muscular activity (i.e., to create an adequate EPSP to fire the neuron). Consequently, you remain asleep while the sun lamp continues slowly to bake your tissue. When you do awaken, in all probability you will have received serious burns.

By inhibiting activation of brain cells, sleep, anaesthetics, and too much liquor prevent adequate stimulation of recipient neurons.

# PROPRIOCEPTORS

The function of proprioceptors is to conduct sensory reports to the CNS from (1) muscles, (2) tendons, (3) ligaments, and (4) joints. Information coming from the proprioceptors is directed both to the conscious and the unconscious portions of the CNS. The prime purpose of the proprioceptive system is to make the CNS aware of limb positions and movements, often called kinesthesis, kinesthetic awareness, or kinesthetic sense. In addition to the simple muscle stretch reflexes, proprioception information is relayed to the cerebellum, which is capable of modifying the action of muscle groups, resulting in smooth, coordinated, accurate movements.

## The Muscle Spindle

In this section we will examine only the proprioceptors found in the muscles themselves, the muscle spindles. We will discuss the other proprioceptors (Golgi tendon organs and joint receptors) in the next chapter.

**Structure of the Spindle.**     The structure of the muscle spindle is given in Figure 5–5. It is nothing more than several modified muscle fibers contained in a capsule, with a sensory nerve spiraled around its center. These modified muscle cells are called *intrafusal fibers* to distinguish them from the regular or *extrafusal fibers.* The center portion of the spindle is not capable of contracting, but the two ends contain contractile fibers. The thin motor nerves innervating the ends are of the gamma type and are thus called *gamma motor neurons.* When they are stimulated, the ends of the spindle contract. The larger motor nerves innervating the regular or extrafusal fibers are called *alpha motor nerves.* When they are stimulated, the muscle contracts in the usual sense.

**Function of the Spindle.**     The spindle is sensitive to length or stretch. Therefore, because the spindle fibers lie parallel to the regular fibers, when the whole muscle is stretched, the center portion of the spindle is stretched also. This stretching activates the sensory nerve located there, which then sends impulses to the central nervous system. In turn, these impulses activate the alpha motor neurons that innervate the regular muscle fibers, and the muscle contracts. If the muscle shortens when it contracts, the spindle also shortens, thus stopping its flow of sensory impulses; the muscle then relaxes.

The spindle is sensitive to both the *rate* of change in length and to the *final length* attained by the muscle fibers. The functional significance of these two types of sensitivity can be illustrated by a muscle engaged in a steady contraction, as when the elbow is flexed steadily against a load (for example, when holding a book). The type of stretch placed on the muscle because of the load is called *tonic stretch* and is concerned with the final length of the muscle fibers. If the load is light, the fibers will be stretched only moderately, and the frequency of discharge of the sensory impulses from the spindle will be low. Thus, only a few motor units are called upon in keeping the load steady.

If there is an unexpected increase in the load being held, such as by adding another book, the muscle will be stretched again. This is evidenced by the fact that the forearm will be lowered owing to the added load. The ensuing reflex contraction initiated by the spindle will reposition the forearm to its original level. However, there will be some overcompensation; that is, at first the contraction will be greater than needed. The greater and more abrupt the increase in load, the greater the frequency of discharge of the spindle, the greater the contraction, and the greater the overcompensation. In other words, with this type of stretch,

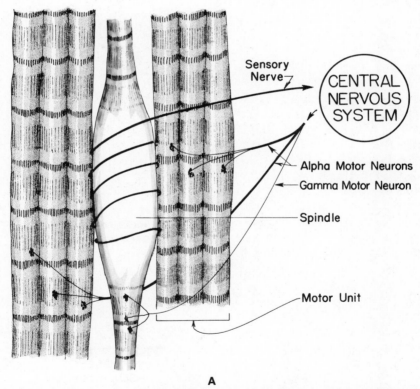

**A**

**Figure 5–5** *A,* Structure of the muscle spindle; *B,* Connections to the central nervous system of the muscle spindle. The spindle is sensitive to stretch. It can be stretched when the entire muscle is stretched or when the gamma motor neurons are stimulated by the motor cortex (gamma loop). In either case, sensory impulses from the spindle are sent to the spinal cord, stimulating the alpha motor neurons, and the muscle contracts. Also, direct stimulation of the alpha motor neurons from the motor cortex is possible.

*Illustration continued on the following page*

called *phasic stretch*, the spindle is responding to the rate or velocity of the change in length and not to the length *per se*. Another example of phasic stretch is given below (stretch reflex).

**The Gamma System.**    There is one other way in which the spindle can be stretched. You will recall (Fig. 5–5) that the contractile ends of the spindle fibers are supplied with motor nerves called gamma motor neurons. These nerves can be stimulated directly by the motor centers located in the cerebral cortex of the brain. When stimulated in this manner, the ends of the spindle contract, thus *stretching* the center portion and stimulating the sensory nerve. In other words, the muscle spindle can be activated by itself, apart from the rest of the muscle. This kind of set-up provides a very sensitive system for the execution of smooth, voluntary movements.

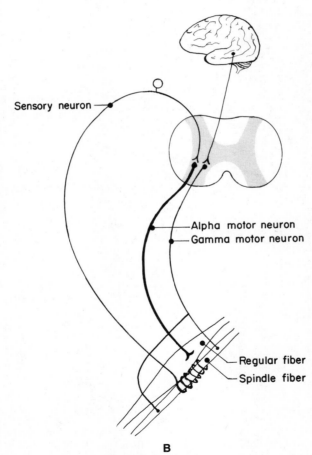

Sensory neuron

Alpha motor neuron
Gamma motor neuron

Regular fiber
Spindle fiber

**B**
**Figure 5–5**  *Continued*

For an example of how the gamma system (sometimes called the gamma loop) works, let's go back to the person voluntarily holding a book in a fixed position (elbow flexed to 90°). We stated that the tonic stretch on the entire muscle created by the load provides information that keeps the load (book) in a relatively fixed position. However, in addition, the gamma neurons are stimulated by impulses sent down directly from the motor cortex. The ends of the spindle contract, the sensory nerve sends impulses back to the central nervous system, and additional information is provided concerning the number of motor units that is required to maintain the original voluntarily initiated position. This additional information provides the refinement that is needed for a smooth rather than a jerky movement.

In summary, there are three ways that the muscle spindle can activate the alpha motor neurons that cause the muscle to contract: (1) by tonic stretch, (2) by phasic stretch, and (3) by the gamma system or gamma loop. All of these controls work together to provide for effective, coordinated, and smooth movement.

### Muscle Tonus

Place your forearm upon the desk in a completely relaxed and slightly flexed position. In feeling the muscles, even though relaxed, you will notice a resiliency rather than a flabbiness. Maintaining this relaxation, have a partner gently extend your forearm (a little powder on the desk will minimize resistance). Your partner will observe a small amount of muscular resistance not related to conscious effort, assuming of course that you are maintaining complete relaxation. This characteristic of resiliency and resistance to stretch in the relaxed resting muscle is called *tonus*.

Now, if you were to sever the efferent or motor nerves (ventral roots) that service this muscle, it would lose tonus and become *flaccid*. Furthermore, if the dorsal roots containing sensory fibers from this muscle were cut, tonus would be obliterated also. Such experiments clearly illustrate that muscular tonus is maintained through reflex activity of the nervous system and is *not* a property of the isolated muscle. Incidentally, muscles with more than normal tone are referred to as *spastic*.

### Stretch Reflex

The basic neural mechanism for maintenance of muscle tonus is the *stretch reflex*. As we have just learned, when a muscle is stretched, impulses are discharged from the muscle spindles. As shown in Figure 5–5, afferent fibers from these spindles enter the spinal cord through a dorsal nerve root and form a synapse with motor nerve cells in the spinal cord. Axons from these motor neurons conduct impulses to the motor endplates in the same muscle fibers, and this activation produces increased tension in the muscle fibers.

You might test your neuromuscular stretch reflexes by exerting a quick forceful tap with a rubber hammer to the tendon. The following is a list of several spinal cord segments associated with their respective muscles:

| MUSCLE | CORD SEGMENTS |
|--------|---------------|
| Biceps Brachii | C5–C6 (fifth and sixth cervical vertebrae) |
| Triceps Brachii | C6–C7 |
| Quadriceps | L2, L3, L4 (second, third, and fourth lumbar vertebrae) |

*Biceps Reflex.* Flex your forearm 90° and have a partner support it; have the partner place his or her thumb over the tendon of insertion of the biceps (tubercle of radius). Now strike the thumb with a mallet; the force is transferred to your biceps tendon. The biceps muscle will contract, flexing the forearm.

*Triceps Reflex.* Support your arm in a similar fashion as in the biceps reflex. The triceps tendon of insertion (olecranon process of ulna) is struck directly with mallet. The triceps will contract, extending the forearm.

*Patellar Reflex.* Sit comfortably on the edge of a table, with your legs dangling and relaxed. Strike the patellar tendon with a sharp blow. The quadriceps femoris muscles will contract, causing extension of the leg.

Stimulation of the spindles by rapping the tendon with a sharp blow conveys information to the CNS, where motor stimuli are relayed to the appropriate muscle and contraction of the muscle is initiated. A positive response (that is, lack of contraction for the specified muscle) is indicative of a malfunction or lesion at the level of the CNS servicing that particular muscle.

## THE NERVOUS SYSTEM AND MOTOR SKILLS

Now we will direct our attention to the motor responses which are fundamental to the execution of motor skills. Figure 5–6 is a cross-sectional diagram of the essential anatomical parts of the spinal cord. The afferent nerve enters the spinal column through the dorsal (rear) root

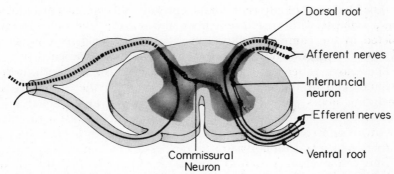

**Figure 5-6**   Essential anatomical parts of the spinal cord. The afferent (sensory) nerve enters the cord through the dorsal root and synapses with internuncial neurons. The efferent (motor) nerve leaves the cord by way of the ventral root to the effector muscle.

and forms synaptic junctions with several neurons (called internuncial neurons). The efferent nerve leaves the spinal cord by way of the ventral root (front) to the effector muscle. Injury to the ventral root (efferent) fibers affects the muscle or muscles supplied with these motor fibers. Severing of the nerve results in total paralysis.

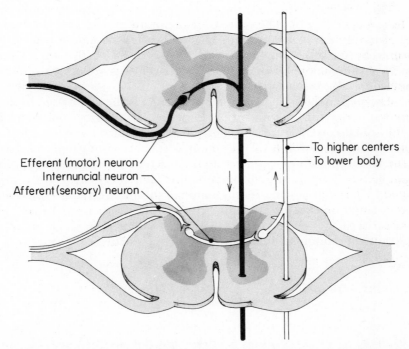

**Figure 5-7**   The majority of afferent fibers entering the cord do not form synapses with efferent fibers and leave at the same level of the cord; rather they split into ascending and descending branches, which travel up and down the cord.

The majority of afferent fibers entering the spinal cord do not form a synapse with an efferent fiber and leave at the same level, as depicted in the common reflex arc; rather, they split into ascending and descending branches which travel up and down the cord (Fig. 5–7). These long reflex paths connect receptors of the feet with those of the hand, and by the same token, the splitting of the ascending and descending fibers allows impulses to be received and discharged as required by the complexity of the movement. Such a vast array of interneurons and connections from the toe to the brain permit the CNS to function as a coordinating unit regardless of movement complexity.

Simple movements such as removing a finger from a heated surface are handled by the spinal cord reflex pattern, whereas the more complicated movements involve higher levels of the cord and brain. Generally speaking, the motoneurons in the spinal cord effect the contraction patterns of the muscles, and the higher centers program the *sequences* of contraction.

## Voluntary Control of Motor Functions

The cerebral cortex and the cerebellum are the centers employed in learning new skills. These areas of the brain initiate voluntary control of movement patterns. Figure 5–8 illustrates the motor area of the brain. The dark shading represents the *pyramidal* or *Betz cells*. Upon electrical stimulation to this area, motor movements are elicited — hence the term *primary motor cortex*.

The pyramidal tract or corticospinal tract is the route used to send impulses from the motor cortex down to the anterior motoneurons of the spinal cord. Figure 5–9 illustrates the area of the body affected when particular portions of the motor cortex are stimulated. The size of the area represented is related to the discreteness of movement. For example, the tongue, thumb, fingers, lips, and vocal cords are represented by large areas where only minimal stimuli are required to contract a single muscle or perhaps even a single fasciculus. In the abdominal area, however, groups of muscles rather than single muscles are contracted upon stimulation of the pyramidal area.

## Premotor Area for Learning Specialized Motor Skills

The area just forward to the motor area is probably the "sports skills area" of the brain. It is believed that this area is especially concerned with the acquisition of specialized motor skills. If a small area is removed, coordinated skill movements are difficult to develop.

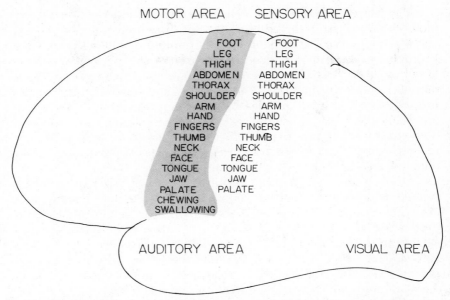

MOTOR AREA        SENSORY AREA

| | |
|---|---|
| FOOT | FOOT |
| LEG | LEG |
| THIGH | THIGH |
| ABDOMEN | ABDOMEN |
| THORAX | THORAX |
| SHOULDER | SHOULDER |
| ARM | ARM |
| HAND | HAND |
| FINGERS | FINGERS |
| THUMB | THUMB |
| NECK | NECK |
| FACE | FACE |
| TONGUE | TONGUE |
| JAW | JAW |
| PALATE | PALATE |
| CHEWING | |
| SWALLOWING | |

AUDITORY AREA        VISUAL AREA

**Figure 5–8**   The motor area of the brain (cortex). The dark shading represents the pyramidal or Betz cells. Upon electrical stimulation to this area, motor movements are elicited—hence the term, primary motor cortex.

**Figure 5–9**   When particular portions of the motor cortex are stimulated, certain areas of the body are affected. The size of the area represented is related to the discreteness of movement. For example, the tongue, thumb, big toe, and lips are represented by large areas where only minimal stimuli are required to contract a single muscle.

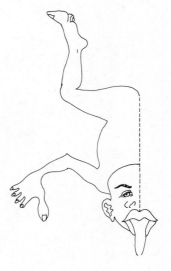

**The Cerebellum.**    The cerebellum receives information when a motor stimulus has occurred regardless of the stimulus source. For example, a voluntary movement such as punting a football is initiated. Impulses are transmitted downward through the pyramidal tract to excite the appropriate muscles. Impulses are also simultaneously transmitted to the cerebellum (Fig. 5–10). As the signals arrive at the muscles, proprioceptors (muscle spindles, Golgi tendon organs, and joint receptors) send the "punting" signal back to the cerebellum. The cerebellum then compares the two sets of information and elicits an impulse (correction factor) from the motor cortex, where the original stimulus was initiated; the movement is then executed.

Here we have an example of one of the many fascinating but extremely complicated feedback circuits that begin in the motor cortex and return to it via proprioceptors and the cerebellum. This servomechanism type of feedback has been compared to control systems such as those used in industry, guided missiles, automatic pilot mechanisms, and anti-aircraft guns. For example, the guided missile continuously transmits radar signals which are received and fed to a computer. The computer which is analogous to the cerebellum, monitors the signals and compares them to a prewritten program. In this manner, it

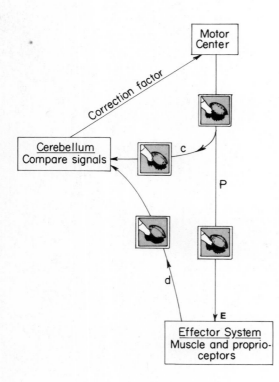

**Figure 5–10** When a voluntary movement such as punting a football is initiated, impulses are transmitted downward through the pyramidal tract (P) and eventually to the muscles (E). Impulses are also transmitted to the cerebellum (C). As the signals arrive at the muscles, proprioceptors send the "punting" signal back to the cerebellum (d). The cerebellum then compares the two sets of information and elicits an impulse (correction factor) from the motor cortex, where the original stimulus was initiated; the movement is then executed.

can detect any errors in the missile's path and radio a correction signal. In somewhat the same fashion, the cerebellum compares the information from the motor cortex to the execution of the football punt. The "error" is calculated by the cerebellum and a correction immediately relayed to the motor cortex.

**Dampening Effect.** It is in the above manner that the cerebellum exerts a dampening effect on such pendular movements as the golf swing and throwing and kicking a ball. As the arm or leg moves, momentum is developed with a resulting tendency for the limb to overshoot its mark. The dampening or "correcting" effect is administered by the cerebellum so that the limb stops at the intended position.

Similarly, the cerebellum predicts eventual limb position. The incoming information from the proprioceptors is used by the cerebellum to guide all body parts during the performance of a skill. Through the motor cortex the cerebellum exerts control over both the antagonist and agonist muscles.

**Perception of Speed.** The cerebellum also allows us to perceive the speed with which we approach objects and with which objects approach us. Without such perception, we would bang into walls and chairs and miss the shuttlecock or tennis lob. For example, the football player, performing an agility run through a maze of blocking dummies, is guided by the cerebellum so that he does not run into a dummy but rather cuts sharply to either the right or the left at the appropriate time.

In addition, the cerebellum aids in establishing equilibrium through interpreting changes as revealed by the semicircular canals in the ears. Just as the cerebellum aids in predicting the speed with which we approach an object, it also predicts body positions as a consequence of rotational movements of the head.

### Sensory Input and Motor Skills

A currently prevalent theory suggests that in the sensory area of the brain, a skill that has been practiced a sufficient number of times becomes memorized and that when the individual wishes to perform the given skill, he or she calls upon this particular motor pattern, which is immediately "replayed." Psychologists have referred to these memorized motor patterns as *engrams*. An engram is a permanent trace left by a stimulus in the tissue protoplasm. By practicing the tennis forehand stroke, for example, this stimulus, over a period of practice sessions, changes the protoplasmic configuration of certain cells in the sensory portion of the brain. The resulting realignment is an engram or a motor memory pattern for that special skill. The engram now becomes a part of the person's sensory portion of the brain and upon the appropriate stimulus can be recalled for use immediately.

The sensory engram involves a proprioceptor feedback servo-mechanism. Neuronal pathways from proprioceptors pass through the cerebellum to the sensory areas of the cerebral cortex and then to the motor cortex. Each center can modify the response to the muscles that perform the motor act. Once learned, the engram is stored and becomes available for use whenever the act is to be performed. In drinking from a glass, the proprioceptors from fingers, hand, and arm convey messages to the CNS. Here the previously stored engram is used as the model. When and if deviations from the stored engram occur, a correction is made through the release of additional motor signals from the motor cortex as "told" to it by the cerebellum.

Engrams for extremely rapid movements are stored in the motor area of the brain and are referred to as *motor engrams.* Engrams stored in the sensory portion of the brain, which are for slower motor acts, operate through the feedback servomechanism previously described in our discussion of the cerebellum; engrams in the motor area (frontal lobe) can be effected without sensory feedback. Typing or rapid movements at the keyboard do not allow sufficient time for a servomechanistic feedback.

### Henry's Memory Drum[1, 2]

Research has cast doubt on the widely accepted theory that motor ability is completely general. This theory states that if one excels in a certain sport, the ability shown there will carry over into other activities. The range of skills displayed by the high school athlete who excels in a number of sports has been cited, although perhaps erroneously, as proof of this theory. Relying on the "obvious," we have permitted ourselves to conclude that motor ability is truly general or nonspecific, whereas the contrary is probably true. Athletes who excel in several sports may owe more to their motivation and to their numerous activity experiences than to any carry-over of acquired skills from one sport to another. Also, they may be endowed with many specific sports aptitudes rather than any great amount of general motor ability.

Research by Franklin Henry and his colleagues at the University of California has shown that the simple ability to perform a given neuromotor skill is no indication that the performer will be equally capable of performing other such skills; that is, motor ability is *specific* to a task rather than *general.*[1, 2] His reasoning led to the theory that neuromotor coordination patterns are stored in the mind on what we might call a memory drum. Whenever a specific movement pattern is needed, the stimulus causes the storage center or memory drum to "play back" the particular learned skill. Hence, the movement is performed automatically. Such learned skills as playing the piano, running, walking, throwing, and eating are all performed without conscious thought; the memory drum simply plays them back on demand.

The entire process might be likened to the functioning of an electronic computer. According to this theory, the program (or recorded movement pattern) has been learned previously and stored on the memory drum (motor memory), ready to be selected and released when needed. Such a program consists of a set of nonconscious instructions that direct the necessary nerve impulses to the appropriate muscles in a coordinated sequence, thus causing the desired movement. The "read-out time," or performance time, varies somewhat, depending on the length and complexity of the movement. A program in process of being "read out" cannot be changed before it has been completed, in conformity with the all-or-none law of physiology. Some of the findings that lend support to this theory are as follows:

1. Individual differences in ability to make a fast arm movement are about 70 per cent specific to the particular movement being made. For example, a person who can perform a certain arm movement rapidly is not necessarily able to perform other movements of the same arm with equal speed.

2. Reaction time lengthens with increased movement complexity.

3. Very low relationships exist between static strength and speed of movement. This seems to indicate that speed of movement depends more upon the quality of the impression on the memory drum than on the muscular strength of the limb.

4. A fast limb movement, once underway, cannot be changed in its direction, nor can it be stopped partway through unless it was originally programmed to be stopped rather than completed.

5. Motor-oriented programming results in slower movement and greater reaction latency than sensory-oriented programming. For instance, concentration on the movement to be made (motor orientation) rather than on the starting signal (sensory orientation) tends to result in *slower* reaction time, as conscious control of motor movement interferes with the reading out of the programmed impulses.

6. The component parts of a skill are first learned discretely and are gradually combined into a continuous pattern on the memory drum. When a skill deteriorates, as is the case in aging or long disuse, one notices that the combined pattern breaks up and reverts to the separate movements.

7. Research over a period of many years has shown that the relationship between motor skills is usually quite low.

# Summary

The central nervous system comprises the brain and spinal cord, the latter extending from the base of the skull to the second lumbar vertebra.

Generally considered by itself, the autonomic nervous system helps to control secretions, urinary output, temperature, sweating, and other involuntary acts.

The sensory nerves are those excited by sound, pain, light, and taste. They bring impulses from the periphery to the CNS for interpretation and response.

A finger being quickly withdrawn from a hot flame as a consequence of a painful sensation exemplifies a simple reflex arc. The sensory signal travels to the spinal cord and makes contact with a motor nerve fiber; the appropriate muscles are stimulated, and the hand is withdrawn.

There are billions of nerve cells throughout the body; connections among them are made through synapses. When an impulse or, more appropriately, a signal arrives at the synapse, it either crosses to the adjoining nerve fiber or it may be inhibited. Such an inhibitory mechanism permits the CNS to select or reject stimuli.

At the neuromuscular junction, where the nerve invaginates the muscle fiber, a similar synaptic arrangement exists. However, all sufficiently strong stimuli are transmitted across the neuromuscular junction, as inhibition does not occur here.

In muscles, tendons, ligaments, and joints are located proprioceptors which transmit information about limb positions to the CNS. These are also called the kinesthetic receptors because they aid in performing body movements.

The learning of a motor skill is a complex and not completely understood process. It takes place in the cerebral cortex and the cerebellum. Signals dealing with the particular skill originate in the motor cortex and are transmitted to the muscles. A "copy" of this information to the muscles is also fed to the cerebellum. As movement of the muscles is initiated, proprioceptors relay the program status back to the cerebellum, which sends a corrected signal to the brain if necessary; the skill is then completed.

Henry's memory drum theory of neuromotor reaction provides some hypotheses about how skills are memorized. Most important evidence supports the concept of specificity, which states that learning of motor skills is specific rather than general. There is little if any carryover from one sport to another unless skills are nearly identical.

In conclusion, we might conjecture about what makes one athlete superior to another. All things being equal, the Olympic athlete, in addition to having good instruction, opportunity, physiology, and motivation, may have inherited a very refined CNS. In particular, he or she may have a more dense proprioceptor system, allowing better kinesthetic interpretation.

## QUESTIONS

1. What are considered to be the three basic functions of the nervous system?

2. Give an example of a sensory receptor and describe how it works.

3. Diagram and label the parts of a nerve cell.

4. What is a reflex arc?

5. How are signals transmitted from one nerve fiber to another?

6. How does inhibition at the neuronal synapse occur? Of what value is the inhibitory mechanism?

7. Diagram the myoneural junction and the related anatomical parts.

8. Explain how a signal is transmitted across the myoneural junction.

9. What are proprioceptors, where are they located, and how do they function?

10. Explain muscle tonus and state the proof we have for its existence.

11. What is the stretch reflex, and how might we test for it?

12. Where is the "sports skills area" of the brain located?

13. Outline the manner in which a voluntary skill is performed.

14. What is meant by the dampening effect exerted through the cerebellum?

15. Define an engram.

16. Outline Henry's memory drum theory of motor learning.

## REFERENCES

1. Henry, Franklin M.: Influence of motor and sensory sets on reaction latency and speed of discrete movements. Res. Quart., Oct., 1960.
2. Henry, Franklin M., and Rogers, Donald E.: Increased response latency for complicated movements and a "memory drum" theory of neuromotor reaction. Res. Quart., Oct., 1960.

## SELECTED READINGS

Best, C. H., and Taylor, N. B.: The Physiological Basis of Medical Practice. 7th ed. Baltimore, Williams and Wilkins Co., 1961.

Eyzaguirre, Carlos: Physiology of the Nervous System. Chicago, Year Book Medical Publishers, 1969.

Gatz, Arthur: Clinical Neuroanatomy and Neurophysiology. 3rd ed. Philadelphia, F. A. Davis Company, 1966.

Guyton, Arthur: Basic Human Physiology: Normal Function and Mechanisms of Disease. Philadelphia, W. B. Saunders Co., 1971.

Mathews, D. K., Stacy, R., and Hoover, G.: Physiology of Muscular Activity and Exercise. New York, Ronald Press, 1964.

Merton, P.: How we control the contraction of our muscles. Sci. Am. 228:30–37, May, 1972.

O'Connell, A., and Gardner, E.: Understanding the Scientific Bases of Human Movement. Baltimore, Williams and Wilkins Co., 1972, pp. 193–232.

# Chapter 6

# SKELETAL MUSCLE: STRUCTURE AND FUNCTION

GROSS STRUCTURE AND FUNCTION
>   Connective Tissues
>   Tendons
>   Blood Supply
>   Nerve Supply
>   Red and White Muscle Fibers

MICROSCOPIC STRUCTURE—THE BASIS FOR CONTRACTION
>   Structure of the Muscle Cell
>   The Sliding Filament Theory

The more than 400 voluntary (skeletal, striated or striped) muscles of the human body constitute about 40 per cent of our total body weight. The muscles are useful because they are able to produce motion, which is the most fundamental function of the muscular and skeletal systems (musculoskeletal system). The action of muscles on the bony levers permits us to stand erect, carry out activities of daily living, and impart movement to other objects. This motion in the musculoskeletal system is governed by the strength of muscles.

For professional people to adequately plan and conduct programs designed to increase muscular strength, endurance, and flexibility, they need a knowledge of the muscles. They should know structure, both gross and microscopic, in order to understand function; and even though it remains a problem for future researchers to answer conclusively, the person dealing with movement should know the most recent views on how a muscle contracts. The purpose of this chapter then, will be to discuss both the structure and function of skeletal muscle.

**Table 6–1   STRUCTURAL UNITS OF SKELETAL MUSCLE AND THEIR CORRESPONDING CONNECTIVE TISSUES**

| STRUCTURAL UNIT | CONNECTIVE TISSUE |
|---|---|
| Muscle Fiber or Cell | Endomysium |
| | Sarcolemma (Cell Membrane) |
| Muscle Bundle (Fasciculus) | Perimysium |
| Entire Muscle | Epimysium |

# GROSS STRUCTURE AND FUNCTION

We will start with a discussion of the so-called gross structures and functions of skeletal muscle.

### Connective Tissues

Skeletal muscle is composed of many thousands of individual contractile fibers bound together by a sheath of connective tissues. That portion of connective tissue which covers each muscle fiber is called the *endomysium.* Just inside and attached to the endomysium is the muscle cell membrane or *sarcolemma.* Since the sarcolemma is *not* a connective

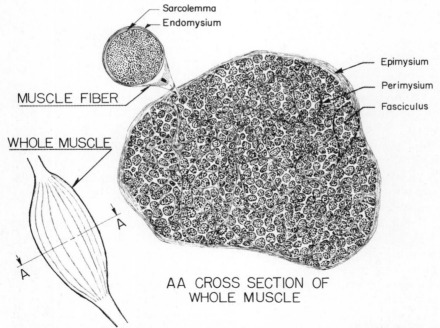

**Figure 6–1**   Relationship between connective tissues and the cell membrane (sarcolemma) of skeletal muscle.

tissue, we will talk more about it later. The inside of the muscle cell is composed of a specialized *protoplasm* called *sarcoplasm* (*sarco* means "flesh"). The muscle cells (fibers) are grouped together to form muscle bundles or *fasciculi*. These bundles, containing various numbers of muscle fibers, are in turn held together by a connective tissue referred to as the *perimysium*. Encasing the entire muscle (or all the muscle bundles) is yet another connective tissue component, called the *epimysium*. The structural units of muscle and their associated connective tissues are given in Table 6–1 and illustrated in Figure 6–1.

## Tendons

The intramuscular network of connective tissues coalesces and becomes continuous with the dense connective tissue of the tendons at each end of a muscle. These tendons are rigidly cemented to the outermost covering of bone, the *periosteum,* and thereby serve to connect the skeletal muscles to the bony skeleton. The muscle fibers themselves do not come into direct contact with the skeleton; thus the tremendous tension developed by muscles is borne entirely by their tendinous attachments. There are several advantages to this arrangement. If muscle fibers were attached directly to bone they would be subject to considerable damage each time the muscle contracted. Tendons not only are much tougher than muscles but are also composed of nonliving fibers. Furthermore, since tendons are stronger than muscles, a relatively small tendon can withstand the tension developed by a relatively large muscle.

## Blood Supply

Muscles are richly supplied with blood vessels. Arteries and veins enter the muscle along with the connective tissues and are oriented parallel to the individual muscle fibers. They branch repeatedly into numerous capillaries and venules, forming vast networks in and around the endomysium. In this manner each fiber is assured of an adequate supply of freshly oxygenated blood from the arterial system and of the removal of waste products such as carbon dioxide via the venous system.

The amount of blood required by skeletal muscle depends, of course, on its state of activity. During maximal exercise the muscles may require as much as 100 times more blood than when resting. Besides the large number of vessels which supply each muscle there are other ways in which this blood flow requirement can be met. For example, the alternating contraction and relaxation of active muscle causes periodic squeezing of the blood vessels. This pumping or milking action speeds up the flow of blood to the heart, thus increasing the amount of fresh blood which can be returned to the muscles. Constriction of the arteries supplying blood to the inactive areas of the body (such as the gut, kidney, and skin) and dilation of those to the active skeletal muscles also aids in regulating muscle blood flow. We will discuss these important mechanisms again in Chapter 10.

## Nerve Supply

The nerves supplying a muscle contain both motor (efferent) and sensory (afferent) fibers. The motor nerves, which when stimulated cause the muscle to contract, originate in the central nervous system (spinal cord and brain). The point of termination of a motor nerve (axon) on a muscle fiber is known as the myoneural or neuromuscular junction or the motor end-plate (see p. 83). Motor nerves constitute about 60 per cent of the nerves which enter the muscle. The sensory nerves, which make up the remaining 40 per cent, convey information concerning pain and orientation of body parts from the muscle sense organs to the central nervous system.

**The Motor Unit.** If we were to count the number of motor nerves entering a muscle and calculate the number of muscle fibers within the muscle, we would find that a great difference exists between the two. There are about a quarter of a billion separate muscle fibers which make up the skeletal musculature in man, but there are only about 420 thousand motor nerves. Inasmuch as the number of muscle fibers greatly exceeds the number of nerve fibers and keeping in mind the fact that every muscle fiber is innervated, we see that the nerve fibers must necessarily branch repeatedly. In other words, a single motor nerve fiber innervates anywhere from 1 to 5 to 150 or more muscle fibers. All the muscle fibers served by the same motor nerve contract and relax at the same time, working as a unit. For this reason, the single motor nerve and the muscle fibers it supplies are called the motor unit (Fig. 6–2).

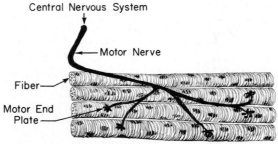

**Figure 6–2** Motor unit of skeletal muscle. A single motor nerve from the central nervous system is shown innervating several muscle fibers through the motor end-plates.

The ratio of muscle fibers innervated by a single motor nerve is not determined by the size of the muscle, but rather by the precision, accuracy, and coordination of its movement. Muscles that are called on to perform fine and delicate work, such as the eye muscles, may have as few as 1 muscle fiber in a motor unit; muscles used for rather heavy work, such as the quadriceps, may have as many as 150 or more muscle fibers per motor unit.

**All-or-None Law.**    A stimulated muscle or nerve fiber contracts or propagates a nerve impulse either completely or not at all. In other words, a minimal stimulus causes the individual muscle fiber to contract to the same extent that a stronger stimulus does. This phenomenon is known as the *all-or-none law.* Because a single neuron supplies many muscle fibers in the formation of the motor unit, it naturally follows that the motor unit will also function according to the all-or-none law. While this law of physiology holds true for the individual muscle fibers and motor units, it does not apply to the muscle as a whole. It is possible for the muscle to exert forces of *graded strengths,* ranging from a barely perceptible contraction to the most vigorous type of contraction, depending on the number of motor units stimulated.

**Muscle Sense Organs.**    There are several types of sense organs in muscle. The pain resulting from exercising too vigorously after long disuse (muscle soreness) or from torn muscle fibers are good examples of muscle sense organs at work. These pain receptors, which are few in number, are found not only in the muscle fibers themselves but also in blood vessels (arteries but *not* veins) that supply the muscle cells and in the connective tissues mentioned earlier that surround the fibers.

The majority of sense organs are concerned with *kinesthesis* or *kinesthetic sense* which, in general, unconsciously tells us where our body parts are in relation to our environment. Their contributions enable us to execute a smooth and coordinated movement no matter whether we are putting a golf ball, hitting a home run or simply climbing an unfamiliar flight of stairs without stumbling. They also help us to maintain a normal body posture. The tendency for the lower jaw to drop, the head to fall forward, and the knees to buckle because of the effects of gravity are all counterbalanced by the so-called antigravity muscles, which relay information regarding position in space.

How do these sense organs or *proprioceptors* function? We can begin to answer this question by first describing how each type of sense organ sends specific sensory information to the central nervous system. For our purposes there are three important muscle sense organs concerned with kinesthesis: *muscle spindles, Golgi tendon organs*, and *joint receptors.*

*Muscle Spindles.*    These are perhaps the most abundant type of proprioceptor found in muscle. Their structure and function are given in some detail in the previous chapter (p. 86). Briefly, muscle spindles send information to the central nervous system concerning the degree

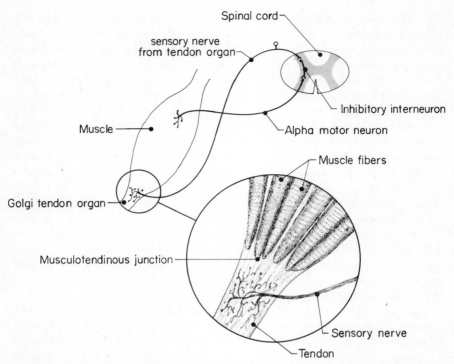

**Figure 6-3** The Golgi tendon organ. When a contracted muscle is forcefully stretched, the sensory nerve of the tendon organ is stimulated. Impulses are sent to the spinal cord, where a synapse is made with an inhibitory interneuron that inhibits the alpha motor neuron, and the muscle relaxes.

of stretch of the muscle in which they are imbedded. This provides the muscles with information, for example, as to the exact number of motor units necessary to contract in order to overcome a given resistance; the greater the stretch, the greater the load, and the greater the number of motor units required. The spindles are important in the control of posture and, with the help of the gamma system, in voluntary movements.

*Golgi Tendon Organs.* These proprioceptors are encapsulated in tendon fibers and are located near the junction of the muscle and tendon fibers (musculotendinous junction). Their structure is shown in Figure 6-3. Like the spindles, the tendon organs are sensitive to stretch. However, they are much less sensitive than the spindles and therefore require a strong stretch before they are activated. Actually, because of their location with respect to the muscle fibers, the Golgi tendon organs are activated mainly by the stretch placed upon them by the contraction of the muscles in whose tendons they lie. Given such a stretch, sensory information is sent to the central nervous system, causing the contracted muscle to relax. In other words, in contrast to the spindles, which are facilitory (that is, they cause contraction), stimulation of the tendon organs results in *inhibition* of the muscles in which they are located. This can be interpreted as a protective function in that during attempts to lift extremely heavy loads that could cause injury, the tendon organs effect a relaxation of the muscles.

A good example of the tendon organs in action is given by "Indian arm-wrestling." It has been suggested that the loss of the contest occurs when the tendon organ inhibition overcomes the voluntary effort to maintain contraction.[11] In addition, the "breaking point" in muscle strength testing might be related to inhibition caused by the tendon organs. If this is the case, maximal strength would be dependent upon the ability to oppose voluntarily the inhibition of the tendon organs.[11]

It should be pointed out that the spindles and tendon organs work together, the former causing just the right degree of muscular tension to effect a smooth movement and the latter causing muscular relaxation when the load is potentially injurious to the muscles and related structures.

*Joint Receptors.* These receptors are found in tendons, ligaments, periosteum (bone), muscle, and joint capsules. They supply information to the central nervous system concerning the joint angle, the acceleration of the joint, and the degree of deformation brought about by pressure. The names of some of the joint receptors are the *end bulbs of Krause,* the *Pacinian corpuscles*, and *Ruffini end organs.* All of this information plus that from other receptors (e.g., sight and sound) is used to give us a sense of awareness of body and limb position, as well as to provide us with automatic reflexes concerned with posture.

### Red and White Muscle Fibers

Not all the muscle fibers of humans or animals have the same metabolic or functional capabilities. For example, while all fibers can perform under both aerobic (endurance) and anaerobic (sprint) conditions, some fibers are better equipped biochemically to work aerobically, whereas others are better equipped to work anaerobically. In humans the aerobic type fibers are called *type I, red, tonic,* or *slow-twitch fibers;* the anaerobic type fibers are called *type II, white, phasic,* or *fast-twitch fibers.*[2, 3, 4, 9]

**Distribution of Red and White Fibers.** The proportions of the different types of fibers in human muscle vary to a great extent. However, generally it can be said that the majority of our muscles contain an approximately equal mixture of red and white fibers, although there are specific muscles that are considered to be predominantly either red or white. For example, the gastrocnemius, latissimus dorsi, biceps brachii and deltoid muscles contain a large percentage of white fibers.

On the other hand, the rectus femoris, soleus, semitendinosus, and rectus abdominis are basically red muscles.[8]

The distribution of red and white fibers in muscles of different groups of athletes is shown in Figure 6–4.[4] The maximal oxygen consumption (max$\dot{V}O_2$) of these groups is indicated on the vertical axis. Notice that the percentage of red or slow-twitch fibers is higher with higher max$\dot{V}O_2$ levels. This makes sense, for we know that the red fiber has a greater potential for aerobic metabolism than does the white fiber. It is also interesting to note that although a greater percentage of white than red fibers might be expected in the muscles of sprinters and weight-lifters, this does not appear to be the case.[4, 13]

There are several questions that need to be asked concerning the relationship between the percentage of red muscle fibers and the max$\dot{V}O_2$: (1) Does training cause an increase in the percentage of red fibers? (2) Is the increase in max$\dot{V}O_2$ that can be induced by training genetically limited by the percentage of red fibers with which one is born? The answer to the first question is no. Actually, the only way to functionally change a white fiber to a red one or vice-versa would be to cross-innervate the two fibers.[12] Cross-innervation means that the nerve

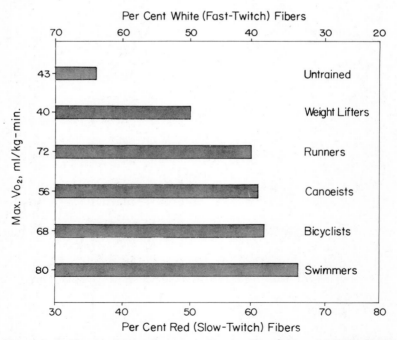

**Figure 6–4** The maximal oxygen consumption (max$\dot{V}O_2$) and the distribution of red and white fibers in muscles of different groups of athletes. Notice that the percentage of red or slow-twitch fibers is higher for higher max$\dot{V}O_2$ values. (Based on data from Gollnick et al.[4])

### Table 6-2   BIOCHEMICAL AND FUNCTIONAL CHARACTERISTICS OF RED AND WHITE MUSCLE FIBERS

| | FIBER TYPE | |
| BIOCHEMICAL CHARACTERISTIC | *Red* | *White* |
| --- | --- | --- |
| Aerobic | | |
| myoglobin* content | high | low |
| fat content | high | low |
| mitochondrial content | high | low |
| oxidative enzyme levels | high | low |
| capillary density | high | low |
| | | |
| Anaerobic | | |
| glycogen content | low | high |
| PC content | low | high |
| glycolytic enzyme levels | low | high |
| speed of contraction | slow | fast |
| fatigue factor | low | high |

*Myoglobin is an oxygen-binding pigment similar to hemoglobin. This is what gives the red fiber its color.

originally innervating one fiber would be transplanted to innervate the other. In other words, the motor nerve to a muscle has an influential effect (called a *trophic effect*) on the eventual functional capabilities of that muscle fiber. As we will discuss later, training causes an increase in the size and capacities of the respective fiber types but not in their number. Thus, in answer to the second question, individual differences in percentage composition of red and white fibers in any given muscle are largely a matter of genetics.

**Functional Differences of Red and White Fibers.** As indicated earlier, red or slow-twitch fibers have a relatively large aerobic capability and a relatively small anaerobic capability compared to the white or fast-twitch fibers. This relationship can be seen by a comparison of the biochemical and functional characteristics of the two fibers (Table 6–2).

The functional significance of the different biochemical and physiological characteristics of red and white fibers is indicated by the fact that white or fast-twitch fibers are preferentially recruited for performing short, high-intensity work bouts such as sprinting. By the same token, the red or slow-twitch fibers are preferentially recruited during long-term, endurance types of activity.[5, 6] This is shown in Figure 6–5, in which the glycogen content of both fiber types of human muscle was qualitatively estimated during sprint and endurance exercises. The glycogen content decreased sooner and to a greater extent in the white fiber during sprint bouts but sooner and to a greater extent in the red fiber during endurance exercise, thus suggesting preferential recruitment.

One other factor is noticeable in Figure 6–5. The initial glycogen level does not limit sprintlike performance, since at exhaustion the

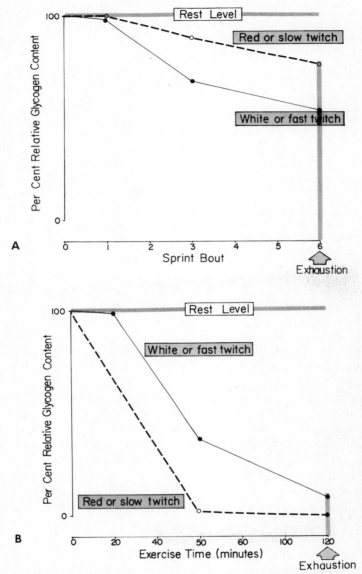

**Figure 6–5** Glycogen content of red (slow-twitch) and white (fast-twitch) fibers during sprintlike exercises (*A*), and endurance-like exercises (*B*). The glycogen content decreased sooner and to a greater extent in the white fiber during sprint bouts but sooner and to a greater extent in the red fiber during endurance exercise. This suggests that the white (fast-twitch) fibers are preferentially recruited for performing short, high intensity work bouts, whereas the red (slow-twitch) fibers are preferentially recruited during long-term endurance types of activities. (Based on data from Gollnick et al.[5, 6])

glycogen content in both fiber types is still substantial. On the contrary, notice that the glycogen, particularly in the red fibers, is completely used up after two hours of exhaustive endurance exercise. In this case, the initial glycogen level limits performance. More will be said about this later (see p. 405).

# MICROSCOPIC STRUCTURE — THE BASIS FOR CONTRACTION

A great deal of information concerning how a muscle contracts has been gathered in the past 15 to 20 years. For the most part, information about the structural changes that occur when a resting muscle cell is actively contracted has been obtained by use of the electron microscope. It is, therefore, imperative that we understand in some detail the microscopic structure of the muscle cell. Then, the theory as to how a muscle contracts will be relatively easy to comprehend.

### Structure of the Muscle Cell

To appreciate the microscopic structure of muscle, we can tease out a fiber from the sartorius muscle of a frog. After placing this single

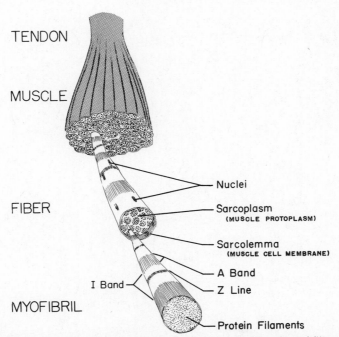

**Figure 6-6** Skeletal muscle showing microscopic delineation of fiber and myofibril. Note the striations in both the fiber and the myofibril; these alternating light and dark bands are caused by the geometric arrangement of the protein filaments.

fiber under a light microscope, we can observe regularly alternating light and dark striations (Fig. 6–6). Because of these striations, skeletal muscle is sometimes referred to as striated or striped muscle. Inside the sarcolemma is the sarcoplasm, which we mentioned earlier. Subcellular components such as nuclei and mitochondria are suspended in this reddish, viscous fluid. The sarcoplasm also contains myoglobin, fat, glycogen, phosphocreatine, ATP, and hundreds of threadlike protein strands called *myofibrils*. It is within these myofibrils that the contractile unit is housed.

**The Myofibrils.** A closer look at the myofibrils (Fig. 6–6) reveals that they also are characterized by alternating light and dark areas. In fact, it is the geometrical arrangement of all these light and dark areas of the myofibrils juxtaposed side by side which gives the fiber its overall striated appearance. The light areas are called I bands, the dark areas A bands. In the middle of each I band is a dark line, the Z line (from the German *zwischen,* meaning "between"). The bands, which are composed of protein filaments, are so named because of what happens to

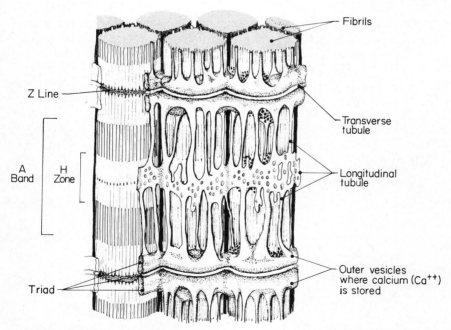

**Figure 6–7** The sarcoplasmic reticulum and transverse tubules form a netlike system of tubules and vesicles surrounding the myofibrils. The outer vesicles store large quantities of calcium ions (Ca$^{++}$), one of the ingredients required for the contractile process. The transverse tubules are concerned with conduction of the nervous impulses deep into the myofibrils. The two outer vesicles and the transverse tubule separating them are known as a triad. (Modified and redrawn from Peachey, L.: The sarcoplasmic reticulum and transverse tubules of frog's sartorius. J. Cell. Biol., 25(3), Part 2:209–231, 1965, p. 222.)

the velocity of a light wave as it passes through them. For example, when a light wave passes through the A band its velocity is not equal in all directions, i.e., it is *anisotropic*. When passed through the I band, the velocity of the emerging light is the same in all directions, and thus is *isotropic*.

**The Sarcoplasmic Reticulum and T-Tubules.**   As shown in Figure 6–7, surrounding the myofibrils is a netlike system of tubules and vesicles, collectively referred to as the *sarcoplasmic reticulum*. The *longitudinal tubules* are so named because they run parallel (longitudinally) to the myofibrils. The longitudinal tubules terminate at either end into vesicles or cisterns sometimes referred to as the *outer vesicles* or *cisterns* (see Fig. 6–7). This reticular pattern is repeated regularly along the entire length of the myofibrils. The outer vesicles of one reticular pattern are separated from those of another by a group of tubules called the *transverse tubules* (because they run transversely to the myofibril), the *T system*, or simply the *T-tubules*. The T-tubules, although functionally associated with the sarcoplasmic reticulum, are known to be anatomically separate from it. They are extensions or invaginations of the muscle cell membrane, the sarcolemma. The two outer vesicles and the T-tubule separating them are known as a *triad*.

The entire function of the sarcoplasmic reticulum and T-tubules is not known. However, it is believed that the triad is of particular importance in muscular contraction. For example, it is thought that the T-tubules are responsible for spreading the nervous impulse from the sarcolemma inward to the deep portions of the fiber. The outer vesicles of the reticulum contain large amounts of calcium ($Ca^{++}$). As the impulse travels over the T-tubules and between the outer vesicles, $Ca^{++}$ is released. We will discuss shortly the importance of both the spreading of the nervous impulse and the release of $Ca^{++}$ in the actual contractile process. Right now, let's go on with the microscopic structure of muscle.

**The Protein Filaments.**   The I and A bands are made up of two different protein filaments, a thinner filament called *actin* and a thicker one called *myosin*. Their arrangement within the myofibrils is shown in Figure 6–8. As can be seen, the I band is composed entirely of the thinner actin filaments. You will also notice that they are not continuous within one *sarcomere*, i.e., between two Z lines. Rather, they are anchored to the Z lines at each end of the sarcomere and partly extend into the A band region. The latter band, although composed mainly of the thicker myosin filaments, therefore contains a small amount of actin. The so-called H zone is due to the slight variation in shading resulting from the absence of actin filaments in the middle of the A band. The Z lines adhere to the sarcolemma, lending stability to the entire structure, and presumably keep the actin filaments in align-

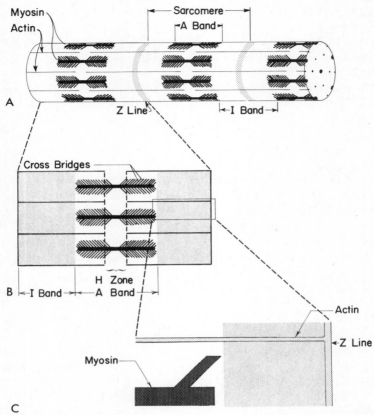

**Figure 6–8** Myofibril—the contractile unit of skeletal muscle. *A,* Note that the A band is composed of two protein filaments (actin and myosin). The I band contains actin filaments only. *B,* A closer look at the myosin filament, which projects in cross-bridging fashion toward the actin filament. The H zone (in the middle of the A band) is a result of the absence of actin filaments. *C,* A magnified view of a single myosin cross-bridge as it projects toward a single actin filament.

ment. The Z lines may also play a role in the transmission of nervous impulses from the sarcolemma to the myofibrils.

A closer look at the actin or thin filament is presented in Figure 6–9. The protein actin consists of globular (spheroidal) molecules linked together to form a double helix. Such a pattern is very similar in appearance to a twisted strand of beads. Although the thin filament is called the actin filament, it actually contains two other important proteins, *tropomyosin* and *troponin*. The tropomyosin is a long, thin molecule that lies on the surface of the actin strand. The ends of the tropomyosin molecules are embedded in globular molecules of troponin (see Fig. 6–9).

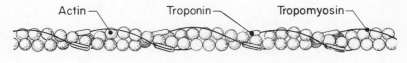

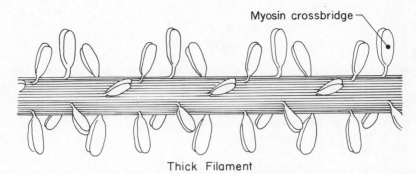

**Figure 6–9** Close-up of actin (thin) and myosin (thick) filaments. The actin filament actually contains two other proteins important in the contractile process, troponin and tropomyosin. The head of the myosin filament is called the cross-bridge. (Modified and redrawn from Murray and Weber.[10])

The myosin filaments have tiny protein projections on each end which extend toward the actin filaments (Fig. 6–9B). These are called *cross-bridges,* and as we shall see, together with the actin filaments they play a very important role in the contraction process.

### The Sliding Filament Theory

The structural arrangement of skeletal muscle presented above has led to a "sliding filament" theory of muscular contraction. As the name of the theory implies, one set of filaments is thought to slide over the other, thus shortening the muscle. This is illustrated in Figure 6–10. Note that the lengths of the actin and myosin filaments do not change during contraction but rather the former merely slide over the latter toward the center of the sarcomere. This leads to a shortening of the I band but not of the A band, and disappearance of the H zone. The sliding filament theory proposes a mechanism somewhat analogous to the way in which a telescope shortens, i.e., the overall length of the telescope (muscle) decreases as one section (actin) slides over the other (myosin), with neither section itself shortening.

The exact manner in which this sliding process is effected has yet to be completely elucidated. However, it is thought that the myosin

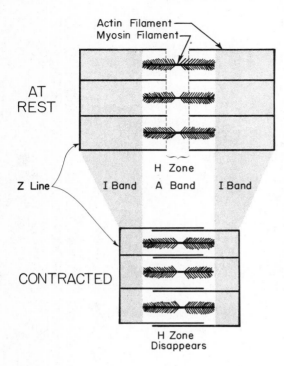

Actin Filament
Myosin Filament

AT REST

Z Line    I Band    A Band    I Band

H Zone

CONTRACTED

H Zone
Disappears

**Figure 6–10** The sliding filament theory. When the sarcomeres of a muscle contract as compared to rest: (1) The H zone disappears because the actin filaments slide over the myosin filaments toward the center of the sarcomere; (2) the I band shortens because the actin filaments attached to the Z lines on either side of the sarcomere are pulled toward the center; (3) the A band does not change in length; and (4) neither the myosin nor the actin *filaments* change in length, because of the sliding or interdigitation mechanics.

cross-bridges form a type of chemical bond with selected sites on the actin filaments. This forms a protein complex called *actomyosin*. When actomyosin is extracted from muscle and ATP is added, it will contract as it does in living muscle.

The mechanical and physiological events underlying the sliding filament theory of muscular contraction can be conveniently divided into five broad phases: (1) rest; (2) excitation-coupling; (3) contraction (shortening and tension development); (4) recharging; and (5) relaxation.

**Rest (Fig. 6–11A).** Under resting conditions, the cross-bridges of the myosin filaments extend toward but do not interact with the actin filaments. An ATP molecule is bound to the end of the cross-bridge. At rest this complex is referred to as an *"uncharged" ATP cross-bridge complex.* Calcium ($Ca^{++}$) is stored in large quantities in the vesicles of the sarcoplasmic reticulum. In the absence of free $Ca^{++}$, the troponin of the actin filament inhibits the myosin cross-bridge from binding with actin; that is, actin and myosin are said to be uncoupled.

**Figure 6–11** Proposed mechanism of the sliding filament theory. *A*, At rest, uncharged ATP cross-bridges are extended, actin and myosin are uncoupled, and Ca$^{++}$ is stored in the reticulum. *B*, During excitation-coupling, stimulation releases Ca$^{++}$, which then binds to troponin, "turning on" actin active sites: actomyosin is formed. *C*, During contraction, ATP is broken down, releasing energy that swivels the cross-bridges; actin slides over the myosin, tension is developed, and the muscle shortens. *D*, During recharging, ATP is resynthesized and actin and myosin uncouple and are recycled. *E*, When stimulation ceases, Ca$^{++}$ is restored in the reticulum by the calcium pump, and the muscle relaxes. (Modified and redrawn from Murray and Weber.[10])

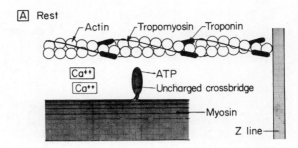

A  Rest

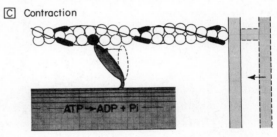

B  Excitation–Coupling

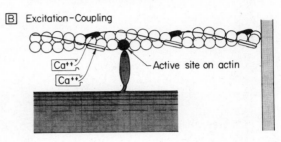

C  Contraction

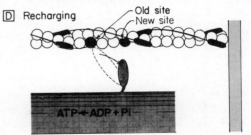

D  Recharging

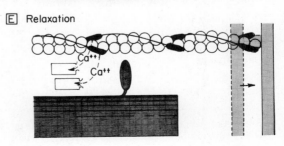

E  Relaxation

**Excitation-Coupling (Fig. 6–11B).**    As we learned from the preceding chapter, when an impulse from a motor nerve reaches the motor end-plate, acetylcholine is released, stimulating the generation of impulses (action potentials) in the sarcolemma of the muscle fiber. These impulses are spread throughout the fiber by way of the T-tubules. En route, they trigger the release of $Ca^{++}$ from the vesicles of the reticulum. The $Ca^{++}$ is immediately bound (taken up) by the troponin molecules on the actin filaments. This results in what is referred to as the "turning on" of active sites on the actin filament. Simultaneously, but in an unknown manner, the "uncharged" ATP cross-bridge complex is changed into a "charged" ATP cross-bridge complex. The "turning on" by $Ca^{++}$ of the active sites on the actin filament and the "charging" of the ATP cross-bridge complex mean that the two proteins are mutually attracted to each other. This results in a physical-chemical coupling of actin and myosin; that is, in the formation of an actomyosin complex. Such a complex, as we will see, is force-generating.

**Contraction (Fig. 6–11C).**    The formation of actomyosin activates an enzyme component of the myosin filament called *ATPase*. ATPase, as you might guess, causes ATP to be broken down into ADP and $P_i$ (inorganic phosphate) with the release of large amounts of energy. This released energy allows the cross-bridge to swivel to a new angle[7] or to collapse[1] in such a way that the actin filament to which it is attached slides over the myosin filament toward the center of the sarcomere. The muscle has developed tension and shortened.

**Recharging (Fig. 6–11D).**    A single myosin cross-bridge may "make and break" with active sites on the actin filaments hundreds of times in the course of a one-second contraction. In order to do this, the myosin cross-bridge must be recharged. The first step in recharging is the breaking of the old bond between the actin and the myosin cross-bridge. This is accomplished by reloading the myosin cross-bridge with a new (resynthesized) ATP molecule. (The resynthesis of ATP was discussed in Chapter 2.) Once a new ATP is reloaded, the bond between the myosin cross-bridge and the active site on the actin filament is broken; the ATP cross-bridge is freed from the actin.* The cross-bridge as well as the active site are thus made available for recycling.

**Relaxation (Fig. 6–11E).**    When the flow of nervous impulses over the motor nerve innervating the muscle ceases, $Ca^{++}$ is unbound from troponin and is actively pumped (calcium pump) back into storage in the outer vesicles of the sarcoplasmic reticulum. Removal of $Ca^{++}$ "turns off" the actin filament, and the ATP cross-bridge complexes are no longer able to form a bond with the active sites. The ATP-

---

*If ATP is not available, as is the case after death, the cross-bridges remain attached to the actin and the muscle is said to be in *rigor mortis*.

**Table 6–3  SUMMARY OF EVENTS OCCURRING DURING MUSCULAR CONTRACTION ACCORDING TO THE SLIDING FILAMENT THEORY**

| | |
|---|---|
| 1. Rest | (a) Uncharged ATP cross-bridges extended |
| | (b) Actin and myosin uncoupled |
| | (c) $Ca^{++}$ stored in sarcoplasmic reticulum |
| 2. Excitation-Coupling | (a) Nerve impulse generated |
| | (b) $Ca^{++}$ released from vesicles |
| | (c) $Ca^{++}$ saturates troponin, turning on actin |
| | (d) ATP cross-bridge "charged" |
| | (e) Actin and myosin coupled $\rightarrow$ actomyosin |
| 3. Contraction | (a) ATP $\xrightarrow{\text{ATPase}}$ ADP + $P_i$ + energy |
| | (b) Energy swivels cross-bridges |
| | (c) Muscle shortens $\rightarrow$ actin slides over myosin |
| | (d) Tension developed |
| 4. Recharging | (a) ATP resynthesized |
| | (b) Actomyosin dissociates $\rightarrow$ actin + myosin |
| | (c) Actin and myosin recycled |
| 5. Relaxation | (a) Nerve impulse ceases |
| | (b) $Ca^{++}$ removed by calcium pump |
| | (c) Muscle returns to resting state |

ase activity of myosin is also turned off, and no more ATP is broken down. The muscle filaments, through elastic recoil, return to their original positions, and the muscle is relaxed.

By way of summary, the contractile events of a muscle can be compared to the firing of a gun.[10] The gun must first be loaded by placing an appropriate cartridge (ATP) in a specific chamber (myosin crossbridge). This combination ("uncharged" ATP cross-bridge) is converted to a readied form by cocking the gun ("charged" ATP crossbridge). When the trigger is squeezed (calcium turning on actin sites), the ATP is rapidly broken down, releasing large amounts of energy. Work is done on the bullet (myosin cross-bridge). The process is completed by ejection of the spent cartridge (ADP + $P_i$) and reloading with another bullet (ATP).

Table 6–3 contains a summary of the sequence of events thought to occur during muscular contraction according to the sliding filament theory.

# SUMMARY

The connective tissues of muscle are the endomysium (fibers), perimysium (bundles) and epimysium (whole muscle). The membrane of the muscle is called the sarcolemma.

The nerves supplying a muscle contain both motor and sensory fibers. The motor nerve and the muscle fibers it supplies are called the motor unit. The most common sense-organs are the muscle spindles, Golgi tendon organs, and joint receptors. Their functions are mainly related to kinesthesis and posture reflexes.

Muscle fibers that have a high aerobic capability are called red or slow-twitch fibers, whereas those with a high anaerobic capability are called white or fast-twitch fibers. During exercise, there is a preferential recruitment of fiber types; red fibers during endurance type exercise and white fibers during sprintlike exercises.

The light and dark striations of the myofibrils are termed the I and A bands, respectively. The bands contain two protein filaments, actin and myosin. Actin filaments also contain the proteins troponin and tropomyosin.

The sarcoplasmic reticulum is a network of tubules surrounding each fiber. It aids in the spreading of the nervous impulse throughout the muscle and in storing and releasing calcium ($Ca^{++}$), both of which are important in the contractile process.

Muscular contraction, according to the sliding filament theory, results when the actin filaments are pulled over the myosin filaments, thus producing tension and shortening of the muscle. Both shortening and tension development are dependent upon the following: (1) the breakdown of ATP for energy; (2) $Ca^{++}$ for activation of the actin filament; and (3) the coupling of myosin to actin.

## QUESTIONS

1. What are the structural units and associated connective tissues of skeletal muscle?

2. Describe the structure and function of a motor unit.

3. What are muscle sense organs, and how do they function?

4. Explain the differences between red and white muscle fibers.

5. What is the functional significance of red and white fibers with respect to sprint and endurance exercises?

6. Draw and label a diagram of a sarcomere. Include the I band, A band, H zone, and Z lines.

7. Describe the structure and function of the sarcoplasmic reticulum and T-tubule system.

8. What proteins make up the thick and thin filaments? What is their functional significance?

9. Define the sliding filament theory of muscular contraction.

10. Describe in detail how the myosin cross-bridges are thought to form a bond with selected sites on the actin filaments during an isotonic contraction.

## REFERENCES

1. Davies, R.: A molecular theory of muscle contraction: calcium dependent contractions with hydrogen bond formation plus ATP-dependent extensions of part of the myosin-actin cross-bridges. Nature, 199:1068–1074, 1963.
2. Dubowitz, V., and Pearse, A.: A comparative histochemical study of oxidative enzymes and phosphorylase activity in skeletal muscle. Histochem., 2:105–117, 1960.
3. Edström, L., and Nyström, B.: Histochemical types and sizes of fibers of normal human muscles. Acta Neurol. Scand., 45:257–269, 1969.
4. Gollnick, P., Armstrong, R., Saubert, C., Piehl, K., and Saltin, B.: Enzyme activity and fiber composition in skeletal muscle of untrained and trained men. J. Appl. Physiol., 33(3):312–319, 1972.
5. Gollnick, P., Armstrong, R., Saubert, C., Sembrowich, W., Shepherd, R., and Saltin, B.: Glycogen depletion patterns in human skeletal muscle fibers during prolonged work. Pflüegers Arch., 344:1–12, 1973.
6. Gollnick, P., Armstrong, R., Sembrowich, W., Shepherd, R., and Saltin, B.: Glycogen depletion pattern in human skeletal muscle fiber after heavy exercise. J. Appl. Physiol., 34(5):615–618, 1973.
7. Huxley, H.: The mechanism of muscular contraction. Science, 164(3886):1356–1366, 1969.
8. Keul, J., Doll, E., and Keppler, D.: Energy Metabolism of Human Muscle. Baltimore, University Park Press, 1972, p. 16.
9. Morris, C.: Human muscle fiber type grouping and collateral re-innervation. J. Neurol. Neurosurg. Psychiat., 32:440–444, 1968.
10. Murray, J., and Weber, A.: The cooperative action of muscle proteins. Sci. Am., 230(2):58–71, 1974.
11. O'Connell, A., and Gardner, E.: Understanding the Scientific Bases of Human Movement. Baltimore, The Williams and Wilkins Company, 1972, p. 209.
12. Romanul, F.: Reversal of enzymatic profiles and capillary supply of muscle fibers in fast and slow muscles after cross innervation. In Pernow, B., and Saltin, B. (eds.): Muscle Metabolism During Exercise. New York, Plenum Press, 1971, pp. 21–32.
13. Saltin, B.: Metabolic fundamentals in exercise. Med. Sci. Sports, 5:137–146, 1973.

## SELECTED READINGS

Huxley, A., and Simmons, R.: Proposed mechanism of force generation in skeletal muscle. Nature, 233(5321):533–538, 1971.
Huxley, H.: The mechanism of muscular contraction. Sci. Am., 213(6):18, 1965.
Huxley, H.: The structural basis of muscular contraction. Proc. Roy. Soc. Med., 178:131–149, 1971.
O'Connell, A., and Gardner, E.: Understanding the Scientific Bases of Human Movement. Baltimore, The Williams and Wilkins Company, 1972, pp. 127–145.
The mechanism of muscular contraction. Cold Spring Harbor Symp. Quant. Biol., Vol. XXXVII, pp. 1–706, 1972.
Weber, A., and Murray, J.: Molecular control mechanisms in muscle contraction. Physiol. Rev., 53(3):612–673, 1973.

_____

# MUSCULAR STRENGTH, ENDURANCE, AND FLEXIBILITY

Our purpose in this chapter is twofold. First, we will investigate in some detail the modern concepts and equipment used in muscular strength and endurance training programs. Second, we will discuss the concept of flexibility as it relates to physical performance.

Coaches and physical educators have always had a prime interest in muscular strength, endurance, and flexibility. Such interest has frequently centered about the following questions:

(1) What is the most effective way in which strength, endurance, and flexibility may be gained?

(2) How long will these gains last, and how may they be maintained?

(3) What physiological and biochemical changes do muscles undergo when they increase in strength and endurance?

(4) Does strength development result in more rapid muscular contractions and therefore in increased power output for the individual?

(5) Do weight training programs and flexibility exercises positively affect sports performance?

Understanding of the most recent developments in muscular training equipment requires a thorough knowledge of the mechanics of muscular contraction. Therefore, we will discuss this topic before examining each of the interesting questions posed above.

# MECHANICS OF MUSCULAR CONTRACTION

The mechanics of muscular contraction involve the principles of levers and moments. A lever is a rigid bar that rotates about a fixed point called a fulcrum. A moment is defined as the perpendicular distance from the line of action of the force to the point of rotation.

## Levers

As shown in Figure 7-1, a muscle can exert its maximal force while in a resting stretched position. As the muscle shortens, less tension or force can be exerted. At about 60 per cent of its resting stretched length, the amount of tension that a muscle can exert approaches zero.* From this observation we might conclude that a per-

---

*The reason for this is related to the fact that the myosin cross-bridges can couple to the active sites of the actin filaments on their side only. With excessive shortening, there is an overlap of actin filaments such that the filament from one side interferes with the coupling potential of the cross-bridges on the other side. Since there are fewer cross-bridges "pulling" on the actin filaments, less tension is developed.

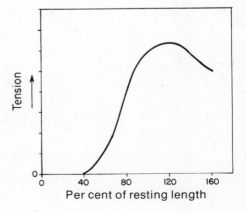

**Figure 7-1** Relationship between tension developed during contraction and muscle length in an isolated muscle. Outside the body, the muscle is strongest at resting length (100 per cent).

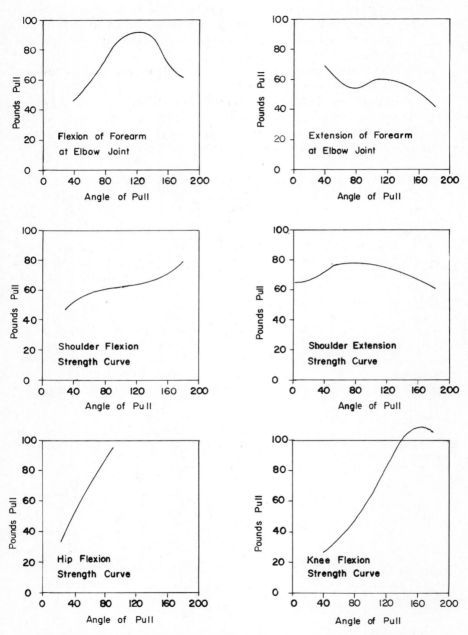

**Figure 7–2**  Relationship between tension (pounds pull) developed during contraction and muscle length (joint angle) for intact muscles. In this case, strength is not always greatest at resting length (180°). For example, the elbow flexor muscles are strongest between 100° and 140°.

son can move the heaviest load while the muscle is on stretch. However, this is not true, because the intact mechanical system with which we move objects involves the use both of muscles for force and bones for levers. It is the arrangement of muscles and bones *together* that determines the final effect.

Figure 7–2 depicts the force exerted by various muscle groups throughout their range of joint motion. For the elbow flexor muscles, you can see that the strongest force is exerted between 100° and 140° (180° is complete extension). At 180° (the position of resting stretch), the muscle group can exert only 64 pounds of force. Why is this so? In any movements throughout the range of motion, the amount of force exerted varies because of the changing moment arms.

Everyone is familiar with the use of levers as aids in performing work, such as in lifting rocks, prying open jelly-jar lids, and opening soft-drink bottles. As mentioned above, a lever is usually a rigid bar (bone), free to rotate about a fixed point or axis called a fulcrum (joint). Theoretically, a lever can be used to lift a load of any size.

The seesaw (Fig. 7–3) is a good example of a lever system, with which a girl on the long end can balance a heavier boy on the short end. If we removed the girl, the boy would cause the teeterboard to rotate in a clockwise direction. To balance this rotary effect, we replace the girl in her original position. The system is once again perfectly balanced, or in equilibrium. The rotary effect just demonstrated is the result of something more than the size of the force or in this case the weight of the subject. If we were to place the girl, who weighs 100 pounds, at the same distance from the fulcrum or axis of rotation as the boy, who weighs 150 pounds, we would observe that the system of

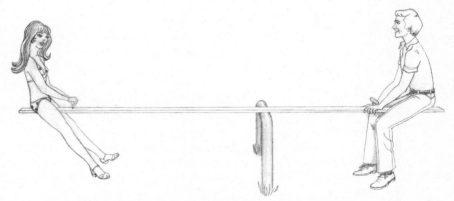

**Figure 7–3** The seesaw, a practical use of moments. The lighter girl on the longer end can teeter with the heavier boy on the shorter end.

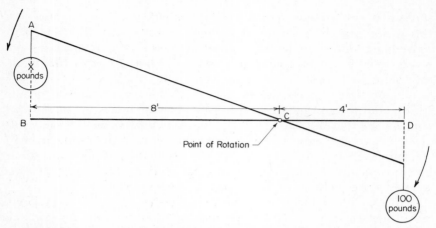

**Figure 7–4**   The sum of the moments about C equals zero; that is, $\Sigma\ M_c = 0$. Can you compute x? The answer is 50 ft.-lb.

levers (teeterboard) is once again out of equilibrium. We may conclude from this simple demonstration that the effectiveness of a given force in producing movement about a point of rotation is determined not by the size of the forces alone or by the distance of the forces from the center of rotation *but by the product of the force and its perpendicular distance to the line of action of the force.*

In Figure 7–4, the perpendicular distance from the point of rotation or axis to the force line of action is CB, not CA. We can observe that AB is the direction of action of the force needed to raise the weight and that BC is the perpendicular distance to this line. The lever arm, or preferably the moment arm of the force, is defined as the perpendicular distance from the axis to the line of action of the force; in this case, BC is the moment arm. The product of the force and its moment arm equals the moment of force, or the torque. When the length of the moment arm is expressed in feet and the force in pounds, the moment of force is reported in foot-pounds.

## Principle of Moments

We are now ready to consider an important concept known as the *principle of moments.* When a body is in equilibrium, the sum of the moments that tend to rotate the system in a clockwise direction equals the sum of the moments that tend to rotate the system in a counterclockwise direction. This may be stated in the following equation:

$$\Sigma\ M_a = 0$$

(The sum of the moments about an axis is equal to zero.)

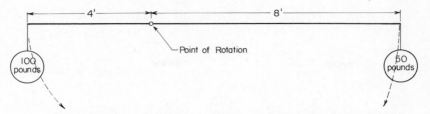

**Figure 7-5**   A system of moments in equilibrium. $\Sigma\,M_a = 0$.

Figure 7–5 illustrates this principle. There are two forces in this particular example, one that tends to rotate the system in a clockwise direction and one that tends to rotate the system in a counterclockwise direction. To meet the condition stipulated by the principle of moments, the sum of the counterclockwise moments must equal the sum of the clockwise moments. The moment tending to rotate the system in a clockwise direction is equal to 8 feet × 50 pounds, or 400 foot-pounds. The product of 4 feet × 100 pounds also equals 400 foot-pounds, the moment tending to rotate the system in a counterclockwise direction.

Figure 7–4 illustrates a problem which requires you to realize that *a moment is defined as the perpendicular distance from the line of action of the force to the point of rotation.* Let us compute the force that would be necessary to balance the 100-pound weight. The moment tending to rotate the system clockwise is equal to 100 pounds × 4 feet, or 400 foot-pounds. The moment tending to move the system in a counterclockwise direction about the fulcrum is equal to 8 feet × $x$, the unknown force. We use 8 feet as the length of one moment arm, because, you will recall, this measure is defined as the perpendicular distance from point of rotation to line of action of the force. Thus:

$$8 \times x = 4 \times 100$$

$$8x = 400$$

$$x = 50 \text{ foot-pounds}$$

The value of the lever is clear, for with a force exerted of 50 pounds, one is able to balance a rock twice as heavy as would be possible without it. Archimedes once said that he would be able to move the world if he had a place to stand.

Thus far, we have dealt only with one force tending to rotate our system clockwise and one force acting in a counterclockwise direction. Figure 7–6 represents several forces acting on a bar, with the distance of the line of action of these forces to the point of rotation indicated.

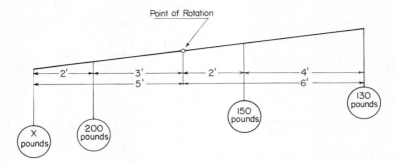

**Figure 7–6** Several forces acting on a bar. How much must force x be in order to maintain the system in equilibrium? See text for answer.

One force is unknown; the problem is to find force $x$, which will maintain the system in equilibrium. To solve this problem we must find all the forces tending to rotate the system clockwise and total them and do likewise for the forces tending to move the system counterclockwise.

On the left of the equation, we have $x \times 5$ ft. $+ 3$ ft. $\times 200$ lb.; on the right, we have 2 ft. $\times 150$ lb. $+ 6$ ft. $\times 130$ lb. or:

$$\text{counterclockwise moments} = \text{clockwise moments}$$

$$x \times 5 + 3 \times 200 = 2 \times 150 + 6 \times 130$$

$$5x + 600 = 300 + 780$$

$$5x = 1080 - 600$$

$$5x = 480$$

$$x = 96 \text{ lb.}$$

### Trigonometry and Forces

In some cases, it may be necessary to compute the length of the moment arm in order to solve the problem. This necessitates the use of the following elementary trigonometric functions (see Fig. 7–7):

Function 1.    Sine $\theta = \dfrac{a}{c}$, or sine $\theta = \dfrac{\text{side opposite}}{\text{hypotenuse}}$

Function 2.    Cosine $\theta = \dfrac{b}{c}$, or cosine $\theta = \dfrac{\text{side adjacent}}{\text{hypotenuse}}$

Function 3.    Tangent $\theta = \dfrac{a}{b}$, or tangent $\theta = \dfrac{\text{side opposite}}{\text{side adjacent}}$

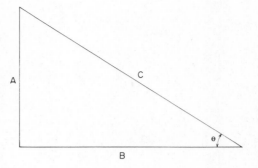

**Figure 7–7** Right triangle. A is side opposite angle Θ; B is side adjacent; and C is the hypotenuse.

In each of the three equations, a knowledge of any two values will enable us to compute the third. For example, let us say that angle theta (θ) equals 52° and side B equals 5 inches; what does side C equal? We should select function 2 for the cosine:

$$\text{Cosine } \theta = \frac{b}{c}$$

$$\text{Cosine } 52° = \frac{5}{c}$$

Referring to Table 7–1 of the trigonometric functions, we find the cosine of angle 52° to be equal to 0.6157. Therefore,

$$0.6157 = \frac{5}{c}$$

$$0.6157c = 5$$

$$c = \frac{5}{0.6157}$$

$$c = 8.1 \text{ inches}$$

Consider the following example of how to make use of the trigonometric functions in the solution of force problems. Figure 7–8 depicts the elbow flexed at a right angle. Let's suppose that the biceps is inserted at an angle of 70° and 3 inches below the joint, or point of rotation. The center of gravity of the forearm is 7 inches from the point of rotation. The problem is to determine how much force the biceps must exert in order to hold the forearm against gravity, assuming that the forearm weighs 8 pounds. AB is the moment arm tending to rotate the system counterclockwise; AC is the moment arm tending to effect

## Table 7–1 TRIGONOMETRIC FUNCTIONS

| Deg. | Sin | Cos | Tan | Cot | |
|------|------|------|------|------|------|
| 0  | 0.0000 | 1.0000 | 0.0000 |        | 90 |
| 1  | 0.0175 | 0.9998 | 0.0175 | 57.290 | 89 |
| 2  | 0.0349 | 0.9994 | 0.0349 | 28.636 | 88 |
| 3  | 0.0523 | 0.9986 | 0.0524 | 19.081 | 87 |
| 4  | 0.0698 | 0.9976 | 0.0699 | 14.301 | 86 |
| 5  | 0.0872 | 0.9962 | 0.0875 | 11.430 | 85 |
| 6  | 0.1045 | 0.9945 | 0.1051 | 9.5144 | 84 |
| 7  | 0.1219 | 0.9925 | 0.1228 | 8.1443 | 83 |
| 8  | 0.1392 | 0.9903 | 0.1405 | 7.1154 | 82 |
| 9  | 0.1564 | 0.9877 | 0.1584 | 6.3138 | 81 |
| 10 | 0.1736 | 0.9848 | 0.1763 | 5.6713 | 80 |
| 11 | 0.1908 | 0.9816 | 0.1944 | 5.1446 | 79 |
| 12 | 0.2079 | 0.9781 | 0.2126 | 4.7046 | 78 |
| 13 | 0.2250 | 0.9744 | 0.2309 | 4.3315 | 77 |
| 14 | 0.2419 | 0.9703 | 0.2493 | 4.0108 | 76 |
| 15 | 0.2588 | 0.9659 | 0.2679 | 3.7321 | 75 |
| 16 | 0.2756 | 0.9613 | 0.2867 | 3.4874 | 74 |
| 17 | 0.2924 | 0.9563 | 0.3057 | 3.2709 | 73 |
| 18 | 0.3000 | 0.9511 | 0.3249 | 3.0777 | 72 |
| 19 | 0.3256 | 0.9455 | 0.3443 | 2.9042 | 71 |
| 20 | 0.3420 | 0.9397 | 0.3640 | 2.7475 | 70 |
| 21 | 0.3584 | 0.9336 | 0.3839 | 2.6051 | 69 |
| 22 | 0.3746 | 0.9272 | 0.4040 | 2.4751 | 68 |
| 23 | 0.3907 | 0.9205 | 0.4245 | 2.3559 | 67 |
| 24 | 0.4067 | 0.9135 | 0.4452 | 2.2460 | 66 |
| 25 | 0.4226 | 0.9063 | 0.4663 | 2.1445 | 65 |
| 26 | 0.4384 | 0.8988 | 0.4877 | 2.0503 | 64 |
| 27 | 0.4540 | 0.8910 | 0.5095 | 1.9626 | 63 |
| 28 | 0.4695 | 0.8829 | 0.5317 | 1.8807 | 62 |
| 29 | 0.4848 | 0.8746 | 0.5543 | 1.1434 | 61 |
| 30 | 0.5000 | 0.8660 | 0.5774 | 1.7321 | 60 |
| 31 | 0.5150 | 0.8572 | 0.6009 | 1.6643 | 59 |
| 32 | 0.5299 | 0.8480 | 0.6249 | 1.6003 | 58 |
| 33 | 0.5446 | 0.8387 | 0.6494 | 1.5399 | 57 |
| 34 | 0.5592 | 0.8290 | 0.6745 | 1.4826 | 56 |
| 35 | 0.5736 | 0.8192 | 0.7002 | 1.4281 | 55 |
| 36 | 0.5878 | 0.8090 | 0.7265 | 1.3764 | 54 |
| 37 | 0.6018 | 0.7986 | 0.7536 | 1.3270 | 53 |
| 38 | 0.6157 | 0.7880 | 0.7813 | 1.2799 | 52 |
| 39 | 0.6293 | 0.7771 | 0.8098 | 1.2349 | 51 |
| 40 | 0.6428 | 0.7660 | 0.8391 | 1.1918 | 50 |
| 41 | 0.6561 | 0.7547 | 0.8693 | 1.1504 | 49 |
| 42 | 0.6691 | 0.7431 | 0.9004 | 1.1106 | 48 |
| 43 | 0.6820 | 0.7314 | 0.9325 | 1.0724 | 47 |
| 44 | 0.6947 | 0.7193 | 0.9657 | 1.0355 | 46 |
| 45 | 0.7071 | 0.7071 | 1.0000 | 1.0000 | 45 |
|    | Cos | Sin | Cot | Tan | Deg. |

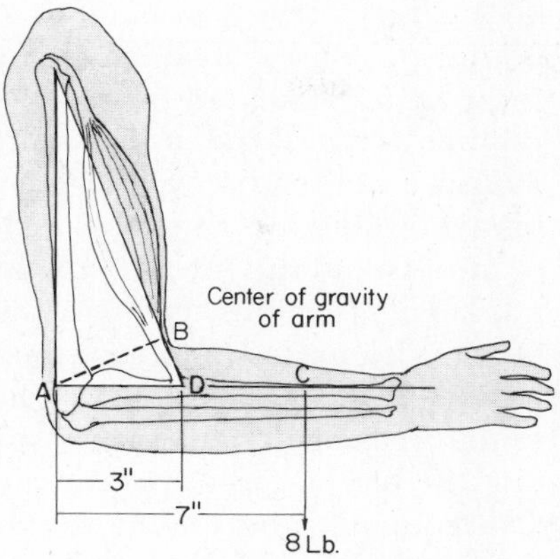

**Figure 7–8**  The elbow is flexed at a 90° angle. The biceps muscle must exert about 20 pounds of force just to hold the forearm against gravity.

movement in a clockwise direction. AC is known; AB must be computed. Knowing the angle BDA, the equation for the sine of $\theta$ may be used.

$$\text{Sine } \theta = \frac{AB}{3}$$

$$\text{Sine } 70° = \frac{AB}{3}$$

$$0.9397 = \frac{AB}{3}$$

$$AB = 0.9397 \times 3$$

$$AB = 2.82 \text{ in.}$$

Now, solving for $\Sigma M = 0$

$$2.82 \text{ in.} \times x = 7 \text{ in.} \times 8 \text{ lb.}$$

$$2.82x = 56$$

$$x = 19.8 \text{ lb.}$$

We see that the biceps must exert almost 20 pounds of force in order to hold a mass of 8 pounds. The smaller the angle at which the biceps is attached, the greater will be the sustaining force required at the origin of the biceps. This fact should be impressive to the physical educator—think how much force is being maintained at the lumbosacral joint in a supine position with the legs held about 10 inches off the floor (leg raises). Calculations reveal this figure to approximate 800 pounds, a conservative estimate for an adult. Furthermore, imagine the force being sustained by the biceps when exerting a force of 60 or 70 pounds as measured at the wrist joint: forces approximating half a ton! Thus we can see how a pitcher, under certain circumstances, can break his arm while throwing a ball. The ability to compute moments helps us to understand the forces being brought to bear at the various joints and muscular insertions during a particular exercise. Such knowledge also helps us to understand that there are limitations to barbell weight-lifting programs. The load (weights) selected must necessarily be related to the weaker muscular positions. For example, recall from Figure 7–2 that the biceps can overcome a greater resistance at 100° than at 180°. Consequently, the muscle is not continuously overloaded throughout the full range of movement. Let's take a look at several types of equipment that have been recently devised to correct some of the limitations associated with barbells.

### The Nautilus Equipment

Figure 7–9 illustrates the Nautilus Hip and Back Machine, which provides stretching in the starting position and appropriate resistance

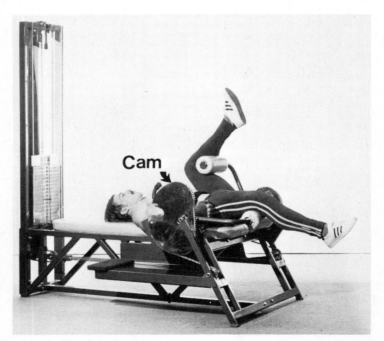

**Figure 7–9** The Nautilus hip and back machine. A cam compensates for the variations in muscular force at different joint angles by changing the moment arm; as a result, the muscle exerts maximal force throughout the full range of motion. (Courtesy Nautilus Sports/Medical Industries, DeLand, Fla.)

throughout the range of motion. The Nautilus equipment (some 17 different machines for various exercises) provides resistance correlated to the force exerted throughout the complete range of motion. Simply, in the joint position at which a muscle can exert its greatest force, the resistance is greatest. How is this accomplished?

A cam (Fig. 7–9) compensates for the variations in force by changing the moment arm, and even though the weights with which the machine is loaded remain constant, the resistance is increased or decreased.

In Figure 7–2 we observed the strength curves for a number of muscle groups at various joint angles. The cams for the Nautilus equipment must be designed in accordance with these curves. As a result, relative resistance occurs throughout the range of motion; the resistance is lowest in the weakest position and highest in the strongest position.

### Mini-Gym and Cybex Equipment

Employing a special mechanical device, the Mini-Gym (Fig. 7–10) and Cybex equipment possess a speed-governor which allows one to preset the speed at which he or she wishes to exercise the muscle group. Applying maximal effort, the machines accelerate to the preset speed. As the muscle continues to contract throughout the range of motion, the speed-governing action of the machine will fluctuate to accommodate the varying force exerted by the muscle. In this manner the device consistently loads the muscle for maximal performance throughout the range of motion once the set speed is obtained by the contracting muscles.

**Figure 7–10** The Mini-Gym. This type of machine uses a speed-governor, which accommodates the load so that the muscle is maximally loaded throughout the full range of motion. (Courtesy Mini-Gym, Inc., Independence, Mo.)

# WEIGHT TRAINING PROGRAMS

In this section, we will concentrate on the various kinds of weight training programs that have been used for the development of muscular strength and endurance. We will start with some basic definitions and then proceed to a discussion of the physiological changes induced by such programs. Finally, we will attempt to answer some of the questions posed earlier, relating strength and endurance to physical performance.

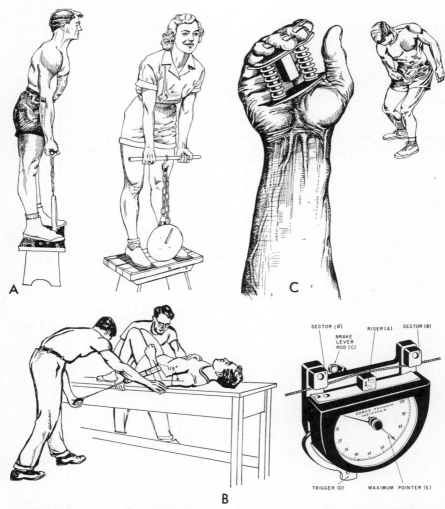

**Figure 7–11**  *A*, Use of dynamometer in measuring back lift strength. *B*, Use of tensiometer in measuring strength of elbow flexors. Right, enlarged view of tensiometer. *C*, Use of manuometer in measuring grip strength. (From Mathews.[47])

## Muscular Strength Defined

Muscular strength may be defined as the force a muscle or, more correctly, a muscle group can exert against a resistance in one maximal effort. Strength is measured in units of pounds or kilograms using a dynamometer, tensiometer, or manuometer (Fig. 7–11). Sometimes, strength is also measured as the maximal amount of weight that can be lifted once by a muscle group throughout the full range of motion.

**Types of Contraction.** There are four basic types of muscular contraction.

*Isotonic Contraction.* This is one of the most familiar types of contraction. It is sometimes referred to as *dynamic contraction.* Actually, the latter term is more accurate, because "isotonic" literally means same or constant *(iso)* tension *(tonic).* In other words, an isotonic contraction, supposedly, is one that produces the same amount of tension while shortening as it overcomes a given resistance. We know, however, from our discussion of the mechanics of contraction, that this is not true for intact muscles; the tension developed by a muscle varies as it shortens over the full range of motion about the joint (see Fig. 7–2). More correctly, a dynamic (isotonic) contraction is one in which the muscle shortens while lifting a *constant* resistance, with the muscular tension varying somewhat over the full range of motion. Another term sometimes used to indicate this type of contraction is *concentric.* This means simply that a muscle shortens during contraction.

*Isometric Contraction.* The term *isometric* literally means same or constant *(iso)* length *(metric).* In other words, a muscle that contracts isometrically is one in which tension is developed but there is no change in the external length of the muscle. The reason that the muscle does not shorten is because the external resistance against which the muscle is pulling is greater than the maximal tension (internal force) the muscle can generate. In an isotonic contraction, where the muscle shortens, the internal force generated by the muscle exceeds that of the external force. Another term used for isometric contraction (although isometric is accurate in its literal derivation) is *static contraction.*

*Eccentric Contraction.* This type of contraction refers to the *lengthening* of a muscle during contraction; that is, during the development of active tension. A good example of an eccentric contraction is as follows: Flex your elbow. Have someone try to extend your forearm by pulling down on your wrist. At the same time, you resist the pull by attempting to flex your elbow. As your forearm is extended, the elbow flexor muscles will lengthen while contracting. This, by definition, is an eccentric contraction. Eccentric contractions are used in resisting gravity, e.g., walking down a hill or down steps.

*Isokinetic Contraction.* During an isokinetic contraction, the tension developed by the muscle as it shortens is *maximal* at all joint angles over the full range of motion. This type of contraction is made possible by specially designed pieces of equipment, such as the Nautilus, the Mini-Gym, and the Cybex, mentioned earlier. Although the machines operate on different principles, they each allow an isokinetic contraction; the Mini-Gym and Cybex on the basis of controlling the speed of contraction and the Nautilus on the basis of changes in the moment arm through specially shaped cams. During exercise with an isokinetic machine, the machine accommodates a resistance equal to the force applied by the muscle group throughout the range of motion. For this reason, an isokinetic exercise is also referred to as an *accommodating resistance exercise.*

The four types of muscular contraction and their definitions are summarized in Table 7–2 (p. 142).

### Muscular Endurance Defined

Endurance is most often spoken of as (1) muscular endurance and (2) cardiorespiratory or cardiovascular endurance. Muscular endurance is usually defined as the ability of a muscle group to perform repeated contractions against a light load for an extended period of time. Arm curls, sit-ups, bench presses, and the use of pulleys with light weights are examples of exercises that involve muscular endurance.

Cardiorespiratory endurance is usually defined as that type of endurance which enables a person to participate in such activities as the 1-mile, 2-mile, and marathon runs.

From these definitions of endurance, one can derive relatively little useful information. To be sure, muscular endurance is more often associated with individual muscle groups, whereas cardiorespiratory endurance reflects total body endurance. Even so, one might ask: Does walking or jogging reflect muscular endurance or cardiorespiratory endurance? Actually, it makes little difference how these activities are classified. What we are truly interested in is improving conditions for participation. Therefore, does it not seem more logical to ask ourselves: What are the primary energy sources involved in the activity, whatever it may be?

Recall from Chapter 2 that there are three energy sources. As a consequence, improving one's ability is dependent first of all upon increasing (through conditioning) the primary energy sources involved for the *specific* activity.

### Physiological Changes Accompanying Increased Strength

Muscular exercise is such a common experience that the more striking effects are evident to all. One need go no farther than the school playground to hear the familiar challenge, "Show us your

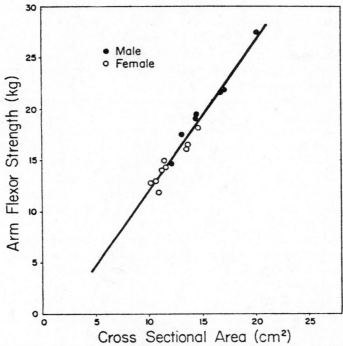

**Figure 7–12**   Relationship between the strength of the arm flexor muscles and their size (cross-sectional area). Notice that the relationship is the same for both men and women. (Based on data from Ikai, M., and Fukunaga, T.: Calculation of muscle strength per unit cross-sectional area of human muscle by means of ultrasonic measurements. Int. Z. Angew. Physiol., 26:26–32, 1968.)

muscle," and witness the youngsters flexing their arms to compare biceps. Indeed, muscle enlargement with a corresponding increase in strength is a commonly observed phenomenon (it was first shown scientifically as early as 1897).[51]

**Hypertrophy.**   The enlargement of muscle that results from weight training programs, is mainly due to an increase in the cross-sectional area of the individual muscle fibers. This increase in fiber diameter is called hypertrophy. In untrained muscle, the fibers vary considerably in diameter. The objective of a strengthening exercise program can be thought of as to bring the smaller muscle fibers up to the size of the larger ones. Rarely do the hypertrophied fibers exceed the cross-sectional area of the already existing larger ones, but a great many more attain this size. The relationship between the strength of a muscle and its cross-sectional area is shown in Figure 7–12. Notice that it is the same for males and females. (For more on this, see p. 464.)

Hypertrophy of individual muscle fibers is attributable to one or more of the following changes:[30A]

(1) Increased number of myofibrils per muscle fiber.[31]

(2) Increased total amount of protein,[32] particularly in the myosin filament.[53]

(3) Increased capillary density per fiber.

(4) Increased amounts (and strength) of connective, tendinous, and ligamentous tissues.

(5) Increased number of fibers, resulting from longitudinal fiber splitting.[28]

(6) Biochemical changes leading to increases in ATP, PC, glycogen, mitochondrion, and various enzymes. (This will be discussed in more detail in Chapter 13, p. 272.)

The changes that contribute most to hypertrophy following weight-training programs are probably the first four listed above. Also, an increased number of capillaries per fiber (number 3 above) is likely to be most closely associated with increased muscular endurance.

The finding of longitudinal fiber splitting in chronically exercised rats (number 5 above) is an interesting phenomenon and deserves further comment. This kind of splitting is shown in Figure 7–13. For nearly 80 years, the increased size of a muscle, as a result of weight training, has been attributed solely to an increase in the diameter of the muscle fibers already present and *not* to an increase in the number of fibers (hyperplasia). Observation of fiber splitting, of course, now casts some doubt on earlier theories about increases in muscle size. The problem is far from resolved; much more research is needed before the importance of such a change can be estimated.

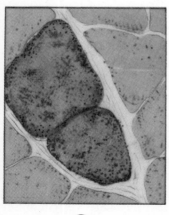 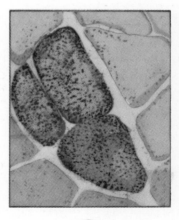

 Ⓑ

**Figure 7–13** Longitudinal fiber splitting. *A,* Prior to chronic exercise stress, there are only two fibers in the bundle located in the middle of the diagram. *B,* After months of exercise training, one of the fibers split, making a total of three fibers. (Redrawn from Edgerton.[28])

**Stimulus for Strength and Endurance Gains.** What causes a muscle to increase in strength and endurance? We have already indicated that muscular hypertrophy involves certain physiological changes that correlate well with an increased capacity of the muscle to exert maximal force as well as to exert submaximal force over an extended period of time. In other words, one of the reasons is related to the increased size of the muscle. In turn, we know that chronic stress or use of the muscles, as would be the case with regularly scheduled weight training programs, is the ultimate stimulus for hypertrophy and increased levels of strength and endurance.

All of the changes described thus far can be said to have occurred in the muscle tissue itself. What about the nervous system? Is it not true that within the body, a muscle voluntarily contracts through the control of the central nervous system? It is interesting that little research has been conducted along these lines. However, there is some evidence to suggest that changes in the central nervous system act as stimuli for gains in both strength and endurance. A good example of this was mentioned in the discussion of the Golgi tendon organs (p. 106). Here we said that the breaking point of strength testing could very well be limited by the inhibiting influence of these proprioceptors.

Another example is given by true stories of extraordinary feats of muscular strength and endurance. These feats usually occur under exceptional circumstances; that is, during frightening or "life-and-death" situations. Nevertheless, they may be interpreted to mean that under normal circumstances, strength and endurance are *inhibited* by the central nervous system.[37] Such feats could be explained on the basis that normally it is not possible, because of central nervous system inhibitions, to activate all of the motor units available within a muscle or muscle groups. Under extreme circumstances, such inhibitions would be removed and thus all motor units activated. A reduction in central nervous sytem inhibition with concomitant increases in strength and endurance would also seem to be a reasonable change that could be learned through weight training programs.

**Weight Training and Body Composition Changes.** For the average college-age male and female, body composition changes following a weight training program will consist of (1) little or no change in total body weight; (2) significant losses of relative and absolute body fat; and (3) a significant gain in lean body weight (presumably muscle mass). More is said about these changes in Chapter 21, page 468.

### The Overload Principle

The physiological principle on which strength and endurance development depends is known as the *overload principle*. This principle states simply that the strength, endurance, and hypertrophy of a muscle will increase only when the muscle performs for a given period of time at its maximal strength and endurance capacity; that is, against work loads that are above those normally encountered. As early as 1919, Lange[40] expressed in the scientific literature the first views on the relationship between muscle hypertrophy and the overload phenomenon:

> Only when a muscle performs with greatest power, i.e., through the overcoming of greater resistance in a unit of time than before, would its functional cross section need to increase.... If, however, the muscle performance is increased merely by working against the same resistance as before for a longer time, no increase in the contractile substance is necessary.

One of the first experimental demonstrations in humans of the overload principle was made by Hellebrandt and Houtz.[33] Some of their results are shown in Figure 7–14. It is clear that the gains in stength and endurance are most pronounced when the muscle is exercised in the overload zone; that is, with resistances far above those normally encountered. Underload, in this case, refers to resistances below those normally encountered by the muscle.

The overload principle, when applied to weight training programs,

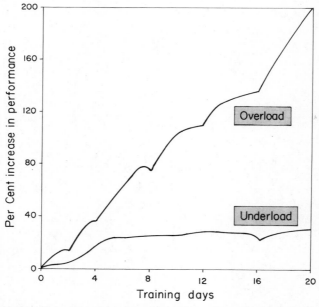

**Figure 7–14** The overload principle. Gains in strength and endurance are most pronounced when the muscle is exercised in the overload zone, i.e., with resistances above those normally encountered by the muscle. (Based on data from Hellebrant and Houtz.[33])

means that the resistance against which the muscle works should be increased throughout the course of the program as the muscle gains in strength and endurance. For this reason, the original version of the overload principle, as first stated by Lange, has been modified to what we now call the principle of *progressive resistance exercise* (PRE).

### Specificity of Weight Training

Experience has taught successful coaches that in order to increase the performance of their athletes, a *specific* training program must be planned for each athlete. In other words, the training programs must be relevant to the demands of the event for which the athlete is being trained. Such demands include (1) the predominant energy system(s) involved, and (2) the movement patterns and the specific muscle groups involved. The first demand will be discussed in more detail in Chapter 12 (see p. 240). The second demand means that gains in strength and endurance will improve skill performance to the greatest extent when the training program consists of progressive resistance exercises that include the muscle groups and simulate the movement patterns most often used during the actual execution of that skill. For example, weight training exercises for improvement in swimming the breast stroke should focus on those muscles and their movement patterns associated with the breast stroke. The same rule would apply to other swimming events and to other events or skills within other sports and activities.

The specificity of weight training is demonstrable in other ways. You will recall from the preceding chapter that fast-twitch or white fibers are preferentially recruited for sprintlike activities and slow-twitch or red fibers for endurance-like exercises. It is easy to see that in order to maximally improve performance in either of these activities, training must be specific to increasing the functional capabilities of the respective fiber types. Also, strength training has been shown to be somewhat specific to the joint angle at which the muscle group is trained.[2, 30] In other words, a muscle group trained, for example, at a joint angle of 115° will not necessarily show increased strength at other joint angles. Specificity is further evidenced by the fact that isometric programs will increase isometric strength more than they will isotonic strength and vice-versa.[5] The same applies to isometric versus isokinetic versus eccentric programs.

Specificity of training is obviously important and should be taken into account when planning a weight training program, whether it be for improvement of athletic or recreational performance.

### Strength and Endurance Programs

Because there are four basic kinds of muscular contraction (see Table 7–2), it is not surprising to find that there are also four types of

**Table 7–2    SUMMARY OF THE TYPES OF MUSCULAR CONTRACTION**

| TYPE OF CONTRACTION | DEFINITION |
|---|---|
| Isotonic, dynamic, or concentric | The muscle shortens with varying tension while lifting a constant load. |
| Isometric or static | Tension develops but there is no change in the length of the muscle. |
| Eccentric | The muscle lengthens while contracting (developing tension). |
| Isokinetic | The tension developed by the muscle while shortening is maximal over the full range of motion. |

strength and endurance programs, each structured around one of the basic contractions. In answering some of the questions posed earlier, we will consider each type of program.

**Isotonic Programs.**    One of the first isotonic progressive resistance programs advocated was that of DeLorme and Watkins in 1948.[24, 25] In setting forth their method of exercises for maximal development of strength, they first established the idea of *repetition maximum (RM)*. A repetition maximum is the maximal load that a muscle group can lift over a given number of repetitions before fatiguing. In their program they used a 10-repetition maximum (10 RM), i.e., the maximal load that can be lifted over 10 repetitions. For each muscle group to be trained, the exercise program consisted of a total of 30 repetitions per training session divided into 3 *sets* of 10 repetitions each as follows:

> Set 1 = 10 repetitions at a load of ½ 10 RM*
> Set 2 = 10 repetitions at a load of ¾ 10 RM
> Set 3 = 10 repetitions at a load of 10 RM

A set is the number of repetitions performed consecutively without resting (in this case, 1 set = 10 repetitions). From day to day the subject tries to increase the number of repetitions while maintaining the same resistance load. When more than 10 repetitions are possible, the load is increased to a new 10 RM load. The most important part of this program is set 3; i.e., 10 repetitions at the full 10 RM load. This represents the greatest resistance for the muscle group. Variations in the warm-up repetitions (sets 1 and 2) do not affect the results appreciably.

DeLorme and Watkins also recommended the training frequency to be 4 consecutive days per week. They found by experience that 5 days per week was usually the heaviest schedule that could be employed without developing serious signs of delayed recovery from the training sessions.

Further research using the principles set forth by DeLorme and

---

*If the 10 RM load were 100 pounds, a ½ 10 RM load would equal 50 pounds.

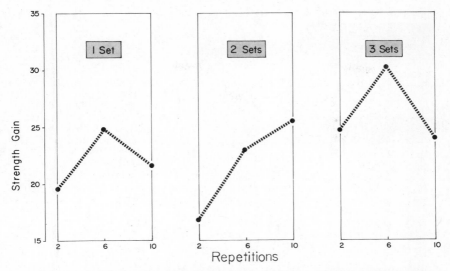

**Figure 7–15** Strength gains resulting from weight training programs consisting of various sets and repetitions. All programs were performed three days per week for 12 weeks. When different numbers of sets are combined with different repetition maximum (RM) loads, several equivalent programs for strength can be developed. (Based on data from Berger.[7])

Watkins was conducted later concerning the optimum number of sets and repetitions that would most effectively increase strength.[3, 4, 5, 6, 10] These studies employed programs with a training frequency of 3 days per week over a duration of 8 to 12 weeks. Some of the results are shown in Figure 7–15. It can be seen that the greatest improvement in strength is obtained from 3 sets, each with a 6 RM load.[4] Generally, it can be said that the optimal number of repetitions maximum lies somewhere between 3 and 9.[6, 69] When different numbers of sets are combined with different RM loads, several equivalent programs for strength can be developed.[3] This is apparent when comparing the mean strength gains from the various programs shown in Figure 7–15.

We can conclude that there is no *single* combination of sets and repetitions that yields optimal strength gains for everyone. Although there is some disagreement regarding the details of a strength training program, there is one agreement in principle: If you want to develop strength, use progressive resistance exercises in the overload zone.

So far we have discussed only isotonic weight training programs that have been shown to improve strength. What about muscular endurance? The "old rule"—strength = low repetitions and high loads, and endurance = high repetitions and low loads—appears still to be valid; but it needs first to be clarified and second extended. Clarification involves the term "low load." We must remember that the progressive overload principle is also a requisite for improvement of muscular

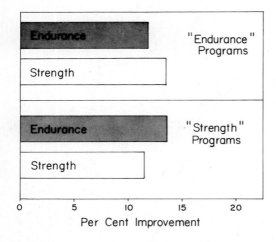

**Figure 7–16** Both muscular strength and endurance can be developed equally from either a low repetition, high load program (so-called strength program) or a high repetition, low load program (so-called endurance program). (Based on data from Clarke and Stull[16] and Stull and Clarke.[60])

endurance. Prolonged repetitions of "underloaded" muscles (see Fig. 7–14) have little effect on endurance.[33]

Extension of the rule is based on the fact that both strength and endurance can be equally developed from either a low repetition and high load program or a high repetition and low load program.[16, 23, 60] This can be seen in Figure 7–16. In this case, both the so-called "endurance" and "strength" programs consisted of 3 training sessions per week for 6 or 7 weeks. Each training session of the "endurance" program[16] consisted of elbow flexion at a rate of 40 repetitions per minute with a load of 11 pounds until exhaustion was reached. The "strength" program[60] consisted of arm curls performed according to the De-Lorme-Watkins progression outlined on page 142.

The implication that can be made from these findings is that the same strength and endurance gains may be achieved in a more economical way by high-intensity, low-repetition techniques. Programs involving a high number of repetitions with low resistance require more time. If time is a factor, the overload technique heretofore considered characteristic of strength training would be preferable.[60]

A basic isotonic weight training program for various muscle groups is given in Appendix D, page 531.

**Isometric Programs.** Just as DeLorme and Watkins did for isotonic programs, Hettinger and Müller[34] in 1953 provided the impetus for the scientific inquiry into and establishment of isometric weight training programs. Their original studies claimed that maximal strength could be gained at a rate of about 5 per cent per week merely by isometrically contracting a muscle group for 6 seconds at ⅔ maximal tension once a day for 5 days per week. Strength gain was unaffected by increasing either the tension (even to maximum) or the number and duration of the contractions. Such findings revolutionized the entire concept of weight training programs.

Their findings concerning strength development and the amount of tension and number and duration of isometric contractions stimulated a great deal of further research both in Europe and in the United States. The results of these studies proved to be inconsistent. Some findings confirmed Hettinger and Müller's original results;[50, 54] others did not.[1, 45, 52, 67] Most interestingly, one of the latter studies was done by Müller himself.[52] His results showed that maximal isometric strength could be developed best by training 5 days per week, with each training session consisting of 5 to 10 maximal contractions held for 5 seconds each.

Again, we see that several types of isometric training programs will yield substantial strength gains. There does not seem to be just one program that will be best for everyone. In addition, it is generally agreed that muscular endurance can be increased through isometric exercises.[14, 17, 18, 56] However, once again the design of such a program varies considerably.

At least two factors related to isometric training programs need to be mentioned at this time. First, we said earlier that the development of strength and endurance is specific to the joint angle at which the muscle group is trained. This, of course, implicates isometric training in particular because of its static nature. Thus, if strength and endurance at different joint angles are desired, and if isometric programs are used, the exercises must be performed at all specified joint angles.

The second factor deals with the changes in blood pressure that accompany weight training exercises. Most muscular contractions and in particular isometric contractions involve what is called a *Valsalva maneuver*. A Valsalva maneuver means making an expiratory effort with the glottis* closed. Since air cannot escape, intrathoracic pressure increases appreciably (even to the point where it can cause the venae cavae, which return blood to the heart, to collapse). This elevated intrathoracic pressure causes systolic and diastolic blood pressures to increase beyond values normally seen during exercise in which a Valsalva maneuver does not occur. Even though the Valsalva maneuver can be avoided by exhaling while lifting or sustaining an isometric contraction, most physicians advise against weight training in general and isometrics in particular as an activity for the postcoronary patient.

**Eccentric Programs.** Weight training programs structured around eccentric contractions are not common. Furthermore, they have not been adopted for use by coaches. What little information is available concerning eccentric programs indicates that while strength gains can be made through such programs,[41] by comparison to other programs they are not as effective.[59] Their use, however, is advocated in therapy and rehabilitation.[57]

---

*The glottis is the space or opening between the vocal cords.

**Isokinetic Programs.** These are the newest type of weight training programs. Because of this, only a few research studies have been conducted using such programs. However, of those that have been done, most indicate that substantial gains in strength and endurance can be made.[49, 62]

In theory, isokinetic exercises should lead to the greatest improvement in muscular performance. For example, as mentioned earlier, the isokinetic principle permits development of maximal muscular tension throughout the full range of joint movement. In other words, a greater number of motor units are activated.[58] As a result, greater demands (greater overload) than were previously possible can be placed on the muscles being exercised.[35]

Numerous coaches have adopted the isokinetic idea and have developed specific weight-training programs structured entirely around isokinetic contractions. One of these coaches is Dr. James Councilman, head swimming coach at Indiana University. He suggests that since swimmers contract their arm muscles isokinetically when pulling through the water, it is important that their weight-training programs on land also be isokinetically oriented.[20, 21, 22, 65]

The special equipment needed for isokinetic exercises (e.g., Nautilus, Mini-Gym, and Cybex) is a potential drawback for the widespread use of the isokinetic program. However, although the Nautilus and Cybex machines are costly, the Mini-Gym is relatively inexpensive. At any rate, all of these corporations have developed numerous isokinetic machines and methods which may be used for strength and endurance development in such specific activities as swimming, running, throwing, putting the shot, volleyball, football, and kicking.*

**Comparison among Programs.** Thus far we have considered the changes in muscular strength and endurance brought about as a result of each of the programs separately. Which program is the best? Again, there is no simple answer to the question. There are research design problems associated with equating the various programs in such a way that the only differing factor is the type of contraction. Further complications result because of specificity. In an attempt to answer the question, some results from comparative studies are presented in Figure 7–17. Figure 7–17A presents a comparison of strength gains resulting from various isotonic programs and one type of isometric program.[7] The exact designs of the isotonic programs are given in the figure. The isometric program consisted of two maximal contractions held for 6 to 8 seconds; each contraction was at a different joint angle. The subjects were college-age males; the training frequency and dura-

---

*For detailed programs write to the following addresses: Nautilus Sports Medical Industries, Box 1783, Deland, Fla., 32720; Mini-Gym, Inc., Box 266, 733½ S. Northern, Independence, Mo. 64051; Cybex Division of Lumex, Inc., Bay Shore, N.Y.

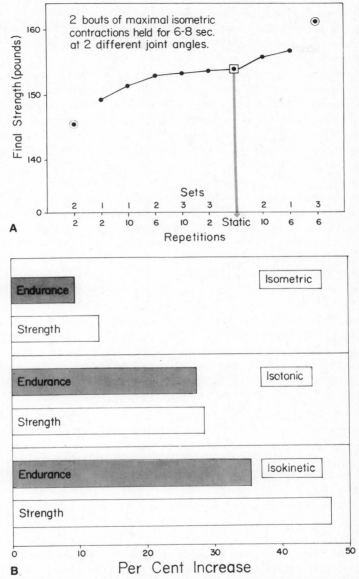

**Figure 7–17** Comparison of different weight training programs. *A,* Comparison of strength gains resulting from various isotonic programs and one isometric program. All programs were performed three days per week for 12 weeks. Only one isotonic program (circled dot to the right) was superior to the isometric program, and the isometric program was superior to only one isotonic program (circled dot at left). *B,* Comparison of isokinetic, isotonic, and isometric programs. All programs were performed four days per week for 8 weeks. The isokinetic program was superior to the other programs in both strength and endurance gains. (Data in *A* from Berger;[4] data in *B* from Thistle et al.[62])

tion were 3 days per week and 12 weeks, respectively, for all programs. Only one isotonic program was superior to the isometric program. By the same token, the isometric program was superior to only one isotonic program. In other words, the two types of programs are quite comparable in this case.

Figure 7–17*B* provides a comparison of isokinetic, isotonic, and isometric programs.[62] The subjects in this study were patients with varying degrees of rehabilitative problems. The training frequency and duration were 4 days per week and 8 weeks, respectively. The programs were consistent with the normal clinical programs; e.g., the isotonic program followed the DeLorme-Watkins technique. In this case, it is easy to conclude that the isokinetic program was clearly superior to the other programs in both strength and endurance gains.

Getting back to the problem of the best program, one has to ask the question, "Best for what?" For the physical educator the answer might be designing a weight training program for students or a particular group in the community. For the coach, it most likely will involve designing a program that will improve performance of a particular athletic skill. These programs will of course be different. However, both can best be designed by considering (1) the overload principle, (2) the specificity of training and (3) the availability of equipment.

**Weight Training and Sports Performance.**  Several of the questions asked at the beginning of this chapter were concerned with strength development and increases in speed of contraction and sports performance. Although a few studies suggest little or no improvement in speed of contraction, most show that strengthening exercises do indeed increase both speed and power of contraction.[8, 15, 46, 70] Incidentally, the fact that speed of contraction is improved by strength training provides evidence that the term "musclebound" has no scientific merit. In addition, research generally demonstrates that specific sports skills such as speed in running, swimming, throwing, speed and force of offensive football charge, and jumping all can be improved significantly through weight training programs.[13, 63, 64]

In a recent review of the research completed on strength development and motor and/or sports improvement, Clarke[19] reached the following conclusions:

(1) Both isometric and isotonic forms of strength training can produce improvements in many motor and sports performances. Although the evidence is at times conflicting, it is generally accepted that progressive weight training programs are superior.

(2) Some studies did not provide adequate overload in applying both isometric and isotonic strength training. In general, exercises confined to single static contractions of short duration or isotonic efforts limited to a single bout were not effective in de-

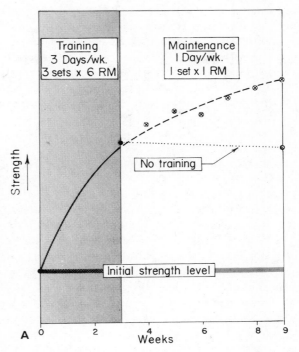

**Figure 7–18** Retention of strength and endurance. *A*, (1) the strength gained during a 3 day per week, 3 week isotonic training program (3 sets of 6 RM) was not lost during a subsequent 6 week period of no training (dotted line); and (2) strength was further improved during a subsequent 6 week training program involving only one set at a 1 RM load performed once a week.

*B*, Retention of muscular endurance. The program was performed 3 days per week for 8 weeks with each session consisting of an exhausting bout of elbow flexions at a work rate of 40 repetitions per minute against an 11 pound load. Although endurance was lost most rapidly during the first few weeks of the detraining (no training) period, after 12 weeks of no training, 70 per cent of the endurance gained was still retained. (Data in *A* from Berger;[6] data in *B* from Syster and Stull[61] and Waldman and Stull.[66])

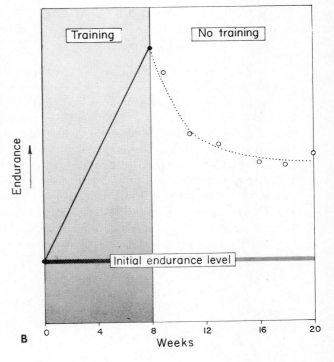

veloping either strength or motor skills. Strenuous resistance exercises of either form are needed for best results.

(3) Fear of musclebound effects from weight training may be laid to rest. The majority of studies show that speed of movement may be enhanced rather than retarded as a consequence of strength development.

(4) Exercise programs designed to strengthen muscles primarily involved in a particular sport can be used as supplements to regular practice in effectively improving the athlete's skills and motor fitness.

**Retention of Strength and Endurance.**    Once desired strength and endurance levels have been attained with a weight training program, how do we retain them? Do we have to continue with the same type of weight training program for an indefinite time? The answer to the last question is no. Let's see why.

It is generally agreed that strength and endurance, once developed, subside at slower rates than they were developed. This can be observed from Figure 7–18. There are two important points to note in *A*. First, strength gained during a three-week isotonic training program consisting of three sets at a 6 RM load, three days per week, was not lost during a subsequent six-week period of no training (detraining). Second, strength was further improved during a subsequent six-week training program involving only one set at a 1 RM load performed once a week.[9] Other studies using both isotonic and isometric programs have confirmed these results.[48, 50, 55, 56] In one study, 45 per cent of the strength gained from a twelve-week program was still retained after one year.[48]

In Fig. 7–18B, the retention of muscular endurance is shown. The training program consisted of three sessions per week for eight weeks, with each session comprising an exhausting bout of elbow flexions at a work rate of 40 repetitions per minute against an 11-pound load. Endurance was lost most rapidly during the first few weeks of the detraining period. However, after twelve weeks of detraining, the loss of endurance was stable and 70 per cent of that gained was still retained.

This information emphasizes that the most difficult phase of the weight training program is the *development* of strength and endurance. Once this has been accomplished, they are relatively easy to retain. As little exercise as once per week or once every two weeks will maintain strength and endurance, provided maximal contractions are used.


# FLEXIBILITY


Along with strength and endurance, flexibility is also an important component of muscular performance. In studying flexibility, we will concentrate our discussion around four topics: (1) definitions (2) structural limits to flexibility, (3) development of flexibility, and (4) flexibility and performance. A review concerning the physiology of flexibility has been written by Holland.[36]

### Definition of Flexibility

In general, flexibility might be described as anything capable of being flexed, turned, bowed, or twisted without breaking. However, two kinds of flexibility, *static* and *dynamic*, have been described.[27]

**Static Flexibility.** The *range of motion about a joint* is defined as static flexibility. Static flexibility can be measured most reliably with an instrument called a flexometer.[42] As shown in Figure 7–19, it has a weighted 360° dial and a weighted pointer that are independently controlled by gravity. While in use, the flexometer is strapped to the segment being tested. When the dial is locked at one extreme position (e.g., full extension of the elbow), the reading of the pointer on the dial is the arch through which the movement has taken place. It is called static flexibility because when the dial is actually read, there is no joint motion.

**Dynamic Flexibility.** This type of flexibility is defined as the *opposition or resistance of a joint to motion.* In other words, it is concerned with the forces that oppose movement over any range rather than the range itself. This type of flexibility is more difficult to measure and as such has been given little attention in physical education and athletics.

### Structural Limits to Flexibility

The structural limits to flexibility are: (1) bone, (2) muscle, (3) ligaments and other structures associated with the joint capsule, (4) ten-

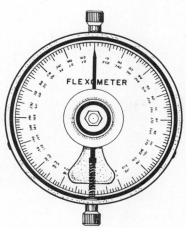

**Figure 7–19** The Leighton flexometer. (From Mathews.[47])

**Table 7–3   RELATIVE CONTRIBUTION OF SOFT-TISSUE STRUCTURES TO JOINT RESISTANCE**[*]

| STRUCTURE | RESISTANCE TO FLEXIBILITY (PERCENTAGE OF TOTAL) |
|---|---|
| 1. Joint capsule | 47 |
| 2. Muscle | 41 |
| 3. Tendon | 10 |
| 4. Skin | 2 |

*Based on data from Johns and Wright.[38]

dons and other connective tissues, and (5) skin. Limitations by bony structures are confined to certain joints, for example the hinge type joint, such as the knee and elbow. However, in all the joints, including the hinge, the so-called soft tissues provide the major limitation to the range of joint movement.

The relative importance of the soft tissues with respect to limiting flexibility is given in Table 7–3. These particular data were obtained from the wrist joints of cats, but they are applicable to humans.[38] The joint capsule and associated connective tissues plus the muscle provide the majority of resistance to flexibility. It should be mentioned that the values were obtained from the mid-range of joint motion. At the extremes of joint motion, the tendons have a more limiting effect. Since flexibility can be modified through exercise, so also can these soft-tissue limitations. The reason for this, at least in part, is related to the *elastic* nature of some of the tissues.

### Development of Flexibility

Flexibility is significant not only in performing certain skills but also recent advances in physical medicine and rehabilitation indicate that flexibility is important to general health and physical fitness. For example, flexibility exercises have been successfully prescribed for

**Figure 7–20** Standing Floor Touch. Place the feet astride and bend at the waist, with the knees straight and the arms and head hanging loosely. Concentrate on relaxing the muscles, and try to touch the floor. This exercise is good for stretching the muscles of the upper back, buttocks, and upper and lower legs.

**Figure 7–21** Sitting Toe Touch. Sit on the floor with the feet spread and reach first for one foot, then the other. Each time you reach, attempt to touch and hold the head and chest to the thigh of the foot for which you are reaching. Although this exercise develops flexibility in the same muscle groups as does the standing floor touch, it places more emphasis on stretching the upper-back muscles.

relief of dysmenorrhea, general neuromuscular tension, and low-back pains.[11, 39] For athletes, if they maintain a satisfactory degree of flexibility, they will be less susceptible to certain muscular injuries.

**Types of Exercise.** The best exercises to use for flexibility are the so-called stretching exercises. A number of these are shown in Figures 7–20 to 7–29. Many variations, which involve similar joints and muscle groups, can also be used.

**Methods of Stretching.** Stretching exercises can be performed in one of two ways: (1) *passively or statically*, and (2) *actively or ballistically*.[26, 68] Static stretching involves stretching without "bobbing" or forcing, followed by holding the final stretched position for a given amount of time. Ballistic stretching involves "bobbing" or active movements. The final stretched position is not held. While both types of stretching will improve flexibility, the static method might be preferred because (1) there is less danger of tissue damage, (2) the energy requirement is

**Figure 7–22** Chest Stretch. Lie face down, with the feet straight and the arms spread. Raise the chest from the floor. Concentrate on arching the upper part of the chest. Hold this position for six seconds. This exercise is excellent for people who have a tendency to slump, because it stretches the muscles of the anterior shoulders and chest.

**Figure 7–23** Alternate Toe Touch. Stand with the feet astride, bend from the waist, and touch the right hand to the left toe and hold. Come to the erect standing position before touching the left hand to the right toe. Continue the exercise, alternating sides. Alternate toe touching stretches the muscles of the shoulders, back, buttocks, and legs.

**Figure 7–24** Waist Bend. Stand with the feet astride and the hands on the hips. Bend forward, head up, and try to attain a position whereby the upper part of the body is parallel to the floor; hold. This exercise is excellent for stretching the muscles of the lower back, upper back, and neck.

**Figure 7–25** Overhead Toe Touch. Lie on the back and raise the feet straight in the air, supporting the hips with the hands. Point the toes and touch first one foot, hold, then the other, to the floor above the head. Excellent for flexibility of the hip joint, upper back, and neck muscles.

**Figure 7-26** Treading. Stand erect, with the weight on the right foot. Place the ball of the left foot on the floor and transfer the weight to it gradually. Alternate by placing the ball of the right foot on the floor and transferring the weight to it from the left foot. Gradually increase the tempo to a slow run. Excellent for flexibility of and for developing proper use of the ankle.

**Figure 7-27** Lower-Leg Stretch. Stand three feet in front of a wall, with the feet two inches apart. Place outstretched hands on the wall, keeping the feet flat on the floor. Move the feet away from the wall, but keep them flat on the floor. This exercise is excellent for stretching the muscles of the lower leg and is practiced a great deal by skiers.

**Figure 7-28** Upper-Chest Stretch. Stand erect, with the feet two to three inches apart, the hands in front, and the elbows raised to the side. While keeping the head up, pull the elbows back. Hold this position. Excellent for stretching the anterior shoulder muscles. A good exercise for people with round upper back.

**Figure 7–29** Spinal Stretch. Place the hands and knees on the floor and hunch the back. Bend the elbows, come slightly forward, and lower the chest toward the floor; return to original position. This exercise will develop flexibility of the spinal column.

less, and (3) there is prevention and/or relief from muscular distress and soreness.[26]

**Design of the Program.**    The frequency and duration of the static program might be 2 days per week for 30 minutes each day. Within five weeks, improvement should be noted.[26] The stretched position should be held for longer periods as the program progresses. For example, at first hold the position for 30 seconds, then after several sessions increase the holding time to a minute. Start by performing each exercise 20 times, then progress to 40.

### Flexibility and Performance

Earlier, we mentioned that flexibility aids the performance of certain skills. Figure 7–30 presents flexion and extension flexibility measurements (with the flexometer) of seven different athletic groups.[43, 44] The following factors concerning flexibility are evident from the figure.

**Specificity of Flexibility.**    The range of motion about a joint is specific in two ways. First, there is a tendency toward a specific pattern of flexibility and selected sporting events. For example, shot-putters and discus throwers have greater flexibility in the wrist than do wrestlers. Second, flexibility is joint-specific. In other words, a high degree of flexibility in one joint does not necessarily indicate a high flexibility in other

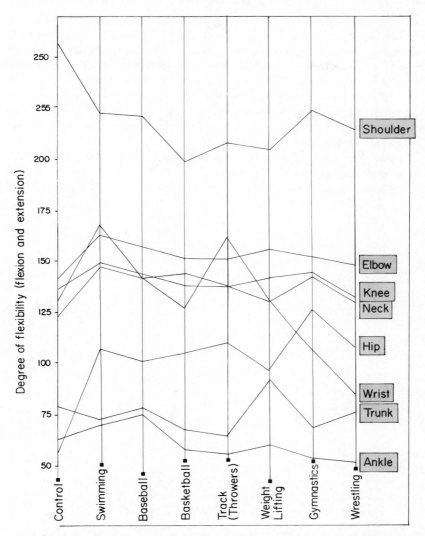

**Figure 7–30** Flexion and extension flexibility measures of seven different athletic groups. For further information, see text. (Based on data from Leighton.[43, 44])

joints. For example, gymnasts can be seen to have above average flexibility in the hip but below average in the ankle.

**Stability versus Flexibility.** Certain joints are structurally very weak. As a result, they are prone to injury. The shoulder is one of these joints. The reason is that the glenoid fossa of the scapula, into which the head of the humerus fits, is very shallow. Its main stability is provided by the surrounding musculature. You will notice that shoulder flexibility in all of the athletic groups shown is below average. This probably reflects an increased muscular strength, which in this case limits flexibility. However, notice that in most other joints, flexibility is at least average or above in those athletes for whom strength is especially important (throwers, weight lifters, gymnasts, and wrestlers). This further refutes the concept of "musclebound."

It should also be mentioned here that excessive flexibility is often indicative of proneness to injury, particularly in contact sports. Thus, flexibility measurements might prove to be a useful screening tool for young prospective football players.

**Warm-up and Flexibility.**   Although this is not shown by the figure, it is probably true that performance of stretching or warm-up exercises that increase flexibility can prevent serious injury during subsequent athletic competition.

## SUMMARY

Understanding of the body's mechanical system helps us to understand the forces acting on various joints; for example, the force sustained by the biceps in lifting 60 pounds approximates half a ton. It also helps us to understand the limitations of barbell weight lifting programs and the ways that the newer equipment compensates for these limitations.

Muscular strength is the force that a muscle group can exert against a resistance in one maximal effort. There are four types of muscular contraction: isotonic, isometric, eccentric, and isokinetic. Muscular endurance is the ability of a muscle group to perform repeated contractions for an extended period of time.

When a muscle gains in strength and endurance, its fibers become larger, or hypertrophied. This can be accomplished through the overload principle by progressive resistance exercises (PRE), by isometric exercises, and/or by isokinetic exercises. Strength and endurance gains are specific.

Lack of well-designed studies makes it impossible to state with certainty which method of training (isotonic, isometric, or isokinetic) is the most effective in producing strength and endurance gains. However, in all probability, machines that allow for accommodating resistance (isokinetic contractions) are better, because the muscle group is afforded maximal or near-maximal resistance throughout the full range of motion. Once gained, strength and endurance are retained for relatively long periods of time.

Although a few studies suggest little or no improvement in speed of contraction, most show that weight training programs do increase both speed and power of contraction. Specific sports skills can also be significantly improved through weight training programs.

Flexibility, the range of motion about a joint, is related to health and, to some extent, to athletic performance. Regularly scheduled programs involving stretching exercises will improve flexibility.

## QUESTIONS

1. Define a moment.

2. A boy weighing 100 pounds sits 5 feet from the fulcrum of a teeterboard. In order to just balance the teeterboard, what must his partner weigh if she sits 4 feet from the fulcrum? (Answer: 125 lb.)

3. The biceps muscle inserts 2 inches below the elbow joint at an angle of 35°. In this position, how much force must be exerted at the origin of the biceps in order for the person to hold a 10 lb. weight in his or her hand, located 20 inches from the elbow joint (fulcrum)? Disregard the weight of the forearm. (Answer: 173.9 lb.)

4. What would be the answer to Question 3 if the forearm weighed 8 lb. and the center of gravity were located 9 in. from the fulcrum? (Answer: 173.9 lb. + 72 lb. = 245.9 lb.)

5. Define the following types of contractions: (a) isotonic, (b) isometric, (c) eccentric, (d) isokinetic.

6. What structural changes are brought about within a muscle as a consequence of a weight training program?

7. What stimulates gains in strength and endurance?

8. Explain the overload principle.

9. Give several examples of the specificity of weight training.

10. Describe how you would structure a weight training program around (a) isotonic exercises, (b) isometric exercises, and (c) isokinetic exercises.

11. Compare the above programs. Which one is the best?

12. How does weight training affect sports performance?

13. How can strength and endurance be retained and/or maintained?

14. What are the structural limitations to flexibility?

15. How can flexibility be gained, and why is it important to health and physical performance?

## REFERENCES

1. Asa, M.: The Effects of Isometric and Isotonic Exercise on the Strength of Skeletal Muscle. Doctoral Dissertation, Springfield College, 1959.
2. Belka, D.: Comparison of dynamic, static, and combination training on dominant wrist flexor muscles. Res. Quart., 39:244–250, 1968.
3. Berger, R.: Comparative effects of three weight training programs. Res. Quart., 34:396–398, 1963.
4. Berger, R.: Effect of varied weight training programs on strength. Res. Quart., 33:168–181, 1962.
5. Berger, R.: Comparison of static and dynamic strength increases. Res. Quart., 33:329–333, 1962.
6. Berger, R.: Optimum repetitions for the development of strength. Res. Quart., 33:334–338, 1962.
7. Berger, R.: Comparison between static training and various dynamic training programs. Res. Quart., 34:131–135, 1963.
8. Berger, R.: Effects of dynamic and static training on vertical jumping ability. Res. Quart., 34:419–424, 1963.
9. Berger, R.: Comparison of the effect of various weight training loads on strength. Res. Quart., 36:141–146, 1965.
10. Berger, R., and Hardage, B.: Effect of maximum loads for each of ten repetitions on strength improvement. Res. Quart., 38:715–718, 1967.
11. Billing, H., and Loewendahl, E.: Mobilization of the Human Body. Palo Alto, California, Stanford University Press, 1949.
12. Byrd, R., and Hills, W.: Strength, endurance, and blood flow responses to isometric training. Res. Quart., 42:357–361, 1971.
13. Campbell, R.: Effects of supplemental weight training on the physical fitness of athletic squads. Res. Quart., 33:343–348, 1962.
14. Clarke, D.: Adaptations in strength and muscular endurance resulting from exercise. *In* Wilmore, J. (ed.): Exercise and Sport Sciences Reviews, vol. 1, pp. 73–102. New York, Academic Press, 1973.
15. Clarke, D., and Henry, F.: Neuromuscular specificity and increased speed from strength development. Res. Quart., 32:315–325, 1961.
16. Clarke, D., and Stull, G.: Endurance training as a determinant of strength and fatigability. Res. Quart., 41:19–26, 1970.
17. Clarke, H. (ed.): Isometric versus isotonic exercises. Phys. Fit. Res. Digest., Series 1, No. 1, July, 1971.
18. Clarke, H. (ed.): Development of muscular strength and endurance. Phys. Fit. Res. Digest, Series 4, No. 1, Jan., 1974.
19. Clarke, H. (ed.): Strength development and motor-sports improvement. Phys. Fit. Res. Digest, Series 4, No. 4, Oct., 1974.
20. Councilman, J.: Isokinetic exercise: a new concept in strength building. Swimming World, 10:4, 1969.
21. Councilman, J.: New approach to strength building. Scholastic Coach, March, 1971.
22. Councilman, J.: Isokinetic exercise. Athletic Journal, 52(6): Feb., 1972.
23. DeLateur, B., Lehmann, J., and Fordyce, W.: A test of the DeLorme axiom. Arch. Phys. Med. Rehabil., 49:245–248, 1968.
24. DeLorme, T., and Watkins, A.: Techniques of progressive resistance exercise. Arch. Phys. Med. Rehabil., 29:263–273, 1948.
25. DeLorme, T., and Watkins, A.: Progressive Resistance Exercise. New York, Appleton-Century-Crofts, 1951.
26. deVries, H.: Evaluation of static stretching procedures for improvement of flexibility. Res. Quart., 33:222–229, 1962.
27. deVries, H.: Physiology of Exercise for Physical Education and Athletics. 2nd ed. Dubuque, Iowa, W. C. Brown Co., 1974.
28. Edgerton, V.: Morphology and histochemistry of the soleus muscle from normal and exercised rats. Am. J. Anat., 127:81–88, 1970.
29. Fox, E., and Mathews, D.: Interval training: Conditioning for Sports and General Fitness. Philadelphia, W. B. Saunders Co., 1974.

30. Gardner, G.: Specificity of strength changes of the exercised and nonexercised limb following isometric training. Res. Quart., 34:98–101, 1963.

30A. Goldberg, A., Etlinger, J., Goldspink, D., and Jablecki, C.: Mechanism of work-induced hypertrophy of skeletal muscle. Med. Sci. Sports, 7(3):185–198, 1975.

31. Goldspink, G.: The combined effects of exercise and reduced food intake on skeletal muscle fibers. J. Cell. Comp. Physiol., 63:209–216, 1964.

32. Gordon, E.: Anatomical and biochemical adaptations of muscle to different exercises. J.A.M.A., 201:755–758, 1967.

33. Hellebrandt, F., and Houtz, S.: Mechanisms of muscle training in man: experimental demonstration of the overload principle. Phys. Ther. Rev., 36:371–383, 1956.

34. Hettinger, T., and Müller, E.: Muskelleistung und Muskeltraining. Arbeitsphysiol., 15:111–126, 1953.

35. Hislop, H., and Perrine, J.: The isokinetic concept of exercise. Phys. Ther., 47:114–117, 1967.

36. Holland, G.: The physiology of flexibility: a review of the literature. Kinesiology Review, 1968, pp. 49–62.

37. Ikai, M., and Steinhaus, A.: Some factors modifying the expression of human strength. J. Appl. Physiol., 16:157–163, 1961.

38. Johns, R., and Wright, V.: Relative importance of various tissues in joint stiffness. J. Appl. Physiol., 17:824–828, 1962.

39. Kraus, H., and Raab, W.: Hypokinetic Disease. Springfield, Ill., Charles C Thomas, 1961.

40. Lange, L.: Uber funktionelle Anpassung. Berlin, Springer Verlag, 1919.

41. Laycoe, R., and Marteniuk, R.: Learning and tension as factors in static strength gains produced by static and eccentric training. Res. Quart., 42:299–306, 1971.

42. Leighton, J.: Instrument and technic for measurement of range of joint motion. Arch. Phys. Med. Rehabil., 36:571–578, 1955.

43. Leighton, J.: Flexibility characteristics of four specialized skill groups of college athletes. Arch. Phys. Med. Rehabil., 38:24–28, 1957.

44. Leighton, J.: Flexibility characteristics of three specialized skill groups of champion athletes. Arch. Phys. Med. Rehabil., 38:580–583, 1957.

45. Liberson, W., and Asa, M.: Further studies of brief isometric exercises. Arch. Phys. Med. Rehabil., 40:330–336, 1959.

46. Masley, J. Hairabedian, A., and Donaldson, D.: Weight training in relation to strength, speed and coordination. Res. Quart., 24:308–315, 1952.

47. Mathews, D.: Measurement in Physical Education. 4th ed. Philadelphia, W. B. Saunders Co., 1973.

48. McMorris, R., and Elkins, E.: A study of production and evaluation of muscular hypertrophy. Arch. Phys. Med. Rehabil., 35:420–426, 1954.

49. Moffroid, M., Whipple, R., Hofkosh, J., Lowman, E., and Thistle, H.: A study of isokinetic exercise. Phys. Ther., 49:735–746, 1968.

50. Morehouse, C.: Development and maintenance of isometric strength of subjects with diverse initial strengths. Res. Quart., 38:449–456, 1967.

51. Morpurgo, B.: Über Aktivitäts-Hypertrophie der willkurlichen Muskeln. Virchows Arch. Pathol. Anat. Physiol., 150:522–544, 1897.

52. Müller, E., and Rohmert, W.: Die Geschwindigkeit der Muskelkraft-Zunahme bei isometrischem Training. Arbeitsphysiol., 19:403–419, 1963.

53. Penman, K.: Ultrastructural changes in human striated muscle using three methods of training. Res. Quart., 40:764–772, 1969.

54. Rarick, G., and Larsen, G.: Observations on frequency and intensity of isometric muscular effort in developing static muscular strength in post-pubescent males. Res. Quart., 29:333–341, 1958.

55. Rasch, P., and Morehouse, L.: Effect of static and dynamic exercises on muscular strength and hypertrophy. J. Appl. Physiol., 11:29–34, 1957.

56. Rasch, P.: Isometric exercise and gains of muscle strength. In Shephard, R. (ed.): Frontiers of Fitness. Springfield, Ill., Charles C Thomas, 1971, Chapter 5.

57. Rasch, P.: The present status of negative (eccentric) exercise: a review. Am. Correct. Ther. J., 28:77, 1974.

58. Rosentsweig, J., and Hinson, M.: Comparison of isometric, isotonic and isokinetic exercises by electromyography. Arch. Phys. Med. Rehabil., 53:249–252, 1972.

59. Singh, M., and Karpovich, P.: Effect of eccentric training of agonists on antagonistic muscles. J. Appl. Physiol., 23:742–745, 1967.

60. Stull, G., and Clarke, D.: High-resistance, low-repetition training as a determiner of strength and fatigability. Res. Quart., 41:189–193, 1970.
61. Syster, B., and Stull, G.: Muscular endurance retention as a function of length of detraining. Res. Quart., 41:105–109, 1970.
62. Thistle, H., Hislop, H., Moffroid, M., and Lowman, E.: Isokinetic contraction: a new concept of resistive exercise. Arch. Phys. Med. Rehabil., 48:279–282, 1967.
63. Thompson, C., and Martin, E.: Weight training and baseball throwing speed. J. Assoc. Phys. Ment. Rehabil., 19:194, 1965.
64. Thompson, H., and Stull, G.: Effects of various training programs on speed of swimming. Res. Quart., 30:479–485, 1959.
65. Van Oteghen, S.: Isokinetic conditioning for women. Scholastic Coach, Oct., 1974.
66. Waldman, R., and Stull, G.: Effects of various periods of inactivity on retention of newly acquired levels of muscular endurance. Res. Quart., 40:396–401, 1969.
67. Walters, C., Stewart, C., and LeClaire, J.: Effect of short bouts of isometric and isotonic contractions on muscular strength and endurance. Am. J. Phys. Med., 39:131–141, 1960.
68. Weber, S., and Kraus, H.: Passive and active stretching of muscles. Phys. Ther. Rev., 29:407–410, 1949.
69. Withers, R.: Effect of varied weight-training loads on the strength of university freshmen. Res. Quart., 41:110–114, 1970.
70. Zorbas, W., and Karpovich, P.: The effect of weight lifting upon the speed of muscular contractions. Res. Quart., 22:145–148, 1951.

# SECTION 3

# CARDIORESPIRATORY CONSIDERATIONS

# Chapter 8

# PULMONARY VENTILATION

MINUTE VENTILATION
Ventilation at Rest
Ventilation During Exercise
Alveolar Ventilation and
Dead Space
Other Lung Volumes and
Capacities
Second Wind
VENTILATORY MECHANICS
Movements of the Thoracic
Cage: The Ventilatory
Muscles
Oxygen Cost of Ventilation
Pressure Changes

In this section, we shall study the functional components of the respiratory and circulatory systems, both at rest and during exercise. Specifically, we shall discuss the changes they undergo and the various mechanisms by which these changes are mediated and regulated. Finally, we shall point out how you can significantly modify or improve these physiological responses through exercise programs. This information should prove to be a valuable contribution to your professional preparation.

In this chapter, we will study the means by which air is moved into and out of the lungs. This rhythmic to-and-fro movement of air is called *pulmonary ventilation*. In studying the materials which follow, you will find it helpful to refer frequently to Appendix A. In this appendix, we have included both a standardized list of cardiorespiratory symbols and typical values for pulmonary function tests most often used by cardiorespiratory physiologists.

## MINUTE VENTILATION

As we all know, ventilation is composed of two phases, one that brings air into the lungs, called *inspiration* or *inhalation*, and one that lets

**165**

air out into the environment, called *expiration* or *exhalation. Minute ventilation* refers to how much air we either inspire *or* expire (but not both together) in one minute. Most often it refers to the amount expired ($\dot{V}E$)* rather than inspired ($\dot{V}I$). This amount can be determined by knowing (a) the tidal volume (T.V.), i.e., how much air we expire in one breath, (b) the respiratory frequency (f), i.e., how many breaths we take in one minute. In other words:

$$\dot{V}E \quad = \quad T.V. \quad \times \quad f$$

$$\text{minute ventilation} = \text{tidal volume} \times \text{breaths per min.}$$

## Ventilation at Rest

Under normal resting conditions, minute ventilation varies considerably from person to person. Usually, we ventilate between 4 and 15 liters per minute (BTPS)* at rest. This varies with body size and is smaller in females and larger in males. Tidal volume and respiratory frequency vary even more than minute ventilation. This is easy to understand, since there are many combinations of tidal volume and frequency that yield the same minute ventilation. At rest, typical values for tidal volume and frequency are 400 to 600 milliliters (ml.) and 10 to 25 breaths per minute, respectively.

## Ventilation During Exercise

Minute ventilation increases during exercise. For the most part, this increase is directly proportional to increases in the amounts of oxygen consumed and carbon dioxide produced per minute by the working muscles. This is shown in Figure 8–1 for trained and untrained young men. Minute ventilation, ($\dot{V}E_{BTPS}$), is disproportional to oxygen consumption ($\dot{V}O_{2STPD}$) only at or near maximal values (Fig. 8–1, *A*). However, this is not the case with respect to carbon dioxide production ($\dot{V}CO_{2STPD}$) (Fig. 8–1, *B*). This indicates that minute ventilation is perhaps regulated more to the need for carbon dioxide removal than to oxygen consumption, at least under maximal exercise. The fact that ventilation increases much more than $\dot{V}O_2$ (indicated by the curved portion of the lines in Fig. 8–1, *A*) also tells us that minute ventilation does not appear to limit the capacity ($\dot{V}O_2$ max) of the cardiorespiratory system.

---

*The procedures for measuring $\dot{V}E$ are given in Chapter 4; those for converting gas volumes to BTPS or STPD in Appendix B.

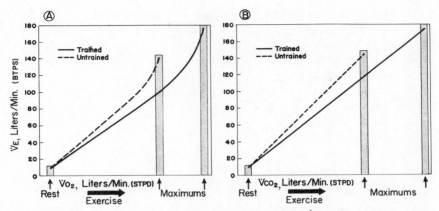

**Figure 8–1**  Effects of exercise on minute ventilation ($\dot{V}E_{BTPS}$) in trained and un-trained subjects. The close relationship of $\dot{V}E$ to $\dot{V}O_2$ is shown in (*A*), and to $\dot{V}CO_2$ in (*B*). Note that $\dot{V}E$ is disproportional to $\dot{V}O_2$, but not to $\dot{V}CO_2$, only at or near maximal values.

Maximal ventilation ($\dot{V}E$ max) due to exercise can reach values as high as 180 and 130 liters per minute (BTPS) in male and female athletes, respectively. This represents about a 25- to 30-fold increase over resting values. Such large increases are made possible by increases in both depth (tidal volume) and frequency of breathing. In untrained men and women, where $\dot{V}O_2$, $\dot{V}CO_2$, and working capacities are lower, $\dot{V}E$ max is also lower. Along with this lower $\dot{V}E$ max is a lower ventilatory efficiency, i.e., untrained men and women have a greater $\dot{V}E$ at a given $\dot{V}O_2$ than trained men and women (Fig. 8–1, *A*).

Ventilation not only varies with work load, but it also varies before, during, and after exercise at any given work load. As shown in Figure 8–2, these changes are as follows:[5]

**Changes Before Exercise.**   Immediately before exercise begins, ventilation increases. This increase obviously cannot be due to anything resulting from the exercise. Therefore, it is most likely due to stimulation from the cerebral cortex resulting from anticipation of the ensuing exercise bout.

**Changes During Exercise.**   During exercise, there are two changes in ventilation:

1. A very rapid increase within only a few seconds after the start of exercise. This is probably related to stimulation arising from the joints resulting from the movement generated by the working muscles.

2. The rapid rise in ventilation soon ceases and is replaced by a *slower rise* which in submaximal exercise (see Fig. 8–2, *A*) tends to level off, i.e., reach a steady-state value. (The ventilations shown

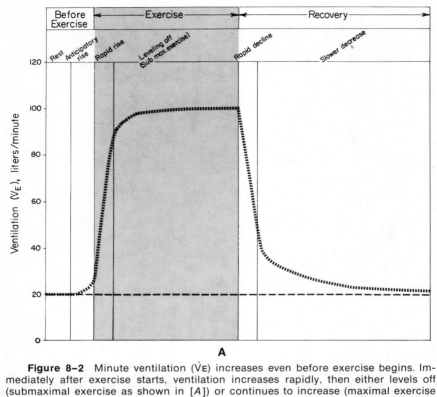

**A**

**Figure 8–2**  Minute ventilation ($\dot{V}E$) increases even before exercise begins. Immediately after exercise starts, ventilation increases rapidly, then either levels off (submaximal exercise as shown in [A]) or continues to increase (maximal exercise as shown in [B]). During recovery, ventilation decreases more rapidly at first, then gradually toward resting values.

*Illustration continued on next page*

in Fig. 8–1, up to maximum, are steady-state values.) In maximal exercise (Fig. 8–2, *B*), this leveling off or steady-state does not occur; rather, ventilation continues to increase until the exercise is terminated. These changes are thought to be stimulated by chemical stimuli, mainly from the carbon dioxide in the blood produced during exercise.

**Changes During Recovery.**   During the recovery period from exercise, there are again two changes:

1. As soon as exercise is stopped, there is a sudden decrease in ventilation. This is because motor activity has stopped, and so has the stimulation from the muscles and joints.

2. After the sudden decrease in ventilation, there is a gradual or slower decrease toward resting values. The more severe the work, the longer it takes for ventilation to return to resting levels. This change is probably related to the decrease in stimulation resulting from a decrease in carbon dioxide production.

A summary of these ventilatory changes is given in Table 8–1. We will discuss their control in more detail in Chapter 11.

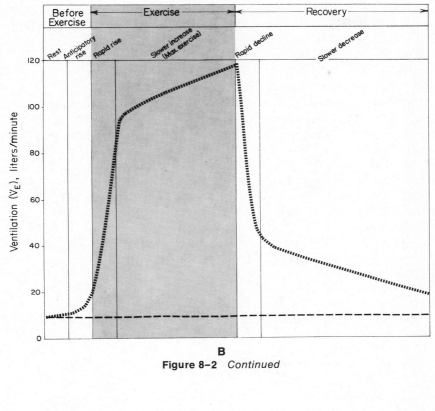

**B**

**Figure 8-2**  *Continued*

## Alveolar Ventilation and Dead Space

Not all the fresh air we inspire per minute takes part in gaseous exchange with the capillaries that perfuse the lungs (referred to as pulmonary capillary blood). Only that portion of fresh air that reaches the

**Table 8-1  VENTILATORY CHANGES BEFORE, DURING, AND AFTER EXERCISE**

| PHASE | CHANGE | CONTROL |
|---|---|---|
| 1. Pre-Exercise | Moderate increase | Cerebral cortex |
| 2. During Exercise | | |
|    Immediate | Rapid increase | Muscles and joints |
|    Later | Steady-state or slower rise | Chemical ($CO_2$) |
| 3. Recovery | | |
|    Immediate | Sudden decrease | Lack of movement |
|    Later | Slower decrease toward rest | Decrease in $CO_2$ |

alveoli, called *alveolar ventilation,* assures adequate oxygenation of and carbon dioxide removal from the pulmonary capillary blood. The alveoli (singular, alveolus) are those tiny, terminal air sacs in the lungs that are in intimate contact with the pulmonary capillaries. The volume of fresh air that remains in the respiratory passages (nose, mouth, pharynx, larynx, trachea, bronchi, and bronchioles) and does not participate in gaseous exchange is referred to as *anatomical dead space.*

The size of the anatomical dead space is difficult to measure in humans, particularly during exercise. However, estimates have indicated that an average resting value is around 0.15 liter in males and about 0.10 liter in females.[2] Since dead space varies somewhat with body size, a rough estimate of dead space in milliliters (ml.) is the body weight expressed in pounds. For example, if you weigh 167 pounds, your respiratory dead space should be close to 167 ml. or 0.167 liter. Of the 0.5 liter of air inspired per breath (tidal volume) at rest, 70 per cent [(0.5 liter − 0.15 liter)/0.5 liter × 100] ventilates the alveoli and 30 per cent remains in the dead space. During exercise, dilation of the respiratory passages may cause anatomical dead space to double, but since tidal volume also increases, an adequate alveolar ventilation, and therefore gaseous exchange, is maintained.

Alveolar ventilation, then, is dependent on three factors: (1) depth of breathing (tidal volume); (2) rate of breathing (frequency); and (3) size of the dead space. Minute ventilation alone does not indicate whether or not alveolar ventilation is adequate. For example, in Figure 8–3, *A, B,* resting minute ventilation is 6.0 liters per minute. However, in Figure 8–3, *A,* tidal volume (TV) is 0.5 liter and respiratory frequency is 12 breaths per minute (0.5 liter per breath × 12 breaths per minute = 6.0 liters per minute). In Figure 8–3, *B,* however, TV is 0.25 liter and frequency is 24 breaths per minute (0.25 × 24 = 6.0 liters per minute). If anatomical dead space (DS) in each case is 0.15 liter then 0.35 liter of fresh air (0.5 − 0.15) will enter the alveoli per breath in (*A*), but only 0.10 liter (0.25 − 0.15) will enter the alveoli in (*B*). This means that alveolar ventilation in (*A*) will be 4.2 liters per minute (0.35 × 12), and sufficient exchange of gases at the alveolar-capillary

---

**Figure 8–3** Effects of tidal volume (TV) and frequency of breathing on alveolar ventilation. The large circles represent alveoli; necks of circles, the respiratory passages or dead space volume (DS); stippled blocks, fresh air (high in $O_2$, low in $CO_2$); shaded areas, alveolar gas (low in $O_2$, high in $CO_2$). Numbers inside blocks represent gas volume, in liters. In (*A*) and (*B*), both minute ventilation and dead space are equal. However, in (*A*) more fresh air reaches the alveoli than in (*B*) because the breaths are deeper but not as frequent. The numbers under the alveoli designate respiratory phases: (1) preinspiration; (2) inspiration; (3) end-inspiration; and (4) end-expiration. (Modified from Comroe et al.[3])

*See illustration on opposite page*

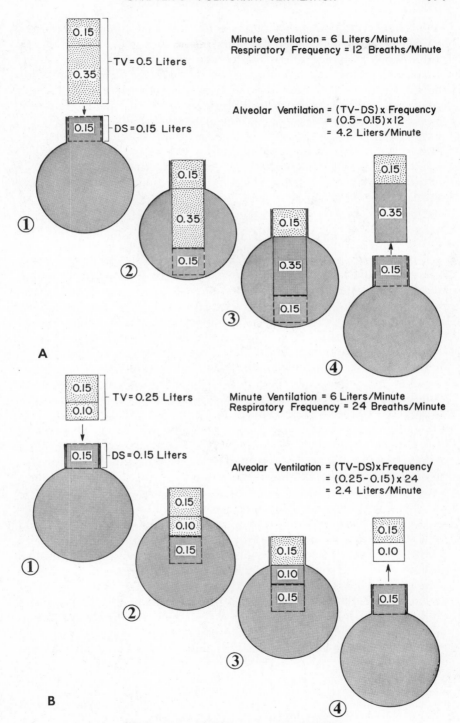

**Figure 8–3**  *See legend on opposite page.*

membranes will be assured. On the other hand, alveolar ventilation in (B) will be reduced to only 2.4 liters per minute ([0.25 − 0.15] × 24), and gaseous exchange will be inadequate.

These relationships point out why doubling DS during exercise does not lead to decreased alveolar ventilation, provided that TV and frequency increase proportionally. For example, if during moderate exercise minute ventilation = 40 liters per minute, TV = 1.6 liters per breath, DS = 0.3 liter per breath, and frequency = 25 breaths per minute, alveolar ventilation would be:

$$(1.6 − 0.3) × 25 = 32.5 \text{ liters per minute.}$$

This indicates that 80 per cent of the fresh air inspired per minute ventilates the alveoli.

## Other Lung Volumes and Capacities

There are a number of other lung volumes with which you should become familiar. Most are used as measures of pulmonary function; therefore, knowledge of them will enable you to better understand respiratory physiology. Furthermore, a few are easily measured with nothing more than a spirometer, and thus you may wish to periodically test the pulmonary function of your athletes.

Table 8–2 contains a list of eight lung volumes or capacities, their definitions, and the approximate changes they undergo during exercise. Also, schematic representations of these volumes at rest, together with their spirographic tracings,* are shown in Figure 8–4, A, B, for untrained and trained young men. As mentioned earlier, the increase in TV during exercise contributes in part to an increase in minute ventilation. During maximal exercise, TV may be five to six times greater than at rest. The increase in TV results from utilization of both the inspiratory reserve volume (IRV) and the expiratory reserve volume (ERV), but probably more of the former than of the latter.

The slight decreases in total lung capacity (TLC) and in vital capacity (VC) during exercise are related to an increase in pulmonary blood flow. This increases the amount of blood in the pulmonary capillaries and thus reduces the available gas volume space. As a result residual volume (RV) and functional residual capacity (FRC) will be slightly increased during exercise. This in turn means that the oxygen and particularly the carbon dioxide levels in the alveoli will fluctuate less and tend toward more constant values. For example, the increased carbon dioxide produced by the working muscles is diluted as it mixes with the large FRC, causing less pronounced changes in alveolar carbon dioxide

---

*Residual volume (and thus functional residual capacity and total lung capacity) cannot be measured directly with a spirometer. Its measurement is more complex and involves gas dilution or wash-out methods.

**Table 8-2  DEFINITIONS OF LUNG VOLUMES AND CAPACITIES AND THEIR CHANGES DURING EXERCISE AS COMPARED TO REST**

| LUNG VOLUME OR CAPACITY | DEFINITION | CHANGES DURING EXERCISE |
|---|---|---|
| Tidal Volume (TV) | Volume inspired or expired per breath | Increase |
| Inspiratory Reserve Volume (IRV) | Maximal volume inspired from end-inspiration | Decrease |
| Expiratory Reserve Volume (ERV) | Maximal volume expired from end-expiration | Slight decrease |
| Residual Volume (RV) | Volume remaining at end of maximal expiration | Slight increase |
| Total Lung Capacity (TLC) | Volume in lung at end of maximal inspiration | Slight decrease |
| Vital Capacity (VC) | Maximal volume forcefully expired after maximal inspiration | Slight decrease |
| Inspiratory Capacity (IC) | Maximal volume inspired from resting expiratory level | |
| Functional Residual Capacity (FRC) | Volume in lungs at resting expiratory level | Slight increase |

levels. We shall see later that changes in carbon dioxide are important in the regulation of pulmonary ventilation.

As shown in Figure 8-4, the various lung volumes measured under resting conditions for the most part (with the exception of TV) are larger in trained than in untrained men.[1] The same holds true for women, although the absolute values are lower for women than for men. The majority of these changes can be attributed to the fact that training results in improved pulmonary function and therefore in

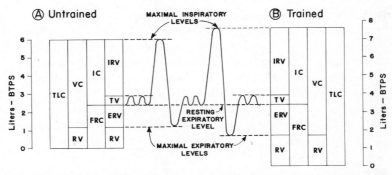

**Figure 8-4** Schematic and spirographic tracings of lung volumes and capacities. The various lung volumes at rest (except TV) are generally smaller in untrained (A) than in trained (B) subjects. For definitions and key to abbreviations, see Table 8-2. (Data for untrained subjects from Comroe et al.[3]; data for trained subjects from Holmgren.[7])

larger lung volumes. This is true even though it has been shown that body size is directly proportional to TLC and VC especially, and that athletes as a group are generally taller and heavier than are their nonathletic counterparts. It should be mentioned, however, that there is very little, if any, correlation between athletic performance and these lung volumes in young (13- to 17-year-olds) boys and girls, provided that body size is taken into consideration.[4]

### Second Wind

A phenomenon usually associated with ventilation is called "second wind." All of us in physical education and athletics have probably experienced the second wind at one time or another. It is generally characterized by a sudden transition from a rather ill-defined feeling of distress or fatigue during the early portion of prolonged exercise to a more comfortable, less stressful feeling later in the exercise. This apparent distress is sensed, so to speak, in a variety of ways, for example, intense breathlessness (dyspnea), rapid, shallow breathing, chest pain, throbbing headache or vertigo and pain in various muscles.[8]

Physiologically, no one knows exactly what causes second wind. In one of the few studies designed to investigate this problem, it was found that second wind was experienced at different times during exercise by different subjects (between 2 and 18 minutes during a 20-minute treadmill run). Also, in 90 per cent of the subjects, second wind was associated with more comfortable breathing, in 70 per cent with relief or partial relief of muscular fatigue or pain in the legs, and in 35 per cent with simultaneous relief from both leg and chest pain. These variable responses lead to the conclusion that second wind does exist.

What then causes second wind? A review of this phenomenon by Dr. R. Shephard of the University of Toronto revealed several possible causes:[14] (1) relief from breathlessness caused by slow ventilatory adjustments early in the exercise; (2) removal (oxidation) of lactic acid accumulated early in the exercise because of delayed blood flow changes in the working muscles; (3) adequate warm-up; (4) relief from local muscle fatigue, particularly of the respiratory muscles (this would also be related to the familiar "pain or stitch in the side"); and (5) psychological factors. Until more definite information is available, it appears that the coach and the athlete alike can do little to accelerate the occurrence of second wind.

## VENTILATORY MECHANICS

Movement of air into and out of the lungs results from changes in intrapulmonary pressure (i.e., the pressure inside the lung), which is produced by variations in the size of the *thoracic cage* or *cavity*. Such variations result from periodic contractions of the respiratory muscles.

### Movements of the Thoracic Cage: The Ventilatory Muscles

In Figure 8–5 are shown the position of the lungs within the thoracic cavity, and the main ventilatory muscles, the *diaphragm* and *intercostal* muscles. It should be pointed out that the lungs themselves are passive contributors to the respiratory movements in that they contain no respiratory muscles.

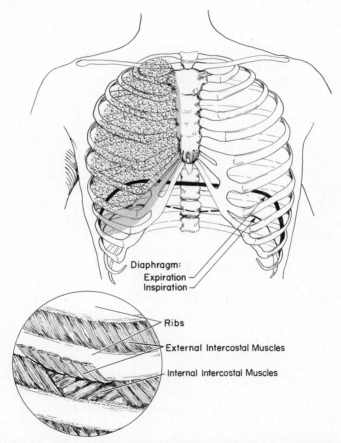

Diaphragm:
Expiration
Inspiration

Ribs
External Intercostal Muscles
Internal Intercostal Muscles

**Figure 8–5**  The ventilatory muscles. The diaphragm and the intercostal muscles (insert) are the principal muscles of respiration. Shaded area represents increase in size of the thoracic cage during inspiration.

**Muscles of Inspiration.** During quiet (resting) inspiration, the size of the thoracic cage is increased longitudinally by contraction of the diaphragm muscle, and transversally and dorsoventrally by contraction of the *external intercostal muscles.* The diaphragm, the principal muscle of inspiration, is a large, dome-shaped muscle innervated by the left and right phrenic nerves. Stimulation of these nerves during inspiration causes the diaphragm to contract or flatten, i.e., its domed portion is lowered. Since it separates the thoracic and abdominal cavities, the longitudinal diameter of the former is increased and the diameter of the latter is decreased. The abdomen therefore protrudes slightly during inspiration. It has been estimated that contraction of the diaphragm contributes between one-fourth and three-fourths of the tidal volume.[6, 15] The intercostal muscles (see insert, Fig. 8–5) lie between successive ribs (*intercostal* means "between ribs") and consist of two layers. The fibers of the external layer (the external intercostal muscles) are so arranged that when they contract the ribs are lifted and rotated, thus increasing the transverse and dorsoventral diameters of the thoracic cavity. These changes in size of the thoracic cage are also shown schematically in Figure 8–5.

The much larger inspired volumes produced by exercise are made possible by contraction of accessory inspiratory muscles, all of which further increase the size of the rib cage.[6] For example, contraction of the *scalene muscles* elevates the first two ribs, and contraction of the *sternocleidomastoid muscles* elevates the sternum (front of thorax). During maximal exercise, contraction of the trapezius and extensors of the back and neck are also thought to facilitate inspiratory movements.

**Muscles of Expiration.** Relaxation of the diaphragm and external intercostal muscles during quiet expiration permits the thoracic cage to return to its original size. In other words, expiration under these conditions is passive and independent of the expiratory muscles. This is so because during inspiration the elastic tissues of the lungs and the walls of the thorax are stretched, thus storing in them potential energy. Therefore, reduction in the size of the thoracic cage during normal expirations is the result of the elastic recoil of these tissues through the release of this stored energy. We shall discuss this in more detail later.

During exercise, expiration is usually active, that is, it is facilitated by contractions of the expiratory muscles, the most important of which are the *abdominal muscles.*[6] These contractions, besides flexing the trunk, depress the lower ribs and increase the pressure inside the abdomen, forcing the diaphragm upward into the thoracic cavity. The *internal intercostal muscles* are also muscles of expiration. Their fibers (see insert, Fig. 8–5) and movements are diametrically opposed to those of the external intercostals; when active, they lower the ribs, moving them closer together. All of these actions aid in reducing the size of the thorax and therefore facilitate the act of expiration. A summary of the major respiratory muscles, and their actions during rest and exercise, is contained in Table 8–3.

## Oxygen Cost of Ventilation

The ventilatory muscles must overcome the elastic recoil of the lungs and thorax and the resistance to air flow offered by the respiratory passages. At rest, the work required in overcoming these forces is minimal because tidal volume and respiratory frequency are also minimal. Furthermore, expiration is passive. Under these conditions, the amount of oxygen consumed by the ventilatory muscles constitutes no more than 1 to 2 per cent of the total body oxygen consumption.

During exercise, increases in tidal volume and frequency and involvement of more respiratory muscles necessarily mean that the oxygen cost of ventilation also increases. In fact, oxygen consumption of the respiratory muscles during heavy exercise may constitute 8 to 10 per cent of the total oxygen consumed by the body.[9, 13] It has been suggested that the increase in total body oxygen consumption above a certain ventilatory rate (around 120 liters per minute) is used exclusively by the respiratory muscles and thus is not available to the other skeletal muscles for performance of mechanical work.[11, 13] Others have suggested that this is true once the cardiac output (amount of blood pumped by the heart in one minute) has reached its limit rather than when ventilation reaches a certain level.[10] In either case, with these

Table 8–3   **THE MAJOR RESPIRATORY MUSCLES DURING REST AND EXERCISE**

| RESPIRATORY PHASE | MUSCLES ACTING DURING REST | ACTION | MUSCLES ACTING DURING EXERCISE |
|---|---|---|---|
| Inspiration | Diaphragm | Flattens | Diaphragm |
| | External intercostals | Raises ribs | External intercostals |
| | | Elevates first and second ribs | Scaleni |
| | | Elevates sternum | Sternocleidomastoids |
| Expiration | None | | |
| | | Lowers ribs | Internal intercostals |
| | | Depresses lower ribs and forces diaphragm into thorax | Abdominals |

limits so high, from a practical viewpoint the oxygen cost of ventilation *per se* does not normally limit most exercise and athletic performances.

**Oxygen Cost of Ventilation and Training.**   It was mentioned earlier that trained individuals have a higher ventilatory efficiency than do untrained persons. A higher ventilatory efficiency means that the amount of air ventilated at the same oxygen consumption level is lower. The $O_2$ cost of ventilation increases greatly with increasing ventilation. Therefore, a lower ventilation, particularly over a prolonged effort (e.g., the marathon) would mean less oxygen to the respiratory muscles and more to the working skeletal muscles.

**Oxygen Cost of Ventilation and Smoking.**   All of us have heard and perhaps used the phrase "smoking causes shortness of breath." The phrase, though colloquial, is essentially correct from a physiological standpoint. Chronic smoking of cigarettes results in increased airway resistance. This in turn means that the respiratory muscles must work harder and thus consume more oxygen in ventilating a given amount of air. As shown in Figure 8–6, during heavy exercise the oxygen cost of ventilation in chronic smokers was found to be on the average two times that of nonsmokers.[12] This was true when only a few cigarettes were smoked within one hour prior to the exercise. In the heaviest smoker (20 to 30 cigarettes per day for 27 years), the difference was nearly four times that of nonsmokers! If no cigarettes were smoked by the smokers for 24 hours prior to exercise, the oxygen cost of ventilation was about 25 per cent lower, but still about 60 per cent higher than in nonsmokers.[12, 13]

This information has two practical implications:

1. The added cost of ventilation caused by the chronic smoking of cigarettes can rob the working muscles of a large percentage of their potential oxygen supply. During maximal exercise, this could lead to a corresponding reduction in performance, and during submaximal exercise to an increase in anaerobic metabolism (L.A. system) and thus early fatigue.

2. A large part of the increase in the oxygen cost of ventilation in chronic smokers can be substantially reduced by a relatively short period of abstinence from cigarettes (24 hours). Therefore, athletes who cannot or will not "kick the habit" permanently can help their performance by not smoking on the day of competition.

### Pressure Changes

We have already stated that ventilation of the lungs is a result of changes in intrapulmonary pressure. The magnitude of these pressure changes and how they are reflected in the lungs by movements of the

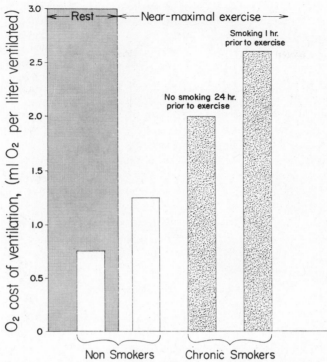

**Figure 8–6** The oxygen cost of ventilation in chronic cigarette smokers is greatly increased during near-maximal exercise, particularly if a few cigarettes are smoked within an hour prior to exercise. Abstinence from smoking 24 hours before exercise decreases the cost of ventilation but does not decrease it to the nonsmokers' levels. (Based on data from Rode and Shephard[12] and Shephard.[13])

thoracic cage are related to the anatomical relationships among the thoracic walls, the diaphragm and outer surfaces of the lungs.

**The Pleural Cavity.** The lungs are not directly attached to the walls of the thorax. Rather, they are "connected" by a thin film of fluid, called *serous fluid*, which covers and is secreted by the inner surfaces of two thin serous membranes, collectively known as the *pleurae* (singular, pleura). The outer surface of one pleura has two "components" — the part that lines the thoracic wall, which is called the *parietal pleura* (*parietal* means "wall"), and the part that covers the diaphragm, which is called the *diaphragmatic pleura*. The outer surface of the other pleura covers the lungs; this is the *visceral pleura* (*visceral* pertains to interior organs). The "potential space" between these two pleurae is called the *pleural cavity*. The thin film of serous fluid is located within this cavity. These relationships are shown in Figure 8–7.

This type of "connection" between the thoracic wall, the diaphragm, and the lungs, is similar to that between two thin, flat pieces of

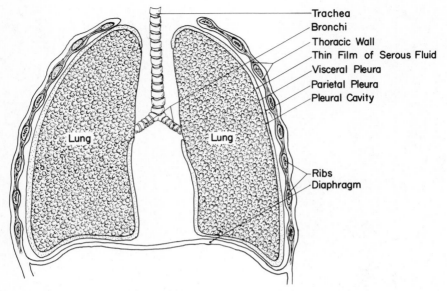

**Figure 8–7**   The pleural cavity.

glass held together by a film of water. While each piece of glass slides easily over the other (the water lubricates the two surfaces), the force required to pull the surfaces apart is considerable. Consequently, lifting one carries the other with it. Through this fluid connection, any movements and resulting pressure changes that occur in the thorax will be reflected directly in the lungs.

**Intrapulmonary and Intrapleural Pressures.**   Expansion of the thorax also expands the lungs. Whenever a volume of gas is suddenly expanded, the gas molecules become farther apart, reducing their pressure. Thus, during inspiration, intrapulmonary pressure is reduced below atmospheric pressure and air flows into the lungs. As air fills the lungs, intrapulmonary pressure rises, and when it is equal again to atmospheric pressure (at end inspiration), air flow ceases. The opposite is true during expiration. Passive or active compression (or both) of the thorax raises intrapulmonary pressure above atmospheric pressure and air flows out of the lungs. At end-expiration, intrapulmonary pressure is again equal to atmospheric pressure, and there is no movement of air.

Changes in intrapleural (or intrathoracic) pressure are similar to those that take place inside the lung. However, intrapleural pressure is *always* lower than intrapulmonary and atmospheric pressures. For example, at the end-expiratory position, intrapleural pressure is about 5 mm. Hg lower than atmospheric pressure. The reason for this is related to the elastic tissues of the lungs and thoracic walls. You will recall that stretching these elastic tissues during quiet inspiration provides all the energy required for the subsequent expiration.

The elastic tissues of the lungs tend to collapse them, i.e., to pull them away from the thoracic wall. This creates the partial vacuum or subatmospheric pressure in the pleural cavity. If this collapsing force were not restrained by an equal and opposite force, the lungs would indeed completely collapse. Such a restraining force is presented by the elasticity of the thoracic walls. In our example (end-expiratory position), the walls of the thorax tend to spring out with the same force as that tending to collapse the lungs. In other words, the elastic forces of the thoracic walls and lungs are equal but opposite at this time. If at any time the restraining force of the thoracic wall is lost (such as would occur by the entrance of air into the pleural cavity), the lung will collapse. This is called *pneumothorax* (see p. 344).

The intrapulmonary pressure, intrapleural pressure, and lung volume changes during inspiration and expiration are summarized in Figure 8–8.

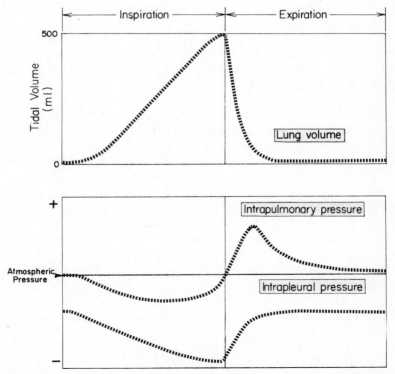

**Figure 8–8** Changes in intrapulmonary and intrapleural pressures and lung volume during inspiration and expiration.

# Summary

The movement of air into and out of the lungs is called pulmonary ventilation. Ventilation is composed of two phases: inspiration and expiration. Minute ventilation is the amount of air we either exhale or inhale in one minute. At rest, this amounts to between 4 and 15 liters. During maximal exercise, this can increase to over 150 liters. Ventilation changes before, during, and after exercise.

Alveolar ventilation assures adequate oxygenation of and carbon dioxide removal from the pulmonary capillary blood. The volume of air that remains in the respiratory passages and does not participate in gaseous exchange is called anatomical dead space. Alveolar ventilation is dependent upon the depth and frequency of breathing and the size of the dead space.

Training improves pulmonary function, as evidenced by the fact that athletes have greater resting and exercising lung volumes than nonathletes. However, these volumes do not necessarily correlate highly with athletic performance.

Second wind is thought to be related to adjustments in ventilation and metabolism made at some time early in exercise. Its exact cause, however, is not known.

The principal muscles of inspiration are the diaphragm and the external intercostal muscles at rest, with added help from the scalene and sternocleidomastoid muscles during exercise. Expiration is passive during rest, and is facilitated by the abdominal and internal intercostal muscles during exercise.

At rest, the oxygen cost of ventilation is negligible. During maximal exercise, the cost increases greatly, but still is not considered to be a limiting factor to performance. On the other hand, chronic cigarette smoking can increase the oxygen cost of ventilation to a point at which it may limit exercise and athletic performance.

Air rushes into the lungs when the intrapulmonary and intrapleural pressures decrease due to contraction of the inspiratory muscles. During expiration, these pressures are reversed and air is forced out of the lung back to the environment.

## QUESTIONS

1. What are the phases of ventilation and what two factors comprise the minute ventilation?

2. How much air do we expire per minute at rest and during maximal exercise?

3. Describe the nature and control of the ventilatory changes: (a) immedi-

ately before exercise, (b) during exercise, and (c) during recovery from exercise.

4. Define alveolar ventilation and dead space, and explain their roles in providing adequate ventilation.

5. Alveolar ventilation depends on what three factors?

6. Define the various lung volumes and discuss how each changes with exercise.

7. Discuss the possible causes of second wind.

8. Name the respiratory muscles at rest and during exercise.

9. Discuss the role of the cost of ventilation with respect to limiting athletic performance. Include the effects of cigarette smoking.

10. Describe the intrapulmonary and intrapleural pressure changes and the movement of air into and out of the lungs.

## REFERENCES

1. Bachman, J., and Horvath, S.: Pulmonary function changes which accompany athletic conditioning programs. Res. Quart., 39:235–239, 1968.
2. Comroe, J.: Physiology of Respiration. Chicago, Year Book Medical Publishers, Inc., 1965.
3. Comroe, J., Forster, R., DuBois, A., Briscoe, W., and Carlsen, E.: The Lung. 2nd ed., Chicago, Year Book Medical Publishers, Inc., 1962.
4. Cumming, G.: Correlation of athletic performance with pulmonary function in 13 to 17 year old boys and girls. Med. Sci. Sports, 1(3):140–143, 1969.
5. DeJours, P.: Respiration. New York, Oxford University Press, 1966.
6. Grimby, G., Bunn, J., and Mead, J.: Relative contribution of rib cage and abdomen to ventilation during exercise. J. Appl. Physiol., 24(2):159–166, 1968.
7. Holmgren, A.: Cardiorespiratory determinants of cardiovascular fitness. Canad. Med. Assoc. J., 96:697–702, 1967.
8. Lefcoe, N., and Yuhasz, M.: The 'second wind' phenomenon in constant load exercise. J. Sports Med. Phys. Fit., 11:135–138, 1971.
9. Otis, A.: The work of breathing. In Fenn, W., and Rahn, H. (eds.): Handbook of Physiology. Sec. 3, Respiration, vol. 1, p. 463, American Physiological Society, Washington, D. C., 1964.
10. Ouellet, Y., Poh, S., and Becklake, M.: Circulatory factors limiting maximal aerobic exercise capacity. J. Appl. Physiol., 27:874–880, 1969.
11. Riley, R.: Pulmonary function in relation to exercise. In Johnson, W. (ed.): Science and Medicine of Exercise and Sports. pp. 162–177, New York, Harper and Brothers, Publishers, 1960.
12. Rode, A., and Shephard, R.: The influence of cigarette smoking upon the oxygen cost of breathing in near-maximal exercise. Med. Sci. Sports., 3(2):51–55, 1971.
13. Shephard, R.: The oxygen cost of breathing during vigorous exercise. Quart. J. Exp. Physiol., 51:336–350, 1966.
14. Shephard, R.: What causes second wind? Phys. Sports Med., 2(11):37–42, 1974.
15. Wade, O.: Movements of the thoracic cage and diaphragm in respiration. J. Physiol. (Lond.), 124:193–212, 1954.

SELECTED READINGS ⎯⎯⎯⎯⎯⎯⎯⎯⎯⎯⎯⎯⎯⎯⎯⎯⎯⎯⎯⎯⎯⎯⎯

Campbell, E.: The Respiratory Muscles and Mechanics of Breathing. Chicago, Year Book Medical Publishers, Inc., 1958.
Grimby, G.: Respiration in exercise. Med. Sci. Sports, 1(1):9–14, 1969.
Guyton, A.: Basic Human Physiology: Normal Function and Mechanisms of Disease. pp. 325–336, Philadelphia, W. B. Saunders Co., 1971.
Milic-Emili, J., Petit, J., and Deroanne, R.: Mechanical work of breathing during exercise in trained and untrained subjects. J. Appl. Physiol., 17:43–46, 1962.

# Chapter 9

# GASEOUS EXCHANGE AND TRANSPORT

We saw from the last chapter that pulmonary ventilation (more accurately, alveolar ventilation) supplies the alveoli with fresh air, which is high in oxygen and low in carbon dioxide content. Venous blood, on the other hand, is low in oxygen and high in carbon dioxide. Thus, gaseous exchange between the air in the alveoli and the venous blood (the alveolar-capillary membrane), loads and unloads the blood with oxygen and carbon dioxide, respectively. After transportation via the circulation, oxygen and carbon dioxide are again exchanged, this time between the tissues (e.g., muscle) and the arterial blood (the tissue-capillary membrane). Here oxygen in the blood is given up to the tissues and carbon dioxide in the tissues is given up to the blood. It is the purpose of this chapter to study both how the gases are exchanged and how they are carried in the blood.

**185**

# GAS EXCHANGE: DIFFUSION

Gaseous exchange at the alveolar-capillary and tissue-capillary membranes takes place through the physical process of diffusion. Diffusion can be defined as the random movement of molecules—in this case, gas molecules. This random movement (sometimes called brownian motion) is due to the kinetic energy of the molecules. Gases tend to diffuse from an area of higher concentration to one of lower concentration.

## Partial Pressure of Gases

We need at this time to go a bit farther with our concept of diffusion. Specifically, we need to know what the *partial pressures* of oxygen ($P_{O_2}$) and carbon dioxide ($P_{CO_2}$) mean with respect to gaseous exchange. Gases consist of discrete particles or molecules. These tiny molecules, although separated by relatively large distances, will occasionally collide with each other (and with the walls of their container) because, as just indicated, each molecule is in a state of random motion. The pressure exerted by a gas is dependent on the number of such collisions; e.g., the greater the number of collisions, the greater will be the pressure.

From what we have said thus far, a higher partial pressure of a gas represents an area of greater molecular activity than does an area in which the partial pressure of that same gas is lower. This means that gases will diffuse from an area of higher to an area of lower partial pressure. The same is true concerning concentration differences; a greater concentration of gas represents greater molecular activity than does one of lower concentration. The relationship between concentration and partial pressure is shown in Figure 9–1. Container *A* holds 100 per cent oxygen. The $P_{O_2}$ is 760 mm. Hg, the same as the total (barometric) pressure since oxygen is the only gas present. Container *B* holds an equal volume of mixed gases, 20 per cent $O_2$ and 80 per cent $N_2$, which is also at a total pressure of 760 mm. Hg. Each of the gases in the mixture will exert a pressure proportional to its respective concentration, the sum of which will equal the total pressure. In other words, the $P_{O_2}$ and $P_{N_2}$ are the same as those which each gas would exert if it alone occupied the entire container. If oxygen alone occupied the entire container (Fig. 9–1, *C*), the number of collisions would be only 20 per cent of that possible in Figure 9–1, *A*, and the $P_{O_2}$ will be correspondingly reduced to 20 per cent of 760 mm. Hg ($760 \times 0.2$), or 152 mm. Hg. The same holds true for nitrogen, as shown in container D; i.e., the $P_{N_2}$ is given by 80 per cent of 760 ($760 \times 0.8$), or 608 mm. Hg. The sum of the two partial pressures equals the total pressure.

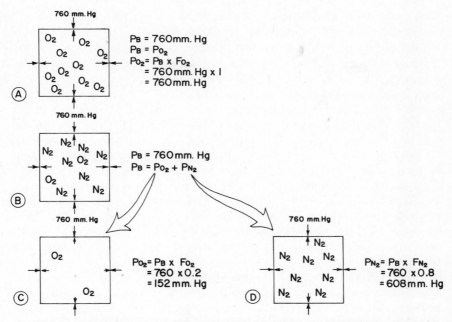

**Figure 9–1** Partial pressure of gases: The partial pressure of a gas is equal to the barometric pressure (PB) times the fractional concentration of that gas. In container *A*, the partial pressure of oxygen ($P_{O_2}$) is equal to the PB because it makes up the entire volume (100 per cent); i.e., its fractional concentration ($F_{O_2}$) is 1. In a mixture, such as the $O_2$ and $N_2$ in container *B*, each gas exerts a partial pressure proportional to its concentration as though it alone (*C* and *D*) occupied the entire volume. In this case, $P_{O_2} + P_{N_2} = P_B$.

The partial pressure of a gas is, then, dependent on (1) the total (barometric) pressure, and (2) the fractional concentration of that gas. If at any time either of these is changed independently of the other, the partial pressure will also change. *The most important factor determining gaseous exchange is the partial pressure gradients of the gases involved.* For example, you shall see in Chapter 16 that the concentration of oxygen at altitude is the same as that at sea level. However, since the total pressure is lower, the $P_{O_2}$ is lower and the taking up of oxygen in the blood is reduced. By the same token, increasing total pressure without reducing the concentration of oxygen (as in scuba diving with air) can increase the $P_{O_2}$ to toxic levels.

## $P_{O_2}$ and $P_{CO_2}$ Gradients in the Body

In order for oxygen to diffuse from the alveoli ultimately into the tissues, the $P_{O_2}$ gradient must decrease from the former to the latter.

The opposite is true for carbon dioxide to diffuse into the blood, i.e., the $Pco_2$ gradient must decrease from the tissues to the alveoli. This is shown in Figure 9–2, *A*. The decrease in $Po_2$ from inspired to tracheal air results from addition of water vapor as air enters the respiratory passages. The partial pressure of water vapor ($PH_2O$) at body temperature is 47 mm. Hg and is independent of the total pressure (see Appendix B). Therefore, the pressure available for oxygen, carbon dioxide, and nitrogen (not shown) is $760 - 47$ mm. Hg, or 713 mm. Hg, and the $Po_2$ is decreased by about 10 mm. Hg. The $Pco_2$ is less affected by $PH_2O$ because its concentration in inspired air is negligible. As moist air enters the alveoli, the $Po_2$ decreases and the $Pco_2$ increases markedly. This results from dilution by the rather large functional reserve volume (see p. 172), in which the $Po_2$ and $Pco_2$ are about 98 and 40 mm. Hg, respectively. After mixing, alveolar $Po_2$ averages 100 mm. Hg and $Pco_2$, 40 mm. Hg. The partial pressures of oxygen and carbon dioxide in the mixed venous blood perfusing the alveoli are 40 and 46 mm. Hg, respectively.

The partial pressure differences between gases in the alveoli and in venous blood means that oxygen will diffuse into venous blood and carbon dioxide into the alveoli. Consequently, venous blood $Po_2$ increases and $Pco_2$ decreases to values approximating those in the alveoli; venous blood is thus arterialized. Blood remains in the pulmonary capillaries for about 0.75 second under resting conditions, as shown in Figure 9–2, *B*. However, the transition from venous to arterial blood is virtually completed within half that time (shaded area). This corresponds to about the length of time blood remains in the pulmonary capillaries during maximal exercise. The $Po_2$ and $Pco_2$ of arterial blood during exercise, then, are maintained or are only slightly reduced, compared to resting values, even though the velocity of blood coursing through the capillaries is greatly increased.

A similar situation exists at the tissue-capillary membranes (Fig. 9–2, *A*). The $Po_2$ of arterial blood is higher than that in the tissues and oxygen diffuses from blood to tissue. The opposite is true for carbon dioxide; the higher $Pco_2$ in the tissues promotes diffusion of carbon dioxide from the tissues to the blood. Consequently, arterial blood is changed back to venous blood and the entire process of gas exchange is repeated over and over. Presumably, the transition from arterial to venous blood also occurs within a few tenths of a second, and is the exact opposite of the transition from venous to arterial blood (Fig. 9–2, *B*). It should be mentioned that the greater the metabolic activity of the tissue, the lower will be the $Po_2$ and the higher the $Pco_2$ in venous blood draining that particular tissue. For example, during exercise the $Po_2$ will be lower and the $Pco_2$ higher in the venous blood from an active skeletal muscle than in venous blood from an inactive tissue, such as the kidney or skin.

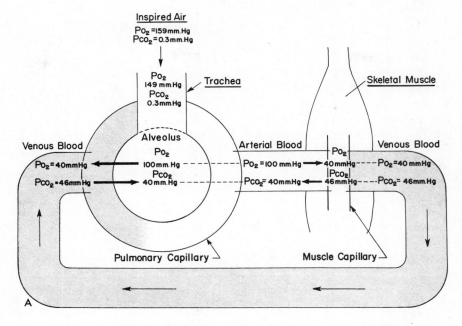

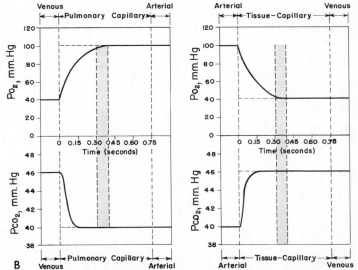

**Figure 9–2**  $Po_2$ and $Pco_2$ gradients and gaseous exchange. In (*A*), the $Po_2$ and $Pco_2$ of inspired air, tracheal air, alveolar gas, venous and arterial blood, and tissue (skeletal muscle) are shown. Exchange (via diffusion) of these gases at the alveolar-capillary and tissue-capillary membranes is always from an area of higher to one of lower partial pressure. The time required to complete these exchanges is shown in (*B*). At rest, blood remains in the pulmonary and tissue capillaries for about 0.75 second, and during maximal exercise between 0.3 to 0.4 second (shaded area).

## Other Factors Affecting Gas Exchange

Besides partial pressure gradients, gaseous exchange can be affected by several other factors. These include (1) the length of the diffusion path; (2) the number of red blood cells or their hemoglobin concentration, or both; and (3) the surface area available for diffusion. Figure 9–3, *A* depicts the diffusion path for oxygen and carbon dioxide at the alveolar-capillary and tissue-capillary membranes. Normally, it is very short, even during exercise. Membrane fibrosis and interstitial edema caused by certain diseases lengthen the path, and diffusion is impaired. You will notice that the diffusion pathways include red blood cells, the transporting vehicles for both oxygen and carbon dioxide. Therefore, variations in their number would obviously affect overall gas exchange.

The surface area available for diffusion at the alveolar-capillary membranes is determined by the number of functional capillaries in

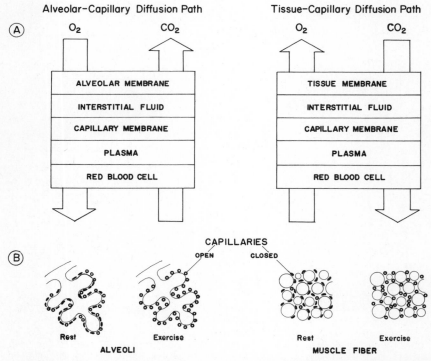

**Figure 9–3** (*A*): Diffusion paths for $O_2$ and $CO_2$ at the alveolar-capillary (left) and tissue-capillary (right) membranes. Normally the lengths of these paths do not limit diffusion. (*B*): Surface area available for diffusion at these membranes is determined by the number of open capillaries in contact with ventilated alveoli (left) and muscle fibers (right). Note large increase in open capillaries during exercise.

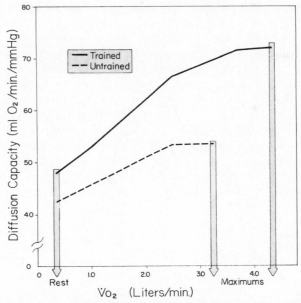

**Figure 9-4**  The pulmonary diffusing capacity for $O_2$ increases during exercise in both trained and untrained subjects. (Based on data from Magel and Andersen.[5])

contact with ventilated alveoli. For example, in Figure 9–3, *B*, the alveoli on the left side of the diagram are all open and are thus ventilated, but not all the capillaries supplying them are open. This is probably a normal situation under resting conditions. An increase in surface area and in diffusion capacity during exercise might occur by increasing the number of open capillaries. In a similar manner, the diffusing surface at the tissue-capillary membranes may be increased by increasing the number of functional tissue capillaries. It has been estimated that an actively contracting muscle has 10 times as many open capillaries as a resting muscle (Fig. 9–3, *B*).

## Diffusion Capacity During Exercise

We just indicated that during exercise there is an increase in surface area and thus in the diffusion of oxygen and carbon dioxide across both the alveolar-capillary and tissue-capillary membranes. The increase in diffusion of oxygen at the alveolar-capillary membrane is shown in Figure 9–4 for trained and untrained young men. This same pattern of change with exercise also applies to trained and untrained females; however, the diffusion values are somewhat lower in magnitude.[3] It can be seen that the diffusion capacity for oxygen increases in nearly a linear (straight line) manner with increasing exercise loads, leveling-off at near maximal efforts.

The trained athletes indicated in Figure 9–4 were male swimmers. In general, it can be said that athletes tend to have larger diffusion capacities at rest and during exercise than nonathletes. This is particularly true for endurance athletes. For example, in Figure 9–5, notice that the diffusion capacity of marathon runners at rest is almost as high as that for untrained men during maximal exercise.[4] Likewise, during maximal exercise the diffusion capacities of oarsmen[9] and endurance swimmers[5, 7] are much higher than their untrained counterparts. It is thought that diffusion capacity *per se* is not directly affected by training,[7, 8, 9] but, rather, training induces larger lung volumes (see p. 173) and thus, in turn, provides a greater alveolar-capillary surface area.[5]

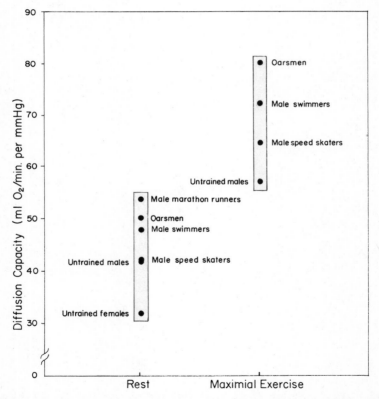

**Figure 9–5** In general, the pulmonary diffusing capacity for $O_2$ in athletes, particularly endurance athletes, is greater at rest and during maximal exercise compared to non-athletes. (Data for untrained females from Fox et al.;[2] untrained males and swimmers from Magel and Andersen[5] and Newman et al.;[7] speed skaters from Maksud et al.;[6] oarsmen from Reuschlein et al.;[9] and marathon runners from Kaufmann et al.[4]).

# GASEOUS TRANSPORT

The oxygen that diffuses from the alveoli to the pulmonary-capillary blood is transported to the tissues, where it is consumed. By the same token, the carbon dioxide that diffuses from the tissues to the tissue-capillary blood is transported to the alveoli, from where it is exhaled. The transport of these gases is the primary function of the cardiovascular or circulatory system. The circulating liquid of this system, the blood, serves as the transport vehicle, the blood vessels act as highways, and the heart provides the force which constantly keeps the blood circulating throughout the lungs and various tissues of the body.

## Transport of Oxygen by Blood

Oxygen is carried both by *plasma* (the liquid portion of the blood) and by *hemoglobin* contained in red blood cells. Oxygen that diffuses into plasma does not undergo any chemical reactions; rather, it is *dissolved* in plasma and is carried in physical solution. The amount carried in this way is, under normal conditions, very small. On the other hand, oxygen that diffuses into the red blood cells *combines chemically* with hemoglobin (Hb) to form what is called *oxyhemoglobin* ($HbO_2$). This binding process increases the oxygen carrying capacity of blood by about 65 times.

### Dissolved Oxygen

The *solubility* (dissolving power) of oxygen in plasma is relatively low. Therefore, very little dissolved oxygen can be transported by plasma to the tissues. For example, at rest, dissolved oxygen contributes only 3 to 4 per cent of the total of 250 to 300 ml. of oxygen required per minute. The percentage is even lower during maximal exercise, when it constitutes less than 2 per cent of the total oxygen required by the working muscles. The amount of oxygen dissolved in plasma is dependent not only on its solubility, but also on its partial pressure. However, even if arterial $Po_2$ is increased by breathing pure oxygen, the amount of oxygen dissolved would still only supply 38 per cent of the total oxygen required at rest and 12 per cent during maximal exercise.

The role played by dissolved oxygen in meeting tissue oxygen demands is therefore not very impressive. What physiological role, if any, does it then play? We can answer this question by first saying that the partial pressure of oxygen in both venous and arterial blood results from the oxygen that is dissolved in plasma. Second, a similar situation exists at the tissues; i.e., tissue $Po_2$ results from the oxygen dissolved in the tissue fluids. The importance of $P_{O_2}$ in gaseous exchange has already been pointed out. Later, you will see that decreases in arterial and tissue $P_{O_2}$ (such as occur at altitude) cause increases in ventilation and red blood cell production, respectively. Both of these changes increase the overall oxygen carrying capacity of the blood when it is vitally needed. These examples illustrate why the concept of dissolved oxygen is an important consideration; its significance is equally great under conditions of exercise and rest.

### Oxyhemoglobin (HbO₂)

The hemoglobin found in red blood cells is a complex molecule containing *iron* (heme) and *protein* (globin). This is shown schematically in Figure 9–6. Hemoglobin's affinity for or ability to combine with oxygen is related to the heme component. Each heme group, of which there are four in each hemoglobin molecule, is capable of combining chemically with one $O_2$ molecule. This means that one Hb molecule is capable of maximally combining with four $O_2$ molecules, i.e.:

$$Hb_4 + 4\ O_2 \rightleftharpoons Hb_4(O_2)_4$$

More simply we can write:

$$Hb + O_2 \rightleftharpoons HbO_2$$

In terms of amount, this turns out to be 1.34 ml. of $O_2$ per gram of Hb. Thus, one gram of Hb becomes *saturated* with $O_2$ when it combines with 1.34 ml. of $O_2$.

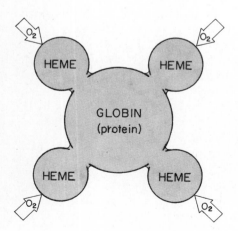

**Figure 9–6** The hemoglobin molecule is composed of a protein called globin and four iron-containing groups called heme. Oxygen is carried by the heme groups, and carbon dioxide is carried by globin.

**$O_2$ Capacity of Hb.** Once we know both the saturation point of hemoglobin and the Hb concentration in blood, we can calculate what is referred to as the *$O_2$ capacity of Hb:*

$O_2$ capacity of Hb (ml. $O_2$/100 ml. blood) = Hb concentration (grams Hb/100 ml. blood) $\times$ (1.34 ml. $O_2$/gram Hb)

Hemoglobin concentration is determined by rupturing the red blood cells so that Hb dissolves uniformly in the fluid portion of the blood sample. The amount of light passed through this fluid is inversely related to the amount of Hb present. At rest and at sea level, there are about 15 grams of Hb present in every 100 ml. of blood (for males, 16 grams per 100 ml., and for females, 14 grams per 100 ml.). Therefore, under these conditions, the $O_2$ capacity of Hb is $15 \times 1.34 = 20.1$ ml. $O_2$/100 ml. blood, or 20.1 volumes per cent.*

During exercise, the Hb concentration of blood increases anywhere from 5 to 10 per cent. This is so, at least in part, because fluid shifts from the blood into the active muscle cells, and *hemoconcentration* results.[1] It is exaggerated during prolonged work in the heat because of further shifts of fluids from the blood to the cell due to excessive sweating. A 10 per cent hemoconcentration during exercise means that there will be about 16.5 grams of Hb per 100 ml. blood instead of the normal 15 grams. The $O_2$ capacity of Hb would in this case increase from 20.1 to 22.1 volumes per cent, a definitely advantageous change.

**Per Cent Saturation of Hb.** There is one more concept concerning Hb which we need to discuss at this time. This is the *per cent saturation of Hb with $O_2$,* abbreviated % $So_2$. It relates the amount of $O_2$ *actually* combined with Hb to the $O_2$ capacity of Hb:

$$\% \ So_2 = \frac{O_2 \text{ actually combined with Hb}}{O_2 \text{ capacity of Hb}} \times 100$$

For example, if your $O_2$ capacity is 20 volumes per cent and the amount of oxygen actually combined with Hb is 10 volumes per cent, then % $So_2$ is $10/20 \times 100 = 50$ per cent. A % $So_2$ of 100 means that the $O_2$ actually combined with Hb is equal to the $O_2$ capacity of Hb. Use of % $So_2$ takes into account individual variations in Hb concentration. The hemoconcentration that occurs during exercise is a good example. In this case, if % $So_2$ is 50 per cent, then the amount of $O_2$ actually combined with Hb would be $22 \times 0.5 = 11$ volumes per cent, rather than 10 volumes per cent. The increase in number of red blood cells, and thus in Hb concentration, during acclimatization to altitude (see page 352) is also another good example of why % $So_2$ is used.

---

*Volumes per cent (vol. %) in this case means milliliters of $O_2$ per 100 ml. blood.

## The Oxyhemoglobin Dissociation (or Association) Curve

Up to now, we have neglected the factors that affect the saturation of Hb with $O_2$. Actually, there are four such factors: (1) the partial pressure of oxygen in the blood; (2) the temperature of the blood; (3) the pH (acidity) of the blood; and (4) the amount of carbon dioxide in the blood. The first of these factors, the $Po_2$ of blood, is of course paramount. However, we will see shortly that the other three factors are also extremely important, particularly during exercise.

The relationships of these factors to % $So_2$ are shown in Figure 9–7. The amount of $O_2$ combined with Hb at the various per cent saturations is also shown, on the right ordinate. These values are based on a Hb concentration of 15 grams per 100 ml. of blood. Such curves are called *oxyhemoglobin (HbO$_2$) dissociation curves*. (They may also be called association curves, but are preferably referred to as dissociation curves). Use of the $HbO_2$ dissociation curve tells us a great deal about gaseous transport. Let us see just what kinds of information it can tell us.

We can start with the single curve shown in Figure 9–7, *A*. This curve is applicable under normal resting conditions, i.e., with blood pH of 7.4, and with temperature of 37° C. Also, keep in mind that at rest the arterial blood $Po_2$ is 100 mm. Hg, whereas the mixed venous blood $Po_2$ is 40 mm. Hg. The first two things we should notice are that the higher the $Po_2$, the greater is the *association* of $O_2$ with Hb ($HbO_2$); and the lower the $Po_2$, the greater is the *dissociation* of $O_2$ from Hb ($Hb + O_2$). For example, at a $Po_2$ of 100 mm. Hg, the Hb in arterial blood is 97.5 per cent saturated with $O_2$. In terms of amount, arterial blood holds $20 \times 0.975 = 19.5$ volumes per cent of $O_2$. Therefore, this amount of $O_2$ is transported to the tissues by each 100 ml. of arterial blood flowing to them.* At a $Po_2$ of 40 mm. Hg, venous blood returning from the various tissues is only 75 per cent saturated; it then holds $20 \times 0.75 = 15$ volumes per cent of $O_2$. The difference between the two, called the *arteriovenous oxygen difference* (a-$\bar{v}$ $O_2$ diff), represents how much oxygen is extracted or consumed by the tissues from each 100 ml. of blood perfusing them. In our present example, the a-$\bar{v}$ $O_2$ diff is $19.5 - 15.0 = 4.5$ ml. of $O_2$ per 100 ml. of blood flow. Most of the oxygen transported by Hb during rest is thus kept in reserve. This will come in handy during exercise, as we shall soon see.

The third thing we should notice is the shape of the curve. The upper part of the curve is almost flat. This means that a large change in

---

*The *total* amount of $O_2$ transported to the tissues per 100 ml. of blood flow is 19.8 volumes per cent; 19.5 volumes per cent via $HbO_2$ plus 0.3 volume per cent dissolved in plasma. For the total $O_2$ content of arterial and venous blood at rest and during exercise, see Table 10–1, page 206.

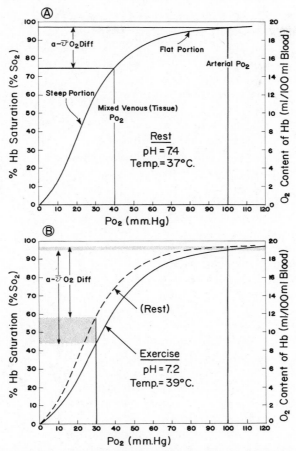

**Figure 9-7** Oxygen transport: The oxyhemoglobin dissociation curve. (A), at rest; (B) during exercise. Such curves give the relationship between $Po_2$ and how much oxygen associates or dissociates with hemoglobin. During exercise, the curve "shifts" to the right and facilitates unloading of $O_2$ to the muscles. For further explanation, see text.

$Po_2$ in this portion of the curve is associated with only a small change in the amount of $O_2$ held by Hb. For example, if arterial blood $Po_2$ were *increased* from the normal 100 mm. Hg (as by breathing pure $O_2$ at sea level), only 0.5 volume per cent of $O_2$ is added to Hb. This plus the additional dissolved $O_2$ represent only an 11 per cent increase in the amount of $O_2$ transported to the tissues. This serves to point out that, normally, arterial $Po_2$ is maintained at close to optimal levels. Use of pure $O_2$ at sea level during exercise, therefore, will not greatly increase $O_2$ transport. On the other hand, if arterial $Po_2$ were *decreased*, e.g., from 100 to 70 mm. Hg (as by ascent to altitude), % $So_2$ would decrease from 97.5 to only 93 per cent, a difference of 1 ml. of $O_2$/100 ml. blood. In this case, the flat upper part of the curve indicates protection against inadequate oxygenation of blood despite large decreases in $Po_2$. During maximal exercise (at sea level), arterial blood $Po_2$ rarely decreases by more than 5 mm. Hg.

The steep middle and lower portions of the curve likewise reflect protective functions, but of a different kind. In this portion of the curve (below a $Po_2$ of about 50 mm. Hg), a small change in $Po_2$ is associated with a large change in Hb saturation. Therefore, a small decrease in *tissue* $Po_2$ enables the tissues to extract a relatively large amount of $O_2$. For example, if tissue $Po_2$ decreased from 40 to 10 mm. Hg, % $So_2$ decreases from 75 to 13 per cent, respectively, a difference of 13.5 ml. of $O_2$ per 100 ml. blood that can be extracted by the tissues. The steep middle and lower portions of the curve, then, protect the tissues by favoring dissociation of $O_2$ from Hb despite small decreases in $Po_2$. During exercise, it has been shown that the $Po_2$ of active skeletal muscles may be lower than 5 mm. Hg.

**The HbO$_2$ Curve During Exercise.**    A fourth consideration is how pH, temperature, and $CO_2$ affect the $HbO_2$ dissociation curve. Increases in blood acidity (which decreases pH), temperature, and $CO_2$ cause a shift of the $HbO_2$ dissociation curve to the right.[10, 11] This is shown in Figure 9–7, *B* (solid line). The curve represented by the dashed line is the same as that in Figure 9–7, *A*, and is included as a basis for comparison. During exercise, increased $CO_2$ and lactic acid production lowers blood pH and increased heat production raises body temperature. Therefore, the "shifted" curve in Figure 9–7, *B*, is applicable under exercise conditions.

What does this shift mean? A close look at the curve reveals that the greatest amount of shift occurs in the steep middle and lower portions, e.g., between 20 and 50 mm. Hg $Po_2$. On the other hand, between 90 and 100 mm. Hg $Po_2$, very little shift occurs. During exercise, these changes are extremely important for two reasons: (1) because more $O_2$ is made available to the tissues at a given tissue $Po_2$; and (2) because the loading of blood with $O_2$ is not greatly affected. For example, suppose that during exercise arterial blood $Po_2$ equalled 100 mm. Hg, and mixed venous blood $Po_2$ equalled 30 mm. Hg. If there were no shift in the $HbO_2$ dissociation curve, the a-$\overline{v}$ $O_2$ diff—i.e., the amount of $O_2$ given up to the tissues—would be $19.5 - 11.6 = 7.9$ ml. per 100 ml. of blood flow. With the shift to the right, as indicated in Figure 9–7, *B*, the a-$\overline{v}$ $O_2$ diff would be $19.0 - 8.8 = 10.2$ ml. of $O_2$ per 100 ml. of blood. This represents nearly a 30 per cent increase in the amount of $O_2$ available to the tissues. During maximal exercise, this shift plus the greatly lowered $Po_2$ of the active muscles may increase the a-$\overline{v}$ $O_2$ diff 3 to 3.5 times that at rest (see Fig. 9–8).

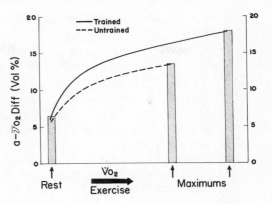

**Figure 9-8** Effects of exercise on arteriovenous oxygen difference ($a$-$\bar{v}O_2$ diff) for trained and untrained subjects. During exercise, the muscles extract a greater amount of $O_2$ from a given quantity of arterial blood. Training improves this capacity.

## Transport of Carbon Dioxide by Blood

Like oxygen, carbon dioxide is carried by the blood in physical solution (dissolved) and in chemical combination. Also, as in $O_2$ transport, the amount of dissolved $CO_2$ constitutes only a small percentage (about 5 per cent) of the total transported; the majority (95 per cent) is carried in chemical combination. However, the chemical reactions which $CO_2$ undergoes (principally in the red blood cells) are quite different from those of oxygen. In blood, $CO_2$ reacts chemically with water to form a weak acid, *carbonic acid*, and with blood proteins (principally, the globin of Hb) to form *carbamino compounds.*

### Dissolved Carbon Dioxide

What was said concerning dissolved $O_2$ is also applicable to dissolved $CO_2$. Briefly:

1. The amount of $CO_2$ dissolved in blood (arterial and venous) and in tissues is dependent on its solubility and partial pressure.
2. Dissolved $CO_2$ is relatively unimportant as a transporting mechanism.
3. Dissolved $CO_2$ determines blood and tissue $P_{CO_2}$ and therefore is important in cardiorespiratory regulating mechanisms.

### Transport of $CO_2$ in Chemical Combination

By far the majority of $CO_2$ is transported in chemical combination. As was previously mentioned, $CO_2$ combines with blood water to form carbonic acid, and with blood proteins to form carbamino compounds.

**Carbonic Acid and the Bicarbonate Ion.** As $CO_2$ diffuses into tissue-capillary blood, it immediately reacts with water in plasma and red blood cells to form carbonic acid ($H_2CO_3$) according to the following reaction:

$$CO_2 + H_2O \rightleftharpoons H_2CO_3$$

In order for this reaction to occur with any great speed, an enzyme called *carbonic anhydrase* is required. In plasma, this enzyme is absent, but in red blood cells, it is highly concentrated. Therefore, the formation of carbonic acid takes place principally within the red blood cells.

As quickly as carbonic acid is formed, it ionizes, i.e., it dissociates into a *hydrogen ion ($H^+$)* and a *bicarbonate ion ($HCO_3^-$)* as follows:

$$H_2CO_3 \rightleftharpoons H^+ + HCO_3^-$$

The complete reaction, then, is more accurately written as:

$$CO_2 + H_2O \rightleftharpoons H_2CO_3 \rightleftharpoons H^+ + HCO_3^-$$

Thus, as shown by this reaction, $CO_2$ is carried in the blood in the form of bicarbonate ions. The double arrows in the equation mean that the reactions are reversible. It proceeds to the right as $CO_2$ is added (by diffusion) to tissue-capillary blood, and it proceeds to the left when $CO_2$ diffuses from the blood into the alveoli. The *formation* of $HCO_3^-$ occurs mostly within the red cell because of the presence of carbonic anhydrase, as mentioned earlier. However, $HCO_3^-$ is *transported* primarily by plasma. This is because as the concentration of $HCO_3^-$ increases in the red cell (but not in plasma) it diffuses into the plasma.*

The $H^+$ ions formed when $H_2CO_3$ dissociates will increase the acidity of venous blood if they are not buffered. (This is one of the reasons why an increase in $CO_2$ production is associated with an increase in acidity.) The small amount of free $H^+$ ions formed in plasma are buffered, i.e., taken out of circulation, by plasma proteins. Inside the red cell, where most of the $H^+$ ions are formed, Hb serves as the buffer. It is interesting to note that Hb is a better buffer than is $HbO_2$. This means that, as $O_2$ dissociates from Hb and diffuses into the tissues, buffering of $H^+$ ions is facilitated. In turn, more $HCO_3^-$ can be formed and more $CO_2$ carried without a substantial change in blood acidity. Furthermore, remember that an increase in blood acidity shifts the $HbO_2$ dissociation curve to the right. This favors not only the release of

---

*As $HCO_3^-$ diffuses from the red cell into plasma, chloride ion ($Cl^-$) diffuses from plasma into the red cell. This is called the "chloride shift" and serves to maintain the ionic balance between the red cell and the plasma.

$O_2$ for tissue use, but also the presence of Hb, which is the better buffer. The increases in both $O_2$ consumption and $CO_2$ production during exercise point out the importance of these mutually beneficial changes.

More about acid-base balance and buffering mechanisms can be found in Chapter 15 (p. 332).

**Carbamino Compounds.** Plasma proteins and Hb, besides serving as buffers, also play another important role in $CO_2$ transport. This role involves their direct chemical reaction with $CO_2$, forming what are referred to as carbamino compounds. In these reactions, $H^+$ ions are also formed and must be buffered, as we previously described.

Formation of carbamino compounds takes place mainly in the red

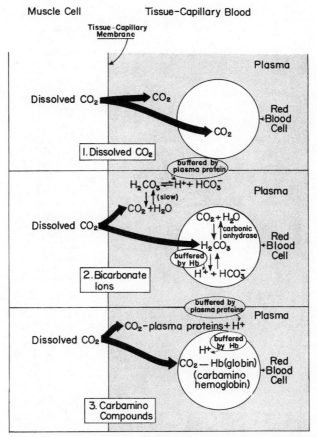

**Figure 9–9**   Carbon dioxide transport. Carbon dioxide is transported in physical solution as dissolved $CO_2$ (1) and in chemical combination as bicarbonate ions (2) and carbamino compounds (3).

blood cells, by the reaction of $CO_2$ with Hb. In this case, the carbamino compound formed is called *carbaminohemoglobin*. Inside the red cells, $CO_2$ reacts with the protein fraction (globin) of the Hb molecule and *not* with the heme or iron group, as is the case with $O_2$. This means that Hb is capable of chemically combining with, and thus transporting, $O_2$ and $CO_2$ simultaneously. However, Hb is capable of combining with more $CO_2$ than $HbO_2$ can. Therefore, as in the case of the bicarbonate ion mechanism, the unloading of $O_2$ to the tissues facilitates the loading of $CO_2$ in tissue-capillary blood, and vice versa.

The transport mechanisms for $CO_2$ as it diffuses from the tissues into tissue-capillary blood are summarized in Figure 9–9. It should be remembered that as $CO_2$ diffuses from the pulmonary-capillary blood to the alveoli, all reactions are reversed, and free $CO_2$ is exhaled.

# SUMMARY

Gaseous exchange at the alveolar-capillary and tissue-capillary membranes is primarily dependent on the partial pressure gradients of the gases involved. In turn, partial pressure of a gas depends on both barometric pressure and the fractional concentration of the gas.

Besides being affected by partial pressure gradients, gaseous exchange can be affected by: (1) the length of the diffusion path, (2) the number of red cells or their hemoglobin concentration or both, and (3) the surface area available for diffusion.

During exercise the diffusion capacity increases because of opening of more alveoli and capillaries, thus increasing the surface area. Generally, athletes have larger diffusion capacities at rest and during maximal exercise than nonathletes.

Oxygen is carried in small amounts in plasma and in large amounts by the red blood cells. In the plasma, it is carried in solution and is responsible for the partial pressure of oxygen in the blood. In the red cell, it is chemically united with hemoglobin. Four factors affect the saturation of Hb with $O_2$: (1) the partial pressure of $O_2$ in the blood, (2) the temperature of the blood, (3) the pH of the blood, and (4) the amount of $CO_2$ in the blood. During exercise, changes in these factors favor the release of $O_2$ to the working muscles. The relationships among these factors may be shown by what is called the oxyhemoglobin dissociation curve.

Like oxygen, carbon dioxide is carried both in physical solution and in chemical combination. By far the greater amount of $CO_2$ is transported in chemical combination, just as with oxygen. Carbon dioxide combines with water in the blood to form carbonic acid and with blood proteins including Hb to form carbamino compounds.

## QUESTIONS

1. What is meant by the partial pressure of a gas?

2. Describe the relationship between partial pressure and concentration of gases.

3. What is the physiological significance of dissolved oxygen and carbon dioxide?

4. Discuss all factors affecting gas exchange.

5. How does diffusion capacity change during exercise?

6. Compare the diffusion capacity of athletes and nonathletes.

7. What effect does training have on diffusion capacity?

8. Explain the hemoconcentration that occurs during exercise.

9. Explain how the $P_{O_2}$ and the $P_{CO_2}$ of arterial blood during exercise are maintained even though the velocity of the blood through the capillaries is greatly increased.

10. What is meant by: (a) the $O_2$ capacity of Hb and (b) the per cent saturation of Hb?

11. Explain the significance of the oxyhemoglobin dissociation curve with respect to gas exchange and transport.

12. During exercise, there are increases in blood acidity, temperature, and $CO_2$. How do these factors affect the dissociation curve?

13. Describe the ways in which $CO_2$ is transported.

14. Relate $CO_2$ transport to acid-base balance.

## REFERENCES

1. Åstrand, P., Cuddy, T., Saltin, B., and Stenberg, J.: Cardiac output during submaximal and maximal work. J. Appl. Physiol., 19:268–274, 1964.
2. Fox, E., Cohen, K., and Stevens, D.: Unpublished data, 1975.
3. Holmgren, A., and Åstrand, P.: $D_L$ and the dimensions and functional capacities of the $O_2$ transport system in humans. J. Appl. Physiol., 21(5):1463–1470, 1966.
4. Kaufmann, D., Swenson, E., Fencl, J., and Lucas, A.: Pulmonary function of marathon runners. Med. Sci. Sports, 6(2):114–117, 1974.
5. Magel, J., and Andersen, K.: Pulmonary diffusing capacity and cardiac output in young trained Norwegian swimmers and untrained subjects. Med. Sci. Sports, 1(3):131–139, 1969.
6. Maksud, M., Hamilton, L., Couths, K., and Wiley, R.: Pulmonary function measurements of Olympic speed skaters from the U.S. Med. Sci. Sports, 3(2):66–71, 1971.

7. Newman, F., Smalley, B., and Thompson, M.: A comparison between body size and lung function of swimmers and normal school children. J. Physiol. (London), 156:9P, 1961.

8. Reddan, W., Bongiorno, F., Burpee, J., Reuschlein, P., Gee, J., and Rankin, J.: Pulmonary function in endurance athletes. Fed. Proc., 22:396, 1963.

9. Reuschlein, P., Reddan, W., Burpee, J., Gee, J., and Rankin, J.: Effect of physical training on the pulmonary diffusing capacity during submaximal work. J. Appl. Physiol., 24(2):152–158, 1968.

10. Shappell, S., Murray, J., Bellingham, A., Woodson, R., Detter, J., and Linfant, C.: Adaptation to exercise: role of hemoglobin affinity for oxygen and 2,3-diphosphoglycerate. J. Appl. Physiol., 30(6):827–832, 1971.

11. Thomson, J., Dempsey, J., Chosy, L., Shahidi, N., and Reddan, W.: Oxygen transport and oxyhemoglobin dissociation during prolonged muscular work. J. Appl. Physiol., 37(5):658–664, 1974.

## SELECTED READINGS

Comroe, J.: Physiology of Respiration. pp. 139–181, Chicago, Year Book Medical Publishers, Inc., 1965.

Comroe, J., Forster, R., DuBois, A., Briscoe, W., and Carlsen, E.: The Lung. 2nd ed. pp. 111–161, Chicago, Year Book Medical Publishers, Inc., 1962.

Forster, R.: Exchange of gases between alveolar air and pulmonary capillary blood: pulmonary diffusing capacity. Physiol. Rev., 37:391–452, 1957.

Slonim, N., and Hamilton, L.: Respiratory Physiology. 2nd ed. pp. 76–96, St. Louis, C. V. Mosby Co., 1971.

Weibel, E.: Morphological basis of alveolar capillary gas exchange. Physiol. Rev., 53(2): 419–495, 1973.

West, J.: Respiratory Physiology—The Essentials. pp. 23–88, Baltimore, The Williams & Wilkins Co., 1974.

# Chapter 10

# BLOOD FLOW AND GAS TRANSPORT

BLOOD FLOW CHANGES
    Cardiac Output During Exercise
    Distribution of Blood Flow
    The Oxygen Transport System
CIRCULATORY MECHANICS:
    HEMODYNAMICS
    Blood Pressure
    Resistance to Flow
    Changes in Pressure and Resistance
    During Exercise

The $O_2$ and $CO_2$ contents of blood at rest and during heavy exercise are shown in Table 10–1. As can be seen, gas transport *per unit volume of blood flow* (in this case, per 100 ml. of blood) increases during exercise. Some of the mechanisms facilitating this increase have already been pointed out. However, these changes alone cannot fully account for the large increases in $O_2$ consumed and $CO_2$ produced by the working muscles on a *per unit of time basis*. For example, as indicated in Table 10–1, $\dot{V}o_2$ at rest is 0.246 liter per minute, and during exercise is 3.2 liters per minute. This represents a 13-fold increase. Yet, during exercise, the amount of $O_2$ extracted by the tissues on an equal blood flow basis (as indicated by the a-$\bar{v}$ $O_2$ diff) is only 3.4 times that at rest (15.86/4.62). This is enough to increase $\dot{V}o_2$ to only $0.246 \times 3.4 = 0.84$ liter per minute.

In order to fully meet the gas transport demands during exercise, two major blood flow changes are necessary: (1) *an increase in cardiac output, i.e., in the amount of blood pumped per minute by the heart;* and (2) *a redistribution of blood flow from inactive organs to the active skeletal muscles.* The object of this chapter will be to provide an understanding of these and other related changes. Our discussion of cardiac output and blood flow changes will be limited to the *left heart and systemic circuit,* i.e., to the flow of arterial blood to and venous blood from the body tissues such as the working muscles. Remember however, that these changes are equally

**Table 10–1 OXYGEN AND CARBON DIOXIDE CONTENT OF BLOOD AT REST AND DURING HEAVY EXERCISE**

| TRANSPORT MECHANISMS | $CO_2$ OR $O_2$ CONTENT (MILLILITERS PER 100 ML. WHOLE BLOOD) | | |
| --- | --- | --- | --- |
| | *Arterial Blood* | *Mixed Venous Blood* | *Difference* |
| Rest ($\dot{V}O_2 = 0.246$ liter per minute; $\dot{V}CO_2 = 0.202$ liter per minute) | | | |
| *Total $O_2$* | 19.8 | 15.18 | 4.62 |
| Dissolved | 0.3 | 0.18 | 0.12 |
| As $HbO_2$ | 19.5 | 15.0 | 4.5 |
| *Total $CO_2$* | 48.0 | 51.8 | 3.8 |
| Dissolved | 2.3 | 2.7 | 0.4 |
| As $HCO_3^-$ | 43.5 | 45.9 | 2.4 |
| As carbamino compounds | 2.2 | 3.2 | 1.0 |
| Heavy exercise ($\dot{V}O_2 = 3.20$ liters per minute; $\dot{V}CO_2 = 3.03$ liters per minute) | | | |
| *Total $O_2$* | 21.2 | 5.34 | 15.86 |
| Dissolved | 0.3 | 0.06 | 0.24 |
| As $HbO_2$ | 20.9 | 5.28 | 15.62 |
| *Total $CO_2$* | 45.0 | 60.0 | 15.0 |
| Dissolved | 2.1 | 3.1 | 1.0 |
| As $HCO_3^-$ | 40.8 | 53.2 | 12.4 |
| As carbamino compounds | 2.1 | 3.7 | 1.6 |

$CO_2$ values at rest from: Davenport.[5]

Hb concentration = 15 grams per 100 ml. whole blood at rest; 16.5 grams per 100 ml. whole blood during exercise (10 per cent hemoconcentration).

great in the flow of blood to and from the lungs, i.e., in the *right heart and pulmonary circuit*. It is easy to visualize what would happen if the outputs of the left and right heart were not equal. In cases in which this does occur, as in cardiac patients with left heart failure, blood accumulates in the lungs, causing pulmonary edema, pneumonia, and even death, if the patient is not treated immediately.

## BLOOD FLOW CHANGES

As previously mentioned, the transport of gases to and from the working muscles involves an increase in cardiac output and a redistribution of blood away from the inactive organs toward the active muscles. Let's see what these changes are and how they are controlled.

### Cardiac Output During Exercise

The increase in cardiac output that occurs during exercise is shown in Figure 10–1, *A*, for trained and untrained male subjects. As would be expected, this increase is closely related to $\dot{V}o_2$ (and thus to workload) over the entire range from rest to maximal values. At rest, there is little difference in cardiac output between trained and untrained subjects, with average values ranging between 5 and 6 liters per minute. However, during exercise requiring a given $\dot{V}o_2$, the cardiac outputs of untrained subjects are sometimes slightly higher than[4, 6, 13, 24] and sometimes the same as[14, 22] those of trained subjects.

Maximal cardiac outputs in trained male subjects can reach values as high as 30 liters per minute. This represents a five- to six-fold increase over resting values. In fact, it is not unusual to find that highly trained athletes, who excel in endurance events and who have exceptionally high aerobic capacities, have maximal cardiac outputs near 40 liters per minute.[7] By the same token, untrained male subjects, who have lower work and aerobic capacities, have lower maximal cardiac outputs (about 20 to 25 liters per minute). In general, we can say that the higher the maximal cardiac output, the higher the aerobic capacity (max $\dot{V}o_2$), and vice versa.

The changes in cardiac output described above for males are similar to those for females.[1, 15] However, it should be mentioned that in comparison with males, females tend to have slightly higher cardiac output when performing work at the same levels of oxygen consumption. This difference amounts to about 1.5 liters per minute; in other words, the cardiac output will be about 1.5 liters per minute higher on the average in females than in males for a given oxygen consumption.[1] The reason for this is probably due to the females' lower oxygen-carrying capacity of blood, resulting from their lower levels of hemoglobin (see p. 460). Also, the maximal cardiac output of both trained and untrained females is generally lower than that of their male counterparts.

These large increases in cardiac output during exercise are brought about through increases in (1) *stroke volume*, i.e., the amount of blood pumped by the heart per stroke or beat; and (2) *heart rate*, the number of times the heart beats per minute. Mathematically, the relationship of cardiac output ($\dot{Q}$) to stroke volume (S.V.) and heart rate (H.R.) is as follows:

$\dot{Q}$ (liters per minute) = S.V. (liters per beat) × H.R. (beats per minute)

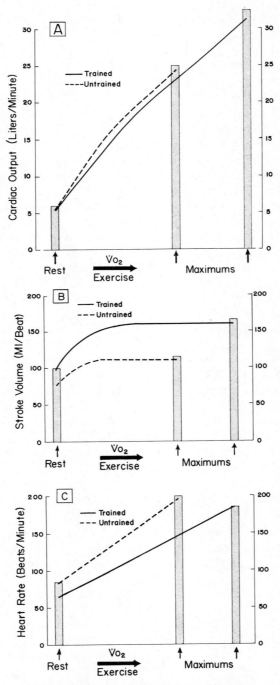

**Figure 10-1**   *See legend on opposite page*

For example, if during heavy exercise stroke volume were 160 ml. (0.16 liter) per beat and heart rate were 185 beats per minute, cardiac output would be:

$$\dot{Q} = 0.16 \text{ liter per beat} \times 185 \text{ beats per minute}$$
$$= 29.6 \text{ liters/minute}$$

**Stroke Volume.** The relationship of stroke volume to exercise $\dot{V}_{O_2}$ is shown in Figure 10–1, *B*. Stroke volume increases during the progression from rest to moderate work, but does not necessarily increase from moderate to maximal work. Thus, in most cases, stroke volume becomes maximal at a submaximal workload when $\dot{V}_{O_2}$ is only about 40 per cent of maximum. This applies both to trained and untrained male and female subjects.

The resting stroke volume of untrained male subjects averages between 70 and 90 ml. per beat with maximal values ranging between 100 and 120 ml. per beat. For trained men, both resting and maximal values are higher, averaging about 100 to 120 ml. and 150 to 170 ml. per beat, respectively. For the highly trained male endurance athletes mentioned earlier, maximal stroke volume may reach or even exceed 200 ml. per beat.

For females, the values for stroke volume are generally lower than those for males under all conditions. For example, at rest, the stroke volume may be between 50 and 70 ml. per beat in untrained females and between 70 and 90 ml. per beat after training. Maximal stroke volumes for untrained and trained females are usually between 80 and 100 ml. and 100 and 120 ml. per beat, respectively. At a submaximal work load requiring the same oxygen consumption, stroke volume will be lower in the female than in the male. Since stroke volume is maximal during submaximal exercise, this difference can be explained by the smaller heart volume of the female.

The mechanism whereby stroke volume is increased during exercise was for a long time thought to be a result of *Starling's law of the heart.* This law states that stroke volume increases in response to an increase in the volume of blood filling the heart ventricle during *diastole* (ventricular relaxation). The increase in *diastolic volume* causes a greater stretch on the cardiac muscle fiber, which in turn promotes a more

---

**Figure 10–1** Cardiac output (*A*), stroke volume (*B*), and heart rate (*C*) during exercise in trained and untrained subjects. Cardiac output and heart rate are closely related to $\dot{V}_{O_2}$ over the entire range from rest to maximal exercise; maximal stroke volume is usually reached at submaximal $\dot{V}_{O_2}$ or exercise. Cardiac output is the product of stroke volume times heart rate.

forceful ventricular systole (contraction). As a result, more blood is ejected, and stroke volume increases. However, more recently it has been shown that diastolic volume does not increase during exercise,[3, 10] and so the significance of this mechanism with respect to increasing the stroke volume is now questionable. Actually, the major role of Starling's law, both at rest and during exercise, is in keeping the outputs of the left and right ventricles in pace with each other, so that blood flow through the systemic and pulmonary circuits is maintained equal.

How, then, does stroke volume increase during exercise? The answer to this question lies in the fact that at rest only about 40 to 50 per cent of the total diastolic volume is ejected during each ventricular systole. This means that, without increasing diastolic volume, a stronger contraction could as much as double stroke volume by more completely emptying the ventricles. In this case, the stronger ventricular contraction, often referred to as an increased *myocardial contractility*, is mediated through nervous and hormonal influences. These will be discussed in greater detail later.

**Heart Rate.** Figure 10–1, *C*, shows that heart rate increases linearly with increasing workload or $\dot{V}o_2$ in both trained and untrained subjects. However, in some cases, this increase may lessen just before maximal values are reached. It should be remembered that once stroke volume becomes maximal (which is usually at submaximal workloads), further increases in cardiac output are possible only through increases in heart rate. Here it is interesting to note that the same nervous and hormonal influences that increase stroke volume also increase heart rate.

Training has a very pronounced effect on heart rate, even at rest. For example, in highly trained athletes of either sex, resting heart rates may be as low as or lower than 40 beats per minute. In contrast, resting heart rates for untrained but healthy individuals may be as high as 90 beats per minute. A slow resting heart rate is characteristic of the trained individual.

· During exercise, the heart rate of a trained subject is also lower at any given $\dot{V}o_2$ than is that of his or her untrained counterpart. However, under these conditions the female has a higher heart rate. This is so because as mentioned before, she also has a greater cardiac output and smaller stroke volume for the same oxygen consumption. (Remember, $\dot{Q} = \text{S.V.} \times \text{H.R.}$). In addition, training also reduces maximal heart rate, e.g., from 200 to about 185 to 190 beats per minute. However, this effect is neither as consistent nor as pronounced as that at a given $\dot{V}o_2$. This is because training also increases work capacity (and max $\dot{V}o_2$); therefore, maximal heart rates in trained subjects are reached at comparatively higher workload and $\dot{V}o_2$ levels.

It should be pointed out that a relatively slow heart rate, coupled with a relatively large stroke volume, indicates an efficient circulatory system. This is true because, for a given cardiac output, the heart does not beat as often. For example, consider a trained subject whose cardiac output during exercise is 20 liters per minute. With a stroke volume of 150 ml. per beat, the heart rate would be:

$$\text{H.R.} = \dot{Q}/\text{S.V. [since } \dot{Q} = \text{S.V.} \times \text{H.R.]}$$
$$= 20 \text{ liters per minute}/0.15 \text{ liter per beat}$$
$$= 133 \text{ beats per minute}$$

On the other hand, an untrained subject with the same cardiac output but with a stroke volume of only 120 ml. per beat would have a heart rate of 167 beats per minute. This also applies under resting conditions. For a given cardiac output, a slower beating heart with a larger stroke volume requires less oxygen.

Measurement of heart rate, either in the laboratory (with an electrocardiograph) or in the field by counting the pulse,* is relatively simple. This simplicity, plus the relationships of heart rate to $\dot{V}o_2$, workload, and training, has made it the single most often used index of circulatory function during exercise. As a coach and physical educator, you can use heart rate responses: (1) as a guide to the severity of any given exercise; (2) in assessing the effects of training; and (3) based on results of the first two, in developing the most effective training programs employing the progressive overload principle (see Chapter 12). It must be emphasized, however, that such criteria should be confined to use on an individual basis since heart rate responses to exercise can and do vary considerably from one person to another.

**Cardiac Output During Prolonged Exercise.**    Changes in cardiac output, stroke volume, and heart rate for short-term exercise (5 to 10 minutes) are shown in Figure 10–2, A. These changes are similar in pattern to those described earlier for oxygen consumption (p. 57) and pulmonary ventilation (p. 167). There is a sharp rise at the onset of exercise followed by a more gradual rise and then a leveling or steady-state plateau. These steady-state levels were shown for several submaximal efforts in Figure 10–1.

During prolonged submaximal work, i.e., work over 30 minutes' duration, cardiac output is maintained over the course of the exercise, but stroke volume and heart rate are not.[8, 23] As shown in Figure 10–2, B, stroke volume gradually decreases and heart rate gradually increases as the exercise progresses. Since the changes are opposite in direction and equal in magnitude, cardiac output remains fairly stable. Thus, in prolonged efforts, it is not surprising to find near maximal

---

*Even your own students (athletes) can measure their heart rates during practice sessions (see Chapter 12).

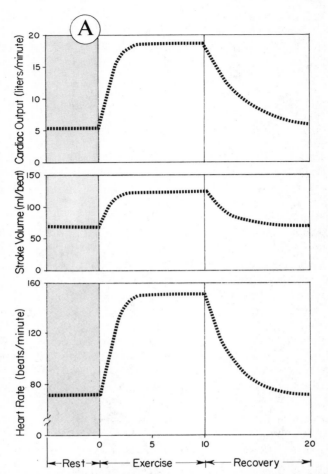

**Figure 10-2** *A,* Pattern of change in cardiac output (top), stroke volume (middle), and heart rate (bottom) during short-term (5 to 10 minutes) submaximal exercise. There is a sharp rise at the onset of exercise followed by a steady state, then a sharp decline as exercise stops. *B,* During prolonged exercise (30 minutes or more), heart rate increases steadily while stroke volume decreases. Since these changes are equal in magnitude and opposite in direction, cardiac output remains stable.

heart rates by the end of the performance. As an example, it has been estimated that during a 2½-hour marathon race, in which the energy requirements are about 75 per cent of maximum, heart rate was maximal for as long as one hour or so.[9]

**Venous Return.**    Regardless of the mechanisms that increase cardiac output during exercise, the heart can pump only as much blood as it receives. For this reason, cardiac output is ultimately dependent on the amount of blood returned to the right heart via the systemic venous system, or, in other words, upon the *venous return.* Thus, an increase in

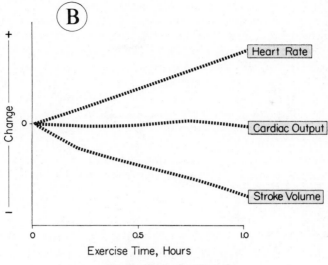

**Figure 10–2** *Continued*

cardiac output of 30 liters per minute or more during maximal exercise means that the venous return must also increase by that amount.

Several mechanisms contribute to increasing the venous return during exercise. One of these, the *muscle pump,* was mentioned briefly in Chapter 6; it is a result of the mechanical pumping action produced by rhythmical muscular contractions. As the muscles contract, their veins are compressed and the blood within them is forced toward the heart. Blood is prevented from flowing backwards because the veins in the limbs contain numerous valves, which permit flow only toward the heart. When the muscles relax, blood fills the veins again and with the next contraction, more blood is forced toward the heart. The muscle pump is important when standing and when walking, running, and performing other, similar exercises during which the muscles alternatively contract and relax. During weight lifting or other types of exercises that require *sustained* muscular effort, the pump cannot operate and venous return is actually hindered.

Another, similar mechanical action that promotes venous return is provided by the *respiratory pump.* With this pump, the veins of the thorax and abdomen are emptied toward the heart during inspiration and refilled during expiration. The reason for this is because the intrathoracic pressure decreases during inspiration (becomes more subatmospheric; see p. 180), and this serves to aspirate the blood in the thoracic veins toward the right heart. The lowering of the diaphragm during inspiration increases abdominal pressure and the veins contained within this cavity are also emptied during inspiration. These pressure effects are reversed during expiration, and the veins fill again with more venous blood. Thus, merely by breathing, venous return is enhanced. This pump is more effective the greater the respiratory rate and depth, such as is the case during exercise.

A third way in which venous return is facilitated during exercise is through *venoconstriction*, i.e., by reflex constriction of the veins draining the muscles. Venoconstriction reduces the volume capacity of the systemic venous system, and, as a result, blood is forced out toward the heart. As we have indicated, this reflex is one of many that is initiated and controlled by the central nervous system during exercise.

### Distribution of Blood Flow

In Figure 10–3 are shown the approximate percentages of the total cardiac output distributed to the skeletal muscles, in comparison to other organs, at rest and during exercise. At rest, only between 15 and 20 per cent of the total systemic flow is distributed to the muscles; the majority goes to the visceral organs (gastrointestinal tract, liver, spleen, kidneys), the heart, and the brain. However, during exercise there is a redistribution of blood flow so that the active muscles receive the greatest proportion of the cardiac output.[11, 18, 19] In fact, during maximal exercise the working muscles may receive as much as 85 to 90 per cent of the total blood flow. This means that, with a cardiac output of 30 liters per minute, more than 25 liters of blood would go to the muscles.

As we mentioned in Chapter 6, this redistribution of blood flow results from (1) reflex vasoconstriction of the arterioles supplying the inactive areas of the body, especially those of the visceral organs and skin, and (2) reflex vasodilation of the arterioles supplying the active

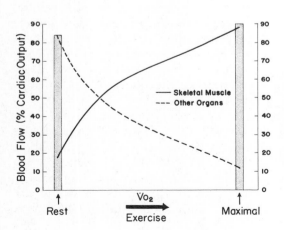

**Figure 10–3** Distribution of blood (per cent of cardiac output) to skeletal muscles and other organs during exercise. During maximal exercise, 80 to 90 per cent of the cardiac output is distributed to the working muscles.

skeletal muscles. As might be suspected, these nervous reflexes are co-ordinated with the nervous and hormonal reflexes mentioned earlier, which increase stroke volume, heart rate, and venous return. Vasodila-tion in the active muscles is also facilitated by increases in local temper-ature, $CO_2$, lactic acid levels, and a decrease in $O_2$, particularly as the exercise continues. Blood flow to the heart (since it too is an active muscle) likewise increases during exercise as a result of vasodilation,[16] whereas that to the brain is maintained at resting levels.[25] It will be pointed out in Chapter 17, that in the heat or when rectal temperature reaches a critical level, blood flow to the skin increases greatly and the amount of blood available to the working muscles is correspondingly reduced.

In the last chapter (p. 196), we said that the difference in oxygen content between the arterial and mixed venous blood (a-$\bar{v}O_2$ diff) rep-resents the amount of oxygen extracted or consumed by the tissues. The more oxygen extracted, the greater is the difference and vice versa. The magnitude of the a-$\bar{v}O_2$ diff is also affected by the distribution of blood flow. This is true because tissues that are more metabolically active (e.g., working skeletal muscle) extract more oxygen from the blood than less active tissues (e.g., skin, gastrointestinal tract, and kidney). If more blood is distributed to the tissues that extract more oxygen and less to those that extract less, then the a-$\bar{v}O_2$ diff will be increased.

Training leads to a larger a-$\bar{v}O_2$ diff in young men,[21] especially during maximal exercise. However, in young women and older men and women, the a-$\bar{v}O_2$ diff does not increase with training.[14, 15] The reason for this is not known. The increase seen in young men is ap-parently caused by a greater extraction of oxygen by the working muscles.[18]

The significance of the redistribution of blood flow with respect to gas transport is impressive. For example, it can be calculated that an additional 540 ml. of oxygen can be transported to the working muscles per minute during maximal exercise without an additional increase in cardiac output.[18] This amounts to about 15 per cent of the total maximal oxygen consumption in normal male subjects.

## The Oxygen Transport System

The increase in cardiac output and the redistribution of blood flow that occur during exercise can best be summarized by developing the concept of the *oxygen transport system*. The components of the system and their interrelationships are as follows:

| $\dot{V}O_2$ | = | S. V. | $\times$ | H. R. | $\times$ | a-$\bar{v}O_2$ diff |
|---|---|---|---|---|---|---|
| oxygen | = | stroke | $\times$ | heart | $\times$ | arterial-mixed |
| transported | | volume | | rate | | venous $O_2$ difference |

You will remember that the stroke volume times the heart rate is equal to the cardiac output. Also, as just mentioned, the a-$\bar{v}O_2$ diff reflects how much oxygen is extracted by the tissues and the redistribution of blood flow away from inactive tissues toward the active muscles.

Some examples of the system at rest and during maximal exercise for trained and untrained male subjects and endurance athletes are given in Table 10–2. Notice how each component contributes toward increasing the amount of oxygen transported to the muscles. Using the untrained subjects as an example, the oxygen transported during maximal exercise is 10 times greater than that found during rest. This increase is accomplished by a 1.5-fold increase in stroke volume, a 2.4-fold increase in heart rate, and a 2.8-fold increase in the a-$\bar{v}O_2$ diff ($1.5 \times 2.4 \times 2.8 = 10$). Also, notice the differences between the trained subjects and the highly trained endurance athletes. The blood flow changes in the trained subjects resulted from a 16-week, 3 days per week training program. The endurance athletes, on the other hand, were international competitors in long-distance and cross-country running and cycling. They were members of the Swedish National teams and had been training for several years. The biggest difference is in the magnitude of the stroke volume. The 16 weeks of training caused about a 13 per cent increase in stroke volume. However, the stroke volume in the endurance athletes is 70 per cent higher than that of the untrained subjects! Such a large difference clearly points out that the most important component of the oxygen transport system is the stroke volume.

# CIRCULATORY MECHANICS: HEMODYNAMICS

So far we have discussed only some of the physiological mechanisms that modify blood flow during exercise. Full comprehension of how these mechanisms produce such changes requires a basic understanding of *the physical laws which govern blood flow.* The study of these physical laws, as they relate to blood flow, is called *hemodynamics.*

There are two major hemodynamic factors which we need to consider: (1) *blood pressure,* i.e., the driving force which tends to move blood through the circulatory system, and (2) *resistance to flow,* i.e., the opposition offered by the circulatory system to this driving force (sometimes referred to as *total peripheral resistance*). The relationship of these factors to blood flow or to cardiac output is as follows:

Cardiac output ($\dot{Q}$) = Blood pressure (P)/Resistance (R).

**Table 10–2  COMPONENTS OF THE OXYGEN TRANSPORT SYSTEM AT REST AND DURING MAXIMAL EXERCISE FOR TRAINED AND UNTRAINED SUBJECTS AND ENDURANCE ATHLETES**

| CONDITION | $\dot{V}O_2$ (ML/MIN.) | = | STROKE VOLUME (LITERS/BEAT) | × | HEART RATE (BEATS/MIN.) | × | A-$\overline{V}O_2$ DIFF (ML/LITER) |
|---|---|---|---|---|---|---|---|
| A. Untrained | | | | | | | |
| 1. Rest | 300 | = | 0.075* | × | 82 | × | 48.8 |
| 2. Maximal Exercise | 3100 | = | 0.112 | × | 200 | × | 138.0 |
| B. Trained | | | | | | | |
| 1. Rest | 300 | = | 0.105 | × | 58 | × | 49.3 |
| 2. Maximal Exercise | 3440 | = | 0.126 | × | 192 | × | 140.5 |
| C. Endurance Athletes | | | | | | | |
| 1. Maximal Exercise | 5570 | = | 0.189 | × | 190 | × | 155.0 |

*Usually expressed in ml. per beat, e.g., 0.075 liters per beat = 75 ml. per beat. (Data for untrained and trained subjects from Ekblom, et al.;[6] data for endurance athletes from Ekblom and Hermansen.[7]

This is the basic hemodynamic equation. We shall be using it and its two other algebraic forms, $P = \dot{Q} \times R$ and $R = P/\dot{Q}$ later on in this chapter. Right now, let us discuss blood pressure and resistance in more detail.

### Blood Pressure

As we have mentioned, pressure is the force that moves the blood through the circulatory system. However, more important is the concept that, as does any other fluid, *blood flows from an area of high pressure to one of low pressure.* For example, as shown in Figure 10–4, blood flows from the left ventricle of the heart into the aorta (the main artery of the systemic circuit) because as the ventricle contracts it exerts a pressure that is higher than that in the aorta. Blood flows from the aorta through the remaining systemic blood vessels (arteries, arterioles, capillaries, venules, and veins, in that order) and finally to the right heart for the same reason—because of the *pressure differential* along the

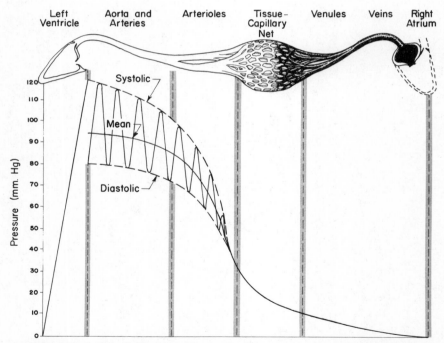

**Figure 10–4** Blood pressure differential along the systemic vascular tree. Blood always flows from an area of high pressure to one of low pressure. Note also that the pressure (and thus the flow of blood) fluctuates in the arteries and arterioles, but that it is steady in the capillaries. Systolic pressure is the highest pressure obtained, diastolic the lowest; the average of the two is the mean arterial pressure.

systemic vascular tree. This is true for pulmonary blood flow as well, except that here the pressures are lower in magnitude.* In other words, blood always flows from an area of higher pressure to one of lower pressure.

**Systolic and Diastolic Pressures.** It is also important to note from Figure 10–4 that the pressure fluctuates in the arteries. The highest pressure obtained is called the *systolic pressure* and the lowest the *diastolic pressure*. As blood is ejected into the arteries during ventricular systole, the pressure increases to a maximum (systolic pressure); as blood drains from the arteries during ventricular diastole, the pressure decreases to a minimum (diastolic pressure). These pressure fluctuations are minimized, and in fact are absent in the capillaries, because the *arteries are elastic* rather than rigid. Thus, their walls stretch during systole and recoil during diastole. The elasticity of the arteries plus an added resistance to flow (mainly in the arterioles) assures a steady flow of blood in the capillaries. This has real meaning, because we know that it is in the capillaries that diffusion of gases and other nutrients takes place.

**Mean Arterial Pressure.** The average of the systemic systolic and diastolic pressures during a complete cardiac cycle (systole plus diastole) is called the *mean arterial pressure.* The mean arterial pressure is one of the most important circulatory pressures because it, more than any other, *determines the rate of blood flow through the systemic circuit.* In our basic hemodynamic equation ($\dot{Q} = P/R$), therefore, it is the mean arterial pressure ($P_{mean}$) that is important.†

### Resistance to Flow

Resistance to blood flow is caused by friction between the blood and the walls of the blood vessels. The greater this friction, the greater the resistance to flow. Vascular friction depends on (1) the viscosity or thickness of the blood, (2) the length of the blood vessel, and (3) the diameter of the blood vessel. For example, an increase in the number of red blood cells, such as occurs at altitude, increases blood viscosity, which in turn causes greater vascular friction and resistance to flow. By the same token, the longer the vessel, the greater the vascular surface in contact with the blood and the greater the resistance.

On the other hand, when the diameter of the vessel decreases (vasoconstriction), resistance to flow increases. This is so because with a

---

*Even though the pressure differential in the pulmonary circuit is lower than that in the systemic circuit, blood flow is the same because pulmonary resistance is also lower ($\dot{Q} = P/R$).

†As we mentioned earlier, it is the pressure differential that determines the rate of blood flow. However, the pressure differential for the entire systemic circuit is $P_{mean}$ minus the pressure in the right atrium. Since the latter is zero, $P_{mean}$ can be used.

smaller diameter, a greater portion of the blood in the vessel is in contact with the walls, and the greater will be the friction. The opposite is true during vasodilation. Actually, *resistance varies inversely to the fourth power of the vessel diameter.* In other words, if the diameter of the vessel doubles, resistance decreases 16 times; if the diameter is halved, resistance increases 16 times! Referring once again to the relationship $\dot{Q} = P_{mean}/R$, we see that for a given $P_{mean}$, substantial blood flow changes can be effected by relatively small adjustments in blood vessel diameter. For this reason, vasoconstriction and vasodilation, which occur primarily in the arterioles, control to a very large extent blood flow through the circulatory system.

### Changes in Pressure and Resistance During Exercise

Shown in Figure 10–5 are the systemic blood pressures *(A)* and resistance *(B)* at rest and during exercise. Systolic and diastolic pres-

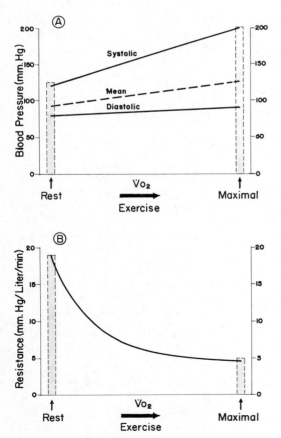

**Figure 10-5** Changes in blood pressure (*A*) and resistance to flow (*B*) during exercise. Blood pressure increases linearly during exercise as a result of an increase in cardiac output (heart rate and stroke volume), whereas resistance decreases because of vasodilation in the active muscles.

sures at rest average around 120 and 80 mm. Hg, respectively, with a mean pressure of about 93 mm. Hg. Although resistance to flow cannot be directly measured in man, it can be calculated from the relationship $R = P_{mean}/\dot{Q}$. Therefore, if cardiac output at rest is 5 liters per minute, the resistance to flow must be 93 mm. Hg/5 liters per minute = 18.6 mm. Hg/liter per minute (Fig. 10–5, *B*).

During exercise, blood pressure increases as a result of the accompanying increase in cardiac output, or more specifically of increases in stroke volume and heart rate brought about by nervous and hormonal influences, as we have previously indicated. Actually, as shown in Figure 10–5, *A*, this affects systolic pressure more than diastolic or mean pressure. The reason for this is because during exercise there is a simultaneous decrease in resistance as a result of vasodilation of the arterioles supplying blood to the active skeletal muscles. This means that more blood will drain from the arteries through the arterioles and into the muscle capillaries, thus minimizing changes in diastolic pressure. In turn, changes in mean arterial pressure will also be minimized. In other words, $P_{mean}$ increases with increasing cardiac output, but decreases with decreasing resistance.

The changes in resistance during exercise are impressive. For example, at maximal exercise, with $P_{mean}$ equal to 126 mm. Hg and cardiac output to 30 liters per minute, resistance would be $126/30 = 4.2$ mm. Hg/liter per min. This represents a 4.5-fold decrease from that at rest.

**Hypertension and Exercise.**   Hypertension refers to high blood pressure, both systolic and diastolic. High blood pressure is associated with a variety of circulatory diseases and, as such, it has been estimated that 12 per cent of all persons die as a direct result of hypertension. Moreover, one out of every five persons can expect to have high blood pressure at some time during their lives.[12]

From our basic hemodynamic equation, we know that the mean arterial pressure is equal to cardiac output times resistance ($P_{mean} = \dot{Q} \times R$). It is easy to see that hypertension is a result of either an increased cardiac output and/or an increased resistance. An increased resistance can be caused by a number of factors, most of which involve the kidneys. However, the most common form of high blood pressure in humans is called *essential hypertension.* It has no known cause and therefore no known cure. It is significant to point out that in this respect, continuous exercise has been shown to reduce resting and exercise blood pressure, particularly in older men[2, 17] and women.[15]

# SUMMARY

In order to fully meet the gas transport demands during exercise, two major blood flow changes are necessary: (1) an increase in cardiac output and (2) a redistribution of blood flow from inactive organs to the active skeletal muscles.

The increase in cardiac output ($\dot{Q}$) with exercise is brought about through increases in stroke volume (S.V.) and in heart rate (H.R.). Their mathematical relationship is: $\dot{Q}$ = S.V. $\times$ H.R. The increase in stroke volume, which reaches maximal levels during submaximal exercise, is a result of greater emptying of the left ventricle. Heart rate increases linearly with increasing work load and $\dot{V}O_2$ in both trained and untrained subjects.

A slow heart rate coupled with a relatively large stroke volume, which is characteristic of the athlete, indicates an efficient circulatory system. For a given cardiac output, a slower-beating heart with a larger stroke volume requires less oxygen.

Cardiac output is ultimately dependent upon the venous return. During exercise, the muscle and respiratory pumps plus venoconstriction help in increasing the venous return.

The redistribution of blood flow that occurs during exercise so that the active muscles receive the greatest proportion of the cardiac output results from (1) reflex vasoconstriction of the arterioles supplying the inactive areas of the body (visceral organs and skin) and (2) reflex vasodilation of the arterioles supplying the active muscles.

The oxygen transport system ($\dot{V}O_2$) is composed of the stroke volume, the heart rate, and the arterial-mixed venous oxygen difference (a-$\overline{v}O_2$ diff). Mathematically, it is defined as: $\dot{V}O_2$ = S.V. $\times$ H.R. $\times$ a-$\overline{v}O_2$ diff. The main difference in the oxygen transport system between trained and untrained subjects is a larger stroke volume.

The study of the physical laws that govern blood flow is called hemodynamics. The two main hemodynamic factors are blood pressure and resistance to flow. The average of the systolic and diastolic pressures during a complete cycle, called mean arterial pressure, determines the rate of blood flow through the systemic circulation. Resistance to flow is caused by friction between the blood and the walls of the vessels. During exercise, blood pressure increases and resistance decreases.

## QUESTIONS

1. What major blood flow changes occur during exercise?

2. How much could we increase our oxygen consumption if the above changes did not occur?

3. Give some values for cardiac output at rest and during maximal exercise for (a) untrained men and women and (b) trained men and women.

4.   Describe the changes in stroke volume and heart rate during exercise.

5.   Describe the differences and similarities between changes in stroke volume and heart rate during short- and long-term exercise.

6.   Explain how the blood flow is redistributed during exercise.

7.   How is the redistribution of blood flow related to the a-$\bar{v}O_2$ diff?

8.   What are the physiological components of the oxygen transport system and give an example of how they are interrelated?

9.   Define blood pressure and explain how and why it changes during exercise.

10.   What is resistance to flow and how is it related to hypertension?

# REFERENCES

1.   Åstrand, P., Cuddy, T., Saltin, B., and Stenberg, J.: Cardiac output during submaximal and maximal work. J. Appl. Physiol., 19:268–274, 1964.
2.   Boyer, J., and Kasch, F.: Exercise therapy in hypertensive men. J.A.M.A., 211:1668–1671, 1970.
3.   Braunwald, E., Godblatt, A., Harrison, D., and Mason, D.: Studies on cardiac dimensions in intact unanesthetized man. III. Effects of muscular exercise. Circ. Res., 13:448, 1963.
4.   Clausen, J.: Effects of physical conditioning. A hypothesis concerning circulatory adjustment to exercise. Scand. J. Clin. Lab. Invest., 24:305, 1969.
5.   Davenport, H.: The ABC of Acid-Base Chemistry. 4th ed., Chicago, University of Chicago Press, 1958.
6.   Ekblom, B., Åstrand, P., Saltin, B., Stenberg, J., and Wallström, B.: Effect of training on circulatory response to exercise. J. Appl. Physiol., 24(4):518–528, 1968.
7.   Ekblom, B., and Hermansen, L.: Cardiac output in athletes. J. Appl. Physiol., 25(5):619–625, 1968.
8.   Ekelund, L., and Holmgren, A.: Circulatory and respiratory adaptation during long-term, non-steady state exercise, in the sitting position. Acta Physiol. Scand., 62:240–255, 1964.
9.   Fox, E., and Costill, D.: Estimated cardiorespiratory responses during marathon running. Arch. Environ. Health, 24:315–324, 1972.
10.   Gorlin, R., Cohen, L., Elliott, W., Klein, M., and Lane, F.: Effect of supine exercise on left ventricular volumes and oxygen consumption in man. Circulation, 32:361, 1965.
11.   Grimby, G.: Renal clearance during prolonged supine exercise at different loads. J. Appl. Physiol., 20:1294–1298, 1965.
12.   Guyton, A.: Textbook of Medical Physiology. 4th ed. p. 304, Philadelphia, W. B. Saunders Co., 1971.
13.   Hanson, J., Tabakin, B., Levy, A., and Nedde, W.: Long-term physical training and cardiovascular dynamics in middle-aged men. Circulation, 38:783–799, 1968.
14.   Hartley, L., Grimby, G., Kilbom, Å., Nilsson, N., Åstrand, I., Ekblom, B., and Saltin, B.: Physical training in sedentary middle-aged and older men. III. Cardiac output and gas exchange at submaximal and maximal exercise. Scand. J. Clin. Lab. Invest., 24:335–344, 1969.
15.   Kilbom, Å., and Åstrand, I.: Physical training with submaximal intensities in women. II. Effect on cardiac output. Scand. J. Clin. Lab. Invest., 28:163–175, 1971.

16. Messer, J., Wagman, R., Levine, H., Neill, W., Krasnow, N., and Gorlin, R.: Patterns of human myocardial oxygen extraction during rest and exercise. J. Clin. Invest., 41:725–742, 1962.
17. Pollock, M., Miller, H., Janeway, R., Linnerud, A., Robertson, B., and Valentino, R.: Effects of walking on body composition and cardiovascular function of middle-aged men. J. Appl. Physiol., 30(1):126–130, 1971.
18. Rowell, L.: Human cardiovascular adjustments to exercise and thermal stress. Physiol. Rev., 54(1):75–159, 1974.
19. Rowell, L., Blackmon, J., and Bruce, R.: Indocyanine green clearance and estimated hepatic blood flow during mild to maximal exercise in upright man. J. Clin. Invest., 43:1677–1690, 1964.
20. Rowell, L., Blackmon, J., Martin, R., Mazzarella, J., and Bruce, R.: Hepatic clearance of indocyanine green in man under thermal and exercise stresses. J. Appl. Physiol., 20:384–394, 1965.
21. Saltin, B.: Physiological effects of physical conditioning. Med. Sci. Sports, 1(1):50–56, 1969.
22. Saltin, B., Blomqvist, G., Mitchell, J., Johnson, R., Wildenthal, K., and Chapman, C.: Response to exercise after bed rest and after training. Circulation, 38 (Suppl. 7):1–78, 1968.
23. Saltin, B., and Stenberg, J.: Circulatory response to prolonged severe exercise. J. Appl. Physiol., 19:833–838, 1964.
24. Tabakin, B., Hanson, J., and Levy, A.: Effects of physical training on the cardiovascular and respiratory response to graded upright exercise in distance runners. Brit. Heart J., 27:205–210, 1965.
25. Zobl, E., Talmers, F., Christensen, R., and Baer, L.: Effect of exercise on the cerebral circulation and metabolism. J. Appl. Physiol., 20:1289–1293, 1965.

## SELECTED READINGS

Berne, R., and Levy, M.: Cardiovascular Physiology, 2nd ed. St. Louis, C. V. Mosby Co., 1972.
Burton, A.: Physiology and Biophysics of the Circulation. Chicago, Year Book Medical Publishers, Inc., 1965.
Carlsten, A., and Grimby, G.: The Circulatory Response to Muscular Exercise in Man. Springfield, Ill., Charles C Thomas, Publishers, 1966.
Guyton, A.: Circulatory Physiology: Cardiac Output and Its Regulation. Philadelphia, W. B. Saunders Co., 1963.
Marshall, R., and Shepherd, J.: Cardiac Function in Health and Disease. Philadelphia, W. B. Saunders Co., 1968.
Rosenbaum, F., and Belknap, E. (eds.): Work and the Heart. New York, Paul B. Hoeber, Inc., 1959.
Rowell, L.: Circulation. Med. Sci. Sports, 1(1):15–22, 1969.
Rowell, L.: Human cardiovascular adjustments to exercise and thermal stress. Physiol. Rev., 54(1):75–159, 1974.

# CARDIORESPIRATORY CONTROL

Control of the cardiorespiratory system is a difficult job. This is true even under resting conditions, but most of all during exercise. For example, we have seen that many respiratory and circulatory adjustments are necessary during exercise in order to meet the increased metabolic demands of the working muscles. Furthermore, to do this most efficiently, all of these adjustments must be controlled and coordinated with each other.

Basically, this difficult job is carried out by the central nervous system through the combined efforts of the *respiratory* and *circulatory centers* located in the brain. These centers constantly receive information concerning the adequacy of gaseous exchange and transport, either directly or from a variety of receptors located throughout the body. Then, using this information as a basis, they elicit, if necessary, regulatory changes in pulmonary ventilation and blood flow.

## SUMMARY OF THE CARDIORESPIRATORY SYSTEM

Let us begin our discussion of cardiorespiratory control by summarizing the function of this system. We see from Figure 11–1 that

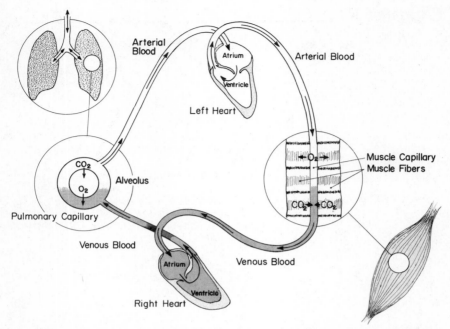

**Figure 11–1** The cardiorespiratory system. The respiratory and circulatory systems work intimately together in meeting, under all conditions, the gaseous exchange and transport requirements of the cells.

the respiratory system first of all provides a means whereby air is moved into and out of the lungs. This rhythmic to-and-fro movement of air is called *pulmonary ventilation.* Next, the oxygen brought in from the outside environment through pulmonary ventilation is made available to the blood by a vast network of capillaries surrounding the 600 million or so tiny closed air sacs or *alveoli* found in the lungs. The blood contained within the capillaries is *venous blood,* which is relatively low in oxygen and high in carbon dioxide content. At the *alveolar-capillary membranes,* oxygen diffuses from the air in the alveoli to the blood in the capillaries, whereas carbon dioxide diffuses in the opposite direction. Thus, the venous blood brought to the alveoli of the lungs via the right heart returns to the left heart as *arterial blood,* high in oxygen and low in carbon dioxide. The alveolar-capillary membranes, then, represent a functional union between the respiratory and circulatory systems.

The next important job, which is the transporting of arterial blood to the body tissues (and ultimately the carrying of venous blood away from the body tissues), is carried out by the left heart and its associated blood vessels. We should remember that the heart represents two pumps, each with its own circuit of blood vessels. The right heart and its blood vessels, as we have already pointed out, are primarily responsible for transporting venous blood to and arterial blood from the lungs (alveoli). This is called the *pulmonary circuit* or *pulmonary circulation*. Maintaining an adequate flow of arterial blood to and venous blood from the body tissues, on the other hand, is the primary function of the left heart and blood vessels. This is called the *systemic circuit* or *systemic circulation*.

Referring again to Figure 11–1, arterial blood in the pulmonary circuit is returned to the left heart, which then pumps it to all the body tissues—for instance, in our example, to the skeletal muscles. At this level, another vast network of capillaries is found. You will recall from Chapter 6 that skeletal muscle is richly supplied with capillary beds, which come into close contact with the individual muscle fibers. It is at these *tissue-capillary membranes* that a second exchange of gases occurs. This time, oxygen diffuses from the blood in the capillaries to the cells of the tissues, and carbon dioxide diffuses in the opposite direction. The exchange of gases at the tissue-capillary membranes converts arterial blood to venous blood. The venous blood is then returned to the right heart, where the entire process of exchange and transportation of gases is repeated over and over again.

Finally, the oxygen delivered via the cardiorespiratory system is utilized by the cells for purposes of supplying energy in the form of ATP. Oxygen utilization and carbon dioxide production by the cell (the aerobic pathway) were discussed in Chapter 2. Now let's answer the question, "How is all this controlled?"

## THE RESPIRATORY AND CIRCULATORY CENTERS

The respiratory and circulatory centers consist of *networks of nerve cells and their connections*. They are located in the brain stem, mainly in an area called the *medulla oblongata*. Anatomically, it is rather difficult to distinguish one center from the other. However, physiologically, it has been shown that electrical stimulation of certain areas in the brain stem primarily affects respiration, whereas stimulation of nearby but different areas primarily affects circulation. The effect on respiration is mainly a change in pulmonary (alveolar) ventilation, i.e., in the rate and particularly in the depth of breathing. Circulatory effects involve changes in heart rate, stroke volume (force of contraction), the distribution of blood to various organs (vasoconstriction and vasodilation), and venous return (venoconstriction). Although these centers affect one system more than the other, they are neurally interconnected, so that each is informed of the other's activity. Therefore, stimulation of one center will, via its connection with the other, affect both ventilation and blood flow. This, of course, makes sense since the functions of these two systems are one and the same.

As we mentioned earlier, the respiratory and circulatory centers receive, evaluate, and send information so that the metabolic needs of each cell are maintained adequately at all times. As part of a control system and under most conditions, this is their main function.

### Stimulation of the Cardiorespiratory Centers

The centers are stimulated by a variety of information, received from all parts of the body, as shown to the left of Figure 11–2. Stimulation refers to an increase in the activity of the nerve cells and connections that make up the centers. As we will see later, this increased activity initiates the regulatory changes in ventilation and blood flow.

**Classification of Stimuli.**   The many *stimuli* shown in Figure 11–2 can be grouped into two classifications, *humoral* and *neural*. Humoral stimuli originate from changes in the physical and chemical properties of blood.* Thus, the centers are supplied with important information

---

*These changes usually mean changes from their normal values at rest.

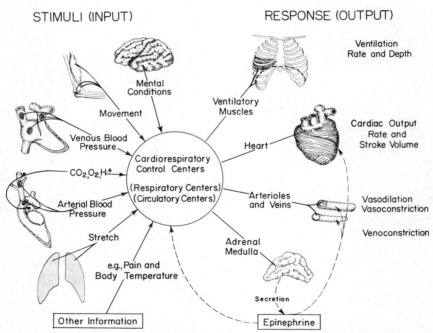

**Figure 11–2**  Nervous control of the cardiorespiratory system. Various kinds of information (stimuli) from all parts of the body are sent to the respiratory and circulatory centers located in the brain stem. Then, using this information, the centers elicit, if necessary, regulatory changes in pulmonary ventilation and blood flow.

concerning changes in: (1) arterial and venous blood pressures and blood temperature (physical changes), and (2) arterial blood $Po_2$, $Pco_2$, and $H^+$ concentration (chemical changes). Neural stimuli, on the other hand, are independent of changes in the properties of blood; rather, they originate from changes that take place in higher brain centers, the lungs, the muscles, joints, tendons, skin, and respiratory passages. The information they provide the centers is concerned with (1) mental conditions, e.g., emotions, and particularly the activity of the motor cortex, (2) inflation and deflation (stretch) of the lungs, (3) limb movement, and (4) intense pain or general discomfort and the presence of respiratory irritants (hence, the cough and sneeze reflexes). While all of these neural stimuli are important, we will be most interested in those from the motor areas of the cortex, the lungs, and the muscles, joints, and tendons.

**Action on the Cardiorespiratory Centers.** As indicated in Table 11–1, stimuli may act upon the cardiorespiratory centers either *directly* or *indirectly*, or both. In the first case, the centers are stimulated directly either via the circulating blood due to increases in temperature, $Pco_2$, and $H^+$ concentration, or via nervous impulses from higher brain centers. Indirect stimulation of the centers occurs *reflexly* via sensory nerves originating in specialized receptors, to which the centers are

**Table 11–1  ACTION OF HUMORAL AND NEURAL STIMULI ON THE CARDIORESPIRATORY CENTERS**

| | **ACTION ON CARDIORESPIRATORY CENTERS** | | | |
|---|---|---|---|---|
| | ***Direct*** | ***Indirect*** | **Receptors** | |
| **STIMULI** | ***(Central)*** | ***(Reflex)*** | *Name* | *Location* |
| A. Humoral | | | | |
| 1. Physical | | | | |
| (a) Increased blood temperature | ✔ | ✔ | Thermoreceptors | Hypothalamus |
| (b) Increased arterial blood pressure | | ✔ | Pressoreceptors, baroreceptors, or stretch receptors | Carotid arteries, aortic arch |
| (c) Increased venous blood pressure | | ✔ | | Vena cavae, right atrium |
| 2. Chemical | | | | |
| (a) Increased arterial blood $Pco_2$, $H^+$ | ✔ | ✔ | Chemoreceptors | Carotid arteries, aortic arch |
| (b) Decreased arterial blood $Po_2$ | | ✔ | | |
| B. Neural | | | | |
| 1. Impulse transmission from higher brain centers | ✔ | | | |
| 2. Inflation and deflation of lungs | | ✔ | Stretch receptors, or mechano-receptors | Lungs (bronchi, bronchioles, alveoli) |
| 3. Limb movement | | ✔ | | Muscles, joints, and tendons |

connected. In this case, the centers are stimulated by an increase in the number of sensory nerve impulses initiated by the receptors as a result of increases in blood temperature, arterial and venous blood pressures, and arterial blood $P_{CO_2}$ and $H^+$ concentrations, a decrease in arterial blood $P_{O_2}$, inflation and deflation of the lungs, and limb movement. The names and locations of the receptors are given in Table 11–1 and are schematically shown in Figure 11–2. Note that increases in blood temperature and arterial blood $P_{CO_2}$ and $H^+$ concentration act on the centers both directly and indirectly. This of course provides additional sensitivity and precision to the controlling mechanism.

**Effects on Ventilation and Blood Flow.** As previously mentioned, stimulation of the cardiorespiratory centers initiates regulatory changes in ventilation and blood flow. Some of these changes, along with their respective stimuli, are contained in Table 11–2. We shall want to study these, as they relate to the control of the cardiorespiratory system both at rest and during exercise. However, before doing so, it is essential that we understand something about the nervous connec-

**Table 11–2  EFFECTS OF VARIOUS STIMULI ON VENTILATION AND BLOOD FLOW**

| | EFFECTS | | |
| | RESPIRATION | CIRCULATION | |
| STIMULI | Ventilation (Rate and Depth) | Heart (Rate and Force) | Blood Vessels |
| --- | --- | --- | --- |
| Decreased arterial $P_{O_2}$ | Increased | Increased | Vasoconstriction |
| Increased arterial $P_{CO_2}$, $H^+$ | Increased | Increased | Vasoconstriction |
| Increased arterial blood pressure | Decreased | Decreased | Vasodilation |
| Increased venous blood pressure | Increased | Increased | Vasoconstriction |
| Inflation of lungs | Inhibits inspiration | Increased | Vasoconstriction |
| Deflation of lungs | Stimulates inspiration | Unknown | Unknown |
| Increased activity of motor cortex | Increased | Increased | Vasodilation in active muscles; vasoconstriction in inactive muscles |
| Increased limb movement | Increased | Increased | Vasodilation in active muscles; vasoconstriction in inactive muscles |
| Increased blood temperature | Increased | Increased | Cutaneous vasodilation |
| Increased norepinephrine and epinephrine from adrenal medulla | Increased | Increased | Vasodilation in active muscles; vasoconstriction in inactive muscles |

tions between the centers on the one hand, and the cardiorespiratory apparatus on the other.

### Innervation of the Cardiorespiratory Apparatus

The innervation of the cardiorespiratory system is shown schematically to the right of Figure 11–2. The motor nerves connected to the ventilatory muscles (see page 175) are called *somatic motor nerves (somatic* means "body"). We know that when they are stimulated they affect both the rate and depth of respiration. In addition, they belong to the *voluntary* nervous system, like those innervating the other skeletal muscles. This explains why we have some voluntary control over ventilation, i.e., why we can alter our ventilatory behavior at will (just as we can alter our motor behavior at will).

The motor nerves innervating the heart and blood vessels, on the other hand, are quite different. This is evidenced by the fact that we do not have voluntary control over the circulatory system. These particular motor nerves belong to the *involuntary* or *autonomic* nervous system and are collectively referred to as autonomic nerves. Those which, when stimulated, cause increased heart rate and stroke volume (greater force of contraction) are called *cardioaccelerator nerves* because of their function, or *sympathetic nerves* because they belong to the *sympathetic division* of the autonomic nervous system. Other autonomic nerves that innervate the heart, the *vagus nerves,* belong to the *parasympathetic division* of the autonomic nervous system. When they are stimulated, heart rate decreases, just the opposite of what happens when the sympathetic nerves are stimulated. This again provides additional precision to the controlling mechanism. For example, increases in heart rate and stroke volume result from either a decreased rate of stimulation of the vagus nerves or an increased rate of stimulation of the sympathetic cardioaccelerator nerves, or both. During exercise, both of these occur simultaneously.*

The motor nerves innervating the smooth muscles of the blood vessels also belong to the autonomic nervous system. They include: (1) sympathetic nerves that go to virtually all arterioles and veins, and which when stimulated cause vaso- and venoconstriction (*sympathetic vasoconstrictor nerves*); and (2) sympathetic nerves that connect *only* to the arterioles of skeletal and heart muscles, and which when stimulated cause vasodilation (*sympathetic vasodilator nerves*).† During exercise, this

---

*At rest, the heart is primarily under the influence of the vagus nerves. The slow resting heart rates of trained subjects are thought to result from increased vagal stimulation (tone). However, the mechanism responsible for this is unknown.

†There are also parasympathetic vasodilator nerves, but they supply only the tongue, salivary glands, external genital organs, urinary bladder, and rectum.

dual nerve supply is in large part responsible for the redistribution of blood to the active muscles and the increase in venous return.

The effects caused by stimulation of these various motor nerves result from the release of chemical compounds at the nerve endings. For example, increases in heart rate, stroke volume, and vasoconstriction are caused by the release of *norepinephrine* from the ends of the sympathetic cardioaccelerator and vasoconstrictor nerves when they are stimulated. We mention this here because of the importance of a group of specialized gland cells found in the medullae (central portions) of the adrenal glands. These cells are similar to the sympathetic nerves just mentioned in that they also release norepinephrine, plus another, similar chemical called *epinephrine* (adrenalin). These two chemicals (in this case called *hormones*) are secreted when their sympathetic nerves are stimulated and are carried in the circulating blood. This occurs during alarm or fright and most importantly before and during exercise. The effects of these hormones on the heart and blood vessels are identical or almost identical to those produced when the sympathetic nerves innervating these tissues are directly stimulated (see Table 11–2). In addition, these hormones increase the metabolic rate of the tissues and the rate and depth of ventilation.

A different chemical, called *acetylcholine*, is released at the ends of the vagus and sympathetic vasodilator nerves and the somatic nerves innervating the ventilatory muscles.

## CARDIORESPIRATORY CONTROL AT REST AND DURING EXERCISE

One of the most important functions of any physiological control system is to maintain certain variables at optimal levels. For example, in Chapter 17, we will see how the thermoregulatory system strives to maintain an optimal body temperature over a wide range of climatic conditions, both at rest and during exercise. In this respect, the cardiorespiratory control system is no different; it too strives to maintain certain variables at optimal levels under all conditions.

From our previous discussions, it is obviously quite difficult to single out any one or even a few cardiorespiratory variables that are, at all times, preferentially maintained at optimal levels. These preferences change, depending on the metabolic needs of the cells from one moment to the next. Actually, with our present knowledge, it is virtually impossible to give an adequate overall explanation of how given levels of ventilation and blood flow are achieved and controlled so as to exactly meet the metabolic needs of any cell under any condition. Furthermore, the respective roles of the many stimuli involved in this control and their interactions are not yet completely known. At best, all we can say is that the final outcome is determined by the stimuli that predominate at any given moment.

All of this serves well to illustrate how complex and how little understood is the control of the cardiorespiratory system. Nevertheless, there are several important concepts concerning this control that we can point out, among them how arterial blood pressure, and arterial blood $Po_2$, $Pco_2$, and $H^+$ concentration are maintained at optimal levels at rest and during exercise. We have chosen these particular variables because more is known about their control than about any others.

### Control at Rest

The most important factors in maintenance of arterial blood pressure, $Po_2$, $Pco_2$, and $H^+$ concentration at optimal levels under resting conditions are changes in these variables themselves. As indicated in Table 11–2, changes in them initiate cardiorespiratory adjustments that affect these changes inversely. For example, an *increased* arterial pressure (e.g., above the 100 mm. Hg normally required at rest) causes decreases in heart rate, stroke volume (force of contraction), and resistance to blood flow (vasodilation). We know from our discussion of hemodynamics that these circulatory adjustments will in turn lead to a *decrease* in arterial pressure.* By the same token, a decrease in pressure below the normal, by causing the opposite circulatory adjustments, will lead to an increase in pressure. In either case, when the pressure returns to its normal (optimal) level, the original stimulus (i.e., a change in pressure) — and thus the whole process — is "turned off." This type of control is sometimes referred to as a *negative feedback mechanism.*

The same type of control mechanism limits changes in the normal levels of arterial blood $Po_2$, $Pco_2$, and $H^+$ concentration. For instance, a decreased $Po_2$ or an increased $Pco_2$ and $H^+$ concentration, or both, causes an immediate increase in alveolar ventilation by increasing primarily the depth of respiration (see Table 11–2). This affects the levels of these variables in the opposite direction.

One other aspect of ventilatory control needs to be mentioned here. Note that inflation and deflation of the lungs does not affect total ventilation, as do the other stimuli. Inflation of the lungs during inspiration causes expiration (i.e., it inhibits inspiration), whereas deflation of the lungs during expiration stimulates inspiration. In other words, these reflexes, initiated via the pulmonary stretch receptors, automatically reinforce the maintenance of a normal respiratory rhythm of inspiration followed by expiration. They provide us the luxury of a normal ventilatory rhythm without continuous conscious effort. This is

---

*Remember: $P_{mean} = \dot{Q} \times R$, and $\dot{Q} = S.V. \times H.R.$; therefore, $P_{mean} = S.V. \times H.R. \times R$.

their main function. They are not directly involved with maintenance of $P_{O_2}$, $P_{CO_2}$ and $H^+$ concentration simply because they are not equipped to supply the respiratory centers with this type of information.

### Control During Exercise

At rest, adjustments in ventilation and blood flow regulate or maintain arterial blood pressure, $P_{O_2}$, $P_{CO_2}$ and $H^+$ concentration at optimal levels. This is also true during exercise, for this is the main function of the cardiorespiratory control system under any condition. However, there is one big difference — at rest, changes in these regulated variables are the predominant stimuli that initiate such adjustments; during exercise, other stimuli predominate. This is easy to see, for many reasons.

First, we know from experience that heart rate and ventilation, for example, increase even before exercise begins, long before changes in pressure or in $P_{O_2}$, $P_{CO_2}$, and $H^+$ concentration can occur. In addition, we now know, from a physiological standpoint, that an increase in heart rate (and in stroke volume) increases arterial blood pressure. If this increased pressure (which is optimal under these conditions), were the predominant stimulus at any time during exercise, heart rate and stroke volume would decrease rather than increase. Likewise, vasodilation would occur in *all* tissues rather than mainly in the active muscles, and the redistribution of blood flow to the latter, which we also know occurs, would not be possible.

Second, changes in arterial blood $P_{O_2}$, $P_{CO_2}$ and $H^+$ concentration would have to be quite pronounced in order to fully account for the large increase in pulmonary ventilation that occurs during exercise. The fact of the matter is that these variables change very little during exercise. This is true except during very heavy or maximal exercise. Under these conditions, $P_{O_2}$ decreases and $H^+$ increases, primarily because of lactic acid formation. In this case, these changes — particularly in $H^+$ concentration — do cause an additional increase in ventilation (see Figure 8–1A, p. 167). On the other hand, arterial blood $P_{CO_2}$ decreases during heavy exercise, and this would tend to decrease ventilation.

Which stimuli, then, predominate during exercise? Unfortunately, all of the stimuli have not as yet been determined. However, there are several that are known to be of primary importance in maintaining certain cardiorespiratory variables at optimal levels. These stimuli include: (1) increased activity of the motor cortex, (2) limb movement, (3) increased $H^+$ concentration (lactic acid formation), (4) increased blood temperature, and (5) increased secretion of norepinephrine and epinephrine from the adrenal medulla. Their effects on ventilation and blood flow are given in Table 11–2. Most of these stimuli (particularly the first four) supply information concerning the intensity of exercise rather than the level or magnitude of any particular cardiorespiratory variable. This enables the resulting adjustments in ventilation and blood flow to keep pace exactly with the increased gaseous exchange and transport requirements of the working muscles.

### Other Control Mechanisms

Nervous control of the cardiorespiratory system is paramount to the overall functional efficiency of this system; for this reason, we have studied it in some detail. However, we must not forget about those cardiorespiratory adjustments that are *not* controlled by the central nervous system. For example, remember that increases in blood temperature, acidity, and $CO_2$ beneficially shift the $HbO_2$ dissociation curve to the right during exercise. Furthermore, these same factors, plus a lowered $P_{O_2}$, also promote local vasodilation of the arterioles supplying blood to the active muscles, an adjustment made by the smooth muscles themselves in response to changes in their local environment. We can also mention the increase in venous return resulting from the mechanical actions of the muscle and respiratory pumps, and the hemoconcentration caused by fluid shifts between the active muscles and the blood. All of these adjustments represent a type of control mechanism that is equally important to the overall efficiency of the cardiorespiratory system, particularly during exercise.

## SUMMARY

During both rest and exercise, control of the cardiorespiratory system is extremely complex. The essential constituents for such control are located in the respiratory and circulatory centers located in the brain stem. Both humoral and neural stimulation of these centers aids in regulating, at all times, such important cardiorespiratory variables as arterial blood pressure and arterial blood $P_{O_2}$, $P_{CO_2}$, and $H^+$ concentration.

Innervation of the cardiorespiratory apparatus involves both the voluntary nervous system (supplying the respiratory muscles) and the involuntary or autonomic nervous system (supplying the heart and blood vessels).

At rest, the most important factors in maintenance of blood pressure, $P_{O_2}$, $P_{CO_2}$, and $H^+$ concentration are changes in these variables themselves (negative feedback).

During exercise, the predominant stimuli are (1) increased activity of the motor cortex, (2) limb movement, (3) increased $H^+$ concentration, (4) increased blood temperature, and (5) secretion of norepinephrine and epinephrine from the adrenal medulla. Other mechanisms include shifts in the $HbO_2$ dissociation curve and in local vasodilation in the muscles.

## QUESTIONS

1. Where are the respiratory and circulatory centers located and what are their main functions?

2. Describe the difference between neural and humoral stimuli and give examples of each.

3. Describe the difference between direct and indirect stimulation of the cardiorespiratory center and give examples of each.

4. Discuss the innervation of the cardiorespiratory apparatus.

5. Outline how ventilation and blood flow are regulated during rest and exercise. How do they differ?

## SELECTED READINGS

Asmussen, E., Johansen, S., Jørgensen, M., and Nielsen, M.: On the nervous factors controlling respiration and circulation during exercise. Acta Physiol. Scand., 63:343–350, 1965.

Asmussen, E., and Nielsen, M.: Cardiac output during muscular work and its regulation. Physiol. Rev., 35:778–800, 1955.

Berne, R., and Levy, M.: Cardiovascular Physiology, 2nd ed., St. Louis, C. V. Mosby Co., 1972, pp. 237–253.

Bevegard, B., and Shepherd, J.: Regulation of the circulation during exercise in man. Physiol. Rev., 47:178–213, 1967.

Burton, A.: Physiology and Biophysics of the Circulation. Chicago, Year Book Medical Publishers, Inc., 1965.

Clausen, J., Trap-Jensen, J., and Lassen, N.: The effects of training on the heart rate during arm and leg exercise. Scand. J. Clin. Lab. Invest., 26:295–301, 1970.

Comroe, J.: Physiology of Respiration. Chicago, Year Book Medical Publishers, Inc., 1965.

Comroe, J., Forster, R., Dubois, A., Briscoe, W., and Carlsen, E.: The Lung. 2nd ed., Chicago, Year Book Medical Publishers, Inc., 1962.

Cunningham, D., and Lloyd, B. (eds.): The Regulation of Human Respiration. Philadelphia, F. A. Davis Co., 1963.

DeJours, P.: Respiration. New York, Oxford University Press, 1966.

Frick, M., Elovainio, R., and Somer, T.: The mechanism of bradycardia evoked by physical training. Cardiologia, 51:46–54, 1967.

Kalia, M., Senapati, J., Parida, B., and Panda, A.: Reflex increase in ventilation by muscle receptors with non-medulated fibers (C fibers). J. Appl. Physiol., 32:189–193, 1972.

Lambertsen, C., Semple, S., Smyth, M., and Gelfand, R.: $H^+$ and $Pco_2$ as chemical factors in respiratory and cerebral circulatory control. J. Appl. Physiol., 16:473–484, 1961.

Rushmer, R.: Cardiovascular Dynamics. Philadelphia, W. B. Saunders Co., 1961.

Slonim, N., and Hamilton, L.: Respiratory Physiology. 2nd ed., St. Louis, C. V. Mosby Co., 1971, pp. 123–142.

Tipton, C.: Training and bradycardia in rats. Am. J. Physiol., 209:1089–1094, 1965.

Yamashiro, S., and Grodins, F.: Optimal regulation of respiratory airflow. J. Appl. Physiol., 30:597–602, 1971.

# SECTION 4

# PHYSICAL TRAINING

*Chapter 12* ———————————————————————

# INTERVAL TRAINING AND OTHER CONDITIONING METHODS

A prime objective of physical educators and coaches is to construct the most effective *individualized* conditioning or training programs for their students and athletes. It is therefore the purpose of this chapter to outline fundamental principles which will help you do just that.

The principles underlying the development of muscular strength, endurance, and flexibility have been discussed in Chapter 7. This presentation will stress the relationship between the particular activity or event you wish to improve and the primary energy source(s) involved. By

**239**

recognizing which of the energy sources are being employed to the greatest extent during a given activity you will be able to prescribe the most effective conditioning regimen.

In starting our discussion, we will outline several general considerations that are applicable to all training and conditioning programs. Then we will move on to the details of specific training regimens, each of which contributes in a unique way to the full development of the energy and performance capabilities of your students and athletes.

## GENERAL CONSIDERATIONS

There are three considerations that are important to all training programs: (1) the basic principles of training; (2) the various training phases; and (3) preliminary activity or warm-up.

### Training Principles

You learned that to develop strength and muscular endurance requires working the muscle at an increasing resistance. As a consequence, the muscle develops in bulk and gains in strength and endurance. In other words, a number of physiological adaptations take place which lead to a greater energy potential within each muscle cell. Thus our basic tenets in any conditioning or training program are to: (1) recognize the major energy source utilized to perform a given activity; and (2) then, through the overload principle, construct a program that will develop that particular energy source more than will any other.

**Specificity of Training.** Tenet (1) above is closely related to what is usually referred to as specificity of training. We mentioned this concept earlier in conjunction with weight training programs (see p. 141). We need to emphasize again that all training programs *must* be specific to developing the energy system or systems predominantly used during performance of the sports activity in question. It should also be pointed out that specificity applies equally to general conditioning programs. In such a case, however, we might be interested in improving fitness only and not necessarily sports performance. In most sports events, one or two energy systems usually are considered when planning the training program. With persons seeking general conditioning, all three systems may be involved, with emphasis perhaps being placed on the system that best meets that person's fitness needs. For example, people recovering from coronary and other related cardiorespiratory diseases would want to emphasize the oxygen system.

**Determining the Predominant Energy System.** How does one know which energy system(s) predominates in various activities and sports? The answer to this question is given by the information contained in Table 12-1. The table illustrates the relationship between track running events and the primary energy-yielding components involved. From this information, it becomes apparent that you as the coach, if training marathon runners, would devote 5 per cent of the training regimen to development of the ATP-PC and lactic acid systems, whereas 95 per cent of the time would be spent on developing the oxygen system.

Table 12-1 was constructed for track events. However, you will notice that the time of performance has been included; this was done for a special reason. Regardless of the event, the time of performance is related to the energy-yielding systems involved. That is to say, if we were discussing a swimming event requiring four to five minutes, reference to the table shows us that the per cent emphasis for training would be as follows: 20 per cent speed, 25 per cent oxygen system, and 55 per cent anaerobic capacity. The point we wish to make is that *the energy sources for a given activity are time-dependent.* Whether a person is chopping wood, shoveling snow, performing calisthenics, running, or swimming for a continuous period of time, the primary source of energy will be dependent upon the performance time.

Using the information given in Table 12-1, it is possible to analyze a number of sports with regard to the per cent emphasis that should be placed on training the various energy systems. The results of these analyses are given in Table 12-2. With these guidelines, specific training programs can be constructed that will lead to maximum increases in performance. We will talk more about this a little later in this chapter. If your favorite sport or activity is not listed in Table 12-2, you can do your own analysis using the information contained in Table 12-1.

**Table 12-1  PER CENT OF TRAINING TIME SPENT IN DEVELOPING THE THREE ENERGY SOURCES FOR VARIOUS TRACK EVENTS***

| EVENT | TIME OF PERFORMANCE (MINUTES:SECONDS) | SPEED (ATP-PC STRENGTH) | AEROBIC CAPACITY (OXYGEN SYSTEM) | ANAEROBIC CAPACITY (SPEED + LACTIC ACID SYSTEM) |
|---|---|---|---|---|
| Marathon | 135:00 to 180:00 | — | 95% | 5% |
| 6 mile | 30:00 to 50:00 | 5 | 80 | 15 |
| 3 mile | 15:00 to 25:00 | 10 | 70 | 20 |
| 2 mile | 10:00 to 16:00 | 20 | 40 | 40 |
| 1 mile | 4:00 to 6:00 | 20 | 25 | 55 |
| 880 yards | 2:00 to 3:00 | 30 | 5 | 65 |
| 440 yards | 1:00 to 1:30 | 80 | 5 | 15 |
| 220 yards | 0:22 to 0:35 | 98 | — | 2 |
| 100 yards | 0:10 to 0:15 | 98 | — | 2 |

*Adapted from Wilt.[30]

## Table 12–2 VARIOUS SPORTS AND THEIR PREDOMINANT ENERGY SYSTEM (S)*

| SPORTS OR SPORT ACTIVITY | % EMPHASIS ACCORDING TO ENERGY SYSTEMS | | |
|---|---|---|---|
| | ATP-PC and LA | LA-$O_2$ | $O_2$ |
| 1. Baseball | 80 | 20 | — |
| 2. Basketball | 85 | 15 | — |
| 3. Fencing | 90 | 10 | — |
| 4. Field Hockey | 60 | 20 | 20 |
| 5. Football | 90 | 10 | — |
| 6. Golf | 95 | 5 | — |
| 7. Gymnastics | 90 | 10 | — |
| 8. Ice Hockey | | | |
| a. forwards, defense | 80 | 20 | — |
| b. goalie | 95 | 5 | — |
| 9. Lacrosse | | | |
| a. goalie, defense, attack men | 80 | 20 | — |
| b. midfielders, man-down | 60 | 20 | 20 |
| 10. Rowing | 20 | 30 | 50 |
| 11. Skiing | | | |
| a. slalom, jumping, downhill | 80 | 20 | — |
| b. cross-country | — | 5 | 95 |
| c. pleasure skiing | 34 | 33 | 33 |
| 12. Soccer | | | |
| a. goalie, wings, strikers | 80 | 20 | — |
| b. halfbacks, or link men | 60 | 20 | 20 |
| 13. Swimming and diving | | | |
| a. 50 yds., diving | 98 | 2 | — |
| b. 100 yds. | 80 | 15 | 5 |
| c. 200 yds. | 30 | 65 | 5 |
| d. 400, 500 yds. | 20 | 40 | 40 |
| e. 1500, 1650 yds. | 10 | 20 | 70 |
| 14. Tennis | 70 | 20 | 10 |
| 15. Track and field | | | |
| a. 100, 220 yds. | 98 | 2 | — |
| b. field events | 90 | 10 | — |
| c. 440 yds. | 80 | 15 | 5 |
| d. 880 yds. | 30 | 65 | 5 |
| e. 1 mile | 20 | 55 | 25 |
| f. 2 miles | 20 | 40 | 40 |
| g. 3 miles | 10 | 20 | 70 |
| h. 6 miles (cross-country) | 5 | 15 | 80 |
| i. marathon | — | 5 | 95 |
| 16. Volleyball | 90 | 10 | — |
| 17. Wrestling | 90 | 10 | — |

*Modified from Fox and Mathews.[15]

**Application of the Overload Principle.** Our second tenet concerns the overload principle. As you will recall from Chapter 7, the progressive overload principle implies that the exercise resistance is maximal and that it is gradually increased as the person's fitness capacity improves throughout the course of the training program. In weight training this was accomplished by establishing the repetition maximum (see p. 142). With training programs consisting of running, cycling, or swimming, the *intensity* of the program rather than the amount of weight lifted is used as the means of progressive overload. One of the best ways to judge the intensity of your training program is by the exercise heart rate response; the higher the heart rate, the greater the intensity. Heart rate guidelines for judging the intensity of your training program, as well as others, will be included in our discussion of the various training methods.

As a simple illustration of how these training principles work together, suppose we wish to develop the speed with which an athlete could run 100 meters. Our first question is, what is the major source of energy for this activity? To run 100 meters as fast as possible requires less than 15 seconds; therefore the athlete is using the ATP-PC system as the predominant energy system. The activity is obviously a power event—a great deal of work is performed in the shortest period of time. We might also refer to this as an activity of high intensity. According to Table 12–2, to increase power output would thus require increasing the rate of utilization of the ATP-PC system, rather than increasing, for example, the aerobic capacity. This could be accomplished through the overload principle by carrying an additional load (i.e., loaded vest) and by sprinting at maximal rates.

You might ask, why not just lift weights? Certainly this will increase the ATP-PC energy resources. This is very true, but remember Henry's Memory Drum theory, which emphasizes the specificity of movement (see p. 96). When you are conditioning an athlete, energy reservoirs are extremely important, but you must remember that a neuromuscular skill is also involved. This is convincingly illustrated by the fact that the speed of performing a flexion movement on one side of the body may be completely independent of the speed in performing an identical movement on the contralateral side, even though the potential energy reservoirs are equal.

We have measured energy reserves of high school and university track and swimming athletes.[4] On occasion we found little if any difference in the energy potential, *but* performance-wise the university athletes were far superior. In other words they were more skillful neuromuscularly and hence used their energy stores more efficiently. Without question, weight training will increase the ATP-PC energy reservoirs, but we cannot disregard the importance of neuromuscular skill in performance.

A young man with good skill proficiency in basketball asked to be placed on a conditioning program. Our first problem was to determine which of his energy resources were weak. In the laboratory we indirectly measured both his aerobic and his ATP-PC capacities. He was average or a little above in regard to aerobic capacity but was extremely poor in the ATP-PC reservoir. We placed him on a high intensity interval training program. This consisted of short sprints of 50 to 220 yards at maximal effort. In six weeks his power output increased almost 20 per cent. We did little if anything to improve neuromuscular skill required of a basketball player. We did, however, provide additional energy potential, which would allow the player to increase performance in the power skills of basketball (i.e., quick starts, jumping).

### Training Phases

It is usual to classify the total training period of athletes into three phases: off-season, pre-season, and in-season. It is also usual for the training programs to vary considerably from phase to phase. Here is what we recommend.

**Off-Season Training.**  Training programs during the off-season are generally nonspecific. Most often they require only that the athlete keep moderately active and, perhaps of most concern, keep his or her body weight at or reasonably near "playing weight."

We suggest that an off-season training program consist of some or all of the following:

1. A weight training program with emphasis placed on increasing strength, muscular endurance, and power in those muscle groups most directly involved in the specific athletic event. Such a program should be based on the principles outlined in Chapter 7.

2. An informal (in other words, not required) eight-week running program of *low intensity* performed no more than twice a week. This kind of program could be administered concurrently with the weight training program. For example, if the latter were conducted on Monday, Wednesday, and Friday, the running program could be performed on Monday and Wednesday or Wednesday and Friday. It makes little difference as to whether the running program is performed before or after the weight training program.

3. Participation in sports activities and recreational games purely for relaxation, pleasure, and enjoyment.

4. Limited participation in the athlete's specific sport in order to develop his or her skill; for example, in basketball such skills would include shooting accuracy, ball-handling (dribbling, passing), pivoting, and so on.

**Pre-Season Training.**  During the pre-season phase (i.e., the 8 to 10 weeks prior to competition), training programs should be designed to increase to a maximum the capacities of the energy systems that are predominant when performing a specific athletic event. *It is during this phase of athletic training that a specific high intensity program should be used.* Examples of pre-season interval training programs for men and women designed to improve primarily the oxygen system are found in Appendix E. Other programs are available.[15] It is hoped, however, that with the information contained in this book, and specifically in this chapter, you will be able to construct your own training program that will best fit the needs of your athletes.

**In-Season Training.** Traditionally, in-season training programs for most sports emphasize skill development. It is generally felt that drills, scrimmages, and competition will maintain the increases in energy capacities that were obtained during the pre-season training program. For the in-season training program, we also agree that in most sports, drills, scrimmages, and regular competition will maintain a high level of fitness throughout the season. However, we emphasize that drills should be used with two main purposes in mind: (1) improvement in skill, and (2) improvement in energy capacity specific to that skill.

Table 12–3 contains a summary of the kinds of programs recommended for the various training phases.

## Preliminary Exercise (Warm-up)

Prior to a heavy workout, preliminary exercises should be performed.[1, 5, 23, 24, 25] There are many physiological reasons for this. For example, increased body and muscle temperatures promote increases in (a) enzyme activity and thus in the metabolic reactions associated with the energy systems; (b) blood flow and oxygen availability; and (c)

### Table 12–3  RECOMMENDED PROGRAMS FOR THE VARIOUS TRAINING PHASES*

| | TRAINING PHASE | |
|---|---|---|
| *Off-Season* | *Pre-Season* | *In-Season* |
| 1. Weight training 8 wks, 3 days per wk | 1. Running** high intensity, 8 wks, 3 days per wk | 1. Skill drills |
| 2. Informal running low intensity, 8 wks, 1 to 2 days per wk | 2. Viewing films, learning strategies, some skill drills | 2. Scrimmages |
| 3. Participation in other sports and games | | 3. Regular competitive performances |
| 4. Limited practice in specific sport for skill development | | |

*Modified from Fox and Mathews.[15]
**The training program should be specific; e.g., swimmers would use a swimming program.

contraction and reflex times.[29] In addition, abrupt, strenuous exercise may be associated with inadequate blood flow to the heart.[3] Preliminary exercise prevents this danger. We recommend inclusion of the following preliminary exercises: (1) stretching exercises for flexibility; (2) calisthenics for development of arm, shoulder, and abdominal strength; and (3) brief and easy activity which you will use during the work interval, thereby placing the body in readiness for maximal effort.

**Stretching Exercises.** Flexibility (stretching) exercises, such as reaching toward the floor without bending the knees, or alternate toe touching, should be performed several times before each workout. These exercises are done (1) to increase the range of motion about a joint, enabling better skill performance; (2) as a precautionary measure against tearing muscle fibers and thus against muscular stiffness and soreness; and (3) as insurance against development of muscular tension in the low back, across the shoulders, and throughout the neck regions. A number of flexibility exercises were given in Chapter 7 (see p. 152). Several or all of these should be performed at least 10 times prior to the workout.

**Calisthenics.** Arm and shoulder girdle strength can be developed effectively through doing pushups, and abdominal strength may be increased through use of bent-knee situps. Running or swimming work intervals certainly develop muscular strength; however, the aforementioned calisthenics will do so more effectively.

In addition to being important for successful athletic performance, satisfactory arm and shoulder girdle strength improve one's appearance; so too with abdominal strength. Even more important, good abdominal strength may serve as an important preventive of low back pain, particularly among the middle aged.

These exercises should, of course, be conducted on a progressive basis, increasing in number and intensity level each week. Intensity of the situp may be increased by exercising on an incline, by holding a weight behind the head, and by increasing speed of performance.

**Easy Work.** It has been said that record performances among athletes have occurred without so-called warm-up. Also, some scientific studies have shown that performances without prior warm-up were no different than after warm-up.[19, 22, 28] Nevertheless, we suggest, whatever the activity, that a few minutes of very moderate rehearsal should occur prior to maximal effort. Why? There are at least three reasons: (1) a person may prevent muscular injury such as tearing muscle fibers ("pulled muscle"); (2) the human machine is perhaps in better physiological preparedness because respiratory and circulatory systems are functioning above resting levels; and (3) psychologically one is ready for maximal or near maximal physical effort.

# INTERVAL TRAINING

Over the past century, there has been a massive assault on athletic performance records. As an example, Figure 12–1 shows the world's best running performances in the 100-meter, 400-meter, 1500-meter, and marathon (42.2 kilometers or 26.2 miles) races since 1900. Notice how sharply the records have fallen. Similar record-breaking trends are common in competitive swimming events as well as in many other sports activities. One of the many factors that undoubtedly has contributed to this phenomenon is improvement in training techniques and methods. Refinement of one such method, interval training (ITP), has probably produced more successful athletes than has any other system of conditioning.

Interval training, as the name implies, is a series of repeated bouts of exercise alternated with periods of relief. Light or mild exercise usually constitutes this relief period. In order to understand why this method of training has been so successful, we will start with a discussion of energy production and fatigue during intermittent work.

## *Energy Production and Fatigue During Intermittent Work*

The information we learned from Chapter 2 concerning energy production during exercise applies, of course, both to work performed intermittently and work performed continuously. However, for our purposes, there is one very important difference.

To illustrate this difference—suppose you ran continuously for as long and as hard as you could for one minute. Then, on another occasion, suppose you ran intermittently, running just as hard as you did continuously, but for only 10 seconds at a time with 30 seconds of rest between each run. If you repeated this six times, you would have performed the same amount of work at the same intensity intermittently as you did continuously (i.e., six runs at 10 seconds each equals one minute of running)—but *the degree of fatigue following intermittent running would be considerably less.*

Let's take another example. This time, suppose you ran an all-out, 5-minute continuous run to exhaustion on one day; then, on another day, you ran five 1-minute intermittent runs at the same speed with 1-minute relief intervals between runs. Again, as before, even though the same amount of work at the same intensity was performed in both types of runs, the *fatigue* following the intermittent runs would be noticeably less. (If you don't believe it, try it.)

Why? The reason for this can be explained physiologically. The answer lies in the different interaction between the ATP-PC and LA systems during intermittent as compared to continuous running. Comparatively, the energy supplied via the LA system will be less and that via the ATP-PC system will be more in the intermittent runs.[16] What this means is that there will be *less lactic acid* accumulated and thus *less fatigue* associated with the intermittent work. This will be true no matter how intense the intermittent work bouts and how long a period they last.

**Replenishing ATP and PC.** How is it possible that the ATP-PC system can supply more ATP and the LA system less ATP during the series of intermittent runs as compared to the continuous run? Didn't we already indicate that the ATP-PC system is exhausted after only a few seconds of all-out running? Yes, we did; however, remember that between each intermittent run there is a *period of relief.* The question that needs answering, then, is, "What, in terms of energy production, is occurring during the relief intervals?"

During the relief intervals, a portion of the muscular stores of ATP and PC that were depleted during the preceding work intervals will be replenished via the aerobic system.[17, 27] This is shown in Figure 12–2. In other words, during the relief intervals, part of the oxygen debt is repaid. Thus, during each run that follows a relief interval, the replenished ATP-PC will again be available as an energy source. Consequently, energy from the LA system will be "spared," so to speak, by that amount, and lactic acid will not accumulate as rapidly nor to as great an extent (see Fig. 12–3). In contrast, during a continuous run,

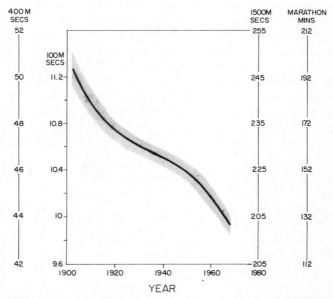

**Figure 12–1** World's best running performances in the 100 meter, 400 meter, 1500 meter and marathon (42.2 kilometers or 26.2 miles) races since 1900. (From Fox and Mathews.[15])

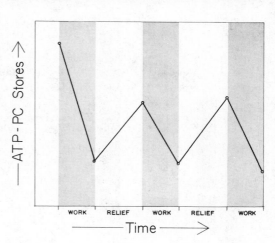

**Figure 12–2** During the relief intervals of intermittent work, a portion of the muscular stores of ATP and PC that were depleted during the preceding work intervals will be replenished via the aerobic system. (From Fox and Mathews.[15])

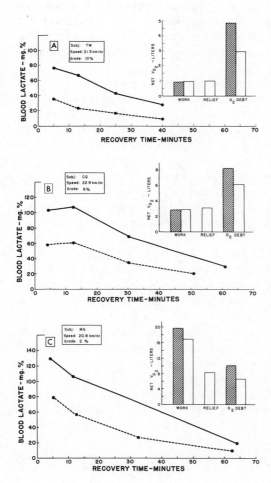

**Figure 12–3** *A*, Blood lactate during recovery from a continuous run (solid line) and interval runs (dashed line) involving the same amount of work. In the continuous run the subject ran for 30 seconds; in the interval run he ran three intervals of 10 seconds each with 20 seconds of rest-relief between intervals. Net $O_2$ consumption ($VO_2$) during work, during the rest-relief intervals, and after work ($O_2$ debt) for the continuous (hatched bar) and interval (open bar) runs are also shown. *B*, similar measurements during and after a continuous run of 60 seconds' duration and an interval run of five 12-second runs with 20 seconds of rest-relief between intervals. *C*, A continuous run of 300 seconds' duration and an interval run of five 60-second runs with 60 seconds of rest-relief between intervals. Symbols the same as in *A*. (From Fox et al.[16]).

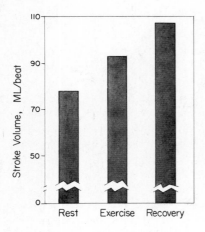

**Figure 12–4** The stroke volume is highest during the recovery period from exercise. During interval training, the stroke volume reaches its highest level many times because of the many relief (recovery) intervals. (Data from Cumming;[9] figure from Fox and Mathews.[15])

the stored ATP-PC will be exhausted within a matter of a few minutes or seconds and will not be replenished until the work is terminated.[17, 18] In this case, energy in the form of ATP from the LA system will be called on early in the run, and LA will rapidly accumulate to exhausting levels.

All of this has real meaning when applied to training, for *the savings in fatigue accompanying intermittent work can be converted to an increase in the intensity of work performed.* This is the single most important feature of intermittent work and as such is the key to the interval training system. It has been shown that an intermittent work level as much as two and one-half times the intensity of the continuous level can be performed before blood lactic acid levels (i.e., fatigue levels) in each are comparable.[2, 6, 16, 21] It has also been shown that the intensity of the work performed during interval training sessions is directly related to the amount of improvement in the energy capacities of the muscles (see p. 293).[12, 13]

The interaction between the ATP-PC and the LA systems during intermittent work also varies slightly according to the type or activity level of the relief interval used. Our discussion thus far has centered around intermittent work using complete rest intervals. During actual interval training, it is recommended that the relief intervals consist of either light or mild work. Later, we will learn when it is best to use one or the other. Right now, the primary difference between intermittent work performed with complete rest intervals as compared to light or mild work-relief intervals is that the blood lactic acid levels will be higher with the latter.[16] This is so because the work performed during the relief interval blocks or partially blocks the replenishment of the ATP-PC stores. Without as much of these stores being renewed, a greater proportion of the energy needed during the work intervals must be supplied via the LA system. In this way, the accumulation of lactic acid will be greater; the harder the work during the relief interval, the greater will be this lactic acid accumulation.

**Stroke Volume During the Relief Interval.** In addition to the important changes that occur with respect to energy production, there is at least one other change that occurs during the relief interval that also contributes to the success of the ITP system. As shown in Figure 12–4, it has been found that the stroke volume of the heart—the amount of blood pumped by the heart at each beat or stroke—is highest not during exercise but during the recovery period from exercise.[9] You will recall from Chapter 10 (p. 216) that the higher the maximal stroke volume, the higher the capacity of the oxygen or aerobic system.[11] This is so because the more blood that is pumped by the heart per beat, the more oxygen that can be transported to the working muscles.

How does this relate to intermittent exercise in general and to interval training specifically? Quite simply, with an intermittent work schedule, there are many "recovery" or relief intervals. Therefore, the stroke volume reaches its highest level many times during the course of an interval training workout. On the other hand, if the work is done on a continuous basis, there is only one relief interval, that which occurs immediately after the workout is over, and only one time during which the stroke volume reaches its highest value. The repeated attainment of peak values of stroke volume over many weeks of interval training provides a good stimulus for improving the maximal stroke volume and thus the capacity of the oxygen system.

Specifically, in regard to the development of the energy systems, intermittent work or the interval training system accomplishes the following:

1. It allows the ATP-PC system to be used over and over. This, in turn, provides an adequate stimulus for promoting an increase in the energy capacity of this system and aids in delaying the onset of fatigue by not delving so deeply into the lactic acid system.

2. With proper regulation of the duration and type of relief interval, the involvement of the lactic acid system will be maximal and thus improved.

3. By working long enough at a sufficient intensity and by improvement in the maximal attainable stroke volume, the aerobic system is developed.

## Interval Training Terms

As mentioned before, interval training is a system of conditioning in which the body is subjected to short but regularly repeated periods of work stress interspersed with adequate periods of relief. It is from these periods of relief that the system derives its name. There are several terms peculiar to describing interval training with which you should be familiar.

*Training.* An exercise program to develop an athlete for a particular event. It involves developing energy potential as well as skill of performance.

*Conditioning.* Primary objective is to develop energy potential through an exercise program; it is not necessarily concerned with skill of performance, as would be the case with training.

*Work Interval.* The portion of the interval training program that consists of the high intensity work effort, for example, a 220-yard run at a prescribed time.

*Relief Interval.* The time between work intervals as well as between sets. The relief interval may consist of (1) light activity such as walking (referred to as rest-relief); (2) mild to moderate exercise such as jogging (referred to as work-relief); or (3) a combination of (1) and (2). The relief interval usually is expressed in relationship to the work interval; together they form the work-relief ratio and may be expressed as follows: 1:½; 1:1; 1:2; or 1:3. A ratio of 1:½ implies that the time of the relief interval is equal to half the time of the work interval; 1:1 indicates that the relief and work intervals are equal; 1:2 indicates that the relief interval is twice as long as the work interval; and 1:3 indicates that the relief interval is three times as long as the work interval. Principles enabling us to note proper work-relief ratios will be explained later in the chapter. With longer work intervals usually a 1:½ or 1:1 work-relief ratio is prescribed; with middle duration intervals a 1:2 ratio, and with shorter work intervals, because of the high intensity, a 1:3 work-relief ratio is prescribed.

*Sets.* A series of work and relief intervals. For example, six 220-yard runs at a prescribed time with designated relief intervals.

*Repetitions.* The number of work intervals within one set. For example, six 220-yard runs may constitute one set and six repetitions.

*Training Time.* The rate at which the work is to be accomplished during the work interval. For example, each 220-yard run might be performed in 33 seconds.

*Training Distance.* The distance of the work interval, e.g., 220 yards.

*Frequency.* The number of times per week for the workout.

*Interval Training Prescription.* Contains pertinent information concerning an interval training workout. It will usually include the number of sets, the number of repetitions, the distance or performance time of the work interval, the training time, and the time of the relief interval. As an example, one set from a prescription for a running program may be written as follows:

SET 1      6 × 220 at 0:33 (1:39)

where:        6 = number of repetitions
         220 = training distance in yards
        0:33 = training time in minutes and seconds
      (1:39) = time of relief interval in minutes and seconds

See Figure 12–5.

### Interval Training Variables

The overload principle as applied to interval training is accomplished through the manipulation of five variables:

(1) Rate and distance of work interval;
(2) Number of repetitions during each workout;
(3) Relief interval or the time between work intervals;
(4) Type of activity during relief interval; and
(5) Frequency of training per week.

There are many advantages to the interval training system as compared to other methods of training. Among these are:

(1) A precise control of the stress;
(2) A systematic day-to-day approach, enabling one to easily observe progress;
(3) More rapid improvement in energy potential than in other methods of conditioning; and
(4) A program that can be performed almost anywhere and that requires no special equipment.

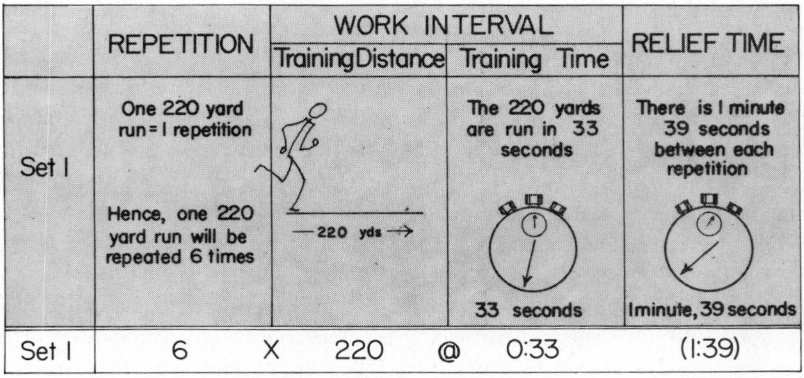

| | REPETITION | WORK INTERVAL | | RELIEF TIME |
| | | Training Distance | Training Time | |
|---|---|---|---|---|
| Set I | One 220 yard run = 1 repetition<br><br>Hence, one 220 yard run will be repeated 6 times | — 220 yds → | The 220 yards are run in 33 seconds<br><br>33 seconds | There is I minute 39 seconds between each repetition<br><br>I minute, 39 seconds |
| Set I | 6 | X    220 | @    0:33 | (1:39) |

**Figure 12–5**   Interpretation of an ITP prescription involving running. (From Fox and Mathews.[15])

## Selecting the Type of Work for the Work Interval

Interval training prescriptions for athletes employ a work interval in which the exercise is specific to that athlete's sport. Swimmers would structure or have their programs developed in accordance with their specific swimming needs, whereas track athletes would employ running.

The type of work chosen for general conditioning is based mainly on preference, since improving a specific sports skill might not be of primary concern. A person could select a single activity that he or she most enjoys, or several activities, e.g., swimming, jogging, jumping rope, cycling, or calisthenics.

## Manipulation of Variables

The variables mentioned previously may be considered in the following manner when constructing the interval program.

**Rate and Distance of Work Interval.** Interval training prescriptions are made up of long duration work intervals performed at low intensities, medium duration intervals performed at moderate intensities, and short work efforts performed at higher intensities. Prescription content depends upon which energy systems are to be enhanced. Thus, for most activities, the interval training prescription can best be written by considering the performance time of the work interval. You will recall that knowing the performance time of an activity allows us to determine the predominant energy system involved (see p. 241). Understanding of the relationship between the predominant energy system and performance time is fundamental in learning how to construct the work intervals of interval training programs.

How is a sufficient rate of work determined? There are several methods by which the proper intensity of the work interval can be calculated:

1. One method, applicable regardless of the type of work or activity used, is based on the *heart rate* response during the work interval. As shown in Table 12–4, for young men and women (less than 20 years old), a heart rate of 190 beats per minute during the work interval would indicate a sufficient work rate. This holds both for athletes and nonathletes. For men and women between the ages of 20–29, 30–39, 40–49, 50–59, and 60–69, heart rates during the work intervals of 180, 170, 160, 150, and 140 beats per minute, respectively, would indicate adequate work rates. The heart rate during the work interval may be estimated by counting the pulse for 6 or 10 seconds immediately after the work interval and multiplying by 10 or 6, respectively (to convert to beats per minute). Accurate pulse counts may be taken at the carotid artery (in the neck) or by holding the hand over the left breast. Use only light pressure at the neck.

2. A second method, again applicable regardless of the type of work, is based on the number of work intervals (repetitions) that can be performed per workout. At a given work rate, if a selected number of repetitions cannot be performed (because of exhaustion), the work rate is too strenuous. On the other hand, if more than the selected number of repetitions can be performed, then that work rate is not sufficiently strenuous. As an illustration, suppose you are using 440 yards as your training distance. The speed of each 440-yard run, therefore, should permit between 6 to 8 repetitions before undue exhaustion.

3. Wilt[30] has worked out a method for determining a sufficient work rate when structuring the *interval training prescription for running* that might be easier than those mentioned above. The times for training distances between 55 and 220 yards should be between 1.5 and 5 seconds slower, respectively, than the best time for those distances measured from running starts. For example, if a person can run 55 yards from a running start in 6 seconds, the training time for this distance would be $6 + 1.5 = 7.5$ seconds. For training distances of 110 and 220 yards, add 3 and 5 seconds, respectively, to the best times taken from running starts.

For training distances of 440 yards, the rate of work would be 1 to 4 seconds less (i.e., the person runs faster) than one-fourth the time required to run a mile. As an illustration, if a person ran the mile in 6 minutes, the average time for each 440 yards would be 90 seconds (360 seconds divided by $4 = 90$ seconds). Therefore, the training time would be between $90 - 4 = 86$ and $90 - 1 = 89$ seconds.

If the training distance is over 440 yards, each 440 yards of that distance should be run at an average speed of 3 to 4 seconds slower than the average 440-yard time in the mile run. For example, in running 880 yards as the training distance, the 6-minute miler would run each 440 yards of the 880 yards in an average time of $90 + 3 = 93$ to $90 + 4 = 94$ seconds.

This method can also be applied to *swimming*. However, the training distances for swimming programs will be one-fourth those used for

### Table 12–4　TARGET HEART RATES DURING ITP WORK INTERVALS (MEN & WOMEN)*

| AGE, YEARS | HEART RATE, BEATS PER MINUTE |
|---|---|
| Under 20 | 190 |
| 20–29 | 180 |
| 30–39 | 170 |
| 40–49 | 160 |
| 50–59 | 150 |
| 60–69 | 140 |

*From Fox and Mathews.[15]

**Table 12–5  GUIDELINES FOR DETERMINING A SUFFICIENT
WORK RATE FOR RUNNING AND SWIMMING
INTERVAL TRAINING PROGRAMS***

| TRAINING DISTANCE (YARDS) | | WORK RATE |
|---|---|---|
| Run | Swim | |
| 55 | 15 | 1½ ⎫ seconds slower than best times from |
| 110 | 25 | 3  ⎬ moving starts |
| 220 | 55 | 5  ⎭ |
| 440 | 110 | 1 to 4 seconds faster than average 440 (run) or 110 (swim) than best times in mile (run) or 440 (swim) |
| 660–1320 | 165–330 | 3 to 4 seconds slower than average 440 (run) or 110 (swim) than best times in mile (run) or 440 (swim) |

*From Fox and Mathews.[15]

running programs. A summary of how to determine a sufficient work rate for running and swimming programs is given in Table 12–5.

**Number of Repetitions.**    The number of repetitions of the work interval is the factor that determines the length of the workout. A total workout distance of between 1.5 and 2 miles will be necessary to achieve maximum improvement. If you should decide to use a training distance of 220 yards on a particular day, it would be necessary to have 12 to 16 repeats. This is the basis upon which the number of repetitions was determined in number 2 above.

**Duration and Type of Relief Interval.**    There are two important considerations when dealing with the relief interval: (1) the time (duration) of the relief interval; and (2) the type of activity during the relief interval.

*1. Time of Relief Interval.*    Recovery heart rate following the work interval is a good indication as to whether or not the individual is physiologically ready for the next work interval or next set. For example, for men and women less than 20 years old, both athletic and nonathletic, the heart rate should drop to at least 150 beats per minute between repetitions and to 120 beats per minute between sets. Recommended heart rate levels between repetitions and between sets for men and women of various ages are given in Table 12–6. Determination of heart rate (pulse) should be made periodically throughout the relief interval by taking 6- or 10-second counts and multiplying by 10 or 6 to convert to beats per minute.

Since it is not always possible to use heart rate as a guide for determining the duration of the relief interval, the work-relief ratio, described earlier (p. 252), can be used. This will guarantee that heart rates will have recovered to or near the values given in Table 12–6.

With longer work intervals (880 yards and over) usually a 1:1 or 1:½ work-relief ratio is prescribed; with middle duration intervals (440 to 660 yards) a 1:2 ratio is used; and with shorter work intervals, because of the high intensity, a 1:3 work-relief ratio is prescribed.

Knowing these work-relief ratios facilitates administration of the interval training program, particularly to groups, as it does not become necessary to time the pulse following each work effort. However, occasional six-second checks must be made toward the end of the relief interval so that work intensity can be increased, decreased, or maintained.

*2. Type of Relief Interval.* What you do during the relief intervals is important, for it also relates to the energy system you may wish to develop. The type of activity may consist of:

1. Rest (i.e., moderate moving about such as walking, or flexing arms and legs; termed "rest-relief")

2. Light or mild exercise including rapid walking and jogging; termed "work-relief"

3. A combination of 1 and 2.

Rest-relief intervals should be used with ITPs designed to modify the ATP-PC energy system. This is so because, during rest-relief intervals, ATP-PC is restored to the muscles and can be used over and over, since it is the prime source of energy for the short exhaustive work intervals. When one is stressing modification of the lactic acid system, work-relief intervals should intervene between work intervals. As you may recall, mild work will inhibit or partially block complete restoration of the ATP-PC energy system. As a consequence, the lactic acid system, rather than the ATP-PC system, is used during subsequent work intervals. Such practice (work-relief) encourages improvement of the lactic acid system. The key to modification of the oxygen system is prevention of lactic acid buildup. Therefore, during the relief interval of a prescription designed for improvement of the oxygen system, rest-relief should prevail.

### Table 12-6  TARGET HEART RATES DURING RELIEF INTERVALS (MEN & WOMEN)*

| | HEART RATE, BEATS PER MINUTE | |
| AGE, YEARS | *Between Repetitions* | *Between Sets* |
|---|---|---|
| Under 20 | 150 | 125 |
| 20–29 | 140 | 120 |
| 30–39 | 130 | 110 |
| 40–49 | 120 | 105 |
| 50–59 | 115 | 100 |
| 60–69 | 105 | 90 |

*From Fox and Mathews.[15]

**Frequency of Training.**   We have found that a 7 to 8 week interval training program with two to three workouts per week is effective in improving all three energy systems.[12, 14] Only minimal further gains will be made over a 13-week program with four or five workouts per week.[14] More will be said concerning frequency of workouts and physiological changes in the next chapter.

## The Group Interval Training Program

Interval training is the method most commonly used by track and swimming coaches to improve the condition and performance of their athletes. As we have stressed, the programs are individually tailored to assure that each athlete receives maximum benefits, depending upon his or her condition and event. Thus the interval training program (ITP) for the sprinter differs from that for the miler; as a matter of fact, in all likelihood it will also differ from one sprinter to another or from one miler to another. For all sports, interval training is a very effective way to train your athletes.[15]

Of considerable additional importance to the physical educator, the ITP, with a minimal amount of time, can also be used to improve the condition of the average person. To do this requires construction of the prescriptions (workouts) on a group basis. Appendix E contains an example of such a program for an 8 week period for both men and women. To administer such a group program one would proceed in the following manner.

The first two weeks will perhaps be the most difficult. Unlike the trained athlete, the nonconditioned individual will be unaccustomed to running; and care must be executed to prevent severe muscle soreness and overindulgence. Your primary objective will be to condition your charges gradually until they can run 1.5 to 2 miles without considerable stress. This should be accomplished in about two weeks with four workouts each week. Running should be easy, allowing the students to select their own paces. Such an approach should enable the participant to be active throughout the entire exercise period. The prescriptions for the first two weeks are given in full in the appendix (p. 538); the first day's prescription is given in Table 12–7.

### Table 12–7   INTERVAL TRAINING PROGRAM PRESCRIPTION, FIRST WEEK

| Day 1 | Repeats (Number) | | Distance (Yards) | | Time | Work Relief Ratio |
|-------|------------------|---|------------------|---|------|-------------------|
| Set 1 | 4 | × | 220 | at | Easy | 1:3 |
| Set 2 | 8 | × | 110 | at | Easy | 1:3 |

**Body of the Training Program.**   After the first two weeks, which should have conditioned the legs sufficiently so that they can stand more strenuous training, sessions should be conducted three times each week, including at least 1.5 to 2.0 miles of running per session. Therefore, during the third week a typical workout prescription might be as follows:

Day 1 Set 1  2 × 660 at 2:15 (4:30)*
      Set 2  2 × 440 at 1:20 (2:40)

(Week 3 in Appendix E)

Day 2 Set 1  4 × 220 at 0:38 (1:54)
      Set 2  4 × 220 at 0:38 (1:54)
      Set 3  4 × 220 at 0:38 (1:54)

Day 3 Set 1  1 × 880 at 3:00 (3:00)

Observe that the total distance for the week is 3¼ miles, with 1¼ miles of longer runs (greater than 440 yd.) and 2 miles of shorter, more intensive sprints (less than 440 yd.).

In keeping with the overload principle, the training process should be accomplished on a progressive basis, with the average workout of each week being more difficult than that of the week before. The progression is accomplished by (1) establishing more intensive work intervals (e.g., running faster); (2) initiating shorter relief intervals (because of the more intensive work interval, the relief interval is necessarily shortened); (3) performing more sets; and (4) a combination of the first three factors. To illustrate, during the last week of an 8 week program, the prescriptions might read as follows:

Day 1 Set 1  2 ×  880 at 2:40 (2:40)
      Set 2  2 ×  440 at 1:16 (2:32)

Day 2 Set 1  4 ×  220 at 0:34 (1:42)
      Set 2  4 ×  220 at 0:34 (1:42)
      Set 3  4 ×  220 at 0:34 (1:42)
      Set 4  4 ×  220 at 0:34 (1:42)

(Week 8 in Appendix E)

Day 3 Set 1  1 × 1320 at 4:24 (2:12)
      Set 2  2 × 1100 at 3:34 (1:47)

Notice that the progression has been accomplished through a combination of the three factors mentioned above. For instance, the intensity of the work interval was increased as reflected by faster running

---

*Work-relief time ratio in minutes:seconds.

times; as a result the duration of the relief interval was reduced; and more sets were performed so that the total distance run per week was increased from 3¼ to 5½ miles.

The response of virtually every person undergoing such a training program is different, and the program frequently has to be adjusted to allow for these differences. However, nearly every person who trains in this fashion benefits from the program, provided that he or she adheres to the above outline.

### Administering the Group Program

**Open Field.** Although the interval program may be conducted either on an open field or a track, it may be easier, in working with larger groups, to run in a field where a 440-yard straightaway can be marked out. All distances up to 440 yards may be performed by having the participants run first in one direction, then in the other, between two lines the desired distance apart. Distances greater than 440 yards may be run around pegs at either end of the 440-yard straightaway.

**Conducting the Program on a 220-Yard Track.** A 220-yard track may be laid out. It may be constructed of cinders or rubberized asphalt. The runs on such a track are laid out as follows:

*55 Yards.* Fifty-five-yard runs are performed on a marked straightaway on the track's infield. Runners go first in one direction, then return to the start on the next run.

*110 Yards.* Runs of 110 yards are executed around one curve of the track from a starting line to marked finish lines in each lane. Runners may then turn around to do the next run in the reverse direction, but each runner stays in his or her own lane.

*220 Yards.* This distance is run in lanes from staggered starting marks to a finish line. The runner in the inside lane runs exactly one lap of the track.

*440 Yards and Up.* All of these training runs are conducted in multiples of 220 yards. The participants start and finish at the same place. Runners are not required to run in lanes.

**Administering the Running Program.** Two persons are needed to conduct the training program, one person being stationed at the start and another at the finish. Each of these people should have a stop watch, preferably one with a split hand. At the beginning of each run, the runners are started with the commands: "Take your marks!", "Get Set!", "Go!" At the command, "Go!" both watches are started. The person at the start times the relief interval and the person at the finish calls off the time in seconds as the runners cross the finish line. The runners themselves are then able to estimate their running times to approximately a half-second.

**Organizing the Workout.** In general, it is easiest to have the runners run in three groups (group *A*, group *B*, and group *C*). Thus, group *A* runs first, then performs the relief interval while groups *B* and *C* are running, then runs again. The time of each group's relief interval is approximately twice the time it takes to complete the succeeding run. This work-to-relief ratio of 1:2 has been found to be satisfactory in that the heart rate of the majority of the group will be at or below the recommended 140 beats per minute before they begin their next work interval. By having four people run in each of the six running lanes in each group, 24 people may be included in each of the three groups, so that a total of 72 people may run at one workout. More may participate by increasing the number of people in each lane. The fastest person, however, must be first in each lane, with the slowest person going last. This is done to make certain that each person can run at his or her own pace.

**Controlling Stress.** It should be remembered that the times included for the various work intervals are only *target* times, and that people vary in their abilities to run. After the first two weeks of the program, the time of each work interval should be individually adjusted, and should be strenuous enough to raise the heart rate to the level recommended in Table 12–4. This may be checked on any individual during the few seconds *immediately* following the work interval by counting the pulse for 10 seconds and multiplying by six to yield a minute rate. If after the first couple of work intervals in a set, the heart rate does not approach the recommended level, the individual should be encouraged to run faster.

In running each set, the runners should be told to maintain an average time by running the first work intervals of a set slightly slower than the target time, and finishing the set with work intervals that are faster than the target times. Thus, a set of six 110-yard runs with a target time of 16 seconds might be run in the following manner:

(1) 17.0 seconds
(2) 16.5 seconds
(3) 16.0 seconds
(4) 16.0 seconds
(5) 15.5 seconds
(6) 15.0 seconds

**Overstress.** Occasionally, a runner will run too hard and will not recover between work intervals as he or she should. When this happens, the individual should wait until the heart rate drops to the level mentioned above. He or she may then run again, but if the heart rate does not recover within the relief interval, the runner should be dropped from the workout for the remainder of the day. Exhaustion is

Table 12-8  PERTINENT INFORMATION FOR WRITING INTERVAL TRAINING PRESCRIPTIONS BASED ON TRAINING TIMES*

| Major Energy System | Training Time (MIN:SEC) | Repetitions per Workout | Sets per Workout | Repetitions per Set | Work-Relief-Ratio | Type of Relief Interval |
|---|---|---|---|---|---|---|
| ATP-PC | 0:10 | 50 | 5 | 10 | | Rest-Relief (e.g., walking, flexing) |
| | 0:15 | 45 | 5 | 9 | | |
| | 0:20 | 40 | 4 | 10 | 1:3 | |
| | 0:25 | 32 | 4 | 8 | | |
| ATP-PC-LA | 0:30 | 25 | 5 | 5 | | Work-Relief (e.g., light to mild exercise, jogging.) |
| | 0:40–0:50 | 20 | 4 | 5 | 1:3 | |
| | 1:00–1:10 | 15 | 3 | 5 | | |
| | 1:20 | 10 | 2 | 5 | 1:2 | |
| LA-$O_2$ | 1:30–2:00 | 8 | 2 | 4 | 1:2 | Work-Relief |
| | 2:10–2:40 | 6 | 1 | 6 | | |
| | 2:50–3:00 | 4 | 1 | 4 | 1:1 | Rest-Relief |
| $O_2$ | 3:00–4:00 | 4 | 1 | 4 | 1:1 | Rest-Relief |
| | 4:00–5:00 | 3 | 1 | 3 | 1:½ | |

*Modified from Fox and Mathews.[15]

the enemy of training. If runners are allowed to exhaust themselves, it may be several days before they are capable of another good workout.

Another problem is soreness. Some fatigue is natural, of course, but exhaustion and soreness, particularly soreness of the hip, thigh, and front of the leg (shin splints) must be guarded against. Soreness is the signal for overstress. It may require medical attention, but whether or not it is treated medically, a person with acute or chronic soreness should not be allowed to run in an interval training program until completely recovered.

## Summary of the Interval Training System

Before going on to other kinds of conditioning methods, let's summarize the interval training system.

1. Determine which energy system(s) needs to be increased.
2. Select the type of activity (exercise) to be used during the work interval.
3. Using Tables 12-8 and 12-9, write the training prescriptions according to the information appearing in the row opposite the major energy systems you wish to be improved. The number of repetitions and sets, the work-relief ratio, and the type of relief interval are all given in the tables. For any activity selected, the training times given in Table 12-8 (second column) may be used. However, if the activity is either running or swimming, it

is more common to use training distance as shown in the second column of Table 12–9.

4. Provide for an increase in intensity (progressive overload) throughout the training program.

# OTHER CONDITIONING METHODS

Although interval training is an excellent system for conditioning athletes of any sport as well as for nonathletes interested in general fitness, it is not the only training method available today. Some of the conditioning methods presented below are also effective in improving specific fitness levels required for many sports and activities. Generally, as was the case with interval training, these methods were developed mainly by track-and-field and swimming coaches to meet the specific needs of their athletes. However, again as with interval training, with some adaptations these methods can be used to bring about the specific changes required to improve the fitness and health of those who use them.

### Continuous Running

This method, as the name implies, involves continuous running (or swimming) for relatively long distances. Wilt[30] classifies continuous running programs into two categories, *continuous slow-running training* and *continuous fast-running training*. We have added a third category, *jogging*. In all cases, the aerobic or oxygen system is the predominant source of

**Table 12–9  PERTINENT INFORMATION FOR WRITING INTERVAL TRAINING PRESCRIPTIONS BASED ON TRAINING DISTANCES***

| Major Energy System | Training Distance Yards | | Repetitions per Workout | Sets per Workout | Maximal Reps per Set | Work-Relief-Ratio | Type of Relief Interval |
|---|---|---|---|---|---|---|---|
| | *Run* | *Swim* | | | | | |
| ATP-PC | 55 | 15 | 50 | 5 | 10 | 1:3 | Rest-Relief (e.g., |
| | 110 | 25 | 24 | 3 | 8 | | walking, flexing) |
| ATP-PC-LA | 220 | 55 | 16 | 4 | 4 | 1:3 | Work-Relief (e.g., |
| | 440 | 110 | 8 | 2 | 4 | 1:2 | light to mild exercise, jogging) |
| LA-$O_2$ | 660 | 165 | 5 | 1 | 5 | 1:2 | Work-Relief |
| | 880 | 220 | 4 | 2 | 2 | 1:1 | Rest-Relief |
| $O_2$ | 1100 | 275 | 3 | 1 | 3 | 1:½ | Rest-Relief |
| | 1320 | 330 | 3 | 1 | 3 | 1:½ | |

*Modified from Fox and Mathews.[15]

**Table 12–10   A BASIC JOGGING SCHEDULE FOR MEN AND WOMEN** *

| STEPS | 1 MILE CHECK TIME (MIN:SEC) | TOTAL TARGET TIME FOR 2 MILES (MIN:SEC) |
|---|---|---|
| 1. Slow walk | 20:00 | 40:00 |
| 2. Alternate ¼ mile slow walk & ¼ mile fast walk | 18:00 | 36:00 |
| 3. Fast walk | 16:00 | 32:00 |
| 4. Alternate 330 yds. fast walk & 110 yds. slow jog | 14:30 | 29:00 |
| 5. Alternate 220 yds. fast walk & 220 yds. slow jog | 13:00 | 26:00 |
| 6. Alternate ¼ mile fast walk & ¼ mile slow jog | 13:00 | 26:00 |
| 7. Alternate ½ mile slow jog & ¼ mile fast walk | 11:30 | 23:00 |
| 8. Alternate ¾ mile slow jog & ¼ mile fast walk | 11:30 | 23:00 |
| 9. Slow jog | 10:00 | 20:00 |
| 10. Alternate ¼ mile fast jog & ¼ mile slow jog | 9:30 | 19:00 |
| 11. Alternate ¼ mile slow jog & ¼ mile fast jog | 9:00 | 18:00 |
| 12. Alternate ½ mile slow jog & ½ mile fast jog | 9:00 | 18:00 |
| 13. Alternate ½ mile fast jog & ¼ mile slow jog | 8:30 | 17:00 |
| 14. Alternate ¼ mile slow jog & ¾ mile fast jog | 8:30 | 17:00 |
| 15. Fast jog | 8:00 | 16:00 |
| 16. Alternate ¼ mile fast jog & ¼ mile faster jog | 7:30 | 15:00 |
| 17. Alternate ½ mile fast jog & ½ mile faster jog | 7:30 | 15:00 |
| 18. Faster jog | 7:00 | 14:00 |

*Modified from Roby and Davis.[26]

energy, and therefore continuous running programs develop endurance capacity (maxVo$_2$).

**Continuous Slow-Running.**   This means running for long distances at a slow speed or pace. This type of running is sometimes referred to as LSD, i.e., long, slow distance. The pace will vary from runner to runner but always should be fast enough to bring the heart rate to 150 beats per minute.[30] The distance covered should be related to the runner's specialty event. Generally, runners should cover between two to five times the distance of their racing event. For example, a miler would cover 3 to 5 miles, a 3-miler 6 to 12 miles, and a 6-miler 12 to 18 miles.[30] Because running such distances is monotonous on a track, they are usually covered over natural terrain (e.g., golf courses or roads).

Continuous slow-running is also used by marathon (26.2 miles) and ultra-marathon (52.5 miles) runners. How does one prepare to run a 52.5 mile race? For one such runner, Ted Corbitt,[7] a typical weekly workout schedule would include a 30-mile run on Sunday, 20 miles each of the other mornings (Monday through Saturday), and an additional 11.6 to 13 miles each evening. This requires an average of four hours each day. Several times each month, Ted runs 62 miles in one day. In a month of training, he is able to cover more than 800 miles, more than most family cars accumulate in the same period! Most of his training distance is covered at a rate of between seven and eight minutes per mile, since very little emphasis is placed on speed.

**Continuous Fast-Running.** This differs from slow running in that the pace is faster, resulting in earlier fatigue, and less distance is covered. As examples, an 880-yard runner might run 3/4 to 1½ miles, repeating the distance one to four times; a 6-miler might run 8 to 10 miles at a steady but fast pace, or run four to five miles on 2 to 3 occasions.[30]

**Jogging.** This is a term used to include all speeds of running, but it usually refers to slow continuous running.[26] Recently, jogging has gained a great deal of popularity, particularly among adults seeking fitness for health reasons. For example, the improvement in the circulatory and respiratory systems resulting from jogging programs serves as a prophylaxis against coronary disease.

Jogging programs, like competitive programs, vary a great deal. A reasonable basic schedule to follow is contained in Table 12–10. Whenever the goal of one step is achieved, no matter how long it takes, the jogger should proceed to the next step. The frequency of the training sessions should be three days per week, jogging two miles at each session.

### Repetition Running

Repetition running is similar to interval training but differs in (a) the length of the work interval, and (b) the degree of recovery between repetitions.[30] The lengths of the work intervals in repetition running are usually between 880 yards and 2 miles, and recovery between repetitions are more complete (e.g., a recovery heart rate well below 120 beats per minute).

There are basically two forms of repetition running:[20, 30]

1. Running one-half the race distance at or faster than race pace. This is repeated so as to accumulate from 1.5 to 2 times the race distance. For example, a 4-minute, 30-second (4:30) miler would run 3 to 4 repeats of ½ mile each at a pace of between 2:10 and 2:15. Remember, the recovery between repetitions should be nearly complete.

2. Running three quarters of the race distance at slower than race pace. Again, repetitions should allow 1.5 to 2 times the race distance. For example, a 10-minute 2-miler might run 2 to 3 repeats of 1½ miles, each at a speed of about 7:48. The pace is determined by taking the average race pace for each ¼ mile plus 3 seconds (in our example, $75 + 3 = 78$ seconds average per 440 yards $\times 6$ quarter-miles $= 7:48$ per 1½ miles).

Repetition running develops either aerobic or anaerobic capacities, depending on whether the pace is slow or fast, respectively.

## Speed Play or Fartlek Training

Speed play or fartlek (a Swedish word meaning "speed play") training is said to be the forerunner of the interval training system. It involves alternating fast and slow running over natural terrain. It can be thought of as an informal interval training program in that neither the work nor relief intervals are precisely timed. Such a program will develop both aerobic and anaerobic capacities. An example of a training schedule for one workout using the fartlek method is as follows:[8]

1. Warm up by running easily for 5 to 10 minutes.
2. Run at a fast, steady speed over a distance of ¾ to 1¼ miles.
3. Walk rapidly for 5 minutes.
4. Practice easy running, broken by sprints of 65 to 75 yards, repeating until fatigue becomes evident.
5. Run easily, injecting 3 to 4 swift steps occasionally.
6. Run at full speed uphill for 175 to 200 yards.
7. Run at a fast pace for 1 minute.
8. Finish the routine by running 1 to 5 laps around the track, depending on the distance run in competition.

## Sprint Training

This type of training is used by sprinters to develop speed (ATP-PC system) and muscular strength.[30] Here, repeated sprints at *maximal* speed are performed. About six seconds are required to accelerate to maximum speed from a static start. Therefore, the sprinter should run at least 60 yards on each sprint in order to experience moving at top speed.[30] Also, because each sprint should be performed at top speed, recovery between repetitions must be complete.

## Interval Sprinting

Interval sprinting is a method of training whereby an athlete alternately sprints 50 yards and jogs 60 yards for distances up to 3 miles.[30] Because of fatigue setting in after the first few sprints, the athlete will not be able to run subsequent sprints at top speed. This factor, plus the relatively long distances covered per training session (up to three miles), makes this type of training system suitable for the development of the aerobic system.

## Acceleration Sprints

As the name implies, acceleration sprints involve a gradual increase in running speed from jogging to striding and finally to sprinting.[10, 30] The jogging, striding, and sprinting intervals may consist of

**Table 12-11  VARIOUS TRAINING METHODS AND DEVELOPMENT OF THE ENERGY SYSTEMS***

| | DEVELOPMENT (PER CENT) | | |
|---|---|---|---|
| TYPE OF TRAINING | *ATP-PC* | *Aerobic System* | *L.A.* <br> *(Anaerobic System)* |
| Interval Training | 10–30 | 20–60 | 30–50 |
| Continuous Slow-Running | 2 | 93 | 5 |
| Continuous Fast-Running | 2 | 90 | 8 |
| Jogging | — | 100 | — |
| Repetition Running | 10 | 40 | 50 |
| Speed Play (Fartlek) | 20 | 40 | 40 |
| Sprint Training | 90 | 4 | 6 |
| Interval Sprinting | 20 | 70 | 10 |
| Acceleration Sprints | 90 | 5 | 5 |
| Hollow Sprints | 85 | 5 | 10 |

*Modified from Wilt.[30]

50-yard to 120-yard segments. In each case, recovery should consist of walking. For example, a sprinter may jog 50 yards, stride 50 yards, sprint 50 yards, walk 50 yards, and then repeat. Because recovery between repetitions is nearly complete, this type of training develops speed and strength. Also, it is a good method to use in cold weather, since the runs are graduated from easy to hard, thus lessening the chances of muscular injury.[10, 30]

### Hollow Sprints

Hollow sprints involve use of two sprints interrupted by a *hollow* period of either jogging or walking. These sprints are performed in repeats; one repetition might include sprinting 60 yards, jogging 60 yards, then walking 60 yards. Similar intervals might include distances up to but not beyond 220 yards.

A summary of the various training methods as they relate to development of the energy systems is given in Table 12–11.

## SUMMARY

The basic tenets in any conditioning or training program are as follows: (1) to recognize the major energy source utilized in performing a given activity and (2) then, through the overload principle, to construct a program that will develop that particular energy source more than will any other. The primary energy system for any activity can be determined on the basis of its performance time. The overload principle requires (1) that the exercise resistance (intensity) be maximal; and (2) that it be increased gradually as fitness improves throughout the course of the training program.

Off-season training should consist mainly of weight training and low intensity running. Pre-season training should contain the high intensity training program, and in-season training should consist mainly of drills, scrimmages, and competitive performances.

Warm-up prior to any training session should include stretching exercises, calisthenics, and easy work.

The interval training system involves repeated bouts of hard work alternated with periods of lighter work or rest. Intermittent work delays fatigue and allows for maximal intensity during the work intervals. Manipulation of the rate and distance of the work interval, the number of repetitions, and the time and type of relief interval provides for a training program that can meet the needs of nearly every person, athlete or nonathlete.

Other training methods include continuous slow-running (LSD), continuous fast-running, jogging, and interval sprinting primarily for development of the oxygen system; and sprint training, acceleration sprints, and hollow sprints primarily for development of the ATP-PC and LA systems. Interval training, repetition running, and speed play (fartlek) training improve both aerobic and anaerobic systems.

## QUESTIONS

1.  Discuss the basic tenets of any conditioning or training program.

2.  How can one determine which energy system(s) predominates in any sport or activity?

3.  What are the phases of athletic training, and what kinds of programs should they contain?

4.  Why is preliminary exercise (warm-up) important from a physiological standpoint?

5.  Describe the ingredients of a good warm-up program.

6.  Define interval training.

7.  Physiologically, explain why intermittent work, and thus the interval training system, is successful in improving all three energy systems.

8.  There are five variables you may manipulate in fulfilling the requirements of the overload principle. Describe each one.

9.  Discuss the method by which you might estimate the training times in running 55 to 1320 yards in an interval training program.

10. In an interval training program, on what do the time and type of relief interval depend?

11. Discuss several different training programs that develop primarily the aerobic system.

12. Discuss several different training programs that develop primarily the anaerobic systems.

## REFERENCES

1. Asmussen, E., and Boje, O.: Body temperature and capacity for work. Acta Physiol. Scand., 10:1–22, 1945.
2. Åstrand, I., Åstrand, P., Christensen, H., and Hedman, R.: Intermittent muscular work. Acta Physiol. Scand., 48:448–453, 1960.
3. Barnard, R., Gardner, G., Diaco, N., MacAlpin, R., and Kattus, A.: Cardiovascular responses to sudden strenuous exercise—heart rate, blood pressure, and ECG. J. Appl. Physiol., 34(6):833–837, 1973.
4. Breiner, A.: A Comparison of High School and College Athletes on Selected Physiologic and Anthropometric Variables. Doctoral Dissertation, The Ohio State University, 1969.
5. Carlile, F.: Effects of preliminary passive warming-up on swimming performance. Res. Quart., 27:143–151, 1956.
6. Christensen, E., Hedman, R., and Saltin, B.: Intermittent and continuous running. Acta Physiol. Scand., 50:269–287, 1960.
7. Costill, D., and Fox, E.: The ultra-marathoner. Distance Running News, 3(4):4–5, 1968.
8. Cretzmeyer, F., Alley, L., and Tipton, C.: Track and Field Athletics. 8th ed. St. Louis, C. V. Mosby Co., 1974.
9. Cumming, G.: Stroke volume during recovery from supine bicycle exercise. J. Appl. Physiol., 32:575–578, 1972.
10. Dintiman, G.: What Research Tells The Coach about Sprinting. Washington, D.C., American Alliance for Health, Physical Education, and Recreation, 1974.
11. Ekblom, B., and Hermansen, L.: Cardiac output in athletes. J. Appl. Physiol., 25:619–625, 1968.
12. Fox, E.: Differences in metabolic alterations with sprint versus endurance interval training. *In* Howald, H., and Poortmans, J. (eds.): Metabolic Adaption to Prolonged Physical Exercise. Basel, Switzerland, Birkhäuser Verlag, 1975, pp. 119–126.
13. Fox, E., Bartels, R., Billings, C., Mathews, D., Bason, R., and Webb, W.: Intensity and distance of interval training programs and changes in aerobic power. Med. Sci. Sports, 5:18–22, 1973.
14. Fox, E., Bartels, R., Billings, C., O'Brien, R., Bason, R., and Mathews, D.: Frequency and duration of interval training programs and changes in aerobic power. J. Appl. Physiol., 38(3):481–484, 1975.
15. Fox, E., and Mathews, D.: Interval Training: Conditioning for Sports and General Fitness. Philadelphia, W. B. Saunders Co., 1974.
16. Fox, E., Robinson, S., and Wiegman, D.: Metabolic energy sources during continuous and interval running. J. Appl. Physiol., 27:174–178, 1969.
17. Hultman, E., Bergstrom, J., and McLennan Anderson, N.: Breakdown and resynthesis of phosphorylcreatine and adenosine triphosphate in connection with muscular work in man. Scand. J. Clin. Lab. Invest., 19:56–66, 1967.
18. Karlsson, J., and Saltin, B.: Lactate, ATP and CP in working muscles during exhaustive exercise in man. J. Appl. Physiol., 29:598–602, 1970.
19. Karpovich, P., and Hale, C.: Effect of warming-up upon physical performance. J.A.M.A., 162:1117–1119, 1956.

20. Kennedy, R.: Track and Field for College Men. Philadelphia, W. B. Saunders Co., 1970.
21. Margaria, R., Oliva, R., diPrampero, P., and Cerretelli, P.: Energy utilization in intermittent exercise of supramaximal intensity. J. Appl. Physiol., 26:752–756, 1969.
22. Mathews, D., and Snyder, H.: Effect of warm-up on the 440-yard dash. Res. Quart., 30:446–451, 1959.
23. Michael, E., Skubic, V., and Rochelle, R.: Effect of warm-up on softball throw for distance. Res. Quart., 28:357–363, 1957.
24. O'Connor, H.: Warm-up as an aid to track performance. Scholastic Coach, 25, 1955.
25. Pacheco, B.: Improvement in jumping performance due to preliminary exercise. Res. Quart., 28:55–63, 1957.
26. Roby, F., and Davis, R.: Jogging for Fitness and Weight Control. Philadelphia, W. B. Saunders Co., 1970.
27. Saltin, B., and Essen, B.: Muscle glycogen, lactate, ATP, and CP in intermittent exercise. In Pernow, B., and Saltin, B. (eds.): Muscle Metabolism During Exercise. New York, Plenum Press, 1971, pp. 419–424.
28. Skubic, V., and Hodgkins, J.: Effect of warm-up activities on speed, strength, and accuracy. Res. Quart., 28:147–152, 1957.
29. Tipton, C., and Karpovich, P.: Exercise and the patellar reflex. J. Appl. Physiol., 21(1):15–18, 1966.
30. Wilt, F.: Training for competitive running. In Falls, H. (ed.): Exercise Physiology. New York, Academic Press, 1968, pp. 395–414.

## SELECTED READINGS

Armbruster, D., Allen, R., and Billingsley, H.: Swimming and Diving. 6th ed. St. Louis, C. V. Mosby Co., 1973.
Councilman, J.: The Science of Swimming. Englewood Cliffs, N.J., Prentice-Hall, Inc., 1968.
Doherty, J.: Modern Track and Field. 2nd ed. Englewood Cliffs, N.J., Prentice-Hall, Inc., 1963.
Doherty, J.: Modern Training for Running. Englewood Cliffs, N.J., Prentice-Hall, Inc., 1964.
Fox, E., and Mathews, D.: Interval Training: Conditioning for Sports and General Fitness. Philadelphia, W. B. Saunders Co., 1974.

———————————————————

# PHYSIOLOGICAL EFFECTS OF PHYSICAL TRAINING

In the previous chapter we discussed some basic principles related to construction of physical training programs. These programs, when applied over a sufficient time period, cause physiological changes that lead to greater energy-yielding capabilities and improved physical performances.

The purpose of this chapter is to explore these changes with respect to the physiological mechanisms involved as well as to the relevant training factors.

## TRAINING EFFECTS

The effects of training can be studied most easily by classifying the changes as follows: (1) those occurring at the tissue level, that is, biochemical changes; (2) those occurring systemically, that is, those affecting the circulatory and respiratory systems, including the oxygen transport system; and (3) other changes such as those concerned with body composition, blood cholesterol and triglyceride levels, blood pressure changes, and changes with respect to heat acclimatization.

## Biochemical Changes

Much new information concerning the effects of physical training at the cellular or biochemical level has been made available only recently. Excellent reviews concerning these changes have been written by Gollnick and Hermansen[35] and Holloszy.[41, 41A]

**Aerobic Changes.**   There are three major aerobic adaptations that occur in skeletal muscle as a result of physical training.

*1. Increased Myoglobin Content.*   Myoglobin content in skeletal muscle has been shown to be substantially increased following training.[64] The training program involved rats and consisted of treadmill running, five days per week for 12 weeks. This response is specific in that the myoglobin increased only in those muscles involved in the training program (leg muscles).

As was mentioned earlier (p. 109), myoglobin is an oxygen-binding pigment similar to hemoglobin. In this respect, it acts as a store for oxygen. However, this is considered a minor function in contributing to the improvement of the aerobic system. Its main function is in aiding the delivery (diffusion) of oxygen from the cell membrane to the mitochondria where it is consumed.

*2. Increased Oxidation of Carbohydrate (Glycogen).*   Training increases the capacity of skeletal muscle to break down (oxidize) glycogen to $CO_2 + H_2O$ with ATP production. In other words, the capacity of the muscle to generate energy aerobically is improved. Evidence for this change is an increase in the maximal oxygen consumption ($max\dot{V}o_2$). More will be said about this later.

There are two major subcellular adaptations that contribute to the muscle cells' increased capacity to oxidize carbohydrate following training: (a) an increase in the *number* and *size* of the *mitochondria* in skeletal muscle fibers;[34, 40, 47] and (b) an increase in the *level of activity* or *concentration* of the *enzymes* involved in the Krebs cycle and electron transport system.[5, 7, 40, 59] Several studies[34, 40, 47] have shown increases in both the number and size of mitochondria following training. For example, in one study involving humans,[47] there was a 120 per cent increase in the number of mitochondria in the vastus lateralis muscle following a 28 week, five day per week training program of distance running and calisthenics. This too is probably a specific response, occurring only in those muscle fibers involved in the training program.

You will recall from Chapter 2 that the many metabolic reactions involved in the Krebs cycle and electron transport system are controlled by the presence of specific enzymes. An increased level of activity of these enzymes as a result of training means that more ATP can be produced in the presence of oxygen. The levels of activity of these enzymes have been shown to double in the course of a 12 week, five day per week training program.[40]

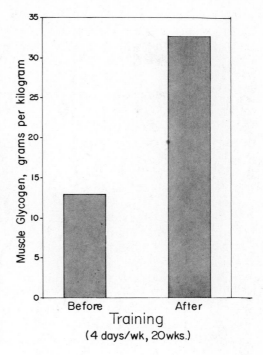

**Figure 13–1** Human skeletal muscle normally contains between 13 and 15 grams of glycogen per kilogram of muscle. After training, this amount has been shown to increase as much as 2.5 times. (Based on data from Gollnick et al.[35])

Aside from the increased ability of muscle to oxidize glycogen, there is also an increase in the amount of glycogen stored in the muscle following training.[35, 36] You will recall from Chapter 2 (p. 19), that human skeletal muscle normally contains between 13 and 15 grams of glycogen per kilogram of muscle. After training, this amount has been shown to increase 2.5 times[35] (see Fig. 13–1). This increase in glycogen storage is due, at least in part, to the fact that training causes an increase in the activity of glycogen synthetase,[80] an enzyme required for the synthesis of glycogen in human skeletal muscle.

The initial level of muscle glycogen is directly related to aerobic or endurance capacity (see p. 405). It is easy to see how the mitochondrial and enzyme changes mentioned above plus the increased glycogen storage in the muscles work together in effectively improving all aspects of the aerobic capabilities of the muscle.

*3. Increased Oxidation of Fat.* Like glycogen, the breakdown (oxidation) of fat to $CO_2 + H_2O$ with ATP production in the presence of oxygen is increased following training.[58, 59] It should be remembered that fat can and does serve as a major source of fuel for skeletal muscle during endurance exercises. Thus, an increased capacity to oxidize fat is a definite advantage in increasing the performance of such activities. Actually, at a given submaximal work load, the trained person oxidizes more fat and less carbohydrate than does the untrained person.[38, 74, 76] During exercise with heavy but submaximal work loads, a greater fat oxidation would mean less lactic acid accumulation and thus less fatigue.

The increase in the muscles' capacity to oxidize fat is related to two factors: (a) training causes a greater release of fatty acids from adipose tissue, i.e., the availability of fats as a fuel is increased; and (b) the activity of the enzymes involved in the activation, transport, and breakdown of fatty acids is increased. This latter factor includes both the enzymes necessary to break down the large fat molecules into smaller units in preparation for entry into the Krebs cycle and electron transport system (called beta oxidation) as well as the enzymes mentioned earlier that work within these latter series of reactions themselves.

The effects of training on the aerobic potential of skeletal muscle are summarized in Figure 13–2.

**Anaerobic Changes.** The anaerobic changes in skeletal muscle resulting from training involve increased capacities of (1) the ATP-PC system; and (2) anaerobic glycolysis, that is, the lactic acid system.

*1. Increased Capacity of the ATP-PC System.* The capacity of the ATP-PC system is enhanced by two major biochemical changes: (a) increased levels of muscular stores of ATP and PC; and (b) an increased activity of a key enzyme, called creatine kinase, in the ATP-PC system.

Muscular stores of ATP have been shown to increase approximately 25 per cent (from 3.8 to 4.8 millimoles per kg. of wet muscle) following a training program of distance-running for 7 months for two to three days per week.[45] Also, the concentration of PC in the muscles

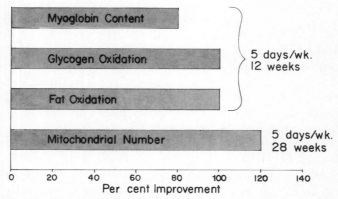

**Figure 13–2**   The effects of training on the aerobic potential of skeletal muscle include increases in myoglobin, glycogen and fat oxidation, and the size and number of mitochondria. (Based on data from Pattengale and Holloszy;[64] Holloszy;[40] Molé et al.;[58] and Kiessling et al.[47])

of boys 11 to 13 years of age increased nearly 40 per cent after four months of training.[22] Since these phosphagens represent the most rapidly available source of energy for the muscle, their increased storage correlates well with the improved execution of activities requiring only a few seconds to perform that is also a consequence of physical training.

As mentioned above, training alters a key enzyme of the ATP-PC system.[79, 82A] You will remember that in the ATP-PC system, ATP is resynthesized from the energy released when PC is broken down. The breakdown of PC is facilitated by an enzyme called *creatine kinase*. In a recent study,[82A] the activity of this enzyme was found to increase by 36 per cent following an eight week training program. Thus, not only is the storage of PC increased by training but also its rate of breakdown is enhanced. These mutually beneficial changes clearly demonstrate that the rapid release of energy by the muscle cell is alterable through proper training programs.

*2. Increased Glycolytic Capacity.* Not nearly as much information concerning the effects of training on the anaerobic pathway (lactic acid system) is available compared to that for the aerobic system. Nevertheless, a number of well-designed studies have indicated that several of the key enzymes that control glycolysis are significantly altered by physical training. For example, the activity of one such enzyme, phosphofructokinase (PFK), which is important in the early reactions of glycolysis, doubled following training in one study[35] and increased by 83 per cent in another.[22] Other important glycolytic enzymes have also been reported to increase following training.[4, 79]

The significance of increased glycolytic enzyme activities is that they speed up the rate and quantity of glycogen broken down to lactic acid. Therefore, the ATP energy derived from the lactic acid system is increased also and thus contributes to the improved performance of activities that depend heavily on this system for energy. Evidence for an increased glycolytic capacity following training is also demonstrable by the ability to accumulate significantly greater quantities of blood lactic acid following maximal exercise (see p. 289).

The changes in the ATP-PC and lactic acid systems as a result of training are shown in Figure 13–3.

**Relative Changes in Red and White Fibers.** The changes just noted do not all occur to the same degree in the red or slow-twitch and white or fast-twitch fibers. There is, in other words, a specific response in red and white fibers with respect to the changes induced by training. Some of these specific changes are as follows:

(1) In the case of aerobic changes, it is fairly well agreed that the aerobic potential of skeletal muscle following training is increased equally in both red and white fibers.[3, 35] This means that the inherent differences in oxidative capacity between the fiber types is not altered

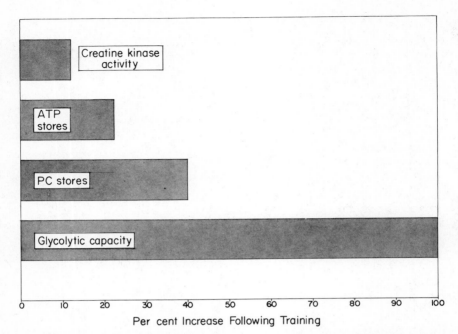

Per cent Increase Following Training

**Figure 13–3** The effects of training on the anaerobic potential of skeletal muscle include increases in creatine kinase activity, muscular stores of ATP and PC, and in glycolytic capacity. (Based on data from Staudte et al.;[79] Karlsson et al.;[45] Eriksson et al.;[22] and Gollnick et al.[35])

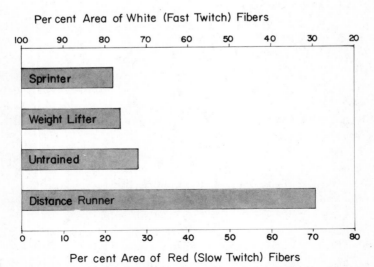

**Figure 13–4** Training produces a selective hypertrophy of red and white skeletal muscle fibers. The red fibers of endurance athletes occupy a greater area of the muscle than do the white fibers. However, the white fibers occupy a greater area in weightlifters and sprinters. (Based on data from Gollnick et al.[36])

### Table 13-1   BIOCHEMICAL CHANGES INDUCED BY PHYSICAL TRAINING

Aerobic Changes
  ↑ ed* myoglobin content
  ↑ ed oxidation of glycogen
    ↑ ed number and size of mitochondria
    ↑ ed activity of Krebs cycle and ETS enzymes
    ↑ ed muscular storage of glycogen
  ↑ ed oxidation of fat
    ↑ ed availability of fats as fuel
    ↑ ed activity of enzymes involved in activation, transport and breakdown of fatty acids
Anaerobic Changes
  ↑ ed capacity of the ATP-PC system
    ↑ ed muscular stores of ATP and PC
    ↑ ed activity of creatine kinase
  ↑ ed glycolytic capacity
    ↑ ed glycolytic enzyme activities
Relative Change in Red and White Fibers
  ↑ ed aerobic capacity equal in both fibers
  ↑ ed glycolytic capacity greater in white fiber
    selective hypertrophy

\* ↑ ed = increased.

by training. In other words, the red or slow-twitch fiber has a higher aerobic capacity compared to the white or fast-twitch fiber after as well as before training.

(2) Changes in the glycolytic capacity appear to be more specific, being greater in the white or fast-twitch fibers.[24, 35]

(3) Evidence suggests that there is a selective hypertrophy of red and white fibers. For example, the red-fibers occupy a greater area of the muscle in endurance athletes than do the white fibers.[36] By the same token, the white fibers occupy a greater area in weight-lifters and sprinters (see Fig. 13-4). This information implies a selective hypertrophy dependent upon the kind of training and/or sports activities performed by the athletes.

A summary of the biochemical changes in skeletal muscle resulting from physical training is given in Table 13-1.

### Cardiorespiratory (Systemic) Changes

The cardiorespiratory (systemic) changes induced by training include those that affect mainly the oxygen transport system. As pointed out in Chapter 10, the oxygen transport system involves many circulatory, respiratory, and tissue level factors, all working together for one common goal—to deliver oxygen to the working muscles. First we will discuss some changes that are demonstrable under resting conditions, and then we will outline the systemic changes that are prominent during submaximal and maximal exercise.

**Cardiorespiratory Changes at Rest.**   There are five main changes resulting from training that are apparent at rest: (1) changes in heart size; (2) a decreased heart rate; (3) an increased stroke volume; (4) increased blood volume and hemoglobin; and (5) changes in skeletal muscles.

*1. Changes in Heart Size.*   It has been known for a long time[50] that the size (volume) of the heart is greater in athletes than in nonathletes (see Table 21–2, p. 472 and Fig. 21–9C, p. 462). However, until recently, not much was known concerning the details of this cardiac hypertrophy because the technique commonly used for its measurement (chest X-ray) is not capable of delineating exact dimensional characteristics of the heart. At present, a noninvasive* technique called echocardiography provides a sensitive means for assessing, among other factors, the size of the cavity of the ventricles and the thickness of the myocardial (heart muscle) wall. One or both of these factors could account for an increase in heart size. Using this method, the following has been found concerning cardiac dimensions of athletes and nonathletes:

(a) The cardiac hypertrophy of endurance athletes (e.g., distance runners and swimmers) is characterized by a *large ventricular cavity* and a *normal thickness* of the ventricular wall.[60, 62] This means that the volume of blood that fills the ventricle during diastole is also larger. We will soon see that this effect causes the stroke volume capabilities of the endurance athlete to be greater than those of the nonathlete as well as those of the nonendurance athlete.

(b) The cardiac hypertrophy of nonendurance athletes, that is, athletes engaged in high-resistance or isometric types of activities such as wrestling and putting the shot, is characterized by a *normal-sized ventricular cavity* and a *thicker ventricular wall.*[60] Therefore, even though the magnitude of the cardiac hypertrophy in these athletes is the same as in endurance athletes, their stroke volume capabilities are no different from those of their nonathletic counterparts.

Previously, it was thought that heredity plays a dominant role in determining heart size. However, it is clear from the above information that differences in cardiac hypertrophy are related to the type of sport or activity performed or trained for by the athlete, thus indicating that heart size is influenced by training. This idea is also supported by the recent finding that heart volume is not as genetically dependent as is, for example, the maximal oxygen consumption.[54] In addition, the heart volumes of nonathletes have increased significantly following several months of physical training.[31] The fact that heart volume does not always increase following physical training[20, 32] suggests that the train-

---

*Noninvasive refers to measurements made from outside the body rather than those made by "invading" the body with hypodermic needles or catheters, for example.

ing program must be intense and that it probably should be maintained over a long period of time, perhaps even years, before the change is effected.

The above information gathered from echocardiography has also provided insight into the types of stimuli required to elicit changes in cardiac function. For example, training for endurance activities usually requires prolonged efforts during which the cardiac output is sustained at high levels.[26] The response to this type of stimulus, which may be called volume stress, is cardiac hypertrophy through an increase in the size of the ventricular cavity. On the other hand, athletes who participate in and train for brief but powerful activities such as wrestling and putting the shot are not subjected to volume stress but rather to intermittently elevated arterial blood pressure similar to that generated during straining. The cardiac hypertrophy in response to this stimulus is a thickening of the ventricular wall.

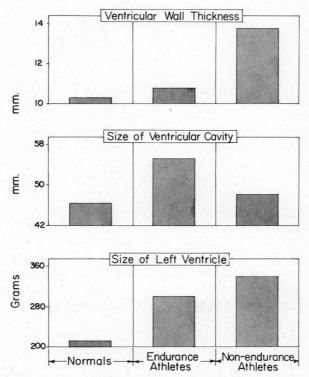

**Figure 13–5**  The cardiac hypertrophy of endurance athletes is characterized by a large ventricular cavity with a normal thickness of the wall. On the other hand, the cardiac hypertrophy of non-endurance athletes is characterized by a thicker ventricular wall with a normal-sized ventricular cavity. (Based on data from Morganroth et al.[60])

We mentioned in Chapter 7 that hypertrophy of skeletal muscle is accompanied by an increase in capillary density. So too is cardiac hypertrophy.[19, 56, 81, 82] Such an effect provides for better blood flow to the heart and most likely serves as a prophylactic treatment against coronary heart disease.

The different types of cardiac hypertrophy resulting from physical training are shown in Figure 13–5.

*2. Decreased Heart Rate.*  The resting *bradycardia* (decreased heart rate) resulting from training is (a) most evident when athletic and nonathletic subjects are compared (see Fig. 13–6*A*); (b) less evident but still clear-cut when sedentary subjects undergo a training program; and (c) least distinct when athletes are studied in the untrained versus the trained state.[30] This information points out that (a) the training bradycardia is dependent upon a long time period (maybe years) of intensive training, and (b) the magnitude of the decrease in resting heart rate produced by training is less when the level of fitness is greater. It should also be noted (see Fig. 13–6*A*) that the magnitude of the bradycardia is the same in endurance and nonendurance athletes. Apparently, neither the different training programs nor the different types of cardiac hypertrophy resulting from them significantly influences the magnitude of the bradycardia.

What causes this training bradycardia at rest? You will recall (p. 231) that the heart is supplied by two major autonomic nerves, the sympathetic nerves, which increase the heart rate, and the vagus nerves (parasympathetic nerves), which decrease the rate when stimulated. With this dual system, the heart rate can be decreased either by: (a) a parasympathetic inhibition (i.e., an increased vagal tone); or (b) a decreased sympathetic influence (drive); or (c) a combination of (a) and (b). The evidence thus far indicates that the resting bradycardia due to physical training is a result of a parasympathetic inhibition.[30, 83, 84]

*3. Increased Stroke Volume.*  Since the resting cardiac output is approximately the same for trained and nontrained subjects, it is easy to see (since Q = S.V. × H.R.) that the resting stroke volume of athletes or trained subjects will be higher than that of their nonathletic counterparts[8, 60] (Fig. 13–6*B*). Notice that the increased stroke volume is most pronounced in endurance athletes. As mentioned earlier, these athletes have an increased ventricular cavity, thus allowing more blood to fill the ventricle during diastole, resulting in a larger stroke volume. Another contributing factor to an increased resting stroke volume following training is an increased myocardial contractility[66] (see p. 210).

The change in resting stroke volume as a result of training is most pronounced when athletes are compared to nonathletes. This again points out that this effect probably requires a long-term intensive training program. Therefore, in some studies in which previously untrained

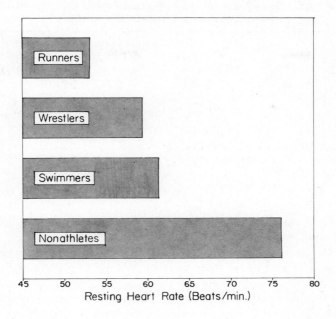

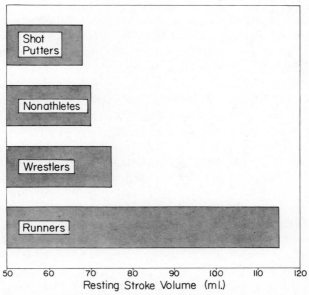

**Figure 13–6** *A,* Training induces a resting bradycardia (a decreased heart rate). *B,* Training induces an increased resting stroke volume. Note that the magnitude of the bradycardia is the same in endurance and non-endurance athletes but that the increase in stroke volume is most pronounced in endurance athletes. (Based on data from Morganroth et al.[60])

**Table 13-2 CHANGES IN HEMOGLOBIN AND BLOOD VOLUME
FOLLOWING PHYSICAL TRAINING**[*]

| VARIABLE | TRAINING STATE | | PER CENT INCREASE |
| --- | --- | --- | --- |
| | *Before* | *After* | |
| Hemoglobin | | | |
| Total, gm. | 805 | 995 | 24 |
| gm./kg. body wt. | 11.6 | 13.7 | 17 |
| Blood Volume | | | |
| Total, liters | 5.25 | 6.58 | 25 |
| ml./kg. body wt. | 75.0 | 90.1 | 20 |

[*]Based on data from Kjellberg et al.[49]

subjects have been trained for only several months, an increased resting stroke volume does not always occur.[20]

*4. Changes in Blood Volume and Hemoglobin.* Both the total blood volume and hemoglobin increase with training.[49, 63] An example of such changes is given in Table 13-2 (see also Table 21-2, p. 472). That the total blood volume and hemoglobin levels are important with respect to the oxygen transport system is evidenced by the fact that they both are closely correlated with the maxV̇o$_2$ (Fig. 21-9, p. 461). Blood volume and hemoglobin also play important roles during exercise at altitude (Chapter 16). In addition, since deep body heat is carried by the blood to the periphery, where it can then be dissipated, blood volume is important during exercise in the heat (Chap. 17).

*5. Changes in Skeletal Muscle.* As previously indicated, hypertrophy of skeletal muscle resulting from weight training programs is generally accompanied by an increase in capillary density. Long-term endurance training, for competition in running, swimming, or cycling, for instance, also causes muscular hypertrophy and increased capillary density in skeletal muscle.[39] This effect is shown in Figure 13-7, which indicates that the muscle fibers of highly trained endurance athletes (maxV̇o$_2$ = 71.4 ml/kg.-min.) were found to be 30 per cent larger than those of a group of untrained subjects (maxV̇o$_2$ = 50.2 ml/kg.-min.) of the same age. In addition, for the athletes it was determined that each muscle fiber was supplied on the average by 1.5 capillaries, whereas for the untrained subjects, the average capillary supply per fiber was only 1 (see Fig. 13-7C). The supply of oxygen and other nutrients to, and the removal of waste products from, the muscle are all enhanced because there are more capillaries per fiber.

A summary of the changes induced by physical training at rest is given in Table 13-3.

**Changes During Submaximal Exercise.** Several important changes in the functioning of the oxygen transport and related systems

A

**Figure 13–7** Training results in hypertrophy of skeletal muscle and increased capillary density. The muscle fibers of the highly trained endurance athletes *(B)* are 30 per cent larger and have 50 per cent more capillaries *(C)* than the fibers of the untrained subjects *(A)*. (Based on data from Hermansen and Wachtlova.[39])

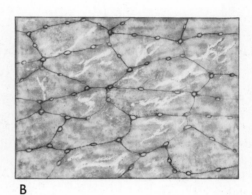

B

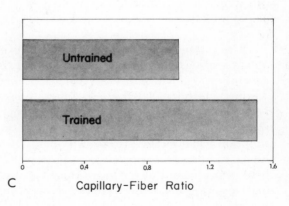

C                    Capillary-Fiber Ratio

following training are evidenced during steady-state, submaximal exercise. These major changes, as shown in Figure 13–8, are as follows:

*1. No Change or Slight Decrease in Oxygen Consumption.* The oxygen consumption during exercise at a given submaximal work load is the same[28, 74] or slightly lower[20, 29] before as compared to after training. The decrease is due to an increase in mechanical efficiency (skill). A

### Table 13-3  CHANGES INDUCED BY TRAINING AT REST

Cardiac hypertrophy
   ↑ ed* ventricular cavity (endurance athletes)
   ↑ ed myocardial thickness (nonendurance athletes)
↓ ed heart rate
   ↑ ed vagal tone (parasympathetic inhibition)
↑ ed stroke volume
   cardiac hypertrophy
   ↑ ed myocardial contractility
↑ ed blood volume and hemoglobin
↑ ed skeletal muscle hypertrophy and capillary density

---

\* ↑ ed = increased;  ↓ ed = decreased.

decrease in oxygen consumption is most pronounced in comparisons of highly trained athletes and untrained individuals. Such a difference is also evident between good and average runners (see Fig. 4–6, p. 61).

*2. Decrease in Lactic Acid Production.*  Training causes a decrease in the accumulation of lactic acid during a given submaximal exercise.[20, 25, 29, 45] This is an important change, since most work, including that performed during training sessions, is to a large extent submaximal. This factor is illustrated in distance running, which requires submaximal effort over extended periods of time. Not only must these runners have a highly developed aerobic power (max$\dot{V}o_2$), but also in order to be successful they must be able to employ a large fraction of that power with minimal accumulation of lactic acid.[17] This allows the runners to maintain a fast pace throughout the race without experiencing early fatigue.

The physiological mechanisms responsible for a decreased accumulation of lactic acid during submaximal work following training are not entirely known. However, a possible mechanism could be a result of some of the biochemical changes discussed earlier that occur in skeletal muscles. For example, since training increases the number and size of muscle mitochondria, the steady state in which oxygen consumption balances the breakdown of ATP to ADP + Pi during exercise will be attained at lower concentrations of ADP + Pi. Since the levels of these phosphagens also control the rate of glycolysis to a large extent, their lower levels after training would cause the rate of lactic acid production to be slower during exercise at the same work load.[41, 42] Later we will see how this relates to differences in changes induced by sprint versus endurance type training programs.

*3. No Change or Slight Decrease in Cardiac Output.*  During submaximal exercise at a given load or $\dot{V}o_2$, the cardiac output of trained subjects is sometimes slightly lower than and sometimes the same as that of untrained subjects (see p. 207). The reason for this discrepancy is not

## STEADY STATE, SUBMAXIMAL WORK

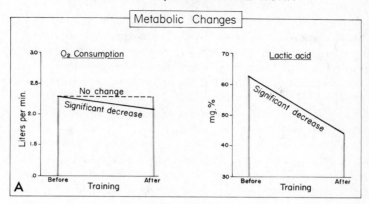

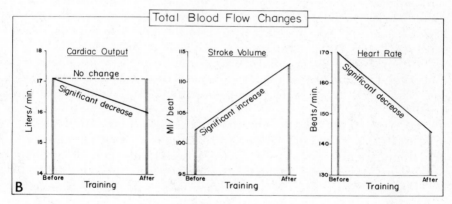

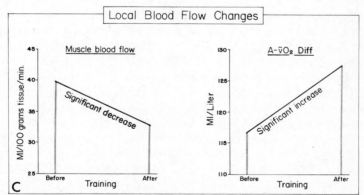

**Figure 13–8**  Important changes in the functioning of the oxygen transport and related systems during submaximal work following training include no change or slight decrease in oxygen consumption; decreased lactic acid production; no change or slight decrease in cardiac output; increased stroke volume; decreased heart rate; and a decreased blood flow per kilogram of working muscle. (Based on data from Ekblom et al.;[20] Frick et al.;[31] and Grimby et al.[37])

known. However, it may be related to the type, intensity, and duration of the training programs involved.

*4. Increased Stroke Volume.*   The stroke volume is increased during submaximal exercise at a given work load following training.[8, 29, 31, 75] As in the case of the increased resting stroke volume, this exercise effect is related mainly to the increased size of the ventricular cavity also promoted by training; the greater the amount of blood filling the cavity, the greater will be the stroke volume. It should also be remembered that one of the most important components of the oxygen transport system is the stroke volume (see p. 215).

*5. Decreased Heart Rate.*   Perhaps the most consistent and pronounced change associated with training is a decreased heart rate during submaximal exercise following training.[20, 27, 28, 29, 30, 31, 76] As in the case of the resting bradycardia, this decrease is most pronounced in comparisons of nonathletic subjects and highly trained athletes. It should also be pointed out again that a slower-beating heart is more efficient, requiring less oxygen than a faster-beating heart at the same cardiac output level (p. 210).

Although the resting bradycardia is caused by a parasympathetic inhibition, the bradycardia during exercise is caused by *a decreased sympathetic drive.*[30] In turn, a decreased sympathetic drive could have two origins:

(a) An *intracardiac mechanism,* that is, an effect directly on the heart muscle itself, may be responsible. For example, we have already seen that training causes an increased stroke volume during submaximal work. Thus, at the same or slightly decreased cardiac output, the need for a higher heart rate through sympathetic stimulation is greatly reduced.[30]

(b) An *extracardiac mechanism,* that is, an indirect effect resulting from alterations in the trained skeletal muscles, may be the cause. For example, we know from Chapter 11 (p. 234) that sympathetic stimulation to the heart can be modified by nervous impulses arising from the muscles and joints and by descending impulses from the motor cortex. A reduced heart rate resulting from these kinds of modifications would mean that the training effect on the heart is secondary to the primary changes occurring in the trained skeletal muscles.[15, 29]

*6. Changes in Muscle Blood Flow.*   Contrary to what you might think, blood flow per kilogram of working muscle is *lower* in trained than in untrained individuals at the same absolute submaximal work load.[37, 41, 51] The working muscles compensate for the lower blood flow in the trained state by extracting more oxygen.[41] This is evidenced by a greater arterial–mixed venous oxygen difference (a-$\bar{v}$ $O_2$ diff.) and may be related to the biochemical changes mentioned earlier that occur in the skeletal muscles.

As previously mentioned, the total blood flow (i.e., cardiac output)

### Table 13-4    CHANGES INDUCED BY TRAINING DURING SUBMAXIMAL EXERCISE

---

No change or slight decrease in $\dot{V}_{O_2}$
↓ ed* lactic acid production
   ↑ ed number and size of mitochondria
No change or slight decrease in cardiac output
↑ ed stroke volume
   cardiac hypertrophy
   ↑ ed myocardial contractility
↓ ed heart rate
   ↓ ed sympathetic drive
↓ ed blood flow per kg. muscle
   ↑ ed oxygen extraction by muscles

---

* ↑ ed = increased;  ↓ ed = decreased.

either remains the same or is slightly lower after training during exercise at the same work load as before training. In the case where the cardiac output is the same, a decreased muscle blood flow would mean that more blood is made available for the nonexercising areas such as the skin. During exercise in the heat, this would be an advantage with respect to heat elimination. On the other hand, a reduced blood flow to the muscles would account for the reduction in cardiac output sometimes observed.

All of the above submaximal exercise changes induced by training tend to reduce the relative stress imposed on the oxygen transport and related systems. In other words, a given amount of submaximal exercise becomes "more submaximal" as a result of physical training. A summary of the changes induced by training during submaximal exercise is given in Table 13-4.

**Changes During Maximal Exercise.**    It is common knowledge that physical training greatly increases maximal working capacity. Some of the physiological changes that are necessary to bring about such an improvement are shown in Figure 13-9.

*1. Increased max$\dot{V}_{O_2}$.*    The effects of training on the amount of oxygen that can be consumed per minute during maximal exercise has been studied extensively; there is little doubt that it is increased with training.[1, 2, 20, 25, 27, 28, 32, 75] The magnitude of the increase in max$\dot{V}_{O_2}$ varies considerably and is dependent upon a number of factors, as we will point out later. However, an average improvement of between 5 and 20 per cent can be anticipated for college-age male or female students following 8 to 12 weeks of training. The max$\dot{V}_{O_2}$ is highest in athletes who compete and train for endurance types of activities.[73]

As you probably know by now, the max$\dot{V}_{O_2}$ is a measure of the functional capacity of the oxygen system, or the cardiorespiratory system, or the oxygen transport system. It is considered by most exercise

MAXIMAL EXERCISE

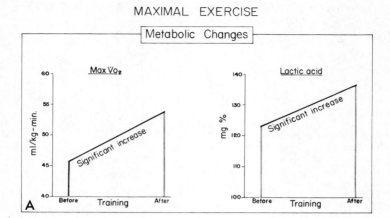

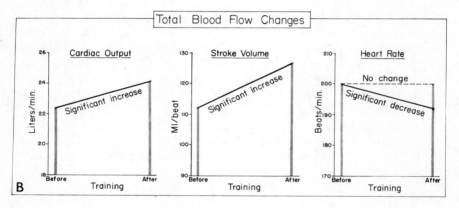

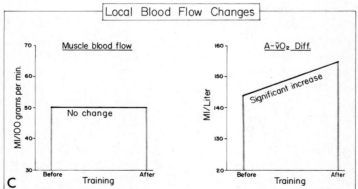

**Figure 13–9** Important changes in the functioning of the oxygen transport and related systems during maximal work include the following: increased max$\dot{V}O_2$; increased lactic acid production; increased cardiac output; increased stroke volume; no change or slight decrease in heart rate; and no change in muscle blood flow per kilogram of working muscle. (Based on data from Ekblom et al.[20] and Grimby et al.[37])

physiologists to be the single most accurate measure of endurance fitness. In Chapter 22, we present several methods for both direct and indirect measurement of the $\text{max}\dot{V}_{O_2}$.

The increase in $\text{max}\dot{V}_{O_2}$ is brought about by two main factors: (a) an increased oxygen delivery to the working muscles through an increased cardiac output; and (b) an increased oxygen extraction from the blood by the skeletal muscles. We will now examine the causes of an increased maximal cardiac output. As mentioned earlier, increased oxygen extraction is related to the biochemical changes that occur in the muscles and that also are a result of training.

A logical question to ask at this time is, "Which factor limits $\text{max}\dot{V}_{O_2}$, the cardiac output or the ability of the skeletal muscles to extract oxygen from the blood?" It is not possible at present to answer this question. For those who wish a review of the subject, start with Dr. Rowell's paper.[71]

*2. Increased Cardiac Output.* As was just indicated, the maximal cardiac output increases with training. The magnitude of change is similar to that of the $\text{max}\dot{V}_{O_2}$. The maximal attainable cardiac output and the $\text{max}\dot{V}_{O_2}$ are directly related; the former is a factor in determining the latter. As would be expected, maximal cardiac output is greatest in highly trained endurance athletes[21] (see p. 207).

The cardiac output, you will recall, is the product of stroke volume and heart rate. Since the maximal heart rate is either unchanged or slightly decreased following training, the increased cardiac output following training is entirely due to an increase in stroke volume.

*3. Increased Stroke Volume.* The increase in maximal stroke volume resulting from training is related to the cardiac hypertrophy and increased myocardial contractility described earlier. A larger ventricular volume coupled with an increased force of contraction allows for a maximal output of blood with each beat.

The single most important feature that distinguishes the athlete who has been training for several years from the sedentary person who has been training for only a few months is the magnitude of the stroke volume.[20, 72] In other words, the stroke volume is a major determinant of the magnitude of the cardiac output and thus of the $\text{max}\dot{V}_{O_2}$.

*4. No Change or Slight Decrease in Heart Rate.* The maximal attainable heart rate is either unchanged or decreases slightly following training. Although the decrease in maximal heart rate is particularly evident in athletes engaged in endurance training,[73] short-term training of previously sedentary subjects can also cause a slight (3 to 10 beats/min.) but significant decrease in maximal heart rate.[20, 27, 28]

A decrease in maximal heart rate with training is probably related to two factors: (a) an increased heart volume due to cardiac hypertrophy; and (b) a decreased sympathetic drive.

*5. Increased Lactic Acid Production.* One of the biochemical changes induced by training is an increase in the glycolytic (lactic acid system) capacity. This increase is evidenced by the ability to produce greater quantities of blood lactic acid during exhaustive maximal work. Thus more ATP energy can be generated through this metabolic pathway, thereby improving the performance or working capacity of activities that rely heavily on this system for energy.

6. *No Change in Muscle Blood Flow.* Even during maximal exercise, the blood flow per kilogram of muscle is no different for the trained or untrained individual.[37] This should not be interpreted to mean that the blood flow to the *entire* working muscle mass is lower after training. In fact, it has been shown that the blood flow to the total working musculature is indeed greater during maximal work following training.[75] How can this apparent contradiction be resolved? The answer lies in the fact that since the maximal work load is greater after training, it is likely that the total muscle mass required to perform the work is also greater. In other words, the increased blood flow is distributed over a larger muscle mass, thus keeping the flow per kilogram of muscle constant.[72]

A summary of the changes induced by physical training during maximal work is given in Table 13–5.

**Respiratory Changes.** So far, we have discussed cardiorespiratory changes resulting from training that are concerned mainly with circulatory functions. What about respiration? In Chapter 8, we presented several respiratory changes that appear to be a result of physical training (see pp. 165–184). Let's review them now.

(1) Maximal minute ventilation is increased following training. Since ventilation is not a limiting factor for the $max\dot{V}o_2$, the increase in maximal ventilation should be considered secondary to the increase in

**Table 13–5  CHANGES INDUCED BY TRAINING DURING MAXIMAL WORK**

↑ ed* $max\dot{V}o_2$
  ↑ ed total blood flow (cardiac output)
  ↑ ed oxygen extraction by muscles
↑ ed lactic acid production
  ↑ ed glycolytic enzyme activities
↑ ed cardiac output
  ↑ ed stroke volume
↑ ed stroke volume
  cardiac hypertrophy (ventricular cavity)
  ↑ ed myocardial contractility
No change or slight decrease in heart rate
  ↑ ed heart volume
  ↓ ed sympathetic drive
No change in blood flow per kg. working muscle
  blood flow distributed over larger muscle mass

* ↑ ed = increased;  ↓ ed = decreased.

$max\dot{V}o_2$. Nevertheless, the increase is brought about by increases in both tidal volume and breathing frequency.

(2) Training causes an increased ventilatory efficiency. A higher ventilatory efficiency means that the amount of air ventilated at the same oxygen consumption level is lower than in untrained individuals. Since the oxygen cost of ventilation increases greatly with increasing ventilation, a greater ventilatory efficiency, particularly over a prolonged effort (e.g., the marathon) would result in less oxygen to the respiratory muscles and more to the working skeletal muscles.

(3) The various lung volumes measured under resting conditions (with the exception of tidal volume) are larger in trained than in untrained individuals. The majority of these changes can be attributed to the fact that training results in improved pulmonary function and therefore in larger lung volumes. It should be mentioned, however, that there is little, if any, correlation between athletic performance and these lung volume changes.

(4) Athletes tend to have larger diffusion capacities at rest and during exercise than do nonathletes. This is particularly true for endurance athletes (see Fig. 9–5, p. 192). It is thought that diffusion capacity *per se* is not directly affected by training but rather that the larger lung volumes of athletes provide a greater alveolar-capillary surface area.

### Other Training Changes

Besides biochemical changes and changes in the cardiorespiratory system, training produces other important alterations. Some of these are concerned with (1) body composition; (2) blood cholesterol and triglyceride levels; (3) blood pressure; and (4) heat acclimatization.

**Changes in Body Composition.**    The changes in body composition induced by training are as follows: (a) a decrease in total body fat; (b) no change or slight increase in lean body weight; and (c) a small decrease in total body weight.[9, 68, 69, 87] For the most part, these changes, particularly that of fat loss, are more pronounced for obese men and women than for the already "lean" individual (see p. 475).

In discussing changes in body composition, it is important to keep in mind that loss of body fat is dependent upon the balance between calories taken in and calories expended (see Chaps. 18 and 22). The significance of this observation is that the caloric cost of running and walking is independent of speed. In terms of how many calories are expended, it is not how *fast* you run or walk, but rather how *far* you travel. Also, it is important to note that (1) more calories are expended when running rather than walking a given distance; and (2) women expend more calories per kilogram of body weight than do men either

### Table 13–6  CALORIC EXPENDITURES FOR WALKING AND RUNNING VARIOUS DISTANCES FOR MEN AND WOMEN*

| DISTANCE | | CALORIC EXPENDITURE, Kcal/kg. BODY WT.** | | | |
| --- | --- | --- | --- | --- | --- |
| | | Walking | | Running | |
| mi. | km. | Men | Women | Men | Women |
| 0.5 | 0.8 | 0.54 | 0.58 | 0.79 | 0.87 |
| 1.0 | 1.6 | 1.08 | 1.15 | 1.57 | 1.73 |
| 1.5 | 2.4 | 1.62 | 1.73 | 2.36 | 2.60 |
| 2.0 | 3.2 | 2.16 | 2.30 | 3.14 | 3.46 |
| 2.5 | 4.0 | 2.70 | 2.88 | 3.93 | 4.33 |
| 3.0 | 4.8 | 3.24 | 3.45 | 4.71 | 5.19 |
| 3.5 | 5.6 | 3.78 | 4.03 | 5.50 | 6.06 |
| 4.0 | 6.4 | 4.32 | 4.60 | 6.28 | 6.92 |
| 4.5 | 7.2 | 4.86 | 5.18 | 7.07 | 7.79 |
| 5.0 | 8.0 | 5.40 | 5.75 | 7.85 | 8.65 |

*Based on data from Howley and Glover.[43]
**To find your total caloric expenditure, multiply the value in the table by your body weight in kilograms (1 kg. = 2.2 lb.).

walking or running a given distance.[43] The approximate caloric expenditures for walking and running various distances are given in Table 13–6.

**Changes in Cholesterol and Triglyceride Levels.**    Regular exercise programs cause decreases in both blood cholesterol and triglyceride levels. This change is particularly apparent in individuals who initially have very high blood levels prior to training[57] (see also p. 475).

**Changes in Blood Pressure.**    Following training, blood pressure at the same absolute work load is lower than before training.[48] Furthermore, individuals with hypertension (p. 475) show significant reductions in resting diastolic and systolic blood pressures as well.[10, 57]

**Changes in Heat Acclimatization.**    Heat acclimatization involves physiological adjustments that allow us to work more comfortably in the heat. As is pointed out in Chapter 17 (p. 381), physical training promotes a high degree of heat acclimatization even if the training sessions are not carried out in hot environments. For example, interval training produces 50 per cent of the total physiological adjustment resulting from heat acclimatization.

The increased heat acclimatization promoted by physical training apparently is stimulated by the large amounts of heat produced during the training sessions. This causes increases in skin and body temperatures comparable to those encountered while working in hot environments.

A summary of the changes induced by training on respiration and other systems is given in Table 13–7.

**Table 13-7   CHANGES INDUCED BY TRAINING ON RESPIRATION AND OTHER SYSTEMS**

Respiratory changes
  ↑ ed* maximal minute ventilation
    ↑ ed tidal volume
    ↑ ed breathing frequency
  ↑ ed ventilatory efficiency
  ↑ ed lung volumes
  ↑ ed diffusion capacity
Other changes
  Changes in body composition
    ↓ ed total body fat
    no change or slight increase in lean body weight
    ↓ ed total body weight
  ↓ ed blood cholesterol and triglyceride levels
  ↓ ed exercise and resting blood pressures
  ↑ ed heat acclimatization

* ↑ ed = increased;  ↓ ed = decreased.

# FACTORS INFLUENCING TRAINING EFFECTS

The effects of training are influenced by many factors, including (1) the intensity of the training sessions; (2) the frequency per week of the training sessions and the duration of the training programs; (3) the type of training program, i.e., the specificity of training effects; (4) genetic limitations; (5) the mode of exercise used during the training program; and (6) maintenance of training effects.

## Intensity of Training

Several studies have shown that with continuous types of training programs, intensity of the training sessions is of paramount importance in guaranteeing maximal gains in fitness.[18, 23, 46, 77, 78] With interval training we have also found this to be true.[16, 27, 28] For example, as shown in Figure 13–10$A$, as the intensity of the training program is increased, the improvement in max$\dot{V}o_2$ is likewise increased.

Two other points are apparent from Figure 13–10$A$. First, the intensity factor as given on the abscissa (horizontal axis) is in relation to the individual's initial fitness level, in this case to the initial max$\dot{V}o_2$. In other words, intensity is relative; what is intense for one person may be easy for another. This is one reason that different people respond differently to similar training programs. Actually, the gains in max$\dot{V}o_2$ are inversely related to the initial max$\dot{V}o_2$ levels, irrespective of the intensity of the training program.[28, 55, 72] This effect is shown in Figure 13–

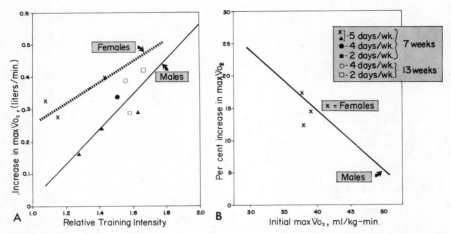

**Figure 13–10** A, The intensity of the training sessions is of paramount importance in guaranteeing maximal gains in fitness; as the intensity of the training program is increased, the improvement in maxV̇o₂ is likewise increased. Note that the improvement in maxV̇o₂ is greater in females than in males at the same relative intensity. B, The gains in maxV̇o₂ are inversely related to the initial maxV̇o₂ levels, irrespective of the intensity of the training program; the lower the initial maxV̇o₂, the greater the improvement with training. (Based on data from Fox et al.[28] and Cohen and Fox.[16])

10B. Thus, the lower the initial maxV̇o₂, the greater the improvement with training.

Second, the improvement in maxV̇o₂ is greater in females than in males at the same relative intensity[16] (see Fig. 13–10A). The reason for this is not immediately apparent. However, it does not seem to be due to the lower initial maxV̇o₂ of the females, since as shown in Figure 13–10B, the relationship between improvement in maxV̇o₂ and initial maxV̇o₂ is the same for men and women. Because of the limited number of training studies conducted on women thus far, the significance of this interesting trend will have to await more extensive studies using women as subjects. For now we can say that females respond to training at least as well, if not better, than do males (see Chap. 21).

So far we have discussed training intensity in relation to changes produced in maxV̇o₂ only. What about other training-induced changes? Are they also related to intensity? For the most part, the answer to the latter question is yes. For example, the biochemical changes referred to earlier are more pronounced in more intensive training programs.[41] Also, as we have emphasized throughout our discussion, the magnitude of most training effects is greatest in the athlete whose competitive training program is very intensive and least in the sedentary individual who has trained only moderately.

We need to point out at this time that there is at least one exception to this intensity rule. The exercise bradycardia induced by training does not appear to be related to training intensity; instead, it is related to the frequency and duration of the training programs. More will be said about this later.

The positive relationship between training intensity and the magnitude of the training effect has been implied for many years. There is a *threshold intensity* of training above which significant gains in fitness occur. This threshold level of intensity varies from individual to individual and is, as we have indicated, related to the initial level of fitness ($\max\dot{V}O_2$) of the participant. How can one determine an individual's intensity threshold? There is no standard answer to this question. However, a starting point that is applicable to most individuals (with the exception of the athlete) would be to exercise at an intensity great enough to raise the heart rate by at least 60 per cent from the resting value to the maximal value.[46] As an example, a young male (18 years old) with a resting heart rate of 70 beats per minute and a maximal rate of 195 beats per minute should start his training program so that the heart rate during exercise is $195 - 70 = 125 \times 0.6 = 75 + 70 = 145$ beats per minute. This equation can serve as a starting point, but remember that the training program must be progressive and that eventually the heart rate during the training sessions or work intervals should be close to that given in Table 12–4 (p. 255) in order to realize maximal training benefits.

## Frequency and Duration of Training

Very few, if any, longitudinal training studies have been conducted; that is, studies in which the same subjects are observed over a prolonged period of time. This particular research design is the only real way to approach the problem of training frequency and duration.

Most of the information concerning the influence of training frequency and duration on training effects has come from studies conducted over relatively short periods of time.[18, 28, 44, 55, 67, 68, 78] Although the results are not clear-cut, most studies show that frequency and duration have some effect on the magnitude of the training results. However, we have found with interval training that frequencies between two and five days per week and durations between 7 and 13 weeks do not significantly affect the gains made in $\max\dot{V}O_2$ (Fig. 13–11). It is quite clear from our interval training studies using college age males that the gain in $\max\dot{V}O_2$ is a function of intensity rather than of frequency or duration (see Fig. 13–10$A$). Others[68] who have used interval training, but with older men as subjects, have shown that $\max\dot{V}O_2$ is greater in more frequent and longer training. Thus age may have a significant influence on training benefits.

Perhaps the most significant effect of frequency and duration is on

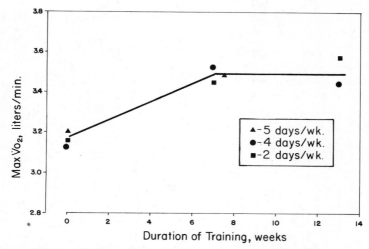

**Figure 13–11** With interval training programs, training frequencies between two and five days per week and training durations between 7 and 13 weeks do not significantly affect the gains made in max$\dot{V}o_2$. (Based on data from Fox et al.[27, 28])

submaximal exercise heart rate. We mentioned earlier that the exercise bradycardia resulting from training is related to the training frequency and duration rather than to the intensity. This observation is illustrated in Figure 13–12, in which the combined effects of frequency and duration of training are expressed as the total oxygen cost during the training program (horizontal axis); the more frequent and longer the training program, the greater the total cost. This effect has also been shown by others.[68] Decreased circulatory stress during the performance of submaximal exercise might prove to be the most important and practical benefit of more frequent and longer duration training programs.

A question often raised concerning training frequency is, "Do multiple daily workouts lead to greater fitness and performance gains?" This question is of particular importance to track and swimming coaches, some of whom advocate two and even three workouts per day. There is no scientific evidence to suggest that multiple daily workouts lead to greater fitness and performance gains. For example, in the few studies conducted on this subject,[61, 85] measurement of several physiological functions (max$\dot{V}o_2$, heart rate, vital capacity, and hemoglobin concentration) plus mile-run times indicated no advantage of two or three workouts per day over one workout per day. In fact, in one of the studies[61] it was even suggested that performances are poorer when the frequency per day of workouts is greater. Therefore, from both a physiological and performance standpoint, multiple daily workouts are not recommended.

Since longitudinal training studies are not available, information

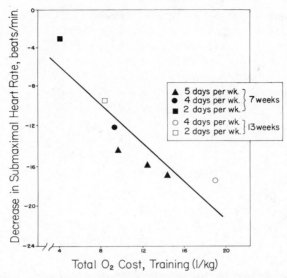

**Figure 13–12**  The most significant effect of training frequency and duration is an exercise bradycardia (decreased submaximal-exercise heart rate). The combined effects of frequency and duration of training are expressed as the total oxygen cost during the training program; the more frequent and longer the training program, the greater the total cost. (Based on data from Fox et al.[28])

concerning prolonged training durations, such as would be the case with many athletes, must come from cross-sectional studies. A cross-sectional study in this case is one in which a comparison is made among different groups of subjects, each of whom has been trained for various durations. Such a comparison is given in Table 13–8. Notice that the greatest difference is in the magnitude of the stroke volume. As mentioned in Chapter 10, this is perhaps the most significant difference be-

**Table 13–8   CROSS-SECTIONAL COMPARISON OF THE EFFECTS OF TRAINING DURATION**\*

| | TRAINING DURATION | | |
|---|---|---|---|
| VARIABLE, MAXIMAL VALUES | *4 Months* | *Several Years* | *Many Years (Champion Athletes)* |
| $\dot{V}o_2$, liters/min. | 3.44 | 4.93 | 5.57 |
| $\dot{Q}$, liters/min. | 24.2 | 28.9 | 36.0 |
| S.V., ml. | 112.0 | 155.0 | 189.0 |
| H.R., beats/min. | 192 | 186 | 190 |
| a-$\bar{v}$ $O_2$ diff., ml./liter | 143.1 | 171.0 | 156.0 |
| heart volume, ml. | 798 | 1070 | 1140 |

\*Based on data from Ekblom et al.,[20] Ekblom and Hermansen,[21] and Saltin.[76]

tween the highly trained champion athlete and the sedentary individual. How much of this difference is due to duration of training or for that matter to any facet of training cannot be determined precisely. While both frequency and duration and intensity of training undoubtedly influence the magnitude of the stroke volume for the champion athlete, genetics, as we will soon see, also is a significant factor. This, of course, points out one of the major drawbacks of cross-sectional studies.

### Specificity of Training Effects

We mentioned in the previous chapter that all training programs must be constructed so as to develop the specific physiological capacities required to perform a given sports skill or activity. This is called specificity of training. The specificity of training is best exemplified by the following examples:

1. *Training effects are specific to the type of exercise performed during the training program.* One group of men was trained for eight weeks, three days per week, on a bicycle ergometer. Another group of men was trained also for eight weeks, three days per week, but this time on a motor-driven treadmill. Each group's $max\dot{V}o_2$ was determined, once using the bicycle and once using the treadmill, both before and after training.[65] The results are shown in Figure 13–13. Notice the specificity of the results for the men who trained on the bicycle ergometer. Although their $max\dot{V}o_2$ was increased significantly as measured by both tests, the increase on the bicycle test was substantially greater. In other words, the cycling training program improved the group's ability to work when cycling more than when running. Similar findings with respect to submaximal heart rate have also been reported.[70] This information demonstrates clearly one aspect of the specificity of training.

It should also be noted that the training effects induced by running are more general than those for cycling, i.e., the $max\dot{V}o_2$ improved to the same extent whether measured on the bicycle or treadmill. This is also useful information, since many training programs are based on running programs even though the sport being trained for does not involve a great deal of running.

2. *Training effects are specific to the muscle groups used during the training program.* A group of male college students was tested on a bicycle ergometer once while performing submaximal exercise with the arms (pedaling with the arms) and once while performing submaximal exercise with the legs (pedaling with the legs), both before and after five weeks of daily interval training. For half of the students, training consisted of pedaling the bicycle with the arms only, whereas the other half pedaled the bicycle with the legs only.[29] The results are shown in Fig-

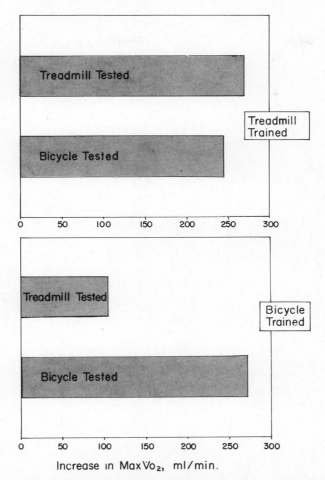

**Figure 13–13** Training effects are specific to the type of exercise performed during the training program. Notice in the lower portion of the figure that the cycling training program improved the group's maxV̇o₂ more when cycling than when running. Notice also that the training effects induced by running are more general than those induced by cycling (upper figure). (Based on data from Pechar et al.[65])

ure 13–14. Notice the specificity of responses. The magnitudes of the post-training changes were always greater when the exercise was performed with the trained rather than the untrained muscle groups (limbs). Again, these results emphasize the specific nature of the physiological changes induced by training. They also indicate that the controlling mechanisms for such changes are to a large extent mediated by the skeletal muscles.

3. *Training effects are specific to the type of training program used.* Two groups of male college students were trained using the interval training

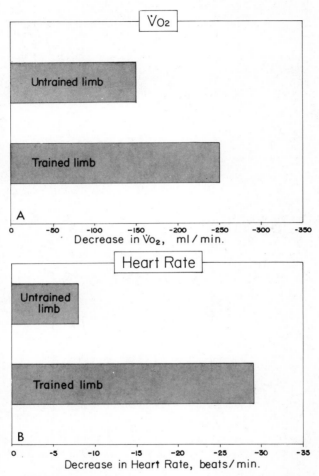

**Figure 13–14** Training effects are specific to the muscle groups used during the training program. Notice that the magnitudes of the post-training changes were always greater when the exercise was performed with the trained rather than with the untrained muscle groups (limbs). (Based on data from Fox et al.[29])

*Illustration continued on the opposite page.*

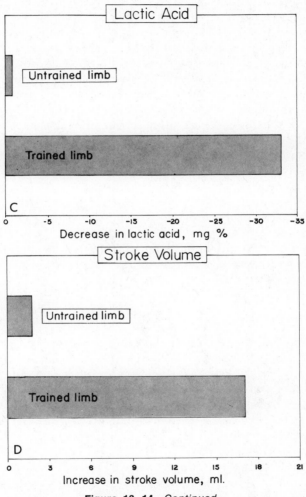

Figure 13–14  *Continued*

method. One group participated in a sprint program consisting of repeated bouts of short (30 seconds) fast runs. The other group used an endurance program consisting of repeated bouts of longer (two minutes) but slower runs.[25] The results, as shown in Figure 13–15, were as follows:

(a) Both groups improved by approximately the same magnitude in max$\dot{V}o_2$.

(b) After training, the endurance group had a much greater *decrease* in lactic acid production during exercise at the same submaximal work load than did the sprint group.

(c) The capacity of the ATP-PC system was significantly increased in the sprint group but not in the endurance group.

(d) Neither group increased the capacity of the lactic acid system.

These results indicate yet another type of specificity. For example, although the max$\dot{V}o_2$ for each group was not much different, the lower accumulation of lactic acid induced by the endurance training would be a definite advantage for athletes training for endurance events, because there would be less fatigue. By the same token, the sprint program would be advantageous for those training for sprints because of the increased capacity of the ATP-PC system. Also, it is significant that neither type of program is suitable for increasing the capacity of the lactic acid system. Apparently, the type of program needed for such a change would involve repeated bouts of runs between 60 and 90 seconds in duration.[25]

## Genetic Limitations

In Chapter 6 (p. 109) and earlier in this chapter (p. 278), we mentioned that certain physiological and functional capacities are to a large extent limited by genetic make-up. For example, even with the best possible training program, the improvement in functional capabilities is ultimately going to be limited by genetic potential. Just recently, this fact has been scientifically demonstrated.[53] For example, one monozygous (identical) twin who was well trained athletically was compared to the other twin, who was sedentary. The results showed that the max$\dot{V}o_2$ of the trained twin was 37 per cent greater than that of the untrained twin. However, the magnitude of the max$\dot{V}o_2$ after training was still within the normal range of values, thus suggesting a genetic limitation.

How heritable are some of the physiological functions that we have been discussing? Again, the information that allows us to answer this question has become available only recently. It has been estimated[52, 54] that the max$\dot{V}o_2$ is 93.4 per cent genetically determined. This estimate is based on differences in intrapair variability measures of the max$\dot{V}o_2$

of monozygous (identical) twins and dizygous (fraternal) twins. As shown in Figure 13–16, the intrapair (twin A versus twin B) variability in max$\dot{V}o_2$ for dizygous twins is much greater than for monozygous twins, as indicated by the wide scatter of points about the diagonal line. If the max$\dot{V}o_2$ values were exactly the same for twin A and twin B, the points would fall on the line. The heritability of the max$\dot{V}o_2$ is not significantly influenced by either sex or age.

In the same manner, the capacity of the lactic acid system and the maximal heart rate have been found to be genetically determined to the extent of 81.4 and 85.9 per cent, respectively. Again, neither age nor sex has a significant influence on the heritability. Other functions that were studied but that did not show significant heritability tendencies were respiratory frequency, tidal volume, respiratory exchange ratio, oxygen pulse,* minute ventilation, and heart volume.[52, 54]

There is an old saying, "Sprinters are born, not made." As we have seen, this statement has some scientific support in that the capacity of the lactic acid system is in part genetically determined. Also, from studies of the heritability of the max$\dot{V}o_2$, it seems appropriate to add a new saying: "Distance runners are born, not made."

## Mode of Exercise

Most exercise activities, when used in a training program structured on the principles set forth in the preceding chapter, will lead to substantial gains in fitness. For example, increases in fitness have been demonstrated for such activities as walking, jogging, running, bicycling, swimming, bench stepping, calisthenics, and skipping rope.

An interesting question in this regard is, "Which mode of exercise leads to the greatest gains in fitness?" In answering this question, we must first be concerned with two factors: (1) the frequency, duration, and most importantly, the intensity of the program; and (2) the specificity of the training results. In other words, as we have seen, the outcome of any training program is greatly influenced by these factors. However, if these factors are held constant, we can answer the question more accurately.

A comparison of training effects on middle-aged males using either running, walking, cycling, jogging, or tennis as an exercise mode is given in Table 13–9.[69, 86] The training intensities of the various programs, as judged by the heart rate response during the training sessions, were comparable except in the tennis group. Here the intensity

---

*Oxygen pulse is the ratio of oxygen consumption ($\dot{V}o_2$) and heart rate (H.R.); i.e., $\dot{V}o_2$/H.R. Since $\dot{V}o_2$ = S.V. × H.R. × a-$\bar{v}$ $O_2$ diff., the oxygen pulse is the product of the stroke volume (S.V.) and the a-$\bar{v}$ $O_2$ diff.

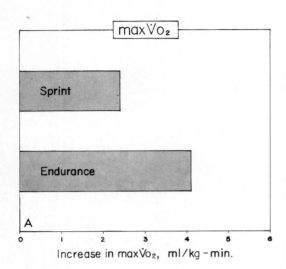

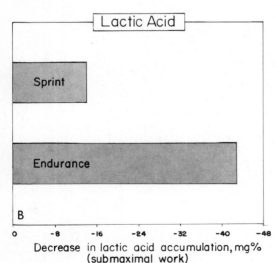

**Figure 13–15** Training effects are specific to the type of training program used. In comparing sprint and endurance training programs: *A*, both groups improved by the same magnitude in maxVo₂; *B*, after training, the endurance group had a greater decrease in lactic acid production during submaximal exercise than did the sprint group; *C*, the capacity of the ATP-PC system was increased in the sprint group only; and *D*, neither group increased the capacity of the lactic acid system. (Based on data from Fox.[25])

*Illustration continued on the opposite page*

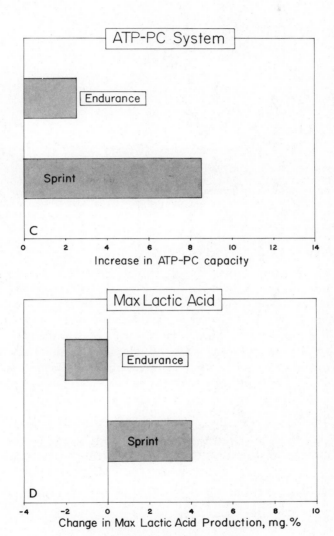

**Figure 13–15**  *Continued*

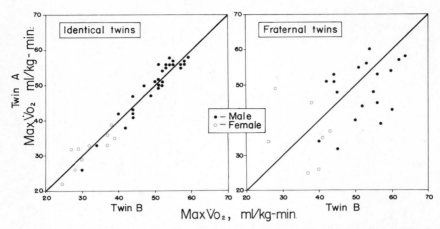

**Figure 13–16**  The max$\dot{V}O_2$ is genetically determined to a great extent. This is shown by the fact that the intrapair (twin A vs. twin B) variability in max$\dot{V}O_2$ for dizygous (fraternal) twins is much greater than for monozygous (identical) twins, as indicated by the wide scatter of points about the diagonal line. If the max$\dot{V}O_2$ values were exactly the same for twin A and twin B, the points would fall on the line. (Based on data from Klissouras et al.[52, 54])

was much lower, which undoubtedly explains why the improvement in max$\dot{V}O_2$ was also much lower compared to the other groups. In addition, the influence of specificity was eliminated by testing the subjects according to their training exercise mode. As can be seen, improvement in max$\dot{V}O_2$ is quite comparable for all exercise modes (with the exception of the tennis group as mentioned above). Similar results were obtained for other related functions, including a significant decrease in per cent body fat from all programs. This information emphasizes again that provided the training program is conducted according to

### Table 13–9  COMPARISON OF TRAINING EFFECTS ON MIDDLE-AGED MALES USING DIFFERENT MODES OF EXERCISE*

| MODE OF EXERCISE | INTENSITY OF TRAINING (% maxH.R.) | TYPE OF TEST | PER CENT INCREASE IN max$\dot{V}O_2$ |
|---|---|---|---|
| Running | 90 | treadmill | 11.7 |
| Walking | 87 | treadmill | 12.4 |
| Cycling | 87 | bicycle | 23.6 |
| Cycling | 82 | bicycle | 17.4 |
| Jogging | 84 | treadmill | 13.3 |
| Tennis | 65 | treadmill | 5.7 |

*Based on data from Pollock et al.[68] and Wilmore et al.[86]  All training programs were three days per week for 20 weeks.

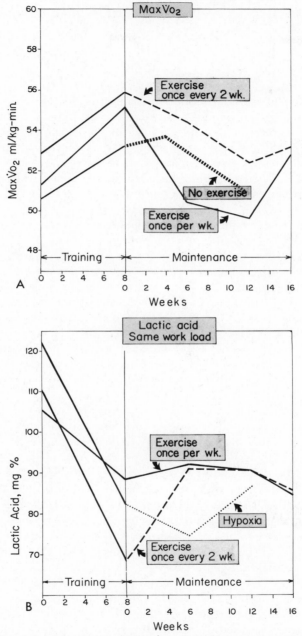

**Figure 13–17** *A,* The gains in maxVo₂ from interval training programs are not maintained by maintenance training programs consisting of frequencies of either once per week or once every two weeks. *B,* One of the most important benefits retained by a maintenance training program is the ability to perform a given submaximal work load with less accumulation of lactic acid. This effect can be maintained by exercise once per week or by weekly exposures to hypoxia. (Based on data from Case;[12] Chaloupka;[13] and Bason et al.[6])

sound principles, its fitness benefits can be realized, regardless of the type of exercise.

## Maintenance of Training Effects

An important consideration in any training procedure is how to effectively maintain the benefits gained from training. Of course, one way to do this would be to train on a regular basis (e.g., three days per week) throughout the year, year after year. However, this remedy is least desirable from the standpoint of economy of time on the part of the participant. Furthermore, a number of beneficial training effects can be maintained for several months with a reduced training frequency. For example, the gains made in max$\dot{V}o_2$ following a five day per week, five week training program could be maintained for an additional five weeks by training only three days per week.[11]

Using interval training we have found that a reduction in training frequency from three days per week to one day per week is also effective in maintaining some, but not all, of the fitness benefits gained during the three day per week program.[13, 14] For example, as shown in Figure 13–17A, the max$\dot{V}o_2$ is not maintained by a training frequency of only one training session per week. Actually, the decrease in max$\dot{V}o_2$ following a one day per week maintenance program is the same as for no maintenance (exercise) program at all. Thus, it appears difficult to maintain the max$\dot{V}o_2$ with a training frequency of only one session per week.

What training benefits can be maintained by a one day per week interval training maintenance program? One of the most important benefits that is maintained is the ability to perform a given submaximal work load with less accumulation of lactic acid. As shown in Figure 13–17B, this effect can be maintained for at least 16 weeks. The prescription for the one maintenance workout per week should be the same as, or nearly identical to, that used during the final week of the regular training program. Notice also that this benefit can be maintained by intermittent exposure to altitude (hypoxia).[6] During the exposures, no exercise is necessary (see p. 357). Also of interest is the fact that the lower lactic acid accumulation cannot be maintained with a maintenance program consisting of a training frequency of only once every two weeks.

The question often arises as to the constituents of a year-round training program. Unfortunately, there is no simple answer to this question. However, based on our results with the interval training system, we would recommend alternating a 7 to 8 week interval training program involving three workouts per week with a 16 week maintenance program involving one workout per week. Such a training sequence should be effective for men and women of all ages as well as for athletes. In fact, when dealing with athletes, the benefits of a preseason training program can most likely be maintained in most sports by conducting gamelike scrimmages one day per week.

## SUMMARY

Biochemical alterations induced by training are as follows:
(1) increased myoglobin content
(2) increased oxidation of carbohydrate (glycogen)
(3) increased oxidation of fat
(4) increased muscular stores of ATP and PC
(5) increased glycolytic (lactic acid system) capacity

Systemic (oxygen transport system) changes induced by training include the following:
(1) At rest:
   (a) cardiac hypertrophy
   (b) decreased heart rate
   (c) increased stroke volume
   (d) increased blood volume and hemoglobin
   (e) hypertrophy of skeletal muscle
(2) During submaximal exercise:
   (a) no change or slight decrease in $\dot{V}o_2$
   (b) decrease in lactic acid accumulation
   (c) no change or slight decrease in cardiac output
   (d) increased stroke volume
   (e) decreased heart rate
   (f) lower blood flow per kilogram of working muscle
(3) During maximal exercise:
   (a) increased $\max\dot{V}o_2$
   (b) increased lactic acid accumulation
   (c) increased cardiac output
   (d) increased stroke volume
   (e) no change or slight decrease in heart rate
   (f) no change in muscle blood flow per kilogram of muscle

Respiratory changes induced by training include:
(1) increased pulmonary ventilation
(2) increased ventilatory efficiency
(3) increased lung volumes
(4) increased diffusion capacity

Other changes resulting from training are:
(1) decreased body fat
(2) decreased blood levels of cholesterol and triglycerides

(3) decreased blood pressure during rest and exercise

(4) increased heat acclimatization

The effects of training are influenced by many factors. Generally, the greater the intensity, frequency, and duration of the training program, the greater will be the improvement in most functions. Training effects are specific to the type of training program used, e.g., running versus bicycling, sprint versus endurance, and arm versus leg training. Genetic limitations are also influential in determining the final magnitude of the training effect. The max$\dot{V}o_2$, the lactic acid capacity, and the maximal heart rate are to a large extent genetically determined.

Most modes of exercise (e.g., walking, jogging, running, bicycling, and swimming), when used in a training program structured on sound principles, will lead to substantial gains in fitness.

A number of beneficial training effects can be maintained for several months with a maintenance training program consisting of only one workout per week.

## QUESTIONS

1. What are the three major aerobic adaptations that occur in skeletal muscle as a result of training?

2. How does an increased myoglobin concentration resulting from training enhance the aerobic system?

3. Discuss the major subcellular adaptations that contribute toward the muscle cells' increased capacity to oxidize carbohydrate and fat following training.

4. List the two major anaerobic adaptations that occur in skeletal muscle as a result of training.

5. Discuss the relative biochemical changes resulting from training in red and white muscle fibers.

6. Discuss the major systemic changes resulting from training that are apparent at rest.

7. What are the major differences between the cardiac hypertrophy in endurance and nonendurance athletes?

8. What physiological mechanism is responsible for the resting bradycardia induced by training?

9. List the changes in the oxygen transport system following training that are evidenced during steady-state submaximal exercise.

10.  What mechanism may be responsible for the decreased lactic acid accumulation during submaximal work following training?

11.  Discuss the intracardiac and extracardiac mechanisms as related to the exercise bradycardia.

12.  List the training effects that are responsible for increases in maximal working capacity.

13.  Discuss the respiratory and other changes induced by training.

14.  In what manner do training intensity, frequency, and duration influence training effects?

15.  Give three examples of the specificity of training effects.

16.  In what manner does heredity influence training effects?

17.  Which mode of exercise leads to the greatest gains in fitness?

18.  What factors should be considered in the development of a maintenance program?

# REFERENCES

1. Åstrand, P.: Experimental Studies of Physical Working Capacity in Relation to Sex and Age. Ejnar, Munksgaard, Copenhagen, 1952.
2. Åstrand, P., Eriksson, B., Nylander, I., Engstrom, L., Karlberg, P., Saltin, B., and Thoren, C.: Girl swimmers. Acta Paediat., Suppl. 147, 1963.
3. Baldwin, K., Klinerfuss, G., Terjung, R., Molé, P., and Holloszy, J.: Respiratory capacity of white, red, and intermediate muscle: adaptive response to exercise. Am. J. Physiol., 222:373–378, 1972.
4. Baldwin, K., Winder, W., Terjung, R., and Holloszy, J.: Glycolytic capacity of red, white, and intermediate muscle: adaptive response to running. Med. Sci. Sports, 4:50, 1972.
5. Barnard, R., Edgerton, V., and Peter, J.: Effects of exercise on skeletal muscle. I. Biochemical and histological properties. J. Appl. Physiol., 28:762–766, 1970.
6. Bason, R., Fox, E., Billings, C., Klinzing, J., Ragg, K., and Chaloupka, E.: Maintenance of physical training effects by intermittent exposure to hypoxia. Aerospace Med., 44(10):1097–1100, 1973.
7. Benzi, G., Panceri, P., DeBernardi, M., Villa, R., Arcelli, E., d'Angelo, L., Arrigoni, E., and Berte, F.: Mitochondrial enzymatic adaptation of skeletal muscle to endurance training. J. Appl. Physiol., 38(4):565–569, 1975.
8. Bevegard, S., Holmgren, A., and Jonsson, B.: Circulatory studies in well trained athletes at rest and during heavy exercise, with special reference to stroke volume and the influence of body position. Acta Physiol. Scand., 57:26–50, 1963.
9. Boileau, R., Buskirk, E., Hortsman, D., Mendez, J., and Nichols, W.: Body composition changes in obese and lean men during physical conditioning. Med. Sci. Sports, 3(4):183–189, 1971.
10. Boyer, J., and Kasch, F.: Exercise therapy in hypertensive men. J.A.M.A., 211:1668–1671, 1970.
11. Brynteson, P., and Sinning, W.: The effects of training frequencies on the retention of cardiovascular fitness. Med. Sci. Sports, 5(1):29–33, 1973.

12. Case, H.: Detraining Following High Volume Interval Training. Doctoral Dissertation, The Ohio State University, 1971.
13. Chaloupka, E.: The Physiological Effects of Two Maintenance Programs Following Eight Weeks of Interval Training. Doctoral Dissertation, The Ohio State University, 1972.
14. Chaloupka, E., and Fox, E.: Physiological effects of two maintenance programs following eight weeks of interval training. Fed. Proc., 34(3):443, 1975.
15. Clausen, J., Trap-Jensen, J., and Lassen, N.: The effects of training on the heart rate during arm and leg exercise. Scand. J. Clin. Lab. Invest., 26:295–301, 1970.
16. Cohen, K., and Fox, E.: Intensity and distance of interval training programs and metabolic changes in females. Unpublished manuscript, 1975.
17. Costill, D., Thomason, H., and Roberts, E.: Fractional utilization of the aerobic capacity during distance running. Med. Sci. Sports, 5(4):248–252, 1973.
18. Davies, C., and Knibbs, A.: The training stimulus: the effects of intensity, duration and frequency of effort on maximum aerobic power output. Int. Z. Angew. Physiol., 29:299–305, 1971.
19. Eckstein, R.: Effect of exercise and coronary artery narrowing on coronary collateral circulation. Circ. Res., 5:230–238, 1957.
20. Ekblom, B., Åstrand, P., Saltin, B., Stenberg, J., and Wallström, B.: Effect of training on circulatory response to exercise. J. Appl. Physiol., 24(4):518–528, 1968.
21. Ekblom, B., and Hermansen, L.: Cardiac output in athletes. J. Appl. Physiol., 25(5):619–625, 1968.
22. Eriksson, B., Gollnick, P., and Saltin, B.: Muscle metabolism and enzyme activities after training in boys 11–13 years old. Acta Physiol. Scand., 87:485–497, 1973.
23. Faria, I.: Cardiovascular response to exercise as influenced by training of various intensities. Res. Quart., 41:44–50, 1970.
24. Fink, W., Costill, D., Daniels, J., Pollock, M., and Saltin, B.: Muscle fiber composition and enzyme activities in male and female athletes. Physiologist, 18(3):213, 1975.
25. Fox, E.: Differences in metabolic alterations with sprint versus endurance interval training programs. In Howald, H., and Poortmans, J. (eds.): Metabolic Adaption to Prolonged Physical Exercise. Basel, Switzerland, Birkhauser Verlag. 1975, pp. 119–126.
26. Fox, E., and Costill, D.: Estimated cardiorespiratory responses during marathon running. Arch. Environ. Health, 24:315–324, 1972.
27. Fox, E., Bartels, R., Billings, C., Mathews, D., Bason, R., and Webb, W.: Intensity and distance of interval training programs and changes in aerobic power. Med. Sci. Sports, 5(1):18–22, 1973.
28. Fox, E., Bartels, R., Billings, C., O'Brien, R., Bason, R., and Mathews, D.: Frequency and duration of interval training programs and changes in aerobic power. J. Appl. Physiol., 38(3):481–484, 1975.
29. Fox, E., McKenzie, D., and Cohen, K.: Specificity of training: metabolic and circulatory responses. Med. Sci. Sports, 7(1):83, 1975.
30. Frick, M., Elovainio, R., and Somer, T.: The mechanism of bradycardia evoked by physical training. Cardiologia, 51:46–54, 1967.
31. Frick, M., Konttinen, A., and Sarajas, S.: Effects of physical training on circulation at rest and during exercise. Am. J. Cardiol., 12:142–147, 1963.
32. Frick, M., Sjögren, A., Persäsalo, J., and Pajunen, S.: Cardiovascular dimensions and moderate physical training in young men. J. Appl. Physiol., 29(4):452–455, 1970.
33. Gollnick, P., and Hermansen, L.: Biochemical adaptations to exercise: anaerobic metabolism. In Wilmore, J. (ed.): Exercise and Sports Sciences Reviews. New York, Academic Press, 1973, pp. 1–43.
34. Gollnick, P., and King, D.: Effect of exercise and training on mitochondria of rat skeletal muscle. Am. J. Physiol., 216:1502–1509, 1969.
35. Gollnick, P., Armstrong, R., Saltin, B., Saubert, C., Sembrowich, W., and Shepherd, R.: Effect of training on enzyme activity and fiber composition of human skeletal muscle. J. Appl. Physiol., 34(1):107–111, 1973.
36. Gollnick, P., Armstrong, R., Saubert, C., Piehl, K., and Saltin, B.: Enzyme activity

and fiber composition in skeletal muscle of untrained and trained men. J. Appl. Physiol., 33(3):312–319, 1972.

37. Grimby, G., Häggendal, E., and Saltin, B.: Local xenon 133 clearance from the quadriceps muscle during exercise in man. J. Appl. Physiol., 22(2):305–310, 1967.

38. Hermansen, L., Hultman, E., and Saltin, B.: Muscle glycogen during prolonged severe exercise. Acta Physiol. Scand., 71:129–139, 1967.

39. Hermansen, L., and Wachtlova, M.: Capillary density of skeletal muscle in well-trained and untrained men. J. Appl. Physiol., 30(6):860–863, 1971.

40. Holloszy, J.: Effects of exercise on mitochondrial oxygen uptake and respiratory enzyme activity in skeletal muscle. J. Biol. Chem., 242:2278–2282, 1967.

41. Holloszy, J.: Biochemical adaptations to exercise: aerobic metabolism. In Wilmore, J. (ed.): Exercise and Sports Sciences Reviews. New York, Academic Press, 1973, pp. 45–71.

41A. Holloszy, J.: Adaptation of skeletal muscle to endurance exercise. Med. Sci. Sports, 7(3):155–164, 1975.

42. Holloszy, J., Oscai, L., Molé, P., and Don, I.: Biochemical adaptations to endurance exercise in skeletal muscle. In Pernow, B., and Saltin, B. (eds.): Muscle Metabolism During Exercise. New York, Plenum Press, 1971, pp. 51–61.

43. Howley, E., and Glover, M.: The caloric costs of running and walking one mile for men and women. Med. Sci. Sports, 6(4):235–237, 1974.

44. Jackson, J., Sharkey, B., and Johnston, L.: Cardiorespiratory adaptations to training at specified frequencies. Res. Quart., 39:295–300, 1968.

45. Karlsson, J., Nordesjö, L., Jorfeldt, L., and Saltin, B.: Muscle lactate, ATP, and CP levels during exercise after physical training in man. J. Appl. Physiol., 33(2):199–203, 1972.

46. Karvonen, M., Kentala, E., and Mustala, O.: The effects of training on heart rate. A longitudinal study. Ann. Med. Exp. Biol. Fenn., 35:307–315, 1957.

47. Kiessling, K., Piehl, K., and Lundquist, C.: Effect of physical training on ultrastructural features in human skeletal muscle. In Pernow, B., and Saltin, B. (eds.): Muscle Metabolism During Exercise. New York, Plenum Press, 1971, pp. 97–101.

48. Kilbom, Å.: Physical training with submaximal intensities in women. I. Reaction to exercise and orthostasis. Scand. J. Clin. Lab. Invest., 28:141–161, 1971.

49. Kjellberg, S., Rudhe, U., and Sjöstrand, T.: Increase of the amount of hemoglobin and blood volume in connection with physical training. Acta Physiol. Scand., 19:146–151, 1949.

50. Kjellberg, S., Rudhe, U., and Sjöstrand, T.: The amount of hemoglobin and the blood volume in relation to the pulse rate and cardiac volume during rest. Acta Physiol. Scand., 19:136–145, 1949.

51. Klassen, G., Andrew, G., and Becklake, M.: Effect of training on total and regional blood flow and metabolism in paddlers. J. Appl. Physiol., 28(4):397–406, 1970.

52. Klissouras, V.: Heritability of adaptive variation. J. Appl. Physiol., 31(3):338–344, 1971.

53. Klissouras, V.: Genetic limit of functional adaptability. Int. Z. Angew. Physiol., 30:85–94, 1972.

54. Klissouras, V., Pirnay, F., and Petit, J.: Adaptation to maximal effort: genetics and age. J. Appl. Physiol., 35(2):288–293, 1973.

55. Knuttgen, H., Nordesjö, L., Ollander, B., and Saltin, B.: Physical conditioning through interval training with young male adults. Med. Sci. Sports, 5:220–226, 1973.

56. Leon, A., and Bloor, C.: Effects of exercise and its cessation on the heart and its blood supply. J. Appl. Physiol., 24(4):485–490, 1968.

57. Mann, G., Garrett, H., Farhi, A., Murray, H., and Billings, F.: Exercise to prevent coronary heart disease. Am. J. Med., 46:12–27, 1969.

58. Molé, P., Oscai, L., and Holloszy, J.: Adaptation of muscle to exercise. Increase in levels of palmityl CoA synthetase, carnitine palmityltransferase, and palmityl CoA dehydrogenase, and in the capacity to oxidize fatty acids. J. Clin. Invest., 50:2323–2330, 1971

59. Morgan, T., Cobb, L., Short, F., Ross, R., and Gunn, D.: Effects of long-term exercise on human muscle mitochondria. *In* Pernow, B., and Saltin, B. (eds.): Muscle Metabolism During Exercise. New York, Plenum Press, 1971, pp. 87–95.

60. Morganroth, J., Maron, B., Henry, W., and Epstein, S.: Comparative left ventricular dimensions in trained athletes. Ann. Intern. Med., 82:521–524, 1975.

61. Mostardi, R., Gandee, R., and Campbell, T.: Multiple daily training and improvement in aerobic power. Med. Sci Sports, 7(1):82, 1975.

62. Nutter, D., Gilbert, C., Heymsfield, S., Perkins, J., and Schlant, R.: Cardiac hypertrophy in the endurance athlete. Physiologist, 18(3):336, 1975.

63. Oscai, L., Williams, B., and Hertig, B.: Effect of exercise on blood volume. J. Appl. Physiol., 24(5):622–624, 1968.

64. Pattengale P., and Holloszy, J.: Augmentation of skeletal muscle myoglobin by a program of treadmill running. Am. J. Physiol., 213:783–785, 1967.

65. Pechar, G., McArdle, W., Katch, F., Magel, J., and DeLuca, J.: Specificity of cardiorespiratory adaptation to bicycle and treadmill training. J. Appl. Physiol., 36(6):753–756, 1974.

66. Penpargkul, S., and Scheuer, J.: The effect of physical training upon the mechanical and metabolic performance of the rat heart. J. Clin. Invest., 49:1859–1868, 1970.

67. Pollock, M.: The quantification of endurance training programs. *In* Wilmore, J. (ed.): Exercise and Sport Sciences Reviews. Vol. 1. New York, Academic Press, 1973, pp. 155–188.

68. Pollock, M., Cureton, T., and Greninger, L.: Effects of frequency of training on working capacity, cardiovascular function, and body composition of adult men. Med. Sci. Sports, 1(2):70–74, 1969.

69. Pollock, M., Dimmick, J., Miller, H., Kendrick, Z., and Linnerud, A.: Effects of mode of training on cardiovascular function and body composition of adult men. Med. Sci. Sports, 7(2):139–145, 1975.

70. Roberts, J., and Alspaugh, J.: Specificity of training effects resulting from programs of treadmill running and bicycle ergometer riding. Med. Sci. Sports, 4(1):6–10, 1972.

71. Rowell, L.: Human cardiovascular adjustments to exercise and thermal stress. Physiol. Rev., 54(1):75–159, 1974.

72. Saltin, B.: Physiological effects of physical training. Med. Sci. Sports, 1(1):50–56, 1969.

73. Saltin, B., and Åstrand, P.: Maximal oxygen uptake in athletes. J. Appl. Physiol., 23:353–358, 1967.

74. Saltin, B., and Karlsson, J.: Muscle glycogen utilization during work of different intensities. *In* Pernow, B., and Saltin, B. (eds.): Muscle Metabolism During Exercise. New York, Plenum Press, 1971, pp. 289–299.

75. Saltin, B., Blomqvist, G., Mitchell, J., Johnson, R., Wildenthal, K., and Chapman, C.: Response to exercise after bedrest and after training. Circulation, Suppl. 7, 1968.

76. Saltin, B., Hartley, L., Kilbom, Å., and Åstrand, I.: Physical training in sedentary middle-aged and older men. II. Oxygen uptake, heart rate and blood lactate concentrations at submaximal and maximal exercise. Scand. J. Clin. Lab. Invest., 24:323–334, 1969.

77. Sharkey, B., and Holleman, J.: Cardiorespiratory adaptations to training at specified intensities. Res. Quart., 38:698–704, 1967.

78. Shephard, R.: Intensity, duration and frequency of exercise as determinants of the response to a training regimen. Int. Z. Angew. Physiol., 26:272–278, 1968.

79. Staudte, H., Exner, G., and Pette, D.: Effects of short-term, high intensity (sprint) training on some contractile and metabolic characteristics of fast and slow muscle of the rat. Pflügers Arch., 344:159–168, 1973.

80. Taylor, A., Thayer, R., and Rao, S.: Human skeletal muscle glycogen synthetase activities with exercise and training. Can. J. Physiol. Pharmacol., 50:411–412, 1972.

81. Tepperman, J., and Pearlman, D.: Effects of exercise and anemia on coronary arte-

ries of small animals as revealed by the corrosion-cast technique. Circ. Res., 9:576–584, 1961.
82. Terjung, R., and Spear, K.: Effects of exercise training on coronary blood flow in rats. Physiologist, 18(3):419, 1975.
82A. Thorstensson, A., Sjödin, B., and Karlsson, J.: Enzyme activities and muscle strength after "sprint training" in man. Acta Physiol. Scand., 94:313–318, 1975.
83. Tipton, C.: Training and bradycardia in rats. Am. J. Physiol., 209:1089–1094, 1965.
84. Tipton, C., Barnard, R., and Tcheng, T.: Resting heart rate investigations with trained and nontrained hypophysectomized rats. J. Appl. Physiol., 26(5):585–588, 1969.
85. Watt, E., Buskirk, E., and Plotnicki, B.: A comparison of single vs. multiple daily training regimens: some physiological considerations. Res. Quart., 44(1):119–123, 1973.
86. Wilmore, J., Davis, J., O'Brien, R., Vodak, P., Walder, G., and Amsterdam, E.: A comparative investigation of bicycling, tennis and jogging as modes for altering cardiovascular endurance capacity. Med. Sci. Sports, 7(1):83, 1975.
87. Wilmore, J., Royce, J., Girandola, R., Katch, F., and Katch, V.: Body composition changes with a 10-week program of jogging. Med. Sci. Sports, 2(3):113–117, 1970.

# SECTION 5

# ENVIRONMENTAL ASPECTS

# DIFFUSION, OSMOSIS, AND DROWNING

If you had knowledge of how, physiologically, a boy practicing football can die from heat stroke, you would never knowingly contribute to such a casualty. As a matter of fact you, being informed, could greatly influence other teachers and coaches. If *all* were informed, there would be no deaths in physical education attributed to heat stroke. By the same token, understanding the physiological sequence in drowning prepares us to handle emergency treatment with a greater depth of understanding. For example, if you should be present at the scene of a near drowning, you would never permit the victim to get up and move about before being taken to the hospital. These are two illustrations as to why you should be informed regarding certain physiological principles which take place at the *cellular* level. The knowledge in this chapter will help you understand important practical problems that will confront you as a coach and physical educator.

Life is maintained at the cellular level, and this maintenance is dependent primarily on the movement of food, electrolytes, and waste products into and out of the cell. When this delicate equilibrium is interrupted, serious consequences prevail and death may occur if the situation is not remedied immediately. Comprehending the principles of cellular exchange is extremely important if the physical educator is to be knowledgeable about his or her profession. For example, the principles of cellular exchange are important in understanding respiration, cellular metabolism, heat stroke, and the sequential events in drowning, as well as important aspects of athletic injuries.

# THE CELL

The interior of the cell is composed of organic and inorganic materials dissolved in $H_2O$: these substances are constantly involved in a myriad of chemical reactions to produce energy and hence maintain life. Outside of every cell is the *interstitial fluid,* whose composition is quite similar to the interior of the cell. Food moves from the blood through the interstitial fluid and into the cell, while waste materials come from the cell through the interstitial fluid into the blood. Forces are constantly at work to maintain this dynamic equilibrium.

*Diffusion, facilitated diffusion, osmosis, electrical potential,* and *active transport* are the forces that allow this delicate balance between the inside and the outside of the cell to be maintained.

## Diffusion

Each molecule is in constant vibration, and as a result, the molecules contained within a given volume will be constantly colliding with one another. The vibrating and colliding result in a mixing of the molecules throughout the system. The movement is caused by the kinetic energy of the particle. This randomness of movement, or *diffusion,* is an excellent mixing device and is the most important means by which particles move into and out of the cell. In diffusion, particles always move from a region of higher concentration to one of lower concentration. For example, oxygen moves from the capillary to the interstitial fluid (lymph surrounding the cell) and from the interstitial fluid into the cell. By the same token, carbon dioxide ($CO_2$) moves from the cell through the interstitial fluid and into the capillaries. There are by far a greater number of oxygen molecules in the blood moving about in random fashion—this is the reason why more will diffuse toward the cell. By the same token, $CO_2$ is produced in the cell and the random motion of these molecules will result in their greater diffusion out of the cell through the interstitial fluid and into the capillaries. When the concentration of molecules is greater on one side of a membrane than on the other, a *diffusion gradient* exists. One might say that the oxygen has a "downhill grade" toward the cell, whereas $CO_2$ would have a "downhill grade" toward the capillary. Figure 14–1 diagrammatically portrays this phenomenon.

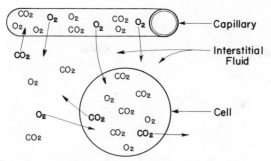

**Figure 14–1** Diffusion between cell and capillary. Because of a higher concentration of $CO_2$ in the cell, more $CO_2$ moves toward the capillary; on the other hand, a greater concentration of $O_2$ in the capillary causes more $O_2$ to move toward and into the cell by diffusion. Water, $CO_2$, and $O_2$ pass freely into and out of the cell.

## Facilitated Diffusion

Each cell is surrounded by a membrane within which is contained a matrix. The matrix is composed of lipids (fats), and therefore is called a lipid matrix (see Fig. 14–2). As we have just seen, in ordinary or free diffusion, carbon dioxide, oxygen, and other compounds such as fatty acids and alcohol (1) pass through the pores of the outer membrane, (2) dissolve into the matrix, (3) diffuse to the inner membrane, and (4) finally pass through the membrane wall into the interior of the cell.

Sugars, such as glucose, however, *do not* dissolve in the lipid matrix. Consequently, they must find some other means of diffusing to the inner membrane wall. It is thought that this is accomplished with the help of an unknown carrier substance. Figure 14–3 shows how it works. The carrier substance (let's call it X) combines with glucose just inside the outer membrane of the matrix, forming a compound we can call glucose X. Since this compound is soluble (dissolvable) in the lipid matrix, the glucose can now diffuse across to the inner membrane of the

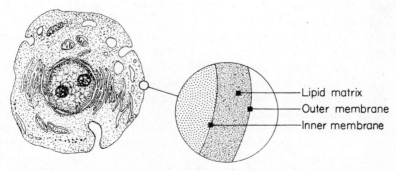

**Figure 14–2** The membrane of a cell is composed of a lipid (fat) matrix.

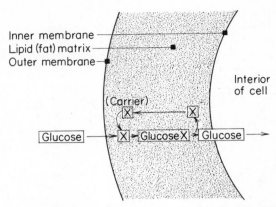

**Figure 14–3** Facilitated diffusion. A carrier substance (X) combines with glucose just inside the outer membrane of the matrix, forming a compound called glucose X. The glucose (now soluble) diffuses across to the inner membrane of the matrix. The carrier then breaks away, and glucose passes into the cell.

matrix. At this point, the carrier substance breaks away and glucose passes to the inside of the cell. The carrier substance then diffuses back across the matrix where it can once again transport more glucose to the inside of the cell. This process is called *facilitated diffusion* because, as we have seen, the carrier substance facilitates the transport or diffusion of glucose into the cell.

## Osmosis

Small molecules and other particles, such as $CO_2$ and $O_2$, pass into and out of the cell membrane through pores, with ease, as was discussed above. However, certain molecules are too large to find passage through the pores of the cell membrane and as a result, too little or too much water moving into or out of the cell may cause it to swell or shrink. The reason for this may be explained in the following manner. Consider a cell with only water on the inside and outside. As water molecules pass easily into and out of the cell through diffusion, there will be an equal number of molecules on either side of the cell membrane—that is, a diffusion gradient does not exist. Now suppose there were a number of large nondiffusible particles (too large to get through the pores) on the outside of the membrane, which would prevent the water molecules from entering the cell. In this situation, the water molecules on the inside would remain continuously in motion and gradually move to the outside of the cell by diffusion. The condition whereby there are a greater number of molecules bombarding one side of the cell membrane than the other is called *osmosis*. Osmosis is a special case of diffusion that occurs when you have: (1) a semipermeable membrane, and (2) a liquid containing particles on either side of the membrane.

Osmosis can be demonstrated using a U-tube with a semipermeable membrane that separates water and a solution of sodium chloride (NaCl). The relatively large sodium ($Na^+$) and chloride ($Cl^-$) ions find it difficult to move through the membrane. Because of the presence of these ions about the membrane, fewer water molecules will come into contact with the membrane and fewer will diffuse through to the other side. The side containing water molecules alone will lose more of these molecules by diffusion as there is nothing to impede their progress through the cell membrane. Water will diffuse to the side of the membrane containing a larger number of $Na^+$ and $Cl^-$ ions and the fewer number of water molecules. In other words, the water diffuses from a higher to a lower concentration. As a consequence of the diffusion of water, pressure will gradually increase on the side of the membrane containing the greater number of $Na^+$ and $Cl^-$ ions because of the weight of the additional amount of water. The buildup in pressure will stop when the force tending to drive the molecules into the compartment is equalized by the force tending to drive them out. This is a hydraulic pressure, which overcomes the tendency of water to diffuse into the compartment of higher concentration of ions. This force is called the *osmotic pressure.*

Figure 14–4 depicts two U-tubes with a semipermeable membrane separating the solutions. In Figure 14–4, the solutions ($A_1$ and $A_2$) on either side of the membrane contain an equal number of $Na^+$ and $Cl^-$ ions. The membrane is not permeable to these ions; however, water will pass through from one side to the other in equal amounts. As a result, the solutions are said to be *isotonic* to each other. In Figure 14–4, side $B_1$ contains fewer $Na^+$ and $Cl^-$ ions as compared to side $B_2$. Gradually more water molecules will diffuse to $B_2$. Solution $B_2$ is said to be *hypertonic* to side $B_1$, which in turn is *hypotonic* to side $B_2$. Practical application of this principle can be observed using red blood cells in three separate saline solutions: (1) a solution isotonic to the internal mixture of the cell; (2) a solution hypertonic to the internal mixture of the cell; (3) a solution hypotonic to the internal mixture of the cell. Can you deduce what would happen to the cell in each of the three conditions? Figure 14–5 contains three test tubes with the aforementioned solutions. Observe what has happened in each instance to the red blood cell. Does this demonstration help explain why a physician uses an isotonic solution when making injections into the bloodstream?

### Electrical Forces

When certain compounds such as NaCl are placed in water they ionize. That is, the sodium breaks away from the chlorine, resulting in a

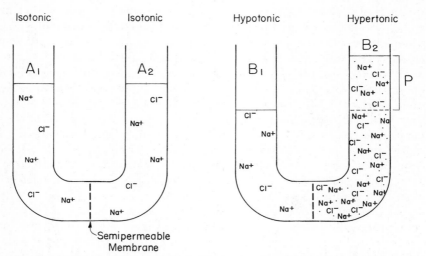

**Figure 14–4** U-tubes with semipermeable membranes separating the solutions. Solutions $A_1$ and $A_2$ contain an equal number of $Na^+$ and $Cl^-$ ions. Water will pass in both directions through the semipermeable membrane in equal amounts; the solutions are isotonic to each other. Solution $B_1$ contains fewer $Na^+$ and $Cl^-$ ions than solution $B_2$. More water molecules will therefore diffuse to solution $B_2$. This will continue until the same number of water molecules are diffusing from $B_2$ to $B_1$, and vice versa. The point at which there exists an equilibrium in diffusion is dependent upon the osmotic pressure, $P$.

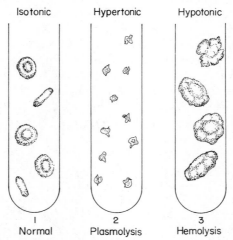

**Figure 14–5** Three test tubes containing isotonic, hypertonic, and hypotonic solutions. In test tube 1 the solution is isotonic, and therefore the cells retain their normal size and shape; in tube 2 the solution is hypertonic to the interior of the cells, causing them to shrink (plasmolysis); and in tube 3 the solution is hypotonic, causing the cells to swell (hemolysis).

positively charged sodium ion (cation) or $Na^+$ and a negatively charged chloride ion (anion) or $Cl^-$. Like charges repel and unlike charges attract. The outstanding difference between the intracellular fluid and the interstitial fluid is the concentration of ions. Sodium, calcium, and chloride concentrations are many times greater outside the cell; on the other hand, potassium, magnesium, and phosphate concentrations are greater inside the cell. As a result of the distribution of these ions, the inside of the cell has a negative charge (of about $-90$ millivolts), whereas the electrical potential of the interstitial fluid is 0. This *electrochemical force* on the inside of the cell tends to attract the positively charged cations into the cell and drive the negatively charged anions out of the cell. For example, $K^+$ would tend to diffuse from the cell because of its high concentration, but the influence of the internal negative charge would cause the $K^+$ to remain within the cell. These two forces (diffusion gradient and electrochemical force) are almost equal, but are sufficiently unequal to favor the movement of $K^+$ from the cell. The opposite is true for $Cl^-$. Chloride ion has a high interstitial concentration, which would cause diffusion into the cell, but the electric forces are sufficient to keep the $Cl^-$ from entering the cell. In other words, the chloride ions inside the cell are in electrochemical equilibrium with those on the outside.

### Active Transport

Sodium is a large ion because it attracts water molecules about its surface. Consequently, even though it is a cation, it experiences difficulty in penetrating the pores of the cell. Although there is a small leakage of sodium into the cell, the number of ions inside the cell remains small, which suggests that a mechanism is in operation that actively removes sodium from the cell. Recollect that when sodium moves from the inside to the outside of the cell it is going against the concentration gradient ("uphill," for sodium is in greater concentration outside the cell). It is also moving against the electrochemical force because the inside of the cell is electrically negative, and unlike charges attract. The explanation for this suggests the presence of an enzyme active in cellular metabolism, which affords the energy to move sodium from the interior of the cell. Exactly how this comes about is unknown, but it is observed that as sodium leaves the cell, $K^+$ enters. This phenomenon, which is referred to as the *sodium-potassium pump*, maintains an equilibrated movement of $Na^+$ and $K^+$ against the diffusion gradient and the electrochemical forces.

Diffusion, both free and facilitated, osmosis (hydraulic pressure), electrochemical potential, and active transport are the forces that move materials into and out of the cell. This is a dynamic process going on continuously. The time factor for a given particle to diffuse from the capillary to the cell and vice versa is measured in microseconds at the cellular level. Upsetting this equilibrium, as was mentioned earlier, results in serious physiological consequences.

# PHYSIOLOGY OF DROWNING

Exploring the physiology of drowning will permit us to see how adverse consequences upset the delicate ionic balance at the cellular level and can cause death if the process is not immediately checked. It should be obvious to us that the sequential events that occur when a person drowns in fresh water will not be the same as those that occur when one drowns in sea water. The reason for this is simply that fresh water is hypotonic, whereas sea water is hypertonic, to the blood. Let us apply what we have learned thus far.

## Drowning in Fresh Water

Even though it is commonly believed that manual resuscitative methods are effective in expelling water from the airway, research has shown that this is not true.[4] Experiments in which dogs have been submerged in fresh water have resulted in the following observations: (1) The dog holds his breath; (2) large amounts of water are swallowed; (3) vomiting occurs; (4) terminal gasping accompanied by flooding of lungs with water (in the neighborhood of 1.5 liters) takes place; and (5) death ensues. This sequence of events is rapid, but survival was usually noted if interruption of the events occurred prior to the stage of terminal gasping. In this case, spontaneous survival was most common, with resuscitative efforts contributing little.[1]

Further experiments have demonstrated that drowning in fresh water results in large volumes of water passing rapidly from the lungs into the blood. It has been found that after 2 minutes of submergence, a dog's blood could contain 51 per cent of the aspirated water.[7] This dilution of blood *(hemodilution)* as a result of increased water volume is called *hypervolemia.* From our knowledge of osmosis we can readily follow the adverse physiological consequences:

(1) The water as it enters the alveoli is hypotonic to the blood (Fig. 14–6A); therefore, through osmosis it will move into the bloodstream. The inaccuracy of such a statement as "The person couldn't have drowned because there wasn't any water in his lungs" should be apparent when drowning occurs in *fresh water.*

(2) The blood is diluted and becomes hypotonic to the cell. It follows that water will diffuse into the red blood cells, causing them literally to burst. This is termed *hemolysis* (see Fig. 14–5), and it occurs in

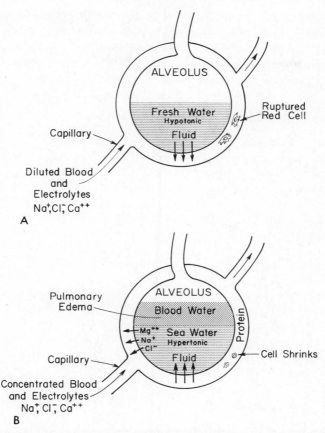

**Figure 14–6**  Alveoli with surrounding capillaries. *A,* During freshwater drowning, water moves into the capillary by osmosis, diluting the blood and electrolytes and rupturing the cells. *B,* During saltwater drowning, blood water moves from the capillaries into the alveoli, causing edema, concentration of blood electrolytes, and cell shrinkage. (Adapted from Redding et al.[2])

such massive proportions that it eliminates the oxygen-carrying capacity of the red blood cells.

(3) The dilution of the blood electrolytes (sodium, chloride, and calcium, in particular) and of plasma proteins, coupled with low oxygen concentration, precipitates *ventricular fibrillation* (irregularity in force and rhythm of the heart, or quivering of the muscle fibers, causing inefficient emptying). It has been demonstrated that fibrillation results from low plasma sodium accompanied by low oxygen tension, both of which occur in freshwater drowning.[6]

Experimentally, a group of scientists prevented ventricular fibrillation in freshwater drowning by intravenous administration of 37 per cent sodium chloride solution. However, if the heart were already fibrillating, immediate administration of the saline failed to reverse the condition. Because the onset of fibrillation is so rapid after submergence in fresh water, the investigators abandoned the technique as not being practical as a resuscitative measure.[6]

### Drowning in Sea Water

As we mentioned earlier, seawater drowning precipitates a different sequence of events because the water (3.5 per cent salts) is hypertonic to blood (0.9 per cent salts).

In saltwater drowning:

(1) Sea water enters the alveoli and salts diffuse into the blood, while water from the blood (blood water) moves into the lungs (see Fig. 14–6B).

(2) The withdrawal of water from the blood causes a rapid rise in plasma sodium concentration.

(3) The number of red blood cells per cubic centimeter of blood (hematocrit value) rapidly increases. The cells undergo plasmolysis, that is, they shrink (Fig. 14–5).

(4) The lungs become full of blood water (pulmonary edema), the systolic blood pressure falls (hypotension), bradycardia (slowing of heart) occurs, and death ensues.

### Emergency Treatment

Investigators have noted that spontaneous breathing movements often did not stop until the heart failed.[3] After immersion in sea water, dogs recovered when water being taken into their lungs was stopped and before profound hypotension occurred. Furthermore (as we have already mentioned), recovery also occurred when freshwater flooding of the lungs did not lead to ventricular fibrillation.

It has been concluded that spontaneous survival is likely in victims of near drowning who are apneic (that is, who have stopped breathing). The following care should be given in such an emergency:[2]

(1) Reoxygenation should be started immediately by means of exhaled air methods (e.g., mouth-to-mouth resuscitation).

(2) Reoxygenation should be continued as soon as possible by means of intermittent positive pressure breathing (IPPB) apparatus with 100 per cent oxygen.

(3) For seawater victims, once IPPB therapy is started it should be continued until a blood specimen demonstrates plasma deficiencies have been corrected.

(4) Intermittent positive pressure breathing treatment using oxygen combined with closed chest cardiac massage is recommended when fibrillation occurs from freshwater drowning. This is preliminary to external electrical defibrillation.

(5) Finally, delayed death after freshwater near-drowning may be averted through subsequent judicious management of massive hemolysis, hypovolemia, electrolyte imbalances and myocardial failure by the attending physician.

### Implications

What does this mean to you, the physical educator, should you be at the scene of a near-drowning? Your training should allow you to perform mouth-to-mouth resuscitation and, if necessary, closed chest cardiac massage prior to arrival of the emergency squad. Remember that the near-drowning casualty should *never* be permitted to move about. The individual should be transported to the hospital, where competent medical attention will permit observation and complete evaluation of the patient's condition before being discharged.

Another potential subject of interest stemming from our discussion of drowning is how to decrease the hazard of drowning in private and public swimming pools (fresh water). For example, we learned that in both fresh and salt (sea) water drownings, gas exchange is prevented. In addition, drowning in fresh water causes hemolysis and hemodilution (hypotonic solution), and drowning in salt water results in plasmolysis and hemoconcentration (hypertonic solution). We saw how the latter changes were instrumental in the eventual death of the drowning victim.

We also learned, however, that in an isotonic solution, blood cells, for instance, are not damaged; that is, they retain their normal size and shape. In other words, there is no net movement of large amounts of water into or out of the cell (see Fig. 14–5). What this implies is that the survival time may be longer if drowned in an isotonic solution* rather than in either fresh or sea water. In mice, this has actually been demonstrated. As shown in Figure 14–7, the survival time of mice (as judged by the time of the last gasp) was significantly increased when drowned in an isotonic solution rather than in either fresh or salt water.[5] While this significant increase amounted to only 15 seconds, remember that these data apply to mice; in humans, because of their much larger size, the increase in survival time would most likely be much greater. Even at that, with at least 15 more seconds: Is it possible that more lives could be saved if our swimming pools were isotonic rather than hypo-

---

*An isotonic solution for humans would contain 0.9 per cent NaCl. (Incidentally, the salt content of sea water is 3.5 per cent.)

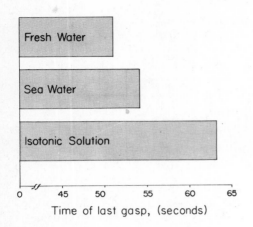

Time of last gasp, (seconds)

**Figure 14–7** Survival times of mice drowned in fresh water, sea water and an isotonic solution. The survival time is significantly greater in the isotonic solution. (Based on data from Standish and Miller.[5])

tonic? Although we recognize that there would be technical and perhaps costly problems associated with maintaining an "isotonic pool," it nevertheless provides some "food for thought."

## SUMMARY

We have observed in this chapter how particles are moved into and out of cells. The information was applied to the sequential events of drowning, both in fresh water and in sea water. We also raised the question of the possibility of saving more lives through "isotonic swimming pools."

In Chapter 17 we will study the sequential events leading to heat stroke. Because of our understanding of osmosis and diffusion, it will be easy for us to follow how a physiological imbalance results from serious body water loss. Because more water than salt is lost during profuse sweating, the concentration of $Na^+$ outside the cell is increased. This is called *hypernatremia*. The water will move from inside to outside the cell; blood water will move to the interstitial spaces; and concentration of $Na^+$ and other electrolytes will be increased.

## QUESTIONS

1. Indicate how oxygen and carbon dioxide move into and out of the cell.

2. Describe the difference between diffusion and osmosis.

3. Why does a physician use a solution isotonic to the blood when making injections into a vein?

4. Why is there a tendency for potassium to remain within the cell and sodium to remain outside the cell?

5. What are the prime forces that move materials into and out of a cell?

6. What are the sequential events in drowning? Where must these events be interrupted if survival is to occur?

7. What are the adverse physiological consequences of drowning (1) in fresh water, and (2) in salt water?

8. If you were present at the scene of a near-drowning, what considerations should be taken into account to insure the best care for the person involved?

9. Explain physiologically how an isotonic swimming pool could potentially save lives from drowning.

## REFERENCES

1. Fainer, D., Martin, C., and Ivy, A.: Resuscitation of dogs from fresh water drowning. J. Appl. Physiol., 12:417–426, 1957.
2. Redding, J., Cozine, R., Voigt, G., and Safar, P.: Resuscitation from drowning. J.A.M.A., 178(12):1136–1139, 1961.
3. Redding, J., Voigt, G., and Safar, P.: Resuscitation from drowning: laboratory evaluation. Anesthesiology, 21:113–114, 1959.
4. Safar, P.: Failure of manual artificial respiration. J. Appl. Physiol., 14:84–88, 1959.
5. Standish, M., and Miller, J.: Drowning in fresh water, Ringer's solution, and sea water: effects of hypothermia. Fed. Proc., 28(2):792, 1969.
6. Swann, H.: Studies in Resuscitation. Air Force Technical Report No. 6696, Wright Air Development Center, Wright-Patterson Air Force Base, Ohio, 1951.
7. Swann, H., and Spafford, N.: Body salt and water changes during fresh and sea water drowning. Texas Rep. Biol. Med., 9:356–382, 1951.

## SELECTED READING

Guyton, A.: Basic Human Physiology: Normal Function and Mechanisms of Disease. Philadelphia, W. B. Saunders Co., pp. 37–47, 1971.

────────────────────────────

# Chapter 15

# EXERCISE AND ACID-BASE BALANCE

ACIDS AND BASES
    Buffers
    pH (Power of the Hydrogen Ion)
RESPIRATORY REGULATION
    Alkali Reserve
THE KIDNEY AND ACID-BASE
    BALANCE
    Alkalosis and Acidosis
ACID-BASE BALANCE FOLLOW-
    ING STRENUOUS EXERCISE

As body fluids become more acidic, muscles lose their contractility. During the metabolism of food, acid metabolites are released within the body; during exercise even more acid is produced. If acids were allowed to accumulate, serious illness and, finally, death would result. So, too, if tissue fluids become too basic (alkaline), illness and death would be consequential.

The body's maintenance of a proper acid-base fluid environment occurs through three mechanisms:

1. Contained within the body fluids are chemicals called *buffers*. These substances react with the acids and bases to maintain a proper acid-base balance; a buffer softens and diminishes the effect when either an acid or a base is added to the body fluids.

2. The *kidney* through a sensor system will excrete urine that is either acidic or basic in order to maintain the correct acid-base environment; and

3. The *respiratory mechanism* aids in regulating the acid-base balance by the amount of carbon dioxide retained or released.

## ACIDS AND BASES

An acid is a chemical compound which in solution gives up hydrogen ($H^+$) ions; a base is one which gives up hydroxyl ions ($OH^-$) when placed in solution. For example:

|                | Acids                              |                | Bases                          |

| Acids | Bases |
|-------|-------|

$$HCl \rightleftharpoons H^+ + Cl^- \qquad\qquad NaOH \rightleftharpoons Na + OH^-$$

$$H_2SO_4 \rightleftharpoons H^+ + SO_4^- \qquad\qquad KOH \rightleftharpoons K^+ + OH^-$$

Strong acids give up relatively more $H^+$ ions than weak acids; strong bases release more $OH^-$ ions than weak bases.

Aqueous (water) solutions contain both $H^+$ and $OH^-$ ions. An acid solution contains more $H^+$ ions, whereas the basic solution contains more $OH^-$ ions. Pure water is neutral since it contains an equal number of $H^+$ ions and $OH^-$ ions:

$$H_2O \rightleftharpoons H^+ + OH^-$$

Consequently, the determinant regarding whether a solution is acidic or basic simply amounts to *the number of $H^+$ ions present*. If the number of $H^+$ ions exceeds the number of $OH^-$ ions, then the solution is acidic, and vice versa.

## Buffers

A buffer system consists of two parts: (1) a weak acid and (2) the salt of that weak acid. Its primary purpose is to maintain a given $H^+$ ion concentration. Examples of buffers are: acetic acid (weak acid) and sodium acetate (salt), carbonic acid (weak acid) and sodium bicarbonate (salt).

In the buffering game, an acid reacts with a salt, resulting in the formation of a stronger salt and a weaker acid. For example, lactic acid (LA) reacting with sodium bicarbonate ($NaHCO_3$) forms sodium lactate (NaLA) and carbonic acid ($H_2CO_3$):

$$LA + NaHCO_3 \leftarrow NaLA + H_2CO_3$$

In the blood, carbonic acid is weak, for it does not yield many $H^+$ ions; also carbonic acid dissociates into water and carbon dioxide, both of which can be readily excreted:

$$H_2CO_3 \rightleftharpoons H_2O + CO_2$$

Sodium bicarbonate easily buffers the strong hydrochloric acid (HCl) with formation of a strong salt (NaCl) and a weak acid ($H_2CO_3$):

$$NaHCO_3 + HCl \rightarrow NaCl + H_2CO_3$$

or

Bicarbonate + strong acid → salt + weak acid

Here, the excessive hydrogen ions dissociated from HCl are by and large removed from the solution in forming carbonic acid. Remember this acid is weak, for it does not dissociate as readily as HCl (i.e., it does not yield as many $H^+$ ions).

Such a buffering system exemplifies the one way in which the body fluids do not become too acidic or basic.

## pH (Power of the Hydrogen Ion)

To express alkalinity or acidity of a solution, one determines the number of $H^+$ ions present. This resulting number is expressed as the pH of that solution or power of the hydrogen ion. Because of the large numbers with which we must deal (e.g., the weight in moles* of the hydrogen ions contained in 1 liter of water), the pH of a liquid is expressed as a negative logarithm to the base 10:

$$pH = -\log [H^+]$$

Where $[H^+]$ equals grams of $H^+$ ions present in one liter of solution.

The concentration of hydrogen ions in pure water is approximately $10^{-7}$ moles per liter (.0000007 moles per liter).

Therefore:

$$pH = -\log [10^{-7}] = -[-7] = 7.0 \text{ (the log of } 10^{-7} = -7)$$

The pH of pure water equals 7; a pH greater than 7 (fewer hydrogen ions) would be considered alkaline; a pH of 7, neutral; and a pH less than 7, acidic.

Adding an acid to a solution lowers its pH because the number of free hydrogen ions increases, while adding an alkali reduces the concentration of the $H^+$ ions because the number of $OH^-$ ions increases, hence increasing the pH.

The range of pH in the body compatible with life is between 7.3 and 7.5 during rest. Exercise will cause the pH to shift toward the acid side; it may go as low as 6.80 during strenuous exercise.[3] Such a low pH is only transitory, for the body's buffering power including the kidney and respiratory systems will become operable and return the pH to normal.

In addition to the bicarbonate buffering system (e.g., $NaHCO_3$), there are the phosphate and protein buffering systems. All the systems work in a similar manner. The phosphate buffers (e.g., $Na_2HPO_4$) are concentrated in the kidneys, while the proteins (e.g., hemoglobin) are contained in the cells and plasma. Since most buffering is performed within the cells, the protein buffers are very important.

# RESPIRATORY REGULATION

The respiratory center of the medulla oblongata in the brain and the chemoreceptors in the aortic arch are sensitive to changes in the hydrogen ion concentration of the blood. An increase in $CO_2$ within the body fluids (which combines with water to form carbonic acid) decreases the pH; elimination of $CO_2$ will cause the pH to rise. The

---

*A mole is the amount of a substance with a weight equal to its molecular weight in grams. One mole of $H_2O$ equals 18 gm. [H = 1; O = 16; therefore, $1 \times 2 + 16 = 18$]

increased $H^+$ ion concentration stimulates the respiratory system, thus increasing ventilation and removing (blowing-off) the $CO_2$. Conversely, a lowered $H^+$ ion concentration will depress the respiratory mechanism. Alterations in the rate and depth of respiration can effect immediate changes in fluid pH. As the pH falls below 7.41, respiration is strongly stimulated. At a pH of 7.20, ventilation increases fourfold; as the pH increases above 7.41, respiration is inhibited; at a pH of 7.50, pulmonary ventilation is reduced by about one-half.

Application of this principle, although dangerous, can be observed in underwater swimmers who hyperventilate preceding a dive. This enables them to hold their breath longer as the stimulus for breathing (presence of $CO_2$) is significantly reduced.

### Alkali Reserve

The degree to which the pH is affected by the buildup of $CO_2$ and subsequent formation of carbonic acid depends upon the amount of $HCO_3^-$ (bicarbonate) available for the buffering operation. When the bicarbonate concentration is equivalent to the dissolved carbon dioxide, tissue pH equals 6.1. Normally, the ratio of the bicarbonate to carbonic acid is 20:1, or a pH of 7.4. An increase in bicarbonate ions causes a rise in pH, while an increase in dissolved $CO_2$ decreases the pH. The amount of bicarbonate available for buffering is called the *alkali reserve*.

Some have conjectured that by taking doses of bicarbonate to increase the alkali reserve, fatigue during heavy work or athletic events would be forestalled. Hopefully, this would be brought about by the increased capacity to buffer lactic acid. Perhaps this is a good idea, but experiments showed such "doping" to be of no value.

## THE KIDNEY AND ACID-BASE BALANCE

The kidney can regulate the $H^+$ ion concentration in a number of ways, but primarily through increasing or decreasing the bicarbonate ion concentration ($HCO_3^-$).

Epithelial cells within the kidney secrete $H^+$ ions. Here, carbon dioxide with an assist from the enzyme carbonic anhydrase combines with water to form carbonic acid.

$$CO_2 + H_2O \xrightarrow{\text{carbonic anhydrase}} H_2CO_3$$

The carbonic acid dissociates into a bicarbonate and a hydrogen ion:

$$H_2CO_3 \rightleftharpoons H^+ + HCO_3^-$$

From the epithelial cell the hydrogen ion is secreted into the tubule of the kidney. As the $CO_2$ concentration in the extracellular fluid increases, so does the secretion of the $H^+$ ions into the tubules. Of course, there is a limit to the $H^+$ ion secretion; secretion stops when the pH of the tubular fluid reaches about 4.5.

It now becomes possible for large numbers of hydrogen ions to tie up the bicarbonate ion in the formation of carbonic acid ($H_2CO_3$). Consequently, few, if any, bicarbonate ions are left to be passed into the urine. However, with each hydrogen ion secreted into the tubule, one hydroxyl ion ($OH^-$) is left within the renal tubule cell. As these $OH^-$ ions accumulate within the cell, the pH commences to rise. At this time, intracellular neutralization occurs; $CO_2$ and water eventually combine with these hydroxyl ions, maintaining the pH.

$$CO_2 + H_2O \rightarrow H_2CO_3 \rightarrow HCO_3^- + H^+$$

These newly formed $HCO_3^-$ ions, along with a sodium ion ($Na^+$), are transported into the peritubular fluid and renal venous plasma to be used as needed.

### Alkalosis and Acidosis

When there are excessive bicarbonate ions in the extracellular fluids, the condition is called alkalosis. These ions enter the tubules and pass on into the urine accompanied by sodium or some other positive ion, (e.g., potassium or $K^+$). Removal of bicarbonate ions from the extracellular fluid shifts the pH toward the acidic side.

When there is an increase in $CO_2$ in the extracellular fluid, acidosis occurs. In this case there is an excessive number of hydrogen ions being secreted in the tubules; these combine with the tubular buffers and are then excreted in the urine.

## ACID-BASE BALANCE FOLLOWING
## STRENUOUS EXERCISE

During maximal exercise of short duration, dramatic changes occur in the acid-base metabolic chemistry due primarily to the production of lactic acid. Anaerobic work which produces lactic acid causes the blood pH to decrease. The amount of acid produced depends upon: (1) the amount of time, (2) work intensity, and (3) muscle mass involved.[2] Within seconds during continuous anaerobic work, lactic acid levels may approximate 180 mg. per cent, with pH values nearing 7.0. Intermittent work may cause the pH to reach 6.80 (one of the lowest values ever recorded) with lactic acid values around 280 mg. per cent.[3]

These values are excessive when one considers that during rest a pH of less than 7.4 indicates that the person is acidotic, while a pH greater than 7.4 indicates that he is alkalotic. The lower limit of pH compatible with life (not exercising) for a few minutes is 7.0 and the upper limit about 7.8.[1]

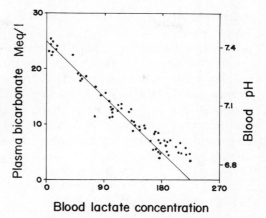

**Figure 15-1** Relationship between blood pH, blood lactate (lactic acid), and plasma bicarbonate following exhaustive exercise. (Based on data from Osnes and Hermansen.[3])

The plasma bicarbonate concentration (normal values 23–28 millimoles (mM.)/liter — women lower than men) has been recorded as low as 2.6 mM./liter. Figure 15-1 illustrates the relationship of blood pH, blood lactate concentration, and plasma bicarbonate following exhaustive work from data by Osnes and Hermansen.[3]

Figure 15-2 illustrates the relationship between blood pH and blood lactate concentration as a consequence of brief, strenuous exercise. Note that the pH values decline toward 6.80 as the blood lactic acid increases to 288 mg. per cent. These are the lowest and highest values, respectively, ever recorded.

## SUMMARY

The kidney, by excreting bicarbonate and/or manufacturing new bicarbonate ions along with its buffering systems, functions to maintain

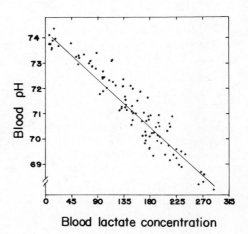

**Figure 15-2** Relationship between blood pH and blood lactate concentration as a consequence of brief, strenuous exercise. Note that the pH values decline toward 6.80 as the blood lactic acid increases to 288 mg. per cent. (Based on data from Osnes and Hermansen.[3])

the power of the hydrogen ion within normal limits. The respiratory system responds at once to abnormal $H^+$ ion concentration by increased or decreased ventilation. The kidneys' response, though extremely effective, may take 10 to 20 hours in regulating acid-base abnormalities.

Immediately following strenuous intermittent exercise of short duration the pH drops to below 7.0, while the lactate concentration in the blood may rise to 288 mg. per cent; plasma bicarbonate concentration may drop as low as 2.6 mM./L. During rest these values could not be sustained and death would ensue; however, during exercise they are tolerated quite well.

## QUESTIONS

1. Define an acid; a base.

2. Describe how a buffer works.

3. What is meant by the power of the hydrogen ion (pH)?

4. Explain how respiration aids in regulating acid-base balance.

5. What is the alkali reserve?

6. Explain the kidney's function in acid-base regulation.

7. Immediately following strenuous exercise of short duration, what happens to the following: pH, plasma bicarbonate, and blood lactate?

## REFERENCES

1. Guyton, A.: Basic Human Physiology: Normal Function and Mechanisms of Disease. p. 305, Philadelphia, W. B. Saunders Co., 1971.
2. Hermansen, L.: Lactate production during exercise. *In* Pernow, B., and Saltin, B. (eds.): Muscle Metabolism During Exercise. New York, Plenum Press, 1971.
3. Osnes, J., and Hermansen, L.: Acid-base balance after maximal exercise of short duration. J. Appl. Physiol., 32(1):59–63, 1972.

## SELECTED READING

Davenport, H.: The ABC of Acid-Base Chemistry. 4th ed., The University of Chicago Press, 1958.

# Chapter 16

# SCUBA AND PERFORMANCE AT ALTITUDE

Scuba (self-contained underwater breathing apparatus) diving, in addition to being fun, offers a wonderful opportunity to learn a great deal about physiology in a very exciting and interesting manner. The physiology of just one dive could actually fill a textbook, and the importance of this information is dramatically illustrated by the fact that if the knowledge is not applied, a single dive could be fatal.

It is not unusual in this jet age for athletic teams to be suddenly whisked to competitions in cities that are at much greater altitudes than the place where the athletes trained. The day of the competition will be too late to wonder about the effects of low pressure and the advisability of administering oxygen to your team; one must plan well in advance.

You are the most logical person in a community to serve as a knowledgeable reference source for those who wish to learn about scuba and performance at altitude. The purpose of this chapter is to provide the knowledge that will allow you to fulfill this function.

# EFFECTS OF CHANGES IN PRESSURE AND TEMPERATURE ON GAS VOLUMES

Comprehension of the physiological factors associated with physical performance below the sea and at altitude absolutely requires knowledge of the gas laws. Familiarity with these laws will help us to make valid judgments regarding how the individual may be physiologically affected, whether skiing in Squaw Valley (altitude of 6000 or more feet) or donning scuba gear and searching the ocean floors.

### Effects of Pressure Changes on Gas Volume

It is quite interesting to note that when you increase the pressure on a given volume of gas, the volume diminishes. Whereas, when you increase the pressure on a given volume of water, the volume remains just about the same. If, for example, a given amount of gas is subjected to twice the pressure, the volume will be *reduced* by one-half. By the same token, if the pressure should be diminished by one-half, the volume will *double*. Water volume is not affected by pressure changes, whereas gas volumes are significantly altered. You will realize shortly that these are important considerations for us to be aware of, particularly in scuba.

### Effects of Temperature Changes on Gas Volume

Gas volume is affected not only by pressure but also by temperature. Heating a gas causes it to expand. As a matter of fact, if you hold pressure on the gas constant and raise the temperature from 0° C. to 100° C., the volume increases almost 37 per cent. However, temperature change has an insignificant effect on the volume of water, just as does pressure change. A more comprehensive treatment of the gas laws appears in Appendix B.

### Weight of Air

Air has weight and at sea level exerts 14.7 pounds of pressure per square inch (psi). As we ascend in altitude, the amount of air above us decreases and, as a result, the pressure diminishes. For example, at 5000 feet the pressure is reduced to 12.2 psi; at 10,000, 10.1 psi, and at 15,000, 8.3 psi. At 60,500 feet, only 1 psi of pressure is exerted by air.

On the other hand, as we descend below the surface of the sea, we have in addition to the 14.7 psi of pressure exerted by the atmosphere, the weight of the water above us. Sea water, because of the salt content, weighs 64 pounds per cubic foot, while fresh water weighs 62.4 pounds per cubic foot. The density* of water, that is, its weight per cubic foot, remains constant as one descends to the ocean depths because, as was mentioned earlier, water is essentially noncompressible. Because of this factor, the weight of water is proportional to the depth. That is, at 33 feet under the surface the weight of water alone will be equal to one atmosphere, or 14.7 psi of pressure. Why is this so?

If the weight of sea water equals 64 pounds per cubic foot, and a diver descends to 33 feet, what is the pressure (or weight of the water) on the diver at this depth in terms of pounds per square inch?

33 feet × 64 pounds per cubic foot = 2112 pounds per square foot
1 square foot contains (12 inch × 12 inch) or 144 square inches
Converting pounds per square foot to pounds per square inch:

$$\frac{2112 \text{ pounds per square foot}}{144 \text{ square inches per square foot}} = 14.7 \text{ psi}$$

Therefore, at a depth of 33 feet, the water would cause a pressure on the diver of 14.7 psi. The total pressure on the diver, or what is referred to as the absolute pressure, will be equal to 29.4 psi because to the weight of the water must be added the weight of the atmosphere (14.7 psi + 14.7 psi). Figure 16–1 depicts the increased pressure as one descends to 99 feet.

## PHYSICAL AND PHYSIOLOGICAL PRINCIPLES OF SCUBA

We have learned: (1) that gas volume is affected by both pressure and temperature; (2) that air has weight, and that the greater the altitude, the less it weighs; (3) that water is noncompressible (at 5000 feet below the surface a cubic foot of water weighs the same as at the surface); and (4) why, at 33 feet below the surface of the sea, the water pressure is equivalent to one atmosphere. It is imperative for us to remember that the body contains air cavities, the most important being

---

*Density equals the mass per unit volume.

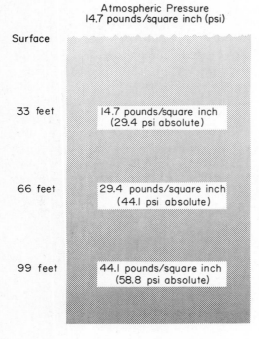

Atmospheric Pressure
14.7 pounds/square inch (psi)

Surface

33 feet    14.7 pounds/square inch
(29.4 psi absolute)

66 feet    29.4 pounds/square inch
(44.1 psi absolute)

99 feet    44.1 pounds/square inch
(58.8 psi absolute)

**Figure 16–1** Depth and pressure relationships. As the diver descends from the surface of the water at sea level to a depth of 99 feet, the absolute pressure increases from 14.7 psi to 58.8 psi.

the lungs; and that the body (with the exception of air cavities) is essentially water and therefore noncompressible.

## Air Embolus (Fig. 16–2)

The term *embolus* comes from the Greek meaning "plug"; it is used in physiology to refer to any material that enters the blood stream and obstructs a blood vessel. We may consider the alveoli of the lungs as millions of small balloons. Let us suppose that, at a depth of 33 feet, a diver inhales a volume of air from his or her tank, holds the breath, and then proceeds to the surface. If the diver should be foolish enough to do this, the lungs would rupture and death would result. This is true because, as we have learned, gas volume is affected by pressure; the volume of gas the diver inhaled at a depth of 33 feet would double by the time he or she reached the surface, causing the alveoli to explode.

Even under 5 feet of water, if a volume of air is breathed from the scuba tank and the breath is held while surfacing, overdistension of the lungs will occur. This in turn can cause rupture of the alveoli and perhaps pulmonary hemorrhage. The more severe rupture results in shattering of lung tissue, capillaries, and veins, and free air may be

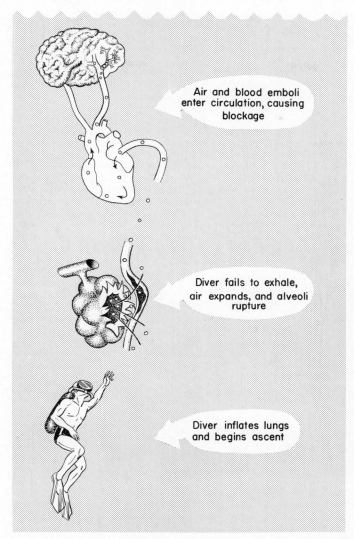

**Figure 16–2**    Formation of emboli as a diver ascends without exhaling.

forced into the capillaries, forming emboli. The emboli may then enter the mainstream of the circulatory system, and the bubbles of air may find their way into the arteries of the heart and brain. As a consequence, circulatory blockage by the emboli and even death may occur. Probably the single most important consideration when giving scuba instruction is that *a diver must exhale as he or she surfaces. NEVER HOLD YOUR BREATH!*

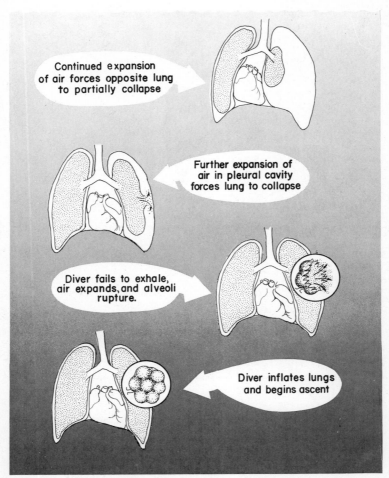

**Figure 16-3** Spontaneous pneumothorax, caused by diver's failure to exhale during ascent.

## Spontaneous Pneumothorax (Spontaneous Entrance of Air into the Pleural Cavity, Fig. 16–3)

Following rupture of lung tissue (alveoli), an air pocket within the chest cavity (intrathoracic space) may form. As the diver continues to ascend, the pressure decreases, and the air that is in the pleural cavity, as a consequence of the lung rupture, will continue to expand, causing the ruptured lung to collapse. In addition, the increasing volume of air will cause the collapsed lung and the heart to be pushed toward the opposite side of the chest. As a consequence, the diver may go into shock, and if the pneumothorax is sufficiently severe, death may result. Treatment requires surgical intervention with a syringe and needle to remove the air pocket.

### Nitrogen Narcosis (Raptures of the Deep, Fig. 16–4)

Nitrogen narcosis is dependent primarily on the depth of the dive and secondarily on the length of time at that depth. Nitrogen narcosis affects the central nervous system: first there is a sense of dizziness, then a slowing of mental processes, euphoria, and a fixation of ideas. The exact cause of these symptoms is difficult to explain. However, it is felt that because nitrogen is quite soluble in fatty tissue, the deeper the diver (i.e., exceeding 100 feet), the more nitrogen is forced into solution within the body. Its effects on the central nervous system are similar to those of alcohol. As a consequence, the "martini rule" has been formulated: 100 feet has the same effect as one martini on an empty stomach; 200 feet, two to three martinis; 300 feet, four martinis; and 400 feet, "tee many martoonis"!

**Figure 16–4** Nitrogen narcosis. Nitrogen has a narcotic effect on the nervous system similar to that of alcohol. Prolonged stay at depth may produce a euphoric condition such as is illustrated by the diver chasing the mermaid.

One must recognize that the effects are quite individualistic and some people may be affected at moderate depths (50 feet or less)—the severity of the symptoms is unique to the individual. The U.S. Navy suggests the maximum depth for scuba should be set at 200 feet, with a practical limiting depth of 130 feet.[17]

### The Bends (Fig. 16–5)

Nitrogen is inert, that is, this gas does not take part in respiration. The amount inhaled is equal to the amount exhaled.[11] As a diver descends the pressure about the diver increases; this increased pressure will force gas into solution within the blood. The deeper the dive and the greater the length of time for the dive, the more gas will go into solution. The same principle prevails in carbonation of soft drinks. The carbon dioxide ($CO_2$) is forced into the liquid under high pressure and the bottle is capped. When the cap is removed, the $CO_2$ escapes into the air in the form of bubbles because of the decreased pressure. Very rapid ascent by a diver to regions of lower pressure is similar to removal of the cap from the soda bottle in that the dissolved gas (nitrogen) is liberated in the form of bubbles. These nitrogen bubbles (gas emboli) may cause circulatory blockage and tissue damage. Pain is usually felt at the joints or ligaments and tendons first, within 24 hours following exposure; indeed, 85 per cent of those suffering from the bends will have symptoms within 4 to 6 hours. There is only one way in which the bends may be successfully treated and that is by recompression. The individual is placed into a chamber into which air is pumped,

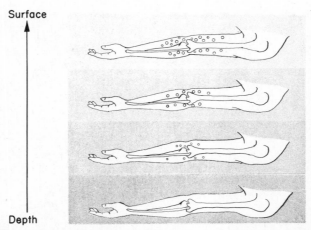

**Figure 16–5**   Bends. Increased pressure forces nitrogen into solution. Decreased pressure releases this nitrogen from solution into the blood and causes formation of gas bubbles in the tissues.

elevating the pressure and hence forcing the nitrogen bubbles back into solution. The diver then undergoes slow decompression, which allows the nitrogen to gradually come from solution (without the formation of bubbles) and be exhaled.

It is obvious that those responsible for the welfare of divers should be aware of the location of the nearest recompression chamber.

The prevention of the bends requires a thorough knowledge of the recommended ascent patterns for divers from various depths who had been submerged for various durations. These data can be found in the United States Navy Diving Manual.[17]

### Oxygen Poisoning (Fig. 16–6)

Breathing of 100 per cent oxygen, and the depth and duration of the dive are factors in the production of oxygen poisoning. As was mentioned earlier, increasing the pressure of a gas over a liquid will cause more of the gas to go into solution. If oxygen is forced into solution, the tissues would first use the oxygen in solution as it is more readily available than is the oxygen carried by the red cell. At the same time, if the red cells are adequately loaded with oxygen, carbon dioxide, which is continually being formed, cannot be removed. Recall that the red cell carries oxygen from the alveoli to the cells and transports $CO_2$ from the cells to the alveoli. Because the red cell cannot dispose of

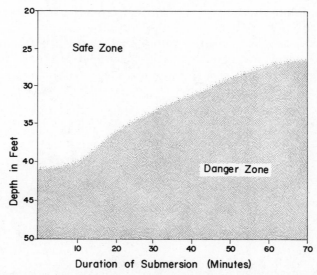

**Figure 16–6** Oxygen poisoning is dependent upon duration of submersion and depth of dive.

the oxygen, it cannot possibly take on the $CO_2$, causing a buildup of $CO_2$ in body tissues. Excess $CO_2$ and $O_2$ in the tissues disturbs cerebral blood flow, resulting in the following symptoms of oxygen poisoning: tingling of fingers and toes, visual disturbance, acoustic hallucinations, sensations of abnormality, confusion, muscle twitching, unpleasant respiratory sensations, nausea, vertigo, lip twitching, and convulsions.

There is no place in amateur diving for the use of pure oxygen. One might might ask why pure oxygen is ever used. Consider the Navy's UDT (Underwater Demolition Team) given a project to destroy an enemy vessel. If you were the man on watch and observed bubbles coming toward your ship, what might you surmise? Quite obviously someone is "up to no good!" Navy divers must use a closed breathing system so that bubbles of expired air do not come to the surface, revealing their presence. The unit works by employing a chemical to absorb the $CO_2$ produced, and returning, hopefully, only oxygen and nitrogen to the tank. Unfortunately, a good chemical for ridding the expired air of all $CO_2$ has not as yet been perfected. The result is a possible buildup of $CO_2$, which may cause the diver eventually to lose consciousness.

### Squeeze (Fig. 16–7)

When the face mask is donned at the surface it contains air at surface pressure. As the diver descends, the water pressure outside increases, causing considerable pressure differential between the inside and outside of the mask. Exhaling occasionally into the mask from the tank will equilibrate the two pressures. If equilibration does not take place, there will be extravasation of blood into the conjunctivae of the eyes; indeed, extreme pressure differential would have a tendency to "suck" the eyes from their sockets. *Quite certainly a person should never wear goggles to dive, as there is no way in which to equilibrate the pressures.*

**Figure 16–7** Squeeze is caused by failure to equilibrate pressures. When the diver fails to equilibrate the pressure between the inside and outside of the mask extravasation of blood into the conjunctivae of the eyes may occur. This is why goggles should not be worn while diving.

*Aerotitis*

The eustachian tube is a small channel connecting the middle ear cavity and the back of the throat. When ascending or descending, one may experience a popping in the ears. The purpose of this tube is to equilibrate the pressure within the ear cavity with the outside. When this passageway is blocked (e.g., because of infection), equilibration is impossible. If you are diving and continue to descend, there will be pain, congestion of mucous membranes, hemorrhage, bleeding into the middle ear, and possible rupture of the ear drum. Consequently, you should never dive when you have an upper respiratory infection because of the possibility of a mucus plug forming in the eustachian tube and preventing equilibration of pressure. As a matter of fact, if during any dive pain is experienced in the ear, the dive should be aborted and the diver should return at once to the surface.

We are well aware that the skull contains a number of sinuses anatomically in communication with our surroundings. The sinuses contain air cavities, and should mucus block the passageways to the outside, pressure changes cannot take place. In such an instance, should you dive or ascend to heights, pain and bloody transudate may ensue.

*New Underwater Breathing Systems*

One of the newer types of breathing systems in open circuit scuba is the cryogenic (relating to production of very low temperature) gear, which uses liquid air (at temperature of $-317.8°$ F.). A great deal more air can be carried liquified than in compressed gaseous form. As a result, one tank will last several hours and weighs approximately one-half of the standard 72 cubic foot bottle. A heat exchanger and a pressure regulator raise the very low liquid air temperature and pressure to those of the surrounding water.

The scuba gear that permits diving to depths of 1000 feet uses a helium-oxygen system. Helium replaces the nitrogen to eliminate problems of the bends and at the same time dilutes the oxygen to avoid oxygen toxicity. The amount of oxygen to be mixed with helium must be regulated with the depth of the dive. By means of regulator valves, the partial pressure of oxygen must approximate that in the air at sea level (21 per cent of 760 mm. of Hg). For example at 100 feet the breathing mixture would be approximately 5 per cent oxygen and 95 per cent helium; whereas at 650 feet, the mixture would be 1 per cent oxygen and 99 per cent helium.

The cryogenic gear using liquid air will undoubtedly replace the present scuba equipment used by the sports diver. Whereas the deep diving gear is extremely expensive (several thousand dollars) it has been developed for use mostly by the Navy in such exploits as the Navy's Sealabs and the Tektite project.

## PERFORMANCE AT ALTITUDE

It is an established fact that at altitudes of over 5000 feet (1524 meters), the ability to perform physical work is affected — the higher the altitude, the more severe the effects. This is illustrated by the data shown in Figure 16–8. In general, one can expect a reduction in endurance capacity as measured by the maximal oxygen consumption (max $\dot{V}o_2$) of 3 to $3\frac{1}{2}$ per cent for every 1000 feet ascended above 5000 feet.[7] Also notice in the figure that work performance and max $\dot{V}o_2$ are reduced by 60 per cent or more at extremely high altitudes, i.e., at around 25,000 feet.[15] Although such reductions in physical performance are quite large as they stand, it should be pointed out that these values were obtained on acclimatized and very fit mountain climbers. Acclimatization, as we will presently discuss, refers to certain physiological adjustments which are brought about through continued expo-

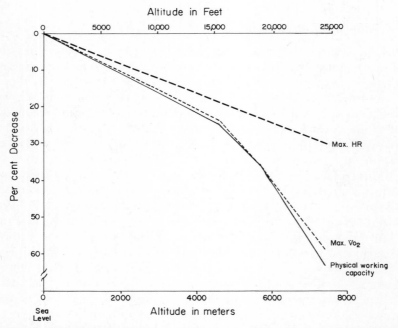

**Figure 16–8** At altitudes of over 5000 feet (1524 meters), the ability to perform physical work is affected. In general, one can expect a reduction in max$\dot{V}o_2$ of 3 to $3\frac{1}{2}$ per cent for every 1000 feet ascended above 5000 feet. Physical working capacity and max$\dot{V}o_2$ are reduced by 60 per cent or more at extremely high altitudes. (Based on data from Pugh.[15])

sure to altitude and which significantly improve performance. For the unacclimatized person, additional oxygen is essential above 18,000 feet (5488 meters).

It is important to point out at this time that although more than approximately 15 million people live at an altitude higher than 10,000 feet (3000 meters), most athletic competition in the United States takes place in areas located below this altitude. This means that since the effects of altitudes below 5000 feet are not great, from a practical standpoint, we need to be concerned mainly with the effects on athletic competition of altitudes between 5000 and 10,000 feet.

### Altitude Acclimatization

The longer you remain at altitude, the better becomes your performance, but it never quite reaches the values that are obtained at sea level. As we have just mentioned, the improved performance during stay at altitude is brought about through *acclimatization.* The number of weeks to acclimatize depends on the altitude—i.e., for 9000 feet, about seven to ten days; for 12,000 feet, 15 to 21 days; and for 15,000 feet, 21 to 25 days. These are only approximations; a great deal depends on the individual. As a matter of fact, a few people will never acclimatize and continue to suffer *mountain or altitude sickness* while at altitude. This happens even with people who were born and raised at altitude. Suddenly, for unknown reasons, they lose their acclimatization and suffer from mountain sickness. The symptoms of altitude sickness include nausea, vomiting, headache, rapid pulse, and loss of appetite.

A word of warning: severe cases of mountain sickness cause symptoms not unlike pneumonia, even at an altitude of 10,000 feet; that is, fever and congestion of the lungs. In more than one instance the diagnosis has been that these persons were suffering from pneumonia and they were given antibiotics, while the persons were left at altitude. As a result, the patients have died. Emergency treatment of severe mountain sickness consists of administering oxygen or removal to lower altitude or both. Services of a physician should be obtained at once.

**Physiology of Acclimatization.**   As we ascend above sea level, the barometric pressure ($P_B$) decreases as the weight of the atmosphere becomes less. The *percentage* of oxygen in the air remains 20.93 per cent, but the number of oxygen molecules per unit volume decreases. This means that, when at altitude, in order to receive the same number of molecules in a breath of air that we receive at sea level, we must breathe more air. The prime reason for lessened performance at altitude is a consequence of lowered oxygen pressure (tension). This lowered oxygen tension results in *hypoxia,* that is, lack of adequate oxygen. Apparently this hypoxia stimulates the acclimatization mechanisms. Depending upon altitude and duration of stay, among the important physiological changes that take place during acclimatization to altitude are:[13]

(1) *Increased pulmonary ventilation (hyperventilation)*. This response is immediate (within a few hours) upon arrival at altitude, being more pronounced during the first few days, then stabilizing after about a week at altitude. The most important result of hyperventilation is an increased alveolar $Po_2$. This ensures a greater saturation of hemoglobin (Hb) with oxygen (see Fig. 9–7, p. 197). Also, you may remember that with hyperventilation, excessive amounts of $CO_2$ are "blown off," thus decreasing both the alveolar $Pco_2$ and the $H^+$ concentration (increased pH).

(2) *Increased number of red blood cells and hemoglobin concentration*. This too is rapid during the first few weeks at altitude, with the increase becoming more gradual thereafter. The function of this response is to increase the oxygen content of the arterial blood.

(3) *Elimination of bicarbonate ($HCO_3^-$) in the urine*. This adjustment requires several days. Although this mechanism *per se* does not enhance oxygen availability, its main function is to maintain blood pH at near-normal values. Remember, with hyperventilation and loss of $CO_2$, the blood pH will tend to increase; elimination of bicarbonate is offsetting, causing a decrease in pH.

(4) *Tissue level changes*. These changes include (a) increased muscle and tissue capillarization; (b) increased myoglobin concentration; (c) increased mitochondrial density; and (d) enzyme changes that enhance the oxidative capacity. Unlike the previously mentioned acclimatization processes, these cellular changes take more time. In fact, they are seen most developed in the long-time resident of high altitude regions.

Unquestionably, these are prime physiological changes that greatly aid in delivering oxygen to the tissues when oxygen is hard to come by (i.e., under hypoxic conditions). When the person returns from a three- to four-week sojourn at altitude, he or she will lose these changes brought about by acclimatization within a period of about two to four weeks.

**Conditioned vs. Nonconditioned Persons.**    Studies have shown that on first arriving at altitude, conditioned subjects have no greater advantage over their nonconditioned contemporaries beyond what they would have at sea level.[3] Fit persons will be able to perform more work, just as they can at sea level, than the unfit, but at a diminished level; they will not acclimatize any more rapidly; nor will they be any more immune to the discomforts of mountain sickness.[4] As a matter of fact, in our altitude studies[3, 4] the most highly trained person became so ill at 12,500 feet we had to remove him to a lower altitude, where he stayed for two days. We then returned him to 12,500 feet for another two weeks, during which time he was a little better off, but not much.

## Athletic Performance at Altitude

Recently, several studies involving both high school and college athletes have been conducted. The results provide important information regarding the effects of training and acclimatization on competitive athletic performances.

**The Lexington-Leadville Study.**[12]   The primary purpose of this very interesting study with high school athletes was to determine whether lifelong acclimatization to altitude would give the native an advantage over the newcomer in regard to track performance. Two groups of athletes were studied:

(1) Five members of the track team of Lafayette High School, Lexington, Kentucky (altitude, 300 meters or 1000 feet); and

(2) Five athletes from Lake County High School, Leadville, Colorado (altitude, 3100 meters or 10,200 feet).

The Leadville students had to be selected from other sports (skiing, basketball, or football) as the high school had no organized track team. They did, however, have four months of training prior to a track meet with the Kentucky high school track team. Table 16–1 contains the physical and physiological characteristics of these young athletes. The interesting thing to note is the unusually high maximum oxygen consumption values these young men obtained while running on a treadmill. The data may be compared with those appearing in Figure 21–7, p. 457.

The experiment consisted of having two track meets between the teams, one in Leadville and the other in Lexington. In Leadville, the competition was held on the twentieth day of residence at altitude for the Kentucky team. Table 16–2 contains the running times for the track events at both altitudes. The Kentucky team (who incidentally were the Kentucky State Champions in 1964) was superior and won the competition at both low and high altitudes. It is apparent from these track times that hypoxia as a consequence of altitude affects the long-term resident just as it does the newcomer during strenuous activity.

### Table 16–1  AVERAGE PHYSICAL AND PHYSIOLOGICAL CHARACTERISTICS OF HIGH SCHOOL ATHLETES*

|  | ATHLETES NATIVE TO 3100 METERS | ATHLETES NATIVE TO 300 METERS |
|---|---|---|
| Age | 17 years | 17 years |
| Height | 176 cm. | 175 cm. |
| Weight | 68 kg. | 66 kg. |
| Max $\dot{V}o_2$ (low altitude) | 66 ml./kg.-minute | 68 ml./kg.-minute |

*From Grover, et al.[12]

Table 16–2   **RUNNING TIMES FOR TRACK EVENTS**
**AT 300 AND 3100 METERS***

| RUNNING DISTANCES | | LEXINGTON TEAM | | LEADVILLE TEAM | |
| | | Altitude (meters) | | Altitude (meters) | |
| | | 300 | 3100 | 300 | 3100 |
| Yards | Meters | Time (min:sec) | | Time (min:sec) | |
|---|---|---|---|---|---|
| 220 | 201 | 0:24.0 | 0:22.4 | 0:25.7 | 0:27.0 |
| 440 | 402 | 0:54.0 | 0:51.0 | 1:03.5 | 0:52.5 |
| 880 | 804 | 2:10.0 | 2:11.5 | 2:24.7 | 2:30.0 |
| 1760 | 1608 | 4:49.0 | 5:10.9 | 5:23.5 | 5:35.0 |

*From Grover, et al.[12]

The athlete or team that is highly successful in competition at sea level should be equally successful at altitude.

The faster times obtained by the Kentucky team in the 220- and 440-yard sprints at altitude may be due in part to the lessened atmospheric density at 3100 meters (about 1/3 less dense than that at sea level).

**The Pennsylvania State University Study.**[6]   A study of equal interest was conducted by E. Buskirk and others of Pennsylvania State University. They took several of Penn State's track men to Nunoa, Peru, which is at an altitude of 13,000 feet (4000 meters). In Figure 16–9 are shown the average decreases in running performance experienced by the runners. The running times were obtained after 40 to 57 days at altitude, that is, after acclimatization had occurred. Notice also that as was the case with the high school runners, the decreases in performance were most pronounced in the longer events, where the oxygen system is the predominant energy pathway.

Following three weeks of residence at altitude, the runners began participating in soccer with the Indian natives. After five weeks of residence the trackmen were as good as the natives, with four of the runners eventually playing on the winning team! During a track meet held at 13,000 feet, the runners won over the best times for the Indians by 1 minute in the 1-mile event and by 2 minutes in the 2-mile event. These results again point out that altitude affects the working capacity of the native in much the same manner as it does the newcomer to altitude.

It is of further interest to note from Figure 16–9 that upon return to sea level the athletes' performances were not improved as a result of training at altitude. As a matter of fact, performance in the 1-mile and 2-mile events was slower the third and fifteenth days after return from altitude.

**The Michigan–Penn State Study.**[10]   In another study by Dr. Buskirk and associates, 12 athletes, some of whom were top-rated

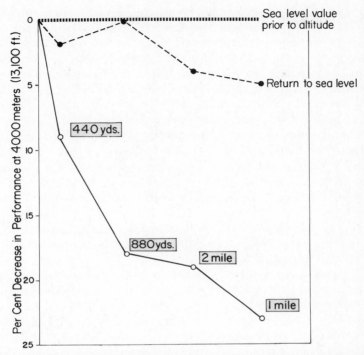

**Figure 16–9** Decreases in running performances at 13,000 feet (4000 meters). Notice that the decreases in performance are most pronounced in the longer events, where the oxygen system is the predominant energy pathway. Notice also that upon return to sea level, the athletes' performances were not improved. (Based on data from Buskirk et al.[6])

middle-distance runners, were studied at various altitudes over a 5 to 6 week period. The results of their time-trials at an altitude of 7500 feet (2300 meters) are shown in Figure 16–10. Three points are worth noting: First, all performances were not quite as good as at sea level. Sec-

**Figure 16–10** Decreases in running performances at 7500 feet (2300 meters). These results indicate that even at moderate altitude, physical performance, particularly if it relies heavily on the aerobic system, will be impaired and will not always improve with acclimatization. (Based on data from Faulkner et al.[10])

ond, the decrease in performance was related, once again, to the duration of the event; the longer the race, the greater the oxygen needed and the poorer the performance. Third, the two and three mile performances were *not* improved with acclimatization as was the performance in the mile run. In relation to this, it is interesting that the maximal aerobic power also did not improve with acclimatization.

These results indicate that even at moderate altitude (7500 feet), physical performance, particularly if it relies heavily on the aerobic system, will be impaired and will not always improve with acclimatization.

**The Ohio State Studies.**[3,4,5]   We studied 25 young college men at Columbus, Ohio (altitude, 750 feet or 230 meters), and at the Barcroft Research Station, White Mountain, California, elevation, 12,470 feet (3800 meters). The following conclusions were reached:

(1) The physical fitness of healthy individuals, measured at sea level, is not a sufficient index of their ability to perform hard physical work at high terrestrial altitudes.

(2) Physical fitness appears to bear no relationship to the occurrence of symptoms of acute altitude sickness. The extremely fit person is as likely to become ill as is the sedentary person.

(3) Ability to perform hard physical work at high altitudes improves markedly during three weeks of continuous residence at such altitudes. It does not, however, approach sea level work capacity during this period of time.

(4) Some subjects, regardless of physical condition, do not tolerate altitude well and may be expected to become ineffective or ill.

(5) All healthy individuals, other than those with a predisposition to altitude sickness, can work steadily for one half hour or more at a level that is roughly half their sea level capacity at 12,500 feet immediately after arrival. Only a minority will be able to sustain one-half hour of work at two-thirds of their sea level work capacity even after eight days at altitude.

### Training and Altitude

When Mexico City (elevation, 7400 feet or 2250 meters) was named as the site for the 1968 Olympic games, coaches immediately asked: How can we train our athletes to best withstand any effects of altitude on their performance? Should they train only at altitude? If so, at what altitude and for how long? Should they train intermittently at altitude and at sea level? Because the answers to these questions were not available, a great deal of research was initiated.

From a theoretical viewpoint, training at altitude could produce more rapid and even greater physiological changes than could train-

**Table 16–3 TIME TRIALS IN RUNNING BEFORE, DURING, AND AFTER TRAINING AT AN ALTITUDE OF 7500 FEET (2300 METERS)***

| EVENT | TIME AT SEA LEVEL (MIN:SEC) | Day 3 | TIME AT ALTITUDE (MIN:SEC) Day 14 | Day 21 | TIME ON RETURN TO SEA LEVEL (MIN:SEC) Day 1 | Day 21 |
|---|---|---|---|---|---|---|
| 880 yd run | 2:41 | 2:48 | 2:38 | 2:37 | 2:32 | 2:32 |
| 1 mile run | 6:07 | 6:30 | — | 6:15 | 5:49 | 5:38 |
| 2 mile run | 13:08 | 13:45 | 13:09 | — | 12:22 | 11:57 |

*Based on data from Faulkner, Daniels, and Balke.[9]

ing at sea level only. The reason for this is that altitude hypoxia is a stress that produces physiological changes (acclimatization) similar to those caused by physical training. For example, total blood volume, hemoglobin, red blood cell count, mitochondrial concentration, and muscle enzyme changes have all been shown to be enhanced in both types of stress. To a certain extent, this idea has been supported experimentally. For example, in a well-controlled study using nonathletes,[16] greater increases in maximal aerobic power were seen when the training sessions were conducted at altitude (7400 to 11,300 feet) rather than at sea level. In addition, we have shown that some effects of eight weeks of interval training can be maintained for an additional 12 weeks by use of two three-hour exposures to a simulated altitude of 15,000 feet (4572 meters). During the exposures, the subjects did not perform any exercise, but merely rested.[2] Other studies[1, 9] have shown improved performances at sea level after training at altitude. Some of the results are given in Table 16–3. However, in these studies, it was not determined whether the increased sea level performances were due to altitude exposure *per se* or to the fact that the subjects eventually increased their fitness level during the conditioning at altitude. In other words, it is possible that their performances would have been improved with further training even at sea level.

It can be seen from Figures 16–9 and 16–10 that in studies involving highly trained athletes, performance on return from altitude was not much different from prior performance at sea level; if anything, some were poorer. This would indicate that for the highly trained athlete, training at and acclimatization to altitude does not improve performance. Also, as already pointed out, maximal aerobic power and performance of these athletes do not always improve with altitude acclimatization. One of the major reasons for this might be that the training programs required for these athletes cannot be sustained at altitude at an intensity and duration commensurate with that at sea level.[14] This can be seen from Figure 16–11, which lists the intensity of the training workouts for six collegiate runners at various altitudes.

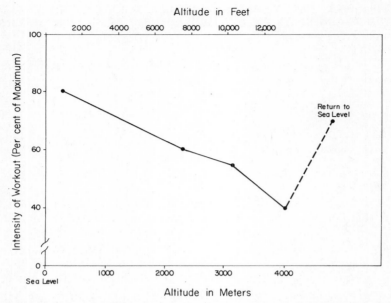

**Figure 16–11**   Intensity of training workouts for six collegiate runners at various altitudes. Even though their coach was present at all workouts, it is clear that altitude greatly reduced their training efforts. (Based on data from Kollias and Buskirk.[14])

Even though their coach was present at all workouts, it is clear that altitude greatly reduced their training efforts.

Training at altitude, therefore, appears to be helpful for unconditioned, nonathletic subjects but not necessarily for highly trained athletes. However, if you wish to train your athletes at altitude for whatever reason, the following guidelines may prove to be helpful:[8]

(1) Adequate training facilities and training atmosphere must be available.

(2) The bulk of time spent at altitude should be at moderate altitude (6500 to 7500 feet).

(3) Short exposures to higher altitude should be included regularly during the general training period at moderate elevation.

(4) Steady altitude exposures should be limited to periods of two to four weeks, with intermittent sea-level or lower elevation trips scheduled to assure maintenance of muscular power and normal competitive rhythm and intensity of effort.

(5) Training at altitude should emphasize maintenance of muscular power yet be geared to include normal or near-normal overall amounts of work.

(6) Important sea level efforts should be scheduled about two weeks after leaving altitude.

## Summary

Scuba is an excellent sport and can be performed without accident, provided that the physiological concepts are understood and applied. Following is a list of guidelines that should be strictly adhered to if one wishes to dive:

(1) Receive competent instruction before going out on your own;

(2) Never dive alone;

(3) Never dive when you have upper respiratory infection;

(4) Do not dive using pure oxygen;

(5) Never ascend faster than do the smallest bubbles from your exhaled air;

(6) Follow very carefully the Navy decompression tables for depths greater than 30 feet;

(7) Know your equipment well;

(8) If you are easily disturbed emotionally, seek some other sport. Panic causes accidents;

(9) Practical limiting depth is 130 feet.

If athletic performance is to take place above 7000 feet, a period of acclimatization is essential. Upon first arrival at altitude the person should move about at any easy pace rather than rest. We have found that acclimatization probably takes place more slowly if the person naps frequently. By the same token, overexertion on first arrival is to be avoided. Excessive hyperventilation, rapid heart rate, and sensation of breathlessness are indications of overexertion. At an altitude between 7000 and 10,000 feet, noticeable improvement will be observed on the second and third days, indicating that acclimatization is taking place.

Performance in events requiring less than 1 minute, such as the 100-yard dash, hammer throw, discus throw, and so forth, will not be affected. For example, a group of 25 university sophomores performed the same number of push-ups at 12,500 feet as they did at 800 feet. This is because such events are primarily anaerobic. Events approaching 2 to 3 minutes or more in duration require considerable aerobic support; here oxygen is absolutely essential and as a consequence, performance in such activities at altitude will be hampered.

In recognition of the added physiological stress caused by hypoxia, one should seriously question the feasibility of holding athletic events that are endurance contests in nature above 7000 feet.

Our attention is directed to the World Olympic Games held in Mexico City in 1968, at an altitude of 7340 feet: (1) Performance in events lasting under 2 minutes was not affected. (2) It has been noted that performance in most Olympic events usually exceeds the records set in previous Olympic Games. This was not so at Mexico in 1968. (3) Far too great a number of athletes competing in events exceeding 2 minutes' duration suffered effects of severe hypoxia.

Training at altitude probably enhances performance at sea level but only in unconditioned, nonathletic individuals. For the highly trained athlete, the training intensity required for maintenance of peak performances cannot be achieved at altitude.

## QUESTIONS

1. Discuss the effects of increasing and decreasing the pressure, while holding temperature constant, on (1) a given volume of water, and (2) a given volume of gas.

2. At 33 feet below the surface of the sea, the weight of water above the diver will be equal to one atmosphere. Why is this true?

3. Describe how a diver may suffer air embolism.

4. What is spontaneous pneumothorax, and how is it treated?

5. What is the effect of nitrogen narcosis on a diver?

6. How may one avoid developing the bends during a dive?

7. What are the physiological principles underlying oxygen poisoning while diving?

8. How does one prevent squeeze while diving?

9. What is the importance of the eustachian tube for one who descends below the surface of the sea or ascends to altitude?

10. Define acclimatization to altitude and discuss the physiology involved.

11. How is performance affected at altitude?

12. How does training at altitude affect performance at altitude and at sea level?

## REFERENCES

1. Balke, B., Nagle, F., and Daniels, J.: Altitude and maximum performance in work and sports activity. JAMA 194:646–649, 1965.
2. Bason, R., Fox, E., Billings, C., Klinzing, J., Ragg, K., and Chaloupka, E.: Maintenance of physical training effects by intermittent exposure to hypoxia. Aerospace Med. 44(10):1097–1100, 1973.
3. Billings, C., Bason, R., Mathews, D., and Fox, E.: Cost of submaximal and maximal work during chronic exposure at 3,800 m. J. Appl. Physiol. 30(3):406–408, 1971.
4. Billings, C., Brashear, R., Mathews, D., and Bason, R.: Medical observations during twenty days at 3800 meters. Arch. Environ. Health. 18:987–995, 1969.
5. Billings, C., Mathews, D., Bartels, R., Fox, E., Bason, R., and Tanzi, D.: The Effects of Physical Conditioning and Partial Acclimatization to Hypoxia on Work Tolerance at High Altitudes. Columbus, Ohio, Ohio State University Research Foundation Report RF 2002-4, June, 1968.

6. Buskirk, E., Kollias, J., Akers, R., Prokop, E., and Picon-Reátegui, E.: Maximal performance at altitude and on return from altitude in conditioned runners. J. Appl. Physiol. 23(2):259–266, 1967.
7. Buskirk, E., Kollias, J., Picon-Reátegui, E., Akers, R., Prokop, E., and Baker, P.: Physiology and performance of track athletes at various altitudes in the United States and Peru. Symposium Proceedings Effects of Altitude on Physical Performance. Chicago, Athletic Institute, 1966.
8. Daniels, J.: Effects of altitude on athletic accomplishment. Mod. Med. June 26, 1972, pp. 73–76.
9. Faulkner, J., Daniels, J., and Balke, B.: Effects of training at moderate altitude on physical performance capacity. J. Appl. Physiol. 23(1):85–89, 1967.
10. Faulkner, J., Kollias, J., Favour, C., Buskirk, E., and Balke, B.: Maximum aerobic capacity and running performance at altitude. J. Appl. Physiol. 24(5):685–691, 1968.
11. Fox, E., and Bowers, R.: Steady-state equality of respiratory gaseous $N_2$ in resting man. J. Appl. Physiol. 35:143–144, 1973.
12. Grover, R., Reeves, J., Grover, E., and Leathers, J.: Muscular exercise in young men native to 3,100 m altitude. J. Appl. Physiol. 22(3):555–564, 1967.
13. Hurtado, A.: Acclimatization to high altitudes. *In* Weihe, W. (ed.): The Physiological Effects of High Altitude. New York, MacMillan Co., 1964, pp. 1–17.
14. Kollias, J., and Buskirk, E.: Exercise and altitude. *In* Johnson, W., and Buskirk, E. (eds.): Science and Medicine of Exercise and Sports, 2nd ed. New York, Harper and Row, 1974, pp. 211–227.
15. Pugh, L.: Muscular exercise at great altitudes. *In* Weihe, W. (ed.): The Physiological Effects of High Altitude. New York, MacMillan Co., 1964, pp. 209–210.
16. Roskamm, H., Landry, F., Samek, L., Schlager, M., Weidemann, H., and Reindell, H.: Effects of a standardized ergometer training program at three different altitudes. J. Appl. Physiol. 27(6):840–847, 1969.
17. U.S. Navy Diving Manual. Washington, D.C., Department of Navy, 1970.

## SELECTED READINGS

Goddard, R. (ed.): The International Symposium on the Effects of Altitude on Physical Performance. Chicago, The Athletic Institute, 1967.
Hegnauer, A. (ed.): Biomedicine Problems of High Terrestrial Elevations. Natick, U.S. Army Research Institute of Environmental Medicines, January, 1969.
Hurtado, A.: Animals in high altitudes: resident man. *In* Handbook of Physiology, Section H. Adaptation to the Environment. Washington, D.C., American Physiological Society, 1964.
Margaria, R. (ed.): Exercise at Altitude. New York, Exerpta Medica Foundation, 1967.
Miles, S.: Underwater Medicine. Philadelphia, J. B. Lippincott Co., 1962.
Pugh, L.: Athletes at altitude. J. Physiol. 192:619–646, 1967.
Weihe, W. (ed.): The Physiological Effects of High Altitude. New York, MacMillan Co., 1964.

# Chapter 17

# HEAT BALANCE: PREVENTION OF HEAT STROKE IN ATHLETICS

Over a 3-year period 7 heat stroke (sunstroke) deaths were reported among high school football players and 5 among college players.[6] Information about the fatalities is assembled in Table 17–1. Three colleges failed to respond to the inquiry; as a consequence, data on only nine players are presented.

All players (including the three not shown) were interior linemen, and seven of the nine were stricken during the first two days of practice. All were clothed in full football equipment. The temperature and relative humidity at the time of the fatalities are indicated in Figure 17–1. The line drawn from 100 per cent relative humidity and 60° F.

Table 17-1  **DESCRIPTION OF HEAT STROKE VICTIMS**

| POSITION | DATE | HOUR | PRACTICE SESSION | AGE (YEARS) | HEIGHT (FEET, INCHES) | WEIGHT (POUNDS) |
|---|---|---|---|---|---|---|
| Guard-Tackle (1)* | 9/25/61 | 2–4 PM | 5th week | 17 | 5′ 11″ | 190 |
| Tackle (2) | 8/21/59 | 4:00 PM | 2nd day | 16 | 6′ 1″ | 185 |
| Tackle (3) | 8/29/60 | 3:30 PM | 1st day | 15 | 6′ 1″ | 180 |
| Guard (4) | 8/27/62 | 5:00 PM | 2nd day | 15 | 5′ 10″ | 165 |
| Tackle (5) | 8/22/62 | 10:00 AM | 1st day | 15 | 6′ 1½″ | 244 |
| Tackle (6) | 10/8/62 | 4:15 PM | 7th week | 15 | 5′ 10″ | 190 |
| Guard (7) | 8/20/59 | 10:00 AM | 1st day | 15 | 5′ 8″ | 180 |
| Guard (8) | 9/1/62 | 5:50 PM | 1st day | 19 | 5′ 11″ | 190 |
| Center (9) | 9/2/62 | 10:00 AM | 1st day | 20 | 6′ 0″ | 200 |

*The numbers in parentheses correspond to the circled numbers in Figure 17–1.
From Fox, et al.[6]

(15.6° C.) to 40 per cent relative humidity and 89° F. (31.7° C.) indicates that the deaths occurred under conditions ranging from either high temperature (dry bulb) and low relative humidity to low temperature and high relative humidity. It should also be noted that five of the casualties were not permitted water during practice but were required to take salt tablets, a practice which is far from being physiologically sound!

More recent data concerning heat stroke occurrences in high school football players[22] and in Marine recruits engaged in heavy physical exercise[14] are also shown in Figure 17–1. Although all of the Marine recruits survived, the two high school football players were less fortu-

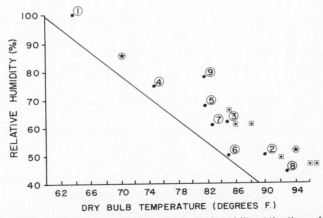

**Figure 17–1** Dry bulb temperature and relative humidity at the time of heat stroke incidences in football players (●, ✦) and Marine recruits (▣). Note that football casualty number 1 occurred at a temperature of 64° F. and relative humidity of 100 per cent. Although the temperature was low, heat could not be lost through evaporation because the atmosphere was saturated with water vapor. (● = data from Fox et al.;[6] ✦ = data from Sohal et al.;[22] and ▣ = data from O'Donnell and Clowes.[14])

nate; they died. It is easily seen that these incidences of heat stroke also occurred under either high dry bulb temperature and low relative humidity or low dry bulb temperature and high relative humidity.

The deaths of these young men were in vain, for all were preventable. Why did they happen? Lack of knowledge as well as misinformation on the part of the coaches contributed to the fatalities. It is our intention in this chapter to insure you well against contributing toward such accidents.

Essentially, what must you understand in order to maintain a team at top level of performance while at the same time eliminating the dangers of heat illness? We should realize, first of all, which basic physiological mechanisms prevail in heat illness; second, how the environmental or weather conditions can significantly contribute to heat illness; and third, which symptoms occur and which vital emergency procedures are required if such accidents should occur. We shall presently make use of the knowledge gained in Chapter 14, especially that regarding movement of water and electrolytes into and out of the cell.

Obviously, during physical activity an athlete sweats. The sweating rate will depend on many factors, among them: (1) the intensity of the activity, (2) the environmental conditions, (3) the physical fitness of the athlete, (4) how accustomed the athlete is to working in the heat (heat acclimatization), and (5) the type and amount of clothing worn.

Before considering these relevant factors, let us in a very general manner examine the sequential events that culminate in heat stroke. We can then return and discuss each of the factors mentioned previously, along with the important considerations that will enable us to protect our athletes.

(1) Sweat is hypotonic to the blood; that is, it contains more water than salt.

(2) We know from Chapter 14 that if one loses more water than salt, the liquid surrounding the cell becomes hypertonic to the interior of the cell.

(3) As a consequence, the water from the interior of the cell will flow out of the cell to maintain osmotic equilibrium.

(4) If the athlete continues to sweat without replacing water, a critical physiological situation will ensue. To maintain the osmotic equilibrium, water must move from the blood. This is true because of the lowered diffusion gradient existing outside the blood vessels. As the blood volume diminishes because of the water moving out, a high concentration of electrolytes will exist in the remaining blood volume.

(5) As water loss becomes excessive, the sweating mechanism is turned off to maintain blood volume. Internal body temperature soars. A conclusive symptom of heat stroke is a body temperature exceeding 104° F. or 40° C. In the Marine recruits referred to earlier, the body

temperatures ranged between 106° F. (41.1° C.) and 110° F. (43.3° C.). The average body temperature was 107.2° F. or 41.8° C.

(6) A high concentration of electrolytes in the blood will interfere with the normal rhythm of the heart, precipitating ventricular fibrillation, heart failure, and death.

This, to be certain, is a simplified outline of the primary physiological factors involved in heat stroke casualty. However, this information will permit us to discuss intelligently measures that will aid us in averting trouble.

## HEAT BALANCE

The heat stroke fatalities listed in Figure 17–1 were all interior linemen. Even the three about whom we failed to obtain complete information played this position. Why are these men most vulnerable? The answer is that they expend a significantly greater amount of energy than do the other players. All of this energy, as you will recall, is liberated as heat from within the body. In order to maintain a constant body temperature, this heat must be dissipated; if it is not, it will be stored by the body, causing the temperature to climb. This is shown schematically in Figure 17–2.

Let us examine the concept of heat balance in a little more detail. As we sit or otherwise use little energy, our body temperature remains at 98.6° F. (37° C.). In other words, the energy we expend in performing light activity is constantly being liberated by the body to the environment so that we maintain heat balance; as a result, our body temperature remains constant.

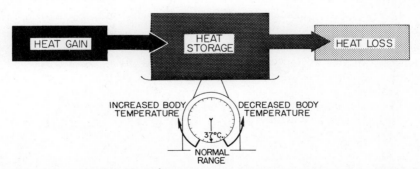

**Figure 17–2** Heat balance. When heat gain and heat loss are equal, the amount of heat stored does not change, and therefore body temperature remains constant. When heat gain is greater than heat loss, body temperature will increase, and vice versa.

## Heat Loss

The body loses heat through *convection, conduction, radiation,* and *evaporation.*

**Convection.** A fan blowing over the surface of the skin removes air warmed by the body and replaces it with cooler air. This is called *convection.* Holding your arm out the window of a moving auto produces the same results. As long as cooler air blows across the surface of the body, heat can be lost. The individual who is running can lose heat by convection just as one can lose heat by standing in a breeze. The amount of heat lost depends on the speed and temperature of the air flow over the surface of the body. Of passing interest might be the mention of the cold air tubes used in glass factories during the summer. The worker may simply reach overhead and direct a fast flow of cold air over the face and neck by means of a tube. A similar cooling device is found on most commercial jetliners.

**Conduction.** Conduction is the transfer of heat between two objects of different temperatures that are in direct contact with each other. The direction of heat flow is always from the warmer to the cooler object. When we touch a piece of ice, for example, heat is conducted from the surface of the hand to the ice, whereas when we touch a hot stove, heat is transferred from the stove to the hand.

**Radiation.** This accounts for about 60 per cent of the heat loss from a nude person resting quietly in a room at 70° F. The principle of radiation is based upon the fact that molecules within a body are constantly vibrating, and as a consequence, heat in the form of electromagnetic waves is continuously being given off. When we are seated in the classroom, for example, we are radiating heat to the walls of the room, while at the same time heat is being radiated from the walls to us. We gain heat through radiation when surrounding objects are warmer than our bodies; we lose heat through radiation when our body temperatures are warmer than surrounding objects. A young man seated in a sweat box with the temperature set at 120° F. would obviously gain more heat from the radiating light bulbs than he could lose through radiation.

By the same token, on the athletic field a considerable amount of heat can be gained from the sun through radiation. This is especially true (1) when there is little or no cloud cover, and (2) between 12:00 noon to 4:00 P.M., as a result of the position of the sun (during this period the radiation from the sun is more concentrated).

**Evaporation.** The major portion of heat loss during exercise is through *evaporation* of sweat from the surface of the skin. Even during resting, what is referred to as *insensible perspiration* aids in ridding the body of the excessive heat being produced. A small amount of extracellular fluid is continually diffusing through the skin and evaporating. As it evaporates rapidly, we do not notice the moisture, hence the term "insensible."

Evaporation is the term applied when a liquid vaporizes. Energy is required for this change and is extracted from the immediate surroundings. This extraction of energy results in cooling. When we work hard and sweat profusely, our bodies will be cooled only if the sweat evaporates; that is, if it changes into a vapor at the surface of the skin. If the sweat cannot evaporate and merely falls to the ground, no cooling of the body can take place. For every gram of sweat evaporated, the body can lose approximately 0.580 kcal. of heat.

### Heat Gain

The unit of heat energy most commonly used is the calorie, which we already defined as the heat required to raise the temperature of 1 gm. of water 1° C. The kilocalorie (kcal.), as the name implies, is the amount of heat required to raise the temperature of 1 kg. of water 1° C. The *specific heat* of water (the heat required to change the temperature of a unit mass of water one degree) is therefore 1 kcal. per kilogram of water per degree Centigrade (1 kcal./kg./°C.). The specific heat of the body tissues (collectively) is 0.83 kcal./kg./°C. That is to say, a person weighing 70 kg. (154 pounds) must "store" 58 kcal. of heat ($0.83 \times 70$) to increase the body temperature 1° C.

As you will recall, the amount of heat or energy produced during metabolism is dependent upon the food being oxidized. A person weighing 70 kg. who is resting quietly consumes between 250 and 300 ml. of oxygen per minute. The caloric equivalent of one liter of oxygen ranges between 4.69 and 5.05 kcal., depending, of course, on the food being metabolized. We realize that a resting person usually oxidizes about 66.6 per cent fat and 33.3 per cent carbohydrate ($R = 0.82$), which means that for each liter of oxygen consumed, 4.83 kcal. of heat will be produced. Heat production of a resting person as a consequence of metabolism would be about 1.45 kcal. (0.3 liter $\times$ 4.83 kcal. per liter of $O_2$) per minute, or 87 kcal. per hour. If no heat were lost, body temperature would increase approximately 1.5° C. in 1 hour or rise from 37.0° C. (normal) to 38.5° C. (that is, 98.6° F. to 101.3° F.). This increase usually does not occur at rest because under most environmental conditions of temperature and relative humidity the 87 kcal. per hour of heat produced can be easily dissipated through convection, conduction, radiation, and evaporation. However, on an extremely hot day the potential rise in body temperature of an athlete whose heat production may be ten to fifteen times that at rest is staggering.

Let us assume that an athlete consumes, on the average, 2 liters of oxygen per minute doing an activity for 1 hour. At the end of this hour the oxygen consumption would equal 120 liters (60 minutes $\times$ 2 liters per minute). Each liter of oxygen, assuming $R$ equals 0.82, would be equivalent to 4.83 kcal. of heat energy. The total heat energy produced would equal 580 kcal. (120 liters × 4.83 kcal. per liter). If no heat were lost at all, how high would the body temperature rise because of the stored heat? Remember, the specific heat of body tissue is 0.83 kcal./kg./°C. If the person weighed 80 kg., the temperature would increase 1° C. for each 66.4 kcal. of heat produced (0.83 kcal./kg./°C × 80 kg.). As the person produced 580 kcal. in 1 hour, the temperature would rise 8.7° C. (580 divided by 66.4)! This simple calculation should make us keenly aware of the extreme importance of maintaining heat balance during activity.

The heat stroke cases plotted in Figure 17–1 were the direct cause of the body's inability to lose heat. At this time it would be wise for us to learn the fascinating manner in which a person regulates his or her internal temperature. The understanding we have of the physical means of losing heat (conduction, convection, radiation, and evaporation), coupled with the knowledge of the thermoregulatory mechanisms, will enable us to judiciously manage our athletes during periods of environmental stress.

## TEMPERATURE REGULATION

The function of the thermoregulatory system is to maintain a relatively constant internal body temperature.* At rest the system strives to keep the temperature at 37° C., which is called the *reference temperature*. Interestingly enough and for reasons not well understood, we will see that during exercise this reference temperature is increased.

The thermoregulatory system uses the following basic components in carrying out its function: (1) thermal receptors or sensors, i.e., organs sensitive to thermal stimuli (heat and cold); (2) thermal effectors or organs that respond to the stimuli sensed by the receptors and which produce regulatory or corrective changes; and (3) a center in the central nervous system that coordinates the incoming information from the receptors with the outgoing regulatory action of the effector organs.

### Thermal Receptors

The human body has at least two thermal receptor areas; one is located in the hypothalamus of the brain (central receptors), the other in the skin (peripheral receptors). Both receptor areas contain two types of sensors, one sensitive to heat, the other to cold. The receptors

---

*Internal body temperature is most frequently measured in the rectum and is sometimes called core temperature. Recently, the temperature of the tympanic membrane (ear drum) has also been used to reflect internal body temperature.

in the hypothalamus are sensitive to small temperature fluctuations (within 0.2 to 0.5° F.) of the arterial blood perfusing them, whereas the skin receptors respond to fluctuations in environmental temperature.

The receptors in the skin, both those that sense cold and those that sense warmth, are thought to consist mainly of free nerve endings. They are located throughout the body surface, usually with more cold receptors than warm. It was once thought that specialized nerve endings, such as the end bulbs of Krause (sensitive to cold) and the brushes of Ruffini (sensitive to heat) also served as thermal receptors. This now seems doubtful. At any rate, both the central and peripheral receptors are neurally connected to the cortex as well as to the regulatory center in the hypothalamus. The cortical connections, from which we consciously perceive warm and cold sensations, provide us with a means for voluntary regulation, such as seeking shaded or sunny areas, initiating or avoiding physical exercise, removing or adding clothing, and stretching out or curling up in warm or cool environments, respectfully. Regulation initiated from the hypothalamus is reflex in nature and thus is involuntary.

## Effectors

The effector organs are the skeletal muscles, the smooth muscles encircling the arterioles that supply blood to the skin, sweat glands, and certain endocrine glands. In a cold environment, the muscles effect shivering, which increases metabolic heat production; at the same time, the arterioles supplying blood to the skin constrict (cutaneous vasoconstriction). In a warm or hot environment, cutaneous vasodilation and sweating occur, as opposed to vasoconstriction and shivering. The importance of vasomotor control (by dilation and constriction) of the arterioles supplying blood to the skin stems from the fact that heat from the body core must first be transported — by circulatory conduction and convection — to the surface before it can be lost to the environment by conduction, convection, radiation, and evaporation. For example, with cutaneous vasoconstriction, skin blood flow is decreased and, hence, so is the transfer of heat from the body core. The opposite is true for cutaneous vasodilation; increased blood flow allows dissipation of more deep body heat to the environment. The secretion of sweat, so important in preventing overheating in man because it eventually vaporizes, comes from an estimated 2,500,000 sweat glands. These glands are very widely distributed over the body surface, being more heavily concentrated on the palms of the hands, soles of the feet, the neck, and the trunk.

The endocrine glands involved in temperature regulation are the thyroid and the adrenal medulla. Over several weeks' exposure to cold, metabolic heat production is increased due to increased output of thyroxin from the thyroid gland. Also during cold exposure, increased levels of epinephrine and norepinephrine from the adrenal medulla cause increased heat production along with increased heat conservation through cutaneous vasoconstriction.

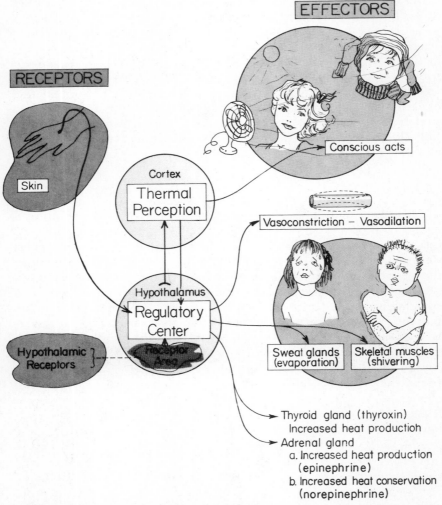

**Figure 17-3**   A summary of the thermoregulatory system. The internal body temperature is measured by receptor organs and compared to a set point (37°C.). If the temperature deviates from the set point, the hypothalamic center automatically relays information to the effector organs, which correct the temperature to the set point value through the mechanisms shown on the right. The return to the set point value then automatically shuts off the effector system. The cortical connections provide us with a means for voluntary regulation of body temperature.

## The Regulatory Center

The responses previously described are coordinated by the thermal regulatory center located in the *hypothalamus.* The role of this center is somewhat analogous to that of a thermostat in a house. The temperature of the room (internal body temperature) is measured by a thermometer (receptor organs) and compared to a set point (37° C.). If the measured temperature deviates from the set point, the thermostat (hypothalamic center) automatically relays information to the heating or cooling systems (effectors), which correct the temperature to the set point value through the mechanisms we have already described. The return to the set point value then automatically shuts off the effector system.

Although the regulatory center responds to both the central and peripheral thermal receptors mentioned earlier, it does so in different ways. We said that the central receptors initiate appropriate effector action after the internal body temperature is compared with a set point temperature, which is usually 37° C. or 98.6° F. The set point, however, can be changed and this is thought to be the major role of the peripheral receptors in temperature regulation. For example, when the skin is warmed, the set point is reduced. In effect, this causes sweating and cutaneous vasodilation and thus body cooling to occur sooner. The opposite is true when the skin is exposed to cold; that is, the set point is increased and increases in heat conservation and heat production occur sooner.

A summary of the thermoregulatory system is shown in Figure 17–3.

# EXERCISE IN THE HEAT AND HEAT DISORDERS

The principal means by which we lose heat during exercise or exposure to heat are: (1) circulatory adjustments of increased skin blood flow resulting from cutaneous vasodilation; and (2) evaporative cooling resulting from increased secretion of sweat. Internal body heat produced mainly by the liver and skeletal muscles is carried by the blood (circulatory convection) to the surface, where conduction, convection, radiation, and particularly evaporation take place. The cooled blood then returns to the warmer core and the cycle is repeated. The body temperature changes that occur during exercise in a comfortable environment (room temperature) are shown in Figure 17–4. Internal or rectal temperature increases to a new level during the first 30 minutes or so of work, and remains at this new level until work is terminated. At the same time, skin temperature decreases slightly primarily as a result of increased convective and evaporative cooling. The net result

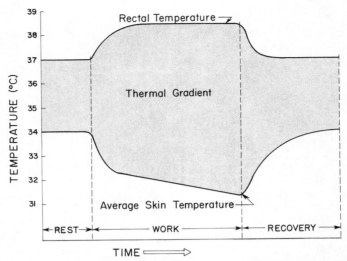

**Figure 17-4** Rectal and skin temperatures during and following 60 minutes of running at six miles per hour. Note that during exercise, rectal temperature increases while skin temperature decreases, thus increasing the thermal gradient between skin and core. Environmental conditions were 25° C. and 35 per cent relative humidity.

of these changes is an increase in the *thermal gradient* between the skin and the core, which facilitates heat loss in the manner previously described.

In a cold or cool environment, exercise that can be maintained for an hour or more is seldom limited by an excessive increase in internal or rectal temperature. Under these environmental conditions, nearly

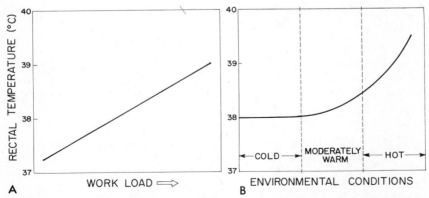

**Figure 17-5** *A,* Relationship between rectal temperature and work rate in a cool environment. Although environmental conditions remain constant, as the work rate increases, the rectal temperature increases proportionately. *B,* At a constant work rate, the rise in rectal temperature is the same in a cool to moderately warm environment, but it rises disproportionately in a hot environment because of the added resistance to heat loss.

all the metabolic heat produced can be easily dissipated by the circulatory and sudomotor (sweating) adjustments referred to earlier. Even in severe, short term work, when heat production may well exceed the heat dissipating capacity made possible by these adjustments, exhaustion usually results from the buildup of anaerobic metabolites (mainly lactic acid) before rectal temperature can reach a limiting or dangerous level. It is important to note that the elevation of rectal temperature during exercise, although proportional to the intensity of work (and therefore to metabolic rate), is independent of environmental temperatures ranging from cold to moderately warm (Fig. 17–5). This means that the rise in rectal temperature during exercise in environments that offer little or no resistance to heat dissipation is due to a higher reference temperature set by the thermoregulatory center in the hypothalamus.

### Exercise in the Heat

Environmental heat reduces the thermal gradient between the environment and the skin surface, and between the skin surface and the body core, thus imposing an added resistance to body heat loss. We have seen that body heat can actually be gained when the temperature of the environment is greater than that of our skin. By the same token, increased humidity imposes a heat loss barrier to the evaporative mechanism by decreasing the vapor pressure gradient between the moisture in the air and the sweat on our skin. When these heat loss resistances are superimposed on the higher reference temperature set by the thermoregulatory center, limitation of work is a direct result of an excessive increase in rectal temperature.

**Circulatory System and Sweating Mechanism.** The reduced thermal and vapor pressure gradients of hot, humid environments greatly increase the demands placed upon the circulatory system and sweating mechanism. This is evidenced by greater increases in heart rate and sweating during exercise in hot as compared to cool environments (Table 17–2). More blood must be circulated and more sweat

### Table 17–2 EFFECTS OF ENVIRONMENTAL HEAT LOADS ON SWEAT RATE AND HEART RATE RESPONSES DURING 15 MINUTES OF MODERATE WORK

| TEMPERATURE, °C. | RELATIVE HUMIDITY, PER CENT | SWEAT RATE, POUNDS PER HOUR | HEART RATE, BEATS PER MINUTE |
|---|---|---|---|
| 22 | 45 | 0.88 | 150 |
| 35 | 50 | 2.2 | 155 |
| 35 | 90 | 3.5 | 165 |

secreted by the sweat glands in order to lose any given quantity of heat. Note should also be made of the effects of hot, dry environments on the magnitude of these responses. Even though the temperature is high, the low relative humidity considerably reduces the heat stress because evaporation of sweat is more efficient. The major circulatory demands while working in the heat are: (1) A large blood flow through the working muscles is necessary to provide for the increased respiratory exchange of $O_2$ and $CO_2$, and to carry away the increased heat produced there; and (2) as previously indicated, a large skin blood flow is also necessary to cool the blood and supply the sweat glands with water. An excellent review of the circulatory adjustments during exercise in the heat has been written by Rowell.[18]

**Water and Salt Requirements.** The high sweat rates required for adequate evaporative cooling during exposure to heat (1 to 3.5 quarts per hour) can lead to excessive losses of water (dehydration) and of salt and other electrolytes. When this occurs, work performance and tolerance to heat are greatly reduced; hyperthermia (excessive internal body temperature) with predisposition to serious disorders is eminent.[4, 5, 8, 15, 19, 21, 23]

*The most serious consequence of profuse sweating is loss of body water.* This leads to a decrease in blood volume[10, 20] and, if severe enough, to a decrease in sweating rate and evaporative cooling. The decrease in

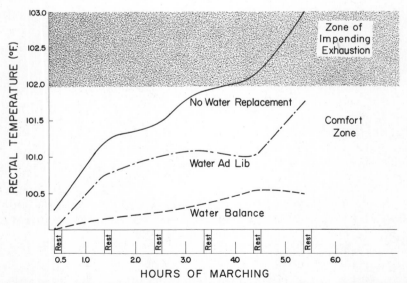

**Figure 17–6** Effects of progressive water and salt deficiencies during intermittent marching in the heat. When water consumption equals sweat loss (water balance) rectal temperature is lowest compared to no replacement and water ad lib. Environmental conditions were 100° F. and 35 to 45 per cent relative humidity. (Adapted from Pitts et al.[14])

blood volume and evaporative cooling, in turn, cause added circulatory strain with eventual circulatory collapse and an excessive rise in rectal temperature. Figure 17–6 shows clearly the effects of progressive water and salt deficiencies during intermittent marching in the heat for a 6-hour period. The best replacement fluid is one that contains as much salt and water as is lost through sweating; that is, about 1 to 2 gm. of salt per liter of water. Several such types of replacement fluids — which have been flavored for palatability — are available commercially. When these liquids are used salt tablets should *not* be taken. Fluids should be administered during as well as after prolonged work bouts in the heat. Adequate hydration by voluntary intake (thirst mechanism) alone takes several days. Therefore, during day-to-day heat exposures it might be necessary to insist on the drinking of some liquid even though there is no apparent thirst.

## HEAT DISORDERS IN ATHLETICS

The seriousness of overexposure to heat is exemplified not only by a decrease in work performance, but also by a predisposition to heat illness. These disorders are categorized in order of ascending severity as: (1) heat cramps; (2) heat exhaustion; and (3) heat stroke. The most frequent common denominators for all of these are: (1) heat exposure; (2) loss of water and salt; and (3) heat storage, usually reflected by high internal (rectal) temperature. However, the single most important factor, from a clinical standpoint, is loss of body water. It is also important to point out that inattention to heat cramps and heat exhaustion can lead to heat stroke and finally to death because of irreversible damage to the central nervous system. Even in those who do recover from heat stroke there often is some permanent damage to the thermoregulatory center in the hypothalamus. As a result of this damage, the hypothalamus loses some of its integrity or ability to regulate body temperature. This is why many who have survived heat stroke are more prone to future heat disorders.

Normally, a person will voluntarily stop working and seek shelter from the heat when either heat cramps or heat exhaustion sets in. However, highly competitive athletes are more vulnerable to heat disorders in general and heat stroke in particular for several reasons: (1) they are highly competitive (motivated) and therefore more likely to overextend themselves; (2) they sometimes are required to wear heavy protective equipment, which adds resistance to heat dissipation; and (3) the coach may deny them water during prolonged contests or practice sessions, which lowers their resistance to heat tolerance. These factors, either singularly or combined, are as pertinent to environmental conditions that are usually considered "comfortable" as they are to hot environments. For example, rectal temperatures equal to or greater than 40° C. (104° F.) are not uncommon, even in athletes who compete at environmental temperatures as low as 5° to 16° C. (41° to 61° F.).

## Football

As discussed earlier, the seriousness of the problem of heat disorders in athletics is best illustrated by the frequency of heat stroke deaths among football players. These deaths resulted from a combination of the factors mentioned above and therefore could have been prevented by the well-informed coach or team physician. You will recall that information about nine of twelve deaths reported between 1959 and 1962 revealed that: (1) All victims were interior linemen, who are probably required to work hardest and longest; (2) most were stricken during the first two days of preseason practice, indicating that they were probably not in good physical condition (see Table 17–1); (3) environmental conditions ranged from high temperature and low relative humidity to low temperature and high humidity (see Fig. 17–1); (4) all players were dressed in full uniform which, by virtue of its weight (6 kg. or 13 pounds), increases the effective work load (metabolism) and interferes with heat dissipation; and (5) most were not permitted to drink water during practice, but were required to take salt tablets. Unfortunately, these situations are typical of those which exist throughout the United States during preseason football practice, both in high school and college.

If it is not obvious to you why these men died needlessly of heat stroke, consider the following illustration. Nine men ran on a treadmill for 30 minutes at 6 miles per hour under three conditions: (1) in shorts only; (2) in a football uniform; and (3) in shorts plus a back pack weighing the same as the uniform (13 pounds). The temperature of the room for all runs was only 78° F., with a relative humidity of 35 per cent—in other words, a normally comfortable situation. As shown in Figure 17–7A, the increase in rectal temperature while wearing the uniform was 1.5 times greater (average, 39.0° C.) than when only shorts were worn.

The weight of the uniform alone, as shown by the increase in rectal temperature while carrying the pack, was as important a factor as was the heat loss barrier imposed by the clothing and protective pads of the uniform. The heat loss barrier of the uniform showed its effect by the excessively high skin temperatures of those areas covered by both pads and clothing, compared with conditions obtained by shorts and shorts plus pack (Fig. 17–7, B). In other words, the uniform prevented the evaporation of sweat, greatly impairing body cooling. Concomitant with this was a twofold greater loss of body water because of profuse

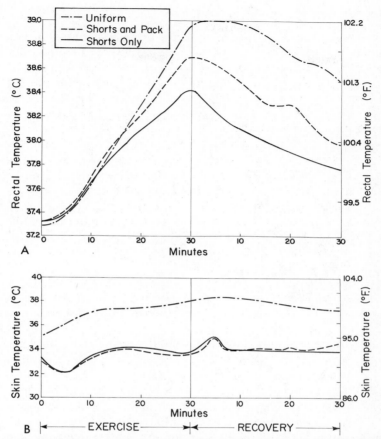

**Figure 17-7** The effects of football uniform on rectal and skin temperatures during 30 minutes of running at six miles per hour. *A,* The uniform retards heat loss, causing rectal temperature to climb during exercise and remain elevated during recovery. *B,* Skin temperatures while wearing the uniform also rise considerably owing to reduction in evaporative cooling. Environmental conditions were 78° F. and 35 per cent relative humidity. (Adapted from Mathews, Fox, and Tanzi.[10])

sweating and a significantly higher heart rate or circulatory strain—both of which reduce tolerance to heat.

Perhaps even more startling was the slow return of rectal temperature during recovery in the uniform, as compared with the other conditions. This is an extremely important point to remember. For example, a sixteen-year-old boy reported to his first football practice on a hot day and was required to wear a complete uniform. After a period of time, he felt ill. The coach placed him in the shade but did not remove his uniform; practice was then resumed and the boy was left unattended. About 2 hours later the boy was found unconscious. He was then taken to the hospital, where he died of heat stroke.

## Other Sports

Serious heat disorders in athletics are not confined to football. Football was merely used as an example. Any sport or physical activity is potentially hazardous insofar as heat illness is concerned. This includes wrestling, for which sport the athlete loses large quantities of water in order to "make weight," and track and field events, particularly those held outdoors. For example, in the 1956 Olympic Games, the marathon was run on a hot (85° F.), humid day. One of the United States marathoners reported that at the start of the race, Emil Zatopek, the great Czechoslovakian runner, said "Today we die!" It was not surprising that a French Algerian, who was heat acclimatized because of his native climate won that particular marathon race.[3]

Concerned by hot weather conditions under which official distance races are sometimes held—and by the growing number of middle-aged and older runners—the American College of Sports Medicine has issued a position statement aimed at preventing heat injuries during distance running.[9] Their statement is as follows:

1. Distance races (16 kilometers or 10 miles) should *not* be conducted when the wet bulb, globe temperature exceeds 82.4° F or 28.0° C. (For calculation of the wet bulb, globe temperature, see page 495).

2. During periods of the year when the daylight dry bulb temperature often exceeds 80° F (27° C), distance races should be conducted before 9 AM or after 4 PM.

3. It is the responsibility of the race sponsors to provide fluids which contain small amounts of sugar (less than 2.5 grams of glucose per 100 ml. of water) and electrolytes (less than 10 milliequivalence or 230 mg. of sodium and 5 milliequivalence or 195 mg. of potassium per liter of solution).

4. Runners should be encouraged to frequently ingest fluids during competition and to consume 400 to 500 ml. (13 to 17 oz.) of fluid 10 to 15 minutes before competition.

5. Rules prohibiting the administration of fluids during the first 6.2 miles (10 kilometers) of a marathon race should be amended to permit fluid ingestion at frequent intervals along the race course. In light of the high sweat rates and body temperatures during distance running in the heat, race sponsors should provide "water stations" at 2- to 2½-mile (3- to 4-km.) intervals for all races of 10 miles (16 km.) or more.

6. Runners should be instructed in how to recognize the early warning symptoms that precede heat injury. Recognition of symptoms, cessation of running, and proper treatment can prevent heat injury. Early warning symptoms include the following: piloerection on chest and upper arms, chilling, throbbing pressure in the head, unsteadiness, nausea, and dry skin.

7. Race sponsors should make prior arrangements with medical personnel for the care of cases of heat injury. Responsible and informed personnel should supervise each "feeding station." Organizational personnel should reserve the right to stop runners who exhibit clear signs of heat stroke or heat exhaustion.

Even ordinary activities, such as cutting the grass on an extremely warm day, can induce heat illness if proper precautions are not taken. In any case, the basic principles underlying prevention of heat disorders are common to all situations.

## PREVENTION OF HEAT DISORDERS

The occurrence of heat disorders can be greatly reduced by: (1) adequate salt and water replacement; (2) acclimatization to heat; and (3) awareness of the limitations imposed by the combination of exercise, clothing, and environmental heat.

### Salt and Water

As we have seen, water and salt replacement during and following work in the heat is absolutely essential (see Fig. 17–6). It is not unusual for an athlete to lose 5 to 10 pounds (mostly water loss, i.e., sweat) during each practice session or during a game. Such large weight losses can occur even when water is available on the field. For example, it has been shown that a college football player (tackle) lost 14 pounds during one fall preseason practice in spite of offering salt and water on the field.[13] It was further shown that the largest weight losses occurred in the tackles, the least in the quarterbacks. These considerable weight losses serve to illustrate the need for the coach to keep daily weight records to prevent progressive day-to-day water and salt depletion. The athletes should be weighed before and after each practice session. If a weight loss of greater than 2 per cent exists before the next scheduled practice, the player should be excused from any further sessions until this weight deficit is reduced.

**Water Replacement.** The availability of water (and salt) should be unrestricted at all times during scheduled practices and games. The "superhydrated" athlete suffers no impairment of efficiency.[2, 8] However, large amounts of water should not be imbibed at any one time since the athlete may feel uncomfortable under these conditions. The best procedure is to schedule frequent water breaks as well as to encourage the drinking of water *ad libitum.*

For athletic teams, water consumption can be facilitated by maintaining several water stations strategically located around the practice field. This allows the player convenient access to water. Frequent trips to the "bucket" and drinking small amounts are ideal. This procedure

## Table 17–3   A GUIDE FOR SALT REPLACEMENT

| Approximate Salt Loss | | | Supplemental Replacement | | |
|:---:|:---:|:---:|:---:|:---:|:---:|
| Water Loss Pounds or Pints | Grams | Grains | Water (Pints) | No. of 7-Grain Salt Tablets* To Be Taken Per Pint of Water Replaced | |
| 2 | 1.5 | 23 | 2 | Diet adequate | |
| 4 | 3.0 | 46 | 4 | Diet adequate | |
| 6 | 4.5 | 69 | 6 | Diet adequate | |
| | | | | *Nonacclimatized* | *Acclimatized* |
| 8 | 6.0 | 92 | 8 | 2 | 1 |
| 10 | 7.5 | 115 | 10 | 4 | 3 |
| 12 | 9.0 | 138 | 12 | 6 | 5 |

*Salt tablets usually come in 7- and 10-grain sizes (15.4 grains equals 1 gm.).

is physiologically more sensible than having a break every hour or so, during which the athlete might gulp copious amounts of water; also, it allows for more efficient use of practice time. Ice water buckets, pressurized garden-spray containers and thermos jugs are containers that can be properly located and adequately maintained.[12]

**Salt Replacement.** A person normally consumes 7 to 15 gm. of salt each day, which is more than adequate. As was previously mentioned, considerable salt is lost through sweating, and when this occurs, supplemental salt is required. Table 17–3 contains a schedule of salt replacement as related to water loss.

From the table, we can see that no supplemental salt is necessary, provided that not more than 6 pounds or 6 pints of water have been lost. This salt loss can be met through the normal diet. It is also interesting to note that as the athlete becomes acclimatized to heat the quantity of supplemental salt can be decreased. This is true because the sweat of an acclimatized individual probably contains less salt. It is extremely important to understand that salt tablets must be taken with an *adequate* amount of water—at least 1 pint of water with each 7-grain tablet. Taking salt tablets without sufficient water can lead to serious medical problems.

### Acclimatization to Heat

Tolerance and ability to work comfortably in the heat are increased through heat acclimatization.[1, 4] It improves the circulatory and sweating responses (see Table 17–4), which facilitate heat dissipation, and thus minimizes changes in skin and rectal temperature. Acclimatization is accomplished by a progressive exercise program performed in the heat for five to eight days. Merely resting in the heat produces

**Table 17–4  PHYSIOLOGICAL ADJUSTMENTS WHILE WORKING IN THE HEAT FOLLOWING ACCLIMATIZATION**

| PHYSIOLOGICAL MECHANISMS | PHYSIOLOGICAL ADJUSTMENTS |
|---|---|
| CIRCULATORY SYSTEM | |
| Pulse rate | Decreased |
| Skin blood flow | (1) time of response increased |
| | (2) more blood available at skin surface |
| Blood volume | Increased |
| Blood pressure | Adequately regulated |
| | |
| SWEATING MECHANISM | |
| Sweat rate | Increased and more rapid response |
| Evaporation | Increased |
| Salt loss in sweat | Decreased |
| | |
| SUBJECTIVE SYMPTOMS | |
| Nausea | Decreased |
| Dizziness | Decreased |
| Syncope (fainting) | Decreased |
| Discomfort | Decreased |

little, if any, tolerance to heat. An example of such a program would be 20 minutes of light work (in shorts), followed by 20 minutes of rest on the first day. Each day the work period, work load, and uniform dress can be increased. On the last day, the work period may be 30 minutes long at full speed and in complete uniform, with rest periods of 10 to 15 minutes. During the rest periods, water or a commercial electrolyte solution should be administered since—in addition to the factors already mentioned—withholding liquids significantly retards the acclimatization process. Such a program serves two purposes: (1) it enhances physical conditioning; and (2) it provides acclimatization to heat.

* The relationship between physical conditioning and heat acclimatization is interesting and deserves further comment. It has been shown that a training program conducted indoors or outdoors during the winter months promotes a high degree of heat acclimatization even though the subjects had not been exposed to environmental heat since the preceding summer.[7, 17] Interval training produces 50 per cent of the total physiological adjustment resulting from heat acclimatization.[7] The great elevation in metabolic rate and therefore in heat production during training causes rectal temperatures to increase close to 40° C. at the end of each workout. Such high rectal temperatures undoubtedly serve as a stimulus for the improvement of the circulatory and sweating adjustments characteristic of the acclimatized individual. Although good physical condition alone does not guarantee acclimatization, it does promote more rapid acclimatization. For example, when some of the men referred to above were subjected to a more severe work-heat stress, further acclimatization occurred within only four days.[16]

## Clothing and Environment

In spite of consideration for the above precautions, heat disorders can occur when the exercise load is superimposed on heat loss resistances induced by environmental conditions or the wearing of necessary protective equipment and clothing required in some activities, or both. For example, we know a nude man exercising in a hot, saturated environment cannot lose a significant amount of heat since all avenues of heat loss are blocked. We have also seen that neither can an exercising person lose a significant amount of heat even in a moderate environment when most of his or her surface (skin) is covered with protective equipment impermeable to sweat (see Fig. 17–7, *B*). Recently a high school football player died from heat stroke during a preseason practice session in which he was required to wear, beneath a full uniform, a rubber sweat suit! Is there any wonder why he died? Regardless of acclimatization and complete hydration, an athlete can suffer heat illness while wearing full equipment if the environmental conditions are severe and the work load is heavy.

**Clothing.** The padding of the football uniform covers 50 per cent of the body, seriously limiting heat loss through evaporative cooling.[11] There are certain considerations of dress that you as the coach can take into account to aid in heat dissipation when weather conditions warrant:

(1) Have your athletes wear short sleeve netted jerseys, loose fitting and light in color, and no stockings;

(2) Remove helmets when feasible;

(3) Use conservative taping on exposed skin surfaces; and

(4) During rest periods, remove as much clothing as feasible to expose skin surface, e.g., raise jersey to expose abdominal area.

**Weather Guide.** Each athlete responds in an individual manner to the various combinations of environmental heat and clothing. Some are able to tolerate fairly heavy heat loads; others are not. Sufficient information is now available for the construction of an environmental guide. This makes it possible for you to make reasonable estimates as to the severity of the climatic conditions as they may affect your athletes.

The football weather guide shown in Figure 17–8 was constructed from the weather data gathered at the time of the heat stroke fatalities shown in Figure 17–1. Note that any combination of environmental conditions in Zone 1 would be considered safe. Under conditions obtaining in Zone 2, all players should be carefully observed for symptoms of heat illness, for example, nausea, profuse sweating, lack of good color, headache, and lack of coordination. When conditions meet those of Zone 3, practice should be postponed, or only moderately light

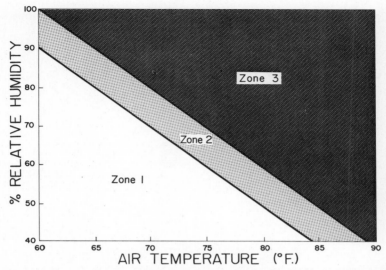

**Figure 17–8** Football weather guide for prevention of heat illness. The combination of relative humidity and air temperature in Zone 1 can be considered safe; for Zone 2, use caution; and for Zone 3, use extreme caution when working in a football uniform.

workouts in shorts should be permitted. Unacclimatized players should be closely observed for the symptoms previously mentioned. Note that all the heat stroke fatalities plus the marine survivors referred to earlier occurred in this zone. It should be mentioned that the marines were wearing the usual fatigue uniforms and were engaged in heavy exercise.

### Emergency Care in Heat Illness

When an athlete exhibits symptoms of heat illness, which have been previously discussed, *immediate* emergency procedures must be initiated. If not, heat stroke, a much more dangerous clinical situation, will follow heat exhaustion. It is not the prerogative of the coach to make a diagnosis, but rather to act at once:

(1) All clothing should be removed without delay;

(2) Immediate cooling with whatever means available — hose, ice water and cold shower are examples;

(3) An emergency vehicle should be called and hospital notified of a possible heat casualty; and

(4) En route, ice water through use of sponge or towels should be continuously applied.

For your knowledge, hospital treatment may consist of immersing the nude athlete in a tub of ice water while attendants rub extremities. Meanwhile, the physician will administer fluids and such drugs as the clinical situation dictates. A rectal thermometer is used to continuously record body temperature, which may go as high as 110° F. When the temperature descends to around 102° F., the patient is removed to a

## 1 ACCLIMATIZATION — GETTING YOUR MEN IN CONDITION

Get your athlete in condition by getting him used to working in heat. Start with light exercise in gym shorts and gradually increase workout time and clothing to full uniform over a 5 day period. Workout sessions starting with 1 hour and working up to 2 hours in 5 days is recommended. Consider 10 minute breaks every 20 minutes of workout.

| Day | 1 | 2 | 3 | 4 | 5 |
|-----|---|---|---|---|---|
| Time in Minutes | 60 | 80 | 100 | 110 | 120 |
| Gear | Shorts | Shorts | Pants | Pants & Helmet | Full Gear |
| Workout | Calisthenics & Jogging | Calis. & Sprints | Sprints & Drills | Sprints & Drills | Practice |

## 2 WEIGHT CHARTS — KEY TO GOOD TRAINING PRACTICE

The weight charts are prepared to help you in your work. Set up a procedure of lining up your men for weigh-in and weigh-out before and after practice or workout. The difference in weight is the athlete's loss of sweat. Replacement of fluid loss is important. Replacement is necessary for performance. At least 80% replacement must be achieved before next practice session.

Wt. Before   Wt. After = Wt. Loss = Sweat = Fluid replacement needed.

## 3 WEIGHT LOSS CHECK — FOCUS ON REHYDRATION NEED

The weight loss check is a convenient, reliable way of keeping tabs on the athlete's rehydration needs. If an athlete is given adequate access to fluids (Gatorade thirst quencher, water) by providing water breaks and encouraged to drink, he may be able to diminish his dehydration and replenish his fluid requirements. Such athletes will not show large losses in weight. If an athlete's weight loss is high, then his rehydration needs are great and should be satisfied. It is better to drink frequently, replace the fluid needed gradually, and maintain maximum rehydration throughout practice workout and game performance.

## 4 WATER REPLACEMENT — MAJOR INGREDIENT OF SWEAT

What goes out as sweat must be put back in the form of a fluid replacement. Since sweating helps to keep our body temperature from becoming excessive, it is in line to sweat, to minimize body temperature rise. Rehydrating the body of fluid lost is one of the best ways of insuring a continued cycle of performance. Rehydration must be encouraged — fluid replacement made available to make up for the fluid lost in sweat.

## 5 SALT REPLACEMENT — THE OTHER INGREDIENTS OF SWEAT

Along with water, when one sweats one loses electrolytes and body salts, primarily sodium chloride. In rehydrating the athlete with the water lost, we must replenish the lost salts as well. Gatorade has been formulated to supply those body salts in their proper ratios with respect to water and rehydration. If you drink water, however, make certain you use the proper ratio of water to salt tablets in order to keep the concentrations in balance. It is easier to stick to Gatorade and have the properly prepared, physiologically sound fluid replacement for your needs. No salt tablets should be used if one is drinking Gatorade.

## 6 WORK-HEAT RELATIONSHIP — ELEMENTARY BUT BASIC FACTS

Work produces heat and increases body temperature. If we were not able to lose the heat produced, our body temperature could go from 98.6°F (normal body temperature) to as high as 114°F (fatal to humans) in one hour. Fortunately, our body has a built-in temperature regulator and control. Our body sweats, loses water and salts and cools the skin while evaporation is taking place. Under normal conditions this cycle and regulation is adequate. In periods of heavy work and/or heavy uniform and insulation, the regulation system needs a helping hand to be able to maintain reasonable temperature control. The properly hydrated athlete in top shape is able to perform to his capacity. Remember that even a 3% weight loss is sufficient to show up significant performance loss. The percent weight loss can easily be calculated.

$$\frac{\text{Wt. loss of athlete}}{\text{Wt. before workout}} \times 100 = \text{Percent wt. loss.}$$

If you want the athlete's best performance, keep a sharp lookout on his heat-work relationship. Give him fluid replacement to help keep that temperature in control. Rehydrate him continually.

## 7 WEATHER EFFECTS — THE OVERLOOKED FACTOR

Hot and humid days can materially contribute to taking the zing out of your athlete's performance. On such days, the dehydration of the athlete is greater. His chances of heat illness are greater and your needs for rehydration are more acute. The use of the wet bulb thermometer is a means of quickly determining what the conditions are on the field during practice or a game. The sling psychrometer (about $15.00) may be purchased at any industrial supply company and assigned to a student manager, trainer or assistant coach. Careful observations of the wet bulb temperature and following the recommendations on the chart, can minimize dehydration. Frequent drinking breaks, fluid drinking encouragement, as well as allowing the body to dissipate heat, will be needed. The higher the temperature, the greater the humidity of the day, the greater is the degree of dehydration. Rehydrate your athletes — do it with Gatorade. It works.

## 8 DANGER SYMPTOMS — KEEP A SHARP LOOKOUT

They say an ounce of prevention is worth a pound of cure. A coach or trainer who is on the lookout for the danger signs will not only catch a situation before it becomes dangerous, but will also recognize that something must be corrected if it is producing such dangerous conditions. He then takes steps to correct the situation. Watch out for Muscle Cramps, Heat Exhaustion, Heat Stroke, Heat Fatigue and Sloppy Coordination. They all spell danger.

## 9 PROPER DRESS — EVERY LITTLE BIT HELPS

Particularly in football, the athlete is forced to wear heavy clothing which retards heat dissipation and acts as an insulator. Whenever and wherever it is possible, the body should be given a chance to throw off heat and become cooler. Clothing which can breathe and ventilate rather than insulate, can be helpful. Loosening the garments when not in action will help to cool. Keep using every means to bring your athlete close to normal body condition.

## 10 EMERGENCY MEASURES

If you practice good performance habits you will cut down on dangerous incidents. When an emergency occurs, however, be prepared to handle it with professional efficiency. Have a telephone handy. Give quick, effective treatment on the spot by cooling the body, removing clothing and applying cold applications such as a sponge, towel or bath in cold water or ice. Transport to a hospital immediately while applying the cold applications. Give the doctor the background information so that he can quickly anticipate what must be done. Even with all this, you must orient and teach all your personnel to carry out such a program when the necessity arises.

**Figure 17–9**  10 Point Fluid Replacement Guide. (Courtesy of Stokely-Van Camp, Inc., P. O. Box 1113, Indianapolis, Ind. 46206.)

bed and covered with blankets. Should the patient remain in the cold bath too long, body temperature will rapidly fall to dangerously low levels, precipitating shock, which might be lethal.

A wise coach and athletic director will not find it necessary to use the protocol outlined previously. If an emergency should occur, a prearranged plan for prompt emergency care and medical assistance regardless of the illness or injury should be available. This includes immediate access to a phone, as well as presence of assistants who are familiar with well thought out and rehearsed printed emergency procedures.

Figure 17–9 is a 10-point fluid replacement and heat guide. The large, colorful chart may be obtained free of charge by writing Stokely-Van Camp, Inc., P.O. Box 113, Indianapolis, Indiana 46206. It would be wise to post such a chart in the locker room or training facility for all participants, coaches, trainers, and athletes to study.

# COLD

A few sports, such as skiing, skating, and even some football games are played in cold weather. However, exposure to cold under these conditions does not usually present a serious problem. This is so for several reasons: (1) adequate clothing for heat conservation is usually worn and (2) as we all know, exercise increases body heat production. Thus, with clothing to prevent large heat losses and exercise to produce more body heat, the effects of cold exposure are not generally felt during athletic performances. Just a few words about cold exposure are necessary.

## Physiological Responses to Cold

Cold, as it cools the skin, causes cutaneous vasoconstriction, significantly reducing the amount of blood circulating in the extremities. This occurs over the entire body, with the exception of the head. Here, the blood supply is not diminished and because of this, on a cold day, a great deal of heat is lost through radiation if the head is not covered.

As the external temperature falls, more blood is forced inward (via vasoconstriction) to maintain proper temperature of the vital organs such as the brain, liver, and kidneys. This causes additional lowered skin temperature particularly at the extremities where the larger surface areas (fingers and toes) more easily lose heat through radiation. It is for these reasons that in severe cold, frostbite (actual freezing of the tissues) most often attacks the toes, fingers, and ears. Both exercise and clothing will help maintain body warmth.

## Exercise

As just mentioned, exposure to cold causes cutaneous vasoconstriction and shivering. The latter can increase metabolism as much as 50 per cent, which in turn furnishes heat for the body. On the other hand, heavy exercise may increase metabolism 700 per cent, with as much as 75 per cent of this available to heat the body. To maintain warmth on a cold day, continue to move about; if in a confined place exercise isometrically. Your activity should be adequate to maintain warmth but not so much that you begin to sweat. Perspiration dampens your clothing. Damp clothing conducts heat away from your body. This is the reason why a person should change clothing, particularly socks and mittens when they become wet. If your activity is so severe that sweating cannot be avoided, then your clothing should be loosened to allow heat and moisture to escape. When you remove your hat, the head becomes an excellent radiator.

## Clothing

Cold weather gear is designed to insulate the skin surface from the outside air. The effectiveness of the insulation is dependent not upon the *type* of material, but rather on its *thickness*. Down, the soft underplumage of birds, has become popular in winter garments because you can achieve the necessary thickness while maintaining a comparatively light weight. For the camper, down-filled clothing and sleeping bags are compressible requiring minimal storage space. Then, too, the resiliency (ease of compression and expansion) aids in keeping the down dry by permitting body moisture to escape.

# SUMMARY

The danger of heat stroke should be of major concern to all coaches and particularly to football coaches. Over the past several years there have been more than a dozen heat stroke fatalities — all needless deaths. By and large, coaches have not been oriented to the fundamental physiological and environmental conditions that contribute to heat illness.

Of prime concern is the understanding of heat balance, that is, the way in which the body may gain or lose heat. Knowledge of these factors, along with the way in which body temperature is regulated, forms the basis for understanding the principles of exercise in the heat and heat disorders.

It is with this knowledge that we can significantly reduce heat disorders, particularly through (1) adequate salt and water replacement; (2) acclimatization to heat; and (3) awareness of the limitations imposed by the combination of exercise, clothing, and environmental heat.

Finally, it is essential for us to understand the emergency care which should be immediately initiated if a heat stroke casualty occurs.

Although some sports are played in cold weather, exposure to cold under these conditions does not usually present a serious problem.

## QUESTIONS

1. Outline the sequential physiological events that occur during heat stroke.

2. Describe the manner by which the body loses heat.

3. Describe in detail how the body may gain heat.

4. How does the thermoregulatory system maintain a relatively constant temperature?

5. Explain the principal means by which we lose heat during exercise or exposure to heat.

6. Explain how salt and water depletion during exercise can lead to serious heat disorders.

7. What procedures would you follow to insure the athlete against heat illness during stressful environmental conditions?

8. How would you regulate salt and water replacement as a consequence of exercising in the heat?

9. Why may the highly competitive athlete be more vulnerable to heat disorders?

10. Describe the pertinent aspects of the experiment discussed in the text that demonstrated the effects of wearing a football uniform on heart rate, water loss, and core temperature.

11. Diagram the weather guide that may be used to estimate severity of climatic conditions.

12. What are the emergency procedures for a heat stroke casualty?

## REFERENCES

1. Bass, D., Kleeman, C., Quinn, M., Henschel, A., and Hegnauer, A.: Mechanisms of acclimatization to heat in man. Medicine, 34:323–380, 1955.
2. Blyth, C., and Burt, J.: Effects of water balance on ability to perform at high ambient temperatures. Res. Quart., 32:301–307, 1961.
3. Buskirk, E., and Bass, D.: Climate and exercise. *In* Johnson, W., and Buskirk, E.

(eds.): Science and Medicine of Exercise and Sports. 2nd ed., pp. 190–205, New York, Harper and Brothers Publishers, 1974.

4. Buskirk, E., Iampietro, P., and Bass, D.: Work performance and dehydration; effects of physical condition and heat acclimatization. J. Appl. Physiol., 12:189–194, 1958.

5. Craig, E., and Cummings, E.: Dehydration and muscular work. J. Appl. Physiol., 21:670–674, 1966.

6. Fox, E., Mathews, D., Kaufman, W., and Bowers, R.: Effects of football equipment on thermal balance and energy cost during exercise. Res. Quart., 37:332–339, 1966.

7. Gisolfi, C.: Work-heat tolerance derived from interval training. J. Appl. Physiol., 35:349–354, 1973.

8. Greenleaf, J., and Castle, B.: Exercise temperature regulation in man during hypohydration and hyperhydration. J. Appl. Physiol., 30:847–853, 1971.

9. Heat peril in distance runs spurs ACSM guideline alert. The Physician and Sportsmedicine, 3(7): 85–87, 1975.

10. Kozlowski, S., and Saltin, B.: Effects of sweat loss on body fluids. J. Appl. Physiol., 19:1119–1124, 1964.

11. Mathews, D., Fox, E., and Tanzi, D.: Physiological responses during exercise and recovery in a football uniform. J. Appl. Physiol., 26:611–615, 1969.

12. Murphy, R.: The problem of environmental heat in athletics. Ohio State Med. J., 59, No. 8, 1963.

13. Murphy, R., and Ashe, W.: Prevention of heat illness in football players. J.A.M.A., 194:650–654, 1965.

14. O'Donnell, T., and Clowes, G.: The circulatory abnormalities of heat stroke. New Eng. J. Med., 287(15):734–737, 1972.

15. Pitts, G., Johnson, R., and Consolazio, F.: Work in the heat as affected by intake of water, salt and glucose. Am. J. Physiol., 142:253–259, 1944.

16. Piwonka, R., and Robinson, S.: Acclimatization of highly trained men to work in severe heat. J. Appl. Physiol., 22:9–12, 1967.

17. Piwonka, R., Robinson, S., Gay, V., and Manalis, R.: Pre-acclimatization of men to heat by training. J. Appl. Physiol., 20:379–383, 1965.

18. Rowell, L.: Human cardiovascular adjustments to exercise and thermal stress. Physiol. Rev., 54(1):75–159, 1974.

19. Saltin, B.: Aerobic and anaerobic work capacity after dehydration. J. Appl. Physiol., 19:1114–1118, 1964.

20. Saltin, B.: Aerobic work capacity and circulation at exercise in man. Acta Physiol. Scand., 62(Suppl. 230):1–52, 1964.

21. Saltin, B.: Circulatory response to submaximal and maximal exercise after thermal dehydration. J. Appl. Physiol., 19:1125–1132, 1964.

22. Sohal, R., Sun, S., Colcolough, H., and Burch, G.: Heat stroke: an electron microscopic study of endothelial cell damage and disseminated intravascular coagulation. Arch. Intern. Med., 122:43–47, 1968.

23. Taylor, H., Henschel, A., Mickelson, O., and Keys, A.: The effect of sodium chloride intake on the work performance of man during exposure to dry heat and experimental heat exhaustion. Am. J. Physiol., 140:439, 1943.

## SELECTED READINGS

Bass, D., and Henschel, A.: Responses of body fluid compartments to heat and cold. Physiol. Rev., 36:128–144, 1956.

Benzinger, T.: Heat regulation: homeostasis of central temperature in man. Physiol. Rev., 49:671–759, 1969.

Mathews, D., Murphy, R., and Fox, E.: Prevention of heat illness in football. Mich. Osteopath. J., 35:9–12, 1970.

Robinson, S.: Temperature regulation in exercise. Pediatrics, 32:691–702, 1963.

# SECTION 6 _____

# NUTRITION AND BODY COMPOSITION

# Chapter 18

# NUTRITION, ATHLETIC PERFORMANCE, AND OBESITY

The only difference between diets for the athlete and the nonathlete should be the number of kilocalories (kcal.) or the amount of energy required by each. Athletes may consume twice the number of kilocalories, depending upon the strenuousness of their sport.

Athletic performance improves with wise nutrition and crumbles with nutritive deficiency. Inadequate water intake has by far the most immediate and serious debilitating effect on performance. An athlete's exploits can be not only improved through proper nutritional practices but harmed through malpractice.

Prevention of obesity achieves greater results than treatment for it. Particularly among pre-adolescent and adolescent children, inactivity is a prime cause of obesity. Our essential concern here is to understand nutrition and its effects upon athletics and obesity.

# ENERGY BALANCE AND COST OF ACTIVITIES

The quantity of food required by an individual above that which is necessary for body maintenance and growth depends upon the amount of physical activity that he or she experiences. Just as an automobile traveling 60 miles each day requires more gasoline than one traveling 30 miles per day, a person walking 20 miles a day requires more food than a person walking 2 miles each day. For body weight to remain constant, food intake must equal energy needs. If, in fact, too much food is consumed, we will gain weight or be in what is referred to as a

**Table 18–1   MEDIAN ENERGY CONSUMPTION AND CORRESPONDING DAILY FOOD REQUIREMENTS (IN KILOCALORIES)**

| SELECTED DISCIPLINES | EXPENDITURE OF ENERGY/KG OF BODY WEIGHT/ DAY (kcal) | AVERAGE BODY WEIGHT (kg) | NORMATIVE DAILY NET NEEDS BASED ON COMPUTED ENERGY REQUIREMENTS (COLUMN 2 × COLUMN 3) (kcal) | NUTRITIONAL, PHYSIOLOGICAL, OPTIMAL DAILY GROSS REQUIRE- MENTS, WITH 10 PER CENT ADDED FOR CONSUMP- TION (kcal) |
|---|---|---|---|---|
| 1 | 2 | 3 | 4 | 5 |
| **Group A** | | | | |
| Cross-country skiing | 82.14 | 67.5 | 5,550 | 6,105* |
| Crew racing | 69.21 | 80.0 | 5,550 | 6,105 |
| Canoe racing | 72.72 | 75.0 | 5,450 | 5,995 |
| Swimming | 69.87 | 76.0 | 5,300 | 5,830* |
| Bicycle racing | 80.39 | 68.0 | 5,450 | 5,995 |
| Marathon racing | 79.07 | 68.0 | 5,400 | 5,940 |
| Average values (men) | | | 5,450 | 5,995* |
| | | Rounded-off norm: 6,000 kcal | | |

Also belonging to sports of group A are skiing, Norwegian combination; middle-distance racing; walking; ice racing; modern pentathlon; equine sports, military; and touring (Alpine climbing).

| | | | | |
|---|---|---|---|---|
| **Group B** | | | | |
| Soccer | 72.28 | 74.0 | 5,350 | 5,885 |
| Handball | 68.06 | 75.0 | 5,100 | 5,610 |
| Basketball | 67.93 | 75.0 | 5,100 | 5,610 |
| Field Hockey | 69.18 | 75.0 | 5,200 | 5,720 |
| Ice Hockey | 71.87 | 68.0 | 4,900 | 5,390 |
| Average values (men) | | | 5,130 | 5,643 |
| | | Rounded-off norm: 5,600 kcal | | |

Also belonging to group B are rugby; water polo; volleyball; tennis; polo; and bicycle polo.

| | | | | |
|---|---|---|---|---|
| **Group C** | | | | |
| Canoe slalom | 67.16 | 68.0 | 4,550 | 5,005 |
| Shooting | 62.71 | 72.5 | 4,550 | 5,005 |
| Table tennis | 59.96 | 74.0 | 4,450 | 4,895 |
| Bowling | 62.69 | 75.0 | 4,700 | 5,170 |
| Sailing | 63.77 | 74.0 | 4,700 | 5,170 |
| Average values (men) | | | 4,590 | 5,049 |
| | | Rounded-off norm: 5,000 kcal | | |

Also belonging to group C are circuit cycle racing (1,000–4,000 meters), fencing, ice sailing, and gliding.

*Table continued on the opposite page.*

*positive energy balance.* On the other hand, if our energy needs exceed that produced by the food we eat, a *negative energy balance* occurs. In this case, the body consumes its own fat, and then protein, with a concomitant loss in body weight.

Table 18–1 contains a number of sports with their respective energy requirements in kcal.* per day. Table 18–2 contains a few

---

*To convert from kcal. to liters of oxygen consumed, divide kcal. by 5.

## Table 18–1  MEDIAN ENERGY CONSUMPTION AND CORRESPONDING DAILY FOOD REQUIREMENTS (IN KILOCALORIES) *(Continued)*

| SELECTED DISCIPLINES | EXPENDITURE OF ENERGY/kg OF BODY WEIGHT/ DAY (kcal) | AVERAGE BODY WEIGHT (kg) | NORMATIVE DAILY NET NEEDS BASED ON COMPUTED ENERGY REQUIREMENTS (COLUMN 2 × COLUMN 3) (kcal) | NUTRITIONAL, PHYSIOLOGICAL, OPTIMAL DAILY GROSS REQUIRE- MENTS, WITH 10 PER CENT ADDED FOR CONSUMP- TION (kcal) |
|---|---|---|---|---|
| 1 | 2 | 3 | 4 | 5 |
| Group D | | | | |
| Sprinting | 61.77 | 69.0 | 4,250 | 4,675 |
| Running: short to middle distances | 65.62 | 65.0 | 4,250 | 4,675 |
| Pole vault | 57.83 | 73.0 | 4,200 | 4,620 |
| Diving | 69.24 | 61.0 | 4,200 | 4,620 |
| Boxing (middle and welter weight: to 63.5 kg) | 67.25 | 63.0 | 4,250 | 4,675 |
| Average values (men) | | | 4,230 | 4,653 |
| | | Rounded-off norm: 4,600 kcal | | |

Also belonging to group D are hurdle races; broad- and high jump; hop-skip-and-jump; ballet swimming; figure skating; figure roller skating; and ski, ski jump, bob sled, and toboganing.

| | | | | |
|---|---|---|---|---|
| Group E | | | | |
| Group I | | | | |
| Judo (lightweight) | 72.92 | 62.5 | 4,550 | 5,005 |
| Weight lifting (light-weight) | 69.15 | 67.5 | 4,650 | 5,115 |
| Javelin | 56.95 | 76.0 | 4,350 | 4,785 |
| Gymnastics with apparatus | 67.14 | 65.0 | 4,350 | 4,785 |
| Steeplechase | 63.96 | 68.0 | 4,350 | 4,785 |
| Ski: Alpine competition | 71.29 | 67.5 | 4,800 | 5,280 |
| Average values (men) | | | 4,508 | 4,959 |
| | | Rounded-off norm: 5,000 kcal | | |
| Group II | | | | |
| Hammerthrow | 62.46 | 102.0 | 6,350 | 6,985 |
| Shot put and discuss | 62.47 | 102.0 | 6,350 | 6,985 |
| | | Rounded-off norm: 7,000 kcal | | |

Also belonging to group E/I are wrestling; automobile rallies; motor racing; gymnastics; acrobatics; parachute jumping; equine sports shows; decathlon; and bicycle gymnastics.

---

*Deviations of a few per cent from the median values are, in the field of biology, to be taken as basically insignificant.

From Encyclopedia of Sport Sciences and Medicine. New York, The Macmillan Co., pp. 1128–1129.

### Table 18-2  APPROXIMATE ENERGY COST OF VARIOUS EXERCISES AND SPORTS

| SPORT OR EXERCISE | TOTAL CALORIES EXPENDED PER MINUTE OF ACTIVITY |
|---|---|
| Climbing | 10.7–13.2 |
| Cycling 5.5 mph | 4.5 |
| 9.4 mph | 7.0 |
| 13.1 mph | 11.1 |
| Dancing | 3.3–7.7 |
| Football | 8.9 |
| Golf | 5.0 |
| Gymnastics | |
| Balancing | 2.5 |
| Abdominal exercises | 3.0 |
| Trunk Bending | 3.5 |
| Arms swinging, hopping | 6.5 |
| Rowing 51 str/min | 4.1 |
| 87 str/min | 7.0 |
| 97 str/min | 11.2 |
| Running | |
| Short-distance | 13.3–16.6 |
| Cross-country | 10.6 |
| Tennis | 7.1 |
| Skating (fast) | 11.5 |
| Skiing, moderate speed | 10.8–15.9 |
| Uphill, maximum speed | 18.6 |
| Squash | 10.2 |
| Swimming | |
| Breaststroke | 11.0 |
| Backstroke | 11.5 |
| Crawl (55 yd/min) | 14.0 |
| Wrestling | 14.2 |

From *Nutrition for the Athlete.* American Association for Health, Physical Education and Recreation. Washington, D.C., p. 26.

sports and exercises in terms of total kcal. expended per minute. Of what value is this information to us? By knowing the energy cost of the activity, we can more judiciously plan our diets to maintain proper energy balance.

For example, a man weighing 68 kilograms and participating in bicycle racing would expend 5450 kcal. (plus 10% utilized in digestion) or 5995 kcal. per day (Table 18–1). A person playing golf uses 5 kcal. per minute (Table 18–2). If that person were to play for three hours, he or she would have expended 900 kcal. of energy (5 kcal. per min. times 180 min.).

These data are approximations and depend upon a number of factors, including the physical condition of the person, his or her degree of skill, and the degree of effort employed. For example, (Table 18–2), 7.1 kcal. per minute are expended for playing tennis. A novice might

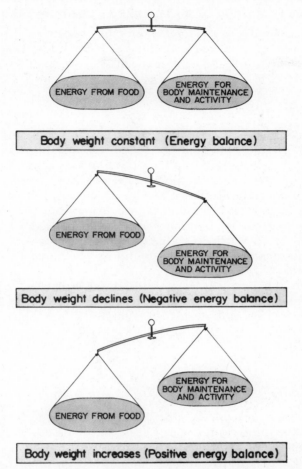

**Figure 18–1**  Relationship of food consumption, energy expenditure, and body weight.

spend considerable time walking after balls, while the expert engages in vigorous rallies. The same would be true for golf. Terrain, skill, and body weight are also important considerations related to the energy cost of the activity. Usually, it costs you more in the rough than on the fairway—in more ways than one!

Figure 18–1 may help in summarizing the relationship of food consumption, energy expenditure, and body weight.

## NUTRIENTS

Essential to the diet are: proteins, fats, carbohydrates, vitamins, minerals, and water. Proteins, fats, and carbohydrates are the only sources of energy; hence, they are called the *energy* nutrients. Devoid of carbon, minerals and water are the inorganic nutrients. Vitamins play a metabolic role in every single cell of the body, the B complex being particularly important in energy metabolism.

## Carbohydrates

Sugars, simple and complex, comprise this nutritional group. Simple sugars such as glucose and fructose, double sugars (disaccharides) sucrose and maltose, and the polysaccharides starch and glycogen are among the important members. Finally, all sugars must be reduced to simple sugars through digestion before being absorbed. Starch is a complex sugar containing numerous glucose molecules. Plants store sugar in this form. Man stores a limited amount of sugar as glycogen in the liver and muscles that is depleted during strenuous muscular activity (see p. 19).

Candy, cake, jam, jelly, honey, and dried fruits are foods containing large amounts of sugar. Wheat, corn, rice, barley, potatoes, and legumes (e.g., peas and beans) are among those foods containing starch.

## Fats

Butter, margarine, vegetable oils, lard, and ice cream are rich sources of fat. Cheese, nuts, meat, eggs, and milk also contain significant amounts of fat.

Fats are spoken of as saturated, unsaturated, and polyunsaturated. Those with chemical structures not permitting the addition of more hydrogen atoms are called saturated (saturated with hydrogen atoms). Those with bonds allowing additional hydrogen are unsaturated and polyunsaturated, depending upon the number of vacant bonds available. Forty to 45 per cent of the total energy intake in the United States is made up of fat nutrients. Unquestionably, eating such a large quantity of fat contributes toward excessive obesity. Nutritionists suggest that 25 per cent fat in our daily diet would be an adequate amount. Some fat in the diet is necessary for essential fatty acids and the fat-soluble vitamins A, D, E, and K.

Essential fatty acids may be important in preventing atherosclerosis. Apparently, these acids are effective in lowering cholesterol concentration in the blood. Vegetable oils contain these essential fatty acids. Use of the polyunsaturated oils, especially those containing linoleic acid, is encouraged; eating saturated fats (animal fat) is discouraged.

## Protein

Proteins are more complex and larger molecules than either carbohydrates or fats. In addition to carbon, hydrogen, and oxygen, proteins contain nitrogen; many contain sulfur, phosphorus, and iron. Proteins, the building blocks of tissue, form a vital part of the nucleus and protoplasm of all cells.

The protein molecule is composed of nitrogenous compounds called amino acids. Through digestion, particular proteins used in cell formation and repair are derived from these amino acids.

Daily protein consumption throughout the world varies from 50 to 300 grams per day, depending primarily on the affluence of the community. Usually, high income families eat more protein.

It is important to remember that muscular work, even of the magnitude to double daily energy requirements, has very little effect on protein metabolism. The United States Food and Nutrition Board suggests a protein allowance of 0.9 grams per kilogram of body weight per day; suggested minimal requirement is 0.35 to 0.5 grams per kilogram body weight. Thus, a person of average physical activity weighing 80 kilograms (176 pounds) would require 72 grams (2.05 ounces) of protein per day (0.9 gm. × 80 kg.). As mentioned above, increased physical activity does not greatly affect protein requirement. Therefore, during training, this amount of protein should also be adequate even during heavy weight (strength) training involving relatively large changes in muscle (protein) mass.

Concurrent with the commencement of training is an increased need for plasma protein and iron.[18] Red cells become fragile, precipitating a transient anemia during the initial stages of heavy conditioning. The situation becomes normal within two weeks provided that protein intake is adequate and iron reserves are normal.

A group from the United Kingdom[14] recommends that protein should yield 10 per cent of the required energy. The following calculations demonstrate this amount of protein in grams.

Required energy yield = 3000 kcal.

Amount of protein: 10% of 3000 = 300 kcal.

One gram of protein yields 4 kcal. of energy, hence $\dfrac{300}{4} = 75$ grams of protein.

As indicated previously, provided that the man weighed 80 kilograms, according to American standards (0.9 gm./kg. body weight) his daily requirement would equal (0.9) × (80) or 72.0 grams of protein.

## Vitamins

Most frequently appearing in the body as enzymes and coenzymes, vitamins act as catalysts. These are inorganic materials in whose presence important chemical reactions occur. For example, most B vitamins function in the energy metabolic cycle; even if only one vitamin is inadequate, the entire chain of chemical reactions ceases; consequently, ATP is not produced. Serious illness and even death may follow.

Vitamins D and A as well as iron are toxic in excessive dosages. Vitamins and minerals exceeding recommended allowances should be taken only under a physician's direction. The far better practice is to eat nutritive meals which include sufficient amounts of minerals and vitamins.

# FOOD REQUIREMENTS

The amount of food necessary each day depends upon a person's energy needs. These energy needs are directly related to: (1) periods of rapid growth, (2) age, and (3) physical activity. During the rapid growing years (12–22 years for boys and 12–18 years for girls), there is a gradual increase in the minimal daily food requirements (see Table 18–3). As we become older, our daily energy needs decrease (Fig. 18–2). The per cent contributions for each of the three foodstuffs are:[8]

| Protein | 14 to 15% |
| Fat | 29 to 30% |
| Carbohydrate | 55 to 56% |

For example, athletes requiring 5000 kcal. per day could have their menu divided as follows:

**Table 18–3   RECOMMENDED DAILY DIETARY ALLOWANCES ESTABLISHED BY THE NATIONAL ACADEMY OF SCIENCES**

|       | AGE (YRS) | WEIGHT (LBS.) | HEIGHT (IN.) | KILO CALORIES | Kcal/lb. |
|-------|-----------|---------------|--------------|---------------|----------|
| Boys  | 10–12 | 77  | 55 | 2,500 | 33 |
|       | 12–14 | 95  | 59 | 2,700 | 28 |
|       | 14–18 | 130 | 67 | 3,000 | 23 |
|       | 18–22 | 147 | 69 | 2,800 | 19 |
| Girls | 10–12 | 77  | 56 | 2,250 | 29 |
|       | 12–14 | 97  | 61 | 2,300 | 24 |
|       | 14–16 | 114 | 62 | 2,400 | 21 |
|       | 16–18 | 119 | 63 | 2,300 | 19 |
|       | 18–22 | 128 | 64 | 2,000 | 16 |

From Nutrition for the Athlete. American Association for Health, Physical Education and Recreation. Washington, D.C., p. 9.

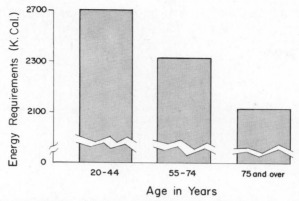

**Figure 18–2**   Daily energy requirements for men ages 20 to 75 years. When body weight is considered, the greatest energy decline occurs at about 60 years of age. (Based on data from McGandy, R., et al.: Nutrient intakes and energy expenditures in men of different ages. J. Gerontol., 21:581.)

| Protein | 700 to 750 kcal. |
| Fat | 1450 to 1500 kcal. |
| Carbohydrate | 2750 to 2800 kcal. |

## Selecting Foods

About 20 years ago, the United States Department of Agriculture suggested four basic food groups from which meals should be selected each day to ensure minimal nutrition:[13] (1) milk, (2) meat, (3) cereals, and (4) vegetables and fruit.

More recently, the American Association for Health, Physical Education and Recreation, in collaboration with the American Dietetic and Nutrition Foundation published, *Nutrition for the Athlete*.[12] The essential food groups in this fine booklet are listed as: milk, meat (fish, poultry, cheese, or eggs), dark green or deep yellow vegetables, citrus fruits, other fruits and vegetables, bread (enriched or whole grain bread), cereal or potatoes and fats (butter, margarine, or other fat spreads).

Table 18–4 contains an extensive list of these foods.

## Number of Meals

The spacing of and number of meals per day which would prove most satisfactory have been inadequately researched. However, using blood glucose levels as a criterion, at least three meals can be considered minimal. Blood sugar levels fall two and one-half to three hours following breakfast causing fatigue and some loss in efficiency.

Nutritive nibbling—not just nibbling—can be interspersed among the three main meals, aiding in the maintenance of proper blood

## Table 18-4   FOODS WHICH WITHIN A GROUP MAY BE EXCHANGED OR SUBSTITUTED FOR EACH OTHER

FOOD GROUPS

MILK

(1 cup whole milk contains 12 grams carbohydrate, 8 grams protein, 10 grams fat, and 170 calories; 1 cup of skim milk contains 80 calories; 1 cup cocoa made with milk contains approximately 200 calories)

1 cup whole milk
1 cup skim milk
½ cup evaporated milk
¼ cup powdered milk
1 cup buttermilk
1 cup cocoa

MEAT GROUP

(1 ounce contains 7 grams protein, 5 grams fat, and 75 calories)

1 ounce lean beef, lamb, pork, liver, chicken*
1 ounce fish—cod, haddock, perch, etc.
1 hot dog
¼ cup tuna, salmon, crab, lobster
5 small oysters, shrimp, clams
3 medium sardines
1 slice cheese
¼ cup cottage cheese
1 egg
2 tablespoons peanut butter

*1 average serving of meat or fish (such as a pork chop or 2 meatballs) is about 3 ounces

DARK GREEN OR DEEP YELLOW VEGETABLES (½ cup is one serving)

Greens and lettuce have very little carbohydrate content. The other vegetables contain approximately 7 grams carbohydrate and 2 grams protein and 35 calories

| | |
|---|---|
| Broccoli* | Greens* |
| Carrots | Beet greens |
| Chicory* | Chard |
| Escarole* | Collard |
| Pepper | Dandelion |
| Pumpkin | Kale |
| Tomatoes* | Mustard |
| Watercress* | Spinach |
| Winter squash | Turnip greens |
| | Lettuce* |

*Low Calorie Vegetables.

CITRUS FRUITS OR SUBSTITUTE (½ cup is one serving)

The carbohydrate is averaged to approximately 10 grams per ½ cup and 40 calories

| | | |
|---|---|---|
| Orange | Grapefruit juice* | Tangerine |
| Orange juice | Cantaloupe* | Tomato juice* |
| Grapefruit* | | |

*Represent low calorie fruits and vegetables

## Table 18-4 FOODS WHICH WITHIN A GROUP MAY BE EXCHANGED OR SUBSTITUTED FOR EACH OTHER (*Continued*)

### OTHER FRUITS AND VEGETABLES

Fruits (½ cup is approximately 10 grams carbohydrate and 40 calories)

| | | |
|---|---|---|
| Apple | Dates | Peach |
| Applesauce | Figs | Pear |
| Apricots | Grapes | Pineapple |
| Banana (½ small) | Grape juice (¼ cup) | Plums |
| Raspberries | Honeydew melon | Raisins (2 tablespoons) |
| Blueberrries | Mango | Pineapple juice (⅓ cup) |
| Cherries | Papaya | Prunes (2 medium) |
| | | Watermelon* |

Vegetables (½ cup is one serving)
The vegetables without the asterisk contain approximately 7 grams carbohydrate, 2 grams protein, and 35 calories

| | | |
|---|---|---|
| Asparagus* | Cucumbers* | Radishes* |
| Beets | Eggplant* | Rutabagas |
| Brussels sprouts* | Mushrooms* | Sauerkraut* |
| Cabbage* | Okra* | String beans* |
| Cauliflower* | Onions | Summer squash* |
| Celery* | Peas, green | Turnips |

*Represents low calorie fruits and vegetables

### BREAD GROUP

(1 slice of bread or 1 substitute contains 15 grams carbohydrate, 2 grams protein, and 70 calories)

| | | |
|---|---|---|
| ½ hamburger bun | ½ cup spaghetti, noodles, macaroni, etc. | ⅔ cup parsnips |
| ½ hot dog bun | | 1 small potato |
| 1 cup popcorn | 2 graham crackers | ½ cup mashed potato |
| 2½″ wedge pizza | 5 saltines | 15 potato chips—1 ounce bag |
| 1 slice enriched bread | 6 round, thin crackers | 6 pretzels, medium, or 20 |
| 1 biscuit or roll | ½ cup beans or peas | thin sticks |
| 1 small muffin | (dried or cooked) | 8 French fries |
| 1 small piece cornbread | (Lima or navy beans, | ½ cup sweet potatoes or |
| ½ cup cooked cereal | split pea, cowpeas, etc) | yams |
| ¾ cup ready-to-eat cereal | ¼ cup baked beans | 1½″ cube sponge or angel |
| | ⅓ cup corn | cake (no icing) |
| | ½ cup rice or grits | ½ cup ice cream (omit 2 fat servings) |

### FAT GROUP

(1 teaspoon fat contains 5 grams fat and 45 calories)

| | | | |
|---|---|---|---|
| Bacon | 1 slice | Cream cheese | 1 tablespoon |
| Butter or margarine or fat spread | 1 teaspoon | French dressing | 1 tablespoon |
| | | Mayonnaise | 1 teaspoon |
| Cream (light) | 2 tablespoons | Oil or cooking fat | 1 teaspoon |
| Cream (heavy—40%) | 1 tablespoon | | |

### SUGARS

(1 teaspoon contains 5 grams carbohydrate and 20 calories)

| | |
|---|---|
| Sugar | Syrup |
| Jelly | Hard candy |
| Honey | Carbonated beverage (¼ cup) |

Salt used in the home should be iodized.

From Nutrition for the Athlete.[12] American Association for Health, Physical Education and Recreation. Washington, D.C.

## Table 18-5   SNACK FOODS AND THEIR APPROXIMATE ENERGY VALUES IN KILOCALORIES (Kcal)

| SNACK FOOD | Kcal |
|---|---|
| Milk Shake (fountain size) | 400 |
| Malted Milk Shake (fountain size) | 500 |
| Sundaes | 215–325 |
| Sodas | 260 |
| Hamburger (including bun) | 360 |
| Hot Dog (including bun) | 210 |
| Pizza (4″–5″ section) | 135 |
| Popcorn, lightly buttered (½ cup) | 75 |
| Nuts (3 tbsp. chopped, or 30 peanuts) | 150 |
| Pound Cake (⅜″ slice) | 140 |
| Cup Cake with frosting (2¾″ diam.) | 185 |
| Layer Cake with frosting (2″ slice) | 370–445 |
| Pancake (4″ diam.) | 60 |
| Waffle (medium, 4½″ × 5½″ × ½″) | 215 |
|     Add 20 Kcals for each teaspoon syrup or sweetening | |
|     Add 45 Kcals for each teaspoon butter or other fat spread | |
| Brownies (2″ × 2″ × ¾″) | 140 |
| Plain Cookie (3″ diam.) | 120 |
| Pie (⅛ of a 9″ pie) | 275–345 |
| Fruit Juice (1 cup) | 110–165 |

From Nutrition for the Athlete. American Association for Health, Physical Education and Recreation. Washington, D.C., p. 19.

glucose levels. Foods without nutritive value should be limited. Always of concern is the problem of obesity when nibbling gets out of hand. Table 18–5 contains a number of snack foods with their caloric equivalents.

A very active person, such as the athlete requiring 5000 or 6000 kcal. per day, may be much better advised to eat four meals, as follows:

|  | kcal.% | Total kcal. |
|---|---|---|
| First breakfast | 21 | 1050 |
| Second breakfast | 14 | 700 |
| Lunch | 27 | 1350 |
| Dinner | 23 | 1150 |
| Snacks | 15 | 750 |
|  | 100 | 5000 |

In addition to maintaining normal blood glucose values, more frequent and smaller meals apparently lead to a more satisfactory level of blood lipids resulting in less deposition of fat.

### Diet Before Activity

Diet must contain adequate carbohydrates as well as vitamins, particularly vitamins C, B, and E. Foods to avoid are those which form gas.

Select items encouraging bowel elimination such as whole kernel breads and fruits. Complete and regular bowel elimination favors the overall health and performance of the athlete; following breakfast is an appropriate physiological time for emptying the bowel.

Performance can be impaired if the athlete has just eaten; generally, there is a feeling of discomfort when one attempts heavy exertion on a full stomach. Fat and meat are slow to digest; consequently, they should not be eaten less than 3 to 4 hours before competing. One to two hours prior to activity, carbohydrates (500 to 600 kcal.) can be taken with no problem; suggested foods: brownies, cookies, dates, hard candy, cake, and figs.

Liquid may be consumed up to 30 minutes before competition without ill effects.[1] Commercial drinks such as Gatorade containing glucose and essential electrolytes may be considered.[17] The cola type of soft drinks (6 oz. bottle) contain 17 grams of carbohydrates producing about 68 kcal. of energy. The endurance athlete should be well hydrated prior to competition.

### Diet During Activity

Maintenance of glucose levels during prolonged physical exertion is necessary. Long-distance cycling, marathon running and long-distance skiing are examples of such activities. Glucose taken in liquid form is recommended when events exceed one hour or more of continuous exertion. Replacement of glucose, electrolytes, and water is the purpose of consumption during these long ordeals. Tennis matches can become marathons, particularly when an individual plays both singles and doubles at one meet. Environmental stress, high temperature, and/or humidity demand that water be replaced in the working athlete if peak performance is to be maintained.

It is important to remember that it is not possible to ingest fluids as rapidly as they are lost (mainly through sweating) during most endurance events. For example, only about 800 ml. per hour of fluid can be emptied by the stomach during distance running, whereas losses amount to 2½ times that or 2 liters per hour.[5] Therefore, endurance athletes must be careful not to ingest fluids at a greater rate than 800 ml. per hour. Otherwise, the fluid retained in the stomach may cause discomfort and possibly hinder performance.

### Diet Following Activity

Following endurance events, serious effort should be made to replace fats, proteins, carbohydrates, vitamins, minerals, and water. One will be in better physiological condition if he or she waits an hour or so before eating a large meal; however, a liquid nutrient may be consumed a few minutes following exertion—a judicious move to stabilize blood glucose. If competition is to be renewed the next day, care must be taken to replenish the energy stores—muscle and liver glycogen (see below). Easily digestible foods should be selected and may include: cream and butter for fat content; carbohydrates in the form of bread, puddings, rice; proteins such as fish, soft-boiled eggs, cheese, and other milk products; and fresh fruit and juices, which are excellent for vitamin C, energy, and liquid replacement.

### Can Diet Affect Performance?

Protein contributes little if anything toward energy required of physical performance. Consequently, steak on the training table has no scientific justification when considered as necessary to increased work performance.

Carbohydrate is the prime source of energy during exhaustive work; both fat and carbohydrate are the sources of energy during steady state activities. The carbohydrate molecule contains more oxygen than fat does. Add to this the fact that carbohydrate is a more efficient precursor of energy than fat (requires less oxygen to produce the same amount of energy); this makes it the preferable energy-producing food. Studies conclusively demonstrate that diets lacking in carbohydrates have deleterious effects on work performance.[2, 3, 9] One study showed that hard work was reduced by 50 per cent with a high fat diet and increased 25 per cent over that with a normal diet when a high carbohydrate menu was employed.[3]

As shown in Figure 18–3, muscle glycogen content is positively related to work performance.[3] Recently, muscle biopsy studies have been used to show the effects of diet on muscle glycogen stores. The procedure involves use of a special needle which is inserted into a muscle under local anesthesia. A portion of the muscle is removed for later analysis. One of the studies[3] went as follows:

Men were administered three diets, following which they performed on a bicycle ergometer to exhaustion. Time to exhaustion on a normal diet was 114 minutes; on a high protein, high fat diet it was 57 minutes; and on a high carbohydrate diet it was 167 minutes. The glycogen content of the quadriceps femoris muscle following the mixed diet was 17.5 grams per kg. of wet muscle before exercise; following three days of a carbohydrate-free diet, it was only 6.3 grams, whereas after the same period of time on a high carbohydrate diet, it was 35.1 grams per kg. of muscle.

In events exceeding 30 to 60 minutes of competition, Åstrand[2] suggests the following regimen to maximally increase muscle glycogen stores:

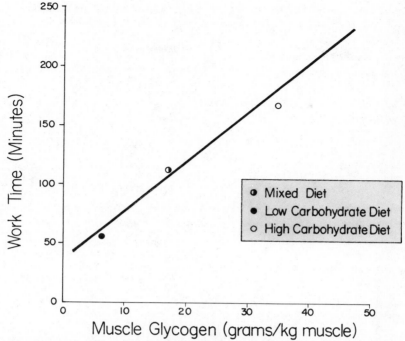

**Figure 18–3** Effects of a mixed diet, a low carbohydrate diet, and a high carbohydrate diet on the initial glycogen content of the quadriceps femoris muscle and the duration of exercise on a bicycle ergometer; the higher the initial muscle glycogen content, the longer the duration of exercise. (Based on data from Bergstrom, et al.[3])

    1. One week before competition, exhaust the muscles primarily involved in your event. This will deplete their glycogen stores. This is required for a subsequent increase in glycogen storage.[4]

    2. The next three days, your diet should include mostly protein and fat. Such will maintain low muscle glycogen.

    3. Following the three days of primarily protein and fat consumption, add large amounts of carbohydrate to the diet. This is in addition to the fat and protein.

    Glycogen stores can exceed 40 grams per kg. of muscle. This conceivably could result in as much as 700 grams of stored glycogen, or 2800 kcal. of ready energy. An average amount for all the muscles of the body would be about 400 grams of glycogen (see p. 19).

    A note of caution is needed here. An increase in muscle glycogen storage also results in an increase in water content of the muscle. Therefore, a feeling of stiffness and heaviness often accompanies large increases in muscle glycogen storage. Consequently, such a practice is

## Table 18–6 DIETS FOR USE IN THE ÅSTRAND REGIMEN FOR ENHANCED MUSCLE GLYCOGEN STORAGE

| DAYS 4–6 BEFORE AN EVENT | DAYS 1–3 BEFORE AN EVENT |
|---|---|
| *High Energy-Low Carbohydrate Diet* | *Very High Energy-High Carbohydrate Diet* |

Breakfast

| | |
|---|---|
| ½ grapefruit or ½ c. grapefruit juice or berries | 1 c. orange or pineapple juice |
| 2 eggs | Hot cereal as desired |
| Generous serving bacon, ham or sausage | Eggs and/or hot cakes |
| Butter or margarine as desired | Generous serving bacon, ham or sausage |
| 1 thin slice whole wheat bread | Butter or margarine as desired |
| 1 c. whole milk or half and half | 2–4 slices whole grain bread |
| | Chocolate or cocoa as desired |

Luncheon and Dinner

| | |
|---|---|
| Clear Bouillon or ½ c. tomato juice | Cream or legume soup or chowder |
| Large serving fish, poultry or liver (>6 oz) | Large serving fish, poultry or liver (>6 oz) |
| Mixed green (only) salad or 1 c. cooked green vegetable | Added beans or fruits |
| Salad dressing, butter or margarine as desired | Salad dressing, butter or margarine as desired |
| 1 c. whole milk or half and half | 1 c. whole milk, half and half, or milkshake |
| Artificially sweetened gelatin with whipped cream (no sugar) | 2–4 slices whole grain bread or rolls or potato |
| | Pie, cake, pudding or ice cream |

Snacks

| | |
|---|---|
| Cheddar cheese | Fruits, especially dates, raisins, apples bananas |
| Nuts | More milk or milkshakes |
| 1 slice whole grain bread | Cookies or candy |
| Artificially sweetened lemonade | |

From Bogert, J., et al.: Nutrition and Physical Fitness. 9th ed., W. B. Saunders Co., p. 487.

only advisable for endurance (30 minutes or more) athletes and *not* for sprinters or those athletes participating in events of short duration.[5]

Table 18–6 is an illustration of diets which may be used in Åstrand's regimen for enhanced muscle glycogen storage.

Minerals and vitamins aid in the regulation of body functions. They are essential to the physiology of nerves, and skeletal and heart muscle. Water is vital not only to performance but to life itself. Its importance is too frequently overlooked by athlete and coach alike. All chemical reactions in the body occur in a water environment. Regulation of body temperature during activity is particularly dependent upon water as it evaporates from the skin. Man may live 30 days without the energy nutrients (carbohydrate, fat, and protein), but dies within five or six days when deprived of water.[16] Optimal physical performance and health are dependent upon body water balance.

Along with water the undigestible portion of vegetable fiber called cellulose, often referred to as roughage, promotes bowel elimination.

Most water is absorbed in the intestine, thus allowing the stool or feces to be lubricated resulting in a more pleasant elimination.

# OBESITY

An unvarnished tale states, "most people become obese because of *physical inactivity*."[11] Such is true for teenagers as well as adults. A study in California revealed 14 per cent of high school seniors (boys and girls) were obese. The need for physical education in elementary, junior, and senior high schools can be substantiated on this verity alone.

Obesity is related to a number of diseases including diabetes, coronary heart disease, psychological disturbances, kidney disease, hypertension, stroke, liver ailments, and mechanical difficulties (particularly, back and foot problems). As a consequence, life expectancy is significantly reduced among the obese population. Excessive obesity may result in as high as 100 per cent increase in mortality over that which might be expected!

## What is Obesity?

Authorities generally concede that the normal body weight between the ages of 25 and 30 years should not be exceeded throughout life. Table 18–7 contains suggested weights based upon a sample of college men and women. A weight in excess of 15 per cent of that regarded as normal would be considered tending toward obesity, whereas 25 per cent above normal is grossly obese.

Buskirk,[7] in addressing the question, "Who is fat?" claims that obesity is difficult to define in quantitative terms. Obesity refers to the above-average amount of fat contained in the body, this in turn being dependent upon lipid content of each fat cell and on the total number of fat cells. Some methods for estimating fat content of the body appear on page 420.

Fat cells (adipocytes) probably increase in number up to early adolescence. Lack of exercise and overeating may stimulate their formation. Obesity, then, is a combination of the number of adipocytes and their lipid content.[15] Obese people have a larger number of fat cells which contain a greater volume of lipids than their lean contemporaries. As a consequence, physical educators should seriously consider that:

1. Prevention of obesity results in greater success than treatment. This is particularly true during pre-adolescence. Evidence suggests that overeating during this period may cause adipocyte hyperplasia

**Table 18–7   SUGGESTED WEIGHTS FOR HEIGHTS OF COLLEGE MEN AND WOMEN**

| HEIGHT (IN.) | MEDIAN WEIGHT (LBS.) | |
|---|---|---|
| | *Men* | *Women* |
| 60 | | 109 ± 9 |
| 62 | | 115 ± 9 |
| 64 | 133 ± 11 | 122 ± 10 |
| 66 | 142 ± 11 | 129 ± 10 |
| 68 | 151 ± 14 | 136 ± 10 |
| 70 | 159 ± 14 | 144 ± 11 |
| 72 | 167 ± 15 | 152 ± 12 |
| 74 | 175 ± 15 | |
| 76 | 182 ± 16 | |

± refers to weight range between 25th and 75th percentile of each height category. For example, 50 per cent of the women sampled at 60 inches weighed between 100 and 118 lbs.

From Bogert, J., et al.: Nutrition and Physical Fitness. 9th ed. W. B. Saunders Co., p. 512.

Measurements—nude.

(an increase in the number of fat cells), thus planting the garden in which obesity may grow and bloom.

2. Exercise keeps total body fat content low and may reduce the rate at which adipose cells accumulate.

3. If a given food intake does not allow weight reduction, then physical activity must be increased for a negative energy balance to occur.

4. Activities must be selected requiring considerable energy expenditure but at the same time within the physical and skill capabilities of the individual.

5. Living habits are developed early, and so the sooner control programs are initiated, the better.

## SUMMARY

The diets of the athlete and the nonathlete should be identical, except for the fact that the athlete usually expends more energy, and consequently, needs greater food intake than the nonathlete. By knowing the energy cost of activities, we can more judiciously plan our diets to maintain proper energy balance.

Proteins, fats, carbohydrates, vitamins, minerals, and water are essential to a person's diet. Deficiencies cause impaired physical performance and disease.

Generally, muscle glycogen stores are not a limiting factor in activities of less than 30 minutes' duration. In longer, more strenuous events, muscle glycogen can become a limiting factor; therefore, proper dietary procedures for increasing the muscle glycogen stores, as outlined in the chapter, should be employed. However, overloading muscles with glycogen may result in a feeling of heaviness or stiffness in the muscles. Consequently, such a practice is not advisable for sprinters or those athletes participating in events of short duration.

Approximately 800 ml. per hour is the maximum amount of fluid that the stomach can empty during prolonged exercise. Therefore, athletes should be careful when taking liquids during such an event as the marathon. Excessive drinking (exceeding 800 ml. per hour) can cause filling of the stomach, accompanied by a feeling of discomfort; therefore, performance may be hindered. The wise plan is to hydrate well and sweeten the athlete prior to competition.

Lack of exercise is the prime cause of obesity in all age groups. Obesity refers to the above average amount of fat contained in the body, this in turn being dependent upon the lipid content of each fat cell and on the total number of fat cells. The prevention of obesity through regular exercise and proper diet is more successful than treatment for it.

## QUESTIONS

1. Is there a difference between the diet of an athlete and the diet of a nonathlete? Explain.

2. What is the value in knowing the approximate energy cost of various activities?

3. What are the essential dietary nutrients?

4. Describe the four basic food groups as suggested by the United States Department of Agriculture.

5. Are there special suggestions you could make in recommending a pregame diet?

6. What would you tell an endurance athlete concerning the intake of fluids (including sugar) during competition?

7. Following competition, should one's diet be modified? Explain.

8. Explain how diet can affect your performance.

9. What is obesity and how may it affect your health?

10. How is obesity best prevented or treated?

## REFERENCES

1. Asprey, G., Alley, L., and Tuttle, W.: Effect of eating at various times on subsequent performances in the 440-yard dash and half-mile run. Res. Quart., 34(3):267–270, 1963.
2. Åstrand, P.-O.: Diet and athletic performance. Fed. Proc., 26:1772, 1967; Nutr. Today, 3(2):9, 1968.
3. Bergström, J., Hermansen, L., Hultman, E., and Saltin, B.: Diet, muscle glycogen and physical performance. Acta Physiol. Scand., 71:140–150, 1967.
4. Bergström, J., and Hultman, E.: Muscle glycogen synthesis after exercise: an enhancing factor localized to the muscle cells in man. Nature, 210(5033):309–310, 1966.
5. Bergström, J., and Hultman, E.: Nutrition for maximal sports performance. J.A.M.A., 221(9):999–1006, 1972.
6. Bogert, J., Briggs, G., and Calloway, D.: Nutrition and Physical Fitness. 9th ed. Philadelphia, W. B. Saunders Co., 1973.
7. Buskirk, E.: Obesity: a brief overview with emphasis on exercise. Fed. Proc., 33(8):1948–1950, 1974.
8. Encyclopedia of Sport Sciences and Medicine. The American College of Sports Medicine. New York, Macmillan Co., 1971.
9. Hultman, E.: Studies on muscle metabolism of glycogen and active phosphate in man with special reference to exercise and diet. Scand. J. Clinc. Lab. Invest., 19(Suppl. 94):1–63, 1967.
10. Hultman, E., and Bergström, J.: Muscle glycogen synthesis in relation to diet studied in normal subjects. Acta Med. Scand., 182:109–117, 1967.
11. Mayer, J.: Overweight: Causes, Cost, and Control. Englewood Cliffs, N. J., Prentice-Hall, Inc., 1968.
12. Nutrition for the Athlete. American Association for Health, Physical Education and Recreation. Washington, D.C., 1971.
13. Page, L., and Phippard, E.: Essentials of An Adequate Diet. Home Economics Research Report No. 3, Washington, D.C., U. S. Department of Agriculture, Government Printing Office, 1957.
14. Recommended Intakes of Nutrients for the United Kingdom. Departments on Public Health and Medicine. Subj. No. 120, London, 1969.
15. Symposium on the Influence of Exercise on the Morphology and Metabolism of the Fat Cell. 20th Annual Meeting of the American College of Sports Medicine, May 7, 1973, Seattle, Washington: *In* Fed. Proc., 33(8):1947–1972, 1974.
16. Water Deprivation and Performance of Athletes. Food and Nutrition Board, Division of Biological Sciences Assembly of Life Sciences, National Research Council, National Academy of Sciences, May, 1974.
17. Witten, C.: The effects of three liquids on exhaustive exercise and absorption following a 2% body weight loss as a result of acute dehydration. J. Sports Med., 12(2):87–96, 1972.
18. Yoshimura, H.: Anemia during physical training. Nutr. Rev., 28:251, 1970.

## SELECTED READINGS

Ahlborg, B., Bergström, J., Ekelund, L., and Hultman, E.: Muscle glycogen and muscle electrolytes during prolonged physical exercise. Acta Physiol. Scand., 70:129–142, 1967.
Bergström, J., and Hultman, E.: A study of the glycogen metabolism during exercise in man. Scand. J. Clin. Lab. Invest., 19:218–228, 1967.
Bergström, J., and Hultman, E.: Synthesis of muscle glycogen in man after glucose and fructose infusion. Acta Med. Scand., 182:93–107, 1967.
Charting the factors of fatness. The Physician and Sportsmedicine, 3(7):57–70, 1975.
Hultman, E.: Muscle glycogen in man determined in needle biopsy specimens. Method and normal values. Scand. J. Clin. Lab. Invest., 19:209–217, 1967.

# Chapter 19

# SOMATOTYPE AND BODY FAT

In this chapter, we have several areas of concentration: (1) the relationship of body build (the somatotype) to performance; (2) the methods of determining total body fat through measuring body density and skinfolds; and (3) the estimation of minimal wrestling weights for high school wrestlers.

## SOMATOTYPE

### The Sheldon Somatotype

Somatotyping deals with the body type or physical classification of the human body. The terms endomorph, mesomorph, and ectomorph are used to describe a person in terms of his or her somatotype. According to Sheldon, included in these three body components are the following characteristics.[11]

*Endomorphy* (the first component) is characterized by roundness and softness of the body. Anteroposterior diameters as well as the lateral diameters tend toward equality in the head, neck, trunk, and limbs. Features of this type are predominance of abdomen over thorax, high square shoulders, and short neck. There is a smoothness of con-

**411**

tours throughout, with no muscle relief. The breasts are always developed, usually as a result of fatty deposit. As Sheldon so aptly states, "the entire trunk gives the impression of being under moderate pneumatic pressure. The buttocks have a round fullness and no noticeable dimpling. The skin is soft and smooth, and rarely is there a great deal of chest hair."

*Mesomorphy* (the second component) is characterized by a square body with hard, rugged, and prominent musculation. The bones are large and covered with thick muscle. Legs, trunks, and arms are usually massive in bone and heavily muscled throughout. Outstanding characteristics of this type are forearm thickness and heavy wrist, hand, and fingers. The thorax is large and the waist is relatively slender. Shoulders are broad, the trunk is usually upright, and the trapezius and deltoid muscles are quite massive.

The abdominal muscles are prominent and thick. The buttocks almost always exhibit a muscular dimpling. The skin appears coarse and acquires deep tan readily, retaining it for a long time.

*Ectomorphy* (the third component) includes, as predominant characteristics, linearity, fragility, and delicacy of body. The bones are small and the muscles thin. Shoulder droop is seen consistently in the ectomorph. The limbs are relatively long and the trunk short; however, this does not necessarily mean that the individual is tall. The abdomen and the lumbar curve are flat, while the thoracic curve is relatively sharp and elevated. The shoulders are mostly narrow and lacking in muscle relief. There is no bulging of muscle at any point on the physique. The shoulder girdle lacks muscular support and padding, and the scapulae tend to wing out posteriorly.

Sheldon's choice of the three body types was made because they exhibit the characteristics of the extreme variants found in the population. Once the components were classified, 4000 males were photographed and classified in accordance with the characteristics of the three basic components. On the basis of this analysis, it was determined that the pure type does not exist, but that each person is made up in part of all three components. That is, each one exhibits in his body makeup a portion of all three components.

Sheldon's method of somatotyping requires a photograph of the individual in three planes (Fig. 19–1). From these three pictures, a number of measurements are taken and, with the aid of tables developed by Sheldon, the somatotype is determined. Numbers one through seven designate the degree of each of the three components; numeral one represents the least amount of the component, while numeral seven the greatest or maximal amount. Thus, a somatotype of 711 would indicate extreme endomorphy; 171, extreme mesomorphy; and 117, extreme ectomorphy.

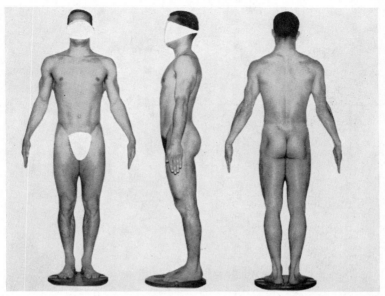

**Figure 19–1** 262 Somatotype: When you watch a baseball game, with possibly 30 players appearing on the field in the course of the afternoon, you can approximately somatotype most of them merely by playing the averages. Probably two thirds of the players are 262's, 263's, or 462's. If it were professional football, the same somatotypes would almost surely predominate, but there would be more 7's in mesomorphy, and in the lines would be six or eight of the heavier extremes such as 371, 471, and even 561 (a heavyweight wrestler somatotype). (Sheldon, W.: Atlas of Men. New York, Harper & Brothers, 1954, p. 120.)

## Heath-Carter Anthropometric Somatotype

Although much of the above description deals primarily with males, recently Heath and Carter have contributed extensively to the field of somatotyping for both men and women. They suggest that there are essentially three methods of obtaining a somatotype rating: (1) an anthropometric rating without a somatotype photograph; (2) photoscopic or inspectional ratings by experienced somatotypers, when age, height and weight, and a standard somatotype photograph are available; and (3) a combination of these two methods, which is the procedure used by Heath and Carter.[4, 5, 8]

To obtain the first component, *endomorphy*, the somatotype rating form shown in Figure 19–2 is used. First sum the obtained values from the following skin fold measurements; triceps, subscapular, and supra-iliac. Procedures for these measurements are shown in Figure 19–3. The sum in our example equals 43.4 mm. The closest value on the total skinfold scale is circled (43.5). Also, the first component for that column is circled (4½).

The second component, *mesomorphy*, is determined also using Figure 19–2 as follows:

**HEATH-CARTER SOMATOTYPE RATING FORM**

NAME D. C. AGE 23-6 SEX: M (F) NO: 96

OCCUPATION Phys. Ed. Student ETHNIC GROUP Cauc. DATE May, 1966

PROJECT: A.T.P. MEASURED BY: L.C.

Skinfolds (mm):
- Triceps = 24.0
- Subcapular = 10.4
- Supraliac = 8.9
- TOTAL SKINFOLDS = 43.4
- Calf = 17.1

TOTAL SKINFOLDS (mm)

| | | | | | | | | | | | | | | | | | | | | | | | | |
|---|---|---|---|---|---|---|---|---|---|---|---|---|---|---|---|---|---|---|---|---|---|---|---|---|
| Upper Limit | 10.9 | 14.9 | 18.9 | 22.9 | 26.9 | 31.2 | 35.8 | 40.7 | 46.2 | 52.2 | 58.7 | 65.7 | 73.2 | 81.2 | 89.7 | 98.9 | 108.9 | 119.7 | 131.2 | 143.7 | 157.2 | 171.9 | 187.9 | 204.0 |
| Mid-point | 9.0 | 13.0 | 17.0 | 21.0 | 25.0 | 29.0 | 33.5 | 38.0 | (43.5) | 49.0 | 55.5 | 62.0 | 69.5 | 77.0 | 85.5 | 94.0 | 104.0 | 114.0 | 125.5 | 137.0 | 150.5 | 164.0 | 180.0 | 196.0 |
| Lower Limit | 7.0 | 11.0 | 15.0 | 19.0 | 23.0 | 27.0 | 31.3 | 35.9 | 40.8 | 46.3 | 52.3 | 58.8 | 65.8 | 73.3 | 81.3 | 89.8 | 99.0 | 109.0 | 119.8 | 131.3 | 143.8 | 157.3 | 172.0 | 188.0 |
| FIRST COMPONENT | ½ | 1 | 1½ | 2 | 2½ | 3 | 3½ | 4 | (4½) | 5 | 5½ | 6 | 6½ | 7 | 7½ | 8 | 8½ | 9 | 9½ | 10 | 10½ | 11 | 11½ | 12 |

- Height (in.) = 64.8
- Bone: Humerus (cm) = 6.05
- Femur = 9.35
- Muscle: Biceps (cm) 29.8−2.4 = 27.4 − (triceps skinfold)
- Calf* = 36.4 − (calf skinfold)
- *38.1−1.7=

| | | | | | | | | | | | | | | | | | | | | | | | | |
|---|---|---|---|---|---|---|---|---|---|---|---|---|---|---|---|---|---|---|---|---|---|---|---|---|
| Height | 55.0 | 56.5 | 58.0 | 59.5 | 61.0 | 62.5 | 64.0↓ | 65.5 | 67.0 | 68.5 | 70.0 | 71.5 | 73.0 | 74.5 | 76.0 | 77.5 | 79.0 | 80.5 | 82.0 | 83.5 | 85.0 | 86.5 | 88.0 | 89.5 |
| Humerus | 5.19 | 5.34 | 5.49 | 5.64 | 5.78 | 5.93 | (6.07) | 6.22 | 6.37 | 6.51 | 6.65 | 6.80 | 6.95 | 7.09 | 7.24 | 7.38 | 7.53 | 7.67 | 7.82 | 7.97 | 8.11 | 8.25 | 8.40 | 8.55 |
| Femur | 7.41 | 7.62 | 7.83 | 8.04 | 8.24 | 8.45 | 8.66 | 8.87 | 9.08 | (9.28) | 9.49 | 9.70 | 9.91 | 10.12 | 10.33 | 10.53 | 10.74 | 10.95 | 11.16 | 11.37 | 11.58 | 11.79 | 12.00 | 12.21 |
| Biceps | 23.7 | 24.4 | 25.0 | 25.7 | 26.3 | 27.0 | (27.7) | 28.3 | 29.0 | 29.7 | 30.3 | 31.0 | 31.6 | 32.2 | 33.0 | 33.6 | 34.3 | 35.0 | 35.6 | 36.3 | 37.1 | 37.8 | 38.5 | 39.3 |
| Calf | 27.7 | 28.5 | 29.3 | 30.1 | 30.8 | 31.6 | 32.4 | 33.2 | 33.9 | 34.7 | 35.5 | (36.3) | 37.1 | 37.8 | 38.6 | 39.4 | 40.2 | 41.0 | 41.8 | 42.6 | 43.4 | 44.2 | 45.0 | 45.8 |

| | | | | | | | | | | | | | | | | | | |
|---|---|---|---|---|---|---|---|---|---|---|---|---|---|---|---|---|---|---|
| SECOND COMPONENT | ½ | 1 | 1½ | 2 | 2½ | 3 | 3½ | 4 | (4½) | 5 | 5½ | 6 | 6½ | 7 | 7½ | 8 | 8½ | 9 |

- Weight (lb.) = 137.0
- Ht. / ∛Wt. = 12.56

| | | | | | | | | | | | | | | | | | | |
|---|---|---|---|---|---|---|---|---|---|---|---|---|---|---|---|---|---|---|
| Upper limit | 11.99 | 12.32 | 12.53 | 12.74 | 12.95 | 13.15 | 13.36 | 13.56 | 13.77 | 13.98 | 14.19 | 14.39 | 14.59 | 14.80 | 15.01 | 15.22 | 15.42 | 15.63 |
| Mid-point | and | 12.16 | 12.43 | 12.64 | 12.85 | 13.05 | 13.26 | 13.46 | 13.67 | 13.88 | 14.01 | 14.29 | 14.50 | 14.70 | 14.91 | 15.12 | 15.33 | 15.53 |
| Lower limit | below | 12.00 | 12.33 | (12.54) | 12.75 | 12.96 | 13.16 | 13.37 | 13.56 | 13.78 | 13.99 | 14.20 | 14.40 | 14.60 | 14.81 | 15.02 | 15.23 | 15.43 |
| THIRD COMPONENT | ½ | 1 | 1½ | (2) | 2½ | 3 | 3½ | 4 | 4½ | 5 | 5½ | 6 | 6½ | 7 | 7½ | 8 | 8½ | 9 |

| | FIRST COMPONENT | SECOND COMPONENT | THIRD COMPONENT | |
|---|---|---|---|---|
| Anthropometric Somatotype | 4½ | 4½ | 2 | BY: L. C. |
| Anthropometric plus Photoscopic Somatotype | | | | RATER: |

**Figure 19–2** Heath-Carter Somatotype Rating Form. (From Mathews, D. K.: Measurement in Physical Education, 4th ed. Philadelphia, W. B. Saunders Co., 1973.)

1. Place an arrow above the column containing the subject's height (or closest approximation*). The arrow in the example has been placed between 64.0 and 65.5.
2. For the two bone measurements (humerus and femur breadth), circle the closest figure in the appropriate row. Where a decision must be made to circle either a higher or a lower number, circle the one which is closer to the height column (noted by arrow). For example, 6.05 cm. width of the humerus occurs at the midpoint between 5.93 and 6.07; consequently, 6.07 cm., the upper limit, was circled.

---

*The height scale is continuous with a distance of 1½ inches between each column. Place your arrow (if necessary, between columns) to represent as accurately as possible the exact height.

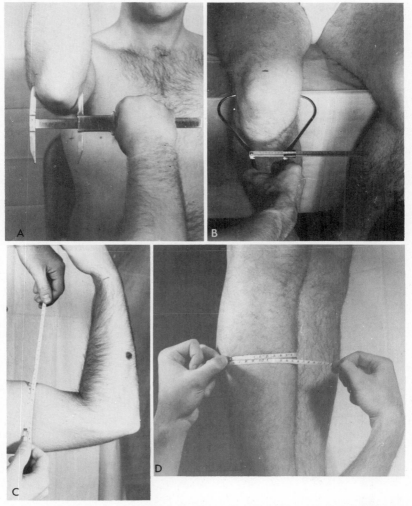

**Figure 19–3**  Measurements necessary for Heath-Carter somatotype. *A,* Humerus breadth; *B,* Femur breadth; *C,* Biceps circumference; *D,* Calf circumference.

*Illustration continued on the following page*

3. Subtract the triceps skinfold from the biceps circumference. To do this, first convert the triceps to centimeters by moving the decimal point one place to the left; e.g., 29.8 cm. − 2.4 cm. (24 mm.) = 27.4 cm.

4. Now subtract the calf skinfold from the calf circumference. Again, change the calf skinfold to centimeters by moving the decimal point one place to the left; e.g., 38.1 cm. − 1.7 cm. (17 mm.) = 36.4 cm.

5. Circle these two corrected measurements (27.4 and 36.4) in their proper rows; e.g., 27.7 and 36.3 are circled.

6. Using the extreme left circled value as the starting column (in our example, both 6.07 and 27.7 appear in the most extreme left column), count the number of columns each other circled value deviates from this starting point. In our example, both the humerus and the biceps measurements deviate zero columns, while the femur measurement deviates three columns and the calf measurement deviates five columns. The average deviation of these measurements equals the total divided by four:

$$\frac{0 + 0 + 3 + 5}{4} = 2.0$$

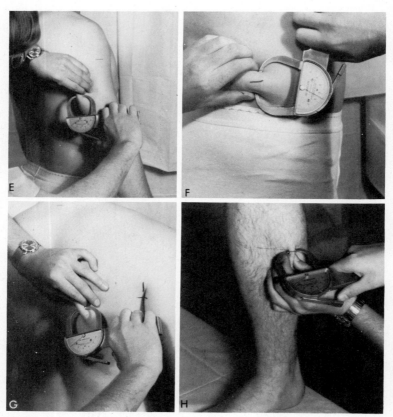

**Figure 19–3** *Continued* E, Skinfold: triceps; F, Skinfold: suprailiac; G, Skinfold: subscapular; H, Skinfold: calf. (Courtesy, E. Churchill et al.[5A])

7. Count the number of columns which the mean deviation (2.0) is to the right of the original starting column and place an asterisk. We placed the asterisk right over 33.9 exactly, indicating 2.0 columns to the right of our starting point.
8. Count the number of columns which the asterisk deviates from the height column (located by the arrow). In our illustration, the number of columns equals 1.5.
9. With this number 1.5 we will now determine the second component. Commencing at 4 in the second component row, count the equivalent number of columns which the asterisk deviates from the height column — which in our example is closest to one. If the asterisk appears to the right of the height column, count the equivalent number of columns to the right of four; if the asterisk appears to the left of four, count the equivalent number of columns below or to the left of four. In our example, the asterisk is to the right of the height column; consequently, we will count one column to the right of four which results in our second component, $4\frac{1}{2}$.

The third component, *ectomorphy*, is obtained by computing the ponderal index, i.e., the height divided by the cube root of the weight (Fig. 19–4), and recording this value. Circle the closest value and note the somatotype in the third component row under the column (Fig. 19–2). In our example, the component 2 appears directly below the 12.54. The complete somatotype equals $4\frac{1}{2}$, $4\frac{1}{2}$, 2. This person is classified as an endo-mesomorph.

## Somatotype and Physical Activity

Somatotyping has been used to describe the type of physique that is most susceptible to various diseases. For example, a number of studies indicate heavily muscular men (mesomorphs) and endo-mesomorphs have a greater predisposition toward coronary artery disease than do ectomorphic types.[9, 13]

Physical educators manifest an interest in somatotyping as a means of relating body type to success in various sports. Figures 19–5 and 19–6 depict the somatotypes of men and women athletes and the various sports in which they excel.

Carter, in reporting on male Olympic athletes, describes the mean somatotype for marathon runners as $1.4 - 4.3 - 3.5$; pole vaulters, $1\frac{1}{2} - 4.8 - 3.2$; and swimmers $2 - 5 - 3$; these somatotypes would be noted collectively as meso-ectomorphs because of the higher meso-morph and ectomorph ratings.[7] The mean somatotype of a varsity football team was found to be $4.2 - 6.3 - 1.4$, which is endo-mesomorphic.[5]

Female swimmers and hockey and softball players are usually endo-mesomorphs. Female gymnasts and skiers are ecto-mesomorphic, while basketball players appear to be endo-mesomorphs. Like the males, female physiques in track and field vary in accordance with the event. Sprinters contain more massive musculature as well as those par-

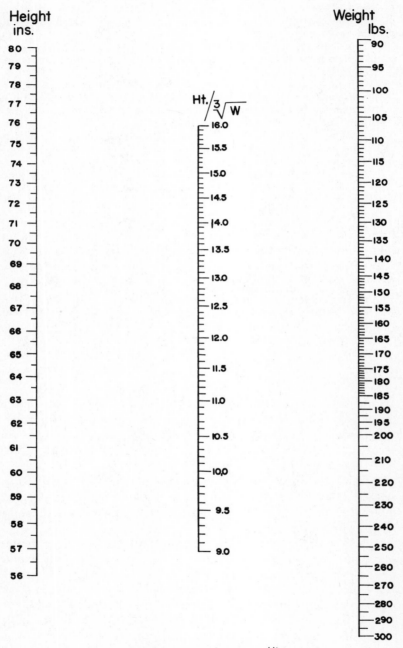

**Figure 19-4**   Ponderal index $\dfrac{Ht.}{\sqrt[3]{W}}$.

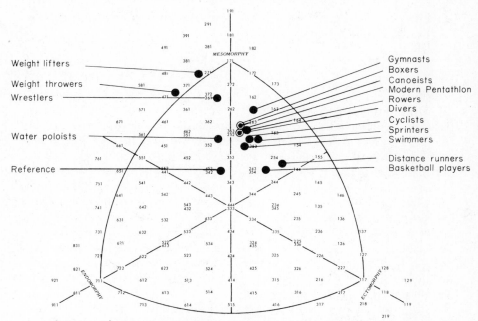

**Figure 19–5** Somatotype distribution of mean somatotypes for various male sports groups and the reference group. (From Garay, A. (ed.): Genetic and Anthropological Studies of Olympic Athletes. New York, Academic Press, 1974, p. 55.)

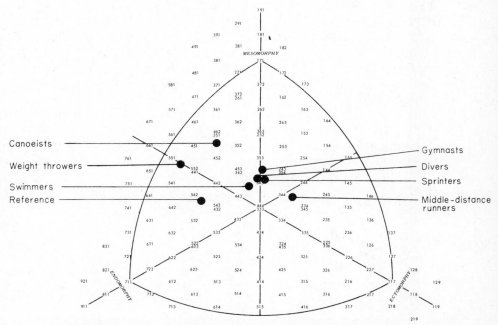

**Figure 19–6** Somatotype distribution of mean somatotypes for various female sports groups and the reference group. (From Garay, A. (ed.): Genetic and Anthropological Studies of Olympic Athletes. New York, Academic Press, 1974, p. 55.)

ticipating in throwing events, while the lithe body prevails in the distance and jumping events.

## BODY FAT

Differences in performance between the male and female can be partially explained by the greater percentage of fat contained in the female body (see p. 451). Body weight of the adult male averages 15 per cent fat, while the female contains about 23 per cent fat. Fat cells do not manufacture ATP for use by the muscles; their primary purpose is to store lipids. Consequently, the greater percentage of fat is detrimental (performance-wise) in two ways: (1) the cells do not contribute toward energy production, and (2) it costs energy to move the fat. For example, a girl weighing 60 kilograms (132 lbs.) would possess approximately 13.8 kilograms (30 lbs.) of fat, while the male of the same weight would possess 9 kilograms (20 lbs.) of fat. During performance, the female would be carrying 4.8 kilograms (10 lbs.) more of non-energy-producing tissue than her male contemporary.

Physically active people possess considerably less total body fat than their less active contemporaries. Table 19–1 contains the results of a number of studies reporting the percentage of fat among male and female athletes.

Buskirk[3] has suggested the following skinfold measurement for classifying male athletes in terms of body fat (see Fig. 19–7):

1. *Triceps.* Back of upper arm over triceps, midway on upper arm; skinfold lifted parallel with the long axis of arm with arm pendant.

2. *Scapula.* Below tip of right scapula; skinfold lifted along long axis of body.

3. *Abdomen.* Five cm. lateral from umbilicus avoiding abdominal crease; skinfold lifted on axis with umbilicus.

According to Buskirk, the scapular skinfold is the single best fold to measure. Classification values can be adjusted in accordance with

### Table 19–1  PER CENT BODY FAT AMONG ATHLETES*

|  | MALE | FEMALE |
|---|---|---|
| Track | 4 – 9.6 | 12–18 |
| Gymnastics | 4.6 | 9–17 |
| Swimming | 7.9 | 19–26 |
| Basketball | 7.9–14.2 | 24 |
| Football | 7.9–14.5 | |
| Baseball | 12 –14.2 | |

*Values reported from a number of studies.

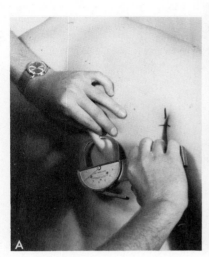
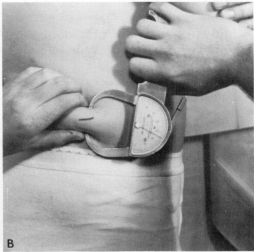
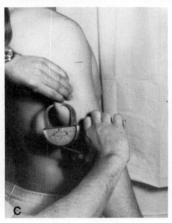

**Figure 19–7**  Skinfold measurements for predicting minimal athletic weight values. *A*, Skinfold: subscapular; *B*, Skinfold: 5 cm lateral from umbilicus; *C*, Skinfold: triceps. (Courtesy, E. Churchill et al.[5A])

### Table 19–2  CLASSIFICATION OF SKINFOLD MEASUREMENTS FOR MALE ATHLETES*

| CLASSIFICATION | | TRICEPS (mm.) | SCAPULAR (mm.) | ABDOMEN (mm.) | SUM (mm.) |
|---|---|---|---|---|---|
| Lean | < 7% fat | < 7 | < 8 | < 10 | < 25 |
| Acceptable | 7–15% fat | 7–13 | 8–15 | 10–20 | 25–48 |
| Overfat | > 15% fat | > 13 | >15 | > 20 | > 48 |

*From Buskirk.[3]

coaches' and physicians' judgments. Table 19–2 contains standards for such skinfold measurements which may be applied to male athletes.

Several methods have been employed to estimate the body's fat content. Measuring the specific gravity is perhaps one of the more valid, but difficult, methods; estimating fat content from a number of anthropometric measures is an easier, though less valid, method.

### Specific Gravity

Specific gravity of a body may be defined as the ratio of its density to the density of water. Density of a body is spoken of in terms of mass per unit volume,

$$D = \frac{M}{V}$$

in which:

$D$ = Density
$M$ = Mass (weight)
$V$ = Volume

For example, the density of water is equal to one gram per cubic centimeter (1 gm./cc.) because one cubic centimeter (cc.) weighs one gram; the density of gold is 19.3 gm./cc. The specific gravity of gold is 19.3. Note that the numbers representing specific gravity are called pure numbers. They merely represent the ratio of the density of a substance to that of water.

**Archimedes' Principle.**   One may determine the specific gravity of an object by using Archimedes' principle, which states that an object immersed in a fluid loses an amount of weight equivalent to the weight of the fluid which is displaced.

$$S.\ G. = \frac{\text{weight of object in air}}{\text{weight of water displaced}}$$

Thus, by weighing an object in air; then immersing the object in water and measuring the weight of the water displaced, the specific gravity of that object could be determined.

Also:

$$S.\ G. = \frac{\text{weight of object in air}}{\text{weight of object in air} - \text{weight of object in water}}$$

As a simple illustration, what would be the specific gravity of an object weighing 200 gm. in air and 120 gm. in water?

$$S.\ G. = \frac{200 \text{ gm.}}{200 \text{ gm.} - 120 \text{ gm.}} = 2.5$$

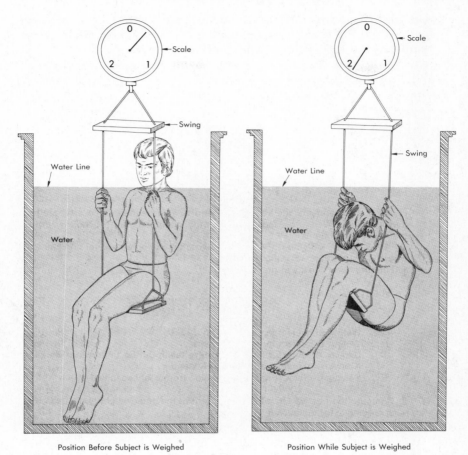

Position Before Subject is Weighed                    Position While Subject is Weighed

**Figure 19–8** Human body volumeter for measuring body density. One could measure either weight of the water displaced by the body or the weight of the body when completely submerged. (From Sinning, W. E.: Experiments and Demonstrations in Exercise Physiology. Philadelphia, W. B. Saunders Co., 1975.)

The density of the object is two and one-half times greater than the density of water; consequently, it would sink.

The volume would be equal to 80 cc. since the weight of the water displaced equals 80 gm. (1 cc. of water weighs 1 gm.)

**Specific Gravity of the Human Body.** Figure 19–8 illustrates a human body volumeter for measuring the body's density. One could measure either the weight of the water displaced by the body or the weight of the body when completely submerged. Fewer technical difficulties are encountered using body weight on land and body weight totally submerged; however, the lungs must be as nearly deflated as possible (maximal expiration) during the underwater weighing, with correction made for the residual volume. The air remaining in the lungs following a maximal expiration (the residual volume) may be estimated for males by multiplying the vital capacity (BTPS) by the constant 0.24 and for females, by the constant 0.28.[16] These values will approximate 1300 ml. for males and 1000 ml. for females.

Once the body weight in air, the weight while totally submerged, and the residual volume are determined, body density (gm./cc.) may be computed by the following formula:[2]

$$D_b = \frac{W_a}{K - R.V.}$$

where:

$D_b$ = body density (gm./cc.)
$W_a$ = weight in air in grams
$K$ = weight in air minus weight in water divided by the density of water at the weighing temperature
$R.V.$ = residual volume in cc.

The amount of fat may be computed by the following formula:[2]

$$\text{per cent fat} = \left[\frac{4.570}{D_b} - 4.142\right] \times 100$$

in which: $D_b$ = body density in gm./cc.

The following data illustrate calculation of body density and percentage of fat (note data are converted to grams [gm.] and cubic centimeters [cc.]).

**Male**

Ht. — 72.1 inches = 183.13 centimeters = 18.31 decimeters
Weight in air = 200 lb. = 90.91 kg. = 90,910 gm.
Weight in water = 4.78 lb. = 2.17 kg. = 2,170 gm.
Density of water at 32° C = .9951 gm./cc.
Vital capacity (BTPS) = 6000 cc.
Residual volume = 0.24 × vital capacity = 0.24 × 6000 cc. = 1440 cc.

$$K = \frac{90,910 - 2,170}{.9951} = \frac{88,740}{.9951} = 89,176.97$$

$$D_b = \frac{90,910}{89,176.97 - 1440} = \frac{90,910}{87,736.97} = 1.0362 \text{ gm./cc.}$$

The amount of fat (%) may be computed as follows:

$$\text{per cent fat} = \left[\frac{4.570}{1.0362} - 4.142\right] \times 100$$

$$= (4.410 - 4.142) \times (100)$$
$$= .268 \times 100 = 26.8\%$$

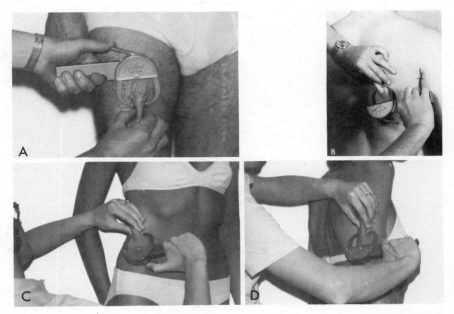

**Figure 19–9** Skinfold measurements required for use with the Sloan-Weir nomogram. *A*, Skinfold: thigh (men); *B*, Skinfold: supscapular (men); *C*, Skinfold: suprailiac (women); *D*, Skinfold: triceps (women).

## Sloan-Weir Nomograms for Predicting Body Density and Total Body Fat

Sloan and Weir, using measurements from two skinfold thicknesses, derived formulas for predicting body density in young men 18 to 26 years and women 17 to 25 years of age.[12] In young men, the best predictions were found to come from a vertical skinfold in the anterior midline of the thigh, halfway between the inguinal ligament and the top of the patella, and the subscapular skinfold running downward and laterally in the natural fold of the skin from the inferior angle of the scapula. In young women, the best predictions were found to come from a vertical skinfold over the iliac crest in the midaxillary line and from a vertical skinfold on the back of the arm halfway between the acromion and olecranon processes measured with the elbow extended. These measurements are shown in Figure 19–9.

By using the formula developed by Brozek et al.,[2] Sloan and Weir could relate total body fat to body density and thus predict body fat from these two skinfold measurements. The formulas and example of the computations appear in Table 19–3, while Figure 19–10 contains the nomograms.

**Table 19-3   SLOAN-WEIR FORMULAS FOR PREDICTING BODY DENSITY AND TOTAL BODY FAT\***

|  | *Female* | *Male* |
|---|---|---|
| Height .... ........................ | 174 cm. | 178 cm. |
| Weight ............................. | 59 kg. | 75.9 kg. |
| Thigh skinfold ...................... | — | 18 mm. |
| Subscapular skinfold ................... | — | 8.5 mm |
| Suprailiac skinfold ................... | 19 mm. | — |
| Triceps skinfold ..................... | 15 mm. | — |
| Actual density ....................... | 1.0524 gm./ml. | 1.0678 gm./ml. |
| (measured by underwater weighing) | | |
| Predicted density .................... | 1.0478 gm./ml. | 1.0693 gm./ml. |
| Fat ................................ | 21.9% | 13.2% |

*Men:* 1.1043 − 0.00133 (Thigh skinfold) − 0.00131 (subscapular skinfold)
    1.1043− .0349 = 1.0692 gm./ml. (Standard error of estimate = 0.0069 gm./ml.)
*Women:* 1.0764 − 0.00081 (suprailiac skinfold) − 0.00088 (triceps skinfold)
    1.0764 − .0286 = 1.0478 gm./ml. (Standard error of estimate = 0.0082 gm./ml.)
Fat Percentage = 4.570/Body density − 4.142 × 100.

*Data by Sloan and Weir and recalculated by L. Laubach of Webb Associates, Yellow Springs, Ohio.

Sloan, A. W. and Weir, J. B. de V.: Nomograms for Prediction of Body Density and Total Body Fat from Skinfold Measurements. J. App. Physiol., Vol. 28, No. 2, February, 1970, p. 221.

# MAKING WEIGHT IN WRESTLING

Understanding the somatotype and anthropometry has important applications to physical education and athletics. Some of these have already been discussed. Another one is making weight in wrestling. Since it is a rather serious problem, let's discuss it in some detail.

The Committee on Medical Aspects of Sports has posed several questions raised by the wrestling community:[6]

1. What are the hazards of indiscriminate and excessive weight reduction?
2. How much weight can a wrestler lose safely?
3. What are defensible means of losing weight?
4. What weigh-in plan would best serve the purpose intended?

Excessive weight loss results in impaired competitive abilities;[10] extreme weight reduction seriously affects health. The wrestler uses a combination of food restriction, liquid deprivation, and dehydration in order to lose weight. Vomiting, the use of hot boxes, rubberized apparel and exercise are among other practices employed. Some studies have shown that weight losses caused by dehydration of three per cent or more result in diminished athletic performance. Prolonged

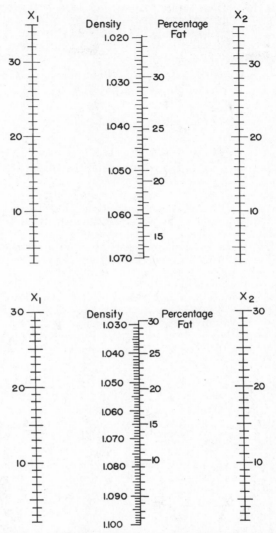

**Figure 19–10** Sloan-Weir nomograms (upper = women, lower = men) for prediction of body density and total body fat from skinfold measurements. (From Sloan, A., and J. Weir: Nomograms for prediction of body density and total body fat from skinfold measurements. J. Appl. Physiol., 28(2):221–222, 1970.)

semistarvation diets, unbalanced diets, and excessive sweating combined with dehydration may cause severe harm to the athlete.

The amount of weight that a wrestler can safely lose should be related to the boy's *effective weight level* (the weight level which yields his best performance) rather than the minimal weight, according to the Committee on the Medical Aspects of Sports. It is difficult to define scientifically the limits of safe weight control. Argument is in favor of a good pre-participation physical. Such a plan commences the weight history which allows the physician a more valid judgment regarding how much weight a boy can safely lose.

The Committee is quick to emphasize that there is no alternative to:

1.  A balanced diet at a sustaining caloric level.
2.  Adequate fluid intake.
3.  High energy output for attaining and maintaining an effective competitive weight.

Finally, the Committee suggests the weight of the wrestling candidates can best be assessed through a natural approach:

1.  Educate youth who are interested in athletics regarding the importance of periodic medical examinations and the advantages of a general, year-round conditioning program for cardiovascular-pulmonary endurance, muscular fitness, and nutritional readiness.
2.  Building on this orientation, assist any aspiring wrestler in an intensive conditioning program related to the demands of wrestling for at least four weeks, preferably six, without emphasis on weight level.
3.  At the end of this period and without altering his daily training routine, take his weight in a prebreakfast, postmicturition state.
4.  Consider this weight his minimal effective weight for competition as well as certification purposes.
5.  Educate the boy and his parents in the concept of defensible weight control to avert fluctuation from his effective weight level.

## The Iowa Studies

Tipton and colleagues at the University of Iowa have performed extensive studies concerning the effect of weight loss in high school wrestlers. Their studies show:[15]

1.  A large number of young athletes lose an excessive amount of weight in a relatively short period of time. This holds true for all classes below 175 pounds. The lightest lose the highest percentage (circa 10%) of body weight during a 17-day period (see Fig. 19–11).
2.  The majority of weight loss occurs immediately preceding the date of certification.
3.  Weight losing methods were suggested by either coach or teammate.
4.  Of the 835 boys measured, the average percentage of fat is 8 per cent, whereas the state finalists (N = 224) had a 4 to 6 per cent body fat content.

Dr. Tipton is particularly concerned with the lack of professional supervision dealing with the method or amount of weight which an athlete should lose. He recommends a body weight containing 7 per cent fat (not less than 5% without medical supervision) and one which does not exceed 7 per cent loss of the initial weight. Ideally, one would predict minimal weight at the beginning of the school year; then under professional guidance, a proper and gradual weight reduction could take place.

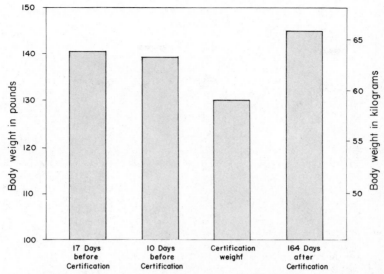

**Figure 19–11** During a 17 day period, 6.8 pounds or 4.9 per cent of the body weight was lost, most of which occurred during the last 10 days. An average increase of 13.6 pounds above the certification weight occurred at the end of the season. (From Tipton, C. M., and T-K Tcheng: Iowa wrestling study. Weight loss in high school students. J.A.M.A., 214:1269–1274, 1970.)

**Predicting Minimal Weight Values.** Research by Dr. Tipton et al.[14] resulted in an equation which allows prediction of minimal weight values. Several anthropometric measurements are obtained six to eight weeks before commencement of the wrestling season. The minimal weights are computed; the results then are used as a screening device along with the physician's judgment concerning the proper minimal weight for the particular boy.

**Anthropometric Measurements** (Fig. 19–12)

1. *Chest Diameter.* Subject stands with both hands on the crests of ilium. Calipers are placed in the axillary region with ends placed on the second or third rib. At the end of expiration, measurement is obtained.

2. *Chest Depth.* Subject stands with right hand behind head. One end of the caliper is placed on the tip of the xiphoid process while the other end is placed over the vertebrae of the twelfth rib. Measurement is taken at end of expiration.

3. *Bi-iliac Diameter.* Distance between most lateral projections of the crests of the ilium is measured.

4. *Bitrochanteric Diameter.* Distance between the most lateral projections of the greater trochanters is measured.

5. *Wrist Diameter.* Distance between the styloid processes of the radius and ulna is measured. Measure both wrists and use their sum.

6. *Ankle Diameter.* The foot is placed on a stool or chair with caliper ends placed over malleoli at an angle of 45 degrees. Measure both ankles and use their sum.

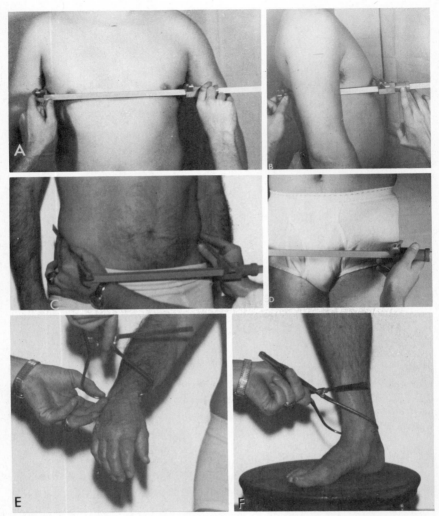

**Figure 19–12** Measurements required for predicting minimal wrestling weight for high school males. *A,* Chest diameter; *B,* Chest depth; *C,* Bi-iliac diameter; *D,* Bitrochanteric diameter; *E,* Wrist diameter; *F,* Ankle diameter. (*A, B, D,* courtesy of E. Churchill et al.[5A])

Data from the above anthropometric measures may then be substituted in one of two formulas, the long form or the short form.

*Long Form.* Minimal weight = 1.84 × (height, inches) + 3.28 × (chest diameter cm.) + 3.31 × (chest depth, cm.) + 0.82 × (bi-iliac diameter, cm.) + 1.69 × (bitrochanteric diameter, cm.) + 3.56 × (both wrists, cm.) + 2.15 × (both ankles) − 281.72. A correlation of .933, with a standard error of estimate of 8.7 pounds was found between this equation and the actual weight of the finalists.

*Short Form.* Minimal weight = 2.05 × (height, inches) + 3.65 × (chest diameter, cm.) + 3.51 (chest depth cm.) + 1.96 × (bitrochanteric diameter, cm.) + 8.02 × (left ankle, cm.) − 282.18. A correlation of .923 with a standard error of estimate of 8.9 pounds was found between this equation and the actual weight of the finalists.

We measured an Ohio State finalist at the beginning of the wrestling season with the following results:

> Wt. = 150 lbs.
> Ht. = 71 in.
> Chest diameter = 25.4 cm.
> Chest depth = 18.5 cm.
> Bitrochanteric diameter = 32.3 cm.
> Bi-iliac diameter = 25.7 cm.
> Wrist diameter (sum of both wrists) = 11.4 cm.
> Ankle diameter (sum of both ankles) = 14.2 cm.

*Minimal Weight (Long Form)*

$$
\begin{aligned}
(1.84) \times (71 \text{ in.}) &= 130.64 \\
(3.28) \times (25.4) &= 83.31 \\
(3.31) \times (18.5) &= 61.24 \\
(.82) \times (25.7) &= 21.07 \\
(1.69) \times (32.3) &= 54.59 \\
(3.56) \times (11.4) &= 40.58 \\
(2.15) \times (14.2) &= \underline{30.53} \\
&\phantom{=}\ 421.96 \\
&\phantom{=}\ \underline{-281.72}
\end{aligned}
$$

Minimal weight = 140.24 lbs.

The boy's predicted minimal weight equals 140.24 lbs. Weighing 150 lbs. at the beginning of the season, this wrestler could lose a maximum of 10 lbs. He actually wrestled at a body weight of 142 pounds.

*Minimal Weight (Short Form)*

$$
\begin{aligned}
(2.05) \times (71 \text{ in.}) &= 145.55 \\
(3.65) \times (25.4) &= 92.71 \\
(3.51) \times (18.5) &= 64.94 \\
(1.96) \times (32.3) &= 63.31 \\
(8.02) \times (7.1) &= \underline{56.94} \\
&\phantom{=}\ 423.45 \\
&\phantom{=}\ \underline{-282.18}
\end{aligned}
$$

Minimal weight = 141.27 lbs.

You can see that the short form produces results almost identical with those of the long form.

# SUMMARY

Endomorph, mesomorph, and ectomorph are the terms employed in describing the somatotype of a person. The endomorph refers to fat; the mesomorph, muscle; and the ectomorph, a body which is lean and fragile.

In addition to studying body types as they are associated with athletic performance, body types have also been related to disease entities; for example, a number of studies associated coronary artery disease more with the mesomorph than with the ectomorph.

Fat content of the body is significantly associated with physical activity. Active people are less obese than sedentary individuals.

Two methods are commonly employed in estimating fat content of the body: (1) measuring the specific gravity of the person, and (2) measuring skin folds to estimate body density.

Considerable attention is being given to the serious malpractices associated with "making weight" in wrestling. This is particularly true for high school wrestlers. Tipton and colleagues have suggested a method using anthropometric measurements whereby minimal wrestling weight can be predicted.

## QUESTIONS

1. Define endomorphy, mesomorphy, and ectomorphy.

2. According to Sheldon's rating form, what would be the somatotype of an extreme endomorph?

3. How do the somatotypes of marathon runners compare with those of football players, according to Carter?

4. Would you consider that female and male somatotypes in comparable sport events are similar?

5. Explain how the difference in track performance between males and females might be partially attributed to the body's fat content.

6. Illustrate how specific gravity determinations are used to compute body fat.

7. How are the Sloan-Weir nomograms used to predict body fat?

8. Compute the percentage of fat of a person whose body density equals 1.0456 gm./cc.

9. The Committee on the Medical Aspect of Sports suggests that the weight of a wrestler can best be assessed through a natural approach. What are some of their suggestions?

10. What are the results of Tipton's studies dealing with weight loss among high school wrestlers?

11. What procedures might be used in predicting minimal weight values for high school wrestlers?

## REFERENCES

1. Brozek, J.: Techniques for measuring body composition. Quartermaster Research and Engineering Center. (A.D. ⟨286506⟩, p. 95, Natick, Mass. January, 1959.
2. Brozek, J., Grande, F., Anderson, J., and Keys, A.: Densitometric analysis of body composition: revision of some quantitative assumptions. Ann. N.Y. Acad. Sci., 110:113–140, 1963.
3. Buskirk, E.: Nutrition for the athlete. *In* Ryan, A., and Allman, F. (eds.): Sports Medicine. p. 146, New York, Academic Press, 1974.
4. Carter, J., and Heath, B.: Somatotype methodology and kinesiology research. Kinesiol. Rev., 1971, pp. 10–19.
5. Carter, J., and Phillips, W.: Structural changes in exercising middle-aged males during a 2-year period. J. Appl. Physiol., 27(6):787–794, 1969.
5A. Churchill, E., McConville, J., Laubach, L., and White, R.: Anthropometry of U.S. Army Aviators—1970. Technical Report 72–52–CE. Natick, Mass., United States Army Natick Laboratories, Dec., 1971.
6. Committee on Medical Aspects of Sports. Wrestling and weight control. J.A.M.A., 201(7):131–133, 1967.
7. Garay, A. (ed.): Genetic and Anthropological Studies of Olympic Athletes. p. 55, New York, Academic Press, Inc., 1974.
8. Heath, B., and Carter, J.: A modified somatotype method. Am. J. Phys. Anthropol., 27(1):57–74, 1967.
9. Parnell, R.: Etiology of coronary heart disease. Brit. Med. J., 1:232, 1959.
10. Ribisl, P.: When wrestlers shed pounds quickly. The Physician and Sportsmedicine, 2(7):30–35, 1974.
11. Sheldon, W.: Atlas of Men. New York, Harper and Brothers, 1954.
12. Sloan, A., and Weir, J.: Nomograms for prediction of body density and total body fat from skinfold measurements. J. Appl. Physiol., 28(2):221–222, 1970.
13. Spain, D., Nathan, D., and Gellis, M.: Weight, body type and the prevalence of coronary atherosclerotic heart disease in males. Am. J. Med. Sci., 245:63–72, 1963.
14. Tcheng, T-K., and Tipton, C.: Iowa wrestling study: anthropometric measurements and the prediction of a "minimal" body weight for high school wrestlers. Med. Sci. Sports, 5(1):1–10, 1973.
15. Tipton, C., and Tcheng, T-K.: Iowa wrestling study. J.A.M.A., 214(7):1269–1274, 1970.
16. Wilmore, J.: The use of actual, predicted and constant residual volumes in the assessment of body composition by underwater weighing. Med. Sci. Sports, 1(2):87–90, 1969.

# SECTION 7

# SPECIAL CONSIDERATIONS

# Chapter 20

# ERGOGENIC AIDS (WORK AIDS)

Problems in Research Design
Steroids
Amphetamines
Blood Doping
Aspartic Acid Salts
Oxygen
Vitamin E

An ergogenic aid, simply defined, is something which improves performance; not only athletic performance, but all physical work as well. Consequently, the industrialist might be as interested in such aids as might be the individual wishing to decrease his or her time in the 100-meter dash.

Frequently, ergogenic aids are thought of only as drugs which may be consumed in order to give the athlete an advantage. This is not necessarily true. Included in the list of ergogenic aids are the following: drugs, music, warm-up, oxygen, vitamins and other nutritional substances such as carbohydrates and water, and even selected psychological phenomena; for example, hypnosis, mental practice, and suggestion. In its broadest sense, one could call anything an ergogenic aid which can be directly related to an increase in work performance.

Ergogenic aids affect different people differently, as might be expected. For some, studies show a positive influence upon work performance and for others, no effect whatsoever. What might prove effective with the athlete may prove inconsequential to the nonathlete and vice-versa. Certain aids may influence a person's endurance performance but may have little or no effect upon activities requiring short bursts of strength and power.

## Problems in Research Design

Unquestionably, the lack of objective and consistent information regarding effects of ergogenic aids is in part attributable to (1) considerable individual physiological and psychological variations among people; and (2) difficulties in developing foolproof research protocol.

For example, a company wished to learn the effects of lighting in an industrial plant on the performance of the workers. As the illumination increased, so did work production. However, as illumination decreased, production did not! Apparently, the results were a consequence of the workers' realizing that they were in an experiment and were not solely because of increased illumination.

Drug studies use placebos in order to deal with possible psychological contaminants. For example, if we tell you that a certain pill will help you to run faster (suggestion), you might run faster simply because of what we have said. Who knows whether it was the pill or the suggestion? A placebo is an inert substance with the identical physical characteristics of the real drug. Thus, in experiments the placebo is administered to half the subjects, while the actual drug is administered to the other half. Neither the investigator nor the subjects knows which is which. Frequently, such a design is referred to as a double-blind study. Even though this design appears to be foolproof, some subjects will react to the placebo, confusing the final results of the study.

Some years ago, we were studying the effects of vitamin E on physical work. By coincidence, one subject in the experiment had been married for about a year. The couple had been attempting to have children, but without success. Halfway through the study, the subject's wife became pregnant. For the remainder of the experiment, this subject went about extolling the virtues of vitamin E, to which he attributed his apparent new-found virility. At the conclusion of this double-blind experiment, the investigator and subject learned that the latter had been taking the placebo! Perhaps the moral of this story for husband and athlete alike might be "It's all in your head"!

The power of suggestion becomes further evident in the following story. A successful high-school football coach seemingly convinced the majority of his team members that by touching a certain stone en route to the playing field, they would be turned into animals of super strength. Upon returning to the locker rooms, they were instructed to touch the stone again; this would convert them to fine gentlemen.

These incidences are merely illustrations that reveal the numerous problems associated with the study of the effects of work aids on performance. We should be alerted to the fact that just because one study shows positive results, it might not necessarily be true or apply to all individuals. The difficulty in experimentally isolating the true effect of any aid is extremely difficult and in many cases nearly impossible.

Today, prime interest in ergogenic aids deals mostly with the effects of drugs on athletic performance and of steroids upon increasing muscle size and strength. Those interested in an elaborate presentation should consult the excellent books *Ergogenic Aids and Muscular Perform-*

*ance,* edited by William P. Morgan (Academic Press, 1972) and *Drugs and Athletic Performance,* by Melvin H. Williams (Charles C Thomas, 1974).

## Steroids

Considerable interest has arisen, particularly among weight-lifters, wrestlers, and those athletes participating in the weight events, regarding the effects of androgenic steroids on performance. The androgenic steroids are derivatives of the male sex hormone, testosterone, secreted by the testicles. Testosterone causes the particular physical characteristics of the male body. Being produced mostly between the ages of 11 and 13, testosterone quickens the onset of puberty and is continually produced throughout life.

Secretion of testosterone causes descent of the testes into the scrotum and enlargement of the testes, penis, and scrotum. It also affects the secondary male characteristics including; (1) distribution of hair, (2) voice, (3) growth and development of bones, and (4) development of musculature following puberty. It is small wonder, therefore, that some drug companies have placed a number of these androgenic steroids on the market in hopes of capitalizing on the athletic market. As Guyton notes, "Testosterone has often been considered to be a 'youth hormone' because of its effect on the musculature, and it is occasionally used for treatment of persons who have poorly developed muscles."[15]

The drug trade names for some of the synthetic testosterone preparations include: Adroyd, Dianabol, Deca-Durabolin, Maxibolin, Nilevar, and Winstrol. These drugs are chemically structured to emphasize the anabolic (protein-building) attributes of testosterone while minimizing the androgenic (producing masculine characteristics) properties.

Recognizing the problems we mentioned earlier in designing scientific studies to probe the effects of these drugs on performance and development of musculature, many have been completed with equivocal results.[4, 9, 11, 13, 18, 27]

It appears that steroids may help performance (strength) and increase lean body (muscle) mass for some but that they are of inconsequential value to others. Perhaps the real issue is that of side effects. Physicians are most concerned with the effects of these drugs on the liver. Under no circumstances should persons with histories of liver ailment involve themselves with steroid experimentation. Women taking steroids have developed acne and exhibited positive symptoms on liver function tests.

## Amphetamines

It generally is reported that amphetamines are the most popular drugs for increasing athletic performance among those inclined toward usage. Amphetamine (Benzedrine being a popular brand) is a synthetic structured drug closely related to epinephrine. Like epinephrine, it produces stimulation of the central nervous system, resulting in increased alertness in motor and physical activity, decrease in fatigue, and sometimes insomnia. Most often there is a rise in blood pressure with increased heart rate and perhaps some irregularities such as extrasystoles (extra beats) and paroxysmal tachycardia (attacks of excessively rapid heart action which occur abruptly and terminate with equal abruptness). Also, there is a moderate rise in metabolism, which may be accompanied by some loss in weight. Excessive dosages result in hyperexcitability and insomnia followed by depression. This may be accompanied by abdominal cramps, hematuria (discharge of blood into the urine), collapse, convulsions, and coma.

Characteristically, amphetamines affect different people differently. For this reason, small doses are administered initially to ascertain individual reactions. Certainly, amphetamines are contraindicated for easily excitable people and for those with high blood pressure.

A number of research studies do not support the popular belief that amphetamines enhance athletic or exercise performance.[14, 20, 23] On the contrary, use of the drug may result in serious illness, particularly while performing strenuous endurance events under hot and humid environmental conditions.[22]

## Blood Doping

Blood doping, the removal and reinfusion of blood, is done to the athlete to increase blood volume (hypervolemia) and/or the number of red blood cells (polycythemia); it is believed that both these effects enhance endurance performance through increasing maximal aerobic power. However, two recent studies of this problem have, again, shown conflicting results. One study showed an "overnight" 23 per cent increase in endurance performance and a 9 per cent increase in maximal aerobic power after reinfusion of red blood cells in normal young men.[7]

The other study compared the effects of injecting whole blood, packed red blood cells, and plasma on the performance of trained male distance-runners. There was no difference in endurance capacity, resting heart rate, and submaximal or maximal heart rate over control values.[28] From this study, it must be concluded that blood doping has little effect on performance of trained athletes.[29]

*Aspartic Acid Salts*

Blood ammonia levels rise following physical activity. The excess ammonia, through a complex series of chemical reactions, is removed from the body by being converted to urea in the liver (urea cycle). It has been conjectured that the weakest part of the cycle is due to limited amounts of aspartic acid (an amino acid). If it were true that excessive amounts of ammonia in the blood cause fatigue, exogenously administered aspartates might clear the blood of ammonia more completely, delaying fatigue and acting as an ergogenic aid.

Studies on humans concerning the performance effects of oral ingestion of aspartic acid salts are rare and, as you might expect, somewhat conflicting in their results. One study[5] concluded that the onset of fatigue in an all-out run was *not* delayed; another[1] indicated that endurance capacity for prolonged exercise (1½ hours) was significantly increased; and a third[10] concluded that there was no difference in fatigue or endurance in weight-lifting activities. It should be noted that none of the studies used athletes as subjects. However, in the first study, where no effects on delaying fatigue were shown, a 7 week physical training program was involved.

In view of the limited research and conflicting results, it is difficult to make any definite judgment relative to the ergogenic merits of aspartic acid salts. However, since the above studies involved different activities performed over different time periods, it is possible that the effects of aspartates vary according to the type and duration of the performance.

An excellent review of the literature on the ergogenic effects of steroids, amphetamines, and aspartic acid can be found in the article by Golding.[12]

*Oxygen*

Studies have been conducted regarding the ergogenic effects of breathing oxygen (1) prior to exercise, (2) during exercise, and (3) during recovery from exercise.

**$O_2$ Breathing Prior to Exercise.** There is some evidence that breathing oxygen immediately prior to exercise has some beneficial effects on performance, provided that the exercise is performed while holding the breath.[19, 30] This effect might be related to the fact that breath-holding time is increased by "blowing off" or washing out carbon dioxide (see p. 352). It is common, for example, to see swimmers hyperventilate (blow off $CO_2$) immediately before the gun goes off. (It should be noted that while this technique may be effective in increasing performance, it is very dangerous in that the possibility of drowning is also increased.)

Studies in which oxygen was breathed prior to a non–breath-holding type of exercise show very little if any effect on performance.[8, 21, 24]

**O₂ Breathing During Exercise.** There is a rather large body of information indicating that breathing oxygen-enriched air (33 to 100 per cent oxygen) has a beneficial effect upon exercise performance.[2, 16, 17, 21] During maximal work, these benefits include a greater endurance capacity, and during submaximal work, lower heart rate, lower blood lactic acid accumulation, and lower minute ventilation have been observed. The mechanisms responsible for these changes are associated with the increased partial pressure of oxygen, which facilitates the transport of oxygen by hemoglobin and in physical solution and by increased diffusion across the alveolar-capillary and tissue-capillary membranes (see p. 186). It must be emphasized here that as an ergogenic aid for the purpose of improving athletic performance, breathing oxygen during exercise is not useful simply because it is not practical.

**O₂ Breathing During Recovery.** We are sure that you have seen oxygen being administered to professional athletes during time-outs or rest breaks. Although there is not a great deal of research on this practice, any beneficial effects, either on the recovery process itself or on performance of a subsequent work bout, are inconsequential.[3, 8, 16, 21] Although there may be a psychological effect, there is no physiological basis for use of oxygen during recovery.

## Vitamin E

Vitamin E appears to be important for normal creatine excretion and for prevention of certain blood disorders, including anemia. Salad oils and margarines, whole grains, liver, beans, fruits, and vegetables contain vitamin E. Wheat germ oil is an excellent natural source. Vitamin E deficiencies are extremely rare.

Even though some studies demonstrate that this vitamin is an ergogenic aid,[6] most research concludes that this is not true;[25, 26] nor does vitamin E reduce heart disease, aid the sex drive, or increase longevity, as some people are inclined to claim.

Recently, Shephard et al.[26] studied 20 swimmers (mostly middle-distance competitors) in an attempt to determine whether athletes need vitamin E supplement. The 20 subjects were divided into ten matched pairs. The study lasted 85 days. Among the findings were the following:

(1) No significant gains in maximum oxygen consumption in either test or control subjects.

(2) Both groups showed a reduction in the lactacid component of the oxygen debt.

(3) Both demonstrated a more rapid pulse recovery rate following maximal effort.

It was concluded that vitamin E supplement has no significant effect as an ergogenic aid.

## SUMMARY

Even though the Olympic Committee disallows drugs, several Olympic athletes have died during competition, the cause of death being use of drugs. In the 1960 Olympic games, two Danish cyclists died of heat stroke following the use of a vasodilator. In 1968, a French basketball player died during a game; he was using an amphetamine.

Dr. Robert Murphy, team physician at The Ohio State University, claims that there is no substitute for athletic ability, superb conditioning, and excellence in coaching to produce a great athletic performance.

Almost all athletic and medical associations, including the International Olympic Committee and the American Medical Association, have outlawed the use of drugs in sports. Athletes known to use them will be banned from competition. Joining such organizations in raising their voices against drug use are coaches, trainers, team physicians, and physical educators. Not only is the practice contrary to the moral code underlying all athletics but also it is injurious to the health of the athlete; even in moderate doses, amphetamines may lead to habituation.

A summary of the effects of some ergogenic aids on performance is given in Table 20–1.

**Table 20–1  SUMMARY OF THE EFFECTS OF SOME ERGOGENIC AIDS ON ATHLETIC AND EXERCISE PERFORMANCE**

| | EFFECTS ON PERFORMANCE | | |
|---|---|---|---|
| ERGOGENIC AID | *Increase* | *No Effect* | *Variable* |
| Steroids | Strength? | | X |
| | Lean body mass? | | |
| Amphetamines | | X | |
| Blood doping | $_{max}\dot{V}O_2$? | | |
| | Endurance? | | X |
| Aspartic acid | Endurance? | | X |
| Oxygen | | | |
| a. Prior to exercise | X – Sprints with breath held | | |
| b. During exercise | X – Endurance | | |
| | Lower submaximal heart rate, lactic acid, ventilation | | |
| c. During recovery | | X | |
| Vitamin E | | X | |

## QUESTIONS

1. Define an ergogenic aid.

2. What are some of the problems associated with obtaining consistent and objective information on the effects of ergogenic aids?

3. How do androgenic steroids affect performance?

4. What are the physiological effects of amphetamines?

5. What is blood doping, and does it improve athletic performance?

6. Explain the effects of aspartic acid salts, oxygen, and vitamin E on athletic performance.

## REFERENCES

1. Ahlborg, B., Ekelund, L. G., and Nilsson, C. G.: Effect of potassium-magnesium-asparate on the capacity for prolonged exercise in man. Acta Physiol. Scand., 74:238–245, 1968.
2. Bannister, R., and Cunningham, D.: The effects on the respiration and performance during exercise of adding oxygen to the inspired air. J. Physiol. Lond., 125:118–137, 1954.
3. Bjorgum, R. K., and Sharkey, B. J.: Inhalation of oxygen as an aid to recovery after exertion. Res. Quart., 37:462–467, 1966.
4. Casner, S., Early, R., and Carlson, B.: Anabolic steroid effects on body composition in normal young men. J. Sports Med. Phys. Fit., 11:98–103, 1971.
5. Consolazio, C. F., Nelson, R. A., Matoush, L. O., and Isaac, G. J.: Effects of aspartic acid salts (Mg + K) on physical performance of men. J. Appl. Physiol., 19:257–261, 1964.
6. Cureton, T. K.: Effect of wheat germ oil and vitamin E on normal human subjects in physical training programs. Am. J. Physiol., 179:628, 1954.
7. Ekblom, B., Goldbard, A., and Gullbring, B.: Response to exercise after blood loss and reinfusion. J. Appl. Physiol., 33(2):175–180, 1973.
8. Elbel, E., Ormond, D., and Close, D.: Some effects of breathing $O_2$ before and after exercise. J. Appl. Physiol., 16:48–52, 1961.
9. Fahey, Thomas D., and Brown, C. Harmon: The effects of anabolic steroids on the strength, body composition and endurance of college males when accompanied by a weight training program. Med. Sci. Sports, 5(4):272–276, 1973.
10. Fallis, N., Wilson, W., Tetreault, L., and LaSagna, L.: Effect of potassium and magnesium aspartates on athletic performance. J.A.M.A., 185(2):129, 1963.
11. Fowler, W. H., Garner, G. W., and Egstrom, G. H.: Effect of an anabolic steroid on physical performance of young men. J. Appl. Physiol., 20:1038–1040, 1965.
12. Golding, L.: Drugs and hormones. In Morgan, W. (ed.): Ergogenic Aids and Muscular Performance. New York, Academic Press, 1972, pp. 367–397.
13. Golding, L., Freydinger, J., and Fishel, S.: Weight, size and strength—unchanged with steroids. The Physician and Sportsmedicine, June, 1974, pp. 39–43.
14. Golding, L. A., and Barnard, R. J.: The effects of d-amphetamine sulfate on physical performance. J. Sports Med. Phys. Fit., 3:221–224, 1963.
15. Guyton, Arthur: Basic Human Physiology; Normal Function and Mechanisms of Disease. Philadelphia, W. B. Saunders Co., 1971, p. 668.
16. Hagerman, F., Bowers, R., Fox, E., and Ersing, W.: The effects of breathing 100 per cent oxygen during rest, heavy work, and recovery. Res. Quart., 39(4):965–974, 1968.
17. Hughes, R., Clode, M., Edwards, R., Goodwin, T., and Jones, N.: Effect of inspired

$O_2$ on cardiopulmonary and metabolic responses to exercise in man. J. Appl. Physiol., 24(3):336–347, 1968.

18. Johnson, L., Fisher, G., Silvester, L., and Hofheins, C.: Anabolic steroid: effects on strength, body weight, oxygen uptake and spermatogenesis upon mature males. Med. Sci. Sports, 4(1):43–45, 1972.

19. Karpovich, P.: The effect of oxygen inhalation on swimming performance. Res. Quart., 5(2):24, 1934.

20. Karpovich, P.: Effect of amphetamine sulphate on athletic performance. J.A.M.A., 170:558–561, 1959.

21. Miller, A.: Influence of oxygen administration on the cardiovascular function during exercise and recovery. J. Appl. Physiol., 5:165–168, 1952.

22. Murphy, R. J.: The problem of environmental heat in athletics. Ohio State Med. J., 59:799, 1963.

23. Ryan, A. J.: Use of amphetamines in athletics. J.A.M.A., 170:562, 1959.

24. Sharkey, B.: The Effect of Preliminary Oxygen Inhalation on Performance in Swimming. Master's Thesis, West Chester State College, 1961.

25. Sharman, I. M., Down, M. G., and Sen, R. N.: The effects of vitamin E on physiological function and athletic performance in adolescent swimmers. Br. J. Nutr., 26:265–276, 1971.

26. Shephard, R., Campbell, R., Pimm, P., Stuart, D., and Wright, G.: Do athletes need vitamin E? The Physician and Sportsmedicine, 2(9):57–60, 1974.

27. Ward, P.: The effect of an anabolic steroid on strength and lean body mass. Med. Sci. Sports, 5(4):277–282, 1973.

28. Williams, M., Goodwin, H., Perkins, R., and Bocrie, J.: Effect of blood reinjection upon endurance capacity and heart rate. Med. Sci. Sports, 5(3):181–185, 1973.

29. Williams, M.: Blood doping—does it really help athletes? The Physician and Sportsmedicine, Jan., 1975, p. 52.

30. Wilmore, J.: Oxygen. *In* Morgan, W. (ed.): Ergogenic Aids and Muscular Performance. New York, Academic Press, 1972, pp. 321–342.

## SELECTED READINGS

Morgan, W. (ed.): Ergogenic Aids and Muscular Performance. New York, Academic Press, 1972.

Williams, M.: Drugs and Athletic Performance. Springfield, Ill., Charles C Thomas, 1974.

# EXERCISE AND TRAINING IN FEMALES

The purpose of this chapter is to emphasize some of the physiological responses of girls and women to both exercise and physical training. It should be made clear from the outset that, in general, the responses of females to exercise and training are *basically* no different from those described elsewhere for boys and men. After all, it must be remembered that the cellular mechanisms controlling most physiological and biochemical responses to exercise are the same for both sexes.

However, there are differences, and they should be recognized mainly as differences in magnitude rather than mechanism.

First we will take a good look at the performance records of men and women. A comparison of these records will provide a basis for our discussion of exercise and training in females with respect to: (1) body size and body composition, (2) the energy systems, (3) muscular strength and function, (4) physical trainability, and (5) gynecological considerations.

## PERFORMANCE RECORDS

Table 21–1 contains the world's best track and field and freestyle swimming performances for men and women up to and including 1974 performances. The differences in performance between the men and women are shown in the table as the *performance ratio*. The performance ratio is nothing more than the women's performance divided by the men's. For example, in the 100-meter dash, the women's time of 10.8 seconds is divided by the men's time of 9.9 seconds, resulting in the performance ratio of 10.8/9.9 = 1.091. An equal performance in any event would set the ratio at one. The performance ratios given in Table 21–1 are all greater than one, meaning that the men's performances are better than the women's.

The above conclusion that the men's performances are better than

**Table 21–1  WORLD'S BEST TRACK AND FIELD AND FREESTYLE SWIMMING PERFORMANCES FOR MEN AND WOMEN**

| Event | Men | Women | Performance Ratio* |
|-------|-----|-------|--------------------|
| | | TRACK AND FIELD | |
| 100 m. | 9.9 sec. | 10.8 sec. | 1.091 |
| 200 m. | 19.8 sec. | 22.1 sec. | 1.116 |
| 400 m. | 43.8 sec. | 49.9 sec. | 1.139 |
| 800 m. | 1 min., 43.7 sec. | 1 min., 57.5 sec. | 1.133 |
| 1500 m. | 3 min., 33.1 sec. | 4 min., 01.4 sec. | 1.133 |
| High jump | 89.75 in. | 75.5 in. | 1.197† |
| Long jump | 350.5 in. | 268.5 in. | 1.307† |
| | | SWIMMING (FREESTYLE) | |
| 100 m. | 51.22 sec. | 56.96 sec. | 1.112 |
| 200 m. | 1 min., 51.66 sec. | 2 min., 03.22 sec. | 1.104 |
| 400 m. | 3 min., 54.69 sec. | 4 min., 15.77 sec. | 1.090 |
| 800 m. | 8 min., 15.58 sec. | 8 min., 47.66 sec. | 1.065 |
| 1500 m. | 15 min., 31.75 sec. | 16 min., 33.95 sec. | 1.067 |

*Women's time divided by men's time.
†Men's distance divided by women's distance.

the women's does not provide any physiological insight into the reason for it. In order to shed more light on this question, let's take a closer look at the performance ratios. In Figure 21–1, we have plotted the performance ratios given in Table 21–1, event by event. In studying the figure, remember that the lower the performance ratio, i.e., the closer the "swimming and running lines" are to the "equal performance line," the closer the performance of the women to the men. The following points should be noticed:

1. The over-all performance by women is closer to the men's in swimming than in either running or jumping.
2. In the running events, the women's performance is closer to the men's in the 100- and 200-meter sprints than in the other events.
3. In the swimming events, the women's performance is closer to the men's in the distance events than in the shorter events.

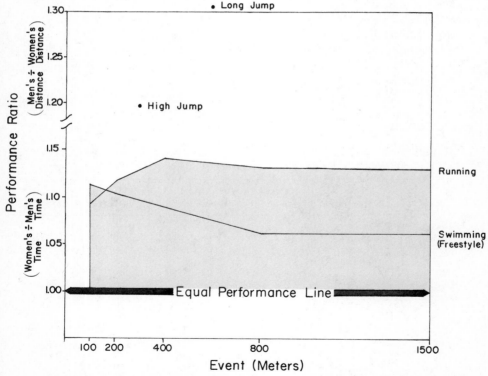

**Figure 21–1** World's best performances by men and women in track and field and freestyle swimming. The performance differences between men and women are given by the performance ratio, i.e., dividing the men's performance time by the women's. Since the performance ratios are all greater than one, the men's performances are better than the women's in all events. See text for further discussion.

4. The worst performances for the women are the 100 meters in swimming, 400 meters in running, and the high jump and long jump.

With these points in mind, let's continue our discussion.

## BODY SIZE AND BODY COMPOSITION

From Figure 21–2, compared with the average adult male, the average adult female:

1. is 3 to 4 inches *shorter*;
2. is 25 to 30 pounds *lighter* in total body weight;
3. has 10 to 15 pounds *more adipose tissue* (fat);
4. has 40 to 45 pounds *less fat-free weight* (mainly muscle, bone, and organs).

In general, these differences refer to both nonathletic and athletic men

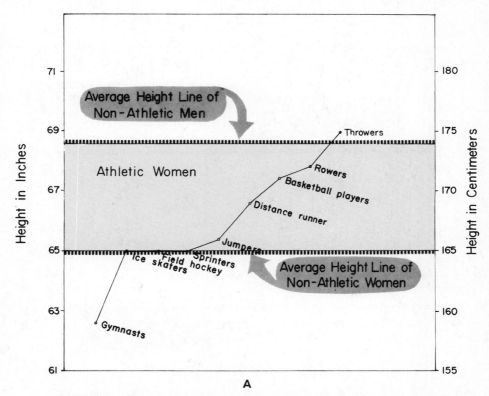

**A**

**Figure 21–2**  Compared with the adult male, the female *A*, is 3 to 4 inches shorter; *B* is 25 to 30 pounds lighter in total body weight; and *C* has 10 to 15 pounds more fat and has 40 to 45 pounds less muscle mass. Also, notice that the biggest female athletes (discus throwers and shot-putters), though larger than nonathletic females are only about the size of average nonathletic males. (Based on data from references 6, 13, 25, 28, 38, 45, 47, 49, 62, 66, 67, and 72.)

*Illustration continued on the following page*

and women.[52] Also, from Figure 21–2, notice that the biggest female athletes (discus throwers and shot-putters), though considerably larger than their nonathletic counterparts, are still only about the size of the average nonathletic male.

### Weight and Height

Some of the performance differences pointed out earlier can be explained, at least in part, by body weight and height differences. For example, let's look at the long jump and high jump. Here, the performance differences are quite large (Table 21–1). However, if the distances jumped are corrected for body weight, the performances are essentially the same (for the high jump, 1.2 vs. 1.3 in./kg. body weight for men and women, respectively, and 4.9 vs. 4.6 in./kg. for men and women, respectively, for the long jump). In the high jump, height is also an important factor because the center of gravity of the body is higher

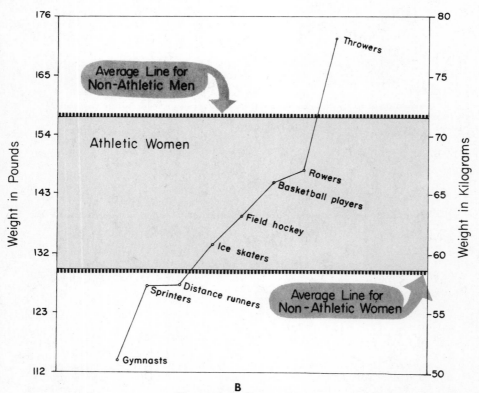

**B**
**Figure 21–2** *Continued*
*Illustration continued on the opposite page*

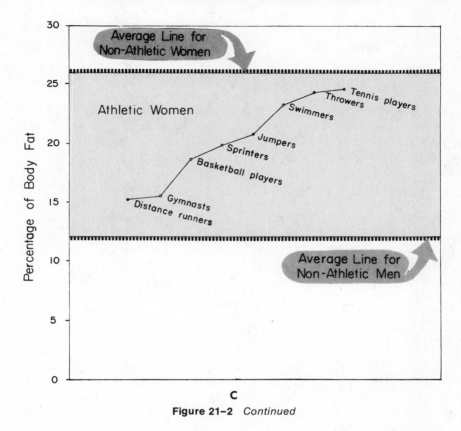

**C**

**Figure 21-2** *Continued*

in men. Although such comparisons may not be completely valid, they do point out nicely the effects of body size on performance.

### Body Fat

We mentioned earlier that in swimming the performance of women is closer to that of men than in running. In swimming, sex differences in body composition tend to be advantageous to the female, whereas in running, the men have the advantage. In water, the greater body fat of the female leads to less body drag, which, in turn, leads to less energy expenditure per unit of distance swum.[58] In other words, women swimming over the same distance as men require 20 per cent less energy per unit body weight. However, in running, the extra body fat of the female becomes a burden by virtue of the fact that it increases the work load. It is analogous to running while carrying a backpack full of bricks!

### Possible Body Structure Differences

The average female has a wider pelvis than the average male. In running, particularly sprinting, this means that the female must shift her pelvis more in order to keep the center of gravity over the weight-bearing foot.[36] As a result, there is greater hip muscle involvement and, thus, a decreased mechanical efficiency during running. Theoretically, this should limit the running ability of the female with respect to the male. However, research findings show that the relationship between width of the hips and running speed is very low and as such should not be a significantly limiting factor from a practical standpoint.[57, 69] This point is well illustrated by the performance ratios shown in Figure 21–1. As already pointed out, the women's performance is closer to the men's in the sprints, in which this limitation would be more apparent than in the other running events.

### Age and Body Size Differences

It is well known that body size differences are minimal in young children, i.e., before the onset of puberty.[2, 21] Thus, it should be instructive with respect to the effects of body size on performance to examine the performance of prepubescent boys and girls. Such performances for freestyle swimming are shown in Figure 21–3. Notice that for the 10-year-old age group, the performance ratios are equal to one or even below. This means that at this young age when body size differences are minimal, the girls' performance is equal to or better than the boys'. Also notice that the performance ratio increases with age, reaching a maximum at about 16 years, at which time body size and composition differences are nearly maximal.

## THE ENERGY SYSTEMS

Of the three energy systems discussed in Chapter 2, only the oxygen (aerobic) system has gained much attention with respect to the female.[3, 15, 18] Even in this, the research is scanty. Almost no research has been conducted with respect to the female's anaerobic capacities (ATP-PC, and L.A. systems). In view of this limited research, a discussion of the energy systems with respect to performance differences might well prove to be enlightening.

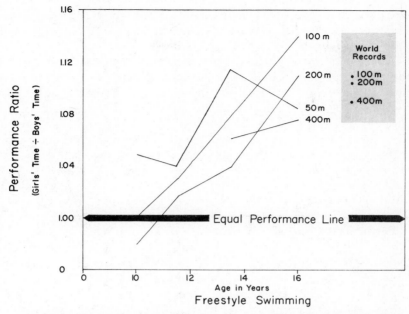

**Figure 21-3** Performance ratios of young boys and girls for freestyle swimming events. At the younger ages, when body size differences between sexes are minimal, girls' performances are equal to or better than boys'. The performance ratio increases with age, however, reaching a maximum at about 16 years, at which time body size and composition differences between sexes are nearly maximal.

## The ATP-PC System

It has been shown that the muscular concentrations of ATP and PC in females are the same as those in males,[33] i.e., about 4 mM/kg. muscle for ATP and 16 mM/kg. muscle for CP (see p. 14). However, because of the smaller total skeletal muscle mass in the female, the total phosphagens available for use during exercise are fewer. Comparisons of the functional capacities of the ATP-PC system between men and women can be made in three ways: first, by alactacid oxygen debt measurements; second, by the Margaria Anaerobic Power Test (see p. 499); and third, by the performance ratios.

**Alactacid O₂ Debt.** You will recall (p. 33) that the maximal alactacid portion of the oxygen debt is associated with regeneration of the total muscular stores of ATP and PC that were depleted during exhaustive exercise. In Figure 21-4 are shown some comparative values for the maximal alactacid oxygen debt capacity between men and women. It can be seen that the lowest values are associated with untrained females and males, whereas the highest values are related to the highly trained oarswomen and oarsmen of the U. S. National

Team. The differences between men and women would be closer if the values were expressed per unit of muscle mass rather than total body weight.

**Anaerobic Power Test.** The stair-climbing test, described in Chapter 22, takes only a fraction of a second and as such indirectly reflects the ability to rapidly utilize the stores of ATP and PC in the leg muscles. These power measurements are shown in Figure 21–5 for males and females from 6 to 25 years old. Notice that there is very little difference between the sexes. Also, though not shown in the figure, the maximal anaerobic power decreases after the age of 25 years for both men and women. The power values are expressed relative to body weight; the total power capability for the average male would be around 2.1 horsepower (HP) and for the average female, 1.7 HP. This difference is due again to the smaller body size of the female.

**Performance Ratios.**   With respect to the performance ratios (Fig. 21–1), it is interesting to note that the best running events for the female in comparison with those of the male are the 100- and 200-

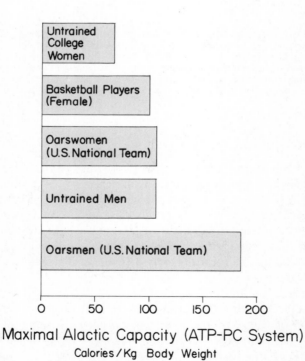

## Maximal Alactic Capacity (ATP-PC System)
### Calories / Kg  Body  Weight

**Figure 21–4** Comparative values for the maximal alactacid oxygen debt capacity between men and women. The lowest values are associated with untrained females and males, whereas the highest values are related to the highly trained oarsmen and oarswomen of the U.S. National Team. (Based on data from Cohen,[9] Diehl,[13] Fox,[22, 23] and Hagerman et al.[28, 29])

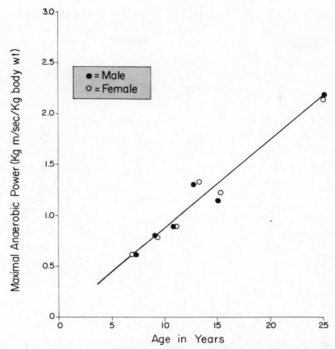

**Figure 21–5**  Anaerobic (ATP+PC) power in males and females. Notice that both men and women fit the same line, indicating that there is very little difference between the sexes. (Based on data from Davies et al.,[12] Kalamen,[37] and Margaria et al.[50])

meter dashes. You will recall that these types of events rely heavily on the muscular stores of ATP and PC for their primary source of energy. This also tends to support the idea that the muscular concentrations of ATP and PC in females are not much different from those of males, and as such should not significantly hinder female performance in those events that require short-term, but high intensity, efforts. The lower total stores of ATP and PC in females appear to be due mainly to their smaller total muscle mass.

### The Lactic Acid System

Females tend to have lower levels of lactic acid in their blood following maximal exercise than do males.[3, 9, 11, 18, 28, 39] Such low lactic acid levels strongly suggest that the capacity of the lactic acid system is also lower in the female. This can be seen in Figure 21–6, in which the capacity of the L.A. system is shown for men and women, both trained and untrained. The values, though expressed as cal./kg. of total body weight, are based on blood lactic acid levels following maximal exercise.

As with the ATP-PC system, one of the reasons for a lower L.A. capacity in the female is the smaller total muscle mass. If the values given in Figure 21–6 were expressed per kg. of total muscle mass, the differences between the sexes would be smaller. However, upon examination of the performance ratios, it becomes quite clear that the worst events, both running and swimming, involve performance times of around one minute (400 meters for running, and 100 meters for swimming). Such events rely heavily on the L.A. system for ATP production. This information indicates that females might be at a slight disadvantage when competing in those events that involve the L.A. system to

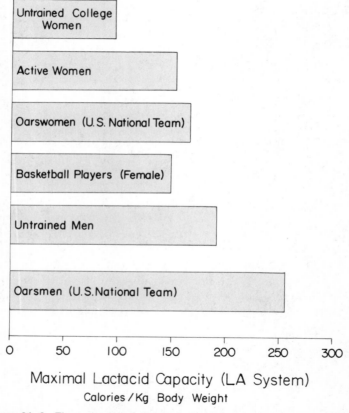

## Maximal Lactacid Capacity (LA System)
### Calories / Kg Body Weight

**Figure 21–6** The capacity of the lactic acid system for men and women, both trained and untrained. Again, the lactic acid capacity is lower in females than in males. While this may be related in part to lesser muscle mass, it points out that females might be at a slight disadvantage when competing in those events that involve the lactic acid system to a large extent. (Based on data from references 3, 9, 11, 13, 18, 22, 28, 29, 39, and 62.)

a large extent. In view of this, we suggest that coaches as well as participants can benefit from training programs that stress the L.A. system (see p. 239).

### The Oxygen (Aerobic) System

As with the two anaerobic capacities mentioned above, the maximal aerobic capacity (max$\dot{V}o_2$) of females is also smaller than that of males (by about 15 to 25 per cent). This is shown in Figure 21–7, in which two points are worth noting:

1. The difference in max$\dot{V}o_2$ between male and female is negligible at the younger ages and most pronounced during the adult, middle-age years. This relationship stems from the fact that, as

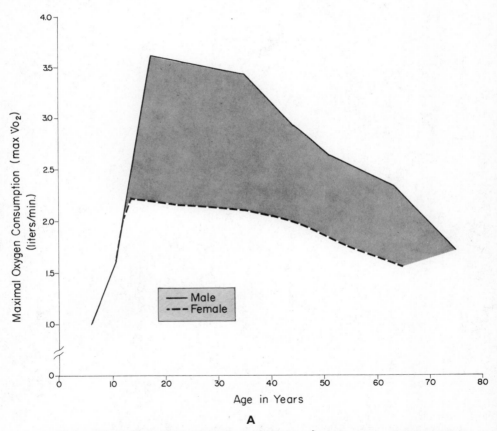

**A**

**Figure 21–7**   The maximal aerobic capacity (max$\dot{V}o_2$) of males and females from 6 to 75 years of age. In *A*, the values are expressed in liters per minute without respect to body size. Note the large sex differences. In *B*, these differences are reduced when max$Vo_2$ is expressed relative to total body weight. (Based on data from Drinkwater et al.,[18] P. Robinson,[62] and S. Robinson.[63])

*Illustration continued on the following page*

mentioned earlier, body size and composition differences between males and females are minimal prior to puberty and maximal during adulthood.

2. The difference in maxV̇o$_2$ between the sexes is smallest when expressed relative to a body size dimension such as body weight (Fig. 21–7B). Again, this goes back to sex differences in body size and composition. Actually, since the metabolism of the working skeletal muscles dictates the size of the maxV̇o$_2$, differences between male and female are minimal when maxV̇o$_2$ is expressed relative to lean body mass[10, 12, 14, 16] and to an even lesser extent when related to active muscle mass.[12] The latter relationship is shown in Figure 21–8. In this case, the maxV̇o$_2$ was measured on a bicycle ergometer and the active muscle

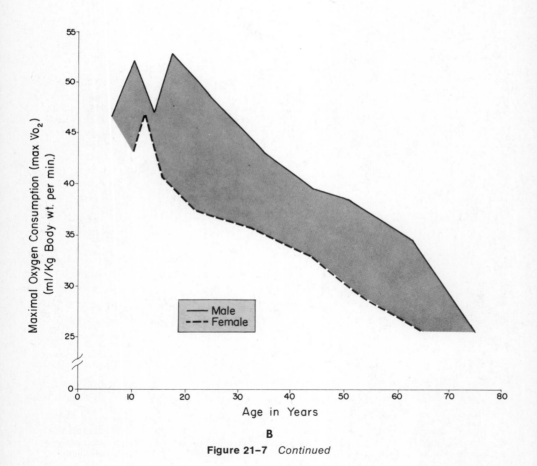

**B**

**Figure 21–7** *Continued*

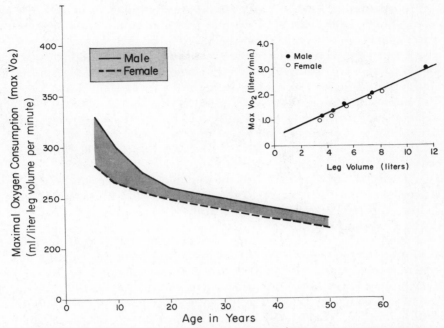

**Figure 21–8**  The maximal aerobic capacity (max$\dot{V}O_2$) of males and females from 5 to 50 years of age. In this case, max$\dot{V}O_2$ was measured on a bicycle ergometer and the active muscle mass estimated by leg volume measurements. Notice how little difference there is between sexes when max$\dot{V}O_2$ is expressed in ml. of oxygen per liter of leg volume. The insert shows the relationship between max$\dot{V}O_2$ in liters per minute and leg volume in liters; both males and females fit the same line. (Based on data from Davies et al.[12])

mass estimated by leg volume measurements. Leg volume is a measure of the volume of leg bone plus the volume of leg muscle. Since leg bone volume does not account for much of the total, leg volume actually reflects leg muscle volume or mass. Notice how little difference there is between males and females at all ages when max$\dot{V}O_2$ is expressed in ml. $O_2$ per liter of leg volume and per minute. Also, the insert shows the relationship between max$\dot{V}O_2$ in liters per minute and leg volume in liters; both males and females fit the same line.

It is important at this time to mention that from a practical standpoint, the only meaningful relationship discussed above is between max$\dot{V}O_2$ and total body weight. This is so because in most exercises and sports activities, the total body weight of the athlete comprises the largest part of the workload. Therefore, there is little question that the female is at a disadvantage in terms of max$\dot{V}O_2$ (see Fig. 21–7B).

**Hemoglobin, Blood Volume, and Heart Volume.**     As you already know, hemoglobin (Hb) is the compound found in red blood cells that carries most of the oxygen from the lungs to the skeletal muscles. Also, the greater the blood volume, the greater the Hb. Thus, both Hb and blood volume are directly related to the amount of oxygen transported, and hence to the functional size of the aerobic or oxygen system, i.e., to the max$\dot{V}o_2$. This is shown in Figure 21–9$A$ and $B$. Notice that the relationships for the male (solid lines) and for the female (broken lines) are the same. This means that everything else being equal, the max$\dot{V}o_2$ of the female would equal that of the male if each were to have the same total Hb and total blood volume.

The total amount of Hb and the total blood volume for the female are less than for the male (see Table 21–2, p. 472), with the differences being about 25 per cent between untrained men and women and only about 12 per cent after each is trained.

The amount of blood capable of being pumped by the heart, that is, the size of the heart, is also an important factor in determining how much oxygen can be transported to the muscles. Therefore, the relationship between heart size (heart volume) and the max$\dot{V}o_2$ is quite good, as is shown in Figure 21–9$C$. Notice once again that the data for both men (filled circles) and women (unfilled circles) fall on the same line. The fact that females have on the average a smaller heart volume than men (see Table 21–2) undoubtedly contributes to their smaller max$\dot{V}o_2$.

For a final look at the oxygen systems, let's go back to the performance ratios. It can be seen (Fig. 21–1, p. 448) that for the distance swimming events (800 and 1500 m.), in which the body size difference is effectively reduced by the water and the energy supplied predominantly by the oxygen system, the females' performance is closer to the men's then under any other set of conditions. From a practical standpoint, this illustrates very nicely the influence of differences in body size and the functional capacities of the female.

# STRENGTH

There are two important questions relative to muscular strength and the female that need answering:
1. What is the magnitude of the difference in strength in various muscle groups between male and female?
2. Does the female have the same potential as the male for strength development, general body composition changes, and muscular hypertrophy (muscle bulk) following a weight training program?

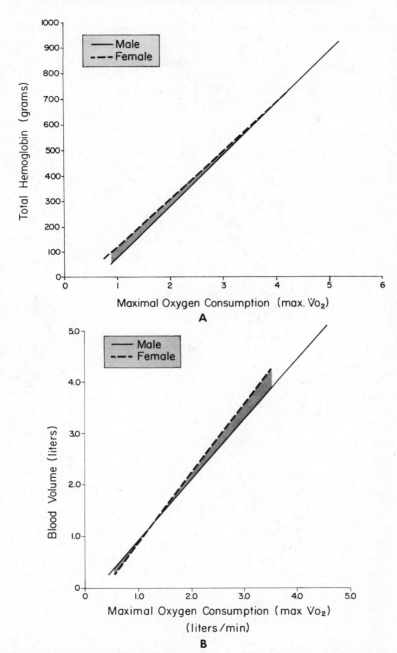

**Figure 21–9**  The total amount of hemoglobin and the blood and heart volumes are directly related to the amount of oxygen transported to the muscles, and hence to the functional size of the aerobic or oxygen system (max$\dot{V}O_2$). These relationships are the same for men and women. (Based on data from Åstrand et al.[4, 5])

*Illustration continued on the following page*

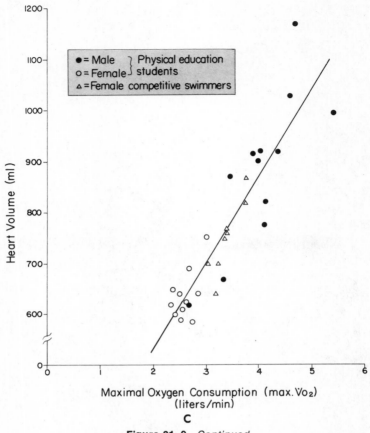

**Figure 21-9** *Continued*

## Strength Differences

Strength differences between male and female should be examined from the standpoint of (1) absolute strength, (2) strength in relation to body size and composition, and (3) strength in relation to muscle size.

**Absolute Strength.** Differences between the sexes in absolute strength, i.e., in pounds pulled or lifted, are shown in Figure 21-10. The differences are expressed in terms of a strength ratio; that is, the absolute strength of the female was divided by the absolute strength of the male—a ratio less than one means the men are stronger. General muscle strength in the female is approximately two-thirds that of the male.[32] However, notice that the strength differences vary among the different muscle groups. For example, in comparison with men, women are weaker in the chest, arms, and shoulders and strongest in the legs.[32, 70] The reason for this is more than likely related to the fact that

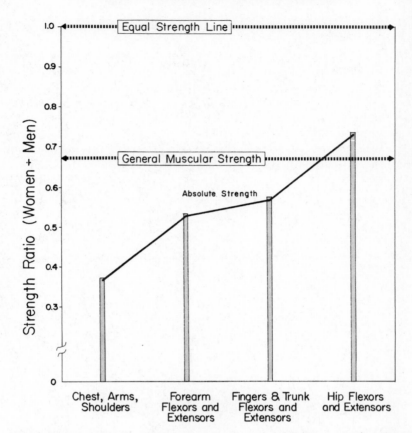

**Figure 21-10** Differences between the sexes in absolute muscular strength. The differences are expressed in terms of a strength ratio (strength of females divided by strength of males); a ratio less than one means the men are stronger. General muscular strength in the female is two-thirds that of the male but varies according to the muscle groups compared. (Based on data from Hettinger[32] and Wilmore.[70])

both sexes use their legs to a similar degree, e.g., standing, walking, running, climbing stairs, and cycling. On the other hand, females, at least heretofore in American society, have had little opportunity to use their upper limb muscles.

**Strength Relative to Body Size.**   Just like the other functional capacities so far discussed, strength differences between male and female are reduced when related to body size. Figure 21-11 shows the strength ratio when strength in both sexes is expressed (a) in terms of total body weight and (b) in terms of lean body mass. Notice that leg strength per unit lean body weight is actually slightly greater in the female than in the male. It should be remembered that lean body weight more closely approximates total muscle mass than does total body weight since lean body weight is calculated as total body weight minus total fat weight.

In addition to total and lean body weights, strength is also related to height.[1] This is particularly true in children of both sexes. For example, there is little or no difference in the strength of the leg muscles in boys and girls from 7 to 17 years of age when expressed relative to body height.

**Strength and Muscle Size.**   So far as is known, strength relative to muscle size (expressed as the cross-sectional area of the muscle) is the same for the male and the female.[32, 35] In other words, the quality of the muscle fibers, as far as the ability to exert force is concerned, is in-

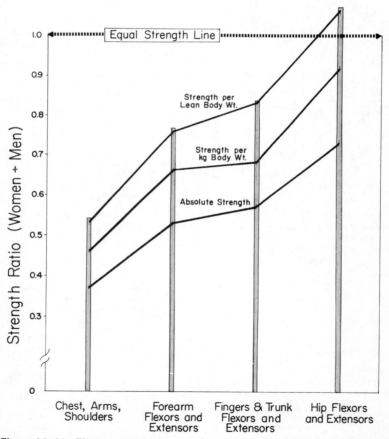

**Figure 21–11**   The strength ratio when strength in both sexes is expressed in terms of total body weight and lean body mass. Strength differences between male and female are reduced when strength is related to body size. (Based on data from Wilmore.[70])

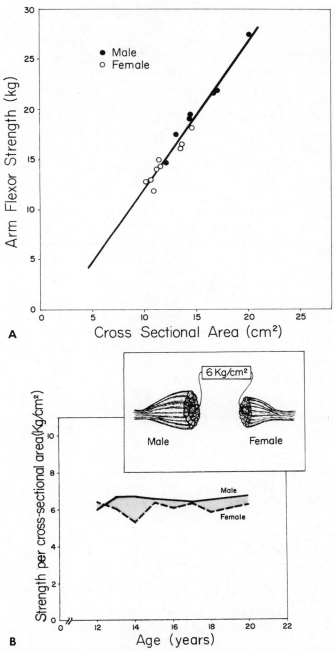

**Figure 21–12**  In *A*, the strength of the arm flexors is plotted against their cross-sectional area; both males and females fit the same line. In *B*, strength per unit cross-sectional area is shown for males and females. Again, there is little or no difference in strength. The insert shows that the force exerted by equally sized muscles is the same in both sexes. (Based on data from Ikai and Fukunago.[35])

dependent of sex. This is shown in Figure 21–12. In Figure 21–12*A*, the strength of the arm flexors is plotted against the cross-sectional area of the flexors. It is easy to see that the relationship between muscle strength and muscle size (cross-sectional area) is excellent. Also, note how both males (filled circles) and females (unfilled circles) fit the same line. In Figure 21–12*B*, strength per unit of cross-sectional area (i.e., the absolute strength of the muscle fibers divided by their cross-sectional area) is shown for males and females of various ages. Again, there is little or no difference between the sexes and little or no difference according to age, at least between 12 and 20 years of age. This means that although the male usually has a larger muscle than the female, the force exerted by equal-sized muscles is the same in both sexes (see Fig. 21–12*B* insert).

The above information, though interesting, is again only practical from the standpoint of absolute strength, that is, strength without respect to muscle or body size. As mentioned before, this is true because in those activities that are at least partially dependent upon strength (such as sprinting or accelerating and jumping), the entire body is involved. The performance ratios tend to bear this out. For example, females are relatively poor in the jumping events. However, when the heights jumped are adjusted according to body size, both sexes are about equal (see p. 450). The same applies to the 100-meter dash. The men's speed per unit of body size is 8.4 meters/min. per kg. body weight, and for the women, 9.5 meters/min. The women are slightly faster when expressed relative to body size.

### Effects of Weight Training

One of the concepts most misunderstood by physical educators, coaches, and parents alike is the effect of a weight training program. This is particularly true regarding the female. The common concept is that although a weight training program increases strength, it also produces bulging muscles that turn into fat when the program is no longer continued. Let's see what the true story is.

**Strength Development.**    It is true that muscular strength in both men and women increases following a weight training program.[6, 32, 51, 70] This is shown in normal college age students in Figure 21–13. The per cent increase in strength for the females in all but one muscle group (the arms) was the same or better than in the males. Although part of this greater relative strength gain can be explained on the basis of the lower initial strength levels of the females, these results indicate that the female can make substantial gains in strength through weight lifting activities. This is an important point, since earlier information indicated that women are less trainable than men with respect to muscular strength.[32] The strength gains shown here

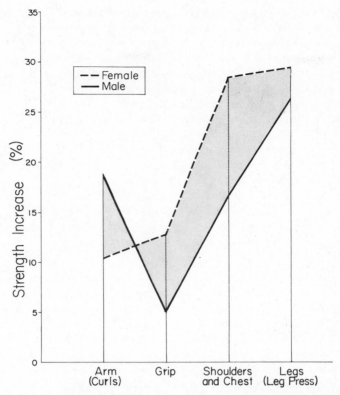

**Figure 21–13**  Both men and women increase in muscular strength following a weight training program. The per cent increase in strength for females in most muscle groups is the same or even better than for males. (Based on data from Wilmore.[70])

were made over a 10-week period, 2 days per week, using the progressive resistance principle. For example, the initial weights were chosen so that the subjects could perform only 7 to 9 repetitions. When the subjects increased in strength to the point where the same weights could be lifted 14 to 16 repetitions, additional weight was added so that only 7 to 9 repetitions could again be performed.

Figure 21–14 also shows the effects of a weight training program on strength gains, but this time for female athletes. The female athletes were nationally prominent track and field and throwing event athletes between the ages of 16 and 23 years. The important point here is that these girls are much stronger than normal girls, but their strength gains are still very substantial, particularly after 6 months of training. This information suggests that weight training programs can and should be used by female athletes who wish to improve their performance in those activities demanding a great deal of strength.

**Weight Training and Body Composition Changes.** For the average college age male and female, body composition changes following a weight training program are as follows:[51, 70]

1. Little or no change in total body weight
2. Significant losses of relative and absolute body fat
3. A significant gain in lean body weight (presumably muscle mass).

An example of these changes is shown in Figure 21–15. Notice that while the changes are similar in both sexes, changes in absolute and relative body fat tend to be slightly greater in the female. On the other hand, the increase in lean body weight (muscle mass) tends to be less in the female than in the male. The changes shown in Figure 21–15 were obtained on the same subjects whose strength gains are shown in Figure 21–13 (10 weeks of training, 2 days per week).

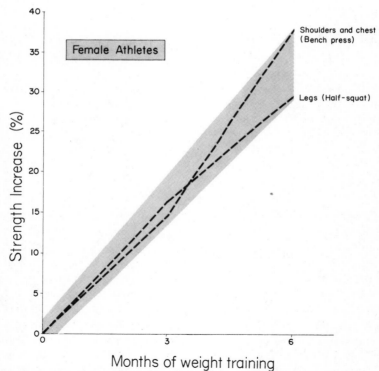

**Figure 21–14** The increase in strength in female athletes. These girls are much stronger than normal girls; yet their strength gains are still very substantial. (Based on data from Brown and Wilmore.[6])

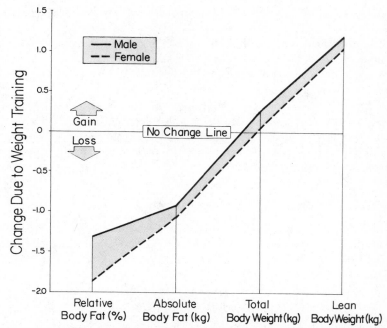

**Figure 21-15** Following a weight training program you could expect, in both sexes, to find little change in total body weight, a loss of body fat, and a gain in muscle mass. Losses in body fat tend to be slightly greater in the female, whereas gains in muscle mass tend to be slightly greater in the male. (Based on data from Wilmore.[70])

Similar changes in body composition have been observed in female athletes following a season of training and competition.[6, 13, 45, 66]

**Muscular Hypertrophy.** Gains in muscular strength are usually accompanied by an increase in the size of individual muscle fibers. While this is true for both the male and female, *it is much less pronounced in the female.*[6, 51, 70, 71] This can be seen from Figure 21–16, where increases in muscular girth are shown for those same subjects whose body composition and strength changes are shown in Figures 21–15 and 21–13, respectively. In every case, increases in muscular girth (circumference) were greater in the male than in the female. Also, the largest increase in muscular size exhibited by the females was 0.6 centimeter or *less than a quarter of an inch*! Such small increases in girth clearly point out that muscular hypertrophy in the female as a result of weight training programs will certainly not lead to excessive muscular bulk or produce a masculinizing effect. Muscular hypertrophy is regulated mainly by the hormone testosterone, which is found in much higher levels in normal men than in normal women. Thus, regardless of strength gains, muscular hypertrophy is less in females than in males.

## PHYSICAL TRAINABILITY

Our discussion of the trainability of the female will be limited mainly to those changes occurring following a physical training program consisting of activities such as running, jogging, swimming, or bicycling. We have already discussed the trainability of the female with respect to muscular strength.

### Training Frequency, Duration, and Intensity

What is presently known concerning training frequency, duration, and intensity has been discussed earlier (p. 293). Again, most of that information was obtained from research on males. A few studies recently conducted on females[9, 19, 27, 31, 39, 64] tend to support the idea that most of this information is applicable to the female.

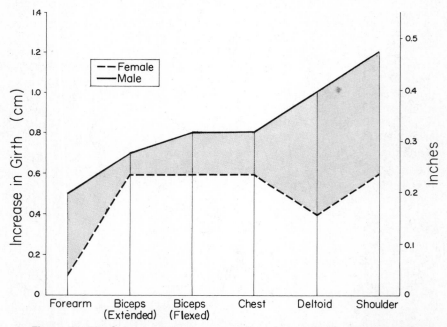

**Figure 21–16** Gains in strength are usually accompanied by increases in muscular size (girth). While this is true for both sexes, it is much less pronounced in the female. (Based on data from Wilmore.[70])

Briefly, the following can be said concerning the frequency, the duration, and the intensity of training programs designed for females.

1. **Frequency.**  For the average, college age female, significant physiological changes can be realized from training programs conducted as few as 2 or 3 times per week.[27, 39, 64] Female athletes usually train 5, even 6, times per week. Although the physiological benefits of more frequent training sessions per week are questionable,[24] more frequent training sessions in this case may be necessary from a skill and/or strategy standpoint.

2. **Duration.**  Significant improvement in fitness has been produced in young sedentary females with as little as 4 weeks of training with 5 training sessions per week.[19] Also, 6 to 7 weeks of training with 2 or 3[39, 64] or 5[9] training sessions per week and 10 weeks with 2 days per week[27] have likewise led to significant improvements in fitness.

3. **Intensity.**  Of all the information obtained on physical training, for both men and women, the intensity of training appears to be most critical in bringing about significant change. There is a *threshold intensity* above which there is significant improvement and below which there is not. This threshold level of intensity varies from individual to individual and is related to the initial level of fitness (conditioning) of the participant (see p. 295).

It becomes obvious from the above discussion that training frequency, duration, and intensity have some degree of interaction. In other words, most of the training effects are dependent upon not one, but a combination of the above variables. Although the exact combination for optional training results is not known, we recommend that training programs for nonathletic, young females be similar to those for nonathletic young males, i.e., at least 7 to 8 weeks in duration, with 2 to 3 training frequencies per week. The intensity of training should increase the participants' heart rates to at least 70 per cent of maximum with higher levels precipitating better results. Also, for young female athletes, training programs similar to those used by men should be followed. As will be discussed later (p. 478), training programs for females should be most intense during the postmenstrual period and less intense during the premenstrual period.[65]

### Physiological Changes Following Training

As already mentioned, there is very little research concerning the female and physical training. However, what little there is supports the idea that, in general, females benefit from training just as males do and that this benefit is brought about through similar physiological changes.[39] This is true for maximal work performance as well as for submaximal efforts.

**Changes and Maximal Work Capacity.**  A summary of the physi-

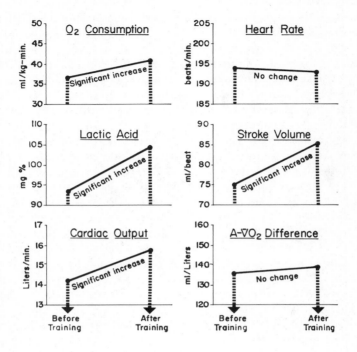

## Maximal Exercise

**Figure 21–17** The physiological changes induced by physical training during maximal work in females are similar to those in males. (Based on data from Kilbom.[39])

**Table 21–2 NORMAL VALUES OF HEMOGLOBIN (Hb), BLOOD VOLUME (B.V.), AND HEART VOLUME (H.V.) FOR TRAINED AND UNTRAINED MEN AND WOMEN**

| SUBJECTS | MEAN AGE (yr.) | Hb (grams) | Hb (gm./kg.) | B.V. (liters) | B.V. (liters/kg.) | H.V. (ml.) | H.V. (ml./kg.) |
|---|---|---|---|---|---|---|---|
| *Untrained* | | | | | | | |
| females | 37.6 | 555 | 8.5 | 4.07 | 62.1 | 560 | 8.5 |
| males | 24.0 | 805 | 11.6 | 5.25 | 75.0 | 785 | 11.2 |
| *Trained* | | | | | | | |
| females | 26.0 | 800 | 12.5 | 5.67 | 88.6 | 790 | 12.3 |
| males | 36.0 | 995 | 13.7 | 6.58 | 90.1 | 930 | 12.7 |

Data from Kjellberg, S., et al.: Acta Physiol. Scand., 19:136, 146, 1949.

ological changes induced by physical training during maximal exercise is shown in Figure 21–17. These changes were obtained on nonathletic normal females (Swedish) between the ages of 19 and 31 years of age.[39] The training programs consisted of riding the bicycle ergometer 2 to 3 days per week for 7 weeks. Each training session lasted 30 minutes and consisted of 6 intervals of bicycling at about 70 per cent capacity for 3 minutes with 2-minute relief intervals. The changes included:

1. A significant increase in the maximal capacity of the oxygen system, i.e., the maximal aerobic power ($max\dot{V}o_2$). Closely related to this change are increases in total blood volume, total hemoglobin, and heart volume (see Table 21–2).
2. A significant increase in the accumulation of lactic acid in the blood following maximal exercise.
3. A significant increase in the maximal cardiac output and stroke volume.

The magnitude of the changes appears comparable with that of males. For example, we have found that the increase in maximal aerobic power is similar in females and males following identical programs of 7 weeks of interval training with 2 training sessions per week.[26, 64] This is shown in Figure 21–18. Notice that the gain in $max\dot{V}o_2$ expressed as ml. $O_2$/kg. body weight per minute (ml./kg.-min.) was the same; however, because the initial $max\dot{V}o_2$ of the females on the average was lower than that of the males (34.8 vs. 44.2 ml./kg.-min., respectively), the per cent increase in $max\dot{V}o_2$, as indicated inside the bars, was higher for the females.

**Changes and Submaximal Exercise Capacity.** As mentioned above, the physiological changes resulting from a physical training pro-

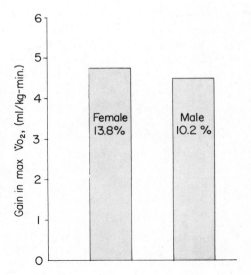

**Figure 21–18** The increase in $max\dot{V}o_2$ is similar in females and males following identical programs of interval training. Expressed in ml. per kilogram of body weight per minute, the gain in $max\dot{V}o_2$ is the same; however, because the initial $max\dot{V}o_2$ of the females was lower, the per cent increase was larger for the females. (Based on data from Fox et al.[24] and Romero.[64])

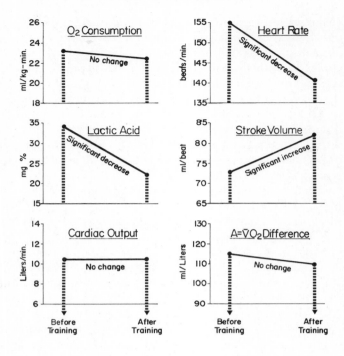

Steady-State Submaximal Exercise

**Figure 21-19** The physiological changes induced by physical training during submaximal work (in this case, 75 watts) in females are similar to those in males. (Based on data from Kilbom.[39])

gram appear to be essentially the same in both sexes with respect to submaximal exercise responses. As illustrated in Figure 21–19, when performing submaximal work of the same intensity before and after physical training (same training program as described above), the most consistent differences are:[39]

1. Little or *no change* in steady-state oxygen consumption ($\dot{V}O_2$).
2. A significant *decrease* in *lactic acid* accumulation following exercise.
3. A significant *decrease* in steady-state *heart rate*.
4. A significant *increase* in steady-state *stroke volume*.
5. Little or *no change* in steady-state *cardiac output* or *arterial-mixed venous blood $O_2$ difference*.

It should be noticed that the above changes are all in the direction of making submaximal exercise a little more submaximal. In other words, training makes submaximal work easier and thus produces less physiological stress. This is an important consideration because most work, including that done during training sessions, is submaximal.

**Biochemical Changes.**    As mentioned on page 272, much new information concerning the effects of physical training at the cellular or biochemical level has only recently been made available. These changes, though determined on male subjects, should be applicable to the female. Also, such changes are presumed to be specific to the type of training program; e.g., so-called sprint training programs mainly bring about anaerobic changes (ATP + PC and L.A. systems), whereas endurance programs mainly bring about aerobic changes (oxygen system). Since the biochemical changes were discussed in detail earlier (see p. 272), only a brief outline will be presented here.

**Anaerobic Changes**

1. An increase in the capacity of the ATP-PC system, by increased stores of ATP and PC in skeletal muscle.
2. An increase in the L.A. system as reflected by:
   a. an increase in glycogen content of skeletal muscle and
   b. an increase in glycolytic enzyme activity of skeletal muscle (mainly in fast twitch fibers).
3. A selective hypertrophy mainly of fast twitch muscle fibers.

**Aerobic Changes**

1. An increase in skeletal muscle myoglobin content.
2. An increase in the capacity of skeletal muscle to utilize (oxidize) carbohydrate and fat (i.e., in the presence of oxygen to break down sugar and fat to $CO_2 + H_2O$ with ATP production). This is facilitated by:
   a. an increase in the number and size of the mitochondria in skeletal muscle fibers and
   b. an increase in the concentration and activity of the enzymes involved in the Krebs cycle, the electron transport system (see p. 16), and the activation, transport, and breakdown of fatty acids.
3. A selective hypertrophy mainly of slow twitch muscle fibers.

**Body Composition Changes.**    The changes in body composition resulting from physical training are similar to those described earlier following weight training. In other words, females can expect (a) a sizable decrease in body fat (e.g., 6 lbs.), (b) a small increase in lean body weight, and (c) a small decrease in total body weight after a physical training program consisting of jogging, walking, and running.[53, 54] These changes, particularly fat loss, are more pronounced for the obese than for the "lean" female. In addition, it is evident that modifications in diet must also be involved in a comprehensive weight loss program in order to obtain an optional weight loss level.

**Other Training Changes.**    With short-term, moderate intensity training programs (7 weeks, 2 to 3 times per week), significant decreases in blood cholesterol, serum iron, and resting as well as exercise systolic and diastolic blood pressures have been noted in young and middle-aged females.[39] The changes in cholesterol and blood pressure

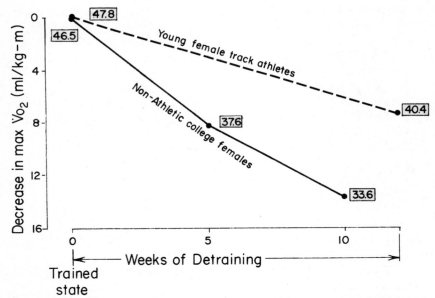

**Figure 21-20** Decrease in max$\dot{V}O_2$ after various weeks of detraining for a group of nonathletic college-age females (solid line) and young female track athletes (dashed line). While max$\dot{V}O_2$ for both groups decreases, the decline for the athletic group is not as great. (Based on data from Drinkwater and Horvath[18] and Fringer and Stull.[27])

are beneficial. However, the lower iron values are not. They probably indicate greater iron consumption through the formation of new red blood cells. Although our own studies[26] do not confirm this finding, such a change should be kept in mind, especially in the training of females who already have large iron losses through menstruation.[68]

**Changes with Detraining.** As you would expect, a period of detraining following a period of training results in a reversal of almost all the changes indicated previously for both men and women. Although this holds true in general for both the nonathlete and athlete, there may be a slower reversal in athletes. For example, Figure 21–20 shows the decrease in maximal aerobic power (max$\dot{V}O_2$) after various weeks of detraining for a group of nonathletic college age females (solid line) and young (15- to 17-year-old) female track athletes (dashed line). Notice that while max$\dot{V}O_2$ for both groups decreases, the decline for the athletic group is not so great. Whether or not this is related to the difference between athletic and nonathletic training programs (the former usually being more difficult) or whether it is due mainly to large individual variations including age cannot be answered with certainty. More research is needed. It should be mentioned here that some *maintenance of training gains* should be possible through a maintenance training program that requires the same intensity of work but less frequent training sessions per week than did the regular training program.[7, 8]

# GYNECOLOGICAL CONSIDERATIONS

There are two important gynecological considerations as they relate to exercise that must be discussed here, namely: (1) menstruation and (2) pregnancy, childbirth, and injuries to the reproductive organs. An excellent review of these factors has been written by Dr. A. J. Ryan.[65]

## Menstruation

There are a number of misconceptions concerning exercise, athletic performance, and menstruation. Let's try to clear up some of them.

**Age of Menarche.**   The age at which menstruation begins (menarche) may be higher in the American female athlete than in her nonathletic counterpart. For example, it has been found that the average age of menarche for a group of nonathletic college age girls was 12.2 years, whereas for a group of college age track and field athletes, it was 13.6 years.[48] On the other hand, age of menarche for Hungarian athletes[20] appears to be little affected by athletic competition, and in Swedish swimmers[5] the age of menarche is slightly earlier than in nonathletes. If American female athletes do indeed mature later than nonathletes, then this would be in opposition to the findings for males. As an example, it is well known that Little League baseball players are much more mature than their nonathletic peers.[30]

There may be a tendency for greater variability of the menstrual cycle later in life for those girls who start sports participation before, rather than after, menarche.[20] Other than this, there does not appear to be a significant relationship between the age of menarche and exercise or sports participation.

**Exercise and Menstrual Disorders.**   Exercise does not appear to significantly affect menstrual disorders. For example, in a group of Swedish elite female swimmers, 81 per cent had regular menstruation at about 4-week intervals. Both the duration of menstruation and the blood loss were no different from that normally found in young girls.[5] Also, out of 557 Hungarian female athletes, 84 per cent showed no change in their menstrual cycles due to sports participation. Of the 16 per cent who did show signs of change, 30 per cent were favorable, whereas 70 per cent were unfavorable. The unfavorable changes were more frequent in the younger than in the older age groups.[20] The menstrual cycle was found to be rhythmic in 61 of 66 female athletes who participated in the 1964 Olympic Games.[73]

#### Table 21–3  PERFORMANCE DURING MENSTRUATION

| | | | PERFORMANCE | | | |
|---|---|---|---|---|---|---|
| CALIBER OF PERFORMANCE | REFER- ENCE | SPORT | *Better* % | *No Change* % | *Poorer* % | *Variable* |
| Olympics | 44 | Track & field | 29 | 63 | 8 | – – |
| Olympics | 34 | Variety | 19 | 43 | 38 | – – |
| Olympics | 73 | Variety | 3 | 37 | 17 | 28 |
| Unspecified | 20 | Variety | 13–15 | 42–48 | 31–38 | – – |
| Unspecified | 4 | Swimming | 4 | 48 | 48 | – – |

Dysmenorrhea (painful menstruation) is probably neither aggravated nor cured by sports participation. If anything, it may be less common in those women who are physically active than in those who are not.[20, 42, 65, 73] However, 30 per cent of a group of competitive swimmers stated that swimming caused pain in the lower part of the abdomen.[5] At any rate, dysmenorrhea, if not severe, should not hinder performance — at least from a physiological standpoint. However, it is recognized that psychological factors also play an important role.

**Performance and Menstruation.**  In Table 21–3 is a compilation of findings obtained from a variety of female athletes relative to their performance during menstruation. In general, these results show that for the majority of young athletes, physical performance itself is not materially affected by the menstrual period. However, there is considerable individual variation. Of those female athletes reporting poorer performances during menstruation, a large percentage were endurance athletes (e.g., tennis players and rowers). Performances for volleyball and basketball players, swimmers and gymnasts were better than for the endurance athletes, but were still below normal. Performances by track and field athletes, especially sprinters, were not affected nearly so much by menstruation as were the performances by other athletes.[20]

There is some evidence that performance levels in the premenstruum (several days before the menstrual flow) and early menstrual period (first two days of the menstrual flow) are characterized by diminished quality and quantity of performance. Improvement is generally shown during the latter part of the cycle, with the best performance occurring in the postmenstrual period, i.e., up to 15 days after the cessation of flow.[20] This kind of information might be useful. For example, training programs should perhaps be most intense during the postmenstrual period with a tapering off during the immediate premenstrual period. It should be mentioned here, however, that these performance variations are not necessarily supported by physiological data. For instance, heart rate and blood pressure do not vary significantly either before or after exercise throughout the menstrual cycle.[61]

**Table 21-4  SURVEY OF OLYMPIC SPORTSWOMEN CONCERNING PARTICIPATION IN TRAINING AND COMPETITION DURING MENSTRUATION**[*]

| | PARTICIPATION (%) | | |
| --- | --- | --- | --- |
| | *Always* | *Sometimes* | *Never* |
| Training | 34 | 54 | 12 |
| Competition | 69 | 31 | |

[*]Data from Zaharieva, E.: J. Sports Med., 5:215–219, 1965.

**Training and Competition During Menstruation.**  Whether or not female athletes should train and/or compete during their menstrual flow (menses) is again an individual matter. As shown in Table 21–4, 69 per cent of the Olympic sportswomen surveyed at the Tokyo games always competed during menstruation. However, only 34 per cent trained during menstruation.[73] Out of the 31 per cent who sometimes competed during menstruation, all competed in major meets, especially those involving team competition. A similar trend was found for a group of young female swimmers; out of 27 girls, only 7 trained during menstruation; whereas all competed if an event coincided with their menstruation.[5]

From a medical standpoint, there is some disagreement regarding sports participation during menses. Some physicians believe that participation (training and competition) should not be allowed in those sports in which there is a greater incidence of menstrual disorders. As mentioned above, these are sports such as skiing, gymnastics, tennis, and rowing. It should be mentioned here that nearly all physicians advise against swimming while menstruating.[5, 20] This is interesting, since it has been determined that during menstruation there is no bacterial contamination of the water in the pool[65] and no sign of any enhanced bacterial infections of the reproductive organs of the swimmers.[5] We agree with Dr. A. J. Ryan that the use of the intravaginal tampon has made it both convenient and comfortable for most female swimmers during menstruation.[65]

From the above information, it is reasonable to suggest that female athletes should be allowed to train and compete in any sport during menstruation provided they know through experience that no unpleasant symptoms will occur and that their performance will not be greatly affected. In addition, it is equally reasonable that no female athlete should be forced or ordered to train or compete during menstruation if, by doing so, she feels uncomfortable and performs very poorly during this time.

## The Breast, Reproductive Organs, Pregnancy, and Childbirth

Earlier, we mentioned that weight training in the female was widely misunderstood by physical educators, coaches, and parents alike. So, too, is the concept of what effects physical activity and athletic participation have on injuries to the breasts and reproductive organs and on pregnancy and childbirth.

**Injuries to the Breast and Reproductive Organs.**    Actually, injuries to the reproductive organs are less frequent and less severe in the female than in the male. The most common injury in the female is to the breasts. For example, repeated blows to the breast can lead to contusions and hemorrhages into the loose fatty tissue. This, in turn, may result in fat necrosis (death of fatty tissue), a condition which clinically is difficult to differentiate from carcinoma or cancer.[42] It is advisable for females to use breast protectors in most sports where there may be body contact.

Injuries to the female genital organs, though rare, are usually confined to minor contusions and lacerations of the external genitalia.[65] The internal organs, i.e., the uterus, fallopian tubes, and ovaries are extremely well protected by virtue of their position deep within the bony pelvis. The only known serious injury to these organs was rupture of the vaginal wall resulting from the forceful entry of water into the vagina following a fall in water skiing.[59] This can result in salpingitis (inflammation of a fallopian tube), pelvic peritonitis (inflammation of the serous membrane lining the pelvis), and vaginal hemorrhage from ruptured uterine arteries. In this regard, it is suggested that rubber wet suits be worn by females when water skiing. Otherwise, participation in physical activities and athletics does not predispose the female to serious or permanent injury to the breasts or reproductive organs.

**Pregnancy and Childbirth.**    There are two schools of thought concerning the effects of athletic participation on pregnancy and childbirth.[20] One opinion is that because of the hypertrophy of the pelvic musculature accompanying sports participation, the muscles become less extensible and thus cause difficulties during labor and delivery.

### Table 21–5    EFFECTS OF ATHLETIC PARTICIPATION ON PREGNANCY AND CHILDBIRTH

| VARIABLE | ATHLETE vs. NONATHLETE |
| --- | --- |
| Complications of pregnancy | fewer |
| Duration of labor | shorter |
| Number of cesarean sections | fewer |
| Tissue ruptures during delivery | fewer |
| Spontaneous abortions | fewer |

The other theory emphasizes the favorable effects on labor and delivery of stronger abdominal muscles. Several surveys have been conducted in order to clarify this issue;[20, 73] the results are given in Table 21–5. In general, it is quite clear that female athletes tend to have fewer pregnancy- and childbirth-related complications than do normal nonathletic women.

There are three more questions relevant to pregnancy and childbirth that need attention: (1) Should female athletes compete during pregnancy? (2) How is performance affected after childbirth? (3) What effects do oral contraceptives (birth control pills) have on performance?

In answering the first question, championship-level athletes have been known to compete during the first 3 or 4 months of their pregnancies and some even up to a few days prior to the onset of labor.[20, 68] Also, the female bronze medalist in swimming in the 1952 Olympics was pregnant.[68] Further, exercise has been shown *not* to constitute a more severe physiological stress during pregnancy than before, provided lifting activities are minimized.[43] Indeed it is recognized that obstetricians frequently prescribe various forms of exercise during pregnancy. This information shows that pregnancy *per se* does not always adversely affect athletic participation or exercise performance. It also shows that the opposite is true; that is, athletics or exercise *per se* do not adversely affect pregnancy. Nevertheless, it must be emphasized that the advisability of participation in athletics and exercise programs during pregnancy should be determined on an individual basis and always with the approval of a physician.

With respect to performance following childbirth, 46 per cent of the female athletes who participated in the Tokyo Olympics (1964) and continued athletic competition after delivery, bettered their results by the end of the first year after childbirth; 31 per cent more bettered their performances between the first and second year after childbirth.[73] Similar results were obtained from other groups of sportswomen.[56, 60] Apparently, childbirth does not limit athletic performance.

Birth control pills have now been used by a great majority of females for a considerable amount of time. Yet the effects of these chemicals (hormones) on athletic performance are still unknown. One study, however, has indicated that females who take birth control pills are less active than those who don't take them.[55] Although much more research is needed to clarify this issue, some medical authorities feel that in light of the already known metabolic effects of these pills, it would be surprising to find no alterations in performance.[68]

## SUMMARY

The purpose of this chapter was to emphasize some of the physiological responses of girls and women to both exercise and physical training.

With respect to world records in track and field and freestyle swimming, performances by men are better than by women. However, the performance of women is closer to men in swimming than in running or jumping. In running, women's performance is closest to men's in sprints, whereas in swimming it is closest in the distance events.

On the average, women are shorter and lighter, with more fatty tissue and less muscle mass than men. This is also true when female athletes are matched against male athletes for any given sport. Some of the performance differences between men and women can thus be explained by these body composition and size differences. This is brought out by the fact that performance and body size differences between prepubescent boys and girls are minimal. It should be remembered that, in swimming, the greater body fat of the female is advantageous.

Females have the same concentrations of muscular ATP + PC as men, but because of their lesser total muscle mass, the total body stores of these phosphagens are smaller. However, female performances in the shortest events (running 100 meters), in which ATP + PC are important sources of energy, are close to the men's performances.

Women tend to have lower levels of lactic acid in their blood following maximal exercise than men. Again, one reason for this is the female's lesser muscle mass. However, the worst events for females compared with those of males, involve performance times of around one minute. This indicates that females may be at a real disadvantage when competing in those events that involve the L.A. system to a large extent.

The maximal aerobic power ($max\dot{V}o_2$) of the female is lower than that of the male. Once again, this difference appears to be due mainly to body size factors, including less hemoglobin and blood volume, and a smaller heart volume. This is illustrated by the fact that differences in $max\dot{V}o_2$ are negligible in young boys and girls, when body size differences are also minimal. When $max\dot{V}o_2$ is expressed relative to body size, particularly with respect to active muscle mass, differences in aerobic power between sexes are small. Performances by females in distance events are relatively good, especially in swimming. In running, since the female must use her total body weight, she is clearly at a disadvantage with respect to $max\dot{V}o_2$.

Although the absolute strength of the female is only about two-thirds that of the male, the quality of the muscle fibers, so far as the ability to exert force is concerned, is independent of sex. With respect to strength development, relative strength increases in the female are the same or even better than in males following similar weight training programs. Also, from a weight training program, females can expect little or no change in total body weight, a decrease in body fat, and an increase in muscle size (hypertrophy). The latter is much less pronounced in the female compared with that of the male, presumably because of lower levels of testosterone. Strength training programs in females do not cause excessive muscular bulk or produce a masculinizing effect.

Present information concerning physical training indicates that training frequency, duration, and intensity have similar effects on both sexes. In other words, comparable physiological and biochemical changes leading to greater working capacity can be produced in both sexes following similar training programs. Minimally, such programs should be 7 to 8 weeks in duration with 2 or 3 training sessions per week and should be intensive enough to raise the heart rate above 70 per cent of the maximum. The only precaution with females is that the training program should be more intense during the postmenstrual period and less intense during the premenstrual period.

Exercise does not appear to have a significant effect on menstrual disorders. In fact, dysmenorrhea is less common in physically active women than in those who are sedentary. For the majority of young athletes, performance is not materially affected by the menstrual period. However, there is some evidence that performance during the premenstruum and early menstrual period is diminished compared with that during the postmenstrual period. Female athletes should be allowed to train and compete in any sport during menstruation, provided that they know that no unpleasant symptoms will occur and that their performance will not be greatly affected.

Serious injuries to either the breasts or external and internal reproductive organs are very rare even in contact sports. Complications of pregnancy and childbirth are fewer in female athletes than in nonathletes. Pregnancy *per se* does not adversely affect athletic participation or exercise performance and *vice versa*. Following childbirth, performance returns or even exceeds previous levels within a year or two. Although the effects of birth control pills on exercise are not known, it is felt that they could alter performance.

## QUESTIONS

1. What track events and freestyle swimming events do women perform best in comparison with men?

2. Describe the differences in body composition and size between men and women and between boys and girls.

3. How are the above differences in body composition and size related to running and swimming performances in adult men and women and in boys and girls?

4. Discuss the similarities and differences between men and women in the physiological capacities of:
   a. the ATP-PC system
   b. the L.A. system
   c. the oxygen system.

5. Relate the similarities and differences in the capacities of the energy systems between the sexes to performance potential.

6. Which muscle groups are strongest and weakest in the female compared with those of the male?

7. Which body size dimensions best relate to muscular strength in both sexes?

8. Compare strength gains and body composition changes in men and women following similar weight training programs.

9. In talking to a group of parents, the question of "muscular bulk" is raised with respect to weight training in females. What would you tell them?

10. What two precautions, different from those for men, should you be aware of when designing and administering physical training programs for women?

11. Design a physical training program for females that would bring about significant physiological change.

12. What physiological and biochemical changes occur in females as a result of physical training?

13. What are the effects of training and athletic participation on menstruation?

14. What are the effects of training and athletic participation on pregnancy and childbirth?

15. What effect does childbirth have on subsequent athletic performance?

# REFERENCES

1. Asmussen, E.: Muscular performance. In Rodahl, K., and Horvath, S.: Muscle As A Tissue. pp. 161–175, New York, McGraw-Hill, 1962.
2. Asmussen, E., and Heebøll-Nielsen, K.: Physical performance and growth in children: influence of sex, age and intelligence. J. Appl. Physiol., 8:371–380, 1956.
3. Åstrand, I.: Aerobic work capacity in men and women with specific reference to age. Acta Physiol. Scand., 49(Suppl.):169, 1960.
4. Åstrand, P. O.: Experimental Studies of Physical Working Capacity in Relation to Sex and Age. Copenhagen, Ejnar Munksgaard, 1952.
5. Åstrand, P. O., Eriksson, B., Nylander, I., Engstrom, L., Karlberg, P., Saltin, B., and Thoren, C.: Girl swimmers. Acta Paediat., Suppl. 147, 1963.
6. Brown, C., and Wilmore, J.: The effects of maximal resistance training on the strength and body composition of women athletes. Med. Sci. Sports, 6:174–177, 1974.

7. Brynteson, P., and Sinning, W.: The effects of training frequencies on the retention of cardiovascular fitness. Med. Sci. Sports, 5:29–33, 1973.
8. Chaloupka, E.: The Physiological Effects of Two Maintenance Programs Following Eight Weeks of Interval Training. Doctoral Dissertation, The Ohio State University, Columbus, Ohio, 1972.
9. Cohen, K.: Metabolic Alterations With Sprint Versus Endurance Interval Training in Females. Doctoral Dissertation, The Ohio State University, Columbus, Ohio, 1975.
10. Cotes, J., Davies, C., Edholm, O., Healy, M., and Tanner, J.: Factors related to the aerobic capacity of 46 British males and females ages 18–28 years. Proc. Roy. Soc. Lond. B., 74:91–114, 1969.
11. Cranford, M.: Blood Lactate Concentrations in Female Athletes Performing Various Types and Intensities of Work. Doctoral Dissertation, The Ohio State University, Columbus, Ohio, 1972.
12. Davies, C., Barnes, C., and Godfrey, S.: Body composition and maximal exercise performance in children. Hum. Biol., 44:195–214, 1972.
13. Diehl, P.: Effects of a Season of Training and Competition on Selected Physiological Parameters in Female College Basketball Players. Doctoral Dissertation, The Ohio State University, Columbus, Ohio, 1974.
14. Döbeln, Von, W.: Human standard and maximal metabolic rate in relation to fat-free body mass. Acta Physiol. Scand., 37(Suppl. 126):1–79, 1956.
15. Drinkwater, B.: Aerobic power in females. J. Phys. Educ. Rec., 46:36–38, 1975.
16. Drinkwater, B.: Physiological responses of women to exercise. In Wilmore, J. (ed.): Exercise and Sport Sciences Reviews. Vol. 1. New York, Academic Press, 1973.
17. Drinkwater, B., and Horvath, S.: Detraining effects on young women. Med. Sci. Sports, 4:91–95, 1972.
18. Drinkwater, B., Horvath, S., and Wells, C.: Aerobic power of females, ages 10 to 68. J. Gerontol., 30(4):385–394, 1975.
19. Edwards, A.: The effects of training at pre-determined heart rate levels for sedentary college women. Med. Sci. Sports, 6:14–19, 1974.
20. Erdelyi, G.: Gynecological survey of female athletes. J. Sports Med., 2:174–179, 1962.
21. Forbes, G: Growth of the lean body mass during childhood and adolescence. J. Pediat., 64:822–827, 1964.
22. Fox, E.: Differences in metabolic alterations with sprint versus endurance interval training. In Howald, H., and Poortmans, J. (eds.): Metabolic Adaptions to Prolonged Physical Exercise. Basel, Switzerland, Birkhäuser Verlag, 1975, pp. 119–126.
23. Fox, E.: Measurement of the maximal alactic (phosphagen) capacity in man. Med. Sci. Sports, 5:66, 1973.
24. Fox, E., Bartels, R., Billings, C., O'Brien, R., Bason, R., and Mathews, D.: Frequency and duration of interval training programs and changes in aerobic power. J. Appl. Physiol., 38(3):481–484, 1975.
25. Fox, E., Billings, C., Bartels, R., Bason, R., and Mathews, D.: Fitness standards for male college students. Int. Z. Angew. Physiol., 31:231–236, 1973.
26. Fox, E., and Cohen, K.: Unpublished data, 1975.
27. Fringer, M., and Stull, G.: Changes in cardiorespiratory parameters during periods of training and detraining in young adult females. Med. Sci. Sports, 6(1):20–25, 1974.
28. Hagerman, F., Fox, E., Connors, M., and Pompei, J.: Metabolic responses of women rowers during ergometric rowing. Med. Sci. Sports, 6(1):87, 1974.
29. Hagerman, F., and Fox, E.: Unpublished data, 1974.
30. Hale, C.: Physiological maturity of little league baseball players. Res. Quart., 27:276–284, 1956.
31. Hanson, J., and Nedde, W.: Long-term physical training effect in sedentary females. J. Appl. Physiol., 37:112–116, 1974.
32. Hettinger, T.: Physiology of Strength. Springfield, Ill., C. C Thomas, 1961.
33. Hultman, E., Bergström, J., and McLennan Anderson, N.: Breakdown and resynthesis of phosphorylcreatine and adenosine triphosphate in connection with muscular work in man. Scand. J. Clin. Lab. Invest., 19:56–66, 1967.
34. Ingman, O.: Menstruation in Finnish top class sportswomen. In Sports Medi-

cine—International Symposium of the Medicine and Physiology of Sports and Athletes. Helsinki. Finnish Association of Sports Medicine, 1952.

35. Ikai, M., and Fukunaga, T.: Calculation of muscle strength per unit cross-sectional area of human muscle by means of ultrasonic measurements. Int. Z. Angew. Physiol., 26:26–32, 1968.

36. James, S., and Brubaker, C.: Biomechanical and neuromuscular aspects of running. In Wilmore, J. (ed.): Exercise and Sport Sciences Reviews. pp. 189–216, vol. 1. New York, Academic Press, 1973.

37. Kalamen, J.: Measurement of Maximum Muscular Power in Man. Doctoral Dissertation, The Ohio State University, Columbus, Ohio, 1968.

38. Katch, F., Michael, E., and Jones, E.: Effects of physical training on the body composition and diet of females. Res. Quart., 40:99–104, 1969.

39. Kilbom, Å.: Physical training in women. Scand. J. Clin. Lab. Invest., 28(Suppl.):119, 1971.

40. Kjellberg, S., Rudhe, U., and Sjöstrand, T.: Increase of the amount of hemoglobin and blood volume in connection with physical training. Acta Physiol. Scand., 19:146–151, 1949.

41. Kjellberg, S., Rudhe, U., and Sjöstrand, T.: The amount of hemoglobin and the blood volume in relation to the pulse rate and cardiac volume during rest. Acta Physiol. Scand., 19:136–145, 1949.

42. Klafs, C., and Lyon, M.: The Female Athlete. St. Louis, C. V. Mosby Co., 1973.

43. Knuttgen, H., and Emerson, K.: Physiological response to pregnancy at rest and during exercise. J. Appl. Physiol., 36:549–553, 1974.

44. Kral, J., and Markalous, E.: The influence of menstruation on sports performance. In Mallwitz, A. (ed.): Proceedings of the 2nd International Congress on Sports Medicine. Leipzig, Thieme, 1937.

45. Lundegren, H.: Changes in skinfold and girth measures of women varsity basketball and field hockey players. Res. Quart., 39:1020–1024, 1968.

46. McNab, R., Conger, P., and Taylor, P.: Differences in maximal and submaximal work capacity in men and women. J. Appl. Physiol., 27:644–648, 1969.

47. Maksud, M., Wiley, R., Hamilton, L., and Lockhart, B.: Maximal $\dot{V}O_2$, ventilation, and heart rate of Olympic speed skating candidates. J. Appl. Physiol., 29:186–190, 1970.

48. Malina, R., Harper, A., Avent, H., and Campbell, D.: Age at menarche in athletes and non-athletes. Med. Sci. Sports, 5(1):11–13, 1973.

49. Malina, R., Harper, A., Avent, H., and Campbell, D.: Physique of female track and field athletes. Med. Sci. Sports, 3:32–38, 1971.

50. Margaria, R., Aghemo, P., and Rovelli, E.: Measurement of muscular power (anaerobic) in man. J. Appl. Physiol., 21:1662–1664, 1966.

51. Mayhew, J., and Gross, P.: Body composition changes in young women with high resistance weight training. Res. Quart., 45:433–440, 1974.

52. Medved, R.: Body height and predisposition for certain sports. J. Sports Med., 6:89–91, 1966.

53. Moody, D., Kollias, J., and Buskirk, E.: The effect of a moderate exercise program on body weight and skinfold thickness in overweight college women. Med. Sci. Sports, 1:75–80, 1969.

54. Moody, D., Wilmore, J., Girandola, R., and Royce, J.: The effects of a jogging program on the body composition of normal and obese high school girls. Med. Sci. Sports, 4(4):210–213, 1972.

55. Morris, N., and Udry, J.: Depression of physical activity by contraceptive pills. Am. J. Obstet. Gynecol., 104:1012–1014, 1969.

56. Noack, H.: Deut. Med. Wochenschr. Cited by Thomas, C. Special problems of the female athlete. In Ryan, A., and Allman, F. (eds.): Sports Medicine, pp. 347–373, New York, Academic Press, 1974.

57. Oyster, N., and Wooten, E.: The influence of selected anthropometric measurements on the ability of college women to perform the 35 yard dash. Med. Sci. Sports, 3:130–134, 1971.

58. Pendergast, D., Wilson, D., diPrampero, P., and Rennie, D.: Energy cost of swimming. Med. Sci. Sports, 6(1):86, 1974.

59. Pfanner, D.: Salpingitis and water-skiing. Med. J. Australia, 1:320, 1964.

60. Pfeiffer, W.: Top performance of women and their influence on constitution, fertility, and proceedings of birth. Rev. Anal. Educ. Phys. Sport, 8:2, 1966.
61. Phillips, M.: Effect of the menstrual cycle on pulse rate and blood pressure before and after exercise. Res. Quart., 39(2):327–333, 1968.
62. Robinson, P.: The Physiological Effects of Chronic Heavy Physical Training on Female Age-Group Swimmers. Doctoral Dissertation, The Ohio State University, Columbus, Ohio, 1974.
63. Robinson, S.: Experimental studies of physical fitness in relation to age. Arbeitsphysiol., 10:251–323, 1938.
64. Romero, L.: The Effects of an Interval Training Program on Selected Physiological Variables in Women. Master's Thesis, The Ohio State University, Columbus, Ohio, 1970.
65. Ryan, A.: Gynecological considerations. J. Phys. Educ. Rec., 46(10):40–44, 1975.
66. Sinning, W.: Body composition, cardiorespiratory function and rule changes in women's basketball. Res. Quart., 44:313–321, 1973.
67. Sinning, W., and Lindberg, G.: Physical characteristics of women gymnasts. Res. Quart., 43:226–234, 1972.
68. Thomas, C.: Special problems of the female athlete. In Ryan, A., and Allman, F. (eds.): Sports Medicine. pp. 347–373, New York, Academic Press, 1974.
69. Thorsen, M.: Body structure and design: Factors in the motor performance of college women. Res. Quart., 35(3)(Suppl.):418–432, 1964.
70. Wilmore, J.: Alterations in strength, body composition and anthropometric measurements consequent to a 10-week weight training program. Med. Sci. Sport., 6:133–138, 1974.
71. Wilmore, J.: Body composition and strength development. J. Phys. Educ. Rec., 46(1):38–40, 1975.
72. Wilmore, J., and Brown, C.: Physiological profiles of women distance runners. Med. Sci. Sports, 6:178–181, 1974.
73. Zaharieva, E.: Survey of sportswomen at the Tokyo Olympics. J. Sports Med., 5:215–219, 1965.

# Chapter 22

# TESTS AND MEASUREMENTS

Tests and measurements constitute a considerable body of knowledge in physical education. At most colleges there is a course requirement in this area for major students; as a consequence we will limit our discussion to tests that are more or less physiologically oriented. For a comprehensive coverage of this broad field there are a number of fine textbooks available (see selected readings).

## BODY WEIGHT

Gain and loss of an athlete's body weight should be of vital concern to the coach. This is a simple measurement to obtain and even though many schools—and trainers of professional teams as well—require weight measurement to be taken religiously, the information frequently is not used to best advantage.

**488**

## Factors Influencing Body Weight Changes

Perhaps we should take a moment to look at the fundamental factors influencing weight changes. First let us consider the question, "Can a person lose *real* weight [fat as distinguished from water loss] through exercise?" The answer is yes, provided that his or her caloric intake remains constant and that the person's physical activity is increased. We should examine this concept in a little more detail. As you will recall, in Chapter 4 we studied caloric values of food (carbohydrates, fats, and proteins). The bomb calorimeter was mentioned as a way in which caloric values of a given quantity and type of food can be determined. If you were to eat 3000 kcal. of food each day and expend 2000 kcal. of energy, your net gain would be 1000 kcal. This would be stored as *fat*. A pound of fat happens to be equivalent to approximately 4000 kcal. At the end of four days you would have gained 1 pound of real weight. Farmers have taken advantage of this fact for years by penning livestock and feeding them well prior to marketing; the result is fat beef or hogs. Conversely if you were to consume 2000 kcal. of food and expend 3000 kcal. of energy doing physical activity, you would lose 1 pound of real weight (fat) in four days.

The simple but extremely important lesson for us to understand is that energy input (food) must equal energy output (physical activity) if real weight is to remain constant. Failure to comprehend and employ this concept with your teams and classes in physical education could possibly jeopardize the health of your students. *Failure to understand the difference between weight loss springing from water loss and real weight loss, and the physiological implications of each, can result in tragedy.*

As an illustration we know of one instance in which a student majoring in physical education, on the second day of football practice in August and in his first coaching position, contributed unknowingly to a heat stroke fatality. A 16-year-old high school student reported to practice considerably overweight. He was instructed to put on a rubberized suit under his football uniform. In somewhat stressful environmental conditions, the boy ran laps and died of heat stroke. The death alone was a tragedy and never should have occurred; a secondary tragedy (and this is a lesson for you) was the reason submitted for placing the uniform over the rubberized suit. The coach thought this would cause the boy to lose *real* weight! We should make it plain at this time there is absolutely no reason whatsoever to wear clothing that makes a person sweat. By this time you should be keenly aware of the fact that sweating is the loss of water and some salt and that these must be replaced to keep the individuals healthy and prepared to compete at their highest level of efficiency. The only physiologically sound reason for use of clothing such as sweat suits during exercise is for warmth. To observe athletes on a hot humid day running about or exercising in a sweat suit with a towel wrapped about the neck (which is quite common), or a person playing handball in a rubberized jacket, clearly demonstrates ignorance on the part of coach or athlete (or both). For success in performance, "keep cool."

Acute exercise of short duration (1 to 2 hours) to be sure results in weight reduction; the weight loss, however, is almost entirely water. To lose real weight (fat) through exercise takes weeks or months. For example, if you were to ride a bicycle at 5 miles per hour for 2 hours you would expend 500 kcal. of energy. It is easy to see that you would have to ride the bike for 16 hours at this speed to lose 1 pound of fat (4,000 kcal./500 kcal. = 8 × 2 hrs = 16 hours). However, if you maintain the same caloric intake (food) and for six months rode the bicycle for 1 hour five times a week, you could lose 7.5 pounds of real weight. Weight can be lost through exercise, but it takes time.

### Recording Body Weight Measurements

The day-to-day weight of a person reflects unerringly metabolic demands, provided, of course, that excessive water loss through exercise or a sweat box is not a factor. An adult's weight may vary from 1 to 3 pounds throughout the day; therefore weight recordings should be made at the same time each day. The person preferably should be weighed nude and dry. Most scales are accurate to a quarter of a pound. Figure 22-1 is an example of a chart that may be used to record day-to-day weight changes.

Youngsters gradually increase in weight to maturity. Therefore, to account for weight changes as a consequence of growth, greater food (energy) intake, as compared to energy expended, must be the rule. Somewhere between the ages of 10 and 16 growth spurts occur. In other words, good nutritional practices must be paramount during this period (see Chapter 18). Severe deviations in weight should result in the person's being referred to a physician. Excessive weight loss among athletes is also indicative of metabolic imbalance and immediate attention must be given these people. As was mentioned in Chapter 17, excessive water loss, reflected in body weight change as a consequence of strenuous activity, should be made up within a 24-hour period. A recent observation showed that the average water loss of the Ohio State University football team during a practice session was just over 5 pounds—the average weight of the team was 206 pounds.[18] The tackles lost 5.7 pounds, while the quarterbacks lost 4.3 pounds. One tackle lost 14 pounds, or 7 quarts of water, which is not compatible with health. This illustrates the importance of supplying adequate water on the field, providing frequent "breaks" so that it may be consumed, and maintaining accurate weight records.

DAYS

| ENVIRONMENTAL CONDITIONS | 1 | | 2 | | | | | |
|---|---|---|---|---|---|---|---|---|
| | AM | PM | AM | PM | | | | |
| DRY BULB | 27°C. | 28°C. | | | | | | |
| WET BULB | 24°C. | 23°C. | | | | | | |
| R. HUMIDITY | 78% | 65% | | | | | | |

| NAME | IN | OUT | IN | OUT | IN | OUT | IN | OUT |
|---|---|---|---|---|---|---|---|---|
| R. BOWERS | 165 | 159 | 160 | | | | | |
| D. CAMAIONE | 150 | 147 | 149 | | | | | |
| D. COSTILL | 170 | 168 | 169 | | | | | |

**Figure 22–1** Daily weight and environmental chart. Note that Bowers lost 6 pounds or a little over 3.5 per cent of his body weight during the morning practice. Because he only regained 1 pound prior to the afternoon session, the coach should postpone or limit his practice. Bowers should have weighed at least 162 pounds prior to the afternoon practice to be within the 2 per cent limit. The other two players are within this limit, allowing unrestricted afternoon practice.

It is a known fact that dehydration by 3 to 4 per cent of the body weight, either by use of a sweatbox or by withholding liquids, will impair performance.[4, 5] To slow down the onset of fatigue and maintain athletes in top shape they must be hydrated adequately.

# TEMPERATURE AND RELATIVE HUMIDITY

We must recognize that *regardless* of heat acclimatization and adequate salt and water intake, environmental conditions may be such as to contribute significantly to heat illness during heavy work. Measurements of temperature and relative humidity will enable the coach and physical educator to make knowledgeable judgments as to the degree of physical activity that should be permitted under any given environmental condition.

*Temperature*

Temperature measurements reflect energy of molecular activity (heat energy). Specifically, a temperature recording measures, with a thermometer, the flow of heat from a place of higher concentration to a place of lower concentration. The thermometers most commonly used contain either mercury or colored alcohol. The scale is arbitrarily set; for example, 0° on the Centigrade scale is the point at which water freezes and 100° C. is the point at which water boils; comparable arbitrary values on the Fahrenheit scale are 32° F. and 212° F., respectively.* As molecular activity increases or decreases, the mercury or alcohol will either expand or contract, respectively. When the height of the column in the thermometer stabilizes, the molecular motions of both the substance being measured and the mercury or alcohol are equal and thus they have the same temperature.

**Dry Bulb Thermometer.** A dry bulb thermometer measures the temperature of the surrounding air. It is the type of thermometer with which you are most familiar.

**Wet Bulb Thermometer.** A wet bulb thermometer consists of a wick wrapped around the bulb of a dry bulb thermometer. The end of the wick is placed in a container of water so that the water creeps up the wick and continually evaporates. The amount of evaporation depends on wind currents and, more importantly, on the amount of water (vapor) in the air. As the water in the wick evaporates, the bulb of the thermometer is cooled just as our skin surface is cooled when sweat evaporates. Therefore a high wet bulb temperature would reflect considerable moisture in the air (little evaporation possible), whereas a low wet bulb temperature shows little moisture (a high rate of evaporation possible). The latter condition is ideal, particularly during strenuous work. As you have already learned, when a large amount of evaporation takes place, there can be adequate cooling of the body.

**Black Bulb Thermometer.** The black bulb thermometer measures radiant energy or solar radiation by a thermometer that is placed in a black globe. The purpose of the black globe is twofold: (1) its black color will absorb radiant energy as contrasted to a shiny or lightly colored substance; and (2) the globe protects the bulb of the thermometer from air movement. You may make this unit as depicted in Figure 22–2 by using a copper toilet float painted black and a dry bulb thermometer. To assemble, drill a hole in the globe (toilet float), place the dry bulb thermometer through a rubber cork, force this into the hole of the globe, and seal—epoxy glue may be used.

---

*Formulas for converting the two scales: $°F. = \frac{9}{5}°C. + 32$; or $°C. = (°F. - 32)\frac{5}{9}$.

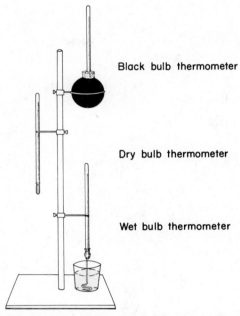

Black bulb thermometer

Dry bulb thermometer

Wet bulb thermometer

**Figure 22-2** An instrument that simultaneously measures solar radiation (black bulb or globe thermometer); air temperature (dry bulb); and relative humidity computed via wet bulb thermometer in conjunction with the dry bulb thermometer. A combination of the three temperatures recorded is used in computing the wet bulb, globe temperature (WBGT) index.

### Relative Humidity

From the standpoint of the earth's weather, water is the most important constituent of the atmosphere. It has been estimated that if all the water in the atmosphere were condensed, it would completely cover the earth with 1 inch of rainfall. Water in the atmosphere exists in three forms: (1) as an invisible gaseous vapor; (2) as rain; and (3) as hail, sleet or snow. The amount of water vapor in the air (humidity) is our immediate concern, for the ability to evaporate sweat during activity is directly related to the amount of water vapor present. Usually the humidity in the air is expressed as a percentage of the amount of moisture the air can maximally hold at any given temperature. This ratio is called *relative humidity*.

$$\text{Relative Humidity} = \frac{\text{Water vapor present}}{\text{Water vapor present when saturated}} \times 100$$

If the relative humidity is 100 per cent (air is maximally saturated with water vapor) the body cannot lose heat through evaporative cooling.

Our present purpose will be to understand how relative humidity can be measured. There are two ways in which this can be done; the most accurate method will be discussed first, as it will lend clarity to the fundamental principles underlying the concept of humidity and its measurement.

**Vapor Pressure.**    The *amount* of vapor in the atmosphere varies considerably in different regions of the country. Around large bodies of water and areas of heavy vegetation there will be more vapor present than in desert regions. The maximal amount of vapor the air can hold at any given period is dependent upon the *vapor pressure* at that time. Vapor pressure is dependent upon temperature alone. That is to say, a liquid at any given temperature is in equilibrium with its own vapor. As many molecules of water are escaping into the surrounding air from the liquid surface as are returning to the liquid. If you were to increase the temperature of the liquid, more molecules would escape, thereby increasing vapor pressure. By the same token decreasing temperature would diminish the number of molecules, hence lessening the vapor pressure. Therefore vapor pressure is the pressure at which a liquid and its vapor can exist in equilibrium at any given temperature (see Table 22–1).

How may we use this information to calculate relative humidity? The method is comparatively simple and may be easily demonstrated. First obtain a metallic vessel, such as a quart aluminum or steel pitcher, containing ice water. Place a thermometer in with the ice and water. At the moment moisture (dew) appears on the outside of the vessel, read the thermometer. The temperature reading is called the *dew point* for it is at this temperature that the air would be completely saturated with vapor. Refer to Table 22–1 and obtain the vapor pressure at this temperature. Read the dry bulb thermometer for the temperature of the ambient air and refer again to Table 22–1 to obtain the vapor pressure

### Table 22–1   VAPOR PRESSURE OF WATER (ABSOLUTE)*

| TEMPERATURE, °C. | VAPOR PRESSURE, MM. OF HG. | TEMPERATURE, °F. |
|:---:|:---:|:---:|
| 5 | 6.51 | 41 |
| 10 | 8.94 | 50 |
| 15 | 12.67 | 59 |
| 20 | 17.50 | 68 |
| 40 | 55.10 | 104 |
| 60 | 149.00 | 140 |

*A liquid at any given temperature is in equilibrium with its own vapor. The pressure corresponding to this concentration of gas molecules is called the vapor pressure of the liquid at the given temperature.

at the particular temperature. The ratio of these two pressures times 100 is the most accurate way in which to determine relative humidity.

$$RH = \frac{\text{Partial pressure of water vapor}}{\text{Vapor pressure at same temperature}} \times 100$$

Given:
    Dew Point = 10° C.
    Dry Bulb = 20° C.

From Table 22–1:
    10° C. = 8.94 mm Hg vapor pressure
    20° C. = 17.5 mm Hg vapor pressure
RH = 8.94/17.5 × 100 = 51 per cent

Your attention is directed to the numerator of our ratio, which reads "*Partial* pressure of water vapor." The reason for this is because at our ambient air temperature of 20° C., this is not the actual vapor pressure but only the partial vapor pressure at this temperature.

Certainly the partial pressure of water vapor cannot be greater than its vapor pressure at any given temperature. When the partial pressure and vapor pressure are equal, the air is saturated and thus the relative humidity would equal 100 per cent.

**Sling Psychrometer.**   A simplified method sufficiently accurate for determining environmental conditions on the athletic field is to use the sling psychrometer (Fig. 22–3). The sling psychrometer contains a wet bulb and a dry bulb thermometer. The instrument is used by dipping the wick of the wet bulb in distilled water and slinging (spinning by handle) the unit for 1.5 minutes. Readings can then be taken and, with the data in Table 22–2, relative humidity computed.

**Wet Bulb, Globe Temperature (WBGT) Index.**   As you could well imagine, the problem of heat illness among our armed forces has been of considerable concern to the military.[16] C. Yaglou of the Harvard University School of Public Health went to work on this problem and found an excellent method of regulating activity in relation to environmental conditions. The information that follows is particularly applicable to unconditioned basic trainees and such military personnel undergoing strenuous physical activity. Remember, the following data and information apply to those men wearing olive green military fatigue uniforms. The standards suggested would not be applicable to men working in full football uniforms as the padding would diminish evaporative cooling more than would be expected from the wearing of army fatigues. Furthermore, the weight of the uniform (about 13 pounds) causes an added work load.

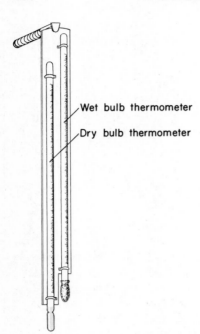

Wet bulb thermometer

Dry bulb thermometer

**Figure 22–3**  Sling psychrometer: an instrument composed of a dry bulb and a wet bulb thermometer, used to measure relative humidity.

The unit for measuring the WBGT index includes a black globe assembly for determining radiant heat; a wet bulb assembly for measuring temperature as affected by wind and humidity; and a dry bulb thermometer for measuring air temperature. Figure 22–2 contains the complete assembly, which, with the assistance of the high school chemistry or physics department, can be constructed for less than $10.

The kit is placed in the open, away from trees, buildings, or other objects that cast shadows on the kit or might influence air movement. The unit should remain in position for at least 30 minutes before readings are made, then all three temperature readings are recorded. To compute the WBGT for green shades of fatigue uniforms, the following formula is employed:

WBGT (° F.) 0.7 × wet bulb temperature
      0.2 × black globe temperature (radiant energy)
      0.1 × dry bulb temperature

Wet bulb =   78° F. × 0.7 = 54.6° F.
Black globe = 130° F. × 0.2 = 26.0
Dry bulb = 104° F. × 0.1 = 10.4
               WBGT = 91.0° F.

**Table 22-2   RELATIVE HUMIDITY FROM WET AND DRY BULB THERMOMETERS (CENTIGRADE SCALE) (DRY BULB, t°C.; WET BULB, t'C.)***

| $\dfrac{t-t'}{t}$ | 1.0 | 2.0 | 3.0 | 4.0 | 5.0 | 6.0 | 7.0 | 8.0 | 9.0 | 10.0 | 11.0 | 12.0 | 13.0 | 14.0 | 15.0 |
|---|---|---|---|---|---|---|---|---|---|---|---|---|---|---|---|
| 16 | 90 | 81 | 71 | 63 | 54 | 46 | 38 | 30 | 23 | 15 | 8 | | | | |
| 17 | 90 | 81 | 72 | 64 | 55 | 47 | 40 | 32 | 25 | 18 | 11 | | | | |
| 18 | 91 | 82 | 73 | 65 | 57 | 49 | 41 | 34 | 27 | 20 | 14 | 7 | | | |
| 19 | 91 | 82 | 74 | 65 | 58 | 50 | 43 | 36 | 29 | 22 | 16 | 10 | | | |
| 20 | 91 | 83 | 74 | 66 | 59 | 51 | 44 | 37 | 31 | 24 | 18 | 12 | 6 | | |
| 21 | 91 | 83 | 75 | 67 | 60 | 53 | 46 | 39 | 32 | 26 | 20 | 14 | 9 | | |
| 22 | 92 | 83 | 76 | 68 | 61 | 54 | 47 | 40 | 34 | 28 | 22 | 17 | 11 | 6 | |
| 23 | 92 | 84 | 76 | 69 | 62 | 55 | 48 | 42 | 36 | 30 | 24 | 19 | 13 | 8 | |
| 24 | 92 | 84 | 77 | 69 | 62 | 56 | 49 | 43 | 37 | 31 | 26 | 20 | 15 | 10 | 5 |
| 25 | 92 | 84 | 77 | 70 | 63 | 57 | 50 | 44 | 39 | 33 | 28 | 22 | 17 | 12 | 8 |
| 26 | 92 | 85 | 78 | 71 | 64 | 58 | 51 | 46 | 40 | 34 | 29 | 24 | 19 | 14 | 10 |
| 27 | 92 | 85 | 78 | 71 | 65 | 58 | 52 | 47 | 41 | 36 | 31 | 26 | 21 | 16 | 12 |
| 28 | 93 | 85 | 78 | 72 | 65 | 59 | 53 | 48 | 42 | 37 | 32 | 27 | 22 | 18 | 13 |
| 29 | 93 | 86 | 79 | 72 | 66 | 60 | 54 | 49 | 43 | 38 | 33 | 28 | 24 | 19 | 15 |
| 30 | 93 | 86 | 79 | 73 | 67 | 61 | 55 | 50 | 44 | 39 | 35 | 30 | 25 | 21 | 17 |
| 31 | 93 | 86 | 80 | 73 | 67 | 61 | 56 | 51 | 45 | 40 | 36 | 31 | 27 | 22 | 18 |
| 32 | 93 | 86 | 80 | 74 | 68 | 62 | 57 | 51 | 46 | 41 | 37 | 32 | 28 | 24 | 20 |
| 33 | 93 | 87 | 80 | 74 | 68 | 63 | 57 | 52 | 47 | 42 | 38 | 33 | 29 | 25 | 21 |
| 34 | 93 | 87 | 81 | 75 | 69 | 63 | 58 | 53 | 48 | 43 | 39 | 35 | 30 | 26 | 23 |
| 35 | 94 | 87 | 81 | 75 | 69 | 64 | 59 | 54 | 49 | 44 | 40 | 36 | 32 | 28 | 24 |
| 36 | 94 | 87 | 81 | 75 | 70 | 64 | 59 | 54 | 50 | 45 | 41 | 37 | 33 | 29 | 25 |
| 37 | 94 | 87 | 82 | 76 | 70 | 65 | 60 | 55 | 51 | 46 | 42 | 38 | 34 | 30 | 26 |
| 38 | 94 | 88 | 82 | 76 | 71 | 66 | 61 | 56 | 51 | 47 | 43 | 39 | 35 | 31 | 27 |
| 39 | 94 | 88 | 82 | 77 | 71 | 66 | 61 | 57 | 52 | 48 | 43 | 39 | 36 | 32 | 28 |
| 40 | 94 | 88 | 82 | 77 | 72 | 67 | 62 | 57 | 53 | 48 | 44 | 40 | 36 | 33 | 29 |

Example: (t) Dry Bulb = 27°

(t') Wet Bulb = 20°

$t - t' = 7°$

R.H. = 52 per cent

*Condensed from U.S. Weather Bureau Bulletin No. 1071.

The following interpretation of the WBGT index is suggested for troops wearing fatigue uniforms. When the temperature exceeds 80° F. discretion should be used in planning heavy exercise for unconditioned personnel. At 85° F. such strenuous exercise as marching at standard cadence should be suspended for unconditioned personnel during their first two weeks of training, and after this period should continue only on a reduced scale; outdoor classes in the sun should be avoided. At 88° F. all physical training should be halted; but trained personnel, after acclimatization, can carry on limited activity up to 90° F. WBGT for periods not exceeding 6 hours a day.

It should be clear to us that ideal appraisal of environmental conditions requires dry, wet, and black bulb temperature measurements. However, considerable knowledge about the environment can be gained from either wet bulb temperature alone or a combination of wet and dry bulb readings. For example, the wet bulb temperature alone has been used to suggest guidelines for environmental heat loads while wearing heavy protective clothing such as a football uniform.[18] Also, for an example of both wet and dry bulb readings, refer to Figure 17–1, page 363. The dry bulb temperature of 64° F. is a comfortable temperature—who would expect a heat stroke casualty on such a day? However note that the humidity was 100 per cent, indicating that absolutely no heat could be lost through evaporative cooling; as a consequence, another boy lost his life.

Figure 17–8 (p. 383) represents a weather guide using the combination of RH and dry bulb temperature. This guide will help you to make valid judgments regarding the existing environmental conditions, strenuosity of football practice, and whether or not the boys should practice in full uniform.

## POWER TESTS

The ability to jump, sprint, put the shot, throw the javelin, or perform fast starts as would be required of backs and linemen are a few examples of athlete's converting energy to power. The ability to develop considerable power is a prime factor in athletic success. Power is performance of work expressed per unit of time. The term *explosive power* has been associated with this anaerobic metabolism and the tests to measure it. However, "explosive" itself connotes power, leaving us to consider the term "explosive power" as redundant. Consequently, we will simply use the term *power test* to reflect such measurement.

As you may recall from Chapter 2, the development of power is related to muscular strength and especially to the amount and rate of utilization of the ATP-PC system. Therefore the tests that follow reflect primarily one's depth and ability to employ the ATP-PC system.

## Sargent Jump

Measuring the difference between a person's standing reach and the height to which he or she can jump and touch (similar to basketball tipoff) has erroneously been used as a power test of the legs. If body weight and the speed in performing the jump are not a part of the measurement, one can't regard this test as a true measure of power. Certainly a 150-pound boy who jumps vertically 2 feet produces less power than the 160-pound boy who jumps 2 feet.

**The Lewis Nomogram.**    In order to make the jump reach test more valid as a measure of leg power, the Lewis nomogram (Fig. 22–4), can be used as follows:

$$\text{Body weight} = 180 \text{ pounds}$$
$$\text{Distance jumped} = \phantom{0}24 \text{ inches}$$

Lay a straight-edge across the nomogram connecting 180 pounds (right column) and 24 inches (left column). Read, from the center column, foot-pounds per second (ft-lb/sec)* as the power output. Note also that the measurements may be either in English or in metric units. In the latter units the body weight in our example would be 82 kg. (1 lb = 0.454 kg), the distance jumped would be equal to 0.61 meters (39.37 in = 1 m), and the power output would be 142 kilogram-meters/second (kg.-m/sec).**

## Margaria-Kalamen Power Test (Fig. 22–5)

R. Margaria[13] suggested an excellent test of power, which has been modified by J. Kalamen,[11] The modification results in greater power output than in Margaria's original test. The subjects stand 6 meters in front of a staircase. At their pleasure they run up the stairs as rapidly as possible, taking three at a time. A switchmat is placed on the third and ninth stair. (An average stair is about 174 mm. high.) A clock starts as the person steps on the first switchmat (on the third step) and stops as he or she steps on the second (on the ninth step). Time is recorded to a hundredth of a second. It is best to administer the test several

---

*1025 ft-lb/sec = 1.8 horsepower (HP). To convert ft-lb/sec to HP, multiply by 0.0018.

**To convert kg.-m/sec to HP multiply by 0.013. For more conversions see Table 4–2, page 47.

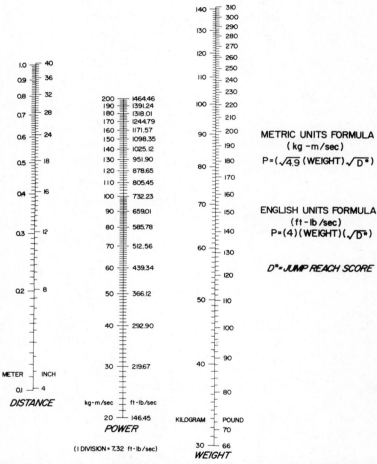

**Figure 22–4**   The Lewis Nomogram. A person's power output can be determined by knowing the score on the jump reach and the body weight. See text for example. (Courtesy, Office of Naval Research.)

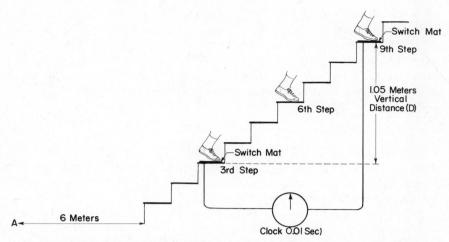

**Figure 22–5**   Margaria-Kalamen power test. Subject commences at point *A* and runs as rapidly as he can up the flight of stairs, taking them three at a time. The time it takes him to traverse the distance between stair 3 and stair 9 is recorded in 0.01 second. The power generated is a product of the subject's weight and the vertical distance *(D)*, divided by the time. An example appears in the text.

times, recording the best score. Power output is computed using the formula:

$$P = \frac{W \times D}{t}$$

in which P = Power
      W = Weight of person
      D = Vertical height between first and last test stairs
      t = Time from first to last test stairs

The test is scored as follows:

W = 75 kg.
D = 1.05 meters
t = 0.49 second
$$P = \frac{75 \times 1.05}{0.49} = 161 \text{ kg.-meters per sec.}$$
P = 161 kg.-meters per sec.

Kalamen,[11] using 23 nonathlete males in service classes at the Ohio State University, obtained a mean power output of 168.5 kg.-meters per second, with a standard deviation of 31. Some standards based on these data, plus those of Margaria et al.,[13] are listed in Table 22–3.

When evaluating seven sprinters from the Ohio State University track team he obtained a mean power output of 200 kg.-meters per second, with a standard deviation of 16. Furthermore, with this test, we have recorded power outputs of professional football players (backs) ranging between 240 and 271 kg.-m/sec.[9] The greater power outputs of these trained athletes contribute evidence of the validity of this test.

## 50-Yard Dash Test

Kalamen[11] obtained a high coefficient of relationship between the time of running the 50-yard dash with a 15-yard running start and the Margaria-Kalamen Power test ($r = 0.974$). This indicates that one could probably substitute the 50-yard dash test and get more or less the same results, eliminating expensive equipment. However, Kalamen obtained an insignificant correlation between the power test and the Sargent Jump Test when merely height of jump was recorded. As mentioned earlier, it is doubtful whether one should use the Sargent Jump Test as a test of power unless speed and weight of the subject are part of the

### Table 22–3  GUIDELINES FOR THE MARGARIA-KALAMEN TEST (ATP-PC SYSTEM)*

| CLASSIFI-CATION | MEN Age Groups (years) | | | | |
|---|---|---|---|---|---|
| | **15–20** | **20–30** | **30–40** | **40–50** | **Over 50** |
| Poor | Under 113** | Under 106** | Under 85** | Under 65** | Under 50** |
| Fair | 113–149 | 106–139 | 85–111 | 65–84 | 50–65 |
| Average | 150–187 | 140–175 | 112–140 | 85–105 | 66–82 |
| Good | 188–224 | 176–210 | 141–168 | 106–125 | 83–98 |
| Excellent | Over 224 | Over 210 | Over 168 | Over 125 | Over 98 |

| CLASSIFI-CATION | WOMEN Age Groups (years) | | | | |
|---|---|---|---|---|---|
| | **15–20** | **20–30** | **30–40** | **40–50** | **Over 50** |
| Poor | Under 92** | Under 85** | Under 65** | Under 50** | Under 38** |
| Fair | 92–120 | 85–111 | 65–84 | 50–65 | 38–48 |
| Average | 121–151 | 112–140 | 85–105 | 66–82 | 49–61 |
| Good | 152–182 | 141–168 | 106–125 | 83–98 | 62–75 |
| Excellent | Over 182 | Over 168 | Over 125 | Over 98 | Over 75 |

*Based on data from Kalamen, J.: Measurement of Maximum Muscular Power in Man. Doctoral Dissertation, The Ohio State University, 1968; and from Margaria, R., Aghemo, P., and Rovelli, E.: Measurement of muscular power (anaerobic) in man. J. Appl. Physiol. 21:1662–1664, 1966.

**kg.-m/sec.

measurement (Lewis nomogram). If timing equipment is available, the Margaria-Kalamen test is superior; if not, the 50-yard dash from a running start may be used.

# TESTS OF MAXIMAL AEROBIC POWER

As was mentioned in Chapter 2, the maximal oxygen consumption test is perhaps the most valid means of determining a person's maximal aerobic power (max $\dot{V}o_2$). It is the first choice in measuring to assess a person's cardiorespiratory fitness.

Maximal oxygen consumption is dependent upon age, sex, and body size and/or composition. These relationships plus average values for different age groups of men and women were given in the previous chapter (see pp. 457–459). Most individuals will reach their maximal aerobic power as a result of growth around 15 to 17 years of age. For the majority of the population, a gradual decline begins around age 30. An average max $\dot{V}o_2$ as measured on the bicycle ergometer, for college men is between 3.0 and 3.5 liters per minute or 41 to 48 ml per kg. per minute.[7] For college women it is between 2.0 and 2.5 liters per minute or 35 to 43 ml per kg. per minute.[1]

## Methods of Directly Assessing Aerobic Power

There are three general methods of appraising maximal oxygen consumption: (1) treadmill (running and walking); (2) cycling (bicycle ergometer); and (3) stepping (step bench). Values of max $\dot{V}o_2$ measured on an inclined treadmill are usually 5 to 15 per cent higher than those obtained on either the bicycle or the step bench.[10, 15] The reason for this might be related to differences in the size of the active muscle mass, this being largest during uphill treadmill running. Another factor might be that cycling leads to localized fatigue, since it mainly involves only the large muscles of the thigh. Such fatigue would occur prior to maximally stressing the circulatory and respiratory systems, thus leading to a smaller max $\dot{V}o_2$.

**Treadmill Methods.** The following are several reliable test procedures that are known to measure a person's max $\dot{V}o_2$.

1. *Mitchell, Sproule, Chapman Method.*[17] In this test the subject walks for 10 minutes at 3 miles per hour (4.8 km. per hour) on a 10 per cent grade. This is a preliminary light exercise period (warm-up) and allows the individual to become adjusted to the equipment. Following a 10-minute rest period, the subject begins running at 6 miles per hour

(9.7 km. per hour) at a 0 per cent grade for 2.5 minutes. The expired gas is collected for purposes of analysis from minute 1:30 to 2:30 of the run. Following the first bout, a 10-minute rest period is allowed. For the next run the speed remains constant, but the grade is elevated to 2.5 per cent. The procedure is repeated until maximal values are obtained.

2. *Saltin-Åstrand Method.*[19]   The subject first performs a 5-minute submaximal bicycle ergometer ride; heart rate and oxygen consumption are measured during the last minute. These data are then used to predict the subject's max $\dot{V}O_2$. This is done by use of a nomogram (see Fig. 22–7, p. 508). From Table 22–4, the predicted max $\dot{V}O_2$ is used to determine the appropriate initial speed and inclination of the treadmill, so that the all-out run will last between 3 and 7 minutes. For example, suppose a subject's predicted max $\dot{V}O_2$ were 45 ml/kg.-min. The starting speed and inclination of the treadmill would be 7.8 miles per hour (12.5 km. per hour) and 5.2 per cent grade, respectively (Table 22–4). Prior to the run, each subject walks for 10 minutes at a workload approximating 50 per cent of his or her predetermined starting load. During the all-out run, the treadmill is elevated 2.7 per cent every 3 minutes until the subject is exhausted. Consecutive one-minute gas collections are started when the heart rate reaches 175 beats per minute.

3. *The Ohio State Method.*[8]   The O.S.U. test is similar to the Saltin-Åstrand method. It includes a 5-minute warm-up walk at 3.5 miles per hour (5.6 km. per hour) on a 10 per cent grade followed by a 4 to 8 minute run to exhaustion. Running speeds usually vary between 6.0 and 9.3 miles per hour (9.6 and 15.0 km. per hour) depending on the anticipated fitness level of the subject. Generally, for untrained college females, the speed is 6.0 miles per hour, for untrained college males, 7.8 miles per hour, and for athletes, 9.3 or 10 miles per hour. In all cases, the treadmill inclination is set initially at a 2 per cent grade and elevated 2 per cent every 2 minutes thereafter. The subject runs to

### Table 22–4   STARTING WORKLOAD USED FOR THE SALTIN-ÅSTRAND MAXIMAL AEROBIC POWER TEST*

| PREDICTED MAX $\dot{V}O_2$, ml/kg.-min. | MEN | | | WOMEN | | |
| --- | --- | --- | --- | --- | --- | --- |
| | *Speed* mi./hr. | km./hr. | *Grade* per cent | *Speed* mi./hr. | km./hr. | *Grade* per cent |
| below 40 | 6.2 | 10.0 | 5.2 | 6.2 | 10.0 | 2.7 |
| 40–54 | 7.8 | 12.5 | 5.2 | 6.2 | 10.0 | 5.2 |
| 55–75 | 9.3 | 15.0 | 5.2 | 7.8 | 12.5 | 5.2 |
| above 75 | 10.9 | 17.5 | 5.2 | | | |

*Modified from Saltin and Åstrand[19] and Åstrand and Rodahl.[2]

exhaustion. Consecutive one-minute gas collections are started when the heart rate reaches 175 beats per minute.

It should be noted that the manner in which the workload can be increased in these tests is either discontinuous, as in the Mitchell, Sproule, Chapman test, or continuous as in the other two tests. Since there are no differences in the max $\dot{V}o_2$ value obtained in the two types of loading,[12, 14] either method can be used. However, the discontinuous method requires more time and in fact often requires several separate trips to the laboratory to complete. In this respect the continuous method is preferable.

**Bicycle Methods.**  Although the treadmill test generally yields higher max $\dot{V}o_2$ values, the bicycle has many advantages as an exercise ergometer: a) it is relatively inexpensive; b) it is, as of the last few years in this country, a familiar exercise for many people and thus less apt to cause apprehension; c) like the treadmill, its results are reproducible; and d) it is portable and therefore usable in field studies.

As with the treadmill test, the bicycle test can consist of either continuous or discontinuous loading; the results are the same.[14] Following are several protocols.

1. *Discontinuous Loading.*  The pedal speed should be 60 revolutions per minute. This frequency elicits the highest max $\dot{V}o_2$ compared to 50, 70, and 80 revolutions per minute.[10] In our laboratory,[6, 7] the subjects perform a series of 5-minute rides with 10-minute rest periods between rides. The initial workload is light—for men, between 125 and 150 watts (750 and 900 kg.-meters per min.)* and for women, between 75 and 100 watts. The workloads in subsequent rides are made progressively heavier according to the subjects' heart rate response to the preceding ride; the lower the heart rate response, the higher the next load (e.g., 50 watts higher. Usually the load increments for both men and women are 20 to 30 watts). The subjects are considered exhausted (usually after 5 or 6 rides) when they can no longer ride for at least 3 minutes at a workload 10 to 15 watts higher than their previous ride. Gas collections can be made during the last minute of each ride.

2. *Continuous Loading.*[14]  The subjects again pedal at 60 revolutions per minute. With a starting load of 150 to 180 watts, the load is increased by 30 watts every 2 minutes until the subject can no longer continue or until the pedal speed drops below 50 revolutions per minute. Gas collections can be made during the last minute of each work increment after the heart rate reaches 175 beats per minute.

In summary, the following can be said concerning direct measurement of maximal oxygen consumption:

   (a) The treadmill elicits higher max$\dot{V}o_2$ values than does the bicycle.

---

*To convert watts to kg.-meters per min., multiply by 6.

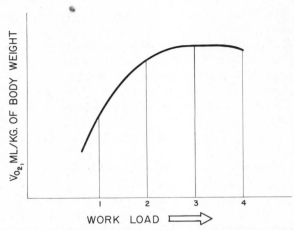

**Figure 22–6** Determining the point at which maximal aerobic capacity has been reached. The primary criterion for such a determination depends upon the individual's inability to consume additional oxygen when the work load is increased. Note also that maximal working capacity may exceed the work load at which maximal oxygen consumption is reached.

    (b) Loading can be either continuous or discontinuous, since both methods yield the same results.
    (c) The length of time for exhaustion should be between 3 and 10 minutes.
    (d) A warm-up bout of exercise is useful psychologically and physiologically and for adjustment to the equipment.

**Criteria for Max $\dot{V}O_2$ Attainment.** How does one know when a subject has reached his or her maximum aerobic power? Figure 22–6 contains the plots for each of the increasing workloads in milliliters per kilogram of body weight per minute. Note that even though the workload was increased, $\dot{V}O_2$ remained constant. As a matter of fact, at the fourth and most severe workload, $\dot{V}O_2$ decreased slightly. The main criterion for determining that maximal aerobic power has been attained, therefore, is a leveling or decrease in $\dot{V}O_2$ with increasing workload. Other criteria are a) volitional exhaustion; b) heart rate in excess of 190 beats per minute; c) a respiratory exchange ratio (R) greater than unity; and d) a blood lactic acid level above 100 mg. per cent.

### Methods of Indirectly Assessing Aerobic Power

    As you may have concluded from the preceding descriptions, direct assessment of max $\dot{V}O_2$ is limited in that the test is difficult, exhausting, and often hazardous to perform regardless of the type of ergometer used. For this reason, several methods for predicting max $\dot{V}O_2$ from submaximal exercise data have been developed. Following are two such methods.

**Åstrand-Åstrand Nomogram.**[1, 3]    This nomogram, shown in Figure 22–7, was the first to be developed for prediction of max $\dot{V}O_2$ from submaximal data. It was originally constructed from data gathered on young (18 to 30 years old), healthy, physical-education students, and it is based on the ideas that 1) heart rate during submaximal cycling and walking increases approximately linearly (in a straight line) with oxygen uptake, and 2) the maximal heart rate of the subjects during this type of maximal work is about 195 beats per minute. Also, the nomogram was said to be more accurate if heart rates between 125 and 170 beats per minute were used to make the predictions of max $\dot{V}O_2$.

Later the nomogram was revised so that now it can be used for male and female subjects 15 years of age or older, and in addition to the treadmill and bicycle, predictions can be made from submaximal heart rate and oxygen consumption data obtained during bench stepping. For subjects older than 25 years, age correction factors must be used; these are given in Table 22–5. The reason for this is that although heart rate and oxygen consumption during submaximal work do not vary greatly with age, max $\dot{V}O_2$ declines with age. Thus, max $\dot{V}O_2$ is overestimated in older subjects.

Here is how to use the nomogram:

1. A workload, either cycling, walking, or running, is selected that will elicit a heart rate of between 125 and 170 beats per minute. If bench stepping is preferred, the bench height should be 33 cm. (13 inches) for females and 40 cm. (16 inches) for males. The stepping frequency should be 30 steps per minute. In all cases, one-minute determinations of heart rate and oxygen consumption are made at some time between minutes 5 and 10 of the work.

2. The heart rate and oxygen consumption data are then applied to the nomogram shown in Figure 22–7 in order to predict the max $\dot{V}O_2$. This is done by connecting, with a straight-edge, the point on the "$\dot{V}O_2$" scale with the corresponding point on the "pulse" (heart) rate scale and the predicted max $\dot{V}O_2$ read from the middle scale. If it is not possible to directly measure the oxygen consumption during stepping or cycling, it can be estimated by reading horizontally from the "body weight" scale (stepping) or "workload" scale (cycling) to the "$\dot{V}O_2$" scale, and then the connections are made from there. Several examples are given in the legend to Figure 22–7.

3. If the subject is older than 25 years, the appropriate age correction factor (given in Table 22–5) must be applied to the predicted max $\dot{V}O_2$ value obtained in the above manner. For example, if the woman whose max $\dot{V}O_2$ was predicted to be 2.4 liters per minute (see legend of Fig. 22–7), were 45 years old, her age-corrected max $\dot{V}O_2$ would be $2.4 \times 0.78 = 1.87$ liters per minute.

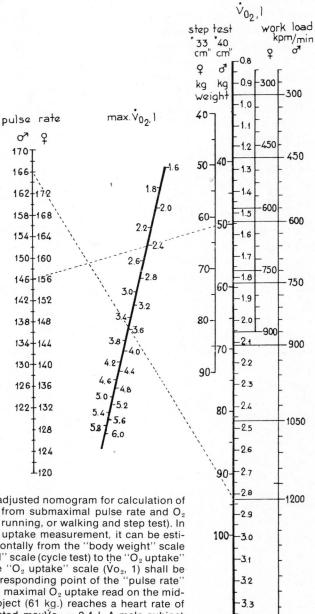

**Figure 22–7** The adjusted nomogram for calculation of aerobic work capacity from submaximal pulse rate and $O_2$ uptake values (cycling, running, or walking and step test). In tests without direct $O_2$ uptake measurement, it can be estimated by reading horizontally from the "body weight" scale (step test) or "work load" scale (cycle test) to the "$O_2$ uptake" scale. The point on the "$O_2$ uptake" scale ($Vo_2$, 1) shall be connected with the corresponding point of the "pulse rate" scale and the predicted maximal $O_2$ uptake read on the middle scale. A female subject (61 kg.) reaches a heart rate of 156 at step test; predicted max$\dot{V}o_2$ = 2.4 I. A male subject reaches a heart rate of 166 at cycling test on a work load of 1200 kpm/min; predicted max$\dot{V}o_2$ = 3.6 I (exemplified by dotted lines). (From Åstrand.[1])

Whenever any variable is predicted rather than measured, the question most often asked is "How accurate is it?" In the case of the Åstrand-Åstrand nomogram, the standard deviation from the measured max $\dot{V}O_2$ is $\pm 15$ per cent. As an example of what this means, for every 1000 persons whose max $\dot{V}O_2$ is predicted to be 3.0 liters per minute, 25 of them will have actual max $\dot{V}O_2$ values less than 2.1 liters per minute and 25 will be greater than 3.9 liters per minute. This clearly points out that such predictions are at best only rough approximations of the true aerobic power. Precise values can be determined only by direct methods.

**The Fox Equation.**[6] More recently, a simple method for predicting max $\dot{V}O_2$ in males has been described. It is based on a linear equation relating the directly measured max $\dot{V}O_2$ to the submaximal heart rate ($HR_{sub}$) response recorded during the fifth minute of bicycle exercise at 150 watts (900 kg.-meters per min.). The equation is

$$\text{predicted max } \dot{V}O_2 \text{ (liters per min.)} = 6.3 - 0.0193 \times HR_{sub}$$

Consider the following example of how to use the equation:

Suppose the heart rate during the fifth minute of cycling at 150 watts is 160 beats per minute. The predicted max $\dot{V}O_2$ would be

$$
\begin{aligned}
\text{pred. max } \dot{V}O_2 &= 6.3 - (0.0193 \times 160) \\
&= 6.3 - 3.09 \\
&= 3.21 \text{ liters per minute}
\end{aligned}
$$

To facilitate use of the equation, we have solved the equation for submaximal heart rates between 100 and 200 beats per minute as given in Table 22–6.

If the subject is older than 25 years, the Åstrand-Åstrand age correction factor (Table 22–5) should be used. In the above example, if

**Table 22–5  AGE CORRECTION FACTORS FOR PREDICTING MAXIMAL AEROBIC POWER\***

| Age, yrs. | Age Correction Factor |
|:---:|:---:|
| 25 | 1.00 |
| 35 | 0.87 |
| 45 | 0.78 |
| 55 | 0.71 |
| 65 | 0.65 |

*From Åstrand.[1]

Table 22–6    PREDICTION OF $\dot{V}o_2$max (l/min.) FROM HEART RATE (beats/min.) AT 150 WATTS (900 kg.-m/min.) ON A BICYCLE ERGOMETER (men only)*

| HR BEATS/ MIN. | $\dot{V}o_2$MAX, LITERS PER MIN. | | | | | | | | | |
|---|---|---|---|---|---|---|---|---|---|---|
| | 0 | 1 | 2 | 3 | 4 | 5 | 6 | 7 | 8 | 9 |
| 100 | 4.37 | 4.35 | 4.33 | 4.31 | 4.29 | 4.27 | 4.25 | 4.23 | 4.22 | 4.20 |
| 110 | 4.18 | 4.16 | 4.14 | 4.12 | 4.10 | 4.09 | 4.07 | 4.05 | 4.03 | 4.01 |
| 120 | 3.99 | 3.97 | 3.95 | 3.93 | 3.91 | 3.89 | 3.87 | 3.85 | 3.84 | 3.82 |
| 130 | 3.80 | 3.78 | 3.76 | 3.74 | 3.72 | 3.70 | 3.68 | 3.66 | 3.64 | 3.62 |
| 140 | 3.60 | 3.58 | 3.57 | 3.55 | 3.53 | 3.51 | 3.49 | 3.47 | 3.45 | 3.43 |
| 150 | 3.41 | 3.39 | 3.37 | 3.35 | 3.33 | 3.32 | 3.30 | 3.28 | 3.26 | 3.24 |
| 160 | 3.22 | 3.20 | 3.18 | 3.16 | 3.14 | 3.12 | 3.10 | 3.08 | 3.06 | 3.05 |
| 170 | 3.03 | 3.01 | 2.99 | 2.97 | 2.95 | 2.93 | 2.91 | 2.89 | 2.87 | 2.85 |
| 180 | 2.83 | 2.81 | 2.80 | 2.78 | 2.76 | 2.74 | 2.72 | 2.70 | 2.68 | 2.66 |
| 190 | 2.64 | 2.62 | 2.60 | 2.58 | 2.56 | 2.54 | 2.53 | 2.51 | 2.49 | 2.47 |
| 200 | 2.45 | | | | | | | | | |

*Based on the equation: $\max \dot{V}o_2 = 6.3 - 0.0193 \times HR_{sub}$. From Fox.[6]

the man were 50 years of age, the age-corrected $\max \dot{V}o_2$ would be 3.21 $\times 0.745 = 2.39$ liters per minute. Notice that the age correction factor of 0.745 was interpolated; this increases the accuracy of predictions.

Again, the question of accuracy comes up. Using 74 subjects, the Fox equation was shown to have a standard deviation of $\pm 0.24$ liters per minute or $\pm 7.7$ per cent. In this case, for every 1000 persons whose $\max \dot{V}o_2$ is predicted to be 3.0 liters per minute, 25 will have actual values less than 2.54 liters per minute and 25 will have values greater than 3.46 liters per minute. While this is more accurate than the Åstrand-Åstrand nomogram, it still should be remembered that it still is only an approximation and that the most accurate $\max \dot{V}o_2$ value will be the one that is directly measured.

# Summary

Weight gain or loss is dependent on energy input (food) and energy output (physical activity). When the two are in equilibrium, weight will not change; when energy input is greater, the person will gain weight; conversely, when energy output is greater, the person will lose weight.

Real weight loss cannot come about through acute exercise sessions. Weight loss during a football practice, for example, is water loss and must be made up; to lose weight through increased energy output requires weeks or months.

There is absolutely no place in athletics for so-called sweat paraphernalia such as sweatboxes, sweat suits, rubber jackets, towels wrapped about the neck and head, and rubberized hoods. The only sound reason for such clothing is for warmth on cold days. The person who believes that by donning a rubber jacket and playing handball he will lose real weight is sadly mistaken.

Measurement of environmental conditions by wet bulb, dry bulb, and black bulb thermometers will permit the computing of relative humidity and the WBGT Index. These indices aid the coach in making judgments regarding the strenuosity of practice.

Using the sweat box and withholding water to cause weight losses greater than 3 per cent significantly retards performance, and precipitates fatigue more rapidly.

Power is essential in athletic performance. It can best be measured by the Margaria-Kalamen Anaerobic Power Test. Other ways are by measuring the time for the 50-yard dash, from a 15-yard running start, and the Sargent jump applied to the Lewis nomogram.

The maximal oxygen consumption test is perhaps the most valid means of determining a person's aerobic capacity. Mean value for college sophomore men is between 3.0 and 3.5 liters per minute, and for females between 2.0 and 2.5 liters per minute. Methods for direct and indirect assessment of $\max\dot{V}O_2$ are given.

## QUESTIONS

1. Describe the difference between *real* weight loss and that which an athlete might lose during practice.

2. Discuss the concept that energy input must equal energy output if body weight is to remain constant.

3. Would you advise the wearing of sweat clothes on hot and humid days? Why?

4. Describe how *real* weight may be lost through exercise.

5. What is the value of recording weight of your athletes?

6. Define relative humidity and indicate how it may be measured.

7. What is solar radiation and how may it be measured?

8. What is vapor pressure and on what is it dependent?

9. Describe the Margaria-Kalamen power test. What energy source does the test purport to measure?

10. Describe the methods of assessing aerobic capacity both directly and indirectly.

## REFERENCES

1. Åstrand, I.: Aerobic work capacity in men and women with special reference to age. Acta. Physiol. Scand., 49, Suppl. 169, 1–92, 1960.
2. Åstrand, P., and Rodahl, K.: Textbook of Work Physiology, p. 617. New York, McGraw-Hill Book Co., 1970.
3. Åstrand, P., and Ryhming, I.: A nomogram for calculation of aerobic capacity (physical fitness) from pulse rate during submaximal work. J. Appl. Physiol., 7:218–221, 1954.
4. Buskirk, E., Iampietro, P., and Bass, D.: Work performance and dehydration; effects of physical condition and heat acclimatization. J. Appl. Physiol., 12:189–194, 1958.
5. Craig, E., and Cummings, E.: Dehydration and muscular work. J. Appl. Physiol., 21:670–674, 1966.
6. Fox, E.: A simple, accurate technique for predicting maximal aerobic power. J. Appl. Physiol., 35(6):914–916, 1973.
7. Fox, E., Billings, C., Bartels, R., Bason, R., and Mathews, D.: Fitness standards for male college students. Int. Z. angew. Physiol., 31:231–236, 1973.
8. Fox, E.: Differences in metabolic alterations with sprint versus endurance interval training. In Howald, H., and Poortmans, J. (eds.): Metabolic Adaptation to Prolonged Physical Exercise. Basel, Switzerland, Birkhäuser Verlag, 1975, pp. 119–126.
9. Fox, E., and Mathews, D.: Interval Training: Conditioning for Sports and General Fitness. Philadelphia, W. B. Saunders Co., 1974.
10. Hermansen, L., and Saltin, B.: Oxygen uptake during maximal treadmill and bicycle exercise. J. Appl. Physiol., 26(1):31–37, 1969.
11. Kalamen, J.: Measurement of Maximum Muscular Power in Man. Doctoral Dissertation, The Ohio State University, 1968.
12. Maksud, M., and Coutts, K.: Comparison of a continuous and discontinuous graded treadmill test for maximal oxygen uptake. Med. Sci. Sports, 3(2):63–65, 1971.
13. Margaria, R., Aghemo, I., and Rovelli, E.: Measurement of muscular power (anaerobic) in man. J. Appl. Physiol., 21:1662–1664, 1966.
14. McArdle, W., Katch, F., and Pechar, G.: Comparison of continuous and discontinuous treadmill and bicycle tests for max$\dot{V}o_2$. Med. Sci. Sports, 5(3):156–160, 1973.
15. McArdle, W., and Magel, J.: Physical work capacity and maximum oxygen uptake in treadmill and bicycle exercise. Med. Sci. Sports, 2(3):118–123, 1970.
16. Minard, D., Belding, H., and Kingston, J.: Prevention of heat casualties. J.A.M.A., 165:1813–1818, 1957.
17. Mitchell, J., Sproule, B., and Chapman, C.: The physiological meaning of the maximal oxygen intake test. J. Clin. Invest., 37:538–547, 1957.
18. Murphy, R., and Ashe, W.: Prevention of heat illness in football players. J.A.M.A., 194:650–654, 1965.
19. Saltin, B., and Åstrand, P.: Maximal oxygen uptake in athletes. J. Appl. Physiol., 23:353–358, 1967.

## SELECTED READINGS

Clarke, H. Harrison: Application of Measurement to Health and Physical Education. 4th ed. Englewood Cliffs, N.J., Prentice-Hall, Inc., 1967.
Consolazio, C. G., Johnson, R. E., and Pecora, L. J.: Physiological Measurements of Metabolic Functions in Man. New York, McGraw-Hill Book Company, 1963.
Mathews, Donald K.: Measurement in Physical Education, 4th ed. Philadelphia, W. B. Saunders Company, 1974.

# APPENDICES

*Appendix A*
## PULMONARY SYMBOLS AND NORMS

*Appendix B*
## THE GAS LAWS

*Appendix C*
## CALCULATION OF OXYGEN CONSUMPTION AND CARBON DIOXIDE PRODUCTION

*Appendix D*
## A BASIC WEIGHT-LIFTING PROGRAM FOR HIGH SCHOOL THROUGH ADULTHOOD

*Appendix E*
## INTERVAL TRAINING PROGRAMS FOR UNCONDITIONED COLLEGE MEN AND WOMEN

# PULMONARY SYMBOLS
# AND NORMS

## 1. SYMBOLS AND ABBREVIATIONS USED
## BY PULMONARY PHYSIOLOGISTS

(Based on report in Federation Proc. 9:602–605, 1950)

Before 1950, each pulmonary physiologist had developed a jargon of his own. In 1950 a group of American pulmonary physiologists, in order to lessen confusion, agreed to use a standard set of symbols and abbreviations. The symbols below are used in equations in this book and in most original articles published since 1950; they cannot be applied to earlier articles.

## Special Symbols

— Dash above any symbol indicates a *mean value*.
· Dot above any symbol indicates a *time derivative*.

## For Gases

| PRIMARY SYMBOLS (Large Capital Letters) | EXAMPLES |
|---|---|
| V = gas volume | $V_A$ = volume of alveolar gas |
| $\dot{V}$ = gas volume per unit time | $\dot{V}_{O_2}$ = $O_2$ consumption per minute |
| P = gas pressure | $P_{A_{O_2}}$ = alveolar $O_2$ pressure |
| $\bar{P}$ = mean gas pressure | $\bar{P}_{C_{O_2}}$ = mean capillary $O_2$ pressure |
| F = fractional concentration in dry gas phase | $F_{I_{O_2}}$ = fractional concentration of $O_2$ in inspired gas |
| f = respiratory frequency (breaths per unit time) | |
| D = diffusing capacity | $D_{O_2}$ = diffusing capacity for $O_2$ (ml $O_2$ per minute per mm. Hg) |
| R = respiratory exchange ratio | R = $\dot{V}_{CO_2}/\dot{V}_{O_2}$ |

---

*From Comroe, J. H., et al.: The Lung, 2nd ed. Chicago, Year Book Medical Publishers, Inc., 1962.

SECONDARY SYMBOLS
(SMALL CAPITAL LETTERS)

EXAMPLES

I  = inspired gas

E  = expired gas
A  = alveolar gas

T  = tidal gas
D  = dead space gas
B  = barometric
STPD = 0°C, 760 mm. Hg, dry
BTPS = body temperature and pressure saturated with water vapor
ATPS = ambient temperature and pressure saturated with water vapor

$F_{I_{CO_2}}$ = fractional concentration of $CO_2$ in inspired gas
$V_E$ = volume of expired gas
$\dot{V}_A$ = alveolar ventilation per minute
$V_T$ = tidal volume
$V_D$ = volume of dead space gas
$P_B$ = barometric pressure

# For Blood

PRIMARY SYMBOLS
(Large Capital Letters)

EXAMPLES

Q  = volume of blood

$\dot{Q}$  = volume flow of blood per unit time

C  = concentration of gas in blood phase

S  = per cent saturation of Hb with $O_2$ or CO

$Q_C$ = volume of blood in pulmonary capillaries

$\dot{Q}_C$ = blood flow through pulmonary capillaries per minute

$Ca_{O_2}$ = ml. $O_2$ in 100 ml. arterial blood

$S\bar{v}_{O_2}$ = saturation of Hb with $O_2$ in mixed venous blood

SECONDARY SYMBOLS
(small letters)

EXAMPLES

a  = arterial blood

v  = venous blood

c  = capillary blood

$Pa_{CO_2}$ = partial pressure of $CO_2$ in arterial blood

$P\bar{v}_{O_2}$ = partial pressure of $O_2$ in mixed venous blood

$Pc_{CO}$ = partial pressure of CO in pulmonary capillary blood

# For Lung Volumes

VC = vital capacity
IC = inspiratory capacity
IRV = inspiratory reserve volume
ERV = expiratory reserve volume

= maximal volume that can be expired after maximal inspiration
= maximal volume that can be inspired from resting expiratory level
= maximal volume that can be inspired from end-tidal inspiration
= maximal volume that can be expired from resting expiratory level

FRC = function residual capacity     = volume of gas in lungs at resting expiratory level

RV   = residual volume     = volume of gas in lungs at end of maximal expiration

TLC = total lung capacity     = volume of gas in lungs at end of maximal inspiration

# 2. TYPICAL VALUES FOR PULMONARY FUNCTION TESTS

These are values for a healthy, resting, recumbent young male (1.7 square meters of surface area), breathing air at sea level, unless other conditions are specified. They are presented merely to give approximate figures. These values may change with position, age, size, sex, and altitude; variability occurs among members of a homogeneous group under standard conditions.

## LUNG VOLUMES (BTPS)

| | |
|---|---:|
| Inspiratory capacity, ml. | 3600 |
| Expiratory reserve volume, ml. | 1200 |
| Vital capacity, ml. | 4800 |
| Residual volume (RV), ml. | 1200 |
| Functional residual capacity, ml. | 2400 |
| Thoracic gas volume, ml. | 2400 |
| Total lung capacity (TLC), ml. | 6000 |
| RV/TLC × 100, per cent | 20 |

## VENTILATION (BTPS)

| | |
|---|---:|
| Tidal volume, ml. | 500 |
| Frequency, respirations per minute | 12 |
| Minute volume, ml. per minute | 6000 |
| Respiratory dead space, ml. | 150 |
| Alveolar ventilation, ml. per minute | 4200 |

### DISTRIBUTION OF INSPIRED GAS

| | |
|---|---:|
| Single-breath test (per cent increase $N_2$ for 500 ml. expired alveolar gas), per cent $N_2$ | <1.5 |
| Pulmonary nitrogen emptying rate (7 minute test), per cent $N_2$ | <2.5 |
| Helium closed circuit (mixing efficiency related to perfect mixing, per cent | 76 |

### ALVEOLAR VENTILATION/PULMONARY CAPILLARY BLOOD FLOW

| | |
|---|---:|
| Alveolar ventilation (liters per minute)/blood flow (liters per minute) | 0.8 |
| Physiologic shunt/cardiac output × 100, per cent | <7 |
| Physiologic dead space/tidal volume × 100, per cent | <30 |

## PULMONARY CIRCULATION

Pulmonary capillary blood flow, ml. per minute ............................. 5400
Pulmonary artery pressure, mm. Hg ............................................. 25/8
Pulmonary capillary blood volume, ml. ......................................... 90
Pulmonary "capillary" blood pressure (wedge), mm. Hg .................. 8

## ALVEOLAR GAS

Oxygen partial pressure, mm. Hg. ............................................... 104
$CO_2$ partial pressure, mm. Hg ...................................................... 40

## DIFFUSION AND GAS EXCHANGE

$O_2$ consumption (STPD), ml. per minute ......................................... 240
$CO_2$ output (STPD), ml. per minute .............................................. 192
Respiratory exchange ratio, R ($CO_2$ output/$O_2$ uptake) .................... 0.8
Diffusing capacity, $O_2$ (STPD) resting, ml. $O_2$ per minute
    per mm. Hg ......................................................................... >15
Diffusing capacity, CO (steady state) (STPD) resting,
    ml. CO per minute per mm. Hg. ............................................ 17
Diffusing capacity, CO (single-breath) (STPD) resting,
    ml. CO per minute per mm. Hg. ............................................ 25
Diffusing capacity, CO (rebreathing) (STPD) resting,
    ml. CO per minute per mm. Hg. ............................................ 25
Fractional CO uptake, resting, per cent ....................................... 53
Maximal diffusing capacity, $O_2$ (exercise) (STPD),
    ml. $O_2$ per minute per mm. Hg. ............................................. 60

## ARTERIAL BLOOD

$O_2$ saturation (per cent saturation of Hb with $O_2$), per cent ............... 97.1
$O_2$ tension, mm. Hg. ................................................................ 95
$CO_2$ tension, mm. Hg. ............................................................... 40
Alveolar-arterial $Po_2$ difference, mm. Hg. .................................... 9
Alveolar-arterial $Po_2$ difference (12–14 per cent $O_2$), mm. Hg. .......... 10
Alveolar-arterial $Po_2$ difference (100 per cent $O_2$), mm. Hg. .............. 35
$O_2$ saturation (100 per cent $O_2$), per cent (+1.9 ml. dissolved
    $O_2$ per 100 ml. blood) ........................................................ 100
$O_2$ tension (100 per cent $O_2$), mm. Hg. ....................................... 640
pH .................................................................................... 7.4

## MECHANICS OF BREATHING

Maximal voluntary ventilation (BTPS), liters per minute .................... 170
Forced expiratory volume, per cent in 1 second ............................. 83
                       per cent in 3 seconds ............................. 97
Maximal expiratory flow rate (for 1 liter) (ATPS), liters per minute ... >400
Maximal inspiratory flow rate (for 1 liter) (ATPS), liters per minute ... >300
Compliance of lungs and thoracic cage, liters per cm. $H_2O$ .............. 0.1
Compliance of lungs, liters per cm. $H_2O$ .................................... 0.2
Airway resistance, cm. $H_2O$ per liter per second ........................... 1.6
Pulmonary resistance, cm. $H_2O$ per liter per second ....................... 1.9
Work of quiet breathing, kg-meter per minute ............................... 0.5
Maximal work of breathing, kg-meter per breath ............................ 10
Maximal inspiratory and expiratory pressures, mm. Hg. .................. 60–100

# THE GAS LAWS

Gas volume is dependent on temperature and pressure. For example, a given number of gas molecules occupies a greater volume at a higher temperature and lower pressure than at a lower temperature and higher pressure. By the same token, an unequal number of gas molecules could occupy the same volume, but only at different temperatures or pressures. In other words, two gas volumes of one liter each could contain an unequal number of gas molecules only if the temperature or pressure of the two volumes were different. On the other hand, whenever the temperature and pressure of two equal volumes of gases are the same, the two volumes will always contain the same number of molecules. For these reasons, respiratory gas volumes *must* be corrected to a reference temperature and pressure so that valid comparisons can be made. Temperature and pressure vary from day to day and from one laboratory to another.

## ATPS CONDITIONS

The conditions of temperature and pressure at the time a respiratory gas volume is measured are abbreviated ATPS. This abbreviation means ambient temperature and pressure, saturated with water vapor. Since most respiratory volumes are measured with a wet spirometer, ambient temperature refers to the temperature of the gas in the spirometer (ts) and ambient pressure refers to the environmental or barometric pressure at the time of the measurement. The volume is also assumed to be saturated with water vapor at spirometer temperature because a wet spirometer is water sealed (see page 59). In other words the gas is collected over water and is assumed to be saturated with water vapor. It is this volume, under various ATPS conditions, which must be corrected to a reference temperature and pressure before any comparisons can be made.

## STPD CONDITIONS

There are two reference conditions of temperature and pressure with which you will be concerned. The first of these is standard temperature and pressure, dry, abbreviated STPD. Standard temperature is 0°C. and standard pressure is 760 mm. Hg. "Dry" means that the volume occupied by molecules of water vapor has been accounted for, i.e., the gas volume at STPD is that volume occupied by all gas molecules except those of water vapor. The number of gas molecules and the volume they occupy under STPD conditions is constant and independent of the particular gas involved. In other words, one mole of any gas (e.g., 32 gm. of oxygen) at STPD contains $6.02 \times 10^{23}$ molecules and occupies 22.4 liters. Therefore, a volume of gas under STPD conditions represents quantitatively the number of gas molecules present. Corrections of gas volumes from ATPS to STPD are made whenever we need to know the *amount* or number of gas molecules, e.g., when calculating the amount of oxygen consumed and the amount of carbon dioxide produced. Such corrections always result in a reduction of volume for several reasons: (1) ambient (spirometer) temperature is higher than 0°C, e.g., from 20° to 25°C.; (2) ambient pressure in most parts of the country is below 760 mm. Hg; and (3) the gas is "dry."

## BTPS CONDITIONS

The other reference point for making gas volume corrections is body temperature and pressure, saturated with water vapor, abbreviated BTPS. Body temperature is 37°C. and body pressure is the same as ambient pressure. Corrections of gas volumes from ATPS (or from STPD, for that matter) to BTPS are made when we are interested in knowing the volume of air that is ventilated by the lungs and not the number of gas molecules present. When air at room temperature (e.g., 22°C.) is inspired, its volume will expand in the lungs as a result of: (1) the increase in temperature (from 22° to 37°C.); and (2) the addition of water vapor molecules because of the increase in temperature. Corrections to BTPS are necessary, therefore, for all respiratory gas measurements dealing with volume only; e.g., vital capacity, tidal volume, minute volume, and maximal breathing capacity.

## CALCULATION OF VOLUME CORRECTIONS

Calculations of gas volume corrections for differences in temperature, pressure, and water vapor are based upon several gas laws irrespective of the specific correction to be made. Remember that correction from ATPS to STPD is made when we are concerned with the amount or number of gas molecules present, such as in calculating oxygen consumption and carbon dioxide production; correction to BTPS is made when we are concerned with the volume occupied by the gas molecules, such as in determining lung volumes.

**Temperature Correction.** Gas volume is directly related to temperature, so that increasing or decreasing the temperature of a gas (at constant pressure) causes a proportional increase or decrease, respectively in volume. This is known as *Charles's Law.* It states that the change in temperature as determined by the ratio of the initial temperature ($T_1$) to that of the final corrected temperature ($T_2$) is equal to the change in volume or the ratio of the initial volume ($V_1$) and the final or corrected volume ($V_2$). In mathematical form:

$$\frac{T_1}{T_2} = \frac{V_1}{V_2} \tag{1}$$

The units for temperature in this case are those of either the Absolute (A.) or the Kelvin (K.) scale, i.e., $273°K. = 0°C.$; $°K. = 273° + °C.$ (e.g., $22°C. = 273° + 22° = 295°K.$).

Rearranging equation (1) to solve for $V_2$:

$$V_2 = \frac{V_1 \times T_2}{T_1} \tag{2}$$

In correcting a gas volume to standard temperature ($0°C.$):

$V_1$ = volume ATPS ($V_{ATPS}$)
$V_2$ = volume corrected to standard temperature ($V_{ST}$)
$T_1$ = absolute spirometer temperature ($273° K. + t s°C.$)
$T_2$ = absolute standard temperature ($273°K.$)

and

$$V_{ST} = V_{ATPS} \frac{273°}{273° + ts} \tag{3}$$

In correcting to body temperature (BT) or $37°C.$, then:

$V_2$ = volume corrected to body temperature ($V_{BT}$)
$T_2$ = absolute body temperature ($273°K. + 37°C. = 310°$)

and

$$V_{BT} = V_{ATPS} \frac{310°}{273° + ts} \tag{4}$$

**Pressure and Water Vapor Corrections.** Gas volume is inversely related to pressure, so that increasing or decreasing the pressure of a gas (at constant temperature) causes a proportional decrease or increase, respectively, in volume. This is known as *Boyle's Law.* It states that the change in pressure as determined by the ratio of the initial pressure ($P_1$) to the final or corrected pressure ($P_2$) is equal to the volume change or the ratio of the final or corrected volume ($V_2$) and the initial volume ($V_1$). In other words:

$$\frac{P_1}{P_2} = \frac{V_2}{V_1} \tag{5}$$

Again, rearranging to solve for $V_2$:

$$V_2 = V_1 \left(\frac{P_1}{P_2}\right) \tag{6}$$

Pressure is measured in millimeters of mercury (mm. Hg).

Correction for water vapor is made along with the correction for pressure even though water vapor pressure is dependent only on temperature. When the gas volume is to be "dried" as in STPD the vapor pressure of water at ambient temperature $T_1$ ($P_{H_2O}$) is subtracted from the ambient or initial pressure ($P_1$) as follows:

$$V_2 = V_1 \left(\frac{P_1 - P_{H_2O}}{P_2}\right) \tag{7}$$

For example, correcting to standard pressure (760 mm. Hg, dry, or SPD), we would have:

$$V_{SPD} = V_{ATPS} \left(\frac{P_1 - P_{H_2O}}{760}\right) \tag{8}$$

When the gas volume is to be saturated, as in BTPS, $P_{H_2O}$ is subtracted from $P_1$ as previously, but in addition the vapor pressure of water at $T_2$ or body temperature ($P_{H_2O}'$) is subtracted from $P_2$ or body pressure. In other words:

$$V_2 = V_1 \left(\frac{P_1 - P_{H_2O}}{P_2 - P_{H_2O}'}\right) \tag{9}$$

The reason why this procedure accounts for the increase in volume due to the addition of water vapor molecules when the temperature is increased to body temperature is because body pressure ($P_2$) obviously must equal ambient pressure ($P_1$), therefore no correction for pressure per se is necessary in going from ATPS to BTPS; i.e., $\frac{P_1}{P_2} = 1$. When $P_{H_2O}$ and $P_{H_2O}'$ are subtracted from $P_1$ and $P_2$, respectively, the resulting ratio, which is greater than 1, is proportional to the increase in volume due to the addition of water vapor molecules.

When correcting to body pressure, saturated with water vapor (BPS):

$$\text{V}_{BPS} = \text{V}_{ATPS} \left( \frac{P_1 - P_{H_2O}}{P_2 - 47 \text{ mm. Hg}} \right) \tag{10}$$

The 47 mm. Hg pressure is the vapor pressure of water at body temperature.

**Combined Correction Factors.** We can now combine the temperature, pressure, and water vapor corrections into one equation for STPD and one equation for BTPS. Correcting from ATPS to STPD, we would combine equation (3) for temperature and equation (8) for pressure and water vapor as follows:

$$\text{V}_{STPD} = \text{V}_{ATPS} \left( \frac{273°}{273° + t_S} \right) \left( \frac{P_1 - P_{H_2O}}{760} \right) \tag{11}$$

Correcting from ATPS to BTPS we would combine equations (4) and (10) for temperature and water vapor pressure, respectively:

$$\text{V}_{BTPS} = \text{V}_{ATPS} \left( \frac{310°}{273° + t_S} \right) \left( \frac{P_1 - P_{H_2O}}{P_2 - 47} \right) \tag{12}$$

## PROBLEMS

Suppose you have collected in a spirometer 100 liters of expired gas. At the time you measured the gas volume, ambient temperature in the spirometer was 22°C., ambient pressure was 747 mm. Hg. and $P_{H_2O}$ at 22°C. is equal to 19.8 mm. Hg.

(1) Correct the volume from ATPS to STPD.
(2) Correct the volume from ATPS to BTPS.
(3) Correct the volume from STPD to BTPS.

## SOLUTIONS

(1) Using equation (11) and substituting, we have:

$$\text{V}_{STPD} = 100 \text{ liters} \left( \frac{273°}{295°} \right) \left( \frac{727.2 \text{ mm.}}{760 \text{ mm.}} \right)$$

$$= 100 \, (0.925) \, (0.957)$$

$$= 100 \, (0.885)$$

$$= 88.5 \text{ liters}$$

(2) Using equation (12) and substituting, we have:

$$V_{BTPS} = 100 \text{ liters} \left(\frac{310°}{295°}\right) \left(\frac{727.2 \text{ mm.}}{700 \text{ mm.}}\right)$$

$$= 100 \ (1.051) \ (1.039)$$

$$= 100 \ (1.092)$$

$$= 109.2 \text{ liters}$$

(3) You can also use equation (12) for this solution but remember; that the gas volume to be corrected is under conditions of STPD and *not* ATPS. Therefore, in equation (12):

(a) V$_{STPD}$ replaces V$_{ATPS}$.
(b) 273° + ts now represents standard temperature, or 273°K. + 0°C.
(c) P$_1$ represents standard pressure, or 760 mm. Hg, and P$_{H_2O}$ at 0°C. is negligible.

Therefore:

$$V_{BTPS} = 88.5 \text{ liters} \left(\frac{310°}{273°}\right) \left(\frac{760 \text{ mm.}}{700 \text{ mm.}}\right)$$

$$= 88.5 \ (1.136) \ (1.086)$$

$$= 88.5 \ (1.233)$$

$$= 109.2 \text{ liters}$$

## *Appendix C*

# CALCULATION OF OXYGEN CONSUMPTION AND CARBON DIOXIDE PRODUCTION

## OXYGEN CONSUMPTION

The amount of oxygen consumed per minute ($\dot{V}O_2$) is equal to the difference between the amount of oxygen inspired ($VI_{O_2}$) and the amount of oxygen expired ($\dot{V}E_{O_2}$) or:

$$\dot{V}O_{2STPD} = \dot{V}I_{O_2STPD} - \dot{V}E_{O_2STPD} \tag{13}$$

In order to use equation (13), the following variables must be measured:

(1) $\dot{V}E$ the volume of air exhaled per minute.
(2) $FE_{O_2}$ the fractional concentration of oxygen in exhaled air.
(3) $FI_{O_2}$ the fractional concentration of oxygen in inspired air.*
(4) $FE_{CO_2}$ the fractional concentration of carbon dioxide in expired air.
(5) $FI_{CO_2}$ the fractional concentration of carbon dioxide in inspired air.*

An *amount* is defined as a volume times a concentration. The volume in this case, as you will recall, is a volume which has been corrected to STPD. All volumes referred to from here on are STPD. In a 100-liter volume of gas containing 20 per cent oxygen ($F_{O_2} = 0.2$) and 80 per cent nitrogen ($F_{N_2} = 0.8$), the *amount* of oxygen is equal to 20 liters (100 liters $\times$ 0.2) and the amount of nitrogen is equal to 80 liters (100 liters $\times$ 0.8). As a result, the amount of oxygen inspired per minute according to equation (13) is equal to:

$$\dot{V}I_{O_2} = (\dot{V}I)(FI_{O_2}) \tag{14}$$

---

*If fresh air (i.e., outside air) is inspired, then $FI_{O_2}$, $FI_{CO_2}$, and $FI_{N_2}$ will be 0.2093, 0.0004, and 0.7903 respectively.

The same is true for the amount of oxygen expired; that is:

$$\dot{V}_{E_{O_2}} = (\dot{V}_E)(F_{E_{O_2}}) \tag{15}$$

Substituting equations (14) and (15) into equation (13), we have:

$$\dot{V}_{O_2} = (\dot{V}_I)(F_{I_{O_2}}) - (\dot{V}_E)(F_{E_{O_2}}) \tag{16}$$

Since $F_{I_{O_2}}$, $\dot{V}_E$, and $F_{E_{O_2}}$ are either known or measured directly, only $\dot{V}_I$ and $\dot{V}_{O_2}$ are unknown. Therefore, we must measure or calculate $\dot{V}_I$ in order to solve equation (16) for $\dot{V}_{O_2}$.

You may at first think that $\dot{V}_I$ equals $\dot{V}_E$, i.e., that the volume we inspire is the same as that which we expire. This is true if, and only if, the amount of $CO_2$ given off is equal to the amount of oxygen consumed. In other words, $\dot{V}_I = \dot{V}_E$ only when $\dot{V}_{CO_2} = \dot{V}_{O_2}$ or when $R = 1$. When more $O_2$ is consumed than $CO_2$ given off, $\dot{V}_E$ is less than $\dot{V}_I$. The opposite is true, i.e., $\dot{V}_E$ is greater than $\dot{V}_I$, when $\dot{V}_{CO_2}$ is greater than $\dot{V}_{O_2}$.

Rather than measuring $\dot{V}_I$ directly, there is a simple method by which we can calculate it accurately. The calculation, sometimes referred to as the Haldane transformation, is based on the fact that the *amount* of nitrogen we inspire is equal to that which we expire, or:

$$(\dot{V}_I)(F_{I_{N_2}}) = (\dot{V}_E)(F_{E_{N_2}}) \tag{17}$$

where: $F_{I_{N_2}}$ = fractional concentration of nitrogen in inspired air.
$F_{E_{N_2}}$ = fractional concentration of nitrogen in expired air.

This relationship holds true because nitrogen is neither consumed nor given off, i.e., it is physiologically inert, and therefore the amounts inspired and expired are essentially equal.*

The fractional concentration of inspired nitrogen is given by the following relationship:

$$F_{I_{N_2}} = 1 - (F_{I_{O_2}} + F_{I_{CO_2}}) \tag{18}$$

and the fractional concentration of expired nitrogen by:

$$F_{E_{N_2}} = 1 - (F_{E_{O_2}} + F_{E_{CO_2}}) \tag{19}$$

---

*Recently, the concept of equality of respiratory gaseous nitrogen in man has been challenged, mainly by one laboratory,[1,3,4,5] and with it the accuracy of calculating oxygen consumption by the Haldane transformation.[2] However, subsequent studies from a number of different laboratories,[7,8,9,10] including our own,[6] have shown that nitrogen differences are small and inconsistent and do not significantly affect oxygen consumption values calculated by assuming nitrogen equality.

These relationships are based on the fact that oxygen, carbon dioxide, and nitrogen are the only gases present, for all practical purposes, in inspired and expired air. The small concentrations of rare gases, such as argon and helium, which are also physiologically inert, are included in the nitrogen fraction. Substituting equations (18) and (19) in equation (17) we have:

$$\dot{V}_I \left[ 1 - (F_{I_{O_2}} + F_{I_{CO_2}}) \right] = \dot{V}_E \left[ 1 - (F_{E_{O_2}} + F_{E_{CO_2}}) \right] \tag{20}$$

Rearranging to solve for $\dot{V}_I$:

$$\dot{V}_I = \dot{V}_E \left[ 1 - (F_{E_{O_2}} + F_{E_{CO_2}}) \right] / \left[ 1 - (F_{I_{O_2}} + F_{I_{CO_2}}) \right] \tag{21}$$

This latter equation (sometimes referred to as the *nitrogen factor*) gives us a simple yet accurate estimate of $\dot{V}_I$.*

By substituting the right side of equation (21) for $\dot{V}_I$ in equation (16) we have the final equation for the calculation of $\dot{V}_{O_2}$:

$$\dot{V}_{O_2} = \dot{V}_E \left[ \frac{1 - (F_{E_{O_2}} + F_{E_{CO_2}})}{1 - (F_{I_{O_2}} + F_{I_{CO_2}})} \right] F_{I_{O_2}} - \dot{V}_E \, F_{E_{O_2}} \tag{22}$$

As mentioned earlier, if fresh air is inspired, then equation (22) will reduce to:

$$\dot{V}_{O_2} = \dot{V}_E \left[ \frac{1 - (F_{E_{O_2}} + F_{E_{CO_2}})}{0.7903} \right] 0.2093 - \dot{V}_E \, F_{E_{O_2}} \tag{23}$$

In the case where $\dot{V}_I = \dot{V}_E$, equation (22) will reduce even further. Substituting $\dot{V}_E$ for $\dot{V}_I$ in equation (16) gives us:

$$\dot{V}_{O_2} = (\dot{V}_E)(F_{I_{O_2}}) - (\dot{V}_E)(F_{E_{O_2}}) \tag{24}$$

Collecting terms, we have:

$$\dot{V}_{O_2} = \dot{V}_E \, (F_{I_{O_2}} - F_{E_{O_2}}) \tag{25}$$

when $\dot{V}_I = \dot{V}_E$.

---

*If $\dot{V}_I$ is measured and $\dot{V}_E$ is to be calculated, which is sometimes the case, then:

$$\dot{V}_E = \dot{V}_I \left[ 1 - (F_{I_{O_2}} + F_{I_{CO_2}}) \right] / \left[ 1 - (F_{E_{O_2}} + F_{E_{CO_2}}) \right]$$

# CARBON DIOXIDE PRODUCTION

Calculation of the amount of $CO_2$ produced per minute is based on the same principles as those used in computing $\dot{V}_{O_2}$. The basic equation is:

$$\dot{V}_{CO_2} = \dot{V}_{E_{CO_2}} - \dot{V}_{I_{CO_2}} \qquad (26)$$

Applying the "amount rule" gives us:

$$\dot{V}_{CO_2} = (\dot{V}_E)(F_{E_{CO_2}}) - (\dot{V}_I)(F_{I_{CO_2}}) \qquad (27)$$

If $\dot{V}_{O_2}$ is calculated first, which is usually the case, then all the factors to the right of equation (27) are known and $\dot{V}_{CO_2}$ can be determined. However, since the amount of $CO_2$ inspired $[\dot{V}_I(F_{I_{CO_2}})]$ is usually negligible (because $F_{I_{CO_2}}$ in inspired air is only 0.0004), equation (27) reduces to:

$$\dot{V}_{CO_2} = (\dot{V}_E)(F_{E_{CO_2}}) \qquad (28)$$

This latter equation is the one most frequently used to calculate $\dot{V}_{CO_2}$.

## PROBLEMS

Suppose you have made a 5-minute collection of expired air from a resting subject breathing fresh air and the following results were obtained:

$V_{E_{ATPS}}$ = 33.5 liters per 5 minutes
$F_{E_{O_2}}$ = 0.1593      $P_B$ = 745 mm. Hg
$F_{I_{O_2}}$ = 0.2093      ts = 24°C.
$F_{E_{CO_2}}$ = 0.0400     $P_{H_2O}$ at 24°C. = 22.4 mm. Hg
$F_{I_{CO_2}}$ = 0.0004     $P_{H_2O}$ at 37°C. = 47 mm. Hg

(1) What is the subject's $\dot{V}_{O_2}$?
(2) What is the subject's $\dot{V}_{CO_2}$?
(3) What is the subject's R?
(4) What is the subject's $\dot{V}_{E_{BTPS}}$?

## SOLUTIONS

(1) To calculate $\dot{V}_{O_2}$, the first thing we must do is to convert $\dot{V}_{E_{ATPS}}$ to $\dot{V}_{E_{STPD}}$. Therefore, from equation (11):

$$\dot{V}_{STPD} = 33.5 \text{ liters} \left(\frac{273°}{297°}\right) \left(\frac{722.6 \text{ mm.}}{760 \text{ mm.}}\right)$$

$$= 33.5 \, (0.919)(0.951)$$

$$= 33.5 \, (0.874)$$

$$= 29.27 \text{ liters per 5 minutes or 5.85 liters per minute}$$

Substituting in equation (23), we have:

$$\dot{V}_{O_2} = 29.27 \text{ liters} \left[\frac{1-(0.1593+0.0400)}{0.7903}\right] \times 0.2093 - [(29.27)(.1593)\,]$$

$$= 29.27 \, (1.0131)(0.2093) - 4.663$$

$$= 6.206 - 4.663$$

$$= 1.543 \text{ liters per 5 minutes, or 309 ml. per minute}$$

(2) For $\dot{V}_{CO_2}$, substitution in equation (28) gives us:

$$\dot{V}_{CO_2} = 29.27 \text{ liters} \, (0.0400)$$

$$= 1.171 \text{ liters per 5 minutes or 234 ml. per minute}$$

(3) The respiratory exchange ratio (R) is defined as $\dot{V}_{CO_2}/\dot{V}_{O_2}$; therefore:

$$\frac{234 \text{ ml. per minute}}{309 \text{ ml. per minute}} = 0.757$$

(4) to calculate $\dot{V}_{E_{BTPS}}$ we would use equation (12):

$$\dot{V}_{E_{BTPS}} = 33.5 \text{ liters} \left(\frac{310°}{297°}\right) \left(\frac{722.6 \text{ mm.}}{698 \text{ mm.}}\right)$$

$$= 33.5 \, (1.044)(1.035)$$

$$= 33.5 \, (1.0805)$$

$$= 36.2 \text{ liters per 5 minutes, or 7.24 liters per minute}$$

## REFERENCES

1. Cissik, J., and Johnson, R.: Myth of nitrogen equality in respiration: its history and implications. Aerospace Med., 43:755–758, 1972.
2. Cissik, J., and Johnson, R.: Regression analysis for steady state $N_2$ inequality in $O_2$ consumption calculations. Aerospace Med., 43:589–591, 1972.

3. Cissik, J., Johnson, R., and Hertig, B.: Production of gaseous nitrogen during human steady state exercise. Physiologist, 15:108, 1972.
4. Cissik, J., Johnson, R., and Rokosch, D.: Production of gaseous nitrogen in human steady-state conditions. J. Appl. Physiol., 32:155–159, 1972.
5. Dudka, L., Inglis, H., Johnson, R., Pechinski, J., and Plowman, S.: Inequality of inspired and expired gaseous nitrogen in man. Nature, 232:265–267, 1971.
6. Fox, E., and Bowers, R.: Steady-state equality of respiratory gaseous $N_2$ in resting man. J. Appl. Physiol., 35(1):143–144, 1973.
7. Herron, J., Saltzman, H., Hills, B., and Kylstra, J.: Differences between inspired and expired volumes of nitrogen in man. J. Appl. Physiol., 35(4):546–551, 1973.
8. Luft, U., Myhre, L., and Loeppky, J.: Validity of Haldane calculation for estimating respiratory gas exchange. J. Appl. Physiol., 34(6):864–865, 1973.
9. Wagner, J., Horvath, S., Dahms, T., and Reed, S.: Validation of open-circuit method for the determination of oxygen consumption. J. Appl. Physiol., 34(6):859–863, 1973.
10. Wilmore, J., and Costill, D.: Adequacy of the Haldane transformation in the computation of exercise $\dot{V}_{O_2}$ in man. J. Appl. Physiol., 35(1):85–89, 1973.

## SELECTED READING

Consolazio, C., Johnson, R., and Pecora, L.: Physiological Measurements of Metabolic Functions in Man. New York. McGraw-Hill Book Company, 1963.

# Appendix D*

# A BASIC WEIGHT-LIFTING PROGRAM FOR HIGH SCHOOL THROUGH ADULTHOOD

Lifting weights is the most effective means of causing muscles to hypertrophy. Selecting weights that cause the muscle to work in the overload zone and then progressively adding resistance as the muscle becomes stronger is the fundamental principle of the progressive resistance exercise program. Exactly what should be the intensity and frequency of the exercise regimen is not known. However, studies show that the heavier the resistance with fewer repetitions, the more significant are the results.

A practical exercise load can be determined by the amount of resistance that will permit raising the weights 10 times. This load is used until 15 repetitions are possible; then more weight is added to reduce the number of repetitions to 10. Exercise should take place at least 3 times a week, with each period averaging 30 minutes to an hour depending, of course, on the person's condition and the speed at which he or she exercises.

Weight training is dynamic in that significant changes take place rapidly. As a result, there are certain precautions that should be taken. Make sure each exercise is performed through complete range of motion; if not, the muscle group will gradually become shortened. The lifts should be executed with as near-perfect body mechanics as possible. Because of the dynamic nature of weight-lifting, muscular imbalances can be developed. Also, causes of poor body mechanics can be easily aggravated through the use of weights. By employing a minimum of 10 repetitions, injury as a result of lifting too much weight will be avoided.

Weight-lifting is an excellent way to develop strength and a better

---

*Modified from Mathews, D. K., et al.: The Science of Physical Education for Handicapped Children. New York, Harper & Brothers, 1962, pp. 287–294.

**531**

looking physique. Contrary to the teachings of some coaches, it has been scientifically demonstrated that weight-lifting, performed in the proper manner, significantly contributes to better performance in athletics.

Following is a general body-building program devised to suit the needs of persons from high school age through adulthood, both male and female. It is simple and extremely effective; exercising 3 times each week will cause noticeable strength gains within a 4-week period. The program can be mimeographed and handed out to the students. One school had the art department make large silhouettes of the lifts to be hung in the weight-lifting room as illustrations of good lifting form.

The proper weight to use when you first start is one with which you can do the exercise *correctly* for 15 repetitions. This weight will differ for each exercise, depending on the strength of the muscles. Each day strive to increase the number of repetitions for the exercise, being careful to use correct form. When you are able to do 20 repetitions, increase the weight 5 pounds. Do this for the first two weeks of training. It is perfectly normal for some muscle soreness and tightness to occur during the first few weeks of training, but this will soon disappear. The weights used will not be heavy enough to cause any injury. After two weeks, use a weight you can properly handle for 10 repetitions, and do not increase the weight until you can do 15 repetitions.

In most exercises you should inhale as you lift the weight and exhale as you lower it. Never hold your breath as you lift, for this increases the blood pressure by compressing the vessels in the chest and neck and may cause you to lose consciousness. All exercises should be done with a regular rhythm. Do not jerk the weight or use momentum to help lift it. When lowering the weight, do not drop it rapidly, but lower it slowly.

The program to follow is described for use with barbells. As was mentioned in Chapter 7, there is now available weight-lifting equipment such as the Nautilus, Mini-Gym, Universal Gym, and others that offer certain advantages over the barbell system with respect to specificity and magnitude of strength gains. However, the exercises given below are basic and therefore applicable, with slight modifications, to use with the latest weight-lifting equipment.

Before every workout, you should spend 5 or 10 minutes doing calisthenics to increase the circulation to the muscles. Cold muscles and stiff joints are more easily injured. The warm-up should consist of calisthenics which will exercise the arms, shoulders, back, and legs.

*1. Warm-up calisthenics:*

A. Arm-swinging
B. Arm-flexing and extending
C. Side-bending
D. Toe-touching
E. Knee-bending

**Figure D–1** Barbell curl.

### 2. Barbell curl (biceps exercise) (Fig. D-1)

Hold the barbell in front of your thighs with palms forward and hands about shoulder width apart. Raise the weight by flexing arms at the elbows until arms are fully bent and the bar is touching the chest. Elbows should be kept at the sides, but should not be braced against the body or moved backward or forward. The bar should be lifted in a continuous motion without jerking or using a backbend. The weight should be lowered slowly in the same manner until arms are *fully extended.*

### 3. Barbell press (triceps and shoulder exercise) (Fig. D-2)

Hold the barbell just in front of your chest, with palms forward and hands shoulder width apart. With a pushing motion, the weight is raised overhead, passing just in front of your face until the arms are fully extended overhead. There should be no backbend or assistance by bending the knees. Knees should be locked, hips forward, and muscles of the buttocks and lower back tensed. Lower the weight slowly to the original position.

**Figure D–2** Barbell press.

**Figure D-3** Sit-up.

### 4. Sit-up (abdominal exercise) (Fig. D-3)

Lie on a mat on your back with feet flat on the floor and knees flexed. Sit up as far as you can, with a curling motion of the trunk, contracting the abdominal muscles as much as possible. Reach forward with the arms as you sit up. Slowly lower to the starting position. To increase the resistance, clasp hands behind the head; and for still more resistance hold a barbell plate behind the head. Do not sit up with a jerking motion. Exhale as you sit up.

### 5. Knee bend (leg exercise) (Fig. D-4)

Place a barbell on your shoulders behind your back. A towel may be used to pad the bar. Have feet spread slightly. Lower to a squatting position until upper leg is parallel to the floor and then immediately rise to the starting position. Look straight ahead as you go down and up as you rise. Do not round your back; keep it as flat as possible. Keep as erect as possible throughout the exercise. Correct form is essential in this exercise to avoid back injury.

### 6. Pullover (chest and shoulder exercise) (Fig. D-5)

Lie on your back on a bench about 9 to 12 inches wide. Hold a barbell above your chest with palms of hands forward and arms locked. Keeping arms locked, lower the weight to a position over your head, at the same time inhaling as deeply as possible. Then raise the weight to the starting position in an

**Figure D-4** Knee bend.

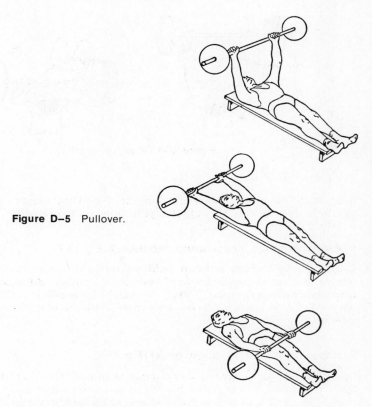

**Figure D–5**  Pullover.

arc and lower it slowly to the thighs. Raise the weight overhead again, repeating the exercise.

## 7. Stiff-legged dead lift (lower back and back of legs) (Fig. D-6)

Hold the weight in front of your thighs with palms to the rear. Keeping knees locked, lower the weight by bending forward at hips until it just touches the

**Figure D–6**  Stiff-legged dead lift.

**Figure D–7**   Press on bench.

floor. Raise the weight by straightening up. Never use weight exceeding body weight in this exercise. Do not attempt to progress too rapidly.

### 8. Press on bench (chest, arms, shoulders) (Fig. D-7)

Lying on your back on a bench, hold a barbell over your chest with arms extended and palms forward toward your feet. Arms should be slightly farther than shoulder width apart. Lower the weight by bending your arms, elbows outward to sides, until it touches your chest. Push the weight up to the starting position.

### 9. Bent rowing motion (upper back) (Fig. D-8)

Grasp the bar with palms back and hands slightly farther than shoulder width apart. The body is bent at the hips to form a right angle, and knees are bent slightly. Keep the back flat. Pull the weight up until it touches the chest just below the nipple line. Do not jerk the weight up or lower the trunk to meet it. Now lower the weight until it is just above the floor and arms are extended.

### 10. Raise on toes (calf) (Fig. D-9)

Place a barbell across your shoulders behind neck. Place toes and balls of feet on the edge of a board 2 to 3 inches high, with heels off the board. Rise up on toes as high as possible. Lower until heels touch the floor. Vary each workout by turning toes in one time, out the next, then straight ahead.

**Figure D–8**   Bent rowing motion.

**Figure D–9** Rise on toes.

### 11. Lateral arm raise (shoulders) (Fig. D-10)

Hold a dumbbell in each hand with palms facing each other and arms hanging at sides. Raise arms sidewards and outwards until they are above the level of the shoulders. Lower to sides. Keep arms extended and locked at elbows.

This regimen is a complete general workout. The exercises are basic ones, of which there are many variations. Many of the barbell exercises can also be done with dumbbells. The beginner should stay on this program for at least six months before varying it. This program will produce results as rapidly as any other program for the beginner. There are hundreds of different exercises that may be performed with barbells and dumbbells, but you must limit yourself to a well-balanced program suited to your needs and available time. Some advanced weight-lifters repeat each exercise three or four times in a workout. This is referred to as doing *sets* of an exercise.

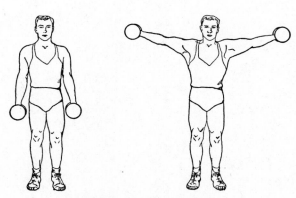

**Figure D–10** Lateral arm raise.

*Appendix E* _____

# INTERVAL TRAINING PROGRAMS FOR UNCONDITIONED COLLEGE MEN AND WOMEN

The times given below are for unconditioned men and women between the ages of 18 to 21 years. Application of the program can be made to various age groups by following the principles as presented in Chapter 12. The programs are given in prescription form, for example:

$$6 \times 220 \text{ at } 0.33 \text{ (1:39)}$$

where 6 = number of repetitions
220 = training distance in yards
0:33 = training time in minutes:seconds
(1:39) = time of relief interval in minutes:seconds

Complete programs for running as well as for most other exercise modes are given in: Fox, E., and Mathews, D.: Interval Training: Conditioning for Sports and General Fitness. Philadelphia, W. B. Saunders Co., 1974.

### MEN

#### WEEK 1

| | | |
|---|---|---|
| Day 1 | Set 1 | 4 × 220 at Easy (1:3)* |
| | Set 2 | 8 × 110 at Easy (1:3) |
| Day 2 | Set 1 | 2 × 440 at Easy (1:3) |
| | Set 2 | 8 × 110 at Easy (1:3) |
| Day 3 | Set 1 | 2 × 440 at Easy (1:3) |
| | Set 2 | 6 × 220 at Easy (1:3) |
| Day 4 | Set 1 | 1 × 880 at Easy |
| | Set 2 | 6 × 220 at Easy (1:3) |

---

*Work-relief ratio

**538**

## WEEK 2

| | | |
|---|---|---|
| Day 1 | Set 1 | 2 × 880 at Easy (1:3) |
| | Set 2 | 2 × 440 at Easy (1:3) |
| Day 2 | Set 1 | 6 × 440 at Easy (1:3) |
| Day 3 | Set 1 | 3 × 880 at Easy (1:3) |
| Day 4 | Set 1 | 1 × 2640 at Easy (1:3) |

## WEEK 3

| | | |
|---|---|---|
| Day 1 | Set 1 | 2 × 660 at 2:15 (4:30)* |
| | Set 2 | 2 × 440 at 1:20 (2:40) |
| Day 2 | Set 1 | 4 × 220 at 0.38 (1:54) |
| | Set 2 | 4 × 220 at 0.38 (1:54) |
| | Set 3 | 4 × 220 at 0:38 (1:54) |
| Day 3 | Set 1 | 1 × 880 at 3:00 (3:00) |

## WEEK 4

| | | |
|---|---|---|
| Day 1 | Set 1 | 3 × 660 at 2:10 (4:20) |
| | Set 2 | 3 × 440 at 1:20 (2:40) |
| Day 2 | Set 1 | 4 × 220 at 0:38 (1:54) |
| | Set 2 | 4 × 220 at 0:38 (1:54) |
| | Set 3 | 4 × 220 at 0:38 (1:54) |
| | Set 4 | 4 × 220 at 0:38 (1:54) |
| Day 3 | Set 1 | 2 × 880 at 2:55 (2:55) |
| | Set 2 | 2 × 440 at 1:20 (2:40) |

## WEEK 5

| | | |
|---|---|---|
| Day 1 | Set 1 | 4 × 660 at 2:05 (4:10) |
| | Set 2 | 2 × 440 at 1:20 (2:40) |
| Day 2 | Set 1 | 4 × 220 at 0:37 (1:51) |
| | Set 2 | 4 × 220 at 0:37 (1:51) |
| | Set 3 | 4 × 220 at 0:37 (1:51) |
| | Set 4 | 4 × 220 at 0:37 (1:51) |
| Day 3 | Set 1 | 2 × 880 at 2:55 (2:55) |
| | Set 2 | 2 × 440 at 1:20 (2:40) |

## WEEK 6

| | | |
|---|---|---|
| Day 1 | Set 1 | 4 × 660 at 2:00 (4:00) |
| | Set 2 | 2 × 440 at 1:18 (2:36) |
| Day 2 | Set 1 | 4 × 220 at 0:36 (1:48) |
| | Set 2 | 4 × 220 at 0:36 (1:48) |
| | Set 3 | 4 × 220 at 0:36 (1:48) |
| | Set 4 | 4 × 220 at 0:36 (1:48) |
| Day 3 | Set 1 | 2 × 880 at 2:50 (2:50) |
| | Set 2 | 2 × 440 at 1:18 (2:36) |

*Minutes:seconds

### WEEK 7

| Day 1 | Set 1 | 2 × 880 at 2:45 (2:45) |
| | Set 2 | 2 × 440 at 1:16 (2:32) |
| Day 2 | Set 1 | 4 × 220 at 0:35 (1:45) |
| | Set 2 | 4 × 220 at 0:35 (1:45) |
| | Set 3 | 4 × 220 at 0:35 (1:45) |
| | Set 4 | 4 × 220 at 0:35 (1:45) |
| Day 3 | Set 1 | 1 × 1320 at 4:30 (2:15) |
| | Set 2 | 2 × 1100 at 3:40 (1:50) |

### WEEK 8

| Day 1 | Set 1 | 2 × 880 at 2:40 (2:40) |
| | Set 2 | 2 × 440 at 1:16 (2:32) |
| Day 2 | Set 1 | 4 × 220 at 0:34 (1:42) |
| | Set 2 | 4 × 220 at 0:34 (1:42) |
| | Set 3 | 4 × 220 at 0:34 (1:42) |
| | Set 4 | 4 × 220 at 0:34 (1:42) |
| Day 3 | Set 1 | 1 × 1320 at 4:24 (2:12) |
| | Set 2 | 2 × 1100 at 3:34 (1:47) |

## WOMEN
### WEEK 1

| Day 1 | Set 1 | 4 × 220 at easy (1:3)* |
| | Set 2 | 8 × 110 at easy (1:3) |
| Day 2 | Set 1 | 2 × 440 at easy (1:3) |
| | Set 2 | 8 × 110 at easy (1:3) |
| Day 3 | Set 1 | 2 × 440 at easy (1:3) |
| | Set 2 | 6 × 220 at easy (1:3) |
| Day 4 | Set 1 | 1 × 880 at easy |
| | Set 2 | 6 × 220 at easy (1:3) |

### WEEK 2

| Day 1 | Set 1 | 2 × 880 at easy (1:3) |
| | Set 2 | 2 × 440 at easy (1:3) |
| Day 2 | Set 1 | 6 × 440 at easy (1:3) |
| Day 3 | Set 1 | 3 × 880 at easy (1:3) |
| Day 4 | Set 1 | 3 × 880 at easy (1:3) |

### WEEK 3

| Day 1 | Set 1 | 2 × 660 at 2:45 (5:30)† |
| | Set 2 | 4 × 110 at 0:25 (1:15) |
| Day 2 | Set 1 | 6 × 220 at 0:45 (2:15) |
| | Set 2 | 6 × 110 at 0:25 (1:15) |

*Work-relief ratio
†Minutes:seconds

Day 3    Set 1    6 × 220 at 0:45 (2:15)
         Set 2    6 × 110 at 0:25 (1:15)

## WEEK 4

Day 1    Set 1     4 × 220 at 0:45 (2:15)
         Set 2     8 × 110 at 0:25 (1:15)
         Set 3    10 ×  55 at 0:10 (0:30)

Day 2    Set 1     2 × 660 at 2:45 (5:30)
         Set 2     3 × 220 at 0:45 (2:15)
         Set 3     3 × 220 at 0:45 (2:15)

Day 3    Set 1     4 × 220 at 0:45 (2:15)
         Set 2     4 × 220 at 0:45 (2:15)
         Set 3     8 × 110 at 0:25 (1:15)

## WEEK 5

Day 1    Set 1     4 × 220 at 0:45 (2:15)
         Set 2     8 × 110 at 0:25 (1:15)
         Set 3    10 ×  55 at 0:10 (0:30)

Day 2    Set 1     2 × 660 at 2:45 (5:30)
         Set 2     3 × 220 at 0:45 (2:15)
         Set 3     3 × 220 at 0:45 (2:15)

Day 3    Set 1     4 × 220 at 0:45 (2:15)
         Set 2     4 × 220 at 0:45 (2:15)
         Set 3     8 × 110 at 0:25 (1:15)

## WEEK 6

Day 1    Set 1     4 × 220 at 0:42 (2:06)
         Set 2     8 × 110 at 0:22 (1:06)
         Set 3     8 × 110 at 0:22 (1:06)

Day 2    Set 1     2 × 660 at 2:40 (5:20)
         Set 2     8 × 110 at 0:22 (1:06)
         Set 3     8 ×  55 at 0:08 (0:24)

Day 3    Set 1     2 × 880 at 4:00 (4:00)
         Set 2     8 ×  55 at 0:08 (0:24)
         Set 3     8 ×  55 at 0:08 (0:24)

## WEEK 7

Day 1    Set 1     2 × 660 at 2:40 (5:20)
         Set 2     6 × 110 at 0:22 (1:06)
         Set 3     6 × 110 at 0:22 (1:06)

Day 2    Set 1     4 × 220 at 0:42 (2:06)
         Set 2     4 × 220 at 0:42 (2:06)
         Set 3     4 × 220 at 0:42 (2:06)

Day 3    Set 1     8 × 110 at 0:22 (1:06)
         Set 2     8 × 110 at 0:22 (1:06)
         Set 3     8 × 110 at 0:22 (1:06)

## Week 8

| Day 1 | Set 1 | 2 × 660 at 2:35 (5:10) |
|-------|-------|-------------------------|
|       | Set 2 | 6 × 110 at 0:20 (1:00) |
|       | Set 3 | 6 × 110 at 0:20 (1:00) |
| Day 2 | Set 1 | 4 × 220 at 0:40 (2:00) |
|       | Set 2 | 4 × 220 at 0:40 (2:00) |
|       | Set 3 | 4 × 220 at 0:40 (2:00) |
| Day 3 | Set 1 | 8 × 110 at 0:20 (1:00) |
|       | Set 2 | 8 × 110 at 0:20 (1:00) |
|       | Set 3 | 8 × 110 at 0:20 (1:00) |

# GLOSSARY

ACCELERATION SPRINT: Sprint in which running speed is gradually increased from jogging to striding and finally to sprinting.

ACCLIMATIZATION: Pertaining to certain physiological adjustments brought about through continued exposure to a different climate, e.g., changes in altitude and heat.

ACETYLCHOLINE (ACh): A chemical substance involved in several important physiological functions such as transmission of an impulse from one nerve fiber to another across a synapse.

ACID: A chemical compound that gives up hydrogen ions ($H^+$) in solution.

ACTIN: A protein involved in muscular contraction.

ACTION POTENTIAL: The electrical activity developed in a muscle or nerve cell during activity or depolarization.

ACTIVE TRANSPORT: The movement of substances or materials against their concentration gradients by the expenditure of metabolic energy.

ADENOSINE DIPHOSPHATE (ADP): A complex chemical compound which, when combined with inorganic phosphate ($P_i$), forms ATP.

ADENOSINE TRIPHOSPHATE (ATP): A complex chemical compound formed with the energy released from food and stored in all cells, particularly muscles. Only from the energy released by the breakdown of this compound can the cell perform work.

ADIPOCYTE: A fat cell; a cell that stores fat.

ADIPOSE TISSUE: Fat tissue.

AEROBIC: In the presence of oxygen.

AEROTITIS: Inflammation or disease of the ear.

AFFERENT NERVE: A neuron that conveys sensory impulses from a receptor to the central nervous system.

ALACTACID OXYGEN DEBT: That portion of the recovery oxygen used to resynthesize and restore ATP + PC in muscle following exercise.

ALKALINE: Pertaining to a base.

ALKALI RESERVE: The amount of bicarbonate (base) available in the body for buffering.

ALKALOSIS: Excessive base (bicarbonate ions) in the extracellular fluids.

ALPHA MOTOR NEURON: A type of efferent nerve cell that innervates extrafusal muscle fibers.

ALVEOLAR-CAPILLARY MEMBRANE: The thin layer of tissue dividing the alveoli and the pulmonary capillaries where gaseous exchange occurs.

ALVEOLAR VENTILATION: The portion of inspired air that reaches the alveoli.

ALVEOLI (plural); ALVEOLUS (singular): Tiny terminal air sacs in the lungs where gaseous exchange with the blood in the pulmonary capillaries occurs.

AMBIENT: Pertaining to the surrounding environment.

AMPHETAMINE: A synthetically structured drug closely related to epinephrine; it produces stimulation of the central nervous system.

ANABOLIC: Protein building.

ANAEROBIC: In the absence of oxygen.

ANATOMICAL DEAD SPACE (DS): That volume of fresh air that remains in the respiratory passages (nose, mouth, pharynx, larynx, trachea, bronchi, and bronchioles) and does not participate in gaseous exchange.

ANDROGEN: Any substance that possesses masculinizing properties.

ANEMIA: A lack of sufficient red blood cells or hemoglobin.

ANTHROPOMETRY: The measurement of the size and proportions of the human body.

APNEA (APNEIC): Cessation of breathing.

AQUEOUS: Pertaining to water.

ARTERIOVENOUS OXYGEN DIFFERENCE (a-$\bar{v}O_2$ diff.): The difference between the oxygen content of arterial and mixed venous blood.

ARTERY: A vessel carrying blood away from the heart.

ATPase: An enzyme that facilitates the breakdown of ATP.

ATP-PC SYSTEM: An anaerobic energy system in which ATP is manufactured when phosphocreatine (PC) is broken down. This system represents the most rapidly available source of ATP for use by muscle. Activities performed at maximum intensity in a period of 10 seconds or less derive energy (ATP) from this system.

ATPS: Ambient temperature, pressure, saturated (see Appendix B, p. 519).

AUTONOMIC NERVOUS SYSTEM: A self-controlled system that helps to control activities such as those involving movement and secretion by the visceral organs, urinary output, body temperature, heart rate, adrenal secretion, and blood pressure.

BAROMETRIC (ATMOSPHERIC) PRESSURE ($P_B$): The force per unit area exerted by the earth's atmosphere. At sea level, it is 14.7 pounds per square inch or 760 millimeters of mercury (mm Hg).

BENDS (DECOMPRESSION SICKNESS): A condition induced by the evolution of nitrogen bubbles resulting from rapid decompression (gas emboli) and which may cause circulatory blockage and tissue damage.

BIOENERGETICS: The study of energy transformations in living organisms.

BIOPSY: The removal and examination of tissue from the living body.

BLACK BULB THERMOMETER: An ordinary thermometer placed in a black globe. The black bulb temperature measures radiant energy or solar radiation and is one of three temperatures used to compute the WBGT index (*see*).

BLOOD PRESSURE: The driving force that moves blood through the circulatory system. Systolic pressure is obtained when blood is ejected into the arteries; diastolic pressure is obtained when the blood drains from the arteries.

BRADYCARDIA: A decreased or slowed heart rate.

BTPS: Body temperature, pressure, saturated (see Appendix B, p. 520).

BUFFER: Any substance in a fluid that lessens the change in hydrogen ion ($H^+$) concentration which otherwise would occur, by adding acids or bases.

CALORIE (cal): A unit of work or energy equal to the amount of heat required to raise the temperature of one gram of water 1°C.

CAPILLARY: A fine network of small vessels located between arteries and veins where exchanges between tissue and blood occur.

CARBAMINO COMPOUNDS. The end product obtained from the chemical combination of plasma proteins and/or hemoglobin (Hb) and carbon dioxide ($CO_2$).

CARBOHYDRATE: Any of a group of chemical compounds, including sugars, starches, and cellulose, containing carbon, hydrogen, and oxygen only. One of the basic foodstuffs.

CARBONIC ANHYDRASE: An enzyme that speeds up the reaction of carbon dioxide ($CO_2$) with water ($H_2O$).

CARDIAC CYCLE: Contraction (systole) and relaxation (diastole) of the heart.

CARDIAC OUTPUT ($\dot{Q}$): The amount of blood pumped by the heart in one minute; the product of the stroke volume and the heart rate.

CARDIORESPIRATORY ENDURANCE: The ability of the lungs and heart to take in and transport adequate amounts of oxygen to the working muscles, allowing activities that involve large muscle masses (e.g., running, swimming, bicycling) to be performed over long periods of time.

CENTRAL NERVOUS SYSTEM: The spinal cord and brain.

CEREBELLUM: That division or part of the brain concerned with coordination of movements.

CEREBRAL CORTEX: That portion of the brain responsible for mental functions, movement, visceral functions, perception, and behavioral reactions, and for the association and integration of these functions.

CHOLINESTERASE: A chemical that deactivates or breaks down acetylcholine.

CONDITIONING: Augmentation of the energy capacity of muscle through an exercise program. Conditioning is not primarily concerned with the skill of performance, as would be the case in training.

CONDUCTION: The transfer of heat between objects of different temperatures in direct contact with each other.

CONTINUOUS WORK: Exercises performed to completion without relief periods.

CONVECTION: The transfer of heat from one place to another by the motion of a heated substance.

COUPLED REACTIONS: Two series of chemical reactions, one of which releases energy (heat) for use by the other.

CROSS-BRIDGES: Extensions of myosin.

CRYOGENIC: Pertaining to the production of low temperatures.

DEHYDRATION: The condition that results from excessive loss of body water.

DENSITY: The mass per unit volume of an object.

DIASTOLE: The resting phase of the cardiac cycle.

DIASTOLIC VOLUME: The amount of blood that fills the ventricle during diastole.

DIFFUSION: The random movement of molecules due to their kinetic energy.

DOUBLE BLIND STUDY: An experimental protocol in which neither the investigators nor the subjects know which group is receiving a placebo and which group the real drug.

DOUGLAS BAG: A rubber-lined, canvas bag used for collection of expired gas.

DRUG: A chemical substance given with the intention of preventing or curing disease or otherwise enhancing the physical or mental welfare of humans or animals.

DRY BULB THERMOMETER: A common thermometer used to record temperature of the air.

DYSMENORRHEA: Painful menstruation.

DYSPNEA: Labored breathing.

ECCENTRIC CONTRACTION: The muscle lengthens while contracting (developing tension).

ECTOMORPHY: A body type component characterized by linearity, fragility, and delicacy of body.

EFFERENT NERVE: A neuron that conveys motor impulses away from the central nervous system to an organ of response such as skeletal muscle.

EFFICIENCY: The ratio of work output to work input.

ELECTRICAL POTENTIAL: The capacity for producing electrical effects, such as an electric current, between two bodies (e.g., between the inside and outside of a cell).

ELECTROLYTE: A substance that ionizes in solution, such as salt (NaCl), and is capable of conducting an electrical current.

ELECTRON: A negatively charged particle.

ELECTRON TRANSPORT SYSTEM (ETS): A series of chemical reactions occurring in mitochondria, in which electrons and hydrogen ions combine with oxygen to form water, and ATP is resynthesized. Also referred to as the *respiratory chain.*

EMBOLUS (singular); EMBOLI (plural): A clot or other plug transported by the blood from another vessel and forced into a smaller one, thus obstructing circulation.

ENDOCRINE GLAND: An organ or gland that produces an internal secretion (hormone).

ENDOMORPHY: A body type component characterized by roundness and softness of the body.

ENDOMYSIUM: A connective tissue surrounding a muscle fiber or cell.

ENERGY: The capacity or ability to perform work.

ENERGY SYSTEM: One of three metabolic systems involving a series of chemical reactions resulting in the formation of waste products and the manufacture of ATP.

ENGRAM: A memorized motor pattern stored in the brain; a permanent trace left by a stimulus in the tissue protoplasm.

ENZYME: A protein compound that speeds up a chemical reaction.

EPIMYSIUM: A connective tissue surrounding the entire muscle.

EPINEPHRINE: A chemical substance involved in several important physiological functions; for example, the chemical transmitter substance at peripheral sympathetic nerve endings.

ERGOGENIC AID: Any factor that improves work performance.

ERGOMETER: An apparatus or device, such as a treadmill or stationary bicycle, used for measuring the physiological effects of exercise.

EVAPORATION: The loss of heat resulting from changing a liquid to a vapor.

EXCITATION: A response to a stimulus.

EXCITATORY POSTSYNAPTIC POTENTIAL (EPSP): A transient increase in electrical potential (depolarization) in a postsynaptic neuron from its resting membrane potential.

EXPIRATORY RESERVE VOLUME (ERV): Maximal volume of air expired from end-expiration.

EXTRACELLULAR: Outside the cell.

EXTRAFUSAL FIBER: A typical or normal muscle cell or fiber.

EXTRASYSTOLE: An extra beat.

FACILITATED DIFFUSION: fusion that takes place with help of a carrier substance.

FASCICULUS (singular); FASCICULI (plural): A group or bundle of skeletal muscle fibers held together by a connective tissue called the perimysium.

FAT: A compound containing glycerol and fatty acids. One of the basic foodstuffs.

FATIGUE: A state of discomfort and decreased efficiency resulting from prolonged or excessive exertion.

FIBRILLATION: Irregularity in force and rhythm of the heart, or quivering of the muscle fibers, causing inefficient emptying.

FLACCID: Lacking muscular tonus.

FLEXIBILITY: The range of motion about a joint (static flexibility); opposition or resistance of a joint to motion (dynamic flexibility).

FLEXOMETER: An instrument used for measuring the range of motion about a joint (static flexibility).

FOOT-POUND: A work unit; that is, application of a one-pound force through a distance of one foot.

FULCRUM: The axis of rotation for a lever.

FUNCTIONAL RESIDUAL CAPACITY (FRC): Volume of air in the lungs at resting expiratory level.

GAMMA MOTOR NEURON: A type of efferent nerve cell that innervates the ends of an intrafusal muscle fiber.

GAMMA SYSTEM (GAMMA LOOP): The contraction of a muscle as a result of stretching the muscle spindle by way of stimulation of the gamma motor neurons.

GLUCOSE: Sugar.

GLYCOGEN: A polymer of glucose; the form in which glucose (sugar) is stored in the body.

GLYCOLYSIS: The incomplete chemical breakdown of glycogen. In aerobic glycolysis, the end product is pyruvic acid; in anaerobic glycolysis (lactic acid system), the end product is lactic acid.

GOLGI TENDON ORGAN: A proprioceptor located within a muscular tendon.

HEAT: A form of energy.

HEAT CRAMPS: Painful muscular contractions caused by prolonged exposure to environmental heat.

HEAT EXHAUSTION: A condition of fatigue caused by prolonged exposure to environmental heat.

HEAT STROKE: A disease caused by overexposure to heat and characterized by high body (rectal) temperature, hot, dry skin (usually flushed), and sometimes delirium or unconsciousness. It can be fatal.

HEMATURIA: Discharge of blood into the urine.

HEMOCONCENTRATION: Concentration of the blood.

HEMODILUTION: Dilution of the blood.

HEMODYNAMICS: The study of the physical laws governing blood flow.

HEMOGLOBIN (Hb): A complex molecule found in red blood cells, which contains iron (heme) and protein (globin) and is capable of combining with oxygen.

HEMOLYSIS: The rupture of a cell, such as the red blood cell.

HOLLOW SPRINTS: Two sprints interrupted by a (hollow) period involving either jogging or walking.

HORMONE: A chemical substance secreted by an endocrine (ductless) gland, which is absorbed into the blood and influences the growth, development, and function of some other part of the body.

HUMIDITY: Pertaining to the moisture in the air.

HYDRAULIC PRESSURE: The force per unit area resulting from a vertical column of water of a certain height.

HYPERNATREMIA: Increased sodium concentration in the blood.

HYPERPLASIA: An increase in the number of cells in a tissue or organ.

HYPERTENSION: High blood pressure.

HYPERTHERMIA: Increased body temperature.

HYPERTONIC: Pertaining to a solution having a greater tension or osmotic pressure than one with which it is being compared.

HYPERTROPHY: An increase in the size of a cell or organ.

HYPERVENTILATION: Excessive ventilation of the lungs caused by increased depth and frequency of breathing and usually resulting in elimination of carbon dioxide.

HYPERVOLEMIA: An increased blood volume.

HYPOTENSION: Low blood pressure.

HYPOTHALAMUS: That portion of the brain that exerts control over visceral activities, water balance, body temperature, and sleep.

HYPOTONIC: Pertaining to a solution having a lesser tension or osmotic pressure than one with which it is being compared.

HYPOXIA: Lack of adequate oxygen due to a reduced oxygen partial pressure.

INERT: Having no action.

INHIBITORY POSTSYNAPTIC POTENTIAL (IPSP): A transient decrease in electrical potential (hyperpolarization) in a postsynaptic neuron from its resting membrane potential.

INSPIRATORY CAPACITY (IC): Maximal volume of air inspired from resting expiratory level.

INSPIRATORY RESERVE VOLUME (IRV): Maximal volume of air inspired from end-inspiration.

INTERMITTENT WORK: Exercises performed with alternate periods of relief, as opposed to continuous work.

INTERNEURON (INTERNUNCIAL NEURON): A nerve cell located between afferent (sensory) and efferent (motor) nerve cells. It acts as a "middleman" between incoming and outgoing impulses.

INTERSTITIAL: Pertaining to the area or space between cells.

INTERVAL SPRINTING: A method of training whereby an athlete alternately sprints 50 yards and jogs 60 yards for distances up to three miles.

INTERVAL TRAINING: A system of physical conditioning in which the body is subjected to short but regularly repeated periods of work stress interspersed with adequate periods of relief.

INTRAFUSAL FIBER: A muscle cell (fiber) that houses the muscle spindle.

ION: An electrically charged particle.

ISOKINETIC CONTRACTION: Contraction in which the tension developed by the muscle while shortening is maximal over the full range of motion.

ISOMETRIC (STATIC) CONTRACTION: Contraction in which tension is developed, but there is no change in the length of the muscle.

ISOTONIC: Pertaining to solutions having the same tension or osmotic pressure.

ISOTONIC CONTRACTION: Contraction in which the muscle shortens with varying tension while lifting a constant load. Also referred to as a *dynamic* or *concentric contraction.*

JOGGING: Slow, continuous running. Also refers to all speeds of running.

JOINT RECEPTORS: A group of sense organs located in joints concerned with kinesthesis.

KILOCALORIE (Kcal): A unit of work or energy equal to the amount of heat required to raise the temperature of one kilogram of water 1°C.

KINESTHESIS: Awareness of body position.

KREBS CYCLE: A series of chemical reactions occurring in mitochondria, in which carbon dioxide is produced and hydrogen ions and electrons are removed from carbon atoms (oxidation). Also referred to as the *tricarboxylic acid cycle (TCA),* or *citric acid cycle.*

LACTACID OXYGEN DEBT: That portion of the recovery oxygen used to remove accumulated lactic acid from the blood following exercise.

LACTIC ACID (LACTATE): A fatiguing metabolite of the lactic acid system resulting from the incomplete breakdown of glucose (sugar).

LACTIC ACID SYSTEM (LA SYSTEM): An anaerobic energy system in which ATP is manufactured when glucose (sugar) is broken down to lactic acid. High intensity efforts requiring one to three minutes to perform draw energy (ATP) primarily from this system.

LEAN BODY MASS (WEIGHT): The body weight minus the weight of the body fat.

LEVER: A rigid bar (such as a bone) that is free to rotate about a fixed point or axis called a fulcrum (such as a joint).

LINEAR: Pertaining to a straight line.

MAXIMAL OXYGEN CONSUMPTION (max$\dot{V}o_2$): The maximal rate at which oxygen can be consumed per minute; the power or capacity of the aerobic or oxygen system.

MEDULLA OBLONGATA: That portion or area of the brain continuous above with the pons and below with the spinal cord and containing the cardiorespiratory control center.

MEMBRANE: A thin layer of tissue that covers a surface or divides a space or organ.

MENARCHE: The onset of menstruation.

MENSES: The monthly flow of blood from the genital tract of women.

MENSTRUATION: The process or an instance of discharging the menses.

MESOMORPHY: A body type component characterized by a square body with hard, rugged, and prominent musculature.

METABOLIC SYSTEM: A system of biochemical reactions which cause the formation of waste products (metabolites) and the manufacture of ATP; for example, the ATP-PC, lactic acid, and oxygen systems.

METABOLISM: The sum total of the chemical changes or reactions occurring in the body.

METABOLITE: Any substance produced by a metabolic reaction.

MITOCHONDRION (singular); MITOCHONDRIA (plural): A subcellular structure found in all aerobic cells, in which the reactions of the Krebs cycle and electron transport system take place.

MOLE: The gram-molecular weight or gram-formula weight of a substance. For example, one mole of glucose, $C_6H_{12}O_6$ weighs $(6 \times 12) + (12 \times 1) + (16 \times 6) = 72 + 12 + 96 = 180$ grams, where the atomic weight of carbon $(C) = 12$; hydrogen $(H) = 1$; and oxygen $(O) = 16$.

MOMENT (MOMENT ARM): The perpendicular distance from the line of action of the force to the point of rotation.

MOTONEURON (MOTOR NEURON): A nerve cell, which when stimulated, effects muscular contraction. Most motoneurons innervate skeletal muscle.

MOTOR END-PLATE: The neuromuscular or myoneural junction.

MOTOR UNIT: An individual motor nerve and all the muscle fibers it innervates.

MOUNTAIN (ALTITUDE) SICKNESS: A condition resulting from exposure to high altitude. Symptoms include nausea, vomiting, headache, rapid pulse, and loss of appetite.

MUSCLE BUNDLE: A fasciculus (*see*).

MUSCLE SPINDLE: A proprioceptor located within an intrafusal muscle fiber.

MUSCULAR ENDURANCE: The ability of a muscle or muscle group to perform repeated contractions against a light load for an extended period of time.

MYOGLOBIN: An oxygen-binding pigment similar to hemoglobin that gives the red muscle fiber its color. It acts as an oxygen store and aids in the diffusion of oxygen.

MYOSIN: A protein involved in muscular contraction.

NECROSIS: Death of a cell or group of cells in contact with living tissue.

NEGATIVE ENERGY BALANCE: A condition in which less energy (food) is taken in than is given off; body weight decreases as a result.

NET OXYGEN COST: The amount of oxygen, above resting values, required to perform a given amount of work. Also referred to as *net cost of exercise.*

NEUROMUSCULAR (MYONEURAL) JUNCTION: The union of a muscle and its nerve. Also referred to as the *motor end-plate.*

NEURON: A nerve cell consisting of a cell body (soma), with its nucleus and cytoplasm, dendrites and axons.

NITROGEN NARCOSIS (RAPTURES OF THE DEEP): A condition affecting the central nervous system (much as does alcohol) due to the forcing (by pressure) of nitrogen into solution within the body; symptoms include dizziness, slowing of mental processes, euphoria, and fixation of ideas.

NOMOGRAM: A graph enabling one to determine by aid of a straight-edge the value of a dependent variable when the values of two independent variables are known.

NOREPINEPHRINE: A chemical substance involved in several important physiological functions; for example, the chemical transmitter substance at peripheral sympathetic nerve endings.

OBESE (OBESITY): Having excessive accumulation and storage of fatty tissue.

OSMOSIS: The diffusion through a semipermeable membrane of a solvent such as water from a lower to a more concentrated solution.

OSMOTIC PRESSURE: The force per unit area needed to stop osmosis.

OVERLOAD PRINCIPLE: Progressively increasing the intensity of the workouts over the course of the training program as fitness capacity improves.

OXIDATION: The removal of electrons.

OXYGEN DEBT: The amount of oxygen consumed during recovery from exercise, above that ordinarily consumed at rest in the same time period. There is a rapid component (alactacid) and a slow component (lactacid).

OXYGEN DEFICIT: The time period during exercise in which the level of oxygen consumption is below that necessary to supply all the ATP required for the exercise; the time period during which an oxygen debt is contracted.

OXYGEN POISONING (TOXIC-

ITY): A condition caused by breathing oxygen under high pressure. Symptoms include tingling of fingers and toes, visual disturbances, auditory hallucinations, confusion, muscle and lip twitching, nausea, vertigo, and convulsions.

OXYGEN SYSTEM: An aerobic energy system in which ATP is manufactured when food (principally sugar and fat) is broken down. This system produces ATP most abundantly and is the prime energy source during long-lasting (endurance) activities.

OXYGEN TRANSPORT SYSTEM ($\dot{V}o_2$): Composed of the stroke volume (S.V.), the heart rate (H.R.), and the arterial–mixed venous oxygen difference (a–$\bar{v}$ $O_2$ diff.). Mathematically, it is defined as $\dot{V}o_2$ = S.V. × H.R. × a–$\bar{v}$ $O_2$ diff.

OXYHEMOGLOBIN ($HbO_2$): Hemoglobin chemically combined with oxygen.

PARASYMPATHETIC: Pertaining to the craniosacral portion of the autonomic nervous system.

PARTIAL PRESSURE: The pressure exerted by a gas in relation to its percentage or concentration in a gas volume.

PERIMYSIUM: A connective tissue surrounding a fasciculus or muscle bundle.

PERIOSTEUM: A fibrous membrane surrounding bone.

PERITONEUM: The thin membrane that secretes serous fluid and lines the walls of the abdominal cavity and encloses the viscera.

PERITONITIS: Inflammation of the peritoneum.

pH: The power of the hydrogen ion; the negative logarithm of the hydrogen ion concentration.

PHOSPHAGEN: A group of compounds; collectively refers to ATP and PC.

PHOSPHOCREATINE (PC): A chemical compound stored in muscle, which when broken down aids in manufacturing ATP.

PLACEBO: An inert substance having the identical physical characteristics of a real drug.

PLASMOLYSIS: The shrinking of a cell such as the red blood cell.

PLEURA (singular); PLEURAE (plural): A thin membrane that secretes serous fluid and lines the thoracic wall (parietal pleura), the diaphragm (diaphragmatic pleura), and the lungs (visceral pleura).

PNEUMOTHORAX: The entrance of air into the pleural cavity.

POLYCYTHEMIA: An increased production of red blood cells.

PONDERAL INDEX: Body height divided by the cube root of body weight.

POSITIVE ENERGY BALANCE: A condition in which more energy (food) is taken in than is given off; body weight increases as a result.

POSTSYNAPTIC NEURON: A nerve cell located distal to a synapse.

POWER: Performance of work expressed per unit of time. For example, if one pound is raised one foot in one second, power is expressed as 1 foot-pound per second.

PRESSURE: Force per unit area.

PROPRIOCEPTOR: Sensory organs found in muscles, joints, and tendons, which give information concerning movements and position of the body (kinesthesis).

PROTEIN: A compound containing amino acids. One of the basic foodstuffs.

PROTON: A positively charged particle.

PSYCHROMETER: An instrument used for measuring the relative humidity.

PULMONARY CIRCUIT: The flow of arterial blood from the heart to the pulmonary (lung) capillaries and of venous blood from the pulmonary capillaries back to the heart.

PYRAMIDAL (CORTICOSPINAL) TRACT: The area in which impulses from the motor area of the cortex are sent down to the anterior motoneurons of the spinal cord.

PYRUVIC ACID (PYRUVATE): The end product of aerobic glycolysis; the precursor of lactic acid (lactate).

RADIATION: The transfer of heat between objects through electromagnetic waves.

RECEPTOR: A sense organ that receives stimuli.

REFLEX: An automatic response induced by stimulation of a receptor.

RELATIVE HUMIDITY: Ratio of water vapor in the atmosphere to the amount of water vapor required to saturate the atmosphere at the same temperature.

RELIEF INTERVAL: In an interval training program, the time between work intervals as well as between sets.

REPETITION: In an interval training program, the number of work intervals within one set. For example, six 220-yard runs would constitute one set of six repetitions.

REPETITION MAXIMUM (RM): The maximal load that a muscle group can lift over a given number of repetitions before fatiguing. For example, a 10 RM load is the maximal load that can be lifted over 10 repetitions.

REPETITION RUNNING: Similar to interval training but differs in the length of the work interval and the degree of recovery between repetitions.

RESIDUAL VOLUME (RV): Volume of air remaining in the lungs at end of maximal expiration.

RESPIRATORY EXCHANGE RATIO (R, RQ): The ratio of the amount of carbon dioxide produced to the amount of oxygen consumed ($\dot{V}CO_2/\dot{V}O_2$).

RESTING MEMBRANE POTENTIAL: The electrical difference between the inside and outside of the cell (i.e., across the cell membrane) at rest.

REST-RELIEF: In an interval training program, a type of relief interval involving moderate moving about, such as walking and flexing of arms and legs.

SALINE: A 0.9 per cent salt solution which is isotonic to the blood.

SALPINGITIS: Inflammation of a fallopian tube.

SARCOLEMMA: The muscle cell membrane.

SARCOMERE: The distance between two Z lines; the smallest contractile unit of skeletal muscle.

SARCOPLASM: Muscle protoplasm.

SARCOPLASMIC RETICULUM: A network of tubules and vesicles surrounding the myofibril.

SECOND WIND: A phenomenon characterized by a sudden transition from an ill-defined feeling of distress or fatigue during the early portion of prolonged exercise to a more comfortable, less stressful feeling later in the exercise.

SEMIPERMEABLE MEMBRANE:

A membrane permeable to some but not all particles or substances.

SENSORY NEURON: A nerve cell that conveys impulses from a receptor to the central nervous system. Examples of sensory neurons are those excited by sound, pain, light, and taste.

SEROUS FLUID: A watery fluid secreted by the pleurae.

SET: In an interval training program, a group of work and relief intervals.

SOMATIC: Pertaining to the body.

SOMATOTYPE: The body type or physical classification of the human body.

SPATIAL SUMMATION: An increase in responsiveness of a nerve resulting from the additive effect of numerous stimuli.

SPECIFIC GRAVITY: The ratio of the density of an object to the density of water.

SPECIFIC HEAT: The heat required to change the temperature of a unit mass of a substance by one degree.

SPECIFICITY OF TRAINING: Principle underlying construction of a training program for a specific activity or skill and the primary energy system(s) involved during performance. For example, a training program for sprinters would consist of repeated bouts of sprints in order to develop both sprinting performance and the ATP-PC system.

SPEED PLAY (FARTLEK TRAINING): Involves alternating fast and slow running over natural terrains. It is the forerunner of the interval training system.

SPIROMETER: A steel container used to collect, store, and measure either inspired or expired gas volumes.

SPRINT TRAINING: A type of training system employing repeated sprints at maximal speed.

STEADY-STATE: Pertaining to the time period during which a physiological function (such as $\dot{V}_{O_2}$) remains at a constant (steady) value.

STEROID: A derivative of the male sex hormone, testosterone, which has masculinizing properties.

STIMULUS (singular); STIMULI (plural): Any agent, act, or influence that modifies the activity of a receptor or irritable tissue.

STPD: Standard temperature, pressure, dry (see Appendix B, p. 519).

STRENGTH: The force that a muscle or muscle group can exert against a resistance in one maximal effort.

STROKE VOLUME (S.V.): The amount of blood pumped by the left ventricle of the heart per beat.

SUDOMOTOR: Pertaining to activation of the sweat glands.

SYMPATHETIC: Pertaining to the thoracolumbar portion of the autonomic nervous system.

SYNAPSE: The connection or junction of one neuron to another.

SYNAPTIC CLEFT: The gap or space between presynaptic and postsynaptic neurons.

SYSTEMIC CIRCUIT: The flow of arterial blood from the heart to the body tissues (such as the muscles) and of the venous blood from the tissues back to the heart.

SYSTOLE: The contractile or emptying phase of the cardiac cycle.

TACHYCARDIA: An increased or rapid heart rate.

TEMPERATURE: The degree of sensible heat or cold.

TEMPORAL SUMMATION: An increase in responsiveness of a nerve, resulting from the additive effect of frequently occurring stimuli.

TESTOSTERONE: The male sex hormone secreted by the testicles; it possesses masculinizing properties.

THERMODYNAMICS: The science of the transformation of heat and energy.

THRESHOLD FOR EXCITATION: The minimal electrical level at which a neuron will transmit or conduct an impulse.

THYROXIN: A hormone secreted by the thyroid gland.

TIDAL VOLUME (TV): Volume of air inspired or expired per breath.

TISSUE-CAPILLARY MEMBRANE: The thin layer of tissue dividing the capillaries and an organ (such as skeletal muscle); site at which gaseous exchange occurs.

TONUS: Resiliency and resistance to stretch in a relaxed, resting muscle.

TOTAL LUNG CAPACITY (TLC): Volume of air in the lungs at end of maximal inspiration.

TRAINING: An exercise program to develop an athlete for a particular event. Increasing skill of performance and energy capacities are of equal consideration.

TRAINING DISTANCE: In an interval training program, the distance of the work interval; e.g., running 220 yards.

TRAINING DURATION: The length of the training program.

TRAINING FREQUENCY: The number of times per week for the training workout.

TRAINING TIME: The rate at which the work is to be accomplished during a work interval in an interval training program.

TROPHIC: Pertaining to nutrition or nourishment.

TROPOMYOSIN: A protein involved in muscular contraction.

TROPONIN: A protein involved in muscular contraction.

VALSALVA MANEUVER: Making an expiratory effort with the glottis closed.

VASOCONSTRICTION: A decrease in the diameter of a blood vessel (usually an arteriole) resulting in a reduction of blood flow to the area supplied by the vessel.

VASODILATION: An increase in the diameter of a blood vessel (usually an arteriole) resulting in an increased blood flow to the area supplied by the vessel.

VASOMOTOR: Pertaining to vasoconstriction and vasodilation.

VEIN: A vessel carrying blood toward the heart.

VENOCONSTRICTION: A decrease in the diameter of a vein.

VENTILATORY EFFICIENCY: The amount of ventilation required per liter of oxygen consumed; i.e., $\dot{V}_E/\dot{V}_{O_2}$.

VISCERA (plural); VISCUS (singular): The internal organs of the body.

VISCERAL: Pertaining to the viscera.

VITAL CAPACITY (VC): Maximal volume of air forcefully expired after maximal inspiration.

VITAMIN: An inorganic material in the presence of which important chemical (metabolic) reactions occur.

WBGT INDEX: An index calculated from dry bulb, wet bulb, and black bulb temperatures. It indicates the severity of the environmental heat conditions.

WET BULB THERMOMETER: An ordinary thermometer with a wetted wick wrapped around the bulb. The wet bulb's temperature is related to the amount of moisture in the air. When the wet bulb and dry bulb temperatures are equal, the air is completely saturated with water and the relative humidity is equal to 100 per cent.

WORK: Application of a force through a distance. For example, application of one pound through one foot equals one foot-pound of work.

WORK INTERVAL: That portion of an interval training program consisting of the work effort.

WORK-RELIEF: In an interval training program, a type of relief interval involving light or mild exercise such as rapid walking or jogging.

WORK:RELIEF RATIO: In an interval training program, a ratio relating the duration of the work interval to the duration of the relief interval. As an example, a work:relief ratio of 1:1 means that the durations of the work and relief intervals are equal.

# NAME INDEX

Numbers in *italics* refer to illustrations;
numbers followed by a (t) refer to tables.

# SUBJECT INDEX

Numbers in *italics* refer to illustrations; numbers followed by a (t) indicate tables.

**565**

## Table 4-2 RELATIONSHIPS AMONG POWER UNITS (POWER EQUALS WORK PER UNIT TIME)

| | HORSE-POWER | KG.-METERS/MINUTE | KG.-METERS/SECOND | FOOT-POUNDS/MINUTE | FOOT-POUNDS/SECOND | WATTS | KCAL./MINUTE | KCAL./SECOND |
|---|---|---|---|---|---|---|---|---|
| 1 horsepower | 1.0 | 4,564.0 | 76.07 | 33,000.0 | 550.0 | 746.0 | 10.694 | 0.178 |
| 1 kg.-meter/minute | 0.000219 | 1.0 | 0.016667 | 7.23 | 0.1205 | 0.16345 | 0.00234 | 0.000039 |
| 1 foot-pound/minute | 0.00003 | 0.1383 | 0.0023 | 1.0 | 0.016667 | 0.0226 | 0.000324 | 0.0000054 |
| 1 watt | 0.001341 | 6.118 | 0.10197 | 44.236 | 0.7373 | 1.0 | 0.014335 | 0.000239 |
| 1 kcal./minute | 0.09355 | 426.78 | 7.113 | 3086.0 | 51.43 | 69.759 | 1.0 | 0.01667 |

## Table 4-1 ENERGY AND WORK UNITS

1 foot-pound = 0.13825 kg.-meter*
1 kg.-meter = 7.23 foot-pounds
1 kcal. = 3086 foot-pounds
1 kcal. = 426.4 kg.-meter

*A kilogram-meter is the distance through which 1 kilogram (2.2 pounds) moves 1 meter (3.28 feet).